THE OXFORD HANDBOOK OF
MEANING IN LIFE

THE OXFORD HANDBOOK OF

MEANING IN LIFE

Edited by
IDDO LANDAU

OXFORD
UNIVERSITY PRESS

Oxford University Press is a department of the University of Oxford. It furthers the University's objective of excellence in research, scholarship, and education by publishing worldwide. Oxford is a registered trade mark of Oxford University Press in the UK and certain other countries.

Published in the United States of America by Oxford University Press
198 Madison Avenue, New York, NY 10016, United States of America.

© Oxford University Press 2022

All rights reserved. No part of this publication may be reproduced, stored in a retrieval system, or transmitted, in any form or by any means, without the prior permission in writing of Oxford University Press, or as expressly permitted by law, by license, or under terms agreed with the appropriate reproduction rights organization. Inquiries concerning reproduction outside the scope of the above should be sent to the Rights Department, Oxford University Press, at the address above.

You must not circulate this work in any other form
and you must impose this same condition on any acquirer.

Library of Congress Cataloging-in-Publication Data
Names: Landau, Iddo, 1958- editor.
Title: The Oxford handbook of meaning in life.
Description: New York : OUP, 2022. | Series: Oxford handbooks series | Includes index.
Identifiers: LCCN 2021054134 | ISBN 9780190063504 | ISBN 9780190063511 | ISBN 9780190063535 | ISBN 9780190063528 (epub)
Subjects: LCSH: Meaning (Philosophy) | Life.
Classification: LCC B105.M4 O94 2022 | DDC 121/.68–dc23/eng/20211123
LC record available at https://lccn.loc.gov/2021054134

DOI: 10.1093/oxfordhb/9780190063504.001.0001

1 3 5 7 9 8 6 4 2

Printed by Integrated Books International, United States of America

Contents

Contributors	ix
Introduction IDDO LANDAU	1

PART I. UNDERSTANDING MEANING IN LIFE

1. The Concept of Life's Meaning THADDEUS METZ	27
2. Subjectivism and Objectivism about Meaning in Life JENS JOHANSSON AND FRANS SVENSSON	43
3. Achievement and Meaning in Life GWEN BRADFORD	58
4. Narrativity and Meaning in Life GALEN STRAWSON	74
5. Meaningfulness and Importance GUY KAHANE	93
6. The Meaning of Life and Death STEVEN LUPER	109

PART II. MEANING IN LIFE, SCIENCE, AND METAPHYSICS

7. The Relevance of Neuroscience to Meaning in Life PAUL THAGARD	127
8. Can Neuroscience Shed Light on What Constitutes a Meaningful Life? P. M. S. HACKER	145

9. Personal Identity and Meaning in Life   159
   MARYA SCHECHTMAN

10. Hard Determinism and Meaning in Life   173
    DERK PEREBOOM

11. Meaning in Life and the Nature of Time   189
    NED MARKOSIAN

PART III. MEANING IN LIFE AND RELIGION

12. The Meaning of Life and Transcendence   205
    JOHN COTTINGHAM

13. Atheism and Meaning in Life   216
    ERIK J. WIELENBERG

14. Theism and Meaning in Life   229
    T. J. MAWSON

15. Mysticism, Ritual, and the Meaning of Life   243
    GUY BENNETT-HUNTER

PART IV. ETHICS AND MEANING IN LIFE

16. Meaning and Morality   263
    TODD MAY

17. Meaning and Anti-Meaning in Life   277
    SVEN NYHOLM AND STEPHEN M. CAMPBELL

18. Forgiveness and Meaning in Life   292
    LUCY ALLAIS

19. Between Sisyphus's Rock and a Warm and Fuzzy Place: Procreative Ethics and the Meaning of Life   308
    RIVKA WEINBERG

20. Nature, Animals, and Meaning in Life   324
    KATIE MCSHANE

PART V. PHILOSOPHICAL PSYCHOLOGY AND MEANING IN LIFE

21. The Experience of Meaning 343
    ANTTI KAUPPINEN

22. Desire and Meaning in Life: Towards a Theory 356
    NOMY ARPALY

23. Love and Meaning in Life 371
    ALAN H. GOLDMAN

24. Meaning in Life and Phoniness 385
    IDDO LANDAU

25. Gratitude and Meaning in Life 401
    TONY MANELA

26. Psychological Approaches to Life's Meaning 416
    ROY F. BAUMEISTER

PART VI. LIVING MEANINGFULLY: CHALLENGES AND PROSPECTS

27. Pessimism, Optimism, and Meaning in Life 431
    DAVID BENATAR

28. The Rationality of Suicide and the Meaningfulness of Life 445
    MICHAEL CHOLBI

29. Suffering and Meaning in Life 461
    MICHAEL S. BRADY

30. Paradoxes and Meaning in Life 475
    SAUL SMILANSKY

31. Education and Meaning in Life 492
    DORET DE RUYTER AND ANDERS SCHINKEL

32. Virtual Reality and the Meaning of Life 508
    JOHN DANAHER

Index 525

Contributors

Lucy Allais works jointly as Professor of Philosophy at the University of the Witwatersrand, Johannesburg, and at Johns Hopkins University. Her publications include 'Wiping the Slate Clean: The Heart of Forgiveness' (*Philosophy and Public Affairs*, 2008), 'Retributive Justice, Restorative Justice, and the South African Truth and Reconciliation Commission' (*Philosophy and Public Affairs*, 2011), and *Manifest Reality: Kant's Idealism and His Realism* (Oxford University Press, 2015).

Nomy Arpaly is a Professor of Philosophy at Brown University. Her publications include *Unprincipled Virtue* (Oxford University Press, 2003) and *In Praise of Desire* (Oxford University Press, 2013) with Timothy Schroeder.

Roy F. Baumeister is a social/personality psychologist and currently president-elect of the International Positive Psychology Association. He has roughly 700 publications, including forty-two books, one of which, *Meanings of Life* (Guilford, 1991), has been cited over 3,500 times in the scientific literature.

David Benatar is Professor of Philosophy at the University of Cape Town, South Africa. His books include *Better Never to Have Been* (Oxford University Press, 2006), *The Second Sexism* (Wiley-Blackwell, 2012), and *The Human Predicament* (Oxford University Press, 2017).

Guy Bennett-Hunter is Executive Editor of the *Expository Times* at the University of Edinburgh, UK. He is the author of *Ineffability and Religious Experience* (Routledge, 2014). Dr Bennett-Hunter is also a degree-qualified psychologist and works clinically as a Psychological Well-Being Practitioner in forensic settings in the northeast of England.

Gwen Bradford is Associate Professor of Philosophy at Rice University, USA. She is the author of *Achievement* (Oxford University Press, 2015), which was awarded the American Philosophical Association Book Prize, as well as various articles about value and well-being.

Michael S. Brady is Professor of Philosophy and Head of the School of Humanities at the University of Glasgow. His research centres on the philosophy of emotion and its links with moral philosophy and epistemology. He is the author of *Emotional Insight: The Epistemic Role of Emotional Experience* (Oxford University Press, 2013), *Suffering and Virtue* (Oxford University Press, 2018), and *Emotion: The Basics* (Routledge, 2018). He has edited six volumes and published numerous journal articles and book chapters.

Stephen M. Campbell is an Assistant Professor of Philosophy at Bentley University. His publications include 'Anti-Meaning and Why It Matters' (*Journal of the American Philosophical Association*, 2015) with Sven Nyholm, 'The Complicated Relationship of Disability and Well-Being' (*Kennedy Institute of Ethics Journal*, 2017) with Joseph Stramondo, and 'Well-Being and the Good Death' (*Ethical Theory and Moral Practice*, 2020).

Michael Cholbi is Professor of Philosophy at the University of Edinburgh. His books include *Suicide: The Philosophical Dimensions* (Broadview, 2011), *Exploring the Philosophy of Death and Dying: Classical and Contemporary Perspectives* (Routledge, 2020), and *Grief: A Philosophical Guide* (Princeton University Press, 2022).

John Cottingham is Professor Emeritus of Philosophy at the University of Reading and an Honorary Fellow of St John's College, Oxford. His books include *The Rationalists* (Oxford University Press, 1988), *Philosophy and the Good Life* (Cambridge University Press, 1998), *On the Meaning of Life* (Routledge, 2003), *The Spiritual Dimension* (Cambridge University Press, 2005), *Cartesian Reflections* (Oxford University Press, 2008), *Philosophy of Religion: Towards a More Humane Approach* (Cambridge University Press, 2014), and *In Search of the Soul* (Princeton University Press, 2020). From 1993 to 2012 he was Editor of the journal *Ratio*.

John Danaher is a Senior Lecturer in the School of Law, NUI Galway, Ireland. He is the coeditor of *Robot Sex: Social and Ethical Implications* (MIT Press, 2017), the author of *Automation and Utopia: Human Flourishing in a World Without Work* (Harvard University Press, 2019), and the co-author of *A Citizen's Guide to Artificial Intelligence* (MIT Press, 2021).

Alan H. Goldman is Kenan Professor of Humanities and Professor of Philosophy Emeritus at the College of William & Mary. He is the author of nine books, the latest being *Reasons from Within* (Oxford University Press, 2010), *Philosophy and the Novel* (Oxford University Press, 2013) and *Life's Values* (Oxford University Press, 2019).

P. M. S. Hacker was a tutorial fellow of St John's College, Oxford from 1966 to 2006, since when he has been an Emeritus Research Fellow. He holds an Honorary Professorship at the Institute of Neuroscience at University College, London. He has published twenty-four books and 165 papers, has written extensively on the philosophy of Wittgenstein, on philosophy and cognitive neuroscience (e.g. *Philosophical Foundations of Neuroscience*, Wiley/Blackwell, 2003, 2nd edition 2021, with M. R. Bennett), and has recently completed a tetralogy on human nature: *Human Nature: The Categorial Framework* (2007), *The Intellectual Powers* (2013), *The Emotions* (2018), and *The Moral Powers* (Wiley/Blackwell, 2021).

Jens Johansson is Professor of Practical Philosophy at Uppsala University, Sweden. He has published essays on a wide range of topics, including the evil of death, the nature of harm, and personal identity, and co-edited *The Oxford Handbook of Philosophy of Death* (Oxford University Press, 2013) with Ben Bradley and Fred Feldman.

Guy Kahane is Professor of Moral Philosophy at the University of Oxford. He is also Fellow and Tutor in Philosophy at Pembroke College, Oxford, and Director of Studies at the Uehiro Centre for Practical Ethics. Kahane's publications include 'Should We Want God to Exist?' (*Philosophy and Phenomenological Research*, 2011), 'Our Cosmic Insignificance' (*Nous*, 2014), 'If Nothing Matters' (*Nous*, 2017) and 'Is the Universe Indifferent? Should We Care?' (*Philosophy and Phenomenological Research*, 2021).

Antti Kauppinen is Professor of Practical Philosophy at the University of Helsinki. His publications include 'Meaningfulness and Time' (*Philosophy and Phenomenological Research*, 2012), 'Meaning and Happiness' (*Philosophical Topics*, 2013), and 'Against Seizing the Day' (*Oxford Studies in Normative Ethics*, 2021).

Iddo Landau is a Professor of Philosophy at the University of Haifa, Israel. His publications include 'The Meaning of Life *sub specie aeternitatis*' (*Australasian Journal of Philosophy*, 2011) and *Finding Meaning in an Imperfect World* (Oxford University Press, 2017).

Steven Luper is a Professor of Philosophy at Trinity University. His publications include *Philosophy of Death* (Cambridge University Press, 2009) and *Mortal Objects* (Cambridge University Press, 2022).

Tony Manela is Assistant Professor of Philosophy at Siena College. He is the author of several articles on gratitude, including 'Gratitude and Appreciation' (*American Philosophical Quarterly*, 2016), 'Negative Feelings of Gratitude' (*The Journal of Value Inquiry*, 2016), and 'Gratitude to Nature' (*Environmental Values*, 2018).

Ned Markosian is a Professor of Philosophy at the University of Massachusetts Amherst. His publications include 'How Fast Does Time Pass?' (*Philosophy and Phenomenological Research*, 1993), 'Simples' (*Australasian Journal of Philosophy*, 1998), 'A Defense of Presentism' (*Oxford Studies in Metaphysics*, 2004), 'Rossian Minimalism' (*Journal of Ethics and Social Philosophy*, 2009), 'Two Puzzles about Mercy' (*Philosophical Quarterly*, 2013), 'A Spatial Approach to Mereology' (in Kleinschmidt, ed., *Mereology and Location*, Oxford University Press, 2014), 'The Right Stuff' (*Australasian Journal of Philosophy*, 2015), and 'Sideways Music' (*Analysis*, 2020).

T. J. Mawson is Dean, Edgar Jones Fellow, and Tutor in Philosophy at St Peter's College, University of Oxford. His publications include *God and the Meanings of Life* (Bloomsbury, 2016) and *Monotheism and the Meaning of Life* (Cambridge University Press, 2019).

Todd May is Class of 1941 Memorial Professor of the Humanities at Clemson University. He is the author of sixteen books of philosophy, including *A Significant Life: Human Meaning in a Silent Universe* (University of Chicago Press, 2015) and *A Decent Life: Morality for the Rest of Us* (University of Chicago Press, 2019).

Katie McShane is a Professor of Philosophy at Colorado State University. Her research is in environmental ethics and ethical theory, with special attention to the place of environmental concerns in theories of value. Her publications include 'Anthropocentrism vs. Nonanthropocentrism: Why Should We Care?' (*Environmental Values*, 2007), 'Anthropocentrism in Climate Ethics and Policy' (*Midwest Studies in Philosophy*, 2016), and 'Against Etiological Function Accounts of Interests' (*Synthese* 2021).

Thaddeus Metz is a Professor of Philosophy at the University of Pretoria, South Africa. His recent publications on life's meaning include *God, Soul and the Meaning of Life* (Cambridge University Press, 2019), 'The Meaning of Life' in T. Crane and E. Mason, eds., *Routledge Encyclopedia of Philosophy* (2020), and 'Supernaturalist Analytic Existentialism' (*International Journal for Philosophy of Religion*, 2021).

Sven Nyholm is Assistant Professor of Philosophical Ethics at Utrecht University. His publications include *Revisiting Kant's Universal Law and Humanity Formulas* (De Gruyter, 2015) and *Humans and Robots: Ethics, Agency, and Anthropomorphism* (Rowman and Littlefield, 2020).

Derk Pereboom is the Susan Linn Sage Professor in the Philosophy Department at Cornell University. He is the author of *Living without Free Will* (Cambridge University Press, 2001), *Consciousness and the Prospects of Physicalism* (Oxford University Press, 2011), *Free Will, Agency, and Meaning in Life* (Oxford University Press, 2014), and *Wrongdoing and the Moral Emotions* (Oxford University Press, 2021).

Doret de Ruyter is Professor of Philosophy of Education at the University of Humanistic Studies in Utrecht, the Netherlands. She is the current president of the Association for Moral Education and Assistant Editor of *The Journal of Philosophy of Education* and of *Theory and Research in Education*. Two of her recent publications are 'Human Flourishing as an Aim of Education' (*Oxford Research Encyclopedia of Education*, 2020) with Lynne Wolbert, and 'Equipping Students with an Ethical Compass' (*Ethics and Education*, 2021) with Lieke van Stekelenburg and Wouter Sanderse.

Marya Schechtman is Professor of Philosophy and an affiliate of the Laboratory of Integrative Neuroscience at the University of Illinois, Chicago. She is the author of *The Constitution of Selves* (Cornell University Press, 1996) and *Staying Alive: Personal Identity, Practical Concerns, and the Unity of a Life* (Oxford University Press, 2014).

Anders Schinkel is Associate Professor of Philosophy of Education at the Vrije Universiteit, Amsterdam, the Netherlands. His publications include *Wonder and Education: On the Educational Importance of Contemplative Wonder* (Bloomsbury, 2021), the edited volume *Wonder, Education, and Human Flourishing: Theoretical, Empirical, and Practical Perspectives* (VU University Press, 2020), and articles on wonder, moral education, environmental education, filial obligations, moral luck, animal ethics, and other issues.

Saul Smilansky is a Professor at the Department of Philosophy, University of Haifa, Israel. He works primarily on normative and applied ethics, the free will problem, and meaning in life. He is the author of *Free Will and Illusion* (Oxford University Press, 2000), *10 Moral Paradoxes* (Blackwell, 2007), and nearly one hundred papers in philosophical journals and edited collections.

Galen Strawson holds the President's Chair of Philosophy at the University of Texas at Austin. His books include *Mental Reality* (MIT Press, 1994) and *Selves* (Oxford University Press, 2009). His most recent books are *The Subject of Experience* (Oxford University Press, 2017) and *Things That Bother Me* (New York Review Books, 2018).

Frans Svensson is a Senior Lecturer of Philosophy at the University of Gothenburg, Sweden. His publications include 'Regimenting Reasons' (*Theoria*, 2005) with Jonas Olson, 'Objections to Virtue Ethics' (*The Oxford Handbook of Virtue*, 2018) with Jens Johansson, and 'Descartes on the Highest Good: Concepts and Conceptions' (*American Catholic Philosophical Quarterly*, 2019). He is currently working on a monograph on the ethical thought of René Descartes.

Paul Thagard is Distinguished Professor of Philosophy Emeritus at the University of Waterloo, Canada. His books include *The Brain and the Meaning of Life* (Princeton University Press, 2010), *Natural Philosophy* (Oxford University Press, 2019), *Bots and Beasts: What Makes Machines, Animals, and People Smart?* (MIT Press, 2021), and *Balance: How It Works, Why It Fails, and What It Means* (Columbia University Press, 2022).

Rivka Weinberg is Professor of Philosophy at Scripps College, Claremont, CA. She is the author of *The Risk of a Lifetime: How, When, and Why Procreation May Be Permissible* (Oxford University Press, 2015). She specializes in ethical and metaphysical issues regarding birth, death, and meaning, and is currently working on a book about death, time, and meaning.

Erik J. Wielenberg is Professor of Philosophy at DePauw University. His publications include *Value and Virtue in a Godless Universe* (Cambridge University Press, 2005), *God and the Reach of Reason* (Cambridge University Press, 2012), and *Robust Ethics: The Metaphysics and Epistemology of Godless Normative Realism* (Oxford University Press, 2014).

INTRODUCTION

IDDO LANDAU

The philosophy of meaning in life[1] has roots in spiritual and religious movements in almost all cultures. Many of the issues dealt with in these movements, such as human vocation, the life worth living, our relation to what is 'greater' than us, and our encounters with suffering and with death, are also discussed (even if in a different manner) in the philosophy of meaning in life.[2] Likewise, many discussions in Western philosophy from its early stages, especially on the good life, can be interpreted as having to do—among other issues—with meaning in life. Meaning in life, or the lack thereof, received much attention in the Romantic movement and, later, in pessimist thought and existentialist philosophy, also becoming a prominent theme in many literary works. In analytic philosophy, however, elaborate discussion of meaning in life is a fairly recent phenomenon. Although there are some early and powerful works on meaning in life by important analytic philosophers such as Russell ([1903] 1985), Schlick ([1927] 1979), Ayer ([1947] 2000), Baier ([1957] 2000), and Hare ([1957] 1972), analytic philosophical research on this topic has propagated only in very recent decades (Metz 2021).

Several possible explanations come to mind for why meaning in life is a young, even if quickly developing, field in analytic philosophy. One is that the excited interest in meaning in life on the part of Romanticism, pessimism, and existentialism dissuaded

---

[1] The expression 'meaning of life', which came into use in the eighteenth century (Landau 1997, 263), has for a long time been employed to relate both to individual people's lives and to the existence of the human race at large as being meaningful. According to a now commonly used terminology, however, meaning *in* life relates to individual people's lives as being meaningful, while meaning *of* life relates to the existence of the human species at large as meaningful. Still, some scholars prefer to use *meaning of life* for both concepts, as was common earlier, or to use other terms entirely. Since most of the essays in this volume focus on meaning in individual human lives, I use *meaning in life* both in the title of this *Handbook* and throughout this Introduction. But much of what is said in the next few paragraphs also holds for the meaning *of* life.

[2] Two very early texts with parts that relate particularly clearly to what we would today call meaning in life are the Epic of Gilgamesh (late second millennium BCE) and Ecclesiastes (ca. 450–200 BCE).

rather than encouraged analytic philosophical discussion of the topic, since meaning in life had become associated with philosophical methodologies from which many analytic philosophers wanted to sharply distinguish their own philosophizing. This was unfortunate, because meaning in life—like love, causality, justice, truth, the mind, progress, and most other philosophical topics—can be discussed both non-analytically and analytically. The prominence of meaning in life in literary works may have had a similar effect, by associating the topic with the sort of emotional and artistic expressiveness that many analytic philosophers wanted to distance from the sober, rational way of philosophizing they espoused. Again, I think this is regrettable since (like many other topics) meaning in life can profit from both artistic and philosophical (including analytic philosophical) attention. Some analytic philosophers may also have refrained from discussing meaning in life as a notion on its own because they missed the distinction between meaning in life and well-being, the happy life, or the flourishing life. That distinction is important: many would agree, for example, that some of the concentration camp inmates that Frankl (1985, 86–98) discusses did succeed in maintaining meaningful lives in the camps notwithstanding the harsh suffering they experienced, although theirs were not, of course, happy lives, flourishing lives, or lives of well-being. Since the distinction is easy to miss (and still requires philosophical attention in order to be recognized), some authors may have satisfied themselves with thinking about the flourishing life or the happy life, failing to see that meaning in life is a distinct topic of its own. Some psychological factors may have been at work here as well. Some of the philosophical discussion of meaning in life touches on questions that may cause psychological discomfort, such as whether life can be meaningful in the face of our eventual death and annihilation, whether our minuteness in comparison to the cosmos renders our lives meaningless, what the goal of our lives might be, and whether we have wasted our lives. Moreover, some philosophical discussions in this field are blatantly pessimistic, again leading to uneasiness. These factors, too, may have led some people to prefer to discuss other topics instead, contributing to the delayed emergence of meaning in life as a research topic in analytic philosophy.

Nevertheless, the analytic philosophical discussion of meaning in life has by now become a thriving field of research. I predict that it will continue to develop, not only because so many interesting topics in it are still waiting to be explored, but also because future technological and environmental changes, posing both great opportunities for enhancing meaning and serious threats to maintaining it, are likely to force us to think much more about meaning in life.

It is my hope that this *Handbook* will not only contribute significantly to the philosophical literature on meaning in life but also motivate future research. The authors represented here aim to survey the literature on the topics they discuss while arguing for their own position. Each chapter breaks new ground, and some of them discuss issues that have never been dealt with before within the research on meaning in life. Many of them discuss the relation between other philosophical topics and meaning in life, showing how they are relevant to each other.

The chapters of this volume are arranged in six parts, according to their interconnecting themes. Some chapters could have been placed into more than one part, and making that decision was to a certain degree arbitrary, but I hope that the divisions I have made will help readers to explore the *Handbook*. The following are short summaries of each of the thirty-two chapters.

PART I: UNDERSTANDING MEANING IN LIFE

Chapter 1: The Concept of Life's Meaning

In the opening chapter of this *Handbook*, Thaddeus Metz discusses what might be called 'the standard view' (in modern analytic discussions) of what makes life meaningful and addresses five challenges to this view. The standard view focuses on individual human lives and their intentional actions that are of high intrinsic value. One challenge to this view suggests that some non-human animals, too, can have meaningful lives. Metz accepts that, in light of this challenge, the standard view should be revised to a degree (for another discussion of this issue see McShane, Chapter 20 of the *Handbook*). A second challenge suggests that not only individual lives, but also organizations, communities, or the human race at large, can have meaningful existence. Here, too, Metz holds that the standard view should be somewhat revised in response. He accepts that some organizations and communities can be seen as having meaningful existence, although he does not think that this is also the case for the human race at large. According to a third challenge, meaning in life has to do primarily with intelligibility or 'making sense', rather than with value. Metz argues that this suggested revision of the standard view should not be accepted. Relatedly, a fourth challenge rejects the view that meaningful lives have to do with positive value, allowing that they could also be of neutral or negative value. Metz presents reasons for also resisting this proposal. Finally, Metz accepts the suggestion that everyday meaning should be distinguished from great meaning (the distinction is especially relevant to the naturalism/supernaturalism debate, since many supernaturalists hold that the spiritual realm is necessary for attaining great meaning in life).

Chapter 2: Subjectivism and Objectivism about Meaning in Life

Jens Johansson and Frans Svensson defend subjectivism about meaning in life—hitherto the less popular alternative in modern analytic discussions. After clarifying the terms they will be using, they point to difficulties in objectivism, focusing on the lack of connection between what (according to objectivism) contributes meaning to life and the attitudes of the person whose meaning in life is enhanced. Johansson and Svensson also argue that hybridism is implausibly exclusivist in holding that activities that have no or only small objective value, such as solving crossword puzzles, can't enhance meaning, even in the lives of people who find these activities deeply fulfilling and rewarding. In defending subjectivism, the authors first answer the epiphany objection, which claims that subjectivism cannot well explain cases in which one realizes that one's life to date has been meaningless. The authors reply that epiphanies also can be made sense of under subjectivism. For example, a pure subjectivist who believes that her love of God made her life meaningful may discover that she was mistaken in thinking that she loved God. Another objection to subjectivism is that it implies that activities that clearly do not make life meaningful should be seen as making it so. Among the five points they raise in reply to this objection, Johansson and Svensson emphasize the difference between meaningfulness and, for example, aesthetic or moral value. Further, they distinguish between different types of positive attitudes that subjectivists may take to make life meaningful. Johansson and Svensson suggest that these and other considerations show subjectivism to be less vulnerable to criticism than are objectivism and hybridism.

Chapter 3: Achievement and Meaning in Life

Gwen Bradford, who presupposes hybridism, focuses on a central element in the objective aspect of meaning in life, namely achievement. Bradford examines cases (such as the one Mill describes in his *Autobiography*) in which, after attaining an achievement of great objective worth, one surprisingly experiences *less* fulfilment than that experienced before the achievement was attained, or even no fulfilment at all. To cope with this problem, Bradford focuses on what she calls self-propagating goals, that is, goals that expand and develop as we progress toward them, thus allowing continuous challenge. Completing such goals is not only technically impossible but also unimaginable. Bradford carefully analyses the self-propagating structure and presents examples of such goals in, among others, the areas of knowledge and art. She copes with objections such as that it is unlikely for achievements to be more meaningful the longer they drag on, that it is irrational to adopt goals that one knows one will never achieve, that self-propagating goals do not allow real progress toward achievement, and that a series of discrete non-self-propagating goals would be as good as a self-propagating goal. Bradford also explains why self-propagating goals are a source of superlative meaning, which leads her to argue that more spheres of human activity than commonly thought allow superlative meaning—it can be found not only in art, knowledge, religion, and political activity, but also in more 'mundane' spheres such as parenting, friendship, farming, homemaking, or bodybuilding. Bradford also notes other important factors, such as the independent value of the activities in question, that influence the degree of meaning in an achievement.

Chapter 4: Narrativity and Meaning in Life

Galen Strawson distinguishes, first, between meaning *of* life and meaning *in* life (he understands these terms differently than is common in the field). The reply to the question 'what is the meaning of life?' is, in Strawson's view, that life has no meaning, while the reply to the question 'what is meaning in life?' is that a necessary and sufficient condition for having a meaningful life is to have an interesting life. Strawson differentiates between meaning in life in general (which needn't be of positive value) and good meaning in life, or good interest, which is of positive value (or at least cannot involve doing anything seriously morally bad). He examines the relation between having a narrative attitude towards life, that is, seeing one's life as having the form of a story or several stories, on the one hand, and, on the other, meaning in life in general and good meaning in life. Strawson is critical of narrativist attitudes towards meaning in life: an interesting life needn't include narrativity, and a life in which there is narrativity needn't be interesting. Thus, narrativity and interest, and therefore narrativity and meaning in life (including good meaning in life), are independent of each other. Narrativity can either contribute to interest (and thus to meaning in life) or decrease it. Seeing one's life narratively, as having the form of a story or several stories, or finding coherence and intelligibility in life, often involves falsification, fantasy, self-deception, and self-alienation. Further, Strawson argues, seeing life as a narrative is natural for some people but unnatural for others. Even when seeing life as a narrative enhances (good) meaning in life, it is only one form, or one source, of such meaning.

Chapter 5: Meaningfulness and Importance

Guy Kahane takes the typical features of meaning to be purposiveness toward valuable, not merely instrumental, goals; transcending in a conscious, engaged way one's mere animal nature to what is external to or larger than oneself; meriting pride and elevation in oneself as well as admiration from others; and perhaps having a subjective attraction toward the valuable goals one engages with and keeping, in this engagement, to morally permissible means. To take something to be important is to take it to merit attention because it makes a significantly large difference (always in comparison to other things). Kahane points out that the extensions of 'meaning' and 'importance' do not completely overlap and the concepts differ. For example, causing, in a non-engaged way, a large difference to which one is not subjectively attracted may bestow importance without bestowing meaning. Likewise, a life dedicated to lovingly raising a family, intense study, or the enjoyment of poetry may be a meaningful life without being an important one. Kahane does, however, point to various ways in which the terms do relate, including that a high degree of importance augments meaning and that superlative meaning involves importance. He also addresses the tension between, on the one hand, the claim that things are important only relative to the contexts they are in and, on the other hand, the claims that importance has its own value and that importance enhances meaning. Further, he considers why, in the face of the relation between importance and meaning, pursuing importance is often seen unfavourably, while pursuing meaning is considered favourably. After critically examining several possible explanations, Kahane suggests that this radical difference in attitudes toward pursuing importance and pursuing meaning may be unjustified.

Chapter 6: The Meaning of Life and Death

Steven Luper starts his discussion by clarifying the relation between meaning and welfare (or well-being). He examines the view that meaning and welfare are similar and argues that they are nevertheless distinct. The distinction between them has to do in part with *achievementism*—Luper's theory of meaning as consisting in people's achieving aims to which they freely and competently devote their lives. This account coheres well with many people's readiness to forgo some elements of their welfare (such as happiness, friendship) in order to attain achievements to which they dedicate their lives. It also explains why animals are not commonly seen as having meaningful lives: Luper points out that animals do not *devote* their lives to a goal and do not *aim* for it. Further, he shows how his account relates to other notions often associated with meaning, such as purpose, direction, identity, and devotion. Luper's characterization of meaning leads him to hold that what gives life positive meaning gives death negative meaning. The reverse is also true: what gives life negative meaning gives death positive meaning. Hence, dying need not undermine meaning. Luper argues that if continued living diminishes meaning in life—when life has negative meaning and, thus, death has positive meaning—people have a reason not to go on living. This implies that suicide, too, does not have to diminish meaning in life, and does not indicate that one's life prior to one's suicide has not been meaningful (Luper's views here are in agreement with Cholbi's in Chapter 28 of this *Handbook*).

PART II: MEANING IN LIFE, SCIENCE, AND METAPHYSICS

Chapter 7: The Relevance of Neuroscience to Meaning in Life

The first two chapters in Part II present opposite views on the relevance of neuroscience to meaning in life. In Chapter 7, Paul Thagard argues that neuroscience can contribute both to the theoretical understanding of life's meaning and to people's practical efforts to enhance meaning in their lives. Thagard criticizes what he sees as Bennett and Hacker's view of philosophy as only a conceptual enterprise, distinct from science. He argues that when characterizing meaning in life we should not seek necessary and sufficient conditions but, rather, examples, typical features, and explanations of the concept, which would allow neurological data to be relevant. Thagard also points out that the notions that psychological discussions of meaning in life commonly employ—coherence, purpose, and value—can profit from neuroscientific explanations. He contends that arguments based on the naturalistic fallacy are problematic and criticizes what Bennett and Hacker have come to call 'the mereological fallacy', that is, the fallacy of attributing psychological attributes (such as pain, emotion, meaning) not to human beings but to body parts such as the brain. Objectivist claims about meaning in life can be based on the fact that people have psychological needs, such as autonomy, competence, relatedness, and beneficence. Such needs have a neural basis, and when they are frustrated, the brain changes and its functioning is damaged. Meaning in life has to do with sensing meaning, which is an emotional reaction that is influenced by neurological events. In Thagard's view, since meaning in life is not a purely philosophical topic, it is unfortunate that psychologists, philosophers, and neuroscientists work separately (for a somewhat similar view about psychology and philosophy, see Baumeister, in Chapter 26 of this *Handbook*), and he recommends that they cooperate more, presenting examples of ways in which such cooperation may be advantageous.

Chapter 8: Can Neuroscience Shed Light on What Constitutes a Meaningful Life?

The opposing view to Thagard's is presented in Chapter 8, where Peter Hacker argues that neuroscience cannot contribute to the understanding of what a meaningful life is. Hacker first clarifies his notion of meaning and meaninglessness in life, pointing out, among other issues, that many of the purposes people pursue are too unimportant to impart meaning to their lives. Meaning in life differs from merely subjective, illusory sensations. The imparting of meaning should be persistent, subsume a sufficient number of subordinate purposes, be of sufficiently high value, and go beyond merely selfish concerns. Indeed, it may well involve self-sacrificial behaviour that undermines one's own flourishing. People can find meaning in, among other things, creative labour, self-realization, developing their talents or capacities, wonder and pleasure in art or in nature, and the manner in which they meet unavoidable suffering or adversity. Hacker argues that, among other errors, those who hold that neurology can teach us what constitutes meaning in life commit the mereological fallacy in ascribing to the brain psychological concepts that make sense only when ascribed to whole human beings. Those holding that neurology can teach us what constitutes meaning in life also wrongly assume that all psychological events must be caused by corresponding representations in the brain and that deep philosophical problems can be solved by discoveries in neuroscience. Furthermore, they equivocate different senses of 'representation', sometimes taking it to signify symbolic representation and at other times to signify a causal correlate. Another mistake is that psychological attributes are taken to be events and states, so that no account is taken of potentialities. Directly engaging with Thagard's work, Hacker argues, among other points, that it is a mistake to see causal explanations as superior to other Aristotelian ones, or to hold that the only alternative to Cartesian dualism is neural naturalism.

Chapter 9: Personal Identity and Meaning in Life

Marya Schechtman explores four ways to think about personal identity and its relation to meaning. According to the first, the *chosen-self view*, people constitute their identity by choosing and committing themselves to certain values and behaviours. These core commitments establish people's personal identity and, by giving their lives purpose and direction, can be seen also as making their lives meaningful. According to the second, the *given-self view*, there is a group of characteristics and values that are natural to people and should be seen as their true identity. Discovering their authentic, genuine selves and following them (or their valuable aspects) allow people to live meaningfully. According to the third, the *episodic view*, some people's lives do not have a set of coherent, diachronically stable commitments (or other qualities) that form a unified self of the type the first two views call for (Strawson elaborates on this view in his Chapter 4 in this *Handbook*). Imposing unified concepts on such lives may reduce options, produce anxiety, and prevent people from being fully present. For such people, meaningfulness will be tied to a rejection of the notions espoused by the first two views and of the notion of personal identity itself. The last type of view Schechtman explores is the one she supports, which is intermediate between the first two (which seem to her too strong) and Strawson's (which seems to her too weak). This view is based on the unity of biological human life. Schechtman discusses its strengths and weaknesses and relates it to a non-traditional notion of meaning in life according to which all lives are meaningful just by virtue of being the singular, irreplaceable events that they are.

Chapter 10: Hard Determinism and Meaning in Life

Many have taken free will, at least in some form and under some understanding, to be necessary for considering life as meaningful and, thus, have considered hard determinism to rule out life's meaning. Derk Pereboom argues, first, against free will, presenting reasons for rejecting both libertarianism and compatibilism. But he argues that life can be seen as meaningful even under hard determinism. He shows, for example, that achievement, based on maintaining the causal efficacy of our deliberation and choice, which are important for a meaningful life, can also make sense in a hard determinist universe (even if this sense of achievement is somewhat diminished in comparison to that under libertarianism). Likewise, love, another important component of meaningful lives, does not presuppose that the beloved must have free will (as can be seen, for example, in parents' love for their babies). Pereboom also discusses ways of determining the lover's love that are not objectionable. Regarding personal relationships in general, he disagrees with the claim that resentment and indignation, which assume moral responsibility that requires desert and free will, are as central to personal relationships as P. F. Strawson famously argues them to be. According to Pereboom, other emotions, which do not presuppose free will, such as moral protest (without anger), or feeling hurt, shocked, disappointed, and morally sad, are also available for personal engagement. He further points out that, according to some views, finding life meaningful has much to do with finding one's place and role in the plan of the universe (for example, in Stoicism), which again does not presuppose free will and is available, in different versions, not only in theistic but also in modern, non-theistic understandings of the plan or the development of human history.

Chapter 11: Meaning in Life and the Nature of Time

Ned Markosian discusses two central theories of time. According to the *static theory of time*, time is in many ways similar to space. Moreover, time integrates with space into a four-dimensional manifold that is called 'spacetime', and physical objects have different temporal parts at different times. Notions such as 'the present moment', 'being past', 'being future', and 'next year' are just part of our subjective perception of time, not the way time really, objectively, is. According to the *dynamic theory of time*, on the other hand, time differs from space and does not integrate with it into a unified 'spacetime' manifold. Physical objects do not have different temporal parts at different times but, when present, are wholly present. The passage of time is real and objective so that some times are past, present, or future. But according to many important theories of meaning in life, meaning has much to do with striving for, or taking action toward, attaining some goals. Such understandings of meaning in life are difficult to make sense of under the static theory of time. The dynamic theory of time, however, is consistent with such understandings of life's meaning. Markosian argues that this is a consideration in favour of the dynamic theory of time. Supporters of the static theory may try to show how it can still cohere with central understandings of meaning in life. But doing so, Markosian claims, will be difficult. Another option for supporters of the static theory is to argue that life is meaningless. Such an argument, however, would differ from those presented by many pessimists about meaning in life, since their arguments, too, often presuppose the dynamic theory of time.

Part III: Meaning in Life and Religion

Chapter 12: The Meaning of Life and Transcendence

John Cottingham presents a distinction between, on the one hand, *transcendentist* perspectives, according to which satisfactory meaningfulness cannot be found only in the human and naturalist spheres, which it is part of being human to long to transcend, and, on the other hand, *immanentist* perspectives, according to which satisfactory meaningfulness may be found in the human and naturalist spheres alone. He argues that life cannot be fully and sufficiently meaningful if this longing for transcendence is not addressed, since the many manifestations of our incompleteness arouse anxiety and yearning for something complete. Because of our limitedness, we cannot answer this yearning only rationally; we can, however, answer it through various spiritual practices that allow us to relate to this yearning not anxiously, but through an expression of joyous hope of reaching the transcendent, complete meaning. These practices are performative rather than theoretical, and express trust, love, and commitment. Cottingham then presents many possible objections to his view and to the practices to which it points: Do they not try to produce meaning where in fact there is none? Do the practices show that there is an overall meaning to human life, or only that it would be good if there were one? Can't the urge toward transcendence be satisfied as helpfully in other, naturalistic ways (for example, by doing good deeds for the sake of other people, participating in innovative and momentous projects, enjoying beauty, and learning)? After explicating these and other objections, Cottingham copes with them one by one to defend the view that lives cannot be satisfactorily meaningful if limited to the immanent sphere, when the urge for transcendence is not acknowledged and addressed.

Chapter 13: Atheism and Meaning in Life

Eric J. Wielenberg argues that life could be meaningful even if there were neither God nor an afterlife. He starts from the notion of a meaningless life and considers what would make it meaningful, identifying features such as love, the reduction of unnecessary suffering in the world, the enhancement of personal psychological harmony and social harmony, responding to one's own suffering with courage and dignity, and (following Metz) orienting one's rationality toward fundamental conditions of the human experience. Wielenberg argues that we would find meaningful lives in which such features are plentiful without any reference to God or an afterlife, which suggests that God and an afterlife are not necessary conditions for having meaningful lives. He accepts that religiousness contributes to meaning, but suggests that it does so because many religions encourage membership in communities, and it is the latter that makes life meaningful. Wielenberg then examines and counters arguments that purport to show that lives cannot be meaningful if there is no God or afterlife, such as that without God or an afterlife all lives eventually end the same way and have no ultimate meaning; that, if there is no God, human lives and the existence of humanity as a whole do not lead to an ultimate goal; that without God and an afterlife, our lives have no infinite meaning and thus no meaning at all; and that without God, objective morality, or objective value in general, is unfounded or implausible. Wielenberg does accept, however, the weaker claim that life would be more meaningful if God and an afterlife were to exist. Thus, the theses that Wielenberg and Mawson (Chapter 14) defend in their chapters are not in conflict.

Chapter 14: Theism and Meaning in Life

T. J. Mawson focuses on one specific type of meaningfulness, namely significance of the valuable type, and defends the view that if God and an afterlife (as understood in the monotheistic traditions) exist, human life is more significant than if God and an afterlife do not exist. The reason for this is that if God and an afterlife exist, our lives have infinite significance, while if God and an afterlife do not exist, our lives can have only finite significance. Mawson argues that if significance is understood subjectively, then under atheism we are subjectively significant to some people for some time, while under theism we are also significant to them in the afterlife for eternity, as well as being significant to God for eternity. If significance is understood objectively, then if God and an afterlife exist, people's lives have infinite value, but they have only limited value if God and an afterlife do not exist. Mawson also discusses Kahane's argument that our lives are more significant under atheism because it implies that humans are the most valuable beings in the universe, while under theism our value is negligible in comparison to that of God. Mawson argues, among other points, that according to the Drake Equation it is probable that there are extraterrestrial beings that are superior to us in the universe, so that we are not the most valuable beings in it. Further, although people don't have much value in comparison to God, they do have much value in comparison to other biological species, and there are reasons for holding that people should be compared to the latter rather than the former. While presenting a beginning of what might be called a theory of comparisons, Mawson also uncovers and discusses many further assumptions and distinctions.

Chapter 15: Mysticism, Ritual, and the Meaning of Life

Guy Bennett-Hunter also discusses transcendence, insufficiency, and spiritual exercises, but in different ways from Cottingham. Bennett-Hunter focuses, from an existentialist-phenomenological perspective, on the mystical experience, or on ineffability, as what constitutes meaning of life and meaning in life. Relying on the work of David E. Cooper, Bennett-Hunter identifies ineffability as a transcendent reality that is inseparable from the events and objects of everyday life, including very mundane ones. Bennett-Hunter emphasizes that this is not a supernaturalist notion but one that transcends the supernaturalist–naturalist distinction, presenting an example from Hugo von Hofmannsthal of what would regularly be seen as a secular experience of ineffability. Thus, understanding meaning in life and meaning of life in terms of ineffability transcends and poses an alternative both to the naturalist and to the supernaturalist philosophical traditions. Likewise, understanding meaning of life and meaning in life through ineffability transcends the distinction between, and poses an alternative to, the subjectivist, objectivist, and hybridist traditional approaches. While explicating his understanding of ineffability and its relation to meaningful lives, Bennett-Hunter also has to cope with various difficulties, one of which is the need to incorporate an experience that transcends the subject–object dichotomy into human experience, which is based on this dichotomy. To address this, he employs an adaptation of Karl Jaspers's theory of ciphers, which are neither representations of the ineffable nor statements about it, and are subjective and objective at once. He gives special attention to rituals as ciphers of ineffability, but holds that both religious rituals and secular works of art can be seen as examples of ciphers and, thus, of experiencing ineffability.

PART IV: ETHICS AND MEANING IN LIFE

Chapter 16: Meaning and Morality

Todd May starts out by examining different aspects of the relation between meaning and morality. Since subjective morality seems implausible to him, he focuses on the relation between objective morality and either subjective or objective meaning. Elaborating on these notions, he argues that the relation between subjective meaning and objective morality is arbitrary. (Thus, May understands subjective meaning differently from Johansson and Svensson in their Chapter 2 and from Arpaly in her Chapter 22 in this *Handbook*.) The relation between objective morality and objective meaning, however, is not arbitrary (although May also distinguishes between lived or experienced relations and theoretical ones). Of these possible combinations, May focuses on the relation between objective morality and objective meaning, while critically engaging with some of Susan Wolf's views on the topic. Among other points, he notes that when discussing the distinction between morality and meaning, Wolf understands the former as a set of impersonal duties toward others; but understanding morality according to virtue ethics approaches would have rendered morality and meaning much closer. May's account of meaning (which is not presented as exhaustive of what makes life meaningful) focuses on what he calls narrative value—a positive value that may be seen as a theme of a sufficiently large segment of a person's life, such as adventurousness, spirituality, or loyalty. Narrative value and morality do not necessarily conflict, but the former is not always in the realm of the morally permissible, and there are cases in which there are tensions between the two. May presents examples that show that the relation between morality and narrative value in a life is determined not only by value, but also by context and by nuances in that life.

Chapter 17: Meaning and Anti-Meaning in Life

Sven Nyholm and Stephen M. Campbell—influenced by the work of Metz and others—suggest that in addition to seeing some lives as meaningful and others as meaningless, certain lives should be characterized as anti-meaningful, that is, as not only lacking any meaning (as *meaningless* may suggest), but as having the opposite quality to that of being meaningful. It would be odd, they argue, to characterize Hitler's life, for example, as just lacking in meaning; it was much worse than that in terms of meaning in life. If degrees of meaning were rated in numbers, Hitler's life would not be appropriately rated with a zero but, rather, with negative numbers. Nyholm and Campbell examine what might justify describing lives as anti-meaningful according to subjectivist, objectivist, and hybrid theories of meaning in life, and distinguish between what they call the *defeater model* and the *counterforce model* of anti-meaning. According to the defeater model, anti-meaning only has the function of offsetting or annulling (positive) meaning, but it does not pose a sphere of meaning on its own. According to the counterforce model, if the anti-meaningful aspects of a person's life outrank the meaningful ones, the person will have, all in all, an anti-meaningful life. While comparing the two models, Nyholm and Campbell also reply to Christopher Woodard's objection that there is no philosophical advantage in accepting the counterforce model of anti-meaning because it does not go beyond the already existing notion of moral badness. Among other points, Nyholm and Campbell emphasize that just noting the moral badness of some actions ignores the difference between the sphere of morality and the sphere of meaning in life, and how the former impacts the latter.

Chapter 18: Forgiveness and Meaning in Life

Lucy Allais, characterizing forgiveness as the release of someone from blame although the blame is seen as warranted, distinguishes between two main types of forgiveness. The first type, *conditional forgiveness*, requires that wrongdoers earn the forgiveness by actions that show that they deserve to be forgiven, such as apologizing, making amends, and proving they have changed. *Unconditional forgiveness* (or *gifted forgiveness*), on the other hand, can be granted independent of such actions. Allais sees both, and especially the latter, as relevant to meaning in life in a number of ways. Among other points she makes, forgiveness allows people to maintain relations of friendship and love, which are highly important for life's meaning, without giving up on what they take to be valuable. Further, forgiveness cuts across the distinction between objective and subjective meaning in life, as it requires both objective moral growth and certain actions, as well as subjective changes that have to do with blaming and caring. Forgiveness also coheres with non-perfectionist views of meaning in life, since it is based on accepting that good relations can be had with flawed people. Especially gifted forgiveness, which goes beyond wrongdoers' demonstration that they deserve to be forgiven, is practiced in trust and hope, viewing people as 'works in progress' that are still open to change, in contrast to the 'closed' way in which things are seen when in despair, which leads to seeing life as meaningless. Moreover, forgiving presupposes P. F. Strawson's *participant view*, which renders irrelevant Thomas Nagel's *view from nowhere* about life's meaning—a view that Nagel and others have taken to jeopardize both meaning in life and meaning of life.

Chapter 19: Between Sisyphus's Rock and a Warm and Fuzzy Place: Procreative Ethics and the Meaning of Life

Rivka Weinberg examines how procreation relates to three types of meaning: Everyday Meaning (the value and significance in our everyday lives in, for example, love, knowledge, and moral behaviour), Cosmic Meaning (our meaningful role in the cosmos), and Ultimate Meaning (the end-regarding justifying reason, or the point, of leading a life at all). She argues that procreation can enhance Everyday Meaning and Cosmic Meaning (Weinberg's views on Cosmic Meaning differ from those of Benatar, Chapter 27, and those of Mawson, Chapter 14, in this *Handbook*, while she seems to be in agreement with Kahane's views on Cosmic Meaning as expressed in his Chapter 5). But Weinberg holds that procreation cannot grant Ultimate Meaning, nor can it save people from Ultimate Meaninglessness. This raises the question of the relative importance of the three types of meaning. Weinberg reflects on the considerations relevant for deciding whether the Ultimate Meaninglessness of a prospective child's life overrides the positive Everyday Meaning and the Cosmic Meaning that procreation allows. She also critically examines the oft-heard view that adoption is a satisfactory (or superior) alternative to procreation. Among other considerations, she argues that not many children are available for adoption; that adoptees often cope with feelings of alienation and rejection; that it is painful for many parents to give up their child for adoption; and that the biological connection in non-adoptive parenthood is significant. Another criticism of procreation compares it to a Ponzi scheme, claiming that earlier procreators enhance meaning in their own lives by exploiting the last descendants in line, who will not be able to procreate. Weinberg points to several important differences between procreation and Ponzi schemes.

Chapter 20: Nature, Animals, and Meaning in Life

Katie McShane argues, first, that the natural world (and especially animals) can be an important source of meaning in human life and, second, that meaning in life is not restricted to human life alone: cognitively sophisticated, emotionally complex, social animals such as wolves and elephants lead lives that, according to many current theories of meaning in life, should be seen as meaningful. McShane is well aware that some theories can be interpreted as presenting standards according to which no animals could be considered as having meaningful lives. However, she points out that adopting such stricter standards would also exclude many human lives from being seen as meaningful. McShane also argues that many discussions of meaning in life are too human-centred. She distinguishes between, on the one hand, leading a meaningful life and, on the other hand, being aware that one is leading a meaningful life. She accepts that animals do not show awareness of the meaningfulness of their lives, but argues that if life is meaningful, this awareness is unnecessary. McShane also examines different subjectivist, objectivist, and hybrid theories of meaning in life, specifying which are consistent with the view that some animals, too, have meaningful lives, and which are not. She calls for a pluralistic understanding of the sources and forms of meaning in life, one in which not only great achievements such as creating excellent art or making important scientific discoveries, but also much more mundane activities such as nursing infants or watching the spring come, are taken to make life meaningful. (Thus, McShane's views here and Luper's views in his Chapter 6 in this *Handbook* differ. McShane's views are closer to those of Metz in his Chapter 1, but are still distinct from them.) McShane argues that this more pluralistic approach to meaning in life is both more plausible in itself and more suitable for conceiving some animals' lives as meaningful.

V: Philosophical Psychology and Meaning in Life

Chapter 21: The Experience of Meaning

For the sake of discussion, Antti Kauppinen brackets questions about the existence and nature of objective meaning in life. Kauppinen draws on philosophical and mostly psychological discussions to focus on three common dimensions of experiencing meaning in life—making sense, purpose, and significance—and then analyses them to specify their pertinent aspects for experiencing meaning. Among other points, Kauppinen relates 'making sense' to what he calls 'narrative justification', which has to do not only with explaining what one does, but also with justifying it. (Here Kauppinen's views are in some disagreement with Strawson's in his Chapter 4 in this *Handbook*.) Kauppinen notes that one can find life intelligible while still feeling that it is meaningless, and suggests that the relevant issue for finding life meaningful is whether one's activities contribute to something one considers worthwhile. The 'making sense' dimension of the experience of meaning is the opposite of disorientation, which can occur after major cultural changes. Purposefulness has much to do with hopefulness and with an enthusiastic, motivated pursuit of goals that are taken to be worthwhile for their own sake. Thus purposefulness, too, must relate to one's values. Significance relates to experiences of fulfilment and pride, to mattering and efficacy in the world, and to purposefully contributing to value that one takes to be final, objective, and beyond oneself. These experiences can be linked to each other: for example, one can see one's motivated pursuit of goals as sensible and as aimed at final, objective aims that will make a difference in the world. Kauppinen holds that, in some sense, it is the experience of significance that is the most basic to experiencing meaning, but that, in another sense, it is the experience of making sense that holds that position.

Chapter 22: Desire and Meaning in Life

Nomy Arpaly focuses on worthwhileness as contributing to meaning in life, and shows how worthwhileness can be explained in terms of people's desires. People's lives are meaningful to them to the extent that they include things that these people desire intrinsically. Satisfying intrinsic desires may involve giving up pleasure or accepting displeasure. Arpaly deals with cases that may challenge this view, such as those in which people obtain all that they want but still feel that life is not meaningful. According to her subjectivist account, if a person is not aware that her desires (for example, for greater social justice) have been fulfilled, her life does not become more meaningful (to her). However, one can also be wrong about the satisfaction of one's desires. People can also have much meaning in their lives without wishing for it or while holding incorrect theories of meaning. Arpaly also addresses the question of whether, in order to have a meaningful life, it is sufficient to have things that one desires (in a certain way), or whether the things that one desires must also be of objective value. She shows how her account can cope with examples that are supposed to prove that hybrid accounts are right: in most cases, people who want to count grass or dedicate their lives to a goldfish may well be wrong about their intrinsic desires, and thus, by Arpaly's account too, their lives are not meaningful. Arpaly also argues that, in general, people can fail to find meaning in their lives because of (among other problems) the difficulty in correctly identifying their intrinsic desires, as well as in satisfying them.

Chapter 23: Love and Meaning in Life

Alan H. Goldman contends that many accounts of love and life's meaning fail to explain well why the former greatly contributes to the latter. He presents an account that he takes to accomplish that. Goldman argues that much in love is not evaluative; one loves one's beloved, not Mother Teresa, although one takes Mother Teresa's life, not the beloved's, to be a paradigm of value. Likewise, once one loves a person, one doesn't trade the beloved for another person with similar but more valuable qualities (for example, someone smarter or more handsome). One can also love one sport or career rather than another without holding that the former is more valuable. Furthermore, Goldman argues that we should understand meaning in life not as based on value but, rather, in a sense closer to the meanings we attach to words through their coherence in sentences, which then have meanings in larger meaningful units. (The same is true, he notes, of musical tones in music and of events in fictional novels.) His model of meaning in life is largely narrativist (and thus in conflict with Strawson's in Chapter 4). For Goldman, the most meaningful events are the pivotal ones that have substantial impact, such as important achievements, births, marriages, and deaths. His non-evaluative understandings of both love and meaning in life help explain why the former can contribute much to the latter. Goldman also takes long-term commitment to be an important quality of love that coheres with the narrativist view of meaning (in which meaningful events are those that relate to many others across extended narratives). Love can be so deeply meaningful in life because it has to do with long-term commitment that impacts narratives in an extended way.

Chapter 24: Meaning in Life and Phoniness

After typifying phoniness, Iddo Landau explains why many take it to undermine life's meaning: among other deficiencies, phoniness inserts falseness into life; conceals the low value of some aspects of life, thus letting them remain unimproved; allows people not to live their own lives; and leads to loneliness and alienation. This holds true under subjectivist, objectivist, and hybrid theories of meaning in life. Those who identify phoniness in themselves or in others and feel that it undermines life's meaning react to it in a number of ways, including self-seclusion, interacting with others in unconventional or rude ways, and undergoing intense experiences. Phoniness and meaninglessness are related in that they share a sensed gap between standards and reality. However, many who react negatively to phoniness may misidentify both its extent and the degree to which it undermines meaning. Among other mistakes, people may misunderstand expressions, misinterpret internal states, undervalue what the expressions refer to, misconceive ambivalence as phoniness, inaccurately take any mistake or action suspected of phoniness to in fact be phoniness, and ignore all the many cases in which people behave non-phonily. Furthermore, life can be both meaningless and phony without being meaningless *because* it is phony; it can be meaningless for other reasons, while the phoniness may not contribute to its meaninglessness but just cover it up. Phoniness (to some degree) can also contribute to meaning in life by allowing moral behaviour, love, teamwork, 'fake it till you make it' dynamics, autonomy, and privacy. Thus, trying to eradicate any phoniness from one's own and others' lives in order to fight meaninglessness or protect meaningfulness is in some cases counterproductive.

Chapter 25: Gratitude and Meaning in Life

Tony Manela emphasizes that although gratitude enhances (and even partly constitutes) meaning in life, it can, in some degrees and forms, also diminish meaning. He starts out by distinguishing between, on the one hand, *gratitude to* (or *prepositional gratitude* or *targeted gratitude*) and, on the other hand, *gratitude that* (or *gratitude for* or *appreciation*). Manela analyses how prepositional gratitude enhances meaning in life in a variety of ways, including increasing self-esteem, motivating moral behaviour, and strengthening personal and social relationships between people. Among other issues, Manela discusses cases in which one's benefactors are inaccessible (for example, because they are deceased or anonymous) and one's gratitude may take the form of 'paying it forward', that is, benefiting others as one has been benefited, in a way that may inspire the benefited people to also continue to 'pay it forward', thus initiating further benevolent acts. Yet Manela also explicates the risks of over-gratitude. He discusses cases in which gratitude can have a negative impact on life's meaning by, for example, limiting autonomy, creating feelings of guilt, burdening people with debts of gratitude, diminishing people's ability to pursue the projects that would have made their lives most meaningful, and prompting people to commit immoral deeds out of gratitude to an immoral benefactor. Manela also explains how appreciation, or *gratitude that*, can enhance meaning in life, suggesting ways of strengthening our appreciation and guarding it. Among other points, he shows that many understandings of the hybrid model of having meaning in life (such as Wolf's 'subjective attraction meets objective attractiveness') seem to consider appreciation as essential to life's meaning. However, Manela is careful to note that there can also be wrong and pathological types of appreciation.

Chapter 26: Psychological Approaches to Life's Meaning

In this chapter, Roy F. Baumeister discusses the relations between psychological and philosophical research on meaning in life, as well as central psychological findings on meaning in life relevant to philosophers writing on the topic. He emphasizes that much of the psychological work on meaning in life examines people's subjective evaluation of their own life's meaning. Thus, it would seem, psychological findings are highly relevant for subjectivist philosophical attitudes toward life's meaning, but are also important for hybridists, as well as for objectivists who take sensed meaning to contribute to life's objective meaning. Baumeister also argues that philosophical research on meaning in life is in turn relevant to psychologists, since, in his view, it has more conceptual rigor than the psychological research on the topic. He also notes that psychological approaches tend to focus on typical and common cases and wonders whether the psychological findings, which have been obtained only in recent decades and mostly in Western countries, can be generalized to other cultures and historical eras. Baumeister recommends that the psychologists and philosophers researching meaning in life interact and familiarize themselves with each other's work, suggesting that both groups would have much to gain from this. Among the psychological findings Baumeister describes as being of interest to philosophers, he mentions that much of what endows people with sensed meaning is common to both humans and animals (community, love, sex, and social status). Sensed meaning is very vulnerable and is easily affected by even very small, trivial manipulations in one's environment. High-level sensed meaning has more to do with emotional and intuitive processes than with deep thought. Searching for meaning does not in itself lead to sensing meaning. Sensed meaning, which should be distinguished from happiness, has much to do with felt purposefulness, value, efficacy or mattering, and coherence or comprehension.

VI: LIVING MEANINGFULLY: CHALLENGES AND PROSPECTS

Chapter 27: Pessimism, Optimism, and Meaning in Life

David Benatar takes lives to have meaning when they have a positive point, purpose, or impact. He distinguishes between meaning from a cosmic perspective and meaning from a variety of terrestrial perspectives, such as the perspective of all humanity, or that of some human groups (for example, Canadians), or that of a single person. He further distinguishes between two questions on which optimists and pessimists might disagree. The first question is whether life has meaning of a certain kind, such as cosmic meaning or individual meaning. The other is whether the absence of meaning of a certain kind is bad or not. Once it is agreed, or supposed, that some type of meaning is missing, the view of whether or not it is bad that that type of meaning is absent is what makes a person a pessimist or an optimist. Benatar holds that some lives have meaning from narrower terrestrial perspectives. Only very few lives (for example, Churchill's, Mother Teresa's) have meaning from the perspective of humanity at large. All lives, however, lack cosmic meaning, since they do not matter for almost all of the cosmos. All in all, then, our lives have only very little meaning. Benatar explains why it is plausible to be sorry for the ways in which our lives lack meaning and copes with objections. One is based on the belief in a God to whom we matter. Another, by Kahane, argues that if humans are the only intelligent beings in the universe, they have huge cosmic significance (this issue is also discussed by Kahane in Chapter 5 and Mawson in Chapter 14 of this *Handbook*). Yet another effort to cope with the lack of cosmic meaning, by Landau, is based on a distinction between standards and perspectives. Benatar explicates these and other efforts to cope with cosmic meaninglessness and replies to them.

Chapter 28: The Rationality of Suicide and the Meaningfulness of Life

Michael Cholbi is careful to distinguish (as does Baumeister in his Chapter 26 in this *Handbook*) between philosophical and empirical-psychological discussions of suicide and of meaning in life. Cholbi claims that the empirical-psychological discussions still suffer from conceptual untidiness and tend to focus on what psychologically *motivates* suicide, rather than on what philosophically *justifies* it. In this chapter, Cholbi focuses on the philosophical justifications. He examines, first, Albert Camus's discussion of suicide and criticizes him for endorsing exaggerated standards for meaningful lives, for holding that at the core our lives are meaningless, and for assuming that only lives that are indispensable to the world's history can become meaningful. Clarifying his own understanding of suicide (which has to do with evaluatively divesting from one's future), Cholbi examines the conditions that would render suicide rational. Unlike some earlier theories of rational suicide, which mostly deal with well-being, Cholbi's theory focuses on meaning in life, using many aspects of Cheshire Calhoun's theory. For Cholbi, reasons to divest from one's future have to do with an absence of current or anticipated meaningfulness, in that people see no point in living through their anticipated future. Cholbi distinguishes, however, between rational and moral reasons for suicide, focusing on the former but noting that the latter might not hold even when the former do. Furthermore, he emphasizes the difficulties in applying the general principles for deciding on suicide to specific cases. He also makes clear that, among other problems that beset such decisions, they may be strongly influenced by depression and other psychological conditions, as well as being complicated by the difficulty in estimating the value of various goals and the probability of success in attaining them in the future.

Chapter 29: Suffering and Meaning in Life

Michael S. Brady emphasizes that suffering—which he understands as the physical or psychological experiencing of unpleasantness that one wishes would cease—often undermines life's meaning. It does so by harming, among other things, people's autonomy, personal relationships, self-respect, and psychological health. Suffering also often curtails the growth of what adds meaning in life, such as intellectual reflection, moral achievement, and artistic creation. Nevertheless, Brady also points to ways in which suffering can enhance or is even necessary for meaning. For Friedrich Nietzsche, suffering allows people (who have the right attitude) to overcome it and, thus, to develop psychological strength, which is a component of meaningful lives. In monotheistic (especially Christian and Islamic) religious thought, suffering is often presented as punishment for people's wrongdoing and, thus, as a way of restoring divine justice. Furthermore, religious thought often considers the acceptance of one's suffering as an apt moral response, a spiritual development, a correct moral attitude, and an opportunity to be forgiven by God and to be rewarded by him in the afterlife. But Brady argues that from secular or agnostic perspectives, too, suffering not only undermines but, under some conditions, enhances life's meaning. Brady takes achievement to be central to life's meaning. This is not only true of outstanding accomplishments that could be attained only by a small number of exceptional people; for a child, learning to tie shoelaces is also an achievement. Following Bradford's work, Brady holds that difficulty is necessary for achievement. Further, Brady argues that difficulty often has to do with suffering. Thus, under secular or agnostic suppositions, too, overcoming suffering is in many cases central to achievement and to meaning in life.

Chapter 30: Paradoxes and Meaning in Life

Saul Smilansky argues that paradoxicality often impacts both meaning in life and meaning of life. After clarifying the sense of 'paradoxicality' that he is using and the notion of an 'existential paradox', Smilansky discusses many examples of paradoxicality, mostly in the moral sphere. For example, the Paradox of Beneficial Retirement suggests that many people who see their profession as a vocation and a source of meaning should nevertheless leave their profession or retire if likely replacements are better at it than they are. Derek Parfit's Repugnant Conclusion suggests that we should prefer a world populated by a huge number of people whose lives just barely have enough meaning to be worth living over a world of fewer people who have highly meaningful lives. Bernard Williams's work on moral luck implies, among other things, that much in our moral status is not up to us and that our evaluation of ourselves is problematic. If it were not for terrible past atrocities, none of the people whose lives are meaningful would have come into existence. The meaningfulness in struggling against phenomena such as hunger, dictatorship, or discrimination will dissipate if the struggle is successful. Smilansky relates these and other instances of life's paradoxicality to claims by Camus and Nagel on life's absurdity, as well as to understandings of meaning in life suggested by Metz, Wolf, and Weinberg. He sees life's paradoxicality as relevant for both subjectivist and objectivist accounts of life's meaning. Smilansky notes that many paradoxes have pessimistic implications and that paradoxicality in general may pose a threat to the notion that life is meaningful. But he points out that some paradoxes have optimistic implications and, in some ways, paradoxicality can also enhance meaning in life. In Smilansky's view, paradoxicality does not, all in all, undermine life's meaning.

Chapter 31: Education and Meaning in Life

Doret de Ruyter and Anders Schinkel do not take meaning in life to be the only or main goal of education. The authors see education's ultimate end as flourishing in general. However, they take meaning in life, alongside other goals, to be important for flourishing. They adopt a hybrid understanding of meaning in life and explicate it as having to do with intelligibility, purpose, and mattering or significance. De Ruyter and Schinkel focus both on family and on school as loci for education to meaning in life. Parents can enhance children's present and future meaning in life by, among other things, helping children develop a sense of who they are, introducing them into the world, setting examples, and presenting outlooks. De Ruyter and Schinkel are well aware that some parents also *diminish* their children's present and future meaning in life, and of the difficult problem of balancing the good of the children, on the one hand, with parents' autonomy to educate their children as they see fit, on the other hand. The authors are also well aware of problems with schools as educators for meaning in life. Educational theories are often lofty, but many classrooms in many schools cannot be described as hospitable environments for discussing or enhancing life's meaning. Nevertheless, the authors hold that it would be odd if schools, which aim, among other goals, to prepare students for life, did not tackle this topic too. Hence, the authors suggest some general strategies for having such education in schools. These include providing service learning (learning combined with actual social service in the community), communicating to students that they matter, and conveying messages about what is of value in life (such as knowledge, caring, and equality).

Chapter 32: Virtual Reality and the Meaning of Life

In the final chapter of this *Handbook*, John Danaher argues against the supposition that it is impossible to find meaning in life in virtual reality. He explains that religion, morality, and many other aspects of meaningful lives also include aspects of virtual reality (understood not only as computer-simulated illusion but, more widely, as projecting our mental world onto the physical world through, for example, our imagination and conceptualization). Furthermore, virtual reality allows for friendship, moral action, the development of abilities, aesthetic enjoyment, and the enhancement of knowledge, all of which are commonly seen as aspects of meaningful lives. Danaher also argues that many of the facets and outcomes of virtual reality are real, rather than illusory. For example, many of our mental reactions to virtual reality experiences are similar to our reactions to experiences incited outside of virtual reality. He is well aware of possible difficulties and dangers in virtual reality, such as those having to do with morality (for example, when people's avatars interact violently with other avatars or with simulated characters and objects). He argues that we can, however, diminish these dangers in virtual reality by applying moral constraints to it. He further argues that although virtual reality may be counterproductive to meaning in life by encouraging passivity, overstimulation, and lack of autonomy, there is nothing in principle nihilistic in virtual reality, and it does not imply or lead to nihilism more than non-virtual reality does. Danaher also acknowledges the danger that virtual reality may lead to social or political fragmentation, for example when people choose to live separately, each in their own virtual world that matches their preferences. But he suggests that this danger may be overestimated and can also be coped with.

ACKNOWLEDGEMENTS

I am grateful to Dorothy Bauhoff, Marie Deer, Saul Smilansky, and Michele L. Waldinger for helpful comments on earlier drafts of the Introduction.

REFERENCES

Ayer, A. J. [1947] 2000. 'The Claims of Philosophy'. *Polemic* 7:18–33. Reprinted in *The Meaning of Life*, ed. E. D. Klemke, 2nd ed., 219–232. New York: Oxford University Press.

Baier, K. [1957] 2000. 'The Meaning of Life'. Reprinted in *The Meaning of Life*, ed. E. D. Klemke, 2nd ed., 101–132. New York: Oxford University Press.

Frankl, V. 1985. *Man's Search for Meaning*. New York: Washington Square Press.

Hare, R. M. [1957] 1972. 'Nothing Matters'. Reprinted in *Applications of Moral Philosophy*, 32–47. London: Macmillan.

Landau, I. 1997. 'Why Has the Question of the Meaning of Life Arisen in the Last Two and a Half Centuries?' *Philosophy Today* 41(2): 263–269.

Metz, T. 2021. 'The Meaning of Life'. In *The Stanford Encyclopedia of Philosophy* (Spring 2021 edition), ed. Edward N. Zalta. https://plato.stanford.edu/archives/spr2021/entries/life-meaning/.

Russell, B. [1903] 1985. 'The Free Man's Worship'. Reprinted in *The Collected Papers of Bertrand Russell, Vol. 12: 1902–14: Contemplation and Action*, ed. R. A. Rempel, A. Brink, and M. Moran, 66–72. London: Allen and Unwin.

Schlick, M. [1927] 1979. 'Vom Sinn des Lebens'. *Symposion* 1: 331–354. Translated by P. Heath as 'On the Meaning of Life', in *Philosophical Papers*, ed. H. L. Mulder and B. F. B. van de Velde-Schlick, vol. 2, 112–129. Dordrecht: Reidel.

PART I

UNDERSTANDING MEANING IN LIFE

CHAPTER 1

THE CONCEPT OF LIFE'S MEANING

THADDEUS METZ

1. INTRODUCING THE STANDARD VIEW OF THE SENSE OF 'LIFE'S MEANING'

IN this chapter, I critically discuss views about what it is that professional English-speaking philosophers in at least the analytic tradition characteristically (if not essentially) mean when speaking of 'life's meaning' and cognate terms such as 'significance', or, closely related, what they have in mind when reflecting on them. When these philosophers debate each other about what, if anything, makes a life meaningful, what are they thinking about such that they are disagreeing about a common subject matter and not speaking past one another? If one philosopher maintains that life is unavoidably meaningless, a second one contends that it is meaningful insofar as it fulfils God's purpose, and a third maintains that it is meaningful if it displays certain virtues, what are they all talking about? What is the shared concept of a meaningful life about which they have competing conceptions?[1]

As I shall demonstrate in the next major section of this chapter (section 2), there has been a standard view of how to analyse the concept of life's meaning. Although philosophers working in the Anglo-American tradition have indeed disagreed about the details, for about fifty years they have by and large contended at least implicitly that talk of 'life's meaning' is about: human persons, and centrally their intentional actions, which exhibit a high final value or strong basic reason that is characteristically present in 'the good, the true, and the beautiful' and absent from the hypothetical lives of Sisyphus

---

[1] For revealing discussion of what those beyond professional philosophers sometimes mean by 'life's meaning', as well as some idiosyncratic usage of the phrase by professional philosophers, see Mawson (2016, esp. 51–68).

or of those in an Experience Machine. That is, a very large majority have maintained that the concept of life's meaning essentially includes something about individual human lives, with a focus on what they do, where what they do is good or choice-worthy for its own sake to a noteworthy degree, and, furthermore, is typified by love/morality, wisdom/enquiry, and the arts/creativity, as well as absent from a life that either rolls a stone up a hill for eternity or is alone in a virtual reality device.[2]

After presenting a variety of analyses of the concept of life's meaning from the past forty years or so and showing that they share the previously noted common ground, I address several challenges to the standard view that have been made in the past five years. Some have contended that it is not merely the lives of human persons that can be sensibly described as being 'meaningful' or not, but also the lives of some animals (section 3). Upon focusing on the lives of human persons, some have argued that it is not merely the life of an individual person that can exhibit meaning, but also the human race as a whole or a sub-group of human beings (section 4). Upon focusing on the life of an individual human person, some have maintained that it is not her decisions that bear the meaning, but instead certain information about her that does (section 5). Upon focusing on the actions of an individual human person, some have made the case that meaningful ones need not exhibit or promote anything of final value, and could instead be neutral or even undesirable in themselves (section 6). Finally, upon focusing on the valuable actions of an individual human person, some have urged us to distinguish between everyday or mundane kinds of meaning and a great meaning that purportedly could come only with the existence of a spiritual realm (section 7). After considering each of these challenges to the standard view, I briefly conclude by summarizing (section 8).

The reader will notice that later sections make assumptions relative to earlier ones; that is merely to organize the debates, and is not meant to imply any judgement about how they are to be resolved. In fact, my current thinking is sympathetic towards some of the preceding challenges to the standard view,[3] while rejecting others. In particular, in this chapter I am inclined to support the ideas that certain animals could have a limited sort of meaning in their lives, that some groups of human beings can exhibit robust kinds of meaning, and that there is an important distinction to be drawn between mundane and great meaning in the life of an individual person. However, I firmly resist the suggestions that meaning always inheres in information about people and never in the actions we take, or that meaning in life need not be positive. I believe that those more radical departures from the standard view are, at this stage of the debate, unwarranted.

---

[2] In claiming that talk of 'life's meaning' inherently involves reflection on the value of an individual life, I am not denying that it has at times been used to connote enquiry into the point of the human race as a whole, which I discuss later (section 4). Often this distinction is now captured with mention of meaning 'in' a life as opposed to the meaning 'of' life as a whole, on which see Seachris (2020, sec. 2). My point is that discussion about the meaning 'of' life has not been salient in the field over the past several decades.

[3] In contrast to some of what I had argued in Metz (2019a).

2. The Standard View of the Concept of a Meaningful Life

In the decades prior to Robert Nozick's (1981, 594–600) influential analysis, English-speaking philosophers had tended to hold that enquiring into life's meaning is equivalent to asking which ends we should strive to achieve, or when it is that we feel satisfied upon having achieved our ends (Ayer 1947; Nielsen 1964; Hepburn 1966). However, virtually no one invokes these accounts any longer. For one, it does not seem conceptually contradictory to hold that meaning inheres in conditions that are not satisfying, e.g., in unpleasant sacrifices for one's children. For another, in order to differentiate meaning from other values such as prudence or right action, we need to know *which* ends that merit pursuit pertain to meaning specifically. Nozick advanced an analysis that avoids these two problems (although he did not represent it as such), which paved the way for what I consider the standard view of the concept of life's meaning.

According to Nozick, when asking about the meaning of anything, one is asking about its relationships with other things. Just as smoke means fire by virtue of the latter having a causal relation with the former, and just as words mean what they do by virtue of referring to things in the world, so a life means something (by definition) insofar as it connects in certain ways with certain things beyond it. In particular, for Nozick a life is more meaningful, the more it is contoured towards final value beyond it, which plausibly captures the good, the true, and the beautiful as potential sources of meaning; they involve relating positively to people, parts of the natural world, and artworks that are good for their own sake. Similarly, neither Sisyphus nor one living in an Experience Machine is transcending his limits to connect with something of final value, aptly making them poor candidates for meaning by Nozick's analysis.

While a number in the field have accepted Nozick's analysis or something close to it (e.g., Levy 2005, 178–180; Waghorn 2014), there have also arisen quite an array of other suggestions about how to analyse the concept of life's meaning. Some suggest that talk of 'life's meaning' is about: pursuing what is worthy of awe and devotion (Taylor 1989, 3–90); seeking out non-trivial purposes (Trisel 2007), perhaps ones beyond our own happiness; leading a life worth living (Landau 2017, 9–12, 15–16); doing what merits esteem or admiration (Kauppinen 2015; cf. Metz 2001, 147–150); displaying narrative qualities in the shape of one's life (Wong 2008); acting on reasons of love (Wolf 2016); acting for good reasons (Visak 2017); making a contribution (Martela 2017); or a cluster of these and perhaps still others (Markus 2003; Metz 2013, 24–35; Martela and Steger 2016).

Those who have proffered such competing analyses of the concept of a meaningful life over the years have naturally argued with each other about which one is strongest, and, as someone who has been party to those debates, I naturally find them important. After all, would it not be fascinating to discover that all philosophical thought about meaning in life is a function of a single property--or not?

However, what I expect is of greater interest to the field, at this stage of reflection, is the fact that these competing accounts of the concept of life's meaning have generally shared a certain approach to it, one that has been questioned in serious ways over the past five years or so. For all the preceding analyses, the relevant life is that of an individual human person, not that of the species. In addition, the principal bearers of the meaning in a person's life are her actions, construed broadly to include not merely choices in a narrow, volitional sense, but also 'judgment-sensitive attitudes' (in the useful words of T. M. Scanlon 1998, 18–22), that is, mental states such as cognition, deliberation, and motivation that are constituted by or can be influenced by rational reflection.[4] Furthermore, those actions are conceived as being positive, as either being good for their own sake or backed by a non-instrumental reason. For a final similarity, the preceding analyses do a reasonable job of both including the sort of value (or reason) particular to the good, the true, and the beautiful and excluding the cases of Sisyphus and the Experience Machine. For instance, on the face of it, making a work of art does, while living in a virtual reality device does not, merit esteem, constitute a good life story, or make a contribution.

In the rest of this chapter, I consider five challenges to the standard view of what is inherent to the concept of a meaningful life. They have appeared recently, and reflection on them should advance the field's understanding of the nature of philosophical enquiry into what, if anything, makes life meaningful.

3. Meaning beyond Human Lives?

According to the standard view of the concept of life's meaning, characteristic human life is what can exhibit meaning or not. That claim should not be understood in a species-ist way—adherents to the standard view would surely accept that meaning could also be present in the lives of alien 'shumans', beings that are like us in terms of function, but are different in terms of surface properties and unable to mate with us. The key point for the standard view is that persons, beings with a certain degree of self-awareness, intelligence, and agency, are what can live meaningful lives, and that non-persons cannot, with philosophers naturally tending to focus on human persons.

Lately, some scholars have argued that, in fact, some non-persons can exhibit meaningfulness. Most powerfully, in my view, they have contended that an animal such as a dog could have a more or less meaningful existence. One intuition is that there is a difference between a dog that sits around all day scratching itself and one that, say, is put into the service of human beings or looks after her pups. The latter benefits others, perhaps consequent to certain intentions, while the former does not

---

[4] One might wonder whether mystical awareness, a prima facie contender for meaningfulness, counts as rational. However, even if this kind of cognition does not involve analysis, it plausibly involves intelligence of some kind insofar as animals lack it. Plus, training is normally understood to be required to get into a position to exhibit this kind of awareness.

(Purves and Delon 2018; Thomas 2018), which marks a difference in significance, so the arguments go.

I have argued elsewhere that these rationales are unsuccessful (Metz 2019a, 406–408), but have since come to believe that another one probably works. One problem with the thought that conferring benefits or doing so consequent to an intention is sufficient for meaning is that it oddly implies that a logically possible source of meaning for a dog would be for it to do much good for others merely because it was forced to, on pain of getting whipped. Beating a dog to the point where it cowers in fear to aid a human does not seem to be a source of meaning for it, not even conceptually—but the preceding accounts of what is sufficient for meaning entail otherwise.

Another problem with the previous rationales is that neither quite supports the idea that animals can have the sort of meaning that human persons can. When it comes to meaning in the lives of human persons, most of us believe that it is appropriate to enhance the meaning of their lives *for their sake*. I do what I can to help my partner find meaningful work at least in large part for her sake, not merely for the sake of others who might benefit as a result. In contrast, when it comes to an animal, we do not readily find reason to enhance meaning in its life for its sake if meaning comes from the animal making others better off. If (intentionally) causing benefits to others were the only source of meaning in an animal's life, we might well act to enhance its meaningfulness, but not obviously for its sake and instead only for those whom we expect would benefit, viz., the humans that a dog serves or the pups that she protects. This difference in the nature of the reason given for action suggests a difference in the type of meaning at stake, and so does not present a real challenge to the standard view.[5]

However, there is plausibly another way that, for instance, a dog could exhibit a meaningful life, which is by being part of a positive relationship, at least with human beings and perhaps also with other dogs. I do not here provide an account of what a positive relationship is, merely noting that conferring benefits is not sufficient for one, as when one gains from fleeting market transactions, and that doing so is also not necessary for one, e.g., when two friends unintentionally harm each other. Although benefiting another is not essential for having a positive relationship with her, doing so is characteristically part of having one, and it might be that positive relationship better captures the sense that animals have meaningful lives than do mere actions that are useful for others. Where a dog and its owner have been in a positive relationship for five years, it is sensible to describe the dog's life as being meaningful to some degree in virtue of that, relative to a stray dog with no such tie. If I had to choose which

---

[5] This point applies with considerable force against those who have recently argued that inanimate objects can exhibit meaning. One has suggested that a sandwich can be significant because of the reactions it arouses in hungry persons or benefits it confers on them (de Muijnck 2013, 1302), while another has contended that gravity is well described as having a '*meaningful* effect on our existence' (Thomas 2018, 284). However, if the terms are aptly used in these contexts, they pick out a property different from the one human beings can exhibit, since no one would sensibly promote a significant sandwich or meaningful gravity for the sake of these *things*.

one to rescue from death, I would save the relational dog instead of the isolated dog, not merely for the sake of the former's owner, but also for its sake and in virtue of the meaning it would continue to have were it reunited with its owner. Both being loved and loving (or something like that, if one demurs from describing it as 'loving') seem to be sources of meaning for a dog.

I am sympathetic to the suggestion that it might be inappropriate to describe a dog as having a 'meaningful life', but it could still be apt to think that it has *some* meaning in its life, even if not enough to count as a life full of meaning. This account plausibly avoids the objections to the previous rationales for the presence of animal meaning, viz., that merely benefiting others, or doing so because of an intention, entails that being threatened to do so is meaning-conferring and cannot capture the intuition that it should be the animal, and not merely the others benefited, for which one has reason to promote meaning in its life.

4. Human Meaning beyond a Person's Life?

For the rest of this essay, I address only human meaning, setting aside the case of animal meaning. When it comes to human meaning, the standard view is that only individual persons can have it. While there has been some debate about whether human non-persons, such as babies (de Muijnck 2013, 1295) and those who are permanently comatose (Thomas 2018, 281–282, 292), can have meaning in their lives, in this section I instead take up the matter of whether human lives beyond those of individuals can matter. Specifically, I address the view that the human race as a whole can be meaningful, after which I consider whether smaller groups of human beings can.

Prior to the twentieth century, use of the phrase 'life's meaning' was often about whether the human race had been created to fulfil a purpose and, if so, what it might be (on which see Tartaglia 2015). Logical positivism was at least partially responsible for having put this view on life support, the thought being that God would explain how humanity could have been assigned a purpose but that God-talk is cognitively meaningless for failing to include perceivable truth-conditions. The demise of positivism has witnessed the rise of more cosmic approaches to meaning, where it is now common to speak of the meaning 'of' human life as a whole as such as opposed to 'in' an individual's life.

According to one approach to the meaning of life, merely having been created by a particular sort of person out of a certain motivation, perhaps by God in order to realize his plenitude or out of love, would be sufficient for the human species to be meaningful to some degree (e.g., Mawson 2016, 57–58, 64–65). By this approach, we need not do anything in order for humanity to be significant; merely having sprung from a certain source is enough.

Now, the standard view implies that the relevant human beings must live one way rather than another in order to be meaningful, say, for connecting with an external value, fulfilling a non-trivial purpose, doing what merits esteem, or acting for reasons of love. It is not obvious whether to change the standard view or to revise the intuition that some meaning in the life of the human species can come from utterly non-volitional sources on its part. One argument in favour of changing the standard view is the fact that some people feel shame for things that have been done to them or for which they are otherwise not at all responsible. Some might feel shame upon learning they were conceived as a product of a rape. If it would not be inappropriate to feel such shame, then, by analogy, it could be appropriate to feel the opposite emotion, viz., esteem, for having been created in a certain way. So, instead of the concept of life's meaning including the idea of *doing* what merits esteem, perhaps it should be changed to the idea of what merits esteem, where the human race having been created in the image of the perfect ground of the universe plausibly counts. Perhaps being the continued object of God's love, regardless of what humanity might do, also merits esteem on its part.

A lingering question, though, is whether being acted upon in these ways would count for all that much. Even if an individual's life would be somewhat less meaningful for having been the product of rape, it would not really impede his ability to live a meaningful life. Analogously, if the existence of the species would be somewhat more meaningful for having been the product of God's loving decision, it would not prevent it from being meaningless in other, substantial ways. Perhaps the degree of meaning involved would be akin to what a dog that is loved by its owner could obtain (cf. section 3).

There is another approach to understanding how the human race as a whole could be meaningful or not, which is to focus on its choices. Here, it is not enough, or even that much, to have been created for a reason or to be loved, but humanity must do something in order to fulfil a purpose. Perhaps its proper aim is to defeat evil, to organize the world so that people have the resources to realize what is highest within them, to meet intelligent alien life, or to love God back with humanity's whole heart.

This approach squares better with the standard view of what meaning-talk is essentially about—it would merely have us shift from individual persons to the species as what is capable of connecting with an external value, fulfilling a non-trivial purpose, doing what merits esteem, etc. However, it is, upon reflection, difficult to see how the human race as a whole could be the agent responsible for such actions. Suppose that humanity at a certain time defeated evil, created global justice, met intelligent aliens, or loved God properly. Why attribute any of those accomplishments to all of the human race as opposed to principally those human beings who were at least alive at the time they were effected? Why think that the species, which includes members who lived more than 50,000 years ago, gets the meaning credit?

I do not mean to suggest that only those alive at the time of, e.g., realizing a just world could obtain meaning from it; for the lives of those who had intentionally contributed to the relevant aim but perished before seeing it realized would be made more significant upon its realization. I am also open to the idea that intending to realize a certain aim is not necessary to obtain meaning from its realization, so long as one were doing what was likely to realize it. Still more, I accept that it could be sensible to attribute a feature to the species despite not every single individual member exhibiting it. The trouble is that many, and probably most, members of the species neither intended to realize the relevant aim, whether it be global justice or love of God, nor did anything substantial to contribute towards its realization. What grounds the attribution of meaning to the entire group of human beings?

One might point out that we often ascribe meaning to the life of an individual in the light of certain actions that he took only at a particular stage. For example, there are those who would maintain that Winston Churchill's life was on balance meaningful because of some of the decisions he made during the Second World War. By analogy, perhaps the life of humanity as a whole can be meaningful because of what it or some of its members did at a certain stage. However, I am concerned that an important disanalogy is the lack of intensional and causal relations amongst a sufficient number of human beings to give credit to the whole for the actions of only some at a particular time. Churchill's life formed a unity, by virtue of continuities amongst mental and bodily events, such that the meaningfulness of what he did at a particular time is sensibly ascribed to his life as a whole. I find it hard to identify relevantly similar continuities amongst, say, the first humans from tens of thousands of years ago, an isolated clan in the Amazon jungle living 300 years ago, and people in twenty-first-century Tokyo.

To sum up, if the reflections here are approximately true, the friend of a cosmic approach to meaning faces a dilemma. On the one hand, it is clear how the human race could have been created by God for a certain reason (setting aside issues about how the spiritual could produce the physical), but it is difficult to see how merely having been caused to exist so as to realize a particular end would be meaningful or enough for a meaningful life, for we normally think that (substantial) meaning is a function of choosing to live one way rather than another, viz., actually realizing a particular end. On the other hand, it is clear how we could choose in ways that effect large-scale changes that are intuitively meaning-conferring, such as advancing global justice, but it is difficult to see how those choices could be properly ascribed to the human race as a whole.

Perhaps this dilemma for the meaning of life theorist obtains only because elements of the standard view unjustifiably continue to frame our thought. If meaning were not a matter of, roughly, an agent's actions having had certain effects, but instead were a certain kind of explanation or narrative, then it would be easier to ascribe meaning to humanity as a whole (Seachris 2009, 2016, 2019; Mawson 2019, 11–16), an approach that I discuss in the next section.

Staying, for now, with the idea that agency of some kind is analytically central to (substantial) meaning, there is on the face of it stronger reason to change the standard view when considering groups of human persons smaller than the species as a whole. Organizations, for instance, plausibly can be bearers of meaning. Consider a non-governmental organization (NGO) that fights famine or a business that aims to sell nutritious, tasty, climate-friendly, and affordable food. At least when these organizations have decision-making structures that are independent of the wills of any specific members, it appears that they can exhibit more or less meaningfulness.

For example, if the NGO did better over time and eventually achieved the fantastic goal of eradicating famine, it would be reasonable to say that the importance or significance of the NGO, as distinct from that of its members' lives, increased and became substantial. Suppose that the intentions of some minority of the NGO's members were not beneficent and that they failed to undertake actions likely to advance famine relief. Such a case brings the distinctness of the NGO's agency into relief; it is reasonably described as having made decisions that are not reducible to those of its members at a given time, and decisions that were furthermore meaningful.

In the light of such cases, I suspect that the individualism characteristic of the standard view is misguided and should be supplemented by a limited form of holism. The prima facie difference between the case of the human race as a whole and an NGO is that the latter might be a person, or, if that is too thick, then at least it is capable of making choices for which it is responsible as distinct from those of its composite members. Insofar as a group can exhibit culpable agency (I do not suggest that such is a necessary condition for any meaningfulness whatsoever––cf. section 3), it can plausibly be characterized as meaningful.

5. Personal Meaning beyond Actions?

Despite being sympathetic to a limited kind of holism, hereafter I focus mainly on individual persons as bearers of meaning, so as to make the discussion tractable. In this section I consider whether the standard view is mistaken for conceiving of individuals' actions as bearers of meaning. According to some philosophers lately, meaning in fact never inheres in what individuals (or groups) do, but instead in certain *interpretations* about them or their actions.

One major motivation for denying that action ever bears meaning and that cognition alone does is an attempt to unify all meaning-talk (Seachris 2019; Thomas 2019). Sometimes we use the word 'meaning' to indicate a substantial result, as in the preceding famine case. Sometimes we use the same word in additional ways, to signify, e.g., what we are communicating ('This sentence means . . .'), what is responsible for another thing ('Smoke means fire'), or what we are trying to achieve ('I did not mean to do that . . .'). If the word 'meaning' meant essentially the same thing in all its various uses, then it would be plausible to maintain that the unifying factor is something pertaining to information that makes sense of a phenomenon.

Applied to life's meaning, the suggestion is that asking about it is by definition a matter of enquiring into whether and how a life is intelligible within a wider frame of reference. Two philosophers have recently said the following of enquiry into life's meaning:

> I am strongly inclined to think that it is a single question, the asking of which reveals our desire to make sense of life and existence. . . . The foci of this sense-making activity, no doubt, include purpose and significance, but it is the sense-making

framework itself—what *makes sense of* these and other existentially weighty matters—that is the meaning of life. (Seachris 2019, 375)

(T)he traditional question is simply a request for the information which constitutes a coherent answer to one or more of a certain set of questions regarding human existence that were salient to the asker. (Thomas 2019, 1555)

By a plain reading of these approaches, the actions of fulfilling a purpose or making a significant difference to the world logically cannot be what exhibit meaning. Instead, what in principle can be meaningful or not is *sense-making information*, perhaps a narrative interpretation of a certain kind (Seachris), or an explanation of various matters concerning what has caused us to exist, what effects we have had on others, what aims we have sought to realize, what the story of our lives has been, and what our lives symbolically represent (Thomas).

I do think that the interpretive or cognitive dimension of meaning has been underappreciated by philosophers, while it has been central to psychological reflection for several decades.[6] There is something right about the views that having a coherent and otherwise plausible belief system can enhance meaning and that not having one can reduce it. Having certain false or unjustified beliefs, e.g., that the devil is making you do something or that the Flying Spaghetti Monster is in charge of the universe, plausibly reduces meaningfulness. In addition, a straightforward explanation of why Albert Einstein's life was particularly meaningful concerns his insight into the nature of the physical world.

We can and should find a way to accommodate these judgements, but without jettisoning the standard view's claim that actions bear meaning. Here is one reason why not (Metz 2019a, 411). Suppose that you hear a child screaming in a house that is on fire, and you risk your life to rescue the child, with success. I presume we agree that there is meaning here, or at the very least that it is logically possible that there is. Now, what could in principle constitute the meaningfulness? It is not so much (or at least not necessarily) that you have fitted this action into a narrative about your life more broadly (Seachris), because you might not have; suppose, for instance, that you have acted out of character on this occasion, or that your discriminatory society does not value heroic rescues of children of this ethnic group. It is also not so much (or at least not necessarily) that you have given an account of the effects of your action or of what your aims were (Thomas), for it is plausibly the effects of the action and the aims behind it themselves that matter, and you might not have bothered to reflect on them either during the rescue or afterward.

I submit that the natural and powerful thing to say about the case is that the heroic risk-taking is what has made your life more meaningful, which entails that a purely cognitive analysis of the concept of life's meaning is too narrow for ruling that out. What the case probably also shows is that meaning-talk is not particularly unified and instead is

---

[6] For citations to some of the relevant psychological literature, see Martela and Steger (2016); Metz (2019a); and Thomas (2019).

a polyseme—what it connotes in the philosophical context of life's meaning is plausibly discontinuous with what it does in the everyday context of language.

How, then, should we understand the logically possible bearers of meaningfulness in a human person's life? The evidence on the table is that beneficent actions, such as saving a child's life, are capable of meaning and that certain kinds of beliefs are, too. What does this mean for the standard view that actions are characteristically what bear meaning? Much depends on precisely what is plausibly meant by 'action' and which beliefs are logically possible contenders for meaningfulness, issues that philosophers of life's meaning have yet to address in depth.

It would be theoretically tidiest if the relevant beliefs invariably involved some kind of deliberation and also some kind of final value (Landau 2017, 12–15, 2020), as might seem to be the case. Meaning plausibly comes neither from believing that a coffee cup is on the table because I have seen one, nor from remembering what I had to eat yesterday, whereas understanding the relative nature of space-time does intuitively count as important knowledge or what could make someone's life more important. Insofar as a broad notion of 'action' includes theoretical reflection that can be good for its own sake, the standard view might be able to accommodate what have up to now been described as 'cognitive' or 'informational' sources of meaning. However, if instead the kinds of beliefs that conceptually are frequently meaning-conferring need not involve the exercise of reason or judgement, then the standard view would probably need to be revised to include a pluralist account of what it is about our lives that can exhibit meaning.

I noted at the start that this section focuses on the lives of individual persons, and not the life of the species. I close it by pointing out that a cognitive construal of the concept of a meaningful life naturally supports cosmic approaches. The human race could sensibly be described as being meaningful insofar as we could (very roughly) understand where it came from and where it is headed (Seachris 2009, 2016, 2019; Mawson 2019, 11–19). I submit, though, that enquiry into the meaning of life is discontinuous with that into meaning in life. That is, the sort of meaning that adherents to the standard view and even many of its critics are trying to capture, which focuses on what an *individual* person should *do* so as to exhibit something *positive* in her life, differs in kind from the cosmic sort of meaning, which is a *story* about the origin and destiny of the human *species* that, as I now discuss, could be *negative*.

6. Actions Conferring Non-evaluative Meaning?

Yet again I begin a section by taking some conditions for granted, in this case that actions are the principal bearers of meaning in a person's life. Another facet of the standard view is that when philosophers disagree about how much meaning arises from what a person does with her life, they are agreeing that they are searching for something positive, normally something good for its own sake (but cf. Visak 2017). Typical is the suggestion that 'meaningfulness is an inescapably evaluative notion; to describe a life as meaningful is at the very least to commend it as a good life' (Cottingham 2013, 180). Specifically, as noted earlier, life's meaning is often by definition thought to be characterized by the superlative final values of the good, the true, and the beautiful. However, some philosophers have recently come to disagree with this common-sense view. For example, it has been suggested that some meanings in a life are 'undesirable' (Mawson 2016, 90; see also 193). Similarly, some say that 'there can exist other kinds of genuine meaning *besides* those which we humans happen to find desirable' (Thomas 2018, 291).

There are a number of theoretical motivations for the revisionism. One suggestion is that meaning need not be positive since it can inhere in the fact of one's life having influenced other lives in substantial ways, where these influences need not have been good. Some ascribe meaning to Hitler's life in virtue of having been responsible for the deaths of so many, while also dramatically having changed the course of history for those who remained alive (e.g., Thomas 2019, 1574). Another supporter of the idea that Hitler's life was meaningful maintains that a chosen life has meaning if it expresses or stands for something, where it might fail to represent something good, as in the case of genocidal anti-Semitism (Mawson 2016, 87–92).

If one denies that actions can, or have to, bear meaning, there is even more conceptual space open for non-evaluative meaning. If one believes that meaning is constituted by a story about why an individual (or the species) was created or where she (or the species) is headed, then there is the real prospect of a neutral or even negative evaluation (e.g., Kiymaz 2019, 150–153). She (or it) might not have been created for a good reason, and she (it) might not be able to look forward to a good ending. Speaking of us and our universe having been created for a purpose, one philosopher remarks, 'If reality is meaningful, then the meaning of human life might be good, bad, or neither' (Tartaglia 2015, 5).

I do not quite suggest that those using the word 'meaningful' to refer to such dimensions of life are misusing the word. However, I submit that, when they use the word in these ways, doing so involves enquiry divergent from what a majority of philosophers have been interested in for several decades (Metz 2019a, 411–412). Adherents to the standard view, and even many of its critics, have been engaging in an essentially evaluative or normative enterprise. They have wanted to know what is good or worth pursuing for its own sake. When we no longer are considering what by definition is positive in those ways, then the subject matter has changed. We are then describing instead of prescribing, or explaining instead of appraising. The revisionists are not so much challenging the standard view of the concept of life's meaning as changing the subject or highlighting an altogether different way to employ the word 'meaningful'.

For analogies, consider terms such as 'human nature', 'person', 'identity', and 'self', which have both evaluative and non-evaluative senses. In metaphysics, for instance, we might enquire into whether selves exist and what they essentially are, whereas in ethics we might want to know how to realize our selves in a desirable way. Just because the word 'self' can be and routinely is used by metaphysicians does not mean that their enquiry should be considered part and parcel of what ethicists are doing. It would be no criticism of an ethical analysis of the concept of self were one to show that metaphysicians use the same word, albeit in different ways. I submit that similar remarks go for the term 'meaningful' and the standard view of what it means.

7. Evaluative Meaning That Is Great?

For a final way that the standard view has been challenged lately, let us focus on an individual person's actions that are inherently positive. Implicit in recent literature has been the suggestion that when thinking about life's meaning, we need to distinguish a normal meaning and a great one, a distinction that the standard view does not draw. I believe the standard view should be revised to do so.

In the meaning of life literature, such a distinction has recently been drawn in the debate between supernaturalists and naturalists, that is, between those who maintain that spiritual conditions such as God or a soul are central to meaning in life and those who deny that and instead maintain that a physical world is at least sufficient for a meaningful life. For most of the modern period, the debate between them had been about the 'extreme' view that a spiritual realm is necessary for our lives to have any meaning in them. However, in the past fifteen years or so, the debate has shifted (on which see Metz 2019b). Since the (stereotypical) lives of Einstein, Picasso, Mother Teresa, and the like were intuitively meaningful even on the supposition of having lived in an atheist world, many supernaturalists now advance a 'moderate' view, that a spiritual realm is necessary for our lives to have an *ultimate* or *great* meaning. For instance, only if one has a soul that enters Heaven could one enjoy an eternally meaningful life (Mawson 2016, 17, 134 144–146, 158), or only if God exists and has assigned one a purpose could one's choices be part of a meaningful plan covering 'the whole universe and all its inhabitants' (Swinburne 2016, 154).

There is important conceptual work yet to be done about how to understand the senses of an 'ultimate' or 'great' meaning that could be available to an individual person in virtue of her actions, probably only within a spiritual realm. Sometimes philosophers conceive of a great meaning quantitatively, with talk of 'more' or 'infinite' meaning, while others think of it qualitatively, with mention of 'deep' or 'higher' meaning, and still others analyse it temporally, with mention of meaning that is 'permanent', 'lasting', or 'eternal' (for citations, see Metz 2019b, 27–28). Are these distinctions exhaustive, or might, say, talk of an 'unlimited' meaning (Nozick 1981, 618–619) signify something else? Are some of these distinctions reducible to others, such that, say, a permanent meaning is nothing more than an infinite meaning? Which of these distinctions is the most valuable or choice-worthy? None of these questions has received a systematic treatment. Insofar as they are coherent, the standard view of the debate about life's meaning should clear space for them.

8. Conclusion

In this chapter I have critically explored what I have called 'the standard view' of the concept of life's meaning, the one common to a very large majority of enquiry on the topic for about fifty years by English-speaking, analytic philosophers. Despite them having disagreed about how to analyse the concept, most have implicitly agreed that meaning-talk is about the actions of individual persons that are desirable or choice-worthy for their own sake, characteristically ones involving the good, the true, and the beautiful, and excluding actions such as rolling a stone forever or living alone in a virtual reality device. I here addressed five reasons for thinking this standard view is inaccurate.

Two of these reasons I rejected. According to one rationale, the standard view incorrectly ascribes meaning to the actions of a person, whereas the sole bearer of meaning is instead certain information about her (or humans more generally) such as a narrative or an explanation. Although I accepted that certain kinds of cognitive states can bear meaning, most clearly ones involving some kind of valuable deliberation, I denied that only they do, arguing that beneficent actions are for instance best understood as being meaningful. According to another rationale, the standard view incorrectly characterizes meaning as essentially positive, e.g., as good for its own sake, whereas it can be neutral or even negative. Although I accepted that it might be useful to use the word 'meaning' to describe certain non-positive conditions, that project is too different from an inherently prescriptive one to justify a change from the standard view of the concept of life's meaning.

However, three of the reasons for revising the standard view I found compelling. Although I suggested that the dominant reason for ascribing meaning to the lives of animals, viz., that they benefit others, is unpersuasive, the idea that they can be party to positive relationships is more persuasive, suggesting that at least a limited kind of meaning is probably available to some of them. Although I found it hard to accept that the human race as a whole could be substantially meaningful merely for having been created in a certain way or that it could be sensibly described as having achieved an end that would make its life meaningful, it was easier to see how meaning could be exhibited by a human sub-group, such as an NGO with a decision-making structure making it responsible for certain policies. Finally, I am inclined to think that the standard view is too narrow for not distinguishing between meaning that is everyday or mundane and a great or ultimate meaning, where enough enquirers into life's meaning have lately become interested in the latter to be explicit when analysing the concept of it.

Here, then, is a long-winded way to capture what a very large majority of philosophical enquiry into life's meaning has been or reasonably could be about: animals (with intentionality), human persons, or human groups (with intentionality), and particularly their actions (which might include intellectual reflection) that are desirable or choice-worthy for their own sake, characteristically ones involving the good, the true, and the beautiful, while excluding actions such as rolling a stone forever or living alone in a virtual reality device, and, in the case of individual persons, potentially exhibiting an intrinsic desirability greater than what is available in day-to-day life on earth. That is what the rest of this book is about.[7]

References

Ayer, A. J. 1947. 'The Claims of Philosophy'. *Polemic* 7: 18–33.
Cottingham, John. 2013. 'Meaningful Life'. In *The Wisdom of the Christian Faith*, ed. P. K. Moser and M. T. McFall, 175–196. Cambridge: Cambridge University Press.
de Muijnck, Wim. 2013. 'The Meaning of Lives and the Meaning of Things'. *Journal of Happiness Studies* 14: 1291–1307.
Hepburn, R. W. 1966. 'Questions about the Meaning of Life'. *Religious Studies* 1: 125–140.
Kauppinen, Antti. 2015. 'Meaningfulness'. In *Routledge Handbook of the Philosophy of Well-being*, ed. Guy Fletcher, 281–291. New York: Routledge.
Kiymaz, Tufan. 2019. 'On the Meaning of "The Meaning of Life"'. *Unisinos Journal of Philosophy* 20: 146–154.
Landau, Iddo. 2017. *Finding Meaning in an Imperfect World*. New York: Oxford University Press.
Landau, Iddo. 2020. 'Is Meaning in Life Based on Value or Intelligibility?' *Psychology Today*, 18 March, https://www.psychologytoday.com/za/blog/finding-meaning-in-imperfect-world/202003/is-meaning-in-life-based-value-or-intelligibility.
Levy, Neil. 2005. 'Downshifting and Meaning in Life'. *Ratio* 18: 176–189.
Markus, Arjan. 2003. 'Assessing Views of Life'. *Religious Studies* 39: 125–143.
Martela, Frank. 2017. 'Meaningfulness as Contribution'. *Southern Journal of Philosophy* 55: 232–256.
Martela, Frank, and Michael Steger. 2016. 'The Three Meanings of Meaning in Life'. *The Journal of Positive Psychology* 11: 531–545.
Mawson, T. J. 2016. *God and the Meanings of Life*. London: Bloomsbury.
Mawson, T. J. 2019. *Monotheism and the Meaning of Life*. Cambridge: Cambridge University Press.
Metz, Thaddeus. 2001. 'The Concept of a Meaningful Life'. *American Philosophical Quarterly* 38: 137–153.
Metz, Thaddeus. 2013. *Meaning in Life: An Analytic Study*. Oxford: Oxford University Press.
Metz, Thaddeus. 2019a. 'Recent Work on the Meaning of "Life's Meaning"'. *Human Affairs* 29: 404–414.
Metz, Thaddeus. 2019b. *God, Soul and the Meaning of Life*. Cambridge: Cambridge University Press.
Nielsen, Kai. 1964. 'Linguistic Philosophy and "The Meaning of Life"'. *Cross Currents* 14: 313–334.
Nozick, Robert. 1981. *Philosophical Explanations*. Cambridge, MA: Harvard University Press.
Purves, Duncan, and Nicolas Delon. 2018. 'Meaning in the Lives of Humans and Other Animals'. *Philosophical Studies* 175: 317–338.
Scanlon, T. M. 1998. *What We Owe to Each Other*. Cambridge, MA: Harvard University Press.

---

[7] I thank Iddo Landau for thoughtful comments on a previous draft of this essay.

Seachris, Joshua. 2009. 'The Meaning of Life as Narrative'. *Philo* 12: 5–23.

Seachris, Joshua. 2016. 'The Meaning of Life and Narratives'. In *God and Meaning*, ed. Joshua Seachris and Stewart Goetz, 13–34. New York: Bloomsbury Academic.

Seachris, Joshua. 2019. 'From the Meaning Triad to Meaning Holism: Unifying Life's Meaning'. *Human Affairs* 29: 363–378.

Seachris, Joshua. 2020. 'The Meaning of Life: Contemporary Analytic Perspectives'. In *The Internet Encyclopedia of Philosophy*, ed. James Fieser and Bradley Dowden. https://iep.utm.edu/mean-ana/.

Swinburne, Richard. 2016. 'How God Makes Life a Lot More Meaningful'. In *God and Meaning*, ed. Joshua Seachris and Stewart Goetz, 149–164. New York: Bloomsbury Academic.

Tartaglia, James. 2015. *Philosophy in a Meaningless Life*. London: Bloomsbury.

Taylor, Charles. 1989. *Sources of the Self*. Cambridge, MA: Harvard University Press.

Thomas, Joshua. 2018. 'Can Only Human Lives Be Meaningful?' *Philosophical Papers* 47: 265–297.

Thomas, Joshua. 2019. 'Meaningfulness as Sensefulness'. *Philosophia* 47: 1555–1577.

Trisel, Brooke Alan. 2007. 'Judging Life and Its Value'. *Sorites* 18: 60–75.

Visak, Tatjana. 2017. 'Understanding "Meaning of Life" in Terms of Reasons for Action'. *Journal of Value Inquiry* 51: 507–530.

Waghorn, Nicholas. 2014. *Nothingness and the Meaning of Life*. London: Bloomsbury.

Wolf, Susan. 2016. 'Meaningfulness: A Third Dimension of the Good Life'. *Foundations of Science* 21: 253–269.

Wong, Wai-hung. 2008. 'Meaningfulness and Identities'. *Ethical Theory and Moral Practice* 11: 123–148.

CHAPTER 2

SUBJECTIVISM AND OBJECTIVISM ABOUT MEANING IN LIFE

JENS JOHANSSON AND FRANS SVENSSON

1. INTRODUCTION

THERE are two main types of theory about what (if anything) makes a life meaningful: *subjectivism* and *objectivism*. According to subjectivism, meaning in a person's life depends at least in part on the person's own concerns: a component of a person's life can contribute meaning to it only if she cares about the component in one way or another. According to objectivism, there is no such dependency: a component of a person's life can contribute meaning to it even if she in no way cares about the component.

Both types of theory have well-known problems. One main problem with objectivist theories is that it seems implausible that knowledge, say, could contribute meaning to the life of a person who is completely indifferent to knowledge. In other words, in objectivist theories there is an unsatisfying *lack of connection* between that which is claimed to contribute meaning to a life and the attitudes of the person whose life it is. Although this complaint may seem to consist in a sheer *denial* of objectivism, we shall see that there is more to it than that.

While subjectivist theories avoid the lack of connection problem, they face others. There are two main types of subjectivism: *pure* subjectivism and *hybridism*. On pure subjectivism, meaning in a person's life depends *only* on her own concerns: all it takes for a component of someone's life to contribute meaning to it is that she cares about the component in some suitable way. Pure subjectivism is strikingly unpopular. One charge that has been levelled against pure subjectivism is that it is incompatible with a certain kind of epiphany, namely, the realization 'that one's life to date has been meaningless' (Wolf 2015a, 96). Another charge is that pure subjectivism has the gravely implausible implication that even the most pointless and unworthy activities—such as 'counting the blades of grass on Harvard Yard' (Smuts 2013, 536), or spending 'day after day, or night after night, in front of a television set, drinking beer and watching situation comedies' (Wolf 2015a, 92)—will automatically contribute meaning to an agent's life so long as she enjoys them.

On *hybridism*, whether something contributes meaning to a person's life depends *both* on her caring about it *and* on its objective value or intrinsic importance. Due to the former element, hybridism avoids the 'lack of connection' problem for objectivism; due to the latter element, it also avoids the 'pointless activities' problem for pure subjectivism. However, hybridism (like objectivism) seems to avoid the latter problem by too wide a margin: it appears implausibly *elitist* or *exclusivist* to rule out that at least *some* of us could acquire meaning to their lives by engaging in intrinsically worthless activities.

This chapter is an opinionated survey of these respective challenges for objectivism, pure subjectivism, and hybridism. Among other things, we shall provide reasons to think that the challenges for pure subjectivism are less serious than they are ordinarily taken to be, and less serious than those that confront objectivism and hybridism.

2. Preliminary Remarks

First of all, we shall offer some initial stage setting.

(a) *Life.* When we talk about meaning in life in this chapter, what we have in mind is meaning in individual human lives. We will thus not be interested in the meaning, if any, of human life as a whole—such as the purpose, if any, for which human life exists or has been created by God.[1] Nor will we be concerned with the meaning that perhaps can be exemplified in the lives of non-human animals or plants (or, for that matter, in the existences of non-living entities).

(b) *Meaning.* It seems clear that meaning, or meaningfulness, is a kind of *value* that a life can have. It would, for example, be absurd to say of someone's life that although it was full of meaning, there was nothing in any way good about it. While there is no need to assume any specific view about the exact nature of this value here, it will prove useful to compare it with some other kinds of value that a life can have.

To begin with, a life's meaningfulness is not the same as its *aesthetic* value. For example, a person who constantly undergoes various harms and misfortunes, and who learns absolutely nothing from them, may well have a life that is devoid of meaning but that also makes for a fascinating story. Indeed, the life's utter meaninglessness may be

---

[1] The question of what is the purpose of human life is perhaps usually thought to belong to the purview of religion. For a discussion of what alternatives there may be for secular thinkers to find a satisfying answer to that question, see e.g. Nagel (2010, chapter 1). For a book-length discussion of purposivism in the universe, see Mulgan (2015).

part of what *makes* the story fascinating. A life's meaningfulness is also distinct from its *moral* value. For example, a life can be morally bad and yet (perhaps for non-moral reasons) full of meaning. After all, a life devoted to reading, scuba diving, and bird watching may well be highly meaningful even if those activities prevent the person from fulfilling her moral duties. It should be noted that distinguishing a life's meaning from its aesthetic and moral value is compatible with saying that aesthetic activities and experiences and moral uprightness can contribute meaning to a life. It is just that when they do, they confer on the person's life not only moral and aesthetic value, but also the *further* value of meaningfulness.

Unlike moral and aesthetic value, meaningfulness seems to be a sort of *prudential* value. If a person's life is meaningful, then it is in some important sense good *for her*; whatever contributes meaning to her life must in some significant sense be *in her own interests*.[2] Meaningfulness, in the relevant sense, is thus plausibly close to *well-being* (or *welfare*)—where well-being is that which utilitarianism asks us to maximize, and that for which standard versions of hedonism and desire satisfactionism, for example, aim to account. Indeed, some might claim that meaningfulness just *is* well-being. While there is no need to settle this issue here, it is worth noting that meaning intuitively requires *depth* in a way that well-being does not. Suppose, for example, that a person's life is replete with pleasant experiences, but that none of these is deeply rewarding for her: she constantly experiences the sort of pleasure that most of us receive from eating candy or drinking soda, but never the sort of deep satisfaction that people tend to receive from the company of friends, from understanding a difficult but important line of reasoning, or from reading a literary masterpiece. A tempting thought is that this person's life scores higher (though perhaps not high) on the well-being scale than on the meaningfulness scale. In that case, meaning cannot be the same as well-being. Of course, it might still be true that anything that contributes meaning to someone's life thereby contributes well-being to it.

A person's life can also have a sort of 'worldly' value: it can contribute to the overall intrinsic value of the world. It can be intrinsically good for the universe, as it were, that a particular life exists. Plausibly, this value, too, is not the same as meaningfulness. In particular, unlike meaningfulness, worldly value is not a sort of prudential value—it is not value *for the person*.

(c) **Reasons**. As just noted, meaning is a sort of prudential value. Now, prudential value gives rise to prudential reasons. Hence, meaningfulness gives rise to prudential reasons. Plausibly, for instance, if an agent faces two alternative courses of action, one of which would result in much more meaning in the agent's life than the other, then she has at least some prudential reason to choose the former course of action rather than the latter. This reason need not be even close to decisive, but it is there.

---

[2] At any rate, surely there is *some* important notion of meaningfulness for which this claim holds. If there are others for which it does not, then those latter notions are simply outside the scope of this chapter.

(d) *Harm*. Prudential value is also intimately related to *harm*. It seems clear, for instance, that one way for an event or state of affairs to harm a person is to prevent something that would make her life go better for her. Given that meaning is a sort of prudential value, then, an event or state of affairs that prevents something that would make her life more meaningful seems to harm her, at least in one respect.

(e) *Components of Lives*. While we formulate objectivism, hybridism, and subjectivism in terms of 'a component of a person's life', not much should be read into this—we use this expression very broadly. For one thing, we are happy to regard things that happen before or after the person's lifetime—such as her being remembered after her death—as components of her life, in the relevant sense. For another, we use the term to cover objects from many different ontological categories, such as actions and other events, processes, facts, properties, and periods of time. Thus if a person eats ice cream this afternoon, then some related components of her life are her act of eating ice cream, the fact that she eats ice cream, and this afternoon. We do not, however, treat non-obtaining states of affairs, or false propositions, as components of a person's life, even if they are 'about' her; the person's winning the lottery is a component of her life only if she actually does win the lottery.

3. Objectivism and the Lack of Connection Problem

Again, what makes a theory of meaning in life objectivist is that it implies that a component of a person's life that she in no way cares about can still contribute meaning to that life.

It is easy to see how one could be drawn to objectivism, even aside from the familiar worries about various versions of subjectivism (section 1). Suppose one starts with the belief that knowledge, say, contributes meaning to a person's life for non-instrumental reasons—that is, whether or not the person's knowledge leads to other valuable things for her, such as professional accomplishments, or admiration from her friends. Then there might seem to be a natural step to the stronger thesis that knowledge contributes meaning entirely on its own—that is, regardless of whatever else the person's life contains. This stronger thesis implies the objectivist claim that knowledge contributes meaning to her life even if she does not care about it.

On the lack of connection objection, however, this goes too far. More exactly, it is implausible to not even demand a connection to the person's own concerns. If the person does not *care* about knowledge, it cannot bestow meaning on her life.

So far, the complaint might amount to little more than a mere *denial* of objectivism, or a mere accusation of unattractiveness. However, we can get more of an *argument* against objectivism by recalling that meaningfulness, like well-being, is a kind of prudential value (section 2). A meaningful life is thus in some important sense good *for* the person living it. Now, a common and plausible view is that prudential value requires a connection with the person's own concerns: only things that somehow resonate with, or have a certain appeal to, the person can make her life good for her. As we might put it, *good for* requires *good to*. While things that leave a person entirely cold might well make her life good in other respects—for example, by contributing aesthetic, moral, or worldly value to it—they do not plausibly make it good *for* her. Hence, they do not make it meaningful, contrary to objectivism.[3]

The lack of connection objection can be further boosted by also recalling that prudential value gives rise to prudential reasons (section 2). Suppose, for instance, that an agent finds nothing at all attractive about knowledge; she is as uninterested in it as most of us would be in counting blades of grass. Suppose that this person faces the choice between acquiring a certain piece of knowledge and not doing so. The choice will not affect other aspects of her life, and her indifference to knowledge will remain whichever alternative she chooses. Given these stipulations, the person intuitively has no *prudential* reason to acquire this piece of knowledge—although she might well have other sorts of reasons to do so, such as moral ones (depending on the circumstances). Similar remarks apply to other candidate meaning-makers, such as friendship and professional accomplishments: an agent has a prudential reason to pursue them only given a proper connection with her own concerns. Since a connection with the person's concerns is thus necessary for prudential reasons, and prudential reasons are necessary for prudential value, and meaning is a prudential value, a connection with the person's concerns is necessary for meaning. This is incompatible with objectivism.

We can also appeal to the relationship between prudential value and harm (section 2). Consider again the case just discussed. Suppose that some event prevents the person from acquiring the piece of knowledge (in which, again, the person has no interest whatsoever). If having this piece of knowledge would contribute meaning and thus prudential value to her life, then this event harms the person. But given the assumptions of the case, the event appears to be completely harmless. And again, the same point applies to other candidate meaning-makers.

It is worth looking at how the lack of connection problem arises for three specific objectivist theories that have recently been proposed by Aaron Smuts, Thaddeus Metz, and Erik J. Wielenberg, respectively. On Smuts's consequentialist view, a person's life is meaningful to the extent that it promotes objective goodness, where the promotion and goodness in question can obtain irrespective of the person's attitudes.[4] For example, finding a cure for cancer would contribute meaning to a scientist's life, no matter what her own concerns happen to be.

To illustrate the counterintuitiveness of this position, consider a variant of the myth of Sisyphus due to Susan Wolf (2010, 21; cf. Smuts 2013, 551). Suppose that Sisyphus is

---

[3] This is a common criticism of objectivist theories of *well-being*. See e.g. Sumner (1996, 42–44, and chapter 3).

[4] Smuts (2013). Consequentialist accounts of meaning in life are defended also in e.g. Audi (2005); Bramble (2015); Singer (1996); and Wells (2015).

entirely indifferent to the well-being of others. Suppose also that his stone rolling keeps scaring off vultures that would otherwise cause much suffering to the inhabitants of the village on the other side of the mountain. Smuts's view implies that Sisyphus's stone rolling thereby contributes meaning to his life. This seems wrong, even if it plausibly adds other kinds of value to it. In particular, while the beneficial effects for the villagers might well provide Sisyphus with a *moral* reason to roll the stone, it does not seem to give him any *prudential* reason to do so. Intuitively, moreover, if some event were to prevent the stone rolling from helping the villagers, then the event would harm *them* but not *Sisyphus*.

In fact, Smuts's view implies that a person's life can be meaningful even if she is unable to care about anything at all. Suppose that someone spends her entire life in a comatose condition, in which she is unable to desire or feel anything. As it happens, however, she has an expression on her face that (for some reason) causes everyone who catches a glimpse of it to experience complete contentment and harmony. Assuming that experiencing complete contentment and harmony is objectively valuable, and that at least some people do catch a glimpse of the expression on the comatose individual's face, this expression contributes meaning to her life on Smuts's view. But in that case, it contributes *prudential* value to her life, which seems wrong. For example, if some event had prevented other people from ever noticing the expression on the person's face, then the event might have harmed *them*, but not *her*.[5]

Both Sisyphus's stone rolling (in the revised version of the myth) and the expression on the comatose individual's face make a positive difference to others. It is important to note that denying that this factor contributes meaning to these two individuals' lives is fully compatible with saying that it does contribute meaning to many other people's lives. After all, many people do care about making a positive difference to others.

Unlike Smuts's account, Metz's and Wielenberg's respective accounts are not consequentialist. On Metz's view, a person's life is meaningful roughly to the extent that it involves orienting her 'rationality towards fundamental conditions of human existence' (Metz 2013, 222). On Wielenberg's view, a person's life is meaningful insofar as she is engaged in intrinsically valuable activities, including 'falling in love, engaging in intellectually stimulating activity, being creative in various ways, experiencing pleasure of various kinds, and teaching' (Wielenberg 2005, 34). Both theories apparently avoid the Sisyphus and coma problems. For both theories involve essential references to activity of some form or another, whereas the comatose individual is as inactive as it gets; similarly, even in the revised version of the myth, Sisyphus is not orienting his rationality towards fundamental conditions of human existence, nor is he engaged in intrinsically (as opposed to instrumentally) valuable activity.

Both Metz's and Wielenberg's views, however, face the lack of connection problem. To deal with both views at once, let us assume that orienting one's rationality toward fundamental conditions of human existence is an intrinsically valuable activity. Suppose

---

[5] For a somewhat similar criticism, see Persson and Savulescu (2019, 227).

that a person finds as little interest in this activity as most of us would in orienting our rationality toward fundamental conditions of the existence of a blade of grass. This activity might still add intrinsic value to the world, and moral value to the person's life (depending on the details of the case)—but given how utterly unrewarding *she* finds it, it does not seem to make her life any better *for her*. Everything else being equal, she seems to have no *prudential* reason for taking part in this activity—and preventing her from doing so would not *harm* her in any way. As a result, while orienting one's rationality toward fundamental conditions of human existence might well contribute meaning to the lives of those who care about this activity, it does not seem to contribute meaning to the lives of those who do not.

Now, some items on Wielenberg's list of intrinsically valuable activities might themselves *contain* a positive attitude. This seems to hold for 'engaging in intellectually stimulating activity', for instance: a person cannot both find something intellectually stimulating and be completely indifferent toward it. This suggests a possible avenue for objectivists. It is open to them to hold that a component of someone's life contributes meaning to it only if the component contains a positive attitude. This non-standard version of objectivism has one important virtue: it avoids the implication that a component of someone's life can contribute meaning to it even if the component has no connection at all to any positive attitude of hers. For example, this version of objectivism does not entail—and indeed, rules out—that knowledge or teaching (another item on Wielenberg's list) can contribute meaning to a person's life even if she does not care about knowledge or teaching, or anything that knowledge or teaching involves. What can contribute meaning, on this view, are things like *the person's having and liking to have knowledge*, and *the person's teaching while finding it rewarding*. For such a state of affairs to obtain, the person needs to have some positive attitude toward knowledge and teaching, respectively.

However, this non-standard version of objectivism, too, faces the lack of connection problem. For in order to count as a version of objectivism, it has to imply that while a component contributes meaning to a person's life only if it *contains* a positive attitude of hers, she need not have any positive attitude toward the attitude-containing component *itself*. For instance, the view will have to imply that things like *the person's being engaged in an intellectually stimulating activity*, and *her having and liking to have knowledge*, and *her teaching while finding it rewarding*, can contribute meaning to her life even if she is completely indifferent toward them. (It seems clearly possible for a person to be indifferent toward a compound of a positive attitude of hers and the object of that attitude.) And the trouble for this view is that, just like standard versions of objectivism, it is in conflict with the plausible idea that meaningfulness is a kind of prudential value, and that a component of someone's life contributes prudential value to that life only if she cares about *that component*. Surely, for example, the attractive claim that 'good for' requires 'good to' (section 3) should be understood as saying that in order for something to be good for a person, *that thing itself* has to be good to her. Given that meaningfulness is a kind of prudential value, then, a component of someone's life contributes meaning to that life only if she cares about *that component*.

4. Hybridism and the Exclusivist Problem

According to hybridism, a component of someone's life contributes meaning to it just in case the component is *both* something that she cares about *and* objectively valuable or intrinsically important. While the second condition is something that most objectivist theories would include, the first, attitudinal condition makes hybridism a version of subjectivism as construed here (see section 1).

There is a great variety of specific positive attitudes to which subjectivists, including hybridists, might appeal. One option, for example, is to focus on attitudes that involve some sort of positive *experience*—such as the attitudes of liking, enjoying, and being pleased. Another option is to focus instead on attitudes like *desires* or *preferences*, or *believing to be good*, which need not involve any positive experiences. Yet other options exist, including ones that combine elements of the two just mentioned.

In any case, the attitudinal requirement makes hybridism immune to the lack of connection problem. Consider, for example, Susan Wolf's version of hybridism, the *fitting fulfillment view*, whose famous slogan is that 'meaning arises when subjective attraction meets objective attractiveness' (Wolf 2015b, 112).[6] A meaningful life, according to Wolf, is one of finding fulfilment in activities of objective worth, or loving engagement in projects that are objectively worthy of love. Since objective attractiveness that is *not* met by subjective attraction fails to yield meaning on this view, Wolf, unlike the objectivist, easily avoids the implication that a person can have a prudential reason to pursue a project that she would find entirely unappealing. Similarly, and again unlike the objectivist, Wolf avoids having to say that the person would be harmed by being prevented from pursuing such a project.

However, Wolf's theory, like all versions of hybridism—and indeed all theories of meaning in life containing the 'objective value or intrinsic importance' requirement—is subject to a related problem, namely, that it is implausibly *elitist* or *exclusivist*. Consider two examples, mentioned by Wolf (2010, 16) and Wielenberg (2005, 34f), respectively, of activities that may be relaxing or enjoyable, but which are also allegedly without objective value and intrinsic importance: solving crossword puzzles and playing video games. Assuming that these activities indeed do lack objective value and intrinsic importance, hybridism implies that they cannot contribute meaning to a life. At first glance, this might seem reasonable. After all, for many people, solving crossword puzzles and playing video games are little more than mere time-killers that do not have any significant link to these individuals' deeper concerns. It does not seem implausible to say that these activities bring no meaning to these lives. (Perhaps the activities still bring

---

[6] For an early defence of a hybrid account, see Hepburn (1966). Hybrid views are also developed in e.g. May (2015) and Flanagan (1996). Kauppinen (2012) defends a view that we believe is, in the end, objectivist, but which is explicitly influenced by Wolf's work in important respects.

some *well-being* to them; see section 2(b).) What does seem implausible, however, is that solving crossword puzzles and playing video games cannot contribute meaning to *any* life—including the life of a person *who finds these activities deeply rewarding and fulfilling*. The complaint is not that the existence or possibility of such a life somehow reveals solving crossword puzzles and playing video games to be objectively valuable or intrinsically important after all. Rather, even granting that they are not, it just seems wrong, and unacceptably elitist or exclusivist, to hold that despite the deep satisfaction the person finds in these activities, they add no meaning to her life.

We are not suggesting that solving crossword puzzles and playing video games contribute meaning to the lives of *all* of those who care deeply about these activities. This is because a person's positive attitudes toward an activity—whether it be reading *War and Peace* or playing *Call of Duty: World at War*—can be *conditional* on the activity's being objectively valuable or intrinsically important. Plausibly, if someone desires to carry out an activity, but only on a certain condition, and that condition fails to obtain, then her desire is not satisfied even if she does carry out the activity (McDaniel and Bradley 2008). Arguably, then, solving crossword puzzles and playing video games do not contribute meaning to the life of someone whose deep concern about these activities is conditional on their possessing objective value or intrinsic importance. However, pointing out this nuance should not be mistaken for providing an adequate response to the exclusivism problem for hybridism. For it seems clear that a person can care deeply about solving crossword puzzles and playing video games *without* this attitude being conditional on the objective value or intrinsic importance of these activities. All that is needed for the exclusivism objection to hybridism is that solving crossword puzzles and playing video games bring meaning to *such* a person's life.

5. Pure Subjectivism and the Epiphany and Pointless Activities Problems

Pure subjectivism is the thesis that meaning in a person's life depends wholly on her own concerns—or more exactly, that a component of a person's life contributes meaning to it just in case she cares about the component in some suitable way.[7] Due to the attitudinal requirement, pure subjectivism avoids the lack of connection problem for objectivism; due to the lack of any additional requirement that the component in question be objectively valuable or intrinsically important, pure subjectivism also avoids the exclusivist problem for hybridism.

We intend the name '*pure* subjectivism' simply to reflect the lack of that additional requirement. We should, however, warn against one misunderstanding to which the name

---

[7] Different variants of pure subjectivism have been defended in e.g. Luper (2014); Svensson (2017); and Taylor (1970).

might give rise. Pure subjectivism is *not* the view, which might be called 'internalism', that meaningfulness is solely a matter of what goes on inside the person's own mind. After all, what pure subjectivism says is that a *component* of someone's life contributes meaning to it just in case she has the relevant sort of positive attitude to it. And, plausibly, many of a person's relevant attitudes—desires, likings, etc.—are directed at states of affairs that concern the world outside of her own mind. If those states of affairs fail to obtain, they are not components of her life (see section 2). The most natural versions of pure subjectivism, then, are 'externalist': they rule out that meaning depends solely on what goes on inside the person's own mind. It is worth adding, however, that pure subjectivists *can* accept internalism, if they like. In particular, an internalist pure subjectivist might contend that the only positive attitudes that matter for meaningfulness are those that can only be directed at one's own mental states. (Presumably, for example, if someone *introspects and appreciates the hedonic qualities of* an object, then that object needs to be a mental state of hers.)

As these remarks illustrate, there are various different ways to be a pure subjectivist. Nevertheless, not many participants in the debate are pure subjectivists. This is mainly due to the 'pointless activities' problem, which we shall consider in subsection 5.2. First, however, we shall discuss another objection.

5.1. The Epiphany Objection

The epiphany objection, as we call it, has primarily been adduced by Susan Wolf. She suggests that by refraining from including any requirement about objective worth, pure subjectivism obliterates the difference between one's life merely *feeling* or *seeming* meaningful to one, and one's life actually *being* meaningful. This difference is crucial, according to Wolf, in order to allow for the possibility of waking up 'either literally or figuratively—to the recognition that one's life to date has been meaningless' (Wolf 2015a, 96). Since such epiphanies are possible, pure subjectivism fails.

It seems to us that pure subjectivism does allow for such epiphanies. Suppose that a person has long believed herself to be participating in various activities, such as close relationships, professional projects, movie watching, and outdoor exercises. Suppose also that she has always had the relevant sort of positive attitudes toward her participating in these activities. Suppose, however, that she has been grossly mistaken in taking herself to be participating in any of them (maybe, for instance, because she is in an 'experience machine'; see Nozick 1974, 42–45). Since what she cares about is actually *being* a participant in these activities—as opposed to merely *believing* herself to participate in them—the objects of her concerns fail to obtain and thus are simply not components of her life (see section 2(e)). Given pure subjectivism, this person's life to date may thus have been meaningless, and the person herself might well come to realize this, once her delusion has been cleared up.

Similar remarks apply even to versions of pure subjectivism that are 'internalist' in the sense suggested earlier. Suppose that a person has always taken pleasure in only one thing, namely, her own love of God—except that she has been mistaken in thinking that she has ever loved God. Maybe her strong wish to love God has fooled her into thinking that she does. Nothing prevents internalist pure subjectivists from saying that since the only thing this person has ever cared about—her love of God—is simply not there, her life until now has been meaningless; and the person might well come to realize this herself, once she discovers her mistake.

There is also the following kind of case. Suppose that pure subjectivism (in any version) is true. Suppose also that a person starts out believing both that objectivism is true and that her life to date has contained plenty of objectively good things, such as knowledge and friendship. Unsurprisingly, then, she does not start out believing that her life is meaningless. Suppose, moreover, that she never has the relevant sort of positive attitude toward any of those things—for instance, she does not take any pleasure at all in knowledge or friendship. One day, however, the person realizes that pure subjectivism is true. This seems to amount to a discovery that her life until now has been meaningless.

A critic might respond that even if the preceding cases show that pure subjectivism is able to accommodate the claim that a person can come to realize that her life to date has been meaningless, it is unable to accommodate the stronger claim that the person can do this by realizing that the objects of her concerns are not *objectively valuable*. It is not clear that this supposed inability makes for a non-question-begging argument against pure subjectivism. But, in any case, it seems to us that pure subjectivism has no such inability—it can accommodate even the stronger claim. For, as pointed out in section 4, desires and other pro-attitudes can be conditional on all sorts of things, including the relevant objects being objectively valuable. It is open to pure subjectivists to say, for example, that if a person has devoted her life until now to playing video games, but has desired to do so only on the condition that playing video games is objectively valuable, and later realizes that playing video games is objectively worthless, she might well thereby also come to realize that her life so far has been meaningless.

5.2. The Pointless Activities Objection

By far the most common objection to pure subjectivist theories is that they have 'seriously counterintuitive implications about which lives count as meaningful' (Metz 2013, 175). On such theories, we could acquire meaning in our lives even from activities such as spending 'day after day, or night after night, in front of a television set, drinking beer and watching situation comedies' (Wolf 2015a, 92), 'collecting rubber bands' (Wolf 2015b, 112), 'memorizing the dictionary' (Wolf 2015b, 112), 'making handwritten copies of *War and Peace*' (Wolf 2015b, 112), 'counting the blades of grass on Harvard Yard' (Smuts 2013, 536), 'collecting bottle tops' (Singer 1996, 113), and 'smoking pot all day' (Wolf 2010, 9). Unlike the activities considered in section 4, that is, solving crossword puzzles and playing video games, which might lack intrinsic significance but still seem to be perfectly reasonable ways of spending at least part of one's time, the activities listed here seem somehow unworthy, absurd, and pointless. It is severely counterintuitive, we are invited to agree, that they could contribute meaning to anyone's life. Pure subjectivism, however, implies that these activities do contribute meaning to the lives of people who have the relevant sort of positive attitudes toward them. Objectivist and hybrid theories, by contrast, have no such consequence.

This objection strikes us as less powerful than it has often been considered to be. Indeed, a promising response to it is implicit in various remarks we have made earlier in this chapter. We want to draw attention to five points in particular.

First, it is again important to remember that desires and similar positive attitudes can be conditional on various things. Suppose that someone devotes all her time to some activity, and strongly desires to do so, but that this desire is conditional on this activity's not being utterly pointless. If the activity *is* utterly pointless, the person's desire is not satisfied (see section 4). In that case, even a pure subjectivist can deny that the activity contributes meaning to the person's life. When imagining a case where someone spends all her time collecting rubber bands, say, it might be easy to implicitly assume that the person bizarrely takes this activity to be objectively worthwhile—and that her desire to perform it is conditional on its being so. But if that is what we are assuming, then the judgement that the activity fails to contribute meaning to the person's life provides no good reason to deny pure subjectivism. Instead, we need to focus on cases where the agent's positive attitudes are *not* conditional on the activity's not being entirely pointless. In such cases, the intuition that the activity fails to contribute meaning to the person's life might be less strong.

Second, as mentioned in section 2, meaningfulness must be distinguished from other kinds of value, such as aesthetic or moral value. A life devoted to collecting rubber bands or memorizing the dictionary is likely to score fairly low on an aesthetic scale; the story of someone spending her days making handwritten copies of *War and Peace* is strikingly worse, from an aesthetic point of view, than is *War and Peace* itself. And such lives will score low on a moral scale as well, in part because they will be of no use to others. Since the lives in question are so glaringly unimpressive in aesthetic and moral respects, it might be easy to let one's aesthetic and moral judgements about them illicitly influence one's judgements about their meaningfulness. When one manages to keep aesthetic and moral considerations out of the picture, it might no longer seem so clear that these lives are meaningless.

Third, recall that both objectivism and hybridism are in tension with the plausible view that meaningfulness is a kind of prudential value, and therefore closely connected with prudential reasons and harm (sections 3–4). The same charge does not seem to apply to pure subjectivism, even with regard to activities such as those presently under consideration. For instance, it does not strike us as implausible to claim that someone who cares deeply about memorizing the dictionary (and whose concern is not conditional on the activity's not being pointless) has some prudential reason to pursue this activity, and that an event that prevents her from doing so harms her. At the very least, that claim obviously respects the close connection between prudential value, and thereby prudential reasons and harm, on the one hand, and the person's own concerns, on the other (section 2). We do not wish to suggest that this constitutes positive support for the thesis that memorizing the dictionary contributes meaning to the person's life—especially since meaningfulness is plausibly not the only kind of prudential value (section 2). However, it is still noteworthy that pure subjectivism, even with regard to activities that are usually taken to be particularly embarrassing for it, performs well in a test that is particularly embarrassing for objectivism and hybridism.

Fourth, pure subjectivists are free to point out that the activities at issue are likely *instrumentally* bad, even in terms of meaning, for the agent. For example, they could stress that constantly collecting rubber bands or drinking beer night after night in front of the TV will be detrimental to other things the agent might, or could come to, care even more about—such as her physical health, her intellectual abilities, and the capacity to initiate and sustain relationships with others. Furthermore, as with most activities, if we engage in them too often, we will likely grow tired of them. If someone spends all of her waking hours making handwritten copies of *War and Peace*, pure subjectivists might reasonably urge her to consider what she will do when that activity loses its grip on her.

Fifth, it is open to pure subjectivists to place some suitable restrictions on the pertinent positive attitudes. In particular, as noted in section 2 (and as implied in section 4), meaningfulness intuitively involves some sort of *depth*. A pure subjectivist could say that merely desiring or liking an activity is not enough for it to add meaning to one's life; the subject needs to somehow find the activity deeply satisfying or rewarding. This general idea can be developed in a variety of ways, depending on what specific kinds of positive attitudes are considered relevant. An 'experientialist' pure subjectivist, for example, could emphasize that the sort of pleasure that most of us receive from eating Mars or drinking Coca-Cola—or that any relatively normal person would at most receive from collecting rubber bands or memorizing the dictionary—simply *feels* very different from the sort of pleasure that we tend to get from intimate conversations with friends, or that a devout Tolstoy reader feels while immersed in *War and Peace*. Only pleasure that feels in this latter kind of way, the experientialist pure subjectivist might say, is relevant to meaning. Similarly, a 'non-experientialist' pure subjectivist could say, for instance, that the attitudes that matter for meaningfulness are desires that are partly constitutive of the inner core of her personality—desires that define who the person truly is, and that she is deeply invested in. Desires that are, in this respect, more superficial are irrelevant. As already indicated, attitudes that satisfy such experientialist or non-experientialist constraints might as a matter of fact tend to be directed at, and attitudes that do not satisfy such constraints might tend not to be directed at, objectively valuable things. But such correlations are surely contingent; someone *could* find collecting rubber bands or memorizing the dictionary deeply rewarding. Once we separate clearly the quality of the *attitude* from the quality of its *object*, it seems far from clear that it is the latter, or the latter together with the former, rather than simply the former, that is relevant to meaning.

6. CONCLUDING REMARKS

In this chapter, we have provided some reasons to think that while the lack of connection problem and the exclusivist problem constitute serious challenges for objectivism and hybridism, respectively, the epiphany and pointless activities problems for pure subjectivism are less serious—and less serious than they are usually taken to be. While these reasons are no doubt non-decisive, they do seem to show it to be a live possibility that pure subjectivism is true.

We shall conclude with a metaethical point. Even if pure subjectivism is indeed true, there is still a clear sense in which meaning in life need not be a subjective matter at all. Again, what pure subjectivism says is that a component of someone's life contributes meaning to that life just in case she has the relevant sort of positive attitudes toward that component. However, *whether that is so* is not thereby something subjective; our attitudes can still be completely irrelevant to the issue of what theory of meaning in life is correct. After all, for all pure subjectivism says, its own truth can be wholly independent of whether anyone believes in it, likes it, desires it to be true, finds it deeply rewarding to contemplate, and so forth. In other words, if pure subjectivism is correct, this can be a purely objective fact.

REFERENCES

Audi, R. 2005. 'Intrinsic Value and the Meaning of Life'. *Philosophical Papers* 34(3): 331–355.
Bramble, B. 2015. 'Consequentialism about Meaning in Life'. *Utilitas* 27(4): 445–459.
Flanagan, O. 1996. *Self-Expressions: Mind, Morals, and the Meaning of Life.* Oxford: Oxford University Press.
Hepburn. R.W. 1966. 'Questions about the Meaning of Life'. *Religious Studies* 1(2): 125–140.
Kauppinen, A. 2012. 'Meaningfulness and Time'. *Philosophy and Phenomenological Research* 84(2): 345–377.
Luper, S. 2014. 'Life's Meaning'. In S. Luper, *The Cambridge Companion to Life and Death,*, pp. 198–212. Cambridge: Cambridge University Press.
May, T. 2015. *A Significant Life: Meaning in a Silent Universe.* Chicago: University of Chicago Press.
McDaniel, K., and B. Bradley. 2008. 'Desires'. *Mind* 117: 267–302.
Metz, T. 2013. *Meaning in Life: An Analytic Study.* Oxford: Oxford University Press
Mulgan, T. 2015. *Purpose in the Universe: The Moral and Metaphysical Case for Ananthropocentric Purposivism.* Oxford: Oxford University Press.
Nagel, T. 2010. 'Secular Philosophy and the Religious Temperament'. In T. Nagel, *Secular Philosophy and the Religious Temperament: Essays 2002–2008,* 3–18. Oxford: Oxford University Press.
Nozick, R. 1974. *Anarchy, State, and Utopia.* New York: Basic Books.
Persson, I., and J. Savulescu. 2019. 'The Meaning of Life, Equality and Eternity'. *The Journal of Ethics* 23: 223–238.
Singer, I. 1996. *Meaning of Life*, Vol. 1: *The Creation of Value.* Baltimore, MD: John Hopkins University Press.
Sumner, W. L. 1996. *Welfare, Happiness, and Ethics.* Oxford: Oxford University Press.

Smuts, A. 2013. 'The Good Cause Account of the Meaning of Life'. *The Southern Journal of Philosophy* 51(4): 536–562.
Svensson, F. 2017. 'A Subjectivist Account of Life's Meaning'. *De Ethica* 4(3): 45–66.
Taylor, R. 1970. *Good and Evil: A New Direction*. New York: Macmillan.
Wells, M. 2015. 'Meaning in Consequences'. *Journal of Philosophy of Life* 5(3): 169–179.
Wielenberg, E. J. 2005. *Value and Virtue in a Godless Universe*. Cambridge: Cambridge University Press.
Wolf, S. 2010. *Meaning in Life and Why It Matters*. Princeton, NJ: Princeton University Press.
Wolf, S. 2015a. 'The Meanings of Lives'. In her *The Variety of Values: Essays on Morality, Meaning, and Love*, pp. 89–106. Oxford: Oxford University Press.
Wolf, S. 2015b. 'Happiness and Meaning: Two Aspects of the Good Life'. In her *The Variety of Values: Essays on Morality, Meaning, and Love*, pp. 107–126. Oxford: Oxford University Press.

CHAPTER 3

ACHIEVEMENT AND MEANING IN LIFE

GWEN BRADFORD

Why Achievement?

UNTIL relatively recently, there was little discussion directly concerning achievement in philosophical literature about well-being or value.[1] But one place where achievement has long been a central part of discussion is in the literature about the meaning of life.[2] In many discussions of meaning in life, achievement, or something very much like it, plays a key role in the account of meaning. Most obviously is Susan Wolf's view that meaning in life amounts to finding fulfilment in projects of 'objective worth'. John Cottingham includes something similar in his account, and there are many other discussions, including one by Neil Levy, which I will discuss in depth shortly.

But for all this, there isn't a lot of discussion about precisely what it is for a project to have 'objective worth'. In this chapter, I'm going to discuss one way in which projects can have objective worth, and why this particular sort of achievement makes them especially rich sources of meaning. I will assume a Wolfian view that worthwhile projects and a subjective sense of fulfilment are components of meaning in life. I will also assume that there is a relationship between 'objective worth' and intrinsic value—to be precise, that having objective worth is the same thing as having intrinsic value. I use 'project' and 'achievement' more or less interchangeably. Even though there may be differences between projects and achievements, what's at stake in this discussion are challenging endeavours that unfold over time, typically with an aim of culminating in an outcome. Given all this, my goal is not to establish that achievements are indeed part of an account

---

[1] The few discussions of achievement and its value include (Hurka 1993); (Keller 2004); (Portmore 2007); (Bradford 2013b, 2015); and (von Kriegstein 2017).
[2] For example, (Wolf 1997); (Cottingham 2003); (Brogaard and Smith 2005); (James 2005); (Levy 2005).

of meaning in life; rather, assuming that they are, I take up the question of which kinds of achievements are the best sources of meaning.

Mill's Crisis

A natural thought is that the achievements that are the most objectively worthwhile and the most significant for meaning are those that accomplish some great good. Projects such as developing a cure for cancer, resolving social injustices, or building schools for needy children are the sorts of achievements that one would expect to find at the centre of an account of projects of objective worthwhileness. No one would deny that these projects are objectively worthwhile and can be superlatively meaningful.

However, that a project results in some great good is neither necessary nor sufficient for it to be meaningful. The crisis suffered by John Stuart Mill as he describes it in his *Autobiography* is a telling illustration. Mill asks himself:

> 'Suppose that all your objects in life were realised; that all the changes in institutions and opinions which you are looking forward to, could be completely effected at this very instant: would this be a great joy and happiness to you?' And an irrepressible self-consciousness distinctly answered, 'No!' At this my heart sank within me: the whole foundation on which my life was constructed fell down. All my happiness was to have been found in the continual pursuit of this end. (Mill [1873] 1989, 112)

Mill subsequently has something of a breakdown, overwhelmed by the sense that his aim has now 'lost its charm' and seems worthless and 'tragic' ([1873] 1989, 112).[3]

There are several lessons we can draw from Mill's crisis. Mill's crisis illustrates that achievements that result in some great good are not sufficient for meaning. Even if a valuable outcome entails that a project is objectively worthwhile, this does not guarantee feelings of fulfilment. Second, it illustrates that there is something significant about the *pursuit* that is distinctive from the finished product when he realizes that his sense of purpose springs from the pursuit of a goal that is far away, independently from the accomplishment of the aim. The pursuit is a source of more significant meaningfulness than the completed accomplishment.

---

[3] Following the passage, Mill asks the following rhetorical question, which I think complicates how we might understand his concerns: 'The end had ceased to charm, and how could there ever again be any interest in the means?' One way of taking the concern is that Mill no longer sees his goals as valuable or worth pursuing, and as a result, the pursuit is uninteresting. This is a different worry than what I take up. I take Mill's concern as the realization that he wasn't driven by the thought that the goal was important to be realized, but driven by the pursuit, illustrating that the pursuit of a goal can be meaningful independently from its accomplishment. Regardless of whether this was precisely what Mill felt, it seems to be an important insight. This seems to be how Levy also understands Mill's crisis, as I discuss later.

This is a surprising insight. The natural thought is that the good that results from an achievement is the source of its objective worth and therefore meaning. But achievements that result in some good—obviously the best sorts of achievements by Mill's utilitarian standards—are not the only or best candidates for achievements that are meaningful. Many paradigmatically valuable achievements don't amount to anything beyond their own execution. In 2015, two mountain climbers scaled the sheer 3,000-foot Dawn Wall of El Capitan at Yosemite, using nothing more than their hands and feet to climb over the course of nineteen days, an achievement for which they were congratulated by the president. This remarkable achievement was clearly valuable and deeply meaningful for the climbers. 'I wanted to see what I was capable of, and this was the biggest canvas,' said one of the climbers.[4] Yet its value has nothing to do at all with any resulting good apart from its own undertaking. Other paradigmatic achievements are similar in this respect, such as running a marathon, learning a new language, or mastering any other difficult hobby.

Philosophical discussions of achievement converge on the observation that achievements are characterized by difficulty (Hurka 1993, 123ff; Keller 2004, 32; Portmore 2007, 3; Bradford 2013b, 2015; von Kriegstein 2017). The challenge, as illustrated by the climbers in Yosemite, is a source of what makes them worthwhile projects, regardless of whether or not they result in some further good.[5] If it were totally effortless to climb a sheer rock face, it wouldn't be the valuable achievement that it is.

Consequently, having a product of independent value is not *necessary* for a project to have objective worth. To be sure, that a project has objective worth does not guarantee that it will be found subjectively fulfilling. But the point here is that projects can be worthwhile solely in virtue of their challenge. If such a worthwhile project is met with subjective attraction by those engaged in it, then it is meaningful.

So far, then, there is something significant about the process of achievement beyond its product. That a project has a discernible valuable outcome is not sufficient for

---

[4] <http://www.nytimes.com/2015/01/15/sports/tommy-caldwell-and-kevin-jorgeson-relax-finally-and-talk-about-climbing-the-dawn-wall.html?_r=0>, <http://news.nationalgeographic.com/news/2015/01/150114-climbing-yosemite-caldwell-jorgeson-capitan/>, retrieved 1 February 2015.

[5] But surely, the obvious objection goes, not every challenging project is worthwhile—what about Rawls's grass counter, or walking from Oxford to London on your hands? But there isn't much principled reason why walking a great distance on one's hands shouldn't be as impressive and worthwhile an achievement as any equally difficult athletic feat, such as running a great distance very quickly, or throwing something very heavy, for which Olympic medals are awarded. A more worrying challenge comes from projects with evil ends. Surely it's incredibly difficult to orchestrate a genocide, but certainly the opposite of 'worthwhile'. Indeed, there are several factors in the overall value of any achievement, and the value of the goal or product of the achievement is among them. Even if the challenging process of an evil achievement has some positive value, it is grossly outweighed by the negative value of the product (Bradford 2015, 160–162). Note that achievements with only slightly evil ends, such as an elaborate art heist, are more palatable candidates for meaningful achievements. Further, the principle of recursion, which I discuss later in this chapter, provides additional value-theoretic resources to capture these intuitions (cf. Bradford 2015, 162ff; Bradford 2013a).

objective worth or meaning, nor is it necessary. Challenge itself appears to be an important source of both objective worth and meaning.

Unimaginable Goals

Another lesson to draw from Mill's crisis is that a process with a certain structure is a particularly good source for meaning. The rough idea is that significantly meaningful achievements are characterized by a structure that is such that completing the goal is *unimaginable*. In this section I elaborate this idea, and motivate the claim that it is achievements with these structures that are exceptionally meaningful.

This idea is suggested by Neil Levy in a paper about meaningfulness in life. This idea is very compelling, and, since Levy doesn't spell out in precise detail exactly what this structure amounts to and why it is so significant for meaning, that is what I would like to do here. Just what exactly is it for the completion of an achievement to be unimaginable? And, more importantly, *why* is this a characteristic of exceptionally meaningful achievements?

Mill's crisis arises when Mill *imagines* his projects completed. So the inspiration for Levy is that 'superlatively' meaningful projects have goals that we cannot 'imagine completing' (Levy 2005, 183).[6] The idea isn't simply that we couldn't imagine completing the goal—I couldn't imagine completing a five-thousand-piece jigsaw puzzle of a sand dune, but that doesn't make it a superlatively meaningful achievement. Nor is the idea that attaining the goal is unimaginable because it is by its nature simply impossible to complete. This would describe Sisyphus's goal, the archetype of meaninglessness.

Rather, the idea is that the project has a certain structure in light of the nature of the goal: the goal develops and expands as we approach it. As we make progress toward the goal, new aspects of the goal emerge and so the pursuit expands. Our understanding of what would amount to completion of the goal changes as we progress; hence, its completion is unimaginable.

Here is how I will put it. Goals are *self-propagating* when the standards for success develop as progress is made toward the goal. These goals are *self*-propagating because the nature of the goal gives the activity of its pursuit this structure. These goals are *propagating* in that they expand and develop. The contention is that this self-propagating structure is a key for projects of exceptional meaning.

The pursuit of knowledge illustrates this structure. The more we explore an area of inquiry and the more we learn about it, the more new questions arise. The boundary, as it were, of what we can know recedes the closer we get to it. A scientist, for example,

---

[6] Levy acknowledges that some superlatively meaningful goals *may* be such that their completion is imaginable, such as 'communion with God' (Levy 2005, 184). Levy says that what distinguishes superlatively meaningful completable goals from those that are not superlatively meaningful is that the accomplishment of the former continues to imbue one's life with meaning.

might have a project to understand some aspect of the natural world. Typically, science progresses by way of studies with findings suitable for publication in academic journals—not expanding goals, but discrete, short-term goals, yet typically these smaller projects are part of a more expansive aim.[7] For the most part, the goals of scientists are broad, and as progress is made on a particular study, the next steps towards the new goal become clear. Hypotheses are confirmed or not, opening and closing different avenues of exploration.

Creative artistic endeavours are also paradigmatically self-propagating. An artist may have a particular vision for a piece, but once the creative enterprise is underway, the conception of the finished product itself is calibrated and refined. On a larger scale, an artist's overall goal may not have a neatly comprehensible finish line. An artist may aim to create a body of work that establishes a certain vision and resonates a certain way with the audience and with art history. Completing this goal isn't something that's neatly imaginable—one can touch it with fingertips, but not envision completion with comprehensive detail from all sides.

This structure can take shape in light of how we understand and set our goals. Goals, after all, can be set by us—we can take on a project and thereby accept certain goals, and so what constitutes the goal is a matter of how we set it.[8] As a result, the degree to which a goal expands in these cases is a function of how we understand our goal. We could, for example, set a goal to learn the number of stars in the Milky Way and google it.[9] This would not be a self-propagating goal. But if the goal is to comprehend the universe in the way made possible by physics as a science, then it would be. Even a slightly more modest project in physics (for example, 'to understand the most elementary constituents of matter') has a goal that is self-propagating in the relevant way.

This structure is a key feature of many projects that are exceptionally meaningful. It's not a necessary feature, since arguably it is possible that achievements can be meaningful, even exceptionally so, without this structure, such as those with very valuable products like developing a cure for cancer. Whether it is sufficient for exceptional meaning depends on some details I won't have time to resolve here.[10] Levy claims that

---

[7] For example, here is the goal of the nuclear and particle physics research lab at Rice University: 'In the Bonner Lab we are trying to understand the most elementary constituents of matter.' The lab then breaks down their goals: 'We attempt to answer such questions as: How did the universe come to be? Are there undiscovered principles of nature?' and so forth, and then finally 'We do so by participating in the experiments that are underway to study these and other questions.' <https://physics.rice.edu/Nuclear.aspx>, retrieved 1 February 2015.

[8] To be precise, *typically* goals are set by us. Sometimes goals are given rather than chosen. Consider, for example, a famous concert pianist, who was forced to practice as a child and now enjoys a successful career. It does seem that for something to count as a goal for you, however, at least some element of your endorsement of it, or taking up of it, is necessary. It is not necessary that we explicitly endorse our goals, however.

[9] This is a surprisingly difficult question to answer, according to space.com, so it can be taken up as a self-propagating goal after all. Estimates are between 100 billion and 400 billion. <http://www.space.com/25959-how-many-stars-are-in-the-milky-way.html>.

[10] One might wonder whether an evil goal that is self-propagating could have exceptional meaning. There are two different lines of argument to support that it could. First, evil projects could have meaning

these achievements are 'superlatively' meaningful, but I will leave open the possibility that other kinds of achievements could be equally or perhaps more meaningful. The claim here is that this structural feature is *typical* of projects that are *exceptionally* meaningful; this structure imbues meaning in a particularly interesting and rich way.

One might draw comparisons to Kieran Setiya's solution to what he calls the 'mid-life crisis', which is a variation or subspecies of a crisis of meaning (Setiya 2014). The crisis Setiya describes is that seeing one's life as an endless stream of projects (even valuable projects) can give rise to a sense of futility, since the aim of each project is its completion. Setiya's diagnosis of the problem is finding value solely in *telic* activities—discrete projects that come to final conclusions: '[t]he way in which you relate to projects that matter most to you is by trying to complete them, and so to expel them from your life. Your days are devoted to ending . . . the activities that give them meaning' (2014, 12). Setiya's prescription is to value instead *atelic* activities—those with *no* built-in end, such as going for an evening stroll, or spending time with friends and family (2014, 13).

Now we can see that Setiya's dichotomy does not exhaust the categorization of project structures. Self-propagating goals avoid the Schopenhauerian paradox of a stack of telic activities, yet develop richness, complexity, and challenge that are not essential to atelic activities. The better resolution, then, to Setiya's midlife crisis is to structure one's aims toward self-propagating goals.

But one might worry that we're in danger of describing the opposite of a meaningful project—doesn't this sound awfully Sisyphean, pursuing a goal that expands almost infinitely, and so its completion recedes further and further?

But the self-propagating structure isn't simply that the goal recedes and is unattainable, which might very well be Sisyphean. Rather, the goal *develops*, and as progress is made toward the goal, new goals emerge, or new aspects of the goal emerge. Think of it as similar to new levels in a game, or new, deeper, and more enriched levels of interpreting poetry or art. The more you accomplish, the more is possible for you to accomplish. As you move along toward the goal, you can turn around and look back and see what you have accomplished from where you started. You can rightly say that you have made progress, you can see what's possible for you now to do would not have been possible earlier. As a philosopher, for instance, you can see that since you started

---

on a certain conception of understanding 'meaning' that includes negative value as a candidate for meaning. This is a surprisingly intuitive position. When asked to generate a list of meaningful events, students in a class I regularly teach typically name far more negative events (World War II, 9/11, funerals) than positive ones. Alternatively, assuming that meaning is related to positive value, one can argue that projects with evil goals can have positive value. Having such a self-propagating structure would be a way that a project with an evil goal could have at least some positive value, even if it is overall negative. Depending how the numbers work out, some evil achievements could have net positive value, and therefore have meaning (assuming meaning is a matter of positive value). Hence evil self-propagating goals *could* have exceptional meaning. However, since on balance some evil self-propagating projects may have more bad than good, this would mean the self-propagating structure is not sufficient for exceptional meaning. The principle of recursion, which I discuss later in this chapter, provides further resources (Bradford 2013a).

in your philosophical studies, you have established and defended some claims, or developed and defended a view. At the very least, your understanding of the space of views on a topic is refined, and the merits and pitfalls of the views are understood more clearly. Further, you can now see the possibility of making new arguments that would not have been possible at the earlier stage. Similarly, a playwright early in his career has only a rudimentary grasp of how to establish character, craft plot, effectively set scenes, and so forth. As he goes along in his career, he develops more sophisticated abilities. His overall goal of developing a corpus of work develops and expands as each new play that he writes is better and better. The plays he writes later in his career wouldn't have been possible for him to write early in his career. As progress is made, new opportunities for progress open up.

Bernard Reginster makes a similar point beautifully, drawing from Goethe's *Faust*, in which the only things Faust will accept in exchange for his soul are, remarkably, insatiable desires. What Faust wants is 'to be moved by desires that are perpetually rekindled, like "trees that every day leaf out anew"' (Reginster 2004, 53).[11] Reginster's argument is that desires of this structure are the Nietzschean antidote to the Schopenhaurian dilemma where life is a pendulum, swinging back and forth between two kinds of misery: the pain of unsatisfied desire on the one hand, and the pain of boredom—lack of desires—on the other. Reginster argues that Nietzsche goes beyond this oscillation by proposing the will to power as the drive for perpetual overcoming of challenge. Reginster illustrates with the pursuit of knowledge: 'It motivates us to solve problems, discover new worlds . . . we would hardly find satisfaction in going again and again over problems that have already been solved . . . the satisfaction of the will to power in the pursuit of knowledge necessarily produces a continuous *self-overcoming* . . . as soon as we attain a certain level of achievement, we proceed to outdo ourselves' (2004, 58). In this sense, what I'm proposing is in this Nietzschean spirit: the most meaningful endeavours are those that afford a wellspring of perpetual challenge.

Yet one might be concerned that there is something perverse about protracted goals. Surely an achievement isn't more meaningful the longer it's dragged out, particularly if the project in question is, say, a cure for cancer.

But of course there are many different reasons why we should undertake projects and many reasons why we should complete them, and the reasons in many of these cases are from sources other than their suitability as sources of meaningfulness in our lives. Additionally, significant meaning can also be found in discrete goals with outcomes of significant value, as acknowledged earlier. The main drawback from discrete goals is illustrated by Mill's crisis. The malaise and let-down from realizing that one's personal fulfilment comes in the pursuit, not the product, means that discrete projects, however significant, are not *perpetual* sources of meaning within one's life. In this respect, projects with self-propagating goals are superior.

---

[11] 'Do you have food that does not satisfy? Or do / You have red gold that will run through / The hand like quicksilver and away? / A game that none may win who play? . . . Show me the fruit that rots on the tree, / And trees that every day leaf out anew!' (Goethe, *Faust*, as quoted by Reginster 2004, 52).

Yet one might argue that pursuit of self-propagating goals is irrational. If it's irrational to adopt impossible aims, such as walking to the moon or making a square circle, and self-propagating goals are impossible, then these projects are irrational.

But what precisely is the concern? It's not irrational to take on goals that are not possible *for you* to complete, since we often work in groups and there is nothing irrational about that; nor is there anything irrational about initiating a project with a plan that is impossible to complete in your lifetime, and could only be completed by others in the future. There is nothing irrational about this at all. Rather, the concern must be that it is irrational to take up self-propagating goals because they are impossible for *anyone* ever to accomplish, such as making a square circle or walking to the moon.

But the self-propagating goals of meaningful achievements are not impossible to accomplish in the way that conceptually or nomologically impossible tasks are impossible. We can't make progress on impossible tasks such as making a square circle, whereas we *can* make progress toward self-propagating goals. The progress that we make toward these goals is genuine, and we accomplish sub-goals along the way. In contrast, there are no sub-goals that contribute to the fulfilment of truly impossible goals. A physicist's overall goal to understand the fundamental particles of the universe might never be reached fully, but publishing a dozen papers reporting some findings is progress in the way that one could not make progress toward, say, walking to the moon. The fulfilment of self-propagating goals is not impossible to conceive in the way that making a square circle is. Completion of a self-propagating goal is not fully graspable, but nevertheless we can conceive it in some sense, enough to touch it with our fingertips even if we cannot wrap our arms around it.

In exceptionally meaningful achievements, a particular conception of what would satisfy completing the goal changes and expands once we draw near to its completion. At any stage along the way what amounts to final completion isn't imaginable with precise detail. Once early sub-goals are completed, these open up the possibility of new goals. Exceptionally valuable achievements are those that have goals that have this self-propagating structure. But what is it about this structure that is so special?

But Why?

The self-propagating structure is significant because of its relationship to a central source of value in projects, namely *challenge*. Challenge is intrinsically worthwhile, as I argued earlier. Given that challenge or difficulty is a central source of value in all achievement, the self-propagating structure therefore provides a perpetual and in some cases limitless source of challenge and therefore value. When paired with subjective attraction, such projects therefore supply a potentially limitless source of meaning.

This, then, is a key way in which the self-propagating structure is characteristic of projects of superlative meaning. The self-propagating structure has instrumental value, insofar as it provides a source of the kind of activity that is itself intrinsically valuable for meaningful projects, namely challenge. That is not to diminish its significance: this structure can, at least in theory, generate infinite intrinsic value.

One might point out that a series of discrete projects pursued in succession could provide just as much valuable activity. But this observation confirms my point precisely: we are asking what projects are sources of superlative meaning, and the fact that one could stack up *several* discrete projects to sum to more meaning than *one* project with a self-propagating goal is no threat to this claim, but rather illustrates it.

Moreover, one can argue that a series of discrete projects would *not* sum to provide just as much valuable activity. Many philosophers argue that long-term projects have *more* value than a sequence of finite but otherwise similar projects. As philosophers such as Antti Kauppinen and Dale Dorsey argue, the *relationship* between the parts of a project imbue it, and therefore one's life, with additional significance (Dorsey 2012, 47–50; Dorsey 2015, 315ff; Kauppinen 2012, 368ff). A project that builds on past towards the future has bolstered coherence and therefore meaning. It is precisely because a long-term project has unifying goals, and builds and develops from past experiences, that the life is imbued with augmented value. So this is another important way in which the self-propagating structure is a source of especially significant meaning.

But of course one might wonder *why*. Is it coherence alone? There is, after all, a long tradition in philosophy of coherence, or unity, augmenting the value of a whole with otherwise diverse parts (see e.g. Moore [1903] 1971, 27; Nozick 1981, 413ff). But can more be said about why this particular kind of unity is also a source of intrinsic value? This is the claim that I am most eager to develop.

The *Amare Bonum* Bonus

In choosing a project that is a renewable source of challenge, and choosing it at least in part for this reason, we choose difficult activity for its own sake. This is good, one might think, because choosing and pursuing something that is good *is itself good*.

There is a tradition of acknowledging a value-theoretic principle that captures this idea. It has been called the principle of recursion by some, or the *amare bonum bonus* by others, and has been acknowledged in one form or another by many philosophers including Aristotle, Moore, Brentano, and Nozick.[12] The idea, in a nutshell, is that, *it is good to love the good*. Given some good object, having a positive attitude toward that object is *itself* good. Positive attitudes here are understood as broadly as possible, and include *loving, taking pleasure in, wishing for, pursuing*, and so forth. The *amare bonum bonus* (ABB) also encompasses the corresponding claims that it is good to hate the bad; bad to hate the good; and bad to love the bad. Likewise, hating is understood broadly

---

[12] For instance, Aristotle, *Nicomachean Ethics*, 1175b25–30, 1174b20–25; Moore ([1903] 1971, 177–178, 204ff); Nozick (1981, 429ff).

as including *avoiding, being pained by, destroying,* and so on.[13] Hurka (2001, 13ff.) crystallizes the principle this way:

(1) Given some base intrinsic good, G, loving G it itself of positive intrinsic value; hating G is of negative intrinsic value;
(2) Given some base intrinsic evil, B, hating B is of positive intrinsic value; loving B is of negative intrinsic value.

Relevant for the discussion here is the first half of ABB—it is good to love the good. So, for ABB to be activated, there must be some intrinsically good base, which is the object of some pro-attitude. In projects with self-propagating goals, the base good is challenging activity, granting that engaging in challenging activity, other things equal, is intrinsically good. In projects with self-propagating goals, we pursue *continued* challenging activity—in other words, we are pursuing a goal that gives us more challenge as we progress. Because our pursuit is at least in part directed toward a good—namely challenge—our activity of pursuit is *itself* intrinsically good. Consequently, we have an additional source of value in projects with self-propagating goals, according to ABB.

Further, since the self-propagating structure is typical of goals that are of independent value, such as the pursuit of knowledge, or creative artistic activity, then in these cases, ABB is activated with respect to these goods. Since knowledge, for example, is intrinsically valuable, ABB entails that the pursuit of knowledge is also intrinsically valuable. The same can be said for creative artistic activity, or any other independently valuable goal. So for any self-propagating goal that is also valuable independently, its pursuit is additionally intrinsically valuable according to ABB.

For these projects with independently valuable goals, as a result, the pursuit is especially valuable, according to ABB. This is because the value accrued by ABB is proportionate to the value of the object. That is, the more valuable the object, the more valuable its pursuit. So a project that has a self-propagating structure *and* has a goal that is independently valuable is all the more valuable.

But one might wonder whether we get some peculiar results considering the structure on its own when it is not part of a project that has significant independent value. One might reasonably point out that it looks as if, for example, playing an infinitely long game of catch might be an example of one of these perpetually difficult and ever-expanding goal activities. Surely playing catch would not be a superlatively meaningful activity.

Now, this doesn't exactly follow. In order for ABB to be activated, the activity must be *sufficiently* challenging so that it is intrinsically good. Catch isn't especially challenging. But we *could* make catch increasingly interesting—several balls at once, greater distance, and strategic bounces. Would a game of Advanced Catch be exceptionally

---

[13] This is not to be confused with fitting attitudes analyses of value, where attitudes towards certain objects are 'fitting' or appropriate in a certain significant way. According to ABB, attitudes themselves are valuable. The base object has prior value, and it grounds the value of the attitude towards it.

valuable? Surely we would not think that someone who chose to dedicate their life to playing Advanced Catch would have a superlatively meaningful life.

Indeed that's true, largely because there are many *more* valuable projects to be pursued. The significance accrued by ABB is, it is reasonable to think, proportionate to the value of the base. The challenge of Advanced Catch may be sufficient to be of some value, but presumably other more challenging activities would be more valuable, not only in virtue of their higher degree of challenge, but also because they may be richer sources of value. But of course to a certain extent, this response concedes that a game of Advanced Catch, or for that matter any other seemingly trivial activity characterized by the self-propagating structure and a certain sufficient degree of difficulty, could be the sort of project that contributes to a meaningful life. This is something I'm willing to embrace, for reasons that emerge soon. In any case, Advanced Catch is not *superlatively* valuable in contrast to other projects, specifically projects that are at least as challenging and also have independent value, such as artistic achievement or scientific inquiry, as well as the self-propagating structure. Having the self-propagating structure is *a* source for superlatively meaningful achievements, but it's not the *only* source. That is, it may be a common feature of superlatively meaningful projects, but it is not *sufficient* for superlative meaning in contrast to other projects.

Independently valuable projects with ever-expanding structures are excellent sources of meaning. This is not a surprising conclusion, but we now have a better understanding of *why* achievements of certain kinds are good candidates for being among the things that make for a meaningful life. In fact, Levy, who suggested the idea with which I began—namely, the idea that achievements with self-propagating structures are the most meaningful—argues that achievements such as intellectual pursuits are the sorts of things that are superlatively meaningful, in contrast to 'downshifting' to a simple life dedicated to raising a family, or moving to the country and farming. A simple life is not superlatively meaningful because it does not have a self-propagating goal.

Exceptionally Meaningful Projects

Now that we have a more detailed account of why the self-propagating goals are a source of superlative meaning, we can see that Levy's claim about so-called downshifting is not right. In the paper where Levy originally sketches out this idea, he argues that 'downshifting' to a simpler life of raising a family or farming, while meaningful, is not 'superlatively' meaningful in the way that, say, philosophy is (Levy 2005, 185). The latter is characterized by the self-propagating structure, while the others are not, argues Levy.[14]

---

[14] Levy also says that exceptionally meaningful projects have 'supremely valuable goods at stake' which further precludes practices such as farming from being superlatively meaningful. Levy also appears to include parenting among such non-superlatively valuable practices (2005, 181, 189). It seems reasonable that supremely valuable goods are at stake in parenting, so even by Levy's own lights it is

Now we can see that this is not true. Because the ever-expanding structure is in part a feature of projects because of the way that we set our goals, a wider range of domains than one might think can be sources of superlative meaning.

When taken up in the right sort of way, many so-called downshifting pursuits *do* have a self-propagating structure that can be superlatively meaningful. Parenting or being a part of a family can have a self-propagating goal. In fact, it seems even more obviously self-propagating than physics. There is no obvious end point, and no maximally good or successful way of loving, caring for, connecting with, and relating to those who are dear to you. There are always new ways to improve your caring endeavours with those whom you love, and always new things to explore and new challenges to meet with your family and loved ones. So it isn't only highfaluting, intellectually lofty projects such as pursuing the philosophical life or being committed to improving social justice that are superlatively meaningful. The range of potential superlatively meaningful projects is much more expansive—successful relationships with friends and family can also be superlatively meaningful in the same way that these other pursuits can.

The same can be said about other seemingly less grand projects. Farming is a prime example of a downshifted lifestyle in Levy's view, but taken in the right way, the goals of farming are self-propagating in a similar way to any creative endeavour. Just as there is no maximally ideal method for doing philosophy, there is no maximally ideal way to cultivate crops or livestock. Methods improve, innovations develop new technology, and new goals open up. One might have thought the goal of farming was obvious: to raise as much crops or livestock as efficiently as possible. But now many farmers have different goals—growing crops that are free of dangerous pesticides, cultivating land with minimal long-term impact on the environment, or treating animals with a certain amount of compassion. There is no final goal to farming and the ideals, methods, and aims shift and develop. This isn't just my 'armchair view' of farming: according to the Agricultural Sustainability Institute at the University of California, Davis, the goals of farming are considerably more complex and sophisticated than feeding more hogs to buy more land: '[p]racticioners of sustainable agriculture seek to integrate three main objectives . . . a healthy environment, economic profitability, and social and economic equity'.[15] Of course there are many different ways to farm, but the important point is that the goals of farming are not obvious, and can be pursued as self-propagating.

The view that I have described here captures more than what one might think would typically be included on a philosopher's account of worthwhile projects that contribute to exceptional meaning in life. Indeed, the most meaningless and seemingly Sisyphean tasks of quotidian life can be exceptionally meaningful when pursued as a self-propagating goal. 'Few tasks are more like the torture of Sisyphus than [housework]', as de Beauvoir observed ([1949] 2011, 474), and yet taken on in a certain way, homemaking eligible for a superlatively meaningful project, although it is clearly categorized among his 'downshifted' pursuits that are not eligible for such meaning.

[15] <https://asi.ucdavis.edu/programs/ucsarep/about/what-is-sustainable-agriculture>, retrieved 24 August 2019.

can become a self-propagating meaningful project. The Ancient Greeks understood the seriousness and complexity that 'household management' can involve—*oikonomikos* is homemaking writ large. Of course, it's hard to imagine this being the case if you live by yourself in a small, sparse apartment, but if we imagine 'household management' to also include raising a large multi-generational family, it can become an increasingly complex undertaking. There are many bills and a budget to balance, a house to maintain, all involving many goals—coordinating schedules, preparing meals, planning projects together, resolving conflicts, developing relationships. There are always new projects to undertake and new methods to explore (Martha Stewart, living proof). It's hard to pin down exactly what the central goal might be ('keep the family happy and healthy', perhaps), and one can easily imagine, like the Agricultural Sustainability Institute, the goals can evolve and develop, as new possibilities open up.

One might think that this is a sort of counterexample to the proposed account of superlatively valuable achievements. De Beauvoir was right. Surely if anything, homemaking is *not* exceptionally meaningful, especially in contrast to, say, pursuing the latest breakthroughs in theoretical physics and so forth.

To be sure, homemaking may be less meaningful than other projects, particularly those with goals that are of greater independent value, and not all goals in homemaking can be self-propagating. But the point is that there is the possibility of an exceptionally meaningful project in homemaking, contrary to what one might think.

The same can be said for trivial pursuits that one might choose to take on as self-propagating goals, such as beer brewing, artisan pottery, elaborate manicures, or bodybuilding. Although there may be some questionable elements involved in the pursuit of some of these goals, and all things considered some pursuits may be less meaningful than others, we should not foreclose the possibility that such pursuits are candidates for superlative meaning in life, since, pursued in a certain way, they may have self-propagating goals which lend them significant meaning.

There are two reasons in particular why I think the meaningfulness of a wide range of projects is worth acknowledging. First, some endeavours that may be seen traditionally as uncultured or menial have rich, independently valuable features that add to their overlooked potential for self-propagating goals. Homemaking, for example, may include not simply household management, but also raising a family or fostering loving relationships. Surely if anything has independent value it would be this. Even in other cases of seemingly trivial pastimes with less obvious independent value, there is a rich world of exploration to be had—to an outsider, something may seem simple or trivial, but to an expert, it is a rich and complex world full of challenge and opportunities for excellence. In some pursuits, this may be exhausted relatively quickly, but one of the wonderful things about human beings is that we can develop ingenuity in just about any domain, and exploit the seemingly simple by uncovering almost unimaginable depths. To be sure, there is more meaning in some projects than in others. Theoretical physics or poetry might have significant independent value, making their pursuit even more valuable than, say, macrame or bodybuilding. But the point is that a far wider range of activities are eligible for superlative meaning than one might have thought.

A second consideration to motivate an all-embracing conclusion with respect to exceptionally meaningful projects concerns the control—lack of, rather—over what we care about. There is only so much control that we have over what sparks our interest—not every activity that would be an appropriate source for fulfilment actually *does* inspire feelings of fulfilment.[16] We have already seen this with Mill, and consider also Tolstoy: his literary career was astounding and might for anyone constitute a source of meaning and fulfilment, but at the time when he wrote *A Confession*, he reveals that it gave him no such feelings at all (Tolstoy [1879] 1987). His life, one might think, had objective meaning but did not have the subjective component of fulfilment that we might think is so crucial for meaningfulness. Because of the diversity of things that spark these feelings and the relatively low degree of control that we have over them, it is a virtue of the proposed view that such a wide range of activities can be appropriate sources for feelings of fulfilment.

Some might see this conclusion as a sort of objection—if elaborate manicures are the only thing that floats your boat, surely pursuit of such a project is not a superlatively meaningful life. Superlative meaning should be reserved for only the highest endeavours, such as philosophy or theoretical physics.

To be sure, if a pursuit exhausts its potential for meaning early on, then that's all you get. Even still, the richness of a project in any domain is at least in part a matter of how its goals are shaped and set by those who pursue it. Wouldn't it be more intellectually generous to admit that I don't know just how deep and rich the exploration of certain domains—such as macrame or bodybuilding—can be? Moreover, it is appealing to have an account that lets lots of people have very meaningful lives, rather than fewer. The world is a more interesting place with more meaningful lives and more diverse pursuits in it.

Let us return to the overall notion that self-propagating goals are superlatively meaningful and consider some further concerns. First, concerning progress: the distinction between the goals of household management or philosophy, say, being either Sisyphean or self-propagating hinges on the possibility of progress. But one might think that progress in self-propagating goals is illusory. The goals may change, but one may question whether there really is progress, and rather see a sort of treadmill of the same sort of thing over again, albeit with different methods, or different variations on the goal in mind, none of which constitutes progress. There might be different ways of doing philosophy, or different aims in farming, but there is no real sense in which these methods or aims are *better* or constitute progress.

This is a real and puzzling concern and something that I don't think I can resolve here. One reason is that the answer will depend on the details of any particular activity, and in some cases, the answer is contentious and complicated (for instance, is there any progress in philosophy?). Whether or not any particular philosopher or farmer is pursuing

---

[16] This point of course has its roots in Frankfurt's observation about the nature and significance of what we care about. We only have so much control over what sparks our care (Frankfurt 1982, 269 ff.).

a self-propagating goal will depend on what they do and how they think about it. A philosopher can plod around and simply try to come up with some decent arguments for a plausible view and set the goal for completion relatively low, or a philosopher can have a self-propagating goal that involves engagement with the larger expanse of the philosophical enterprise. So whether or not one's project has a self-propagating goal is in part a function of how one sets one's goals. But of course this leaves the question open as to whether anyone can pursue philosophy or farming or similar endeavours with a self-propagating goal. It seems to me that at least in one sense one can—namely, in the sense that we can improve and refine our methods. Consider a virtuoso violinist at the height of her career. One might think her goals are simply to maintain her performance abilities. But we can quite easily imagine her with self-propagating goals, constantly refining her technique and interpretation of pieces, streamlining her practice regimen, cultivating new musical relationships. Consider Glenn Gould's two recordings of the Goldberg variations, bookending his career and manifesting his endless pursuit of the refinement of interpretation and performance. In philosophy, even if your theories are ultimately barking up the wrong tree, at the very least a philosopher can indeed have self-propagating goals of improving argumentative prowess, refining the space of views, and developing new sources for creative insights.

One might think that this amounts to a weakness of the view. We are relinquishing the 'objective worthwhileness' of meaningful projects by making too much rely on the way a goal is set and how it is pursued. One might think that this gives the view a kind of subjectivity which one might find objectionable. The appeal, after all, of including 'projects of objective worth' as part of an account of meaning in life is that there is something about the projects that is *objectively* worthwhile—that is to say, set independently from how we understand them.

But this contrast is mistaken because the worthwhileness of projects with self-propagating goals is indeed objective. The self-propagating structure from which significant meaning can be found is a matter of the structure itself. The structure imparts meaning objectively, that is, independently from any particular attitudes towards it. Attitudes partly generate the structure, but the structure itself is significant, independently from our attitudes towards it and so is in this respect objective. This remains true even if we are not making progress in all the ways we might think we are.

There is another respect in which goals are subjective which I take to be part of the appeal of the view. Because goals are shaped by those who pursue them, whether or not and to what extent a project is meaningful is a matter of how its goals are taken up. This not only allows for an appealing plurality of meaningful projects, but it also incorporates the significance of personal investment in meaning. Our personal investment in our projects matters for meaning, and for how projects that matter *to us* make our lives meaningful. Achievements therefore incorporate both objective and subjective components in an appealing way. This point highlights one of the reasons that achievement is suited particularly well to be an element of a meaningful life—it includes both objective and subjective elements, and as a result a meaningful life not only is a matter of personal investment and significance, but also is subject to an objective reckoning. Not just anything goes, but, on the other hand, just about anything can go, when taken up in the relevant way.

There is far more to be said, of course, but we will have to leave it here. I have explored an account of the characteristics of the most meaningful achievements, and have discussed that there is a far wider array of meaningful achievements than we might have originally thought. Whether or not this chapter constitutes one of them, I can't be entirely sure, but I am certain that the many questions left unexplored tell of a self-propagating goal, more than I could possibly accomplish.

References

Aristotle. 1999. *Nicomachean Ethics*. Indianapolis: Hackett.
de Beauvoir, Simone. [1949] 2011. *The Second Sex*. New York: Vintage.
Bradford, Gwen. 2013a. 'Evil Achievements and the Principle of Recursion'. In *Oxford Studies in Normative Ethics*, vol. 3, ed. Mark Timmons. Oxford: Oxford University Press. 79–97.
Bradford, Gwen. 2013b. 'The Value of Achievements'. *Pacific Philosophical Quarterly* 94: 204–224.
Bradford, Gwen. 2015. *Achievement*. Oxford: Oxford University Press.
Brogaard, Berit, and Barry Smith. 2005. 'On Luck, Responsibility, and the Meaning of Life'. *Philosophical Papers* 34(3): 443–458.
Cottingham, John. 2003. *On the Meaning of Life*. London: Routledge.
Dorsey, Dale. 2012. *The Basic Minimum*. Cambridge: Cambridge University Press.
Dorsey, Dale. 2015. 'The Significance of a Life's Shape'. *Ethics* 125: 303–330.
Frankfurt, Harry. 1982. 'The Importance of What We Care About'. *Synthese* 5: 257–272.
Hurka, Thomas. 1993. *Perfectionism*. Oxford: Oxford University Press.
Hurka, Thomas. 2001. *Virtue, Vice, and Value*. Oxford: Oxford University Press.
James, Laurence. 2005. 'Achievement and the Meaningfulness of Life'. *Philosophical Papers* 43(3): 429–442.
Kauppinen, Antti. 2012. 'Meaningfulness and Time'. *Philosophy and Phenomenological Research* 84(2): 345–377.
Keller, Simon. 2004. 'Welfare and the Achievement of Goals'. *Philosophical Studies* 121(1): 27–41.
Levy, Neil. 2005. 'Downshifting and Meaning in Life'. *Ratio* 18(2): 176–189.
Mill, John Stuart. [1873] 1989. *Autobiography*. London: Penguin.
Moore, G. E. [1903] 1971. *Principia Ethica*. Cambridge: Cambridge University Press.
Nozick, Robert. 1981. *Philosophical Explanations*. Cambridge, MA: Harvard Belknap.
Portmore, Douglas. 2007. 'Welfare, Achievement, and Self-Sacrifice'. *Journal of Ethics and Social Philosophy* 2(21): 1–28.
Reginster, Bernard. 2004. 'Happiness as a Faustian Bargain'. *Daedalus* 133(2): 52–59.
Setiya, Kieran. 2014. 'The Mid-Life Crisis'. *Philosophers' Imprint* 14(31): 1–18.
Tolstoy, Leo. [1879] 1987. *A Confession and Other Religious Writings*, trans. Jane Kentish. London: Penguin.
von Kriegstein, Hasko. 2017. 'Effort and Achievement'. *Utilitas* 29(1): 27–51.
Wolf, Susan. 1997. 'Happiness and Meaning'. *Social Philosophy & Policy* 14(1): 207–225.
Wolf, Susan. 2010. *Meaning in Life and Why It Matters*. Princeton, NJ: Princeton University Press.

CHAPTER 4

NARRATIVITY AND MEANING IN LIFE

GALEN STRAWSON

Life . . . is a bowl that one fills and fills and fills.

—Virginia Woolf[1]

1

It's traditional to start with the question

Q1: What is the meaning of life?

—understood as a question about human life. It always makes my mind go blank. Then a negative answer comes. Life is what it is and it has no meaning, any more than a randomly selected volume of air has meaning.

Suppose one had to give a positive answer. I've wondered about this a few times, but nothing has ever stuck. Every time I've considered the question, I've had to start again from nothing. This has just happened again. This time it strikes me that the answer 'It has no meaning' isn't negative or disappointing but positive—celebratory. It is, perhaps, the only answer to that question that sufficiently recognizes the value of life and the nature of its value—apart from being true.

---

[1] Woolf (1939, 64). When I cite a work I give the date of first publication or composition; the page or section reference is to the edition listed in the bibliography. In the case of quotations from languages other than English I cite a standard translation but don't always use it. I use **bold italics** to mark an author's emphasis and *italics* to mark my own.

I've recently learnt how to give a different positive answer, but I'll save it for the end.

2

Some say it's helpful to rephrase Q1 as

Q2: What is the point or purpose of life?

I don't find that this helps. I think that the answer to Q2 must be of the same general form as the answer to

Q3: What is the point or purpose of the universe?

And I think the correct answer to Q3 is plain. 'It has none. It just is.' Any other answer diminishes the 'implacable grandeur' of reality[2]—apart from being false. The existence of the universe may have value, but it doesn't have meaning. So too the existence of life may have value, but it doesn't have meaning.

Someone might use 'the meaning of life' to mean, in effect, the value of life. That would be remarkably unhelpful. If one's question is about the value of life, one needs to make this clear and ask 'What is the value of life?'

Fortunately, I don't think this is what most people mean by 'meaning'. Some think that life has value because—or if, or if and only if—it has meaning. I think they're wrong, because I think that life, like the lilies of the field,[3] has no meaning. But at least they don't mean 'value' by 'meaning'.

It seems better to ask

Q4: What is meaning in life?

—a point well made by Susan Wolf (2010), and acknowledged in the title of this book. I can't really make sense of Q1 except as a mind-blurring version of Q4. I feel much the same about an individualized version of Q1:

Q5: What is it for a life (an individual life as a whole) to have meaning?

I do, though, know something negative about Q1/Q5. No plausible answer can have the consequence that a magnificently artistically creative life is bound (or even likely) to have more meaning-of-life meaning (whatever that might be) than the life of a member

---

[2] Camus (1936–1937, 2006, 125). I think the same goes for the question 'What is the meaning or point or purpose of God?', whether or not one believes in God.

[3] *Matthew* 6:28. The most accurate translation is simply 'wild flowers'.

of a family of subsistence farmers, or indeed that the former life has (meaning-of-life) meaning in some special way that the latter doesn't or can't. The artistic life may be deeply different from the georgic life, but the former can't have meaning-of-life meaning in some way—some qualitative manner—which is fundamentally different from the way in which the latter does. Even though it's intensely unclear what it means to speak of a life as having meaning-of-life meaning, it seems clear that there aren't different fundamental ways of having it—let alone better or worse ways.

3

The mind-blanking question, Q1, isn't Socrates' question:

Q6: How should one live?

—understood in the standard way as a question about how one should live if one wants to live a good life.[4]

Question: 'True—but mightn't a positive answer to Q1 help in some way with Q4?'
Reply: I don't know, because I don't yet know what a positive answer to Q1 would look like.
Question: 'Wouldn't an answer to Q4 (What is meaning in life?) help with Q6?'
Reply: I don't think so. Certainly the answer I'm going to give isn't going to help (see section 6). As far as I can see, there may be a great deal of meaning (meaning-in-life meaning) in a life that counts as extraordinarily bad according to all ordinary ways of understanding Socrates' question.

From now on I'll call meaning-in-life *Meaning*, 'meaning' with a capital 'M', in order to distinguish the meaningfulness that is supposed to be in question when we talk of meaning *in* life, not only from any dubious meaning-*of*-life meaning, but also from any meaning of the sort language has, and any other sort of meaning, real or supposed. So the general question is now this: What is Meaning? And the particular question for this chapter is:

Q7: What (if anything) does Meaning have to do with narrativity?

4

Well, what is narrativity? I'll use the word *Narrativity* with a capital 'N' as a name for a psychological trait. If one is naturally given to Narrativity, if one is a Narrative type, if one is *Narrative*, as I will simply say, then there's a key respect in which

---

[4] i.e. a life that is a good example of the kind of thing it is, i.e. a human life, in the way that a good knife is a good example of the kind of thing it is—a knife.

one naturally experiences or conceives of one's life (one's existence) as having the form of a story, or perhaps a collection of stories, and—in some manner—lives in and through this conception.

What is it like to live one's life in this way? I don't know. Many people think they do know, and I'm going to take the basic viability of the notion for granted. It does appear to capture something important about the way some people live their lives, or at least about the way they think they live their lives (to think one lives one's life in this way may be part of what it is to do so). In other writings I've tried to add body to the preceding definition of Narrativity by quoting people who not only think that we're all naturally Narrative, but also think that we ought to be.[5] Illustration by quotation seems the best idea, when trying to explain what Narrativity is supposed to be, and I'll do it again here.

'Our identities consist of the stories we tell about ourselves' (Jonathan Franzen, *The Guardian* 4 November 2017). 'Each of us constructs and lives a "narrative" . . . this narrative *is* us, our identities' (Sacks 1985, 110). 'We all live out narratives in our lives and . . . understand our own lives in terms of the narratives that we live out' (MacIntyre 1981, 197/212). 'We must inescapably understand our lives in narrative form' (Taylor 1989, 52). 'We are all storytellers, and we are the stories we tell' (Josselson, Lieblich, and McAdams 2006, 3). Life is 'an *activity and a passion in search of a narrative*' (Ricoeur 1990, 29). 'We make sense of our lives not just by ferreting out the facts, but by turning them into stories, so we can bring past events to life' (Simic 2011, 23). 'Self is a perpetually rewritten story'; 'in the end, we *become* the autobiographical narratives by which we "tell about" our lives' (Bruner 1994, 53; 1987, 15). 'Each person's individual identity *is*, or *depends on*, an understanding he has of his life in narrative form, as a development from his past towards his future prospects, ending in his death' (Davenport 2012, 2).

These people think that Narrativity is psychologically inevitable. They also think that it is a good thing. Others think that it's not inevitable, but still essential to a good life: 'an unnarrated life is not worth living' (Kearney 2002, 14).

Jean-Paul Sartre famously disagrees:

> a man is always a teller of stories, he lives surrounded by his own stories and those of other people, he sees everything that happens to him *in terms of* these stories and he tries to live his life as if he were recounting it.
> But one has to choose: to live, or to tell stories. . . . (1938, 64)

In Sartre's view, it seems, Narrativity is anti-life. It is, inevitably, inauthenticity, bad faith, *mauvaise foi*. The novelist Julian Barnes seems as suspicious of it as Sartre when he writes of 'the narratives we turn our lives into' (2008, 152). In the same vein, the novelist and philosopher (and Sartre scholar) Iris Murdoch finds that 'man is a creature who makes pictures of himself, and then comes to resemble the picture' (1957, 75).

---

[5] See e.g. Strawson (2004, 2007, 2020). Advocates of Narrativity may also think that a non-Narrative life would be bound to fail to have meaning in the mysterious meaning-of-life sense of 'meaning'.

This, for her, is a large part of the reason why 'the self, the place where we live, is a place of illusion' (1967, 93). Narrativity may be a fecund source of Meaning, but it's likely to be junk Meaning.

In the standard case, Narrativity involves taking up some relatively large-scale or overarching perspective on oneself and one's life. Some Narrative people may have a strong sense (accurate or not) of the shape of their life considered as a whole: it's a play with seven acts, according to Jaques in Shakespeare's play *As You Like It*, Act 2, Scene 7. That conception of life may be relatively rare, however. Others may live their lives more like a weekly comic. There are profound individual differences, and they're open to empirical investigation.

Narrativity also appears to require that one take up some sort of external stance vis-à-vis oneself. One might say that it requires taking up a second- or third-personal stance to oneself—even if one continues to use the first-person pronoun in one's thought about oneself. ('I'm such a fool!', instead of 'You fool!' addressed to oneself.) Such externality carries a suggestion of alienation—self-alienation. But there can also be value in looking at oneself from the outside.[6] Externality of this sort is in fact a special kind of internality.[7]

True enough. The present point is that even if this kind of self-relation has value, and contributes significantly to Meaning, it doesn't require Narrativity. One can think about life, and about oneself, and one's actions, and do it well, without doing so in a Narrative way.

Some Narrative types, I suspect, do live their lives like a weekly comic. It's always a story, perhaps an adventure story, perhaps perfectly glum, perhaps ruefully humorous.[8] People like this may not engage in any clear larger or overarching Narrative self-construal, although there are of course deep objective continuities in any life (same body, same family, usually same basic beliefs and preferences, usually same occupation, same address), which run through the weekly instalments.

Many find that they're captured by some ruling idea for a fortnight or so, an idea that they live through and that seems at the time the key to things. Then another idea comes along.[9] In some, this happens mainly when they're young. In others it continues

---

[6] See recent discussion of the possible benefits of 'illeism'—the practice of referring to oneself in the third person.

[7] When Robert Burns writes, 'O wad some Power the giftie gie us/To see oursels as ithers see us!' (1786), his idea is that this would correct false self-regard ('It wad frae monie a blunder free us,/An' foolish notion'). For many, though, the problem is the opposite: they lack, quite wrongly, any feeling of self-worth. This can be an excess of something otherwise attractive: self-deprecation. But it can also be a form of pride—pride in the bad sense.

[8] Cf. *Bridget Jones's Diary*. Some people present themselves in this way on Facebook.

[9] 'Gladly we would anchor, but the anchorage is quicksand. This onward trick of nature is too strong for us. . . . Once I took such delight in Montaigne that I thought I should not need any other book; before that, in Shakspeare; then in Plutarch; then in Plotinus; at one time in Bacon; afterwards in Goethe; even in Bettine; but now I turn the pages of either of them languidly, whilst I still cherish their genius' (Emerson 1844, 476). Compare Sterne's *Tristram Shandy*.

throughout life. Often enough, a book or a film or a song sweeps someone into a new view—a new aspiration, a new commitment, a new detachment—for two or three days. One doesn't have to be a Narrative type for this to be so.

5

So much for quotation. Let me now, in an attempt at further clarification, name and state eight plain truths about human life which might at first be thought to support the view that we're all naturally Narrative (and ought to be). I take it that none of them supports the Narrative view, and that one of the best ways to get a fix on what Narrativity is supposed to be is to start from the thought that it is—must be—something essentially more than what is expressed by these eight truths.

(1) *Locke*: All ordinary people fulfil a fundamental condition on what it is to be a person, a condition that is explicitly stated in Locke's famous definition of a person. They can 'consider [themselves] as [themselves], the same thinking thing, in different times and places' (Locke 1694, 2.27.9). They are in other words fully self-conscious beings (where to be fully self-conscious is to be able to think about oneself thought of explicitly *as* oneself), and their self-consciousness has significant temporal extent.[10]

(2) *Self-history*: Almost all ordinary people have a reasonably good grasp of their own history—basic facts about their own life. They possess a more or less adequate 'self-history', a basic 'self-chronicle', where the word 'history' signifies basic factual accuracy.

I say 'almost all' because there are people whose memory of their own pasts is so garbled that they can no longer be said to have an adequate self-history, although they're not classified as mentally unwell.[11] Using the term 'self-biography' to mean a person's set of beliefs about their lives, we can say that such people have a self-biography even if they don't have a self-history, because their self-biography is so dramatically at odds with their actual history.

(3) *Timeline* (or *Dante*): All ordinary people know how old they are, more or less precisely, and they know where they are on the timeline of human life—between life and death—however much or little it matters to them.

---

[10] In fact, one can be fully self-conscious even if one has an extremely short memory span and very little conception of the future. As it stands, Locke's definition implies that a person must have a more considerable temporal range.

[11] Some 'people ... come to believe their own stories by constantly repeating them' (Leibniz 1704, 2.27.16). 'Liars ... by the frequent repetition of their lies, come at last to believe and remember them, as realities' (Hume 1739–1740, 1.3.9.19).

(4) *Knowledge 101*: In our world, one thing leads to another in a highly regular fashion. We are constantly and vividly aware of this. Our lives are set among, and involve, vast series of complexly causally connected happenings in time, coherent, sequentially structured, developmental processes, shorter or longer—from making coffee to writing PhD theses or bringing up children—nearly all of which have relatively well-defined beginnings and ends and typical intermediate stages, and are clearly understood by us to have this form.

The next three points expand aspects of *Knowledge 101*:

(5) *Explanation*: Causal knowledge, causal explanation, is fundamental to our lives. Causal explanation almost invariably involves temporal order.[12] Causation is the 'because something is, something else must be' relation (Kant 1781–1787, B288). It's an understanding of how one thing leads to another or connects to another.

We're sometimes said to be Narrative because 'narrative explanation' is fundamental to our lives, but 'narrative explanation' very often turns out to be nothing other than explanation—causal explanation: this happened because that happened. Causal explanation almost invariably involves reference to temporal order, as just remarked, and sometimes, it seems, mere awareness of temporally ordered connection is taken—quite wrongly—to be enough for Narrativity.

(6) *Psychology*: A vast number of significant and interesting facts about human beings' lives are facts about their psychological states—their hopes, fears, beliefs, desires, goals, memories, intentions, and so on. Vast numbers of these psychological states involve explicit representations of connections between past and future states of the world and in particular past and future parts of one's own life. Vast numbers of these psychological states are crucially involved in the vast numbers of regular sequences and processes that structure a person's life.

(7) *Action*: Vast numbers of the sequences and processes mentioned in the description of the ordered temporal complexity of our lives in (4) play out as they do because of psychological states mentioned in (6): wants, needs, intentions, likes and dislikes, goals, dreams, hopes, fears, suspicions, superstitions, and so on. Vast numbers of them also involve intentional action on our part, and almost all intentional action involves some anticipation, thinking ahead, planning, knowledge of steps to be taken, calculation of possible consequences, *what if?* thinking. It involves causal-temporal thinking, causal-temporal-psychological thinking:

---

[12] Why not 'invariably'? A cannon ball sitting on a springy cushion is the cause of the dent in the cushion.

thinking that has causal matters and temporal matters and psychological matters as part of its content. We engage in such thinking all the time.

(8) adds little to (1) and (7), but it is perhaps worth listing separately:

(8) *Temporality*: We all experience ourselves temporally simply in living from moment to moment as we do, when making coffee, remembering one thing, anticipating another. We experience ourselves temporally even when we're absorbed in what we're doing, living—as we say—wholly in the moment.

I take it that (1)–(8) are accurate descriptions of all or almost all ordinary human beings, but that none of the eight, either singly or jointly with any of the others, implies being Narrative. *Narrativity* is something essentially over and above (1)–(8). If it were not—if any one or any combination of (1)–(8) sufficed for Narrativity—then the claim that all human beings are Narrative would be perfectly trivial.[13]

I hope that this section and the last give a sufficient indication of what it is to be Narrative. I am in any case going to assume an understanding of the notion that is sufficient for considering the relation between Meaning and Narrativity. It's certainly not true that all human beings are naturally Narrative. Nor is it true that they all ought to be. Some people are naturally non-Narrative; some are profoundly anti-Narrative.[14]

6

The question is this:

Q7: What does Meaning have to do with Narrativity?

Is one of them integral to the other? Is either of them necessary or sufficient for the other?

I think not. It seems plain that Meaning has something essentially to do with *being interesting*—I'll call this 'Interest' for short. Such Interest is surely necessary for Meaning:

(1) [Meaning → Interest][15]

and arguably sufficient:

(2) [Interest → Meaning].

---

[13] This section draws on Strawson (2020), where the list is developed in more detail.
[14] I argue for this in Strawson (2004) ('Against Narrativity').
[15] I use '→' to mean 'entails' or 'necessarily involves'.

I think, on reflection, that Interest is indeed sufficient for Meaning, and so both necessary and sufficient:

(3) [Interest ↔ Meaning].

And this suggests, although it doesn't entail, that they're the same thing:

(4) [Interest = Meaning].

Certainly (4) seems the best explanation of (3), if (3) is true. And if (4) is true, then

Q7: What is the relation between Narrativity and Meaning?

is the same as

Q8: What is the relation between Narrativity and Interest?

I think (4) is true, and I'm going to assume it is in order to see what follows.[16] I'm going to assume that (4) is true although it builds in (2), which clashes directly with a standard assumption about Meaning: the assumption that lives with high Meaning will be lives that we judge to be good lives in the wide Socratic ethical sense. I'm not worried by the clash because I think the assumption is false.

What's the answer to Q7/Q8, given (4)? It seems plain to me that one can live a fabulously interesting and profoundly picaresque life with no natural thought of one's life as a narrative or development or 'story'. I think of my friend Bruce Chatwin.[17] So it's plain that

(5) [Interest → Narrativity]

is false. And the converse of (5), i.e.

(6) [Narrativity → Interest]

is also plainly false. Sisyphus the Bored could be a profoundly Narrative type without his life being interesting either to him or anyone else.[18]

---

[16] Obviously it doesn't conflict with the fact that a long book can be entirely linguistically meaningful while being incredibly boring (every sentence reads 'Grass is green').

[17] The view that this is the deep form of his life isn't undermined by his lifelong interest in nomadism (it is if anything confirmed); nor by the fact that a childhood experience provides the original motive for his trip to Patagonia (Chatwin 1977, ch. 1).

[18] Sisyphus is condemned for all eternity to roll a boulder up to the top of a hill, only to have it slip from his grasp before he gets there, so that he has to begin all over again.

If this is right, Meaning doesn't require Narrativity. Narrativity and Meaning = Interest are 'doubly dissociable', as psychologists say. Each can exist without the other, and they can vary independently of the other even when they co-occur.

It may be, though, that Narrativity can increase Interest, and hence Meaning—even if not necessarily for the better. This is something that needs to be considered. It may also be that Narrativity can decrease Interest, and hence Meaning. Sisyphus the Bored might be much better off without constant vivid narrative awareness of the terrible sameness of his life. His best hope is to follow Epictetus, and find freedom in full acceptance of what he cannot change. He needs a very stiff dose of what is now called 'adaptive preference formation'.

Might it not be that Narrativity is in general *more likely* to increase Interest, and so Meaning, than decrease it? It's possible, but I doubt it. If it were more likely to increase Interest than decrease it, might this not be a point in its favour? I very much doubt it. Even if Interest is a good thing, all other things being equal, it can easily be a bad thing. Narrativity can be the more interesting in proportion as it's more self-deceived, and self-deception is very rarely good. More simply, terrible things can be extremely interesting. I don't mean that they can be fascinating to learn about, although they can. Nor do I mean that being interesting is a good or redeeming feature of terrible experiences—a mitigating factor. The Interest of something terrible can reside wholly in its terribleness and thus have no positive value. It can be all bad. It's true that we ordinarily use 'interesting' as a term of commendation, but there's no necessary link between Interest and positive value.

This is hardly surprising, on the present terms, given that Interest = Meaning, and that there's no necessary link between Meaning and positive value. A clinically depressed person's narrative obsession with the course of his life might be intricate and florid in its narrative detail, and in that sense extremely interesting; but not good. Rowland Mallet makes the required point to his cousin Cecilia in Henry James's *Roderick Hudson*:

> True happiness, we are told, consists in getting out of one's self; but the point is not only to get out—you must stay out; and to stay out you must have some absorbing errand.[19]

7

Interest is short for being *interesting*. We think of this as a more or less objective property that things may have or lack. Being *interested* is different—an explicitly subjective matter.

It's obvious that the two things can come apart. When Sisyphus is neurologically rigged in such a way that he finds his life inexhaustibly absorbing, we think he's just

---

[19] *Roderick Hudson* (1875, ch. 1). The connection with Susan Wolf's account of Meaning is clear.

wrong. Even so, it seems that Interest isn't really an objective property. You may be enthralled by things I find dreary, and vice versa, and neither of us need be making any mistake. Most of us find chess pretty interesting, but it might bore an omniscient creature. There's a poignant discussion of this by William James in his paper 'On a Certain Blindness in Human Beings', in which he quotes at length from Robert Louis Stevenson's luminous essay 'The Lantern-bearers'. 'The ground of a man's joy,' as Stevenson says, 'is often hard to hit.'[20]

Is it true that Interest isn't an objective property? I sometimes feel uncertain about this. Some Terran works of art seem objectively and irreducibly full of Interest. The Martians, however, may sincerely disagree, and I'll assume here that Interest is ultimately subjective. It doesn't matter in the end, because I don't think we can connect Narrativity positively to Interest whether we take Interest to be objective or subjective. Either way, Narrativity is neither necessary nor sufficient for Interest.

Meaning = Interest, then, is no more likely to be good than bad. A life that lacked it could be a great deal better than one that had it, even if uninterestingness is always *prima facie* bad. 'May you live in interesting times!' is used as a curse, whatever its disputed origins. If Job's ingeniously varied tortures had continued indefinitely, his life would have continued to be remarkably interesting, and so highly Meaningful, given that Interest = Meaning; but also hellish. Hitler's life was extremely interesting, full of Meaning.

8

I've already reached my main conclusion. Narrativity is neither necessary nor sufficient for Meaning—meaning in life. I've taken it that Meaning is no more likely to be good than bad. I think it's important to begin in this way—treating the word 'Meaning' (like its original, plain old 'meaning') as an evaluatively neutral term. But let me now to introduce a term for *good* Meaning—$Meaning^G$ ('G' for good)—and ask a new question:

Q9: What is the relation between Narrativity and $Meaning^G$?

This, after all, is the question that interests many. And many, perhaps, think that the answer to Q9 is that Narrativity is necessary for $Meaning^G$—that

(7) [$Meaning^G \to$ Narrativity]

even if no one thinks that

(8) [Narrativity $\to Meaning^G$].

---

[20] Stevenson (1888, 247).

I disagree, for reasons that should already be apparent, but it may be helpful to say a little more.

What is Meaning^G? Given (4), it's good Interest—Interest^G. What are its varieties? The question provokes a familiar set of answers. Some may think that Meaning^G (Interest^G) can't involve doing anything morally bad. I'll accept this here, if only for brevity and purposes of argument, and put aside an old acquaintance who once told me about his time smuggling gold across the India–Pakistan border, taking off in a small plane in one country, and parachuting into the other. It was, he said, incredibly exciting.[21]

What are the possible forms of human life high in Meaning^G? Susan Wolf uses 'meaning in life' to mean Meaning^G when she says that 'meaning in life arises when subjective attraction meets objective attractiveness, and'—she adds—'one is able to do something about it or with it' (2010, 26). Subjective interest must couple with an objectively worthwhile pursuit.

This seems as good a proposal as any, and the only question remaining is the range of worthwhile pursuits. Here there is perhaps a danger of being too restrictive. We mustn't I think propose any sort of 'lexical ordering', a ranking that places one kind of life pursuit (say art) inflexibly above another (say farming or fishing). We shouldn't rule out intensely hedonistic lives. For any human activity, there are some who have an extraordinary gift for it. So it is that some are brilliant at pleasure, indefatigable pleasure virtuosos. Their hedonism may overflow with Interest^G (Meaning^G), and it need not be at anyone else's expense.

Objection: 'No. These people are *lotos-eaters*; and the lotos-eating life lacks Meaning^G.'

Reply: Lotos-eating is often taken to imply a wasted life, but there's more to pleasure than lotos-eating.[22] A person may live a simple and unreflective life of extraordinary, Bombadilian, never diminishing joy in the natural world.[23] Another may live a life of extraordinary sexual intensity, never-staling engagement in sexual love, astonishing 'multi-level interpersonal awareness' (Nagel 1969, 50). When Enobarbus says of Cleopatra that

Age cannot wither her, nor custom stale
Her infinite variety,

he takes her Interestingness to be grounded in her defects:

> Other women cloy
> The appetites they feed, but she makes hungry
> Where most she satisfies, for vilest things
> Become themselves in her, that the holy priests
> Bless her when she is riggish.[24]

---

[21] For some connected issues, see Bernard Williams's discussion of Gauguin's life (Williams 1976).

[22] We can put aside a central feature of the original story—the fact that Odysseus and his men were in effect Circe's prisoners.

[23] Cf. Tom Bombadil in Tolkein (1954–1955).

[24] *Antony and Cleopatra*, Act 2, Scene 2. Riggish: 'esp. of a woman: sexually immodest, promiscuous; wanton' (*OED*).

Variety, however, isn't necessary when it comes to not going stale. Unvarying custom has its own astonishing intensities, as much in sex as in other things. The highest reaches of sexual love aren't in tension with fidelity; they're unattainable without it. This isn't in any sense a matter of constraint. It's like squares having four sides.

Objection: 'You're trying to cast doubt on the idea that Meaning^G requires Narrativity, but you're not really thinking things through. Take your own case of long-term sexual love—or perhaps any real love. It essentially involves Narrativity, an explicit sense of a shared past. A Narrative outlook is an essential prerequisite of the most intense forms of interpersonal intentionality, the core of sexual love.'[25]

Reply: This may well seem true to people who are themselves naturally Narrative. Non-Narratives know it's false. Perhaps it *is* true for Narratives. Good—so long as they don't start claiming that Narrative sexual love is essentially higher or deeper than non-Narrative.

Debate here is almost certainly fruitless; there are areas of life in which we perfectly misunderstand one another. This is almost always because we assume that others experience things more or less as we do.[26] I suspect that this is one of those cases, cases in which we are mistaken because we can't really believe or imagine that others are completely different from ourselves, not *really*—and we're wildly wrong (sometimes comically, often tragically). There are things I read about what other human beings like, and feel, things that I take myself to have good and even decisive reason to believe to be true, that I can't really believe—not *really*. In the present case the mistake is about the way the past works—functions—in love and friendship. Its good effects can be invisible, and involve no explicit memory. It can function like musicians' or athletes' intense rehearsals, which are vividly alive in their present performance even when they have no memory of specific past practice sessions.

The past, then, can be very important in the complete absence of Narrativity. That's one point. There's another, no less central: the past needn't be of any importance. Why was Michel de Montaigne's friendship with Étienne de la Boétie perfect? 'Because it was him, because it was me.'[27] There are vertiginous and immediate (and unchosen) affinities between human beings—*Wahllosverwandtschaften* (apologies to Goethe). Profound friendship doesn't require any ability to recall past intense shared experiences, nor any tendency to accord them a particular importance. It's shown in how one is in the present. Montaigne finds that he is 'better at friendship than at anything else', although 'there is nobody less suited than I am to start talking about memory. I can find hardly a trace of it in myself; I doubt if there is any other memory in the world as grotesquely faulty as mine is!'[8]

---

[25] See Nagel (1969); Scruton (1986). The landscape of interpersonal intentionality has some sharply distinct peaks. It can be peculiarly intense, on at least one dimension, the first time two people have sex.

[26] There are many variants of this psychological formation: in some cases, of course, we assume commonalty of experience only with people of the same sex or same sexual orientation or....

[27] Montaigne (1563–1592, 1.28), trans. Screech (1991, 212).

The same goes for sexual love. The Narratives are wrong about love and friendship. Even if they'd been right, their point wouldn't have touched the lover of the natural world (or great cities, or algebraic topology . . .). Deepening knowledge of something may vastly deepen the pleasure it gives, but deepening knowledge doesn't require Narrativity, which is—by definition—an attitude to one's own life. It's not required for a pleasurable sense of history (pleasure in ruins), pleasure in the seasons, pleasure in the grandeur of evolution. Even if one feels a connection with one's personal past, it needn't be distinctively Narrative in character. Certainly it needn't involve any sense of one's personality, either explicit or implicit, as persisting and developing over time. Like Goronwy Rees, I have no such sense:

> For as long as I can remember it has always surprised and slightly bewildered me that other people should take it so much for granted that they each possess what is usually called 'a character'; that is to say, a personality with its own continuous history. . . . I have never been able to find anything of that sort in myself.
> How much I admire those writers who are actually able to record the growth of what they call their personality, describe the conditions which determined its birth, lovingly trace the curve of its development. . . . For myself it would be quite impossible to tell such a story, because at no time in my life have I had that enviable sensation of constituting a continuous personality. . . . As a child this did not worry me, and if indeed I had known at that time of *Der Mann ohne Eigenschaften*, the man without qualities, I would have greeted him as my blood brother and rejoiced because I was not alone in the world; as it was, I was content with a private fantasy of my own in which I figured as Mr. Nobody.[28]

9

Objection: 'You've focused on the example of love and friendship. They're interesting subjects, but you're missing the central point. Narrative experience has great and special Interest/Meaning in and of itself—great Interest^G/Meaning^G.'

Reply: Certainly this may be so for some. Narrativity can take its place alongside a multitude of other possible sources of Meaning^G.

Objection: 'You're not getting it. It's not just that Narrative experience is a source of Meaning^G. It's a unique source. It confers Meaning^G on life in an unmatchable way. It *constitutes* Meaning^G in a foundational manner. Life is indeed, as Ricoeur says, "an *activity and a passion in search of a narrative*" (1990: 29). This fact about life places a fundamental constraint on Meaning^G. It must involve Narrativity.'

Reply: We disagree. Ricoeur's claim seems to me to be flat false considered as a factual claim, and an appalling idea considered as a general recommendation about

---

[28] Rees (1960, 9, 10).

how to live. Good for some, possibly, but bad for others. Some seem to think that Narrativity is a necessary part of a good religious life, including perhaps Alasdair MacIntyre and Charles Taylor. This seems another great mistake, a product of severely constricted vision connected, as often as not, to a fantasy of Quest. It's tightly linked to the point that almost everything that passes for religious belief in human beings is really all about self; a point that holds quite independently of William James's observation that 'religion, in fact, for the great majority of our own race *means* immortality, and nothing else'.[29] On the whole, Narrativity is more likely to lead to a uniquely repugnant pseudo-religious life à la Kierkegaard.[30] Genuine religious belief must I think erode Narrativity.

Every human life can be the subject of a good and narratively well-constructed biography. My advice is to let the narrative take care of itself; you can be sure it will.

Objection: 'Can't you see that one's "experiences must be actively unified, must be gathered together into the life of one narrative ego by virtue of a story the subject tells that *weaves* them together, giving them a kind of coherence and intelligibility they wouldn't otherwise have had. [For] this is how the various experiences and events come to have any real meaning at all . . .''?'[31]

Reply: This is dreadful stuff. The 'must' is wrong if it's an ethical, good-life 'must'. It might be true that weaving one's experiences together gives them a kind of coherence and intelligibility they wouldn't otherwise have had, but this, again, can so very easily be a bad thing, involving lashings of falsification and fantasy—bottomless, invisible, utterly irremediable self-deception, self-alienation. 'The search for unity is deeply natural, but like so many things which are deeply natural may be capable of producing nothing but a variety of illusions' (Murdoch 1969, 76). It is perhaps our fate as human beings that this is far more likely to happen than not. Here again, though, there may be spectacular individual differences. Some may be quite free of it.

Suppose we put the normal case (the case of self-deception) aside, and imagine a case in which the coherence and intelligibility that someone discovers in their own life is not fantasy. Suppose we add that the revelation of it is, for the person in question, a

---

[29] James (1902, 524). It's entirely unsurprising, indeed predictable, given the chaotics of human psychology, that hysterical self-concern can be lived delusionally as concern with God.

[30] Kierkegaard has many truly remarkable things to say, but he is perfectly wrong in his conception of God and the religious life: hysterical, infantile, offensive, nauseating—as he himself might have observed. 'The orthodox', he writes, 'are generally rather assiduous in adding "with God's help" to nearly everything they say and everything they do. Basically they don't mean anything much by it, which is why their cackling is so loud. I believe, silently, deeply, and inwardly that God is helping me; therefore I do not dare to say it, lest God becomes angry, as if I were showing off, lest God cease helping me' (1848, 424). Here he hasn't even taken the first baby steps. Further proof is provided by a remark by 'Anti-Climacus' that is characteristic of many others in Kierkegaard's writings: 'everyone arrives in eternity bringing with them and delivering their absolutely account of every least insignificance which they have committed or have left undone . . . the judicial report follows straight after every fault, and the guilty must write it themselves. But it is written with sympathetic (invisible) ink and only becomes thoroughly clear when it is held up to the light in eternity—while eternity holds audit over the consciences' (1849, 124).

[31] Shoemaker (2005, n.p.), reporting a view in order to criticize it.

wonderful thing. Is it then unmatchable, as Meaning^G, a necessary component of the highest grade of Meaning^G, top-quality, Triple-A Meaning^G?

No. It's one form of Meaning^G among others. Plutarch thinks that

> [t]he foolish overlook and neglect good things even when they are present, because their thoughts are always intent upon the future; but the wise by remembrance make even those benefits that are no longer at hand vividly existent for themselves. So the present good, which permits us to touch it only for the briefest period of time, and then eludes our perception, seems to fools to have no further reference to us nor to belong to us at all. As in that painting of a man twisting rope in Hades, who allows a donkey grazing near by to eat it up as he plaits it, insensible and thankless forgetfulness steals upon most people and takes possession of them, consuming every past action and success, every pleasant moment of leisure, companionship and enjoyment. Forgetfulness does not allow life to become unified, as when past is interwoven with present. Instead, separating yesterday from today as though it were different, and also tomorrow, it immediately makes every event to have never happened because it is never recalled.... Those in the Schools who deny growth and increase, on the ground that Being is in continual flux, turn one into ... a series of persons different from oneself. So too, those who do not preserve or recall former events in memory, but allow them to flow away, make themselves deficient and empty each day and dependent on tomorrow—as though what had happened last year and yesterday and the day before had no relation to them, and had never happened at all (c. 100: 214–217 (473B–474B)

Plutarch has, perhaps, no inkling of Montaignian liberation. He's less inclined to fly in the moment with Marcus Aurelius or the Earl of Shaftesbury or Walter Pater. He's surely right that memorious Narrativity is, for some, a particularly rich source of pleasure: not to be wasted. It doesn't follow that it's necessary to a good life. Those who don't enjoy it, or who just don't do it, are not therefore 'deficient and empty'. They simply have other interests and pleasures. All experience of meaning in life lies in the quality of experience in the present moment. Certainly you can enjoy thinking narratively about yourself. That is one thing you can do in the living moment of experience. There are other things.

10

I began with a negative answer to Q1, the old and now discarded question 'What is the meaning of life?': 'It has no meaning.' I suggested that this grammatically negative answer was ethically positive: celebratory; indispensable to understanding the value of life. Recently, however, I learnt a grammatically positive answer from the Italian comedian Corrado Guzzanti. 'What is the meaning of life?' 'The meaning of life is life.' (*Qual è il senso della vita? Er senso della vita è la vita.*)

In full the quotation runs as follows. 'The meaning of life is life. The end of life—he means death—is the end.' (*Er senso della vita è la vita. Er fine della vita è la fine.*) This seems the sum of wisdom on the question of the meaning of life. I think that the grammatically negative and grammatically positive answers are in effect equivalent, but Guzzanti puts it much better.[32]

The question of how to live, the question of flourishing, is a different question. It has, I think, no detailed general answer, because people are so different from each other. If you say (not at all unreasonably) that Aristotle made a good start on a general answer with his four 'cardinal virtues': (i) temperance, (ii) justice, (iii) practical wisdom, and (iv) courage, I'll reply, as I've done before, that there are people who live profoundly worthwhile lives and inspire deep love and respect, although they're (i) rackety, (ii) partial, (iii) muddle-headed, and (iv) comically faint-hearted.[33]

References

Barnes, Julian. 2008. *Nothing to Be Frightened Of*. London: Cape.
Bruner, Jerome. 1987. 'Life as Narrative'. *Social Research* 54: 11–32.
Bruner, Jerome. 1994. 'The "Remembered" Self'. In *The Remembering Self: Construction and Accuracy in the Self-Narrative*, ed. U. Neisser and R. Fivush, 41–54. Cambridge University Press.
Burns, R. [1786] 1994. 'To a Louse, on Seeing One on a Lady's Bonnet at Church.' In R. Burns, *Poems*, ed. H. W. Meikle and W. Beattie, 3rd ed. Harmondsworth: Penguin.
Camus, Albert. [1936-7] 2006. 'L'été à Alger'. In his *Œuvres complètes I : 1931–1944*. Paris: Gallimard, 117–27.
Chatwin, Bruce. 1977. *In Patagonia*. London: Jonathan Cape.
Davenport, John. 2012. *Narrative Identity and Autonomy: From Frankfurt and MacIntyre to Kierkegaard*. London: Routledge.
Emerson, Ralph Waldo. [1844] 1983. 'Experience', in *Ralph Waldo Emerson: Essays and Lectures*. New York: Library of America, 469–492.
Franzen, Jonathan. 2017 'Is it too late to save the world?' *The Guardian*, 4 November.
Hume, David. [1739–1740] 2000. *A Treatise of Human Nature*, ed. D. F. Norton and M. Norton. Oxford: Clarendon Press.
Hume, David. [1748–1751] 1975. *An Enquiry Concerning Human Understanding*, ed. L. A. Selby-Bigge and P. H. Nidditch. Oxford: Oxford University Press.
James, Henry. [1875] 1983. *Roderick Hudson*. In *Henry James: Novels 1871–1880*. New York: Library of America.
James, William. [1899] 1983. 'On a Certain Blindness in Human Beings'. In *W. James Talks to Teachers on Psychology: And to Students on Some of Life's Ideals*. Cambridge, MA: Harvard University Press, pp 132–149.
James, W. [1902] 1988. *The Varieties of Religious Experience* in *William James: Writings 1902–1910*. New York: Library of America.

---

[32] I've recently learnt that Goethe said something similar—'the purpose of life is life itself' ('Der Zweck des Lebens ist das Leben Selbst')—in a letter to Johann Meyer, in February 1796.
[33] See Strawson (1990). My thanks to Andrea Altobrando and Iddo Landau.

Josselson, Ruth, Amia Lieblich, and Dan McAdams. 2006. 'Introduction'. In *Identity and Story: Creating Self in Narrative*, ed. R. Josselson, A. Lieblich, and D. McAdams, 1–11. American Psychological Association.
Kant, I. [1781–1787] 1996. *Critique of Pure Reason*, trans. W. S. Pluhar. Indianapolis: Hackett.
Kearney, R. 2002. *On Stories*. London: Routledge.
Kierkegaard, S. [1848] 2011. 'Journal NB5'. In *Kierkegaard's Journals and Notebooks*, Volume 4: *Journals NB–NB5*, ed. N. Cappelørn et al. Princeton, NJ: Princeton University Press, 283–366.
Kierkegaard, S. [1849] 1980. *The Sickness unto Death*, trans. H. V. Hong and E. H. Hong. Princeton, NJ: Princeton University Press.
Leibniz, Gottfried. [c. 1704] 1996. *New Essays on Human* Understanding, ed. and trans. J. Bennett and P. Remnant. Cambridge: Cambridge University Press.
Locke, John. 1694. *An Essay Concerning Human Understanding*, 2nd ed. London: Dring and Manship.
MacIntyre, Alasdair. 1981. *After Virtue*. London: Duckworth.
McAdams, Dan. 2019. 'First we invented stories, then they changed us: The Evolution of Narrative Identity'. *Evolutionary Studies in Imaginative Culture* 3: 1–18.
Montaigne, Michel de. [1563–1592] 1991. *The Complete Essays*, trans. M. A. Screech. London: Penguin.
Murdoch, Iris. [1969] 1970. 'On "God" and "Good"'. In I. Murdoch, *The Sovereignty of Good*, 46–76. London: Routledge and Kegan Paul.
Murdoch, Iris. [1957] 1997. 'Metaphysics and Ethics'. In Murdoch, *Existentialists and Mystics*, 59–75. London: Penguin.
Murdoch, Iris. [1964] 1970. 'The Idea of Perfection'. In Murdoch, *The Sovereignty of Good*, 1–45. London: Routledge and Kegan Paul.
Murdoch, Iris. [1967] 1970. *The Sovereignty of Good over Other Concepts: The Leslie Stephen Lecture 1967* in *The Sovereignty of Good*, 77–104. London: Routledge and Kegan Paul.
Nagel, Thomas. 1969. 'Sexual Perversion'. *Journal of Philosophy* 66: 5–17.
Plutarch. [c. 100 CE] 1939. 'On Tranquillity of Mind'. In Plutarch, *Moralia VI*, trans. W. C. Helmbold. Cambridge, MA: Harvard University Press, 167–241.
Rees, Goronwy. 1960. *A Bundle of Sensations*. London: Chatto & Windus.
Ricoeur, Paul. [1990] 1992. *Oneself as Another*, trans. Kathleen Blamey. Chicago: Chicago University Press.
Rilke, Rainer Maria. [1910] 1983. *The Notebooks of Malte Laurids Brigge*, trans. S. Mitchell. New York: Random House.
Sacks, Oliver. 1985. *The Man Who Mistook His Wife for a Hat*. London: Duckworth.
Sartre, Jean-Paul. [1938] 1996. *La nausée*. Paris: Gallimard.
Scruton, Roger. 1986. *Sexual Desire*. Weidenfeld and Nicolson.
Shaftesbury, Earl of. [1698–1712] 1900. 'Philosophical Regimen'. In *The Life, Unpublished Letters, and Philosophical Regimen of Anthony, Earl of Shaftesbury*, ed. B. Rand. New York: Macmillan, 1–272.
Shakespeare, W. [1599] 2016. *As You Like It*. In *The New Oxford Shakespeare: Modern Critical Edition: The Complete Works*. Oxford: Oxford University Press.
Shakespeare, W. [1607] 2016. *Antony and Cleopatra*. In *The New Oxford Shakespeare: Modern Critical Edition: The Complete Works*. Oxford: Oxford University Press.
Shoemaker, David. 2005–2019. 'Personal Identity and Ethics'. *The Stanford Encyclopedia of Philosophy*, ed. Edward N. Zalta, https://plato.stanford.edu/archives/win2019/entries/identity-ethics/.

Simic, Charles. 2011. 'Grass: The Gold and the Garbage'. *New York Review of Books*, March 24.

Stevenson, R. L. [1888] 1911. 'The Lantern-Bearers'. In *The Travels and Essays of Robert Louis Stevenson*. New York: Scribner, 235–249.

Strawson, Galen. 1990. 'Inside the moral maze', review of *Pagan Virtue* by John Casey, *The Times Literary Supplement*, October 11, 1093–1094.

Strawson, Galen.[2004] 2008. 'Against Narrativity'. In G. Strawson, *Real Materialism and Other Essays*, 189–207. Oxford: Oxford University Press.

Strawson, Galen. 2007. 'Episodic Ethics'. In *Narrative and Understanding Persons*, ed. D. Hutto, 85–115. Cambridge: Cambridge University Press.

Strawson, Galen. 2008. *Real Materialism and Other Essays*. Oxford: Oxford University Press.

Strawson, Galen. 2020. 'On the Use of the Notion of Narrative in Ethics and Psychology'. In *The Natural Method: Essays on Mind, Ethics, and Self in Honor of Owen Flanagan*, ed. E. Nahmias, T. Polger, and W. Zhao 119–155. Cambridge, MA: MIT Press.

Taylor, Charles. 1989. *Sources of the Self*. Cambridge: Cambridge University Press.

Tolkein, John R. R. 1954–1955. *The Lord of the Rings*. London: Allen and Unwin.

Williams, Bernard. [1976] 1981. 'Moral Luck'. In his *Problems of the Self*, 20–39. Cambridge: Cambridge University Press.

Wolf, Susan. 2010. *Meaning in Life and Why It Matters*. Princeton, NJ: Princeton University Press.

Woolf, Virginia. [1939] 1972. *Moments of Being*. London: Hogarth Press.

Woolf, Virginia. [1939] 1978. 'A Sketch of the Past'. In *Moments of Being*, ed. with an introduction by Jeanne Schulkind, 64–159. London: Hogarth Press.

CHAPTER 5

MEANINGFULNESS AND IMPORTANCE

GUY KAHANE

HUME wrote that he feels 'an ambition to arise in me of contributing to the instruction of mankind, and of acquiring a name by my inventions and discoveries' (Hume 2000, 176). He elsewhere described this ambition as his 'ruling passion' (Hume 1985, xl).[1]

We can understand this ambition in more than one way. Although this isn't a term that he uses, we can interpret Hume as wanting to make these major inventions and discoveries in order to make his life more meaningful—to give his life a purpose and a point. People who made great intellectual breakthroughs, such as Einstein and Darwin, are often presented as paradigms of a superlatively meaningful life, alongside people like Gandhi and Cezanne, who led moral struggles or created works of great aesthetic value (see Wolf 2012).

Whether or not we want to say that Einstein, Darwin, Gandhi, and Cezanne led deeply meaningful lives, it cannot be denied that these figures are immensely important. And it is also natural to read Hume as wanting to achieve something similarly important on the grand scale, and in this way to become important himself—to acquire a name for himself.

This chapter will be concerned with the relation between meaning and importance. While a great deal has been written recently about what is required for a life to be meaningful, parallel questions about importance are almost entirely ignored.[2] This may be, in part, because while we admire people who transform their lives in the quest for deeper meaning, we tend to regard the craving for importance with suspicion. The pursuit of

---

[1] It is 'literary fame' that Hume describes as his ruling passion, but I take it that he is describing the same aim.

[2] Harry Frankfurt is one exception, though his focus is on what's important *to* people (see Frankfurt 1988). Frankfurt (1999) discusses a more objective notion of importance and also briefly distinguishes between meaning and importance (85); but his argument is premised on a purely subjective understanding of meaningfulness. For another prior discussion of importance, see Williams (2011, 182ff.)

meaning is associated with self-transcendence; the craving for importance sounds embarrassingly egocentric. Meaning just seems, well, more important.

But importance is often ignored not because it comes out badly in the contrast with meaning, but because the two are conflated. For example, Nozick often uses 'meaning', 'significance', and 'importance' interchangeably (Nozick 1981, 603–604; though see Nozick, 1989), and Metz explicitly writes that we are using synonymous terms when we describe a life as 'meaningful, 'important' or 'significant' (Metz 2013, 18, 22), while Benatar thinks that, although there are subtle differences between these notions, they can be used more or less interchangeably (Benatar 2017). If this is right, then to say that Hume was seeking meaning and to say that he was seeking importance are to say (more or less) the same thing.

We shall see, however, that under plausible accounts of these notions, meaning and importance are rather different things. The desire for importance reflects a distinct existential concern, and satisfying that concern may even be a distinctive good. Moreover, when importance also meets the conditions for meaningfulness it can amplify the meaningfulness of a life, and importance on a grander scale may be necessary for superlative meaningfulness. Finally, at their best, both the desire for importance and that for meaningfulness combine outward-looking and self-regarding aspects.

I. Concepts

Let me first explain how I will understand the notion of meaning. With others, I will focus on the notion of a meaningful life, or what some call meaning *in* life, rather than on what, if anything, is the meaning *of* human life. Talk about meaningfulness is rather nebulous, and it's doubtful it has a single common content. But following Metz (2013), I think we can identify several features that are common to most core uses of the term—features that are present, in particular, in the clearest paradigms of meaningful lives, in lives of moral heroism, intellectual discovery, and artistic creativity.

The first feature is purposiveness or point: for a life to have meaning it needs to involve valuable goals that are sought non-instrumentally, for their own sake. These are typically also sought for one's own sake—a meaningful life is good for us—yet must be distinguished from the good of pleasure or mere happiness; while a meaningful life can also be happy, it needn't be (Wolf 2012). The second feature is that for our lives to have meaning they need to transcend our mere animal nature (Metz 2013), and to connect to something of value that is larger than, or at least external to, ourselves (Nozick 1981, 601, 610). And that connection needs to be of the right kind: it shouldn't be accidental, but must involve our agency and conscious engagement. Some would add that we need to be subjectively attracted to the value in question (Wolf 2012). Others, that this value must be positive, and that our engagement with it must be achieved via morally permissible means (Metz 2013). Finally, a life that is meaningful and the acts that make it so are such that they merit certain attitudes: a sense of pride, fulfilment, and elevation in the person leading the life, and admiration from others (Kauppinen 2012; Metz 2013). There are no uncontroversial accounts of meaning—for example, as I understand the preceding reference to external value, it excludes purely subjective accounts of meaning, and this account obviously doesn't tie meaning to anything supernatural. But I think this is nevertheless one of the *least* controversial accounts of meaning on offer.

Turn now to importance. We routinely describe things as important, and do so in very many contexts. We speak, for example, of what is important to prepare for an exam, about an important invention, about what is important for some person, as well as about grand 'world historical' importance. As these examples suggest, importance is relative to a context or domain (that of academic success, mathematical inquiry, a person's life, world history). What are we saying when we say that something is important, relative to some domain? To describe something as important is to say two things (Kahane 2014; Kahane, 2021b): first, that this thing merits attention, and should be given weight, in that context; and, second, that it merits such attention and weight *because* it makes a significant difference in that context. Importantly, both claims have a *comparative* dimension: things merit more attention and concern *compared to* other things belonging to the relevant domain. And they merit that because they make *more* of a difference to the domain compared to these other things. In this way, 'important' operates in a similar manner to gradable adjectives such as 'big': compared to us, the Earth is immensely big, but when placed in the context of the solar system, let alone the universe as a whole, the Earth is infinitesimally small. In the same vein, my migraine counts as important in the context of the other annoyances of a mundane afternoon, yet fades into insignificance when placed in the context of a year, let alone my whole life, or if I am at the hospital, surrounded by grievously ill people.

Now to say that something is important because it makes a significant difference admittedly comes close to being circular—close to saying it must make an *important* difference (Frankfurt 1999). But we can unpack this. Things are more or less important in virtue of making *more* of a difference, compared to other relevant things; and when something makes *enough* of a difference we often describe it, in categorical terms, as simply important.

Some things are intrinsically good or, to use a more precise term, have *final* goodness. Others are good only instrumentally, in virtue of bringing about something else that has final value, or good only relative to some standard. Happiness is a final good, but a good paperclip is good only relative to the function that paperclips serve, or instrumentally good, when you need to keep paper together. We can draw a similar distinction between ways of being important. When we say that it's important to know something for an exam, or that something plays an important role in explaining, say, an earthquake, these things merit attention, and should be given weight, only if we want to do well in that exam, or are interested in explaining that phenomenon. But some things aren't important only in this conditional sense: it is important, period, that Apartheid in South Africa was abolished; this is something that matters impartially, regardless of anyone's interests and aims. That importance shares this distinction with the concept of good is not accidental: when things are simply important, in this way, this is because they make a difference not just to some arbitrary standard or goal, but to something with final value, to something that matters in itself.

Notice, however, that even when importance is unconditional in this way, it is still relative to a domain. A severe but local flooding may be extremely important, period, for a town, but unimportant at the level of the entire country, let alone relative to world history. A useful heuristic for determining how important something is in a given context is to ask how much comparative space would be given to it in an account of that context or domain—say, someone's biography, or a textbook on the subject (Kahane 2014; Benatar 2017). Since concrete bearers of value have a spatio-temporal location, it is common to discuss importance in relation to spatio-temporal regions of the world: a county, a country, an epoch, all the way up to the entirety of human history. Far less often, we also consider how important things are on the 'grand scheme of things', from a frame of reference that considers *everything* in the universe (Kahane 2014; Kahane, 2021b).

Now when something is important, we can also describe it as significant; certainly (holding the domain fixed) the important cannot be *in*significant. When something has meaning, it *signifies* something. Talk about significance can thus refer either to importance or to (one common sense of) meaning. This isn't accidental: just as a sign points to something beyond it, something important makes a difference to something beyond it. It's not surprising, then, that when people ask whether their life is meaningful, or has any significance, they sometimes just mean to ask whether it is important in some sense. However, we should be careful to distinguish between importance, or significance in the sense of importance, from meaning in life. If the accounts sketched previously are even remotely in the right direction, it should be clear that the two notions are far from synonymous. For example, it's just obvious that Hume is an extremely important figure in Western philosophy; I'm also *inclined* to think that his life was highly meaningful, but this isn't as obvious.

Still, even if the two terms mean different things, their extensions might overlap, or nearly overlap, and I already mentioned that many paradigms of meaningfulness also possess great importance. In considering this possibility, it may be useful to consider so-called consequentialist accounts of meaning in life (e.g. Singer 1993). According to such accounts, a life is meaningful to the extent that it makes the world overall better. This property is very close to importance in the unconditional sense I defined earlier. But the two don't fully overlap: the degree to which one's life had good consequences is neither relative nor comparative in the way importance is, and such consequentialist views don't usually make claims about reasons for attention by others. Still, some of the reasons commonly given for rejecting consequentialist accounts of meaning (e.g. Metz 2013) are also reasons for thinking that meaning and importance can come apart in both directions.

Consider first that acting in ways that bring about something important, on however great a scale, isn't sufficient for meaningfulness since, as we saw, it also matters how one connects to external value. Whereas mere causation of a large difference in value is sufficient to endow something with importance, meaningfulness also requires engaged, directed agency and, on some views, also subjective attraction. Think of Nagel's famous example of absurdity: your trousers falling as you are being knighted (Nagel 1971). We can easily conceive of such a royal embarrassment as having a massive positive impact—suppose it somehow ended a bloody war. From a moral perspective, you might even be glad that this wardrobe malfunction happened to you. But such absurdity would not endow your life with more meaning. It wouldn't make you proud, or call for admiration from others. Quite the opposite.

Even conscious choice, in line with your deepest values, might not be enough. Think of Nozick's idea of a 'result machine', a device 'which produces in the world any result you would produce and injects your vector input into any joint activity....' (Nozick 1974, 44). If you got hold of such a device, you could do incredibly important things—cure cancer or bring about world peace. But it's doubtful that pressing these buttons would endow your life with much meaning (Metz 2013). Meaning, unlike importance, seems sensitive to effort and difficulty, and to the degree to which you engage with the value you bring about.

Another difference between importance and meaningfulness is that the difference in value that underlies the importance of what we do, or of our very existence, includes our own happiness, whereas, as we saw, our happiness isn't a source of meaning. To be sure, in the vast majority of cases this difference would not matter since we nearly always acquire importance, on any broad scale, largely via our effects on others, often on very many others. But in principle one's own happiness may be sufficient for importance. Think here of another of Nozick's thought experiments: the 'utility monster', someone who can generate vastly more utility compared to others (Nozick 1974). By funnelling resources to itself, such a utility monster could make a great difference to overall value and therefore it, and its happiness, would be of great importance. But this wouldn't make its life more meaningful.

So importance isn't sufficient for meaningfulness. This is compatible with importance being a necessary condition for meaningfulness—perhaps importance overlaps with meaning if we require that the importance in question involves making a positive difference to value that excludes our own happiness, a difference that is achieved via morally permissible means and which reflects our intentions, involves our close engagement, is the object of our subjective attraction, etc. Mintoff (2008), for example, asserts that activities must be perceived as important to be perceived as meaningful.

Whether this is correct depends on what domain of importance we have in mind. Nearly everything is important relative to some arbitrary context, so this suggestion would be trivially true if we place no constraint on the relevant domain. But if we have in mind importance on some large scale, this is surely wrong. Many would agree that to lovingly raise a family or to be an unusually generous, caring person is a way of leading a perfectly meaningful life, even if these lives have little impact beyond a small circle of people—that is to say, these lives wouldn't normally be described as important, since that would require at least impact on a larger community, if not on something even larger (of course these people and the things they do may be of immense importance to, and for, some particular people, and we can describe them as important if we make that local context explicit). Such lives, while not possessing greater importance in any interesting sense, *exhibit* or *realise* certain values to a high degree even if they do not *bring about* (and thus make a difference to) a great quantity of value. Such lives can seem more meaningful than, say, the life of a wealthy person of limited aesthetic sensibility who, through her extensive philanthropy, nevertheless makes a massive difference to art in her city, and would thus count as important on a much larger scale (Metz 2013).

We can also endow our lives with meaning, not by bringing about or realizing value, but by properly *appreciating* the value already out there. A life devoted to the intense study and enjoyment of the very best poetry can be full of meaning yet would, again, not count as important in any interesting sense. Arguably, if God exists, then the kind of meaning that people derive from worshipping him is of this form. Indeed, religious traditions often emphasise our insignificance on the grand scale of things, yet this doesn't prevent them from being seen as sources of deep meaning—worshippers receive meaning, not from being or doing anything important, but from connecting to *something else* of extraordinary importance.

II. Values

With these accounts of meaning and importance in hand, we can now ask whether they are actually worth having—whether there's any value in having a meaningful life, or being important. There are, of course, those who regard talk about meaning in life as hopelessly obscure, or who see meaningfulness merely as something that some of us need to be happy. But, with others, I will assume that having a life that is meaningful is valuable in itself—that it has *final* value. Since some lives are more meaningful than others, these lives possess more of that value. When a life is meaningful, that makes the world better. But I doubt that anyone seeks to add meaning to their lives because they want the world to have more meaning in it. We seek meaning for our own sakes—leading a more meaningful life is better *for us*, and some would even add that a meaningless life isn't worth living.

When philosophers defend the final value of meaning, they usually do so by appealing to examples. The life of, say, Leonardo da Vinci is appealing, that of Sisyphus not so much. This, however, leaves open the question of *why* meaningfulness is non-instrumentally good for us. It is generally hard to explain why some property has final value: to see why pain is bad, for example, you just have to feel it. But we can sometimes make it more intelligible why (or how) something is a good thing. In the case of meaningfulness, we can try to do so by asking why we would even want our lives to have the core features we highlighted earlier: non-hedonic purposiveness, connecting to something larger than ourselves, and meriting esteem and admiration.

In one way, to say that meaning gives our life a purpose by giving us a worthwhile goal that is distinct from the pursuit of happiness is just to say what the relevant value is *not*. But we can make progress by asking why mere contentment isn't enough. Many reject hedonism because they are impressed by Nozick's 'experience machine' thought experiment—involving an instrument that can perfectly simulate whichever life you may desire (Nozick 1974). To refuse to plug in suggests that we want more from life than a series of experiences, however pleasurable. We also want, as Nozick puts it, some relation to external reality. In a way, for the hedonist, the whole world *just is* a kind of experience machine: so far as our own good is concerned, the entirety of the vast universe around us matters only instrumentally, as a potential source of pleasurable inner experiences. And if we could get these experiences (or more pleasurable ones) without the world, then nothing would be lost. But this seems to misrepresent the relation between our good and the world.

This takes us straight to the second feature: connecting to something larger than ourselves. This shouldn't be taken too literally—hugging a massive rock won't make our lives better. The idea is rather that we need to link to something valuable that is external to the self (Wolf 2012). Now, one way of introducing the moral standpoint is to highlight that we aren't alone in the world, that we are surrounded by numerous others of equal moral value. But while morality may be one source of meaning, meaningfulness can also be derived from non-moral sources, and is not itself a moral value. The claim is rather that it's good *for us* to connect to something else that is *independently* good. *We* need a world (or the world). Or rather, we need a world containing other things of value. Many of these will be of vastly greater value than our own (whether individually, or when pooled together), but it seems plausible that we can derive meaning from relating to something of equal or even lesser value (Wolf [2012] gives the example of taking care of an animal.)[3]

By linking to something external of value, to something beyond our experiences, we transcend our mere animal selves. Importantly, however, that transcendence must be limited. Some traditions recommend losing ourselves in something larger, or even erasing the self altogether. Perhaps that would be good, but it cannot be good for us, since there would be no us left to benefit from such transcendence. As I understand it, even though to seek meaning is inherently world-oriented, it remains a form of self-concern.[4]

The link to pride and admiration brings out another way in which meaningfulness is both world-oriented and self-concerned. By connecting to value external to us, we also give reasons to others, who survey the scene from an external standpoint, to feel admiration for us and what we do (Wolf 2012). And we have reason to feel pride *for* doing something that merits such a response from others. In other words, we have partial—indeed self-focused—reasons to do things that call for appreciation from a

---

[3] Metz (2013) complains that when accounts of meaning appeal to external value in this way, they fail to confront the task of specifying what that value is. But it's not the business of an account of meaning to tell us what things possess value—that's the job of general axiology.

[4] This is compatible with thinking that sacrificing one's life can endow a life with greater meaning. Such acts get their value precisely because the self that is being sacrificed *is* important as such. There isn't this meaning to self-sacrifice by a member of some 'hivemind'.

thoroughly impartial standpoint. We want to do things that should matter to others; and that requires, at least in potential, someone external to us. By contrast, our happiness is self-contained; it doesn't call for any distinctive response from others (Metz 2013). And it's not just that we don't deserve special credit just in virtue of feeling satisfied. While our pleasurable experiences are in one sense the closest thing to us, they at the same time lack any distinctive trace of the self; one's delightful experience of eating a ripe peach could have just as easily been located in someone else, in anyone else. Our meaningful acts are different: while essentially directed outwards, they also express an individual self.

In short, the idea is that it is personally good for us to relate to an external good that is *independent* of our own good (though which could, potentially, be realized *in* us), and to do so in such a way that our relating to that external good merits positive appreciation from an external—an impartial—standpoint.

Turn now to importance. I cannot just assume that importance has value, let alone final value. I'm not aware of anyone defending the value of importance and, no doubt, many will doubt it has any. Yet, with Hume, plenty of people clearly strive to do something important on a large, or even grand, scale. Even if we end up dismissing such aims, we should first try to understand them.

It may seem implausible that importance on a large scale is always desirable. The Genoese sailors who brought the Black Plague to Europe changed the course of history, but having such a horrific impact isn't something anyone should wish for themselves. As we saw, even having a great positive impact needn't be desirable. The person who stops a vicious war by inadvertently making a fool of himself needn't overall regret what happened, if this was the only way to stop the bloodshed, but that's because that's so obviously good for so many others. But it is harder to see what's in it for *them*. If anything, we will probably want to say that this humiliation made their life worse.

What about intentionally making a great positive difference? In considering this question, we need to set aside the first-order value that is necessarily involved in making a great positive difference—say, in finding a cure for cancer. The numerous lives that would be saved by such a discovery obviously add up to an enormous amount of final value, but that value helps explain why a cure for cancer *is* important but in no way shows that this importance itself adds any further value. Now given that it will do so much good, the discovery will count as having considerable *instrumental* value. But we're asking about final value and, in one good sense, instrumental value isn't even real value; it doesn't add to the overall value of the world. It's also irrelevant if the effort to discover such a cure is said to have *moral* value, since we're asking whether it's good for *you* to do something important, and, anyway, many important contributions aren't in the moral domain. Finally, we should similarly set aside the instrumental benefits of making some important contribution. Einstein's discoveries earned him fame, respect, and various material benefits. But while such benefits no doubt help fuel the striving for importance, surely importance is often enough sought for its own sake, and we are asking whether *that's* worth seeking, regardless of the side benefits (which are anyway not due to importance itself but to *socially perceived* importance).

The question then is whether and why having (or doing things of) great instrumental value, compared to others, might make your own life *non*-instrumentally better for *you*.[5] What we said earlier suggests that in cases where importance doesn't meet the conditions for meaningfulness—for example, by being negative, or by not involving the agent's agency and attitudes in the right kind of way—importance doesn't seem desirable (or seems undesirable). Now we saw earlier that importance isn't necessary for meaningfulness. But it might be suggested now that meaningfulness is necessary for *importance* to have any value.

If meaningfulness is valuable, and valuable even without importance, then isn't meaningfulness doing all the evaluative work? Let's suppose for now that it is correct that meaningless importance isn't of benefit, and even that it is meaningfulness that is the true bearer of value. It might still be the case that importance on a large scale *amplifies* meaningfulness and thereby increases its value. We can actually venture a stronger hypothesis: that what we can call 'important meaningfulness' is the primary, and perhaps only, source of truly superlative meaning.

We can first support this hypothesis by example. The standard paradigms of a deeply meaningful life—the Mandelas, Einsteins, and Picassos—also happen to be people who are incredibly important on the grandest human scale. We can also support the hypothesis by argument. Meaningfulness involves a connection to external value. That value, we saw, needn't be larger than one's own, or even large in any other sense, though it also mustn't be negligible. But that claim was just that great value isn't *necessary* for meaningfulness, a claim that is compatible with thinking that, *when* you do something meaningful, the greater the difference to value that you make, the more meaningful your life is. Wolf (2012) says that what matters for meaning is the quality, not quantity, of one's contribution. But if by 'quality' she means value, then it should presumably still matter *how much* value one brings about.[6]

We saw that there are ways of leading meaningful lives without doing anything interestingly important. One was to realize, in our life and actions, some value to a high degree. But it's doubtful that the degree of value one could realize in this local way could compare to the value one can influence via grandly important deeds. To be sure, one might hold that a life with superlative meaning must also itself realize value to a high degree—think again of the example of the influential cultural philanthropist who herself lacks aesthetic understanding. And paradigms of superlative meaningfulness do seem to meet this condition. Yet they *also* involve great impact, so this is compatible with our hypothesis.

The other way to attain meaningfulness without impact was to be engaged in intense appreciation of existing value. And surely there is a vast amount of value one could engage with in this way, vaster than the amount of value even highly impactful figures can bring about. But first, it's doubtful that we can engage with that value with the requisite

---

[5] Setting aside the unusual cases where one's own value drives the difference one makes.
[6] Wolf (2012, 37) seems to agree when she speaks about a 'proportionality condition', though she only discusses cases where one engages with too little value.

intensity; flipping through all the art books in the world is presumably not quite enough. Second, many would hold that it's just more important to bring about great value than to appreciate existing value (better to change the world than to interpret it).[7]

When we tried to explain why meaningfulness is valuable, we highlighted the idea of connecting to something larger, and wanting what one does to merit appreciation from an impartial perspective. When meaningfulness combines with importance, these aims can be realized to a fuller degree. We saw that if we want to reconcile talk of connecting to something larger than ourselves with our judgments about which lives seem meaningful, we need to understand such talk metaphorically, not even as referring to something with greater value, but simply to something of independent value. But bringing in importance allows us to take such talk literally: to be important on a large scale literally is to make a contribution to something far larger than oneself—the greater the scale, the greater the spatio-temporal size of the thing one affects. And that thing's overall value will almost always be far greater than yours, or even that of your total contribution.

The same goes for the esteem one can get from doing things that will be appreciated from an impartial perspective. The meaningful merits admiring appreciation: confronted with an extraordinarily generous and caring person, we should respond with admiration. But such lives, as meaningful as they may be, don't call for special notice when we survey the larger landscape because they don't make enough of a difference to overall value, compared to others. There is so much of value all around and we cannot attend to it all. But the important, by definition, stands out.

We can go even further. I want to suggest that importance on a larger scale can address a distinctive existential concern, the wish for one's existence to matter. Some might prefer to say that this concern relates to a further sense of meaningfulness. But since this concern is about one's importance, a notion that is distinct from meaningfulness as defined earlier, it seems to me better not to mix the two. (I suspect that this mix-up is one reason why consequentialist accounts of meaning remain appealing despite their obvious shortcomings.)

---

[7] It might be objected that some traditions highlight paradigms of meaningfulness that lack external impact: think of isolated religious ascetics devoted exclusively to seeking enlightenment or attaining mystic union with God. And there's also the tradition that regards the contemplative life as the best and, presumably, as also superlatively meaningful (see also Mintoff 2008). In reply, consider first that such lives are rarely mentioned as clear paradigms of supreme meaning in current discussion; so these aren't uncontroversial examples. This is probably because that discussion largely assumes a secular standpoint, which takes us to the second point: it's far less obvious that such lives would count as possessing deep meaning if, in fact, the experienced union with God was illusory. If so, then this counterexample is compatible with thinking that great importance is necessarily for superlative meaningfulness within a naturalist framework. Third, we needn't even concede that such cases aren't taken to involve great importance *within* the relevant tradition. To begin with, spiritual exemplars often have profound impact on other believers. And even if they don't, their seemingly passive worldly stance might mask the great impact they are assumed to make in some spiritual dimension. Finally, the utility monster example demonstrates that great importance needn't involve great causal impact. If, say, mystic union with God has immense intrinsic value, then attaining such a rare state could make more difference to value than, say, writing the Great American Novel. I'm grateful to Iddo Landau for pressing this counterexample.

As with meaningfulness, it's easier to understand what it is we want exactly when we consider its complete absence. When people worry that they are utterly insignificant, they worry that what they do, even their very existence, makes little or no difference to the world around them. As Nagel (1987) puts it, '[l]ooking at [one's life] from the outside, it wouldn't matter if you had never existed'. If you make no difference, then removing you from the world seems to make no difference. You might, in your own corner, be leading a blissfully happy and even meaningful life. But just as the world is redundant for the happy hedonist, to feel insignificant is to feel that you are redundant to the world. Now putting things in such blunt words is an exaggeration. If you didn't exist, the physical order would be somewhat different. And since you and what you do *are* of value, there would also be less value in the world if you weren't here. So such angst shouldn't be understood to reflect doubt about one's value. It is concerned with importance: your value, and the difference to overall value that you make, just isn't enough to merit notice except at the most local of levels (Kahane 2014). Meaningfulness satisfies the self's need for an external world; but when you are important, then the world needs *you*, so to speak.[8]

Imagine Napoleon, restless like a caged lion on St. Helena. He has formed a surprisingly deep friendship with a guard, he discovers a hitherto unsuspected talent for carpentry. His life is not only pleasant but meaningful, if not in any superlative sense. Yet he may still feel his life now lacks the substance it had before. What he does now is unimportant, beyond the modest local context. So much less is at stake. It seems to me that what our imagined Napoleon feels he lacks isn't for his life to be even more meaningful, but to be important, and thus to matter, on a grander scale.[9]

But if importance addresses a distinct existential concern, shouldn't it *always* be good to have it? This needn't follow, but I think there's at least some plausibility to this idea. Let us return to examples of importance without meaningfulness. Imagine, for example, being the tall lady with the feathered hat standing in front of the diminutive Giuseppe Zangara, preventing him from assassinating President-elect Franklin D. Roosevelt.[10] The feathered lady doesn't deserve any credit for saving Roosevelt—it's hard to see why the accident of being there, and being tall enough, would make her life more meaningful. But her presence was important, very important. She changed the

---

[8] It might be tempting to think that importance seems to have distinctive value because important acts are also achievements, and achievement is valuable. But that's unlikely. First, while it is often incredibly hard to do something important on the grand scale, importance itself requires neither effort nor difficulty (think again of the 'result machine'). Second, on some influential accounts of achievement, the value of the product of an achievement is irrelevant to the value of the achievement itself. But if so, then, third, it's odd that people strive for importance when there are far easier ways to realize the value of achievement.

[9] Since the moral character, and upshot, of many of Napoleon's acts were of morally ambiguous character at best, it's far from clear whether his life as emperor possessed much, let alone superlative, meaningfulness, though presumably this is a worry he didn't share.

[10] To clarify: the feathered lady is my invention, though Zangara's short stature did made it hard for him to aim at Roosevelt.

course of world history. She enjoys a kind of 'prudential luck', and can even feel a kind of pride in the grand impact she had, even if it's a very different pride than that merited by achievements attributable to our agency. To be sure—as in the case of the trouser-less knighting—there are cases where other features of the situation make it, from your personal perspective, overall undesirable. But I wouldn't entirely rule out that there is nevertheless something in it for you even here.

Zangara's motives remain somewhat obscure, but there are plenty of recorded cases of people who, say, attempt to assassinate the famous as a perverse way of 'making a name for themselves' (the ancient arsonist Herostratus achieved his goal of going down in history by burning down the temple of Artemis at Ephesus—by me writing these words, and by you reading them, we further satisfy Herostratus's ambition). That such acts are morally obscene goes without saying. But might they still be good for the perpetrators? Our answer to that will presumably be the same as to the parallel question about the meaningfulness of Hitler's life (and Hitler was, of course, incredibly important).

There is one issue we still need to address. If importance amplifies meaning, or even carries its own value, how does that work given that things can be important to different degrees relative to different domains? I'm not yet sure how to answer this. One way to go is to say that it is the absolute amount of value one brings to the world that matters, not the comparative difference in value one makes to a domain. This purely consequentialist property is distinct from importance on some larger scale, though the two would broadly overlap. While I agree that this absolute factor is part of the picture, I don't think it's all that matters. For example, we cannot fully assess Botticelli's contribution if we don't know about Leonardo da Vinci, Michelangelo, and others; and Botticelli's contribution would have been different if, say, there had been no Leonardo, even holding influence fixed. So I think importance matters too, not just absolute impact. Now in some cases, there may be subjective or even objective factors that single out a specific domain of influence—someone may belong to a specific tradition, or aim to make an impact on philosophy. But someone who discovers a cure for cancer has made more of a mark than someone who overhauled his local country club, even if the latter deeply desired to make such an impact. A more attractive approach would identify the largest scale on which someone makes a sufficient difference to value; the value to them would be a function of their degree of importance on that scale, weighted by the size of the domain. But I don't pretend that this is a full solution—it faces, for example, the old dilemma between being a small fish in a big pond or a big fish in a small one.

But why should we seek to make an important difference on the largest scale we can if, when we are regarded from a cosmic standpoint that encompasses everything, we would still remain utterly insignificant? To begin with, if some greater value is far from reach, it hardly follows that anything less is nothing at all. And it's actually unclear that we are so insignificant on the cosmic scale. More expansive frames of references are spatiotemporally bigger, but what makes them more expansive is not their size per se, but that they encompass more of what there is of value. But if the vast universe that surrounds us is empty of value—because there is no intelligent life beyond our little planet—then, collectively, we would be the most valuable things in the universe and our acts, and our very existence, would therefore make a great difference to the value of the cosmos—indeed, they would decide that value. We would, despite appearances, be of immense cosmic significance. And a surprising upshot of this is that the few people who make or made a great difference here on Earth—including many of those familiar paradigms of meaning—would thereby also count as having immense cosmic significance *qua* individuals.[11]

III. Motives

I have argued that importance can amplify meaningfulness and may be required for superlative forms of meaningfulness, and more tentatively that it may also have value independently of meaningfulness. Why then does the pursuit of meaning seem noble, while the striving for importance seems unseemly, even ignoble?

To seek meaning is to seek to transcend the self and its petty concerns. And I wrote earlier that, by contrast, the striving for importance can seem embarrassingly egocentric. But this contrast is mistaken. As we saw, meaningfulness cannot involve the erasure of the self—it is at once outward-looking and self-concerned. It isn't, in this respect, different from importance which similarly requires a relation to external value—and, in most cases, to far more of the external world and the things of value it contains. And while to do something important is to do something that merits attention from others, this again marks no relevant difference since to do something meaningful is similarly to do something that merits others' admiration (and there's no admiration without attention).

One difference between meaning and importance is that meaningfulness attaches to lives, while importance can attach directly to persons. But I suspect that this is only a superficial linguistic difference. We admire the person leading a meaningful life, not their life, and, conversely, it makes perfect sense to describe a life as important.

Still, talk about a deeply meaningful life and talk about a Very Important Person evoke very different associations. This is in part, I think, because the people who are regarded, or treated, as important—think of all those 'influencers'—are often not really important at all—don't merit all that attention. In part, because importance is often associated with superficial benefits: with fame, adulation, power, material advantage, and the like; a meaningful live obviously doesn't confer such benefits. And it doesn't help that people who regard themselves as grandly important can be bad company; the self-important often forget that having an impact doesn't make you *morally* more important than others, let alone justify treating others as inferiors.

---

[11] I spell out this argument in far greater detail in Kahane (2014; 2021b). For criticism, see Benatar (2017), but Benatar's criticism suffers from his conflation of meaningfulness and importance, and from his mistaken assumption that importance on a given scale requires great causal impact on that scale. For my reply to Benatar, see Kahane (2021b).

However, there's no inherent link between perceived importance and arrogance; again, many paradigms of meaningfulness are also important, and know they are. And those who seek importance needn't be aiming at its more superficial rewards (which often enough don't arrive anyway). To be sure, there are enough people who seek fame and fortune, and doing something important can be a means to such an end; such people would presumably forget all about importance if they had a shortcut to fame. But when Hume says he desires to acquire a name for himself, it's natural to interpret him as wanting to be known *for* the genuinely important 'inventions and discoveries' he has made—wanting to receive *deserved* fame. And it is the making of a contribution itself that may be at the foreground, even if accompanied by the further preference that, *if* he succeeds, he'd also like his achievements to be fittingly recognised.[12] And the core aim would still be achieved even if one's contributions were forgotten or misattributed.

Is such an aim still unattractive? It might be argued that although there's a self-regarding component to the seeking of both meaningfulness and of importance, there is nevertheless an important difference in emphasis. When you seek meaning, you seek to connect to value *other* than yourself. When you seek importance, *you* seek to be the one who made a mark, to be the one to whom much of the value around can be attributed. However, while there is this difference in emphasis, I'm not yet sure that it could justify seeing the seeking of meaning as a virtue, of importance as a vice. We see it as perfectly respectable to pursue one's happiness so long as this is done via morally permissible means. Why is it just fine to want there to be as much value as possible *inside* your life, so to speak, yet unseemly to want to be responsible for as much value as possible *out there*?

Perhaps the problem is precisely that, in the latter case, the focus should be on that first order value, not on the self. You should want to cure cancer not in order to *be* important, but because curing cancer *is* incredibly important—because what's important are all those lives that will be saved, all the agony avoided. That's clearly right, but the cancer researcher's focus needn't be on her importance, but on her *doing* something important (to be important just is to have done, or otherwise brought about, important things). This is still self-regarding: one does want *oneself* to have found that cure, not merely, impersonally, for such a cure to be found. But that's no different from wanting one's life to be meaningful; we're not trying to impersonally maximise meaning in the world. Moreover, to want to be the one to find the cure, or to create a great work of art, isn't the same as wanting it to be *only* you who would do so. No, one wants a cure for cancer to be found, period, and by anyone, while also strongly preferring that *if* it gets found, this will be via one's own efforts.

In any event, the claim that aiming at importance is unattractive is only a claim about motivation, about what we should aim at; it is perfectly compatible with still thinking that importance has final value, or amplifies it. Moreover, in cases where we

---

[12] See also Chappell (2011). For further discussion of the relation between importance and fame, see Kahane (2021a).

gain importance inadvertently, it anyway doesn't matter what we aim at, and when we achieve it in meaningful ways, why can't we aim at meaningfulness instead?

However, the quest for meaning also has a problem with self-regard. The problem has a familiar structure. We saw that the idea behind meaning is to transcend the self by connecting it to something external of value. But if we care about that external good only for the sake of the good this does for us, then that external good is just an instrument in the service of that internal good. We haven't really transcended the self. To focus too much on meaningfulness is thus to undermine it—meaningfulness is self-effacing; someone who greedily seeks ever more sources of meaning has missed the point. With meaning then, as with importance, the focus should be on the external value with which we wish to connect—on people, ideas, art, etc.—not on the benefit to us of connecting to it. And as Wolf (2012) points out, those whose lives are already deeply meaningful rarely talk about meaning; they are absorbed instead in their outward-focused projects. The people who talk about meaning are often those who feel that it is missing from their lives. But does this mean that when such people seek to find meaning, they are bound to fail? This depends. To say that you want more meaning can mean that you want this personal good, meaning, that is achieved by connecting to external value. Such an aim may indeed be self-undermining. But it can also just mean that you want to connect to such external value, with the ensuing personal good only as a foreseen side effect. Still, it would be even better, so far as meaning is concerned, if we simply felt the independent pull of that external value.

References

Benatar, D. 2017. *The Human Predicament*. Oxford: Oxford University Press.
Chappell, T. 2011. 'Glory as an Ethical Idea'. *Philosophical Investigations* 34: 105–134.
Frankfurt, H. 1988. 'The Importance of What We Care About'. In his *The Importance of What We Care About*. Cambridge: Cambridge University Press, pp. 80–94.
Frankfurt, H. 1999. 'On The Usefulness of Finals Ends'. In his *Necessity, Volition, and Love* Cambridge: Cambridge University Press, pp. 82–94.
Hume, D. 1985. *Essays Moral, Political, and Literary*, revised edition, ed. E. F. Miller Indianapolis, IN: Liberty Fund.
Hume, D. 2000. *A Treatise of Human Nature*, ed. D. Norton and M. Norton. Oxford: Oxford University Press.
Kahane, G. 2014. 'Our Cosmic Insignificance'. *Noûs* 48: 745–772.
Kahane, G. 2021a. 'Importance, Fame, and Death'. In M. Hauskeller, ed., *Death and Meaning*, Royal Institute of Philosophy Supplement, 90, 33–55.
Kahane, G. 2021b. 'Importance, Value, and Causal Impact'. *Journal of Moral Philosophy*. doi: https://doi.org/10.1163/17455243-20213581
Kauppinen, A. 2012. 'Meaningfulness and Time'. *Philosophy and Phenomenological Research* 84: 345–377.
Metz, T. 2013. *Meaning in Life*. Oxford: Oxford University Press.
Mintoff, J. 2008. 'Transcending Absurdity'. *Ratio* 21: 64–84.
Nagel, T. 1971. 'The Absurd'. *Journal of Philosophy* 68: 716–727.

Nagel, T. 1987. *What Does It All Mean?* Oxford: Oxford University Press.
Nozick, R. 1974. *Anarchy, State and Utopia.* New York: Basic Books.
Nozick, R. 1981. *Philosophical Explanations* Oxford: Clarendon Press.
Nozick, R. 1989. *The Examined Life.* New York: Simon & Schuster.
Parfit, D. 1984. *Reasons and Persons.* Oxford: Clarendon Press.
Singer, P. 1993. *How Are We to Live? Ethics in an Age of Self-Interest.* Melbourne: Text.
Williams, B. 2011. *Ethics and the Limits of Philosophy.* Abingdon: Routledge.
Wolf, S. 2012. *Meaning in Life and Why It Matters.* Princeton, NJ: Princeton University Press.

CHAPTER 6

THE MEANING OF LIFE AND DEATH

STEVEN LUPER

Do we have reason to live? If so, do we live for that reason? The answer is not so clear. It is not as if, after giving it some thought, we opt to start living, then, after some time passes, opt to stay alive, until finally, at some point, we call it quits. We are around long before we notice it, and live a good while by default, without having chosen to begin or to continue our existence, and without looking for grounds for such choices. In time, we find ourselves carried forward in the grip of ambitions whose significance we take largely for granted, like dogs chasing cats. We may go on the same way, and reach the end of our days without ever deciding whether to live or die. We might instead wake one day and ask ourselves whether there is any reason to stay alive. We could end our search with an assuring answer, say that days spent raising children or writing a book are days well spent. But the inquiry is perilous; if our expectations are unrealistic, we are unlikely to reach answers, and without them it may be difficult to live by default again. As well, we may conclude that we have no reason to live, or even that we have reason *not* to live—reason to die.

Wherever our inquiry takes us—whether it frees us to return to our lives or it prompts us to end them—we appear to be concerned with the meaning of our lives, for meaning is often thought to be what gives us reason to live.

But what is meaning? One clue is the very fact that it is something that gives us reason to live (although, as will emerge, what gives us reason to live need not confer meaning on our lives), and we have a very clear reason to live on when the life in prospect is good for us. So perhaps we should say that life has meaning in virtue of the package of things that make it good for us. I will discuss the view that meaning and welfare (well-being) are the same thing in the next section. I think it points us in the right direction, since meaning is prominent among the things that make life worthwhile. However, I will argue, in the following section, that meaning and welfare are distinct. In itself, what gives life meaning makes it better for us, but some things help make (continued) life worth having without conferring meaning on it. In a further section, I will defend a more specific account, *achievementism*, according to which the meaning of my life consists in my achieving the things I devote it to.[1] Achievements are part, but only part, of what makes my life go well. I will follow up, in the penultimate section, with an attempt to clarify how meaning bears on life and on death. In my view, the meaning of life stands in opposition to that of death and vice versa. Other things being equal, what gives us reason to *live on* gives us reason *not to die*, and what gives our lives positive meaning gives our deaths negative meaning. The reverse is true as well: what gives us reason to die gives us reason not to live on, and what gives death positive meaning gives life negative meaning.

Meaning as Welfare

Is meaning really, at bottom, just the same thing as welfare? To decide whether these may be equated, I will need to clarify the nature of welfare. I will do so in this section. We can evaluate the equation in the subsequent section.

I take it that individuals (any sentient creatures) may fare well or ill over time, and that what varies thereby—rising when times are good and falling when times are bad—is their welfare level. Certain things we may call 'goods' are good for us in themselves; their accrual makes us better off, other things being equal. There are also things that we may call 'evils' that are bad for us in themselves. Their accrual makes an individual worse off—again other things being equal. (In order to avoid using the term 'bad' as a count noun I here use the term 'evil' as a synonym for 'bad'.) Accordingly, I will have a positive welfare level over some interval of time if and only if the goods I accrue over that interval outweigh the evils, and a negative welfare level if and only if the evils outweigh the goods. My welfare level will be 0— neither positive nor negative—if and only if I am capable of accruing goods or evils but any goods I accrue are exactly offset by the evils and vice versa. The welfare level I accrue over the course of my entire life we may call my lifetime welfare level.

Drawing on the notion of a welfare level, we can specify when it is that an event (or action—I assume that actions are events) is overall good for me—that is, good for me all things considered:

---

[1] I first defended achievementism in Luper (2014). Compare the account that Derek Parfit called the 'Success Theory' (1984, 494). Laurence James (2004, 429–430) argues that 'other things being equal, a life with some achievements in it is more meaningful than one without any achievements', but adds that achievements are not 'the only things that can make a life meaningful (nor are they sufficient)'. Simon Keller (2004, 30) argues, in effect, that achievements are welfare makers, but does not defend the view that achievements boost meaning: 'There are things apart from the achievement of goals that make a life go well, and . . . one of those things may well be the living of a life that is meaningful or worthwhile.' In a later essay (2016, 279) he entertains the possibility that 'achievement imbues live with meaning'.

> An event is overall good (bad) for me if and only if, and to the extent that, it makes my lifetime welfare level higher (lower) than it otherwise would be.[2]

It makes good sense to favour things that are overall good for me, such as trips to the dentist, even though they may involve some evils, such as pain. (Of course, it is prudent for me to rank the alternatives that are open to me in terms of how likely each is to maximize my lifetime welfare level. Whether an event is overall good for me depends on the particulars of my circumstances. These might include the fact that I am prone to make bad choices.)

I said that welfare may be positive, negative, or neutral. The same would be true of meaning if it were the same thing as welfare. The goods that make for a higher, more positive welfare level would also make for a higher, more positive meaning level, while the evils that make for lower welfare would make for negative meaning. As well, the degree or sum of meaning accrued over one stretch of my life might differ significantly from the degree accrued over other stretches. Patches of my life might have great meaning, while others have just the opposite. Accordingly, we would take the following view concerning meaning:

> My life over a stretch of time has *positive* meaning (a positive meaning level) if and only if, and to the extent that, my welfare level over that time is positive (the goods outweigh the evils), and *negative* meaning if and only if, and insofar as, my welfare level over that time is negative (the evils outweigh the goods). Otherwise (assuming I am capable of accruing goods or evils at all), my life has a level of meaning equal to 0.

(I would be tempted use the terms *meaning*, *absurdity*, and *meaninglessness* to mark the three-way distinction among positive, negative, and neutral meaning, were the term *absurdity* not already widely used for the condition in which a life lacks meaning.)

Having introduced the notion of a meaning level, we may follow up by introducing a notion we may call *meaningfulness*, which would play a role similar to that of the notion of overall goodness. That is, we could stipulate that:

> An event is positively (negatively) *meaningful* for me if and only if, and to the extent that, it makes my lifetime meaning level higher (lower) than it otherwise would be.[3]

---

[2] For some purposes it can be useful to state the account as follows:

An event E is overall good (bad) for S if and only if the intrinsic value for S of the actual world is greater (less) than the intrinsic value for S of the closest world in which E does not occur.

[3] More precisely:

for any subject S, an event is positively (negatively) meaningful for S if and only if, and to the extent that, it makes S's lifetime meaning level higher (lower) than it otherwise would be, as opposed to (e.g.):

Summing up, if we equate meaning with welfare we might also distinguish, in a preliminary way, between meaning and meaningfulness. The first of these, (positive) *meaning*, full stop, corresponds to the (positive) elements of our welfare. We derive a certain sort of benefit from accruing this sort of meaning at or over time. Meaning is good for us *in itself*. It benefits us directly. By contrast, (positively) *meaningful* things benefit us in an indirect way that corresponds to the benefit (harm) involved in something's being overall good (bad) for us.

Welfare as an Element of Meaning

So much for clarifying welfare and what equating it with meaning would involve. Now let us see if we want to equate the two. To that end, let us consider a possible alternative, namely, that meaning consists in more than my welfare—that although what boosts my welfare also gives my life more meaning, as the equation implies, the reverse is not true. Some things give my life more meaning without boosting my welfare.

We can state the alternative view more clearly if we coin the term *meaning makers* for the items that, added to my life, give it a positive or negative meaning level, and the term *welfare makers* for the goods and evils that make for my life's *welfare* level. The simple equation identifies the two, while the alternative we are placing on the table says that although all welfare makers are meaning makers, welfare makers are not the sole meaning makers.

We should reject this view. I suggest that, whatever else we might think about meaning, it is something that makes life directly better for those who accrue it. More precisely, my thought is this:

Accruing a positive (negative) meaning maker is good (bad) in itself for its bearer.

From this assumption, it follows that all meaning makers are welfare makers, so nothing can give my life more meaning without boosting my welfare.

Is there a way around the objection I just stated? It might seem so. Why not do this: (1) distinguish among ways in which my life may be directly improved; (2) designate some of these as improvements that do not boost my welfare; (3) equate my prudential interests with what does boost my welfare; and (4) claim that I derive meaning from at least some of the non-prudential improvements? If we make these moves, we can insist that acquiring meaning is indeed always beneficial to me but sometimes only in the specified, welfare-unrelated, way, so it does not always give me prudential reason

for any subject S, S's *action A* is positively (negatively) meaningful for S if and only if, and to the extent that, A makes someone's (anyone's) lifetime meaning level higher (lower) than it otherwise would be.

to live. For example, we might say that my (having and) exercising the moral virtues is a meaning maker that directly improves my life but not my welfare (although it might indirectly improve both my own welfare and that of other people). We would have divided meaning makers into two sorts: welfare makers and the welfare-unrelated meaning makers.

However, we should meet this rejoinder with scepticism. There may well be reasons to insist that what directly improves my life need not raise its welfare level. For example, we might insist that nothing qualifies as a welfare maker unless constituted entirely by features that are intrinsic to me (Mark Bernstein [1998, 19] and Walter Glannon [2001, 138] defend this view), or contained entirely within my life (whatever that means). Pleasure qualifies. The friendship I form with my neighbour does not. Yet both are good for me in themselves. We might also want to deny that our welfare level could shift (say, because a loved one suffers or dies) without our noticing it (because we are away spelunking at the time). That said, I know of no good reason to insist that accruing things that are good for me in themselves need not be in my prudential interests (other things equal). Indeed, the idea strikes me as incoherent.

If I am right about that, then even if we admit that improving my life and raising my welfare level come apart, we can accept the simple equation with only minor revision. Instead of identifying meaning with welfare, and meaning makers with welfare makers, we can equate meaning with prudence, and positive (negative) meaning makers with the things that are good (bad) for us in themselves, including friendships, and say that a life's meaning level is determined by these (Moritz Schlick [1979] took this view). It follows that what gives my life meaning is in my prudential interests.

In my view, we gain nothing by prizing welfare and prudential interests apart, so in what follows I will apply the term 'welfare maker' to the things that directly improve lives, not to some narrower subset, and I will assume that meaning makers are themselves things that directly improve lives.

Accepting this claim—all meaning makers are welfare makers—does not force us to deny that I have non-prudential reasons to live. (Nor does it rule out the possibility that some feature of *another* person—say the pleasure that another accrues—is a welfare maker for me, although, of course, we might want to deny this possibility on other grounds.) Earlier I noted that we have reason (it need not be a matter of duty) to further the interests of others; assuming that helping someone else need not benefit us, then it can give us non-prudential reason to live.[4] What we *do* have to say is that advancing these—non-prudential—reasons for living will not raise my meaning level.[5] (This point is obscured by a fact I will emphasize later, namely that my life may accrue meaning by

---

[4] We may have moral reasons to live, but morality and prudence are frequently at odds, and the former trumps the latter. So living out of a sense of duty does not confer meaning on life.

[5] Peter Singer (1993, 331–335) appears to reject this claim, but it is hard to tell, since, like many theorists, he tells us how to gain meaning (how to make life 'meaningful')—namely, by putting aside our own interests and helping others—without getting around to telling us what meaning *is*. Perhaps he thinks that meaning is a welfare maker for us, but the most efficient way to accrue it is by helping others.

virtue of my achieving aims that concern matters that, in themselves, would make no meaning for me.) Nevertheless, my living in such a way as to advance the interests of others may be meaningful for *them*—it may augment *their* meaning makers—and that is something I have good reason to do. In many cases, as concerns friends, for example, the distinction will hardly matter to me, since the difference between my interests and theirs is unimportant to me, and I am apt to ignore the boundary separating me from them.[6]

Achievementism

Let us pause to take stock. The goal is to work out how meaning and welfare are related. One possibility, we said, is that they are identical. We would reject this possibility if we concluded that welfare is an element of meaning—that although (1) what boosts my welfare also gives my life more meaning, nevertheless (2) what gives my life more meaning need not boost my welfare. However, we just rejected this view, since we rejected (2), so the simple equation is still on the table. Nevertheless, we have made progress, for the fact that meaning boosts welfare implies that the only alternative to the simple equation is that meaning is an element of welfare—that although, contrary to (2), what gives my life more meaning *does* boost my welfare, nevertheless (1) is also false—not everything that boosts my welfare gives my life more meaning. So if we can show that there are some welfare makers that are not meaning makers, we may conclude that meaning is an element of welfare.

To show that what boosts my welfare need not add meaning to my life, we need only note that, other things being equal, enjoying myself boosts my welfare level yet does not add meaning to my life. If further argument is needed, we might cite Robert Nozick's thought experiment in which our brains are attached to a machine that gives us a constant, maximally pleasant stream of experiences for the rest of our lives, and we are oblivious to what is really going on around us (1974, 42–45). Suppose we stipulate that how happy we are over our lives is determined by how much pleasure and pain we accrue, with pleasure boosting our happiness level and pain lowering it. Then spending our

---

[6] Our way of thinking about meaning has another salient consequence, namely, nothing can accrue meaning unless it is capable of having a welfare level (of course, something that lacks a welfare level may be meaningful to something with one). Individual sentient beings qualify. Not so things such as worlds, sentient beings as a collective, humanity, peoples, or families. (Don't we better a world by adding goods to it or removing evils from it? Not literally. Perhaps it is better that there be more good than less, or that more goods exist than less, but when we speak of bettering the world, we mean either that the world becomes more suitable for its sentient inhabitants (assuming that aesthetic value is wholly instrumental), which is to make *them* better off, not the world, or that the world becomes a better exemplar of its kind, roughly in the way that a car qua car is better if there is oil in the engine. Metaphorical talk aside, however, the evil in a world does not make it less sound as a world, and placing a good into the world— that is, bringing a good into existence—does not benefit the world, or make it a more sound world, any more than my enjoying a meal at home benefits or betters my house.)

lives in Nozick's machine would make us very happy. Yet our lives, spent attached to the machine, would lack something highly significant, despite the surfeit of happiness. What we detect is the absence of meaning, which suggests that happiness is not a form of meaning. Note, too, that in ordinary life it is not uncommon to find ourselves sacrificing our happiness for the sake of accomplishments that we take to confer meaning on life, so not only is happiness not a sort of meaning, it is of much less importance to us than meaning.

We now have a case for the view that meaning is an element of welfare, and Nozick's thought experiment suggests that at least some welfare makers, namely varieties of experiences, such as serenity, fulfilment, passion, and bliss, are not meaning makers, so only some welfare makers are meaning makers.[7] Left open, however, is the possibility that the meaning makers include some selection of welfare makers other than experiences. The welfare makers might be such things as virtues, achievements, friendships, and loving relationships. Perhaps some further restrictions apply as well, such as moral permissibility.[8]

However, I am inclined to think that there is only one sort of meaning maker, namely achievements. More precisely, the view I would defend, achievementism, holds that my life has meaning if and only if, and to the extent that, I achieve the aims that I devote it to, freely and competently. Achievements are the positive meaning makers that serve to raise my life's meaning level, while failures are negative meaning makers that lower it. Things are positively meaning*ful* for me just to the extent that they make my lifetime meaning level higher (by virtue of my achieving things or avoiding failure) than it otherwise would be. Things are negatively meaningful for me just to the extent that they make my lifetime welfare level lower (by virtue of precluding my achieving things or by virtue of increasing my failures) than it otherwise would be.[9] (We can distinguish among different versions of achievementism, one that says that any accomplishments are potential meaning makers, others that filter out some accomplishments. I will not take a position here [I say more in Luper 2014], but I am inclined to think that only the things to which I devote my life as a whole, or at least significant stretches of it [say my remaining days], count as potential meaning makers. This assumption explains why meaning is an issue

---

[7] It does not rule out the possibility that experiences of some sort are necessary for meaning.

[8] Iddo Landau (2011, 312–313) says that a life is not 'meaningful' unless it meets 'a certain threshold of value or worth'. If we counter that achievements are among the goods on Derek Parfit's (1984, 493) Objective List, as I am inclined to think, Landau would reply that achievements do not confer meaning, or that nothing is an achievement if it is immoral, or that extreme moral disvalue undercuts the positive value and meaning of an achievement. In explaining her formula for meaning—'meaning arises when subjective attraction meets objective attractiveness'—Susan Wolf (1997, 211) allows that a project may confer meaning despite having moral disvalue but requires that it have some other sort of objective value (even though presumably this would be less important than *moral* value). It would seem that being on the Objective List does not suffice. Otherwise, achievements would automatically meet her formula.

[9] Something can be negatively meaningful for me by virtue of preventing me from taking on an aim that I otherwise would have achieved. If I never take on the aim, I do not fail at an attempt to achieve it (I do not accrue that intrinsic evil), but I do not gain a success I otherwise would have gained.

for, and available to, only creatures capable of grasping, and taking a critical stance on, their life as a whole.)

If meaning is an element of welfare, achievementism presupposes that my achievements boost my welfare. But do they? Fulfilling a *desire* may well benefit me, but, if so, won't that be because I desire something beneficial to me, such as a good meal? It is true that in many if not most cases I benefit from fulfilling a desire precisely because I wanted something that *itself* was good for me. However, achievement is no ordinary form of desire fulfilment. Take the case in which I devote my life to crossing one sort of flower with another. The hybrid itself may or may not benefit me. Accomplishing something I devote my life to is good for me in itself.

Achievementism has considerable plausibility on its face. It is not unusual for people to sacrifice their happiness, friendships, and other elements of welfare for the sake of achieving things to which they devote their lives; the special place of achievement in our lives supports equating it (and not other welfare makers) with meaning.[10]

More can be said in its favour. One advantage of achievementism is that it makes it clear why the notion of *purpose* is commonly linked to that of meaning: I attain meaning by achieving some aim to which I devote my life. The achievements supply the contents of meaning, and give life direction. Thereby, my life acquires an *end* in a sense that is quite different from its coming to an end: I give it a purpose. This will seem problematic only if we assume that the point or purpose of one thing must be something else with its own point or purpose. But we should avoid this assumption, which starts us down a regress that undermines the very notion of a purpose. There is nothing problematic about an end or aim with no end beyond itself (Luper 1992), and other things will have an intelligible purpose to the extent that they are the means to someone's ends. This is true of one's own life: giving it a meaning gives it a purpose, namely the accomplishment of the aims to which it is devoted.

Achievementism also makes it clear why it is questionable that the lives of non-human animals (with possible exceptions) have meaning, even though it is unquestionable that many of them—the sentient ones—may fare well or ill. Many non-human animals form desires—the desire to eat, the desire to flee—whose fulfilment may or may not enable them to live well. But the fulfilment of desires does not require devoting life to anything and is not the same thing as the achievement of aims. Aims are desires, but not all desires are aims. In desiring that something be the case, I may or may not intend to bring it about. For example, because I live in twenty-first-century America, it would make no sense for me to attempt to fulfil my desire to visit other galaxies, as I am powerless to do anything about it. Although I want to go, it makes no sense to make the journey an aim of mine. As well, it makes little sense to speak of an aim in the case that the fulfilment of my desire requires little or no action on my part. For example, while I desire that the sun will continue to shine, it is no aim of mine: the sun will shine no

---

[10] Camus said we must imagine Sisyphus happy. We should not. By hypothesis, his rock rolling caused him punishing misery. Still, if we posit a Sisyphus who devoted his life to rock rolling, we may well view him as *proud*, accomplishing what he set out to achieve.

matter what I do. If, now, I devote my life, or some substantial part of it, to the achievement of some aim, I must have the capacity to survey my life as a whole, and decide what it is to be for, what direction it will take, and, as far as we know, this is something that only human beings can do. That said, it would not be surprising if it were to turn out that some other sorts of animals had the capacities—such as self-awareness and the ability to take a critical stance on their life as a whole—which enable them to give their life meaning. And even among human beings, the exercise of these capacities is not inevitable. Many people take no interest in their life as a whole. By default, their life, as a whole, lacks meaning.

A further advantage of achievementism is that it illuminates how meaning and identity may be related. What gives a person's life meaning cannot literally give that person an identity—not if the identity in question is numerical identity. It is impossible for something to exist for a time and then acquire its numerical identity. But instead of using the term 'identity' for the conditions that are necessary and sufficient for our existence over time, we might instead use it for some or all of the conditions that bear on whether we *want* to exist, whether our continued existence matters to us. I would not want to exist in just any circumstances; for example, I would not wish to stay alive if I were the only person left in the world, or if my faculties were quickly failing. Call something a *critical feature* if the prospect of never acquiring it or the prospect of its irretrievable loss would leave me indifferent at best about my continued existence (or worse: wishing it were ended). These critical features reveal who or what I wish to be. We might say they constitute my *critical identity*, or my *critical self*.

Devoting my life to something may help me to shape my critical self, for I may make my success at that task one of my critical features. It is possible for me to survive the failure of such a defining task, as my critical features are not constitutive of my numerical identity. However, such a failure will strike me, phenomenologically, as death. Or perhaps it will strike me as worse than death, as the source of especially great anguish, precisely because it is I whose efforts have proven to be futile. Perhaps I might later recover, and devote my life to some new task; if so, it may seem as if I am a different self.

But doesn't achievementism face glaringly obvious objections? Doesn't it imply that I might give my life meaning by advancing aims that are dull and repetitious, or self-centred, or self-destructive, or even completely immoral? Doesn't it imply that pursuits—i.e. journeys as opposed to arrivals—do not confer meaning? On balance, these are not really objections to the view. Here's why.

Consider the last reservation. It is true that the pursuit of an aim is different from its achievement, and that one might never achieve what one sets out to do, but we should not equate meaning with the pursuit of our aims, as the teleological account of meaning (compare Quinn 1997) would have it. If that account were correct, failing to achieve our aims would not matter to us. Yet clearly we pursue an aim in order to achieve it. The point is obscured, I think, by the fact that we sometimes take pursuits *as* aims. For example, I might take, as an aim, learning about, or studying, the Milky Way, which is an aim I achieve by engaging in a pursuit. If given an elixir that bestows eternal life, it would be natural for me to take on more pursuits as aims.

Now consider the possibility of devoting my life to something dull and repetitious. The characterization of my task as 'dull' and 'repetitious' suggests that I am doing something wholly worthless and hence meaningless. But even something dull and repetitious would accrue a distinctive sort of value if indeed I make it the centrepiece of my life, for it matters in itself that I achieve what I set out to do with my life. That said, it would be odd in the extreme to devote my life to something like this. My achievements are not the only things that are good for me. Hence, in shaping my life and choosing my aims, I will want to take the other elements of my welfare into account. In particular, I will want to be able to take pride in what I do, which boosts my self-esteem, and while a degree of pride is appropriate when I accomplish what I set out to do, that benefit will be undermined if I consider what I do to be unchallenging. Also, my well-being will be impaired if I saddle myself with a stultifying aim. There is an excellent reason not to do something dull and repetitious, other things being equal: it is boring. Going to the other extreme is also ill advised: it is all too easy to have overly elevated expectations concerning our achievements. If we aspire to things that will leave a mark on eternity, as perhaps Tolstoy did when he questioned the meaning of his life, we are tilting at windmills.

Achievementism is also consistent with my living in relative solitude, and setting myself goals that call for going it alone, giving my life a meaning solely about myself, or even goals that are morally questionable. These choices, too, are short-sighted. Consider the last of them. Conceivably, I could accrue meaning by taking on unsavoury aims (just as I could amuse myself doing things that are twisted). It would put me in violation of my moral obligations, so it is not an option, but that is because it is wrong, not because I would not accrue meaning. Even a morally neutral pursuit will be objectionable, if it leads me to neglect my duties (Williams 1979). As for the other choices: we have already noted that there are things outside of my own life that are directly worth caring about, and that I may bring into my arena of interests simply by devoting my life to them. We can add that, in setting goals, there is no reason to assume that I must go it alone. I may join with other like-minded persons, and we can set ourselves collective goals. My efforts to achieve the collective goals will matter to the others, and success counts as a win for each of us.

Death

Recapping briefly, I have argued that meaning makers are welfare makers, and that my life's meaning level is determined by the positive and negative meaning makers I accrue. What counts as being meaningful to me does so if and only if and to the extent that it makes my life's meaning level higher than it otherwise would be. If achievementism is also true, achievements are the sole positive meaning makers, while failures are the sole negative meaning makers.

Given this framework, it is possible to draw several conclusions concerning the relationship between meaning and death.

First, in itself, the fact that we will die does not prevent our lives from having positive meaning. People may live well and achieve a great deal before they die—their life as a whole might be overall good and successful—so the lives of mortals may display high levels of meaning. It is also true that our mortality does not stop our lives from having negative meaning. How well we live, and the degree of meaning our life comes to have, depends on many factors, over many of which we have little control. Our prospects for living well are especially vulnerable to chance. Those who are born with debilitating, incurable illnesses have low prospects, while good health and abundant resources better position people to flourish. Assuming that achievementism is true, we have far more control over whether we will attain meaning than over whether we will live well, since we decide what we will set out to achieve, and we can adjust our ambitions so that they are realistic given our foreseeable circumstances (Luper 2012 and 2014).

Second, while we may conceive of people who live well forever and who accrue substantial meaning while doing so, it may also be true that the lives of some people, if extended long enough, would be bad, and their meaning level negative (Williams 1973). (Even if the first stretch of a life were good, as a whole that life would be bad if the evils accrued over the long run swamped the goods accrued during the first stretch.) However, the matter is complicated in this way: we cannot fail at what we do not attempt, so if, at some point, we accomplish what we set out to do, and never take on anything else, our meaning level will not fall, no matter how much longer we live. Still, this would be an odd way to prevent the meaning level of life from dropping into negative territory.

Third, dying at some time may or may not be negatively meaningful for those who die then. Just as we may assess the meaningfulness for me of living on in terms of the way it affects my lifetime meaning level, so we may assess the value for me of *not* living on—of dying at some time, perhaps at my own hand—the same way:[11]

> Dying at a particular time is positively (negatively) meaningful for me if and only if, and to the extent that, it makes my lifetime meaning level higher (lower) than it otherwise would be.

I suppose that if I am not alive then I (may be said to) fail to live on without dying. Let us put aside that possibility, and focus on cases in which I fail to live because I die. Then we may conclude that if living on would be positively meaningful for me, then dying at that time would be negatively meaningful for me, and vice versa. Something similar is true of mortality and immortality: being mortal is positively (negatively) meaningful for me if and only if, and to the extent that, my lifetime meaning level is higher (lower) than it would be were I immortal.

---

[11] Rationally ending one's life does not commit one to the judgment that one's life lacks meaning—that, as a whole, it is not significant.

In this way, meaningfulness is like overall goodness, as it is also true that if living on would be good for me, then dying at that time would be bad for me, and vice versa. Some have challenged this latter claim, however. Typically, they do so in an attempt to rescue the position of Epicurus. Epicurus claimed that dying never harms nor benefits those who die—dying is a matter of indifference (Epicurus 1966). Yet indifference about dying commits us to indifference about living on. Since it is absurd to say that living on is always a matter of indifference, Epicurus's stance on dying is mistaken (Luper 1985). Some commentators (John Fischer [2019] is the latest example; he credits the influence of Rosenbaum [1989] and Heschenov [2007]) instead say that Epicurus can sensibly affirm the goodness of living while retaining his indifference about dying. Such theorists might be tempted to say something similar in response to my claim about meaningfulness, as my account implies that if dying at some time is neither negatively nor positively meaningful for us, then the same goes for living on. The response might be that although dying at some time is neither negatively nor positively meaningful for us, the same need not be true of our living on.

But we cannot plausibly say that living on is sometimes good for us yet dying is always a matter of indifference. Just about no one (Miguel de Unamuno [1954] is a noteworthy exception) will accept the idea that dying is a matter of indifference in a case in which it saves us from an eternity of unmitigated agony. It benefits us to the extent that it precludes our suffering (even though, while dead, we are not in the least grateful for escaping misery), in which case living on would have been bad for us. By parity of reasoning, it follows that dying may be bad for us[12] in virtue of its precluding happiness (even though, while dead, we do not in the least resent not being happy), in which case living on would have been good for us. So if in some set of circumstances living on would be good for us, then dying at that time would be bad for us—*not* a matter of indifference.

On behalf of Epicurus, Fischer responds this way:

> The Epicurean may hold that [a hermit who is completely indifferent to dying] has good reason to reject suicide. The hermit may well prefer continued life to death, because he deems pleasure good....
>
> You might wonder: if life is good, then isn't death worse? Isn't it bad to end up with the worse alternative? An Epicurean would reply that if life is good, then it is indeed better than death. So if one has a choice between a good life and death, it makes sense to choose life. But it is in general not true that if *A* is better than *B*, then *B* is bad. It is better to be given a million dollars than half a million, but getting half-million dollars is not too shabby! (Fischer 2019, 44–45)

It would be difficult for Epicureans to convince competent people who are truly suicidal not to kill themselves. Such people are apt to think their options come in shades of misery: some options lessen their suffering, others worsen it, and one ends it. None of the existing options rises above the *x*-axis, where life is worthwhile; in that sense, none is

---

[12] As several theorists have argued, including Nagel (1970).

good. But the hermit that Fischer imagines is not like this. Not being suicidal, he believes that the life that is yet to come would be good for him. Yet Fischer claims, on behalf of Epicurus, that such a person may be indifferent to dying.

Consider whether and why we might come to judge that dying is good for us. If the suffering it precludes is slight enough, we might hesitate to say that dying is 'good' for us, even while being happy to say that dying is 'better' for us and living on 'worse' for us. It would hardly be accurate to describe our attitude as one of indifference, however, if we *do* prefer to die. What is more, we have only to imagine that the amount of suffering at stake is high enough (think Prometheus) for our hesitation to vanish. This is true, in any case, unless we adopt something like the view that, to be good for us *full stop*, something must bring us things that are good in themselves. On this one-sided view, dying (like being unconscious while undergoing surgery) cannot *possibly* be full-stop good for us, even though it might be vastly better than living on. Similarly, while we might hesitate to say that dying is 'bad' for us if only a little happiness is at stake, our reservation (but not Epicurus's) would go away if enough were at stake—unless we adopt a one-sided view on which to be full-stop bad for us is to bring us things that are bad in themselves.

I doubt Fischer would encourage us to adopt either one-sided view. (For further discussion, see Luper 2012.)

Closing Thoughts

Many widely discussed views of meaning are inconsistent with the story I have defended. What should we make of these? I will not attempt to discuss them all, but, in closing, I do want to say a little about how some of them relate to mine.

Take views according to which meaning consists in some fact or insight. Even though such views imply that meaning is distinct from welfare in general and achievement in particular, they typically focus on some insight specifically because it bears on our welfare in an especially significant way.

By way of illustration, consider Arthur Schopenhauer's claim that 'nothing else can be stated as the aim of our existence except the knowledge that it would be better for us not to exist' (Schopenhauer, 1958, 605), which seems to equate meaning with the insight that it would have been better had we never existed. One reason Schopenhauer gave (1962, 215–227) for deploring life was that (to restate his point) while there are negative welfare makers there are no positive welfare makers, roughly because suffering is the sole negative welfare maker and happiness is no more than the absence of suffering. Here he deliberately reversed a strategy used by Augustine and others in response to the problem of evil: claiming that evil is no more than the absence of goodness. For Schopenhauer, the best life is one in which we suffer as little as possible, which means it is best not to live at all. Life is necessarily an evil, and goodness is banal. While Schopenhauer did not do so, he easily could have put his point this way: there are only negative meaning makers, so the life with the greatest meaning is the life that ends soonest. The view opposite to

Schopenhauer's would be that there are positive welfare makers but no negative welfare makers, so the worst life is one devoid of positive welfare makers, death is necessarily an evil, and evil is banal.

In deliberate opposition to Schopenhauer, whom he initially admired, Friedrich Nietzsche defended a version of achievementism. Nietzsche urged us to strive for greatness, and identified greatness with achievement, in the pursuit of which we should be willing to endure (meaningful) suffering (Nietzsche 1983, 125–195). Behind this thought was the conviction that we affirm life most (and will death least) ardently when we aspire to greatness, and, by our example, move others to do the same.

While never existing was Schopenhauer's focus, other writers have linked death to the meaning of life because of the bearing death has on our welfare. For example, Bernard Williams (1973, 82) claimed that 'death gives the meaning to life'. His point was that death allows us to escape the consequences of lingering long after we are done with life. Williams's claim seems to be related to an aphorism attributed to Franz Kafka: 'the meaning of life is that it ends'.[13] Kafka's point seems to be that because of the fact of death (life's ending) there is a limit to how good and how bad life can be for us, precisely because it ends. On one hand, the end may come before we are done with life; on the other, it may come later than we may have wished.[14]

References

Bernstein, Mark. 1998. *On Moral Considerability: An Essay on Who Morally Matters*. Oxford: Oxford University Press.
Camus, Albert. 1955. *Myth of Sisyphus*, trans. J. O'Brien. London: H. Hamilton.
Epicurus. 1966. 'Letter to Menoeceus'. In *Greek and Roman Philosophy after Aristotle*, ed. J. Saunders. New York: Free Press, pp 49–52.
Fischer, John Martin, ed. 1993. *Metaphysics of Death*. Stanford, CA: Stanford University Press.
Fischer, John Martin. 2019. *Death, Immortality, and Meaning in Life*. Oxford: Oxford University Press.
Glannon, Walter. 2001. 'Persons, Lives, and Posthumous Harms'. *Journal of Social Philosophy* 32: 127–142.
Herschenov, David. 2007. 'A More Palatable Epicureanism'. *American Philosophical Quarterly* 44(2): 171–180.
James, Laurence. 2004. 'Achievement and the Meaningfulness of Life'. *Philosophical Papers* 34: 429–442.
Keller, Simon. 2004. 'Welfare and the Achievement of Goals'. *Philosophical Studies* 121:27–41.
Klemke, E. D., and Stephen Cahn. 2008, *The Meaning of Life*. Oxford: Oxford University Press.
Landau, Iddo. 2011. 'Immorality and the Meaning of Life'. *Journal of Value Inquiry* 45: 309–317.
Luper, Steven. 1985. 'Annihilation'. *The Philosophical Quarterly* 37(148): 233–252. Reprinted in *Metaphysics of Death*, ed. John Martin Fischer, 269–290. Stanford, CA: Stanford University Press, 1993.

---

[13] As far as I know, the aphorism does not appear in any of Kafka's publications.
[14] I thank Rachel Johnson and Iddo Landau for insightful comments on a previous draft.

Luper, Steven. 1992. 'The Absurdity of Life'. *Philosophy and Phenomenological Research* 52: 1–17.
Luper, Steven. 2012. 'Exhausting Life'. *The Journal of Ethics* 16(3): 1–21.
Luper, Steven. 2014. 'Life's Meaning'. In *Cambridge Companion to Life and Death*, ed. S. Luper. Cambridge: Cambridge University Press, pp 198–212.
Nagel, Thomas. 1970. 'Death'. *Noûs* 4(1): 73–80.
Nietzsche, Friedrich. 1983. *Untimely Meditations*, trans. R. J. Hollingdale. Cambridge: Cambridge University Press.
Nozick, Robert. 1974. *Anarchy, State and Utopia*. New York: Basic Books.
Parfit, Derek. 1984. *Reasons and Persons*. Oxford: Oxford University Press.
Quinn, P. 1997. 'The Meaning of Life According to Christianity'. Reprinted in *The Meaning of Life*, ed E. D. Klemke and Stephen Cahn, 35–41. Oxford: Oxford University Press, 2008.
Rosenbaum, Stuart. 1989. 'Epicurus and Annihilation'. *Philosophical Quarterly* 39: 81–90.
Schlick, Moritz. 1979, 'On the Meaning of Life'. In *Philosophical Papers*, ed. H. L. Mulder and B. F. van de Velde-Schlick. Dordrecht: D. Reidel, pp 112–129.
Schopenhauer, Arthur. 1958. *The World as Will and Representation*, Vol. II, trans. E. F. J. Payne. New York: Dover Publications.
Schopenhauer, Arthur. 1962. 'On the Suffering of the World'. In *The Will to Live: Selected Writings of Arthur Schopenhauer*, ed. Richard Taylor. New York: Frederick Ungar, pp 215–227.
Singer, Peter. 1993. *Practical Ethics*, 2nd ed. Cambridge: Cambridge University Press.
Unamuno, M. 1954. *Tragic Sense of Life*, trans. J. E. Crawford Flitch. New York: Dover Publications.
Williams, Bernard. 1973. 'The Makropulos Case: Reflections on the Tedium of Immortality'. In B. Williams, *Problems of the Self*. Cambridge: Cambridge University Press, pp 82–100.
Williams, Bernard. 1979. 'Moral Luck'. In B. Williams, *Moral Luck*, Cambridge: Cambridge University Press, 20–39.
Wolf, Susan. 1997. 'Happiness and Meaning: Two Aspects of the Good Life'. *Social Philosophy and Policy* 14: 207–225.

PART II

MEANING IN LIFE, SCIENCE, AND METAPHYSICS

CHAPTER 7

THE RELEVANCE OF NEUROSCIENCE TO MEANING IN LIFE

PAUL THAGARD

SCIENTIFIC investigations of human and animal brains have achieved substantial progress in recent decades. Many new tools for experimental studies have been developed, including functional magnetic resonance imaging (fMRI), optogenetics, transcranial magnetic stimulation, and multi-cell recording. There have been correlative advances in theoretical understanding of how brains work through methods such as computational modelling and network analysis. Neuroscience is having a major impact on many areas of psychology, including cognitive, developmental, social, and clinical.

But does any of that research matter for philosophical investigations of meaning in life? We can distinguish three answers:

Neuro-neutral: Neuroscience is irrelevant to questions about meaning in life so it can be safely ignored.
Neuro-negative: Neuroscience is relevant to meaning in life only as a warning about how meaning can be distorted or destroyed by excessive attention to scientific findings about the mind.
Neuro-positive: Neuroscience has findings that contribute to philosophical understanding of meaning in life and to guiding people about how to have meaningful lives.

This chapter defends the neuro-positive view after critiquing the two alternatives. It shows how neuroscience helps to answer questions about the meaning of meaningfulness, the characteristics of meaningful lives, the objectivity of life's meaning, strategies for obtaining meaning, and changes in life's meaning that occur with aging.

Neuro-Neutral: Neuroscience Is Irrelevant to Meaning in Life

Several philosophical doctrines challenge the relevance of neuroscience to issues about meaning in life, including dualism, multiple realizability, the naturalistic fallacy, and the mereological fallacy. A dualist might say that mind and body are distinct kinds of entities, and meaning in life belongs to the mind and not to the body that includes the brain. So we should be able to investigate meaning in life just by introspection and thought experiments, ignoring what neuroscience tells us about the brain.

The first problem with this argument is that the evidence for dualism is weak and shrinking fast. The major ground for defending dualism is that consciousness is an essential feature of mind that is beyond scientific explanation and requires the postulation of a non-physical mind or soul. But neuroscientific explanations of consciousness including qualitative experience are increasingly proposed, e.g. by Dehaene (2014), Thagard (2019a, c), and Tononi et al. (2016). Already there are sophisticated neural explanations of many important psychological phenomena such as perception, memory, and inference (e.g. Banich and Compton 2018; Eliasmith 2013). Dualism is not yet refuted, but it is on the run.

Moreover, even if dualism were true, neuroscience could still be relevant as a source of biological inputs to the mind. Dualists have never been able to explain how physical bodies interact with non-material minds, but they grant that bodies do affect the mind, for example when a stubbed toe causes pain. The brain moderates such effects and so might be relevant to ways that the body has some influence on life's meaning. Hence dualism does not imply the neuro-neutral view, although it does presume that meaning is primarily spiritual.

Even a materialist might deny the relevance of neuroscience to meaning by invoking the argument from multiple realizability that became popular in the philosophy of mind through the work of Jerry Fodor (1975) and Hilary Putnam (1975). This non-dualist claim is that the study of minds is independent of the study of brains because mental phenomena can be realized in different physical substrates such as computers and space aliens, not just in brains. So meaning in life is independent of brains.

Multiple realizability became much less plausible in the 1980s and 1990s through the rise of cognitive neuroscience that has transformed cognitive psychology and other areas. In practice, it matters a lot to psychology how different kinds of mental phenomena are processed in the brain (Bechtel and Mundale 1999; Sober 1999; Thagard 1986, 2022). Hence arguments from multiple realizability do not support the brain-independence of meaning in life.

The third philosophical position that might be taken to challenge the relevance of neuroscience to meaning in life is the so-called naturalistic fallacy that claims it is a mistake to try to explain normative concepts such as *good* in terms of descriptive concepts such as *pleasure* (Ridge 2019). You cannot derive an 'ought' from an 'is'. Questions about meaning in life are normative concerning how people ought to conduct their lives and so cannot be deduced from any amount of findings about how brains work.

The first response to this argument is that it is just dogma to assert the independence of the normative from the descriptive. The relation between them need not be strict deduction, but rather a matter of inductive reasoning based on coherence, for example between the vital biological and psychological needs of all humans and judgements about what is good for them (Thagard 2019c). The burden is on advocates of the neuro-positive view to show precisely how neuroscience is relevant to meaning in life, but connections cannot be ruled out as fallacious a priori.

The fourth philosophical position that marks neuroscience as irrelevant to meaning in life is what Bennett and Hacker (2003) call the 'mereological fallacy'. They claim that conceptual analysis shows that psychological predicates apply only to whole human beings, not to body parts such as the brain. Therefore it is a mistake to ascribe psychological concepts such as *mind*, *pain*, *emotion*, and *meaning* to brains. In general, Bennett and Hacker see philosophy as a conceptual enterprise distinct from science, so neuroscience cannot tell us anything about meaning in life.

This view of philosophy has many problems. First, it assumes that psychology depends on a set of concepts that are embedded in ordinary language, but language and its concepts are subject to substantial change resulting from scientific advances (Thagard 1992, 2012, 2014a). For example, the common expression 'the sun rises' is misleading since Copernicus showed that the earth rotates around the sun. Advances in neuroscience are leading psychologists and people in other fields to change their concept of mind beyond what was assumed in twentieth-century philosophy. Contrary to Wittgenstein (1968), philosophy does not 'leave everything as it is' but needs to cooperate with science in an integrative and dynamic enterprise to increase understanding of how minds are and ought to be (Thagard 2019c).

The investigation of meaning in life is part of this enterprise. The cognitive sciences reject the dogma of restricting psychological predicates to whole human beings and make progress by identifying mechanisms with highly relevant parts that include brain areas, sensory organs, neurotransmitters, and hormones. Like the naturalistic fallacy, the so-called mereological fallacy is merely a tactic to block productive inquiry.

Neuro-Negative: Neuroscience Reduces Meaning in Life

The neuro-negative view is that neuroscience is only relevant to meaning in life because the scientific study of the brain diminishes meaning. Caruso and Flanagan (2018) use the term 'neuroexistentialism' for anxiety concerning whether advances in neuroscience and other areas of biology undermine conceptions of persons with purpose and meaning. One source of the reduction of meaning comes from scientific rejection of religion, which many people think is the basis of life's significance. Another threat comes from philosophical arguments that explaining the mind by brain processes is incompatible with free will, which is essential for meaningful action.

Religious Objections

For many people, meaning in life comes from a religious source such as a loving God, an afterlife with eternal rewards, and a supportive church community. Religion meshes with the dualist view that mind is a spiritual soul rather than a material brain. Advances in neuroscience encroach on this spiritual view of mind and therefore threaten dualism and the religious views that cohere with it. Neuroscience blends with materialism, which implies that there is no soul, no God, no afterlife, and therefore no meaning. Writers including Dostoevsky, Tolstoy, and Cottingham (2003) have all worried that without religion life becomes meaningless.

There are several problems with making meaning dependent on religion (see Metz 2013 for a full discussion). First, evidence for the existence of God is scant, and faith is a poor method for acquiring reliable beliefs (Thagard 2010a). Hence religion is a shaky foundation for establishing meaning in life and encourages the bullet-biting conclusion that life is indeed meaningless. Reason might turn out to justify the denial of meaning in life, but the nihilistic path through the failure of religion is easily avoided.

Second, even highly religious people find non-theological sources of meaning in their lives, such as families, jobs, and good deeds. Few people besides reclusive monks and nuns are content with religion as their only meaningful activity.

Third, there are more than a billion people in the world who are not at all religious, but most find lives they consider meaningful through families, jobs, and good deeds that are also sources of meaning for religious people. Therefore, even if neuroscience threatens the plausibility of religion, we should not conclude that it reduces meaning in life.

Free Will

If the mind is the brain, as many neuroscientists assume, then free will is threatened. People's actions result from the physical process of neurons' firing rather than from the soul's free choice. If free will is an illusion, then the sense of autonomy that makes people's choices meaningful is bogus, so meaning goes out the window.

In response, some philosophers, such as Daniel Dennett (2003), argue that free will is actually compatible with findings about the brain, but I have my doubts (Thagard 2019a, 2019c). The more we know about how brain areas interact to produce neural firings that generate actions, the more implausible becomes the traditional idea of free choice. Nevertheless, there is a remaining idea I call 'freeish will' that retains the key characteristics of autonomy concerning absence of internal mental illness and external coercion. Freeish will, based on a rich understanding of how brains produce action, is compatible with revised conceptions of autonomy, purpose, and moral responsibility. Neural determinism does not imply fatalism. Therefore, like rejection of religion, rejection of free will is not a threat to meaningful lives viewed from a scientific perspective. So the neuro-negative view is implausible.

NEURO-POSITIVE: NEUROSCIENCE ENHANCES MEANING IN LIFE

Defending the neuro-positive view requires specifying ways in which neuroscience helps people to understand the nature of meaning in life and helps people to achieve it. I describe contributions to (1) characterizing the concept of a meaningful life, (2) explaining the features of meaningful lives such as value, (3) connecting subjective and objective aspects of meaning in life, (4) developing strategies for aiding people in achieving meaningful lives, and (5) understanding how life's meaning changes with age.

The Concept of a Meaningful Life

Despite extensive writings in philosophy and psychology, no one has succeeded in providing necessary and sufficient conditions for the concepts *meaning in life, meaning of life*, or *meaningful life* (Metz 2013; Hill 2018). The failure is not surprising because such analysis always succumbs to counterexamples or circularities (Thagard 2019c). The assumption that concepts have strict definitions was challenged philosophically by Wittgenstein's (1968) idea of family resemblances and Putnam's (1975) idea of stereotypes, giving rise to claims about meaning as a cluster concept (e.g. Metz 2013). The philosophical challenge was strengthened by numerous psychological studies that show people working with concepts using typical features, examples, and explanations rather than defining conditions (Murphy 2002).

Computational neuroscience provides a unified account of all of these aspects of concepts using Chris Eliasmith's (2013) hypothesis that brains represent the world using semantic pointers, which are neural representations that can be formed by sensory inputs but also can be combined into new representations that go beyond the senses. Blouw, Solodkin, Thagard, and Eliasmith (2016) use computational modelling to show that construing concepts as semantic pointers can explain experiments interpreted as showing that concepts are based on standard examples (exemplars), typical features (stereotypes or prototypes), and explanations.

This theory of concepts supports a new method of characterizing concepts that I call three-analysis (Thagard 2019a). Instead of the futile task of finding strict definitions, we can characterize a concept more naturally by giving its exemplars, typical features, and explanatory uses. Table 7.1 applies this method to the concept *meaningful life*, first by

Table 7.1 Analysis of the Concept *Meaningful Life* Using the Method of "Three-Analysis"

Exemplars	Confucius, Charles Darwin, Albert Einstein, Mahatma Gandhi, Nelson Mandela, Florence Nightingale, Pablo Picasso, Mother Teresa, Leo Tolstoy, etc.
Typical features	Purpose, value, coherence, felt sense, reflection, loving, engagement, significance, pursuit, search
Explanations	Explains: why some people have better lives than others, why some people feel that their lives are deficient
	Explained by: mental, neural, and social mechanisms of cognition, emotion, and communication

Method source: Thagard (2019a).

giving a list of people generally thought to have lives full of meaning. You can easily enhance this list with personal examples such as family members who led rich lives. Exemplars help to pin down a concept even when there is disagreement about which features are necessary, sufficient, or typical.

My list of typical features summarizes aspects of meaning in life emphasized by philosophers and psychologists such as: Baumeister and von Hippel (2020); Heintzelman and King (2014); Hill (2018); King, Heintzelman, and Ward (2016); Landau (2017); Martela and Steger (2016); Metz (2013); Thagard (2010a, 2019c), and Wolf (2010). Recognizing these features as merely typical avoids the tyranny of finding necessary and sufficient conditions, in accord with the overlapping similarities of Wittgenstein's family resemblances and Putnam's stereotypes.

The features can be recognized in most of the exemplars. For example, Charles Darwin (1958) had work and family purposes that he had good reason to value. Reflecting on his life, he felt a sense of worth and coherence in what he had accomplished through significant and engaging activities such as loving his work and his family. I include pursuit and search among the features of a meaningful life because striving to accomplish valuable purposes is itself a contribution to meaning.

Psychologists have found that an important function of concepts is providing explanations (Murphy and Medin 1985). For example, the concept *giraffe* serves not only to describe giraffes but also to explain puzzling facts, for example why some zoo animals are eating leaves off the top of trees. The concept of *meaningful life* also has explanatory functions, for example in answering questions about why some people's lives seem to be substantially better or worse than others. People with severe depression have negative moods that result in part from feeling worthless and lacking any meaningful pursuits. In contrast, people thrive because they have coherent purposes and values that constitute a meaningful life.

Concepts not only explain, but can also *be* explained by underlying mechanisms. For the concept of a meaningful life, the relevant explanations are neural and social as well as mental, as I show in the following. In sum, the neuroscience-derived theory of concepts that unifies exemplars, typical features, and explanations provides a novel and deep way of understanding the concept of a meaningful life. Moreover, neuroscience provides ways of understanding the features that are typical of life's meaning.

Neuroscience Explains the Features of Meaningful Lives

The philosophers and psychologists who mention purpose, value, coherence, reflection, feeling, and love as features of meaning in life take them for granted, rather than explaining how they work in people's minds. I included in my list of explanations relevant to meaningful lives not only what meaningful life explains, but also what explains meaning in life, which I audaciously suggested was a combination of mental, neural, and social mechanisms. Mechanisms are combinations of connected parts whose interactions produce regular changes (Bechtel 2008; Craver and Darden 2013; Glennan 2017; Thagard 2019c). I now describe how neural mechanisms help to explain purpose, value, and coherence, leaving the other typical features for future work.

Informally, a purpose is a goal that serves as a reason for doing something, but what is a goal? Thagard (2019a, 186) explains goals as semantic pointers that bind together two other neural representations, one for a situation to be achieved, such as buying food, and the other for an emotional attitude toward that situation akin to wanting or desiring. In turn, emotions are semantic pointers that combine neural representations of (1) the situation that the emotion is about, (2) an appraisal of the relevance of that situation to the person's goals, and (3) bodily changes such as heartbeat and hormone levels. This theory of purposes as goals can explain how they lead to action (Schröder, Stewart, and Thagard 2014).

What are values? This question is usually dodged by philosophers and psychologists, but not by economists who identify values with preferences understood as observed choices (Hausman 2011). Psychologically, this is crudely behaviouristic compared to the view that values are mental states that cause preferences (which are also mental states) that cause behaviours such as choices. For example, one of my political values is democracy—government by the people through their elected representatives. My mental representation of this value combines a concept and emotions. The concept of democracy includes a set of exemplars such as Canada, typical features such as voting, and explanations such as that democratic countries produce happier people. For me, the main emotions associated with democracy are liking, wanting, and fearing its eclipse by autocrats. Possessing the value of democracy causes some behaviours such as voting, but a person can still have the value without its leading to specific behaviours.

A neural theory of values arises from understanding them as semantic pointers that bind together representations of concepts such as democracy (combining exemplars, typical features, and explanations) with emotional attitudes (combining appraisal and physiology). Thus neuroscience can explain how purposes and values operate in the brains and minds of people searching for meaning in their lives.

The topic of coherence rarely figures in philosophical discussions of meaning in life, even though it has long been important in epistemology. But psychological discussions of meaning emphasize coherence as a longing that people have for their lives to be comprehensible and to make sense (Hill 2018; Martela and Steger 2016). This feature of meaning in life as making sense connects with linguistic meaning as we expect words, sentences, paragraphs, and larger pieces to make sense. It is not accidental that around 80 percent of the more than 100 languages used in Google Translate are like English in using the same word for the meaning of lives and the meaning of words (exceptions include Chinese and Russian).

But what is coherence? Epistemological discussions usually mention consistency but are vague about what else is relevant. In contrast, a theory and computational model of coherence has been based on neural networks (Thagard 1989, 2000, 2019c). Comprehensibility requires various representations of a situation to fit together; for meaning in life, these elements include goals, values, and beliefs. Some elements cohere in that they are mutually supporting, for example when a goal of becoming a financial entrepreneur fits with a major goal of becoming rich. But other elements are incoherent with each other, for example wanting to be an entrepreneur and wanting to help the poor. In a computational neural network, elements can be represented by artificial neurons or groups of neurons, and coherence between elements can be captured by excitatory links through which one neuron increases the firing of another neuron. Incoherence between elements can be captured by inhibitory links between neurons through which one neuron decreases the firing of another neuron. Many computer simulations of realistic cases show that this model of coherence applies to many comprehensibility problems in science and everyday life. It would be an interesting exercise to model in detail coherence and lack of it in psychological studies concerning meaning in life.

In sum, understanding of purpose, value, and coherence can all be deepened by neuroscientific explanations.

The Objectivity of Meaning in Life

The problem of meaning in life has both descriptive and normative aspects. The descriptive problem concerns what people think makes their lives meaningful. Psychologists are largely concerned with this subjective problem and sometimes distinguish descriptive 'meaning in life' from the normative philosophical problem of 'meaning of life' which concerns what actually makes lives meaningful (e.g. Hill 2018). But philosophers such as Wolf (2010) and Landau (2017) take meaning *in* life to be a normative problem also. Sometimes philosophers take meaning in life to be about meaning in the lives of individual people, in contrast to meaning of life as concerned with the whole human race. But I think that questions about the meaning of life for all people and meaning in life for individuals are answerable in the same way, by identifying objective sources of meaning for all.

Accordingly, I take 'meaning in life' and 'meaning of life' to concern the same descriptive and normative problems. The descriptive problem concerns people's subjective sense of what seems to give them meaning in their lives, whereas the normative problem concerns what objectively provides meaning and what people ought to do if they want to achieve such meaning.

However, philosophers have had difficulty establishing objectivity. Wolf (2010) merely hopes that some sense can be made of objective meaning in life. Metz (2013) says that meaning concerns what is 'fundamental' to human life but does not spell this out. Landau (2017) emphasizes the relevance of value to understanding meaning in life but does not provide an account of objective value.

Contrary to what is claimed by the naturalistic fallacy, neuroscience helps to bridge the gap between the subjective and the objective. Boyd (1988) suggests that moral realism, which says that ethical claims can be as objectively true or false as scientific claims, can be achieved by recognizing that people have biological and psychological needs that result from underlying mechanisms. These mechanisms explain why satisfying those needs is good for people. Boyd did not spell out the relevant needs and mechanisms, but neuroscience fills in the crucial gaps. Other philosophers have looked to needs (as opposed to subjective whims, wants, and interests) to provide the connection between the descriptive/subjective and the normative/objective (Orend 2002; Thagard 2010a, 2019c; Wiggins 1987).

To begin, consider biological needs. Well-known biological mechanisms explain why oxygen, water, food, and shelter are needs rather than wants, because without them people die. Without oxygen, people's lungs, hearts, and brains stop working, leading to death in a few minutes, in ways well explained by mechanisms of respiration, blood oxidation, and brain functioning. These mechanisms show that oxygen is an objective need of humans, not just a subjective want.

Analogously, a substantial body of research has established that the major psychological needs of humans across cultures are autonomy (feeling that actions are self-chosen), competence (feeling of efficacy and mastery over one's activities), and relatedness (feeling of belonging with others) (Ryan and Deci 2017). Moreover, achieving these needs predicts high ratings of meaningfulness in surveys (Martela, Ryan, and Steger 2018). A fourth predictive factor is beneficence—being good to others. Martela, Ryan, and Steger (2018, 1279) conclude that 'when an individual is able to find ways of self-expression through satisfaction of autonomy and competence, and self-transcendence through satisfaction of relatedness and beneficence, then that life should be filled with meaning and truly a life worth living.' This research, however, does not connect psychological needs to underlying mechanisms as required for Boyd's version of moral realism.

Thagard (2019c, 162–164) makes these connections. Neural and molecular mechanisms explain why social isolation cripples lives through impacts on the amygdala, ventral, striatum, and orbitofrontal cortex, including epigenetic changes in gene expressions that can contribute to heart attacks. Hence relatedness is a vital need, not just a want for which other wants could be substituted. Similarly, lack of autonomy through control by others and lack of competence through failures in work cause stress with elevated cortisol levels that have negative effects on brain functioning and overall health. Autonomy in the sense of being able to make choices uncontrolled by others is compatible with what I called freeish will operating in the brain. Hence autonomy, competence, and relatedness are not only psychological and social needs, but are also tied to biological mechanisms involving the brain.

In sum, psychological needs and neural mechanisms provide the non-deductive links between subjective and objective meaning. Meaning in life is the pursuit of satisfaction of vital needs for oneself and others, including psychological needs that depend on brain mechanisms.

Strategies for Achieving a Meaningful Life

According to Epicurus (quoted in Lucretius 1969, 22):

> Vain is the word of a philosopher by whom no human suffering is cured. For just as medicine is of no use, if it fails to banish the diseases of the body, so philosophy is of no use, if it fails to banish the suffering of the mind.

This insistence is too hard on philosophy which addresses important epistemological and metaphysical questions that are not directly relevant to suffering. But many ethical questions are highly relevant to suffering and can be addressed by philosophy in alliance with psychology. A sound theory of life's meaning should help people to improve their lives.

One philosophical strategy for helping people is to rebut sceptical arguments that life has no meaning at all. Landau (2017) usefully responds to claims that meaning is undermined by the inevitability of death, the enormity of the universe, relativism, determinism, and chance. More positively, he offers (278–279) wise practical advice, including:

- Avoid perfectionism and do not try to achieve the impossible.
- Treat yourself well.
- Recognize that life is not a dress rehearsal, so seek meaning now.
- Work.

Nevertheless, most people who have issues about meaning in their lives consult psychologists rather than philosophers.

Clinical psychologists are increasingly aware of the relevance of meaning in life to people's mental and physical well-being (Hill 2018). People who are depressed have feelings of worthlessness and hopelessness that imply that their lives are bereft of meaning. The other major malady treated by psychotherapists is anxiety, which can be tied to fears that life is lacking in value and direction.

Hill provides a rich model for how psychotherapists can deal with clients who have concerns about meaning in their lives. Her first recommendation is that therapists should first have sorted out how they feel about meaning in their own lives. Research has shown that successful therapy depends less on the theoretical approach of the therapist than on the establishment of a therapeutic alliance with the client based on empathy and trust (Flückiger, Del Re, Horvath, and Wampold 2018; Larocque and Thagard, forthcoming). Therapists who do not understand the meaning in their own lives will have difficulty establishing the desired alliance with clients who are troubled about meaning.

Hill (2018, 83) provides a list of questions that therapists can pose to clients based on key features of meaning in life—felt sense, what matters, goals, and sources. Therapists might ask broadly about a felt sense of having meaning, e.g. 'Tell me about what meaning you have in your life'. Therapists might also ask about mattering, e.g. 'What are you doing that makes a difference or is worthy?' Therapists might also ask about goals, purpose, and aspirations, e.g. 'When do you feel most engaged in life?' Finally, therapists might ask about sources of meaning, e.g. 'What are you most passionate about doing in your life?'

Hill also suggests interventions for helping people explore meaning in their lives, including restating their concerns, reflecting on their feelings, and disclosing the therapist's own struggles with meaning. Such disclosure furnishes analogies to guide the client's thinking and also shows empathy for the client's problems. Hill provides advice about how to help clients gain insights about their understanding of the meaning in their lives and how to help them reinterpret and revise their views.

Hill provides case examples of clients who sought help from psychotherapists in dealing with issues about meaning in life. Bruce was a man in his mid-sixties who was having difficulties with retirement, his troubled long-term marriage, and health problems. With the therapist he talked about faith, spirituality, his need for freedom, and his attraction to another woman. The therapist helped him to gain clarity about his spiritual struggles and to sort out what he wanted.

Psychotherapy always deals with emotions, which is where neuroscience becomes relevant. Here are some ways in which emotions are relevant to questions about life's meaning:

(1) The sense of meaning is an emotional reaction, positive if life seems meaningful but negative if meaning is lacking.
(2) Feeling bereft of meaning goes with severe emotions such as depression and anger.
(3) Increases or decreases in feelings about meaning go with emotions such as happiness, sadness, and fear.
(4) Contributors to meaning such as love, work, and play are accompanied by emotions such as infatuation, lust, admiration, excitement, enthusiasm, and joy.
(5) Acquiring increased or decreased amounts of meaning in life requires emotional change.

Hence determination of how to enhance meaning in life requires understanding of emotions to which neuroscience contributes.

Psychologists disagree about how to explain emotions (Keltner, Oatley, and Jenkins 2018). The most popular theories view emotions as either (1) cognitive appraisals of the extent to which a situation meets a person's goals, (2) physiological responses to situations, (3) culturally and linguistically constructed responses to situations, or (4) innate neural responses to situations. Computational neuroscience shows how *all* of these can be accommodated in a brain model that views emotions as semantic pointers that combine appraisal, physiology, and culture (Kajic, Schröder, Stewart, and Thagard 2019; Thagard 2019a). Hence neuroscience is crucial to explaining emotional aspects of the pursuit and achievement of meaning in life.

Similarly, emotional change of the sort involved in increasing life's meaning can be explained by psychological processes resulting from neural mechanisms. For example, a psychotherapist working with a client suffering from depression with feelings of worthlessness and hopelessness can help the client reduce these emotions and enhance positive ones such as confidence, joy, and hope. According to the semantic pointer theory of emotions, emotional change requires integrated changes in cognitive appraisal, physiology, and cultural interpretation (Thagard, Larocque, and Kajić, 2022). Interpretation and appraisal can be changed through methods such as psychotherapy, and physiology can be changed through methods such as antidepressant medication and exercise. Hence neuroscience is relevant to explaining both the occurrence and alteration of emotions that increase meaning in human lives.

Introducing psychology and neuroscience into deliberations about meaning in life does not obviate philosophy, which remains relevant because of its normative contribution. A purely descriptive approach to values would accept clients' claims that their lives are meaningful because of practices such as collecting beer bottle caps or having violent sex with strangers. Philosophy is crucial to finding meaning in life because of assessment of the legitimacy of different values. Thagard (2010a) summarized objectively desirable values in the slogan that the meaning of life is love, work, and play, because these three contribute to satisfaction of the vital psychological needs of relatedness, competence, and autonomy. This slogan provides a concise answer to what provides purpose and value to a great many people without having to deal with the abstractness of concepts like relatedness. Coherence comes when people understand that their actions are motivated by the legitimate pursuit of love, work, and play and when they are able to achieve a reasonable balance among these pursuits. As in the case of Bruce, meaning-in-life problems sometimes concern finding balance among difference values.

The relevant mental mechanism for working out conflicts among different goals is emotional coherence among actions and goals, which can also be modelled using neural networks (Thagard 2006). Actions cohere with goals that they accomplish, such as when getting a university degree coheres with the goal of getting a good job. Actions can be incoherent with each other, for example when studying is incompatible with working or travelling. Representing actions and goals by artificial neurons produces a neural network that efficiently computes the comparative emotional value of different options.

I am not proposing a simplistic division of labour where psychology and neuroscience are subjectively descriptive and philosophy is objectively normative. Philosophy should be informed by descriptive empirical studies, and psychology and neuroscience are relevant to normative conclusions by identifying universal human needs. Philosophy and science can effectively cooperate to address questions about meaning and many other questions in epistemology, metaphysics, and ethics (Thagard 2019c).

Aging and Meaning in Life

The presence and search for meaning are not constants across the lifespan of people, but change as people move through childhood, adolescence, adulthood, and old age. What matters to young children is obviously different from what matters to the elderly. Love, work, and play take on different forms and degrees of importance as people age because of shifts in needs for relatedness, competence, and autonomy. Neuroscience helps to explain these shifts as the result of changes in brains that occur as people age.

Psychologists have documented some of the changes that take place as people age. Steger, Oishi, and Kashdan (2009) report that meaning in life is important to overall well-being at many stages, but find differences in people's ratings of how meaning is present in their lives versus how much they are searching for meaning. Individuals at later life stages reported more meaning and less searching, where more searching correlates with less well-being. Carstenson (2019) describes the 'paradox of aging' that older people tend to have greater emotional well-being despite physical decline and shrinking social networks.

Major transitions in life's meaning include going from adolescence to adulthood and from adulthood to old age, both attended by major changes in the brain. Arain et al. (2013, 449) summarize the vulnerabilities of the adolescent brain that can lead to impulsive behaviours concerning food, alcohol, sex, and sleep habits. Myelination that improves connectivity between different brain areas is incomplete because of immaturity and the effects of sex hormones. Excitatory neurotransmission based on glutamate predominates over inhibitory effects of gamma-aminobutyric acid (GABA). An immature limbic system and prefrontal cortex can contribute to social maladjustments.

By their mid-twenties, most people have become more responsible with respect to love and work with less engagement in impulsive play. This transition results from neural changes including reduced hormonal effects and fuller myelination, making for more efficient communication between cortical and emotion-dominated non-cortical areas. So changes in life's meaning between adolescence and adulthood have a component to be explained by neuroscience.

From people's twenties to their sixties, brain functioning declines only slightly in the absence of diseases such as early onset Alzheimer's and strokes. But from the mid-sixties onwards, the news is grim with respect to overall intelligence and general brain operation. Documented declines include reduced brain volume involving number and size of neurons, decline in white matter (the connections between neurons), decreases in dopamine receptors important for motivation and learning, declines in other neurotransmitters such as glutamate and serotonin, and reduction in functional connectivity (Buchman et al. 2014; Sala-Llonch, Bartrés-Faz, and Junqué 2015). Psychological effects include decline in working memory, long-term memory, and speed of processing.

Not surprisingly, aging of brain and body leads most people to retire from full-time work, requiring major changes in purpose, value, and coherence. The need for competence can be satisfied by pursuits other than work, such as hobbies and social recreations. Relatedness also shifts after completion of raising children to interests in friends and grandchildren. Autonomy increases through lack of work constraints but diminishes because of physical limitations. The balance among work, love, and play shifts, with play taking over some of the time and importance of work.

How is the increased meaning consistent with brain decline in aging? Park and Reuter-Lopez (2009, 183) assert: 'Little doubt exists that the extent of cognitive and structural decline is substantial. Nevertheless, people generally function remarkably well even into advanced old age, and do so even in the presence of a great deal of pathology as discovered at autopsy.' They explain this result by *scaffolding*, an ongoing adaptive process in the neocortex that results in new circuits that compensate to some extent for neural decline. Scaffolding enables people to increase meaning in their lives because they still have enough cognitive capacity to enjoy reduction in pressures from work and child-rearing while pursuing activities in line with valuable purposes. Levitin (2020) provides valuable advice based on neuroscience on how to continue having an enjoyable and meaningful life in old age through diet, exercise, sleep, and cognitive enhancement.

Hence for both adolescence and old age, understanding shifts in the meaning of lives requires attention to neuroscience. Old age can also bring increasing concern with death, which looks very different from a neuroscience perspective than from a religious, dualist perspective. The scientific view that minds expire when brains die cancels fear of eternal suffering in favour of Epicurus's view that after death there is nothing and therefore nothing to be feared. Neuroscience encourages the reassuring view that meaning in life is not an infinite issue.

Nagel (1970) claims that death is an evil because the loss of life permanently deprives people of valuable experiences. We can reasonably feel regret for people who die young that they were robbed of years of meaningful activities. But from the scientific perspective that personhood stops when the brain ceases, we can be assured that dead people have no regrets about their deprivations. It is reasonable to fear the suffering that often precedes death, but neuroscience encourages the conclusions that dying and being dead are not scary.

Meaning in Life as an Interdisciplinary Project

I have supported the neuro-positive claim that neuroscience enhances meaning in life by showing how it contributes to understanding the concept of a meaningful life, the features of meaningful lives, the objectivity of meaning, ways of finding meaning such as psychotherapy, and changes in meaning that come with aging. These five considerations complement my responses to arguments for neuro-neutral and neuro-negative views, which face the challenge of finding alternative ways of illuminating the concept, features, objectivity, strategies, and changes of meaning in life.

My discussion of meaning in life weaves together discussions from philosophy, psychology, and neuroscience, but such connections are unusual. The philosophers I mentioned almost never cite psychologists and vice versa. Moreover, the philosophers and psychologists who discuss meaning are equally remiss in ignoring neuroscience.

My five ways in which neuroscience is relevant justify the conclusion that the study of meaning in life is not a purely philosophical project, but should be pursued as an interdisciplinary collaboration of the sort that is common in cognitive science (Thagard 2005, 2010b). Cognitive science is the interdisciplinary study of mind and intelligence, embracing psychology, neuroscience, computational modelling, anthropology, and philosophy. Combining disciplines encourages experimental, theoretical, and practical progress on topics such as perception, cognition, language, and emotion, but also can enhance the investigation of meaning in life. None of the five fields of cognitive science is reducible to the others, but they can productively collaborate by integrating both ideas and methods.

Psychology can continue to conduct behavioural experiments and surveys that collect information about what people value in life, but also develop theories concerning mental mechanisms—representations and processes that explain how people are thinking when they pursue meaning. Psychological research can also investigate further what aspects of human lives amount to needs rather than wants.

Neuroscience can expand the experimental investigation of meaning through techniques such as brain scans, and deepen accounts of mental processing by neural mechanisms that describe how groups of neurons organized into brain areas produce cognition and emotion required for pursuit of meaning. I have shown five ways in which neuroscience is relevant to the investigation of meaning in life, but there are probably others that operate in concert with psychological and philosophical considerations.

Computational modelling spells out the mental and neural mechanisms for meaning in sufficient detail that they can operate in simulations that help to show whether the proposed mechanisms are adequate to explain the relevant phenomena such as value and coherence. Computational ideas turn vague psychological and neural speculations into precise theories about mind and meaning.

Anthropology brings a cross-cultural perspective on meaning in life to avoid the overgeneralization of findings about meaning in life from societies that are WEIRD

(Western, educated, industrial, rich, and democratic; Henrich, Heine, and Norenzayan 2010). There are thousands of different cultures in the world, and a full account of meaning in life should cover the whole range.

Philosophy contributes, not by asserting conceptual truths based on biased thought experiments, but by being more general and more normative than the other fields. Thought experiments have been widely used in discussions of the meaning of life, but they are a highly subjective, circular, and unreliable practice that should not be confused with evidence (Thagard 2014b). Making up stories can be a useful way to generate hypotheses, but the evaluation of those hypotheses should be connected to empirical evidence.

Generality in philosophy comes by tying together empirical and theoretical insights from psychology, neuroscience, computer modelling, and anthropology. Normativity comes by reflecting on what meaning in life ought to be, rather than just what people take it to be. Objectivity arises not from a priori intuitions but from coherent reflections on empirical findings and vital needs that cross the traditional descriptive/normative boundary. Thus meaning in life can best be investigated by interdisciplinary research that combines neuroscience with philosophy and the other fields of cognitive science.

References

Arain, M., M. Haque, L. Johal, P. Mathur, W. Nel, A. Rais, . . . S. Sharma. 2013. 'Maturation of the Adolescent Brain'. *Neuropsychiatric Disease and Treatment* 9: 449–461.

Banich, M. T., and R. J. Compton. 2018. *Cognitive Neuroscience*, 4th ed. Cambridge: Cambridge University Press.

Baumeister, R. F., and W. von Hippel. 2020. 'Meaning and Evolution: Why Nature Selected Minds to Use Meaning'. *Evolutionary Studies in Imaginative Culture* 4: 1–18.

Bechtel, W. 2008. *Mental Mechanisms: Philosophical Perspectives on Cognitive Neuroscience*. New York: Routledge.

Bechtel, W., and J. Mundale. 1999. 'Multiple Realizability Revisited: Linking Cognitive and Neural States'. *Philosophy of Science* 66: 175–207.

Bennett, M. R., and P. M. S. Hacker. 2003. *Philosophical Foundations of Neuroscience*. Oxford: Blackwell.

Blouw, P., E. Solodkin, P. Thagard, and C. Eliasmith. 2016. 'Concepts as Semantic Pointers: A Framework and Computational Model'. *Cognitive Science* 40: 1128–1162.

Boyd, R. N. 1988. 'How to Be a Moral Realist'. In *Essays on Moral Realism*, ed. G. Sayre-McCord, 181–228. Ithaca, NY: Cornell University Press.

Buchman, A. S., L. Yu, R. S. Wilson, P. A. Boyle, J. A. Schneider, and D. A. Bennett. 2014. 'Brain Pathology Contributes to Simultaneous Change in Physical Frailty and Cognition in Old Age'. *Journal of Gerontology A: Biological Sciences Medical Sciences* 69(12): 1536–1544.

Carstensen, L. L. 2019. 'Integrating Cognitive and Emotion Paradigms to Address the Paradox of Aging'. *Cognition and Emotion* 33(1): 119–125.

Caruso, G. D., and O. Flanagan, eds. 2018. *Neuroexistentialism: Meaning, Morals, and Purpose in the Age of Neuroscience*. New York: Oxford University Press.

Cottingham, J. 2003. *On the Meaning of Life*. London: Routledge.

Craver, C. F., and L. Darden. 2013. *In Search of Mechanisms: Discoveries across the Life Sciences*. Chicago: University of Chicago Press.

Darwin, C. 1958. *The Autobiography of Charles Darwin and Selected Letters*. New York: Dover.
Dehaene, S. 2014. *Consciousness and the Brain: Deciphering How the Brain Codes Our Thoughts*. New York: Viking.
Dennett, D. 2003. *Freedom Evolves*. New York: Penguin.
Eliasmith, C. 2013. *How to Build a Brain: A Neural Architecture for Biological Cognition*. Oxford: Oxford University Press.
Flückiger, C., A. C. Del Re, B. E. Wampold, and A. O. Horvath. 2018. 'The Alliance in Adult Psychotherapy: A Meta-analytic Synthesis'. *Psychotherapy* 55(4): 316–340.
Fodor, J. 1975. *The Language of Thought*. New York: Crowell.
Glennan, S. 2017. *The New Mechanical Philosophy*. Oxford: Oxford University Press.
Hausman, D. M. 2011. *Preference, Value, Choice, and Welfare*. Cambridge: Cambridge University Press.
Heintzelman, S. J., and L. A. King. 2014. 'Life Is Pretty Meaningful'. *American Psychologist* 69(6): 561–574.
Henrich, J., S. J. Heine, and A. Norenzayan. 2010. 'The Weirdest People in the World?' *Behavioral and Brain Sciences* 33(2–3): 61–83.
Hill, C. E. 2018. *Meaning in Life: A Therapist's Guide*. Washington, DC: American Psychological Associaton.
Kajić, I., T. Schröder, T. C. Stewart, and P. Thagard. 2019. 'The Semantic Pointer Theory of Emotions'. *Cognitive Systems Research* 58: 35–53.
Keltner, D., K. Oatley, and J. M. Jenkins. 2018. *Understanding Emotions*, 4th ed.. New York: Wiley.
King, L. A., S. J. Heintzelman, and S. J. Ward. 2016. 'Beyond the Search for Meaning: A Contemporary Science of the Experience of Meaning in Life'. *Current Directions in Psychological Science* 25(4): 211–216.
Landau, I. 2017. *Finding Meaning in an Imperfect World*. New York: Oxford University Press.
Larocque, L., and P. Thagard. Forthcoming. 'Explaining the Psychotherapeutic Alliance Using Cognitive, Emotional, and Social Mechanisms'.
Levitin, D. J. 2020. *Successful Aging: A Neuroscientist Explores the Power and Potential of Our Lives*. New York: Dutton.
Lucretius. 1969. *On the Nature of Things*. London: Sphere books.
Martela, F., R. M. Ryan, and M. F. Steger. 2018. 'Meaningfulness as Satisfaction of Autonomy, Competence, Relatedness, and Beneficence: Comparing the Four Satisfactions and Positive Affect as Predictors of Meaning in Life'. *Journal of Happiness Studies* 19(5): 1261–1282.
Martela, F., and M. F. Steger. 2016. 'The Three Meanings of Meaning in Life: Distinguishing Coherence, Purpose, and Significance'. *The Journal of Positive Psychology* 11(5): 531–545.
Metz, T. 2013. *Meaning in Life: An Analytic Study*. Oxford: Oxford University Press.
Murphy, G., and D. Medin. 1985. 'The Role of Theories in Conceptual Coherence'. *Psychological Review* 92: 289–316.
Murphy, G. L. 2002. *The Big Book of Concepts*. Cambridge, MA: MIT Press.
Nagel, T. 1970. 'Death'. *Nous* 4: 73–80.
Orend, B. 2002. *Human Rights: Concept and Context*. Peterborough: Broadview.
Park, D. C., and P. Reuter-Lorenz. 2009. 'The Adaptive Brain: Aging and Neurocognitive Scaffolding'. *Annual Review of Psychology* 60: 173–196.
Putnam, H. 1975. *Mind, Language, and Reality*. Cambridge: Cambridge University Press.
Ridge, M. 2019. 'Moral Non-naturalism'. In *Stanford Encyclopedia of Philosophy*, edited by Edward N. Zalta. Retrieved from https://plato.stanford.edu/entries/moral-non-naturalism/.
Ryan, R. M., and E. L. Deci. 2017. *Self-determination Theory: Basic Psychological Needs in Motivation, Development, and Wellness*. New York: Guilford.

Sala-Llonch, R., D. Bartres-Faz, and C. Junque. 2015. 'Reorganization of Brain Networks in Aging: A Review of Functional Connectivity Studies'. *Frontiers in Psychology* 6: 663.

Schröder, T., T. C. Stewart, and P. Thagard. 2014. 'Intention, Emotion, and Action: A Neural Theory Based on Semantic Pointers'. *Cognitive Science* 38: 851–880.

Sober, E. 1999. 'The Multiple Realizability Argument against Reductionism'. *Philosophy of Science* 66(4): 542–564.

Steger, M. F., S. Oishi, and T. B. Kashdan. 2009. 'Meaning in Life across the Life Span: Levels and Correlates of Meaning in Life from Emerging Adulthood to Older Adulthood'. *The Journal of Positive Psychology* 4(1): 43–52.

Thagard, P. 1986. 'Parallel Computation and the Mind-Body Problem'. *Cognitive Science* 10: 301–318.

Thagard, P. 1989. 'Explanatory Coherence'. *Behavioral and Brain Sciences* 12: 435–467.

Thagard, P. 1992. *Conceptual Revolutions*. Princeton, NJ: Princeton University Press.

Thagard, P. 2000. *Coherence in Thought and Action*. Cambridge, MA: MIT Press.

Thagard, P. 2005. *Mind: Introduction to Cognitive Science*, 2nd ed. Cambridge, MA: MIT Press.

Thagard, P. 2006. *Hot Thought: Mechanisms and Applications of Emotional Cognition*. Cambridge, MA: MIT Press.

Thagard, P. 2010a. *The Brain and the Meaning of Life*. Princeton, NJ: Princeton University Press.

Thagard, P. 2010b. 'Cognitive Science'. In *Oxford Handbook of Interdisciplinarity*, ed. R. Frodemena, J. T. Klein, and C. Mitcham, 234–245. Oxford: Oxford University Press.

Thagard, P. 2012. *The Cognitive Science of Science: Explanation, Discovery, and Conceptual Change*. Cambridge, MA: MIT Press.

Thagard, P. 2014a. 'Explanatory Identities and Conceptual Change'. *Science and Education* 23: 1531–1548.

Thagard, P. 2014b. 'Thought Experiments Considered Harmful'. *Perspectives on Science* 22: 288–305.

Thagard, P. 2019a. *Brain-Mind: From Neurons to Consciousness and Creativity*. New York: Oxford University Press.

Thagard, P. 2019b. *Mind-Society: From Brains to Social Sciences and Professions*. New York: Oxford University Press.

Thagard, P. 2019c. *Natural Philosophy: From Social Brains to Knowledge, Reality, Morality, and Beauty*. New York: Oxford University Press.

Thagard, P. (2022). 'Energy requirements undermine substrate independence and mind-body functionalism'. *Philosophy of Science*.

Thagard, P., L. Larocque, and I. Kajić (2022). 'Emotional Change: Neural Mechanisms Based on Semantic Pointers'. *Emotion*.

Tononi, G., M. Boly, M. Massimini, and C. Koch. 2016. 'Integrated Information Theory: From Consciousness to Its Physical Substrate'. *Nature Reviews Neuroscience* 17(7): 450–461.

Wiggins, D. 1987. *Needs, Values, Truth*. Oxford: Basil Blackwell.

Wittgenstein, L. 1968. *Philosophical Investigations*, trans. G. E. M. Anscombe, 2nd ed. Oxford: Blackwell.

Wolf, S. R. 2010. *Meaning in Life and Why It Matters*. Princeton, NJ: Princeton University Press.

CHAPTER 8

CAN NEUROSCIENCE SHED LIGHT ON WHAT CONSTITUTES A MEANINGFUL LIFE?

P. M. S. HACKER

1. MEANING IN LIFE

WE commonly wonder, especially in adolescence and in old age, what the meaning of life is. Does life have a meaning, or is all vanity and vexation of spirit? One may satisfy one's basic needs for food, drink, clothing, and dwelling, and one's relative social needs for whatever is deemed necessary to live a tolerable life in one's society, yet have nothing to live for. One may lead a life of pleasure and enjoyment, and yet find no meaning in one's hedonistic life. One cannot find happiness in life if one finds no meaning in it. A life devoid of meaning is a life without happiness. But one may find meaning in one's life and in one's activities without finding happiness. For the meaning one finds in life may be given by one's vocation, by the goals one pursues in the course of one's commitments and dedication to a given social role or one's role in the community, and so forth. But one may pursue such goals while being lonely, afflicted by sorrow and unhappiness. Indeed, like Viktor Frankl in the concentration camps (Frankl [1946] 1984, 55–57, 87–89), one may find meaning in one's suffering, in one's ability to maintain one's self-respect and integrity in the face of the horrors of hell on earth.

Goals may be *regulative* or *terminative*. Regulative goals, such as being a good doctor, teacher, or spouse, have no consummation or termination. Terminative goals have a terminus, which, if attained, are *achievements*. Pursuit of a voluntarily chosen goal or purpose does not imply that one finds meaning in doing so. Many of the purposes we pursue in the course of our lives are mere amusements that are too unimportant in the long run to impart meaning to our lives, even though they may mean something to one at the time. In such cases, one may say that the pursuit and achievement of such goals lacks depth and does not touch one's soul. For a purpose to lend meaning to our lives it must typically be continuous or recurrent (as in a vocation) and subsume a multitude of subordinate purposes. A doctor may find meaning in his life from curing and caring for his patients, but not usually from curing one patient. However, it is possible for an individual act alone to suffice to give one's life meaning, e.g. if it is an exceptional act of self-sacrifice. What one finds meaningful in life and what gives one's life meaning is something one finds valuable, something one cares about and that matters to one. It must be serious and not frivolous or trivial. It must transcend selfish and self-centred concerns. Its pursuit must be an expression of one's nature as well as a determinant of one's nature. It must play a role in one's conception of oneself and it must determine in part one's relationship to others and to one's life. However, not all our goals are benevolent or value neutral. Evil purposes cannot give meaning to one's life, although evil doers may have the illusion that they do.

Having *a meaning* must be distinguished from having *meaning*. The former can be denominated 'transitive meaning', inasmuch as the question 'What is the meaning of such-and-such?' can be answered by specification of what it means. By contrast, 'intransitive meaning' cannot be so specified. The phenomenon of intransitive meaning is familiar to us from aesthetics: a musical phrase played one way may be quite meaningless, played another way it has meaning, it says something—although one cannot say what it means. This is not an instance of ineffable meaning, but of *intransitive meaning*. It means itself, one might say—just listen to it. So we may characterize someone's self-sacrificial deed (e.g. Sidney Carton's sacrifice of his life to save Charles Darnay in Dickens's *Tale of Two Cities*) as lending meaning to his or her life. But if asked what is the meaning of their deed, there is no informative answer (although doing the deed may, in another sense of 'meaning', mean that the agent is a saint or a hero).

We must further distinguish between *something's meaning something to a person*, and something *lending meaning to a person's life*. Many *achievements* may mean something to a person without being of sufficient significance to lend meaning to their life, such as winning in some competitive activity at school or passing an examination. To be sure, they may value the achievement, but it need not colour their life and their assessment of their life. But some achievements may, e.g. winning a gold medal at the Olympics or being awarded the Nobel Prize. Many activities may mean something to one, often a great deal, but *need not* make one's life meaningful. So, for example, nature means a great deal to a nature lover, as music means a great deal to music lovers, and ballet to balletomanes. Such passions need not be such as to lend meaning to one's life, although they may endow one's life with subjective meaning, as in the case of Marius the Epicurean, or his creator, the aesthete Walter Pater (Pater [1885] 1985). But it is moot whether it makes his life meaningful. So too, one's youthful 'pleasure friendships', as Aristotle (2000 [fourth century BCE], 143–182; *Nicomachean Ethics* VIII–IX) called them, certainly mean something to one when one goes out on the razzle, but it is only long-term, deeply held, cherished friendships of kindred spirits that contribute meaning to one's life, as did Montaigne's friendship for de la Boètie (Montaigne [1580]

1965, 135–144; *Essays* I, 28). So too, a relationship to another person, the love one bears another person, may be so deep that one may avow that without that person life would have no meaning for one. The former kind of friendship has only subjective meaning, the latter both subjective and objective.

Individual things, both physical objects, pictures or paintings, and places may mean much to one because of their associations or their history. One may treasure them because they belonged to one's parents or grandparents, or because they were given one by someone one dearly loved, or because they had a special role in one's childhood or youth. Such items have *sentimental meaning*, which is perfectly authentic (and should not be confused with sentimentality).

Non-transitive meaning is an axiological and cultural notion with far-reaching ramifications. It is essentially tied to value and valuation, and it is subject to both misjudgement and corruption. Someone may be much taken with kitsch and value it highly. Such putative works of art are worthless, even though they are widely admired by fashionable critics and museum curators to whom they evidently mean something and evidently strike them as meaningful. This is *illusory meaning*, for it rests foursquare on bad taste, on misjudgement and misguided valuation. Something similar arises in the case of non-transitive meaning in life, in judgements concerning a meaningful life, and in finding meaning in life. For here too we must distinguish what is objective from what is subjective and what is authentic from what is illusory. Torquemada may well have felt that his life had meaning because he had burnt so many hundreds of heretics at the stake. Adolf Eichmann felt that he had failed in his mission, since only six million Jews were slaughtered by the Nazis. Had he succeeded in slaughtering all ten and a half million Jews in Europe and occupied Russia, he avowed, he would have died a happy man. It was the murder of Jews that he thought gave his life meaning. This is one form of *illusory meaning*, and it is a mark of an evil conscience. Far from exculpating a wicked or evil person, it is an aggravating condition. Nothing that is evil can give meaning to a person's life, for evil is a paradigm of disvalue. To live an evil life is not to live a worthy life. But for someone to live a meaningful life *is* for that life to be worthy. If an evil person conceives of an evil goal as something meaningful (as Eichmann did), that is an illusion, no matter how devotedly he strives for it and how much personal sacrifice he makes to achieve it. To pursue evil ends, one must have a disjunctive range of deadly vices: cruelty, callousness, arrogance, sadism, rapacity, deception, and dishonesty. For the vices form an interconnected family no less than do the virtues, and an evil person cannot have only one deadly vice. It is, however, striking that illusory meaning, i.e. meaning that rests on false or incoherent beliefs, *can* impart intrinsic meaning to a person's life and make it genuinely meaningful, as is exemplified in the lives of contemplative Buddhist monks or Christian anchorites such as Julian of Norwich. They do no harm, and their beliefs, though false, are not wicked. It is clear that their lives are subjectively meaningful. But they are also objectively meaningful. They are self-transcendent lives, they achieve tranquillity of spirit which informs their lives and constitutively determines their relationships to others and to the world.

2. Meaninglessness in Life

Outside philosophy seminars and writings, we rarely speak of the meaning of life or describe someone as having led a meaningful life. We are much more likely to speak of someone as having led a worthwhile life, a full life, or a well-spent life. But it is common to speak of life being meaningless, of lacking any sense of purpose, of someone's no longer being able to see the point and purpose of life. Furthermore, unlike enjoying oneself, there are no distinctive behavioural criteria other than avowal for finding meaning in one's life or in life in general or for living or having lived a meaningful life. But the common criteria for finding no meaning in life, for living a meaningless life, for finding no purpose in one's life, are various forms of depressed behaviour, of sadness, misery, frustration, aimlessness, boredom, and lack of gaiety and joy. One might go so far as to say that there is a distinctive phenomenon of loss of meaning, but none of finding meaning in one's life and activities. This runs parallel to the phenomena of leading an unhappy life as opposed to the absence of phenomena of leading a happy life (not to be confused with cheerfulness). This suggests that it is meaninglessness that has primacy, i.e. that to clarify what it is for things in life to have meaning and for a person's life to be meaningful, the notion of loss of meaning must first be examined. This parallels the fact that there can be a science of misery but no science of happiness, for misery incapacitates and can *sometimes* be treated pharmacologically or psychiatrically, whereas no one is incapacitated by happiness and it requires no treatment.[1] Loss of all sense of meaning in life may well be pathological and stand in need of treatment inasmuch as it is characteristic of severe depression. But it may equally well be a symptom of a crisis in life and a sign of an ill-spent life in pursuit of misguided goals, or of the shattering of all one's dreams. It can be remedied only by a change in one's mode of life, not by science.

Loss of a sense of meaning is a common phenomenon in the lives of human beings. It is characteristic of our age, beset as it is with alienation, anomie, and depression. But, to be sure, the sentiment is as old as articulate humanity. It was given brilliant poetic expression in *Ecclesiastes* in which 'vanity of vanities, all is vanity' is the recurrent refrain of the book. It was given powerful dramatic expression by Shakespeare in *Hamlet*, and autobiographical expression in John Stuart Mill and above all by Tolstoy in *A Confession*:

---

[1] Of course, there is a flourishing branch of psychology known as happiness studies, replete with journals. But any putative science that claims that its hard data are people's replies to questionnaires asking them to rank their happiness on a scale from 1 to 10 has the plausibility of a science of beauty the hard data of which are answers to questionnaires asking people to rank the beauty of paintings on a scale of 1 to 10, and to compare the beauty of Beethoven's Fifth with Raphael's *Donna Velata* and the beauty of the Himalayas. Happiness studies is an illusory science, resting on deep misconceptions about happiness and its quantification (see Hacker 2020, chs. 9–10).

> ... I experienced moments of perplexity and arrest of life, as though I did not know how to live; and I felt lost and became dejected. But that passed, and I went on living as before. Then these moments of perplexity began to recur oftener and oftener, and always in the same form. They were always expressed by the questions: What is it for? What does it lead to?
>
> ...
>
> I felt that what I had been standing on had collapsed and that I had nothing left under my feet. What I had lived on no longer existed, and there was nothing left.
>
> ...
>
> My life came to a standstill. I could breathe, eat, drink and sleep, and I could not help doing those things; but there was no life, for there were no wishes the fulfilment of which I could consider reasonable. If I desired anything, I knew in advance that whether I satisfied my desire or not, nothing would come of it. Had a fairy come and offered to fulfill my desires, I should not have known what to ask ... I could not even wish to know the truth, for I guessed of what it consisted. The truth was that life is meaningless. (Tolstoy [1879] 1971, 15, 17)

This wonderfully expresses what Iddo Landau (2017, 230–242) has felicitously named 'numbness to meaning' or 'numbness to value'.

An overwhelming sense of the meaninglessness of life in general or of one's own life in particular may have psychological or intellectual roots. The psychological roots may be grief, profound disappointment, realization of the vanity of one's goals, suffering, and the spectacle and experience of human savagery. The intellectual roots include the insignificance of man in the face of the immensity and indifference of the universe, the brevity of human life in comparison with cosmic time, the 'death of God', the ephemeral character of all human deeds, the tedium and futility of the endless cycle of generations, the seventeenth-century discovery of solar-centrism and the nineteenth-century discovery of evolution which jointly destroyed the illusion that man is at the centre of the universe and of divine attention, recognition of human mortality and the loss of faith in an afterlife in which the good will be rewarded and the wicked punished, the terrible cycle of human suffering, an existential sense of the absurdity of human life, and so on.

There is no such thing as *the* meaning of life. Once Divine cosmic plans are laid aside, once 'God is dead', it is evident that life as such has no meaning. Nor does it lack meaning, any more than the Pacific Ocean, an eruption of Vesuvius, and an eclipse of the sun either have or lack meaning. Similarly, life as such has no purpose—it may indeed be wonderful, but it plays no role in any cosmic drama. Similarly there is no such thing as *the* meaning of animal life in general and human life in particular. Their evolutionary development was haphazard, guided neither by extrinsic purpose, design, nor entelechy. But human beings, unlike mere animals, may find meaning in a multitude of things, activities, relations, experiences, and deeds. So, too, human beings can live meaningful lives, and some of the items that they find meaningful may lend meaning to their lives.

No doubt there are many different ways in which one may classify, with an appropriate degree of generality, what kinds of items make life worth living and endow a person's life with meaning. The following is merely one possibility among others:

(1) Acts and activities that transcend one's selfish and self-centred concerns. This is above all evident in love and pursuit of value: transcendence of self in loving relationships and in cherished friendships, dedication to justice and to the welfare of others, and so forth.
(2) Self-realization, i.e. the development of one's talents in worthy pursuits and worthy social roles (including familial ones), and the development of the distinctive human powers of reason in the quest for knowledge and understanding.
(3) Creative labour, ranging from the most mundane (such as lovingly preparing a special dinner for one's family) to the most sublime (such as writing good poetry, creating wondrous gardens, composing great music).
(4) Cultivation of one's sense of wonder and delight in nature and in art.
(5) The meaning that can be found in suffering, in the manner in which a person meets overwhelming adversity without flinching, in retention of inner autonomy.

There are no mysteries about how to live a meaningful life—it is above all blinkers that stand in one's way, misfortune that drains one's spirits, haplessness, and weakness of the will. The blinkers are the deadly human vices of selfishness, such as greed, lust, envy, jealousy, and the equally deadly vices of cruelty, hatred, callousness, or indifference to the suffering of others, arrogance, and the intellectual flaws of stupidity, ignorance, and lack of understanding, as well as the character failing of laziness (lack of persistence, commitment, and hard work). The misfortunes are lack of parental love, grinding poverty, oppression, insecurity, ignorance, illness and decrepitude, and so forth. The haplessness consists of absence of opportunities, lack of education, and failure to find support from the well-established.

3. The Brain and Finding Meaning in Life

The twenty-first century is evidently going to be the century of biological sciences. Among these, neuroscience is already preeminent. The development of cognitive neuroscience, especially since the introduction of non-invasive techniques of investigating brain processes, has seemed complementary to the parallel developments in cognitive, or more properly computational, psychology. This accidental historical convergence has lent plausibility to each of the two different subjects. Both cognitive neuroscientists and computational psychologists commit the mereological fallacy with respect to the human brain, ascribing psychological attributes of human beings to brains, which are merely parts of human beings.[2] The hypothesized computations of cognitive psychology seem to be given unique concrete realization in the neural networks of the human brain. The black box that is postulated by computational psychology to mediate between stimulus input and responsive output seems no longer black, since we can peer into it by means of fMRI (functional magnetic resonance imaging). A veritable eruption of fMRI research ensued—more than half a million papers being published in the mere three decades since the technique was invented by Seiji Ogawa in 1990. It gave many the illusion that one could actually see neural activity in the brain, whereas what one can actually see is no more than an algorithmically constructed computer image of blood-oxygenation level in the course of blood flow in the brain. It is striking that in recent years Ogawa has expressed doubts about the application and interpretation of the technique he invented. Like Brunner's warnings, so too doubts about fMRI and its significance have not generally been heeded so far.

It is widely assumed among cognitive neuroscientists that every mental attribute must have a neural representation, and hence that there can be no psychological state or event that is not caused by a corresponding representation in the brain. It is presupposed that causal explanation is the sole form of satisfactory explanation of states and events. It is taken for granted that deep philosophical problems can be solved by neuroscientific discoveries. The assumption and its consequence fail to register an equivocation on 'representation', sometimes signifying no more than a causal correlate and at others signifying a symbolic representation. It is also assumed that psychological attributes are one and all states or events, wholly forgetting the role in our psychological economy of first- and second-order powers, of potentialities and susceptibilities or liabilities. It is far from clear what can be the 'representational' correlate of a first- or second-order ability: Is there a neural correlate of one's ability to learn German (which is a second-order ability: i.e. an ability to acquire an ability)? Or of one's ability to speak German (which is a first-order ability)? Or of one's understanding of German? The causal presupposition rides rough shod over Aristotle's distinction between four kinds of 'because-s' (*aitia*—misleadingly translated as 'causes'), i.e. four kinds of explanation: efficient causal explanation; material explanation by reference to the constitutive matter of which a thing is made or consists; a formal explanation by reference to the logical or conceptual features of the item (paradigmatic in geometry); and final or teleological explanation by reference to purpose, reason for acting, thinking or feeling, intention or goal. These need not be incompatible even in a single case, each explanation-type disclosing different explanatory features.

Professor Paul Thagard, in his book *The Brain and the Meaning of Life* (2010) avers that his goal is to show that experimental psychology and neuroscience can contribute answers to central philosophical questions about the meaning of life. His book is a clear and simplified presentation of judgements characteristic of many neuroscientists and it

---

[2] The mereological fallacy in neuroscience and cognitive psychology is the mistake of ascribing attributes to parts of an animal or human being that can only intelligibly be ascribed to the animal or human being as a whole. More generally, it is the fallacy of ascribing to parts properties of wholes of which they are parts, as when one ascribes keeping time to the fusée of a clock, or flying to the engines of an aeroplane.

has done the service of bringing such conceptions into view. For only if they are clearly laid out can one confront them.

I shall sketch the trajectory of his argument:

- Neuropsychological theories are now sufficiently powerful to make it plausible that minds are brains. The mind is what the brain does. Hence thoughts and feelings are just biological processes. The main rival to this doctrine is dualism, according to which the mind is the soul.
- Neural explanations of perception are sufficiently rich to justify thinking of perception as a brain process.
- Memory involves laying down engrams in the brain that can be stored and subsequently retrieved by the occurrence of experiences that have neural representations similar to the stored engram.
- Emotional feelings are the result of parallel brain processes involving cognitive appraisal of circumstances and internal perceptions of the states of our bodies: a Jamesian view shared by numerous neuroscientists.
- Decision-making is a neural selection of action based on emotionally marked neural representations of desirable states of affairs. Hope is a brain process that combines cognitive appraisal and physiological perception to produce a positive feeling about future goal satisfaction.
- Inference and so reasoning are neural processes involving parallel interactions among neural populations, not just a step-by-step linguistic procedure.

These points set out the contours of *neural naturalism*, a doctrine widely embraced in one form or another by the majority of leading cognitive neuroscientists (e.g., Crick 1995; Damasio 1996; Edelman 1994; Edelman and Tononi 2000; Koch 2004; Libet 1993; Gazzaniga 2011; Zeki 2009; Kandel 2007). It advances the view that psychological attributes can be fully explained in neuroscientific terms, and that the ultimate explanation of human psychology and behaviour lies in cognitive neuroscience.

With this array of background presuppositions, it is hardly surprising that it should be thought that neuroscience can resolve questions concerning the meaning of life. It is suggested, platitudinously, that human beings find meaning in their lives in three domains. First, love, or to be more explicit, human relationships such as love (romantic, marital), cherished friendships, and family relationships. Second, work, or the activities of one's vocation in life in which one can exercise one's skills and talents. Third, play, or better, one's manifold recreational activities, both social and solitary. It is the task of neuroscience to explain why such goals and activities make a person's life meaningful. It has already made great strides in that direction. The completion of this task will finally resolve the problems of the meaning of life that have long dogged philosophers.

Something matters to a human being if their brain representation of it includes associations that generate positive emotions.[3] Life is meaningful if one has goals that

---

[3] Thagard should have added 'or negative'.

are emotionally valued mental representations of situations consisting of patterns of neural activity. So, in the case of love, it has been established that viewing photographs of someone loved produces increased activity in the ventral tegmental area and nucleus accumbens. These areas are also activated by reward-producing drugs such as cocaine that similarly lead to exhilaration, on the one hand, or sleeplessness and loss of appetite, on the other.

It has also been alleged that there are 'play circuits' within the brain, the activation of which can cause joy. For there are distinct neural systems devoted to the generation of 'rough-and-tumble' play both in rats and in humans. Rough-and-tumble play involves somatosensory information processing in the midbrain, thalamus, and cortex. The chemicals released include acetylcholine, glutamate, and opioids. The evolutionary warrant of such play among animals and humans is its function in developing physical skills, in learning to fight, in establishing social hierarchies, and in bonding. Why is it fun? Because of its neurochemical effects. More sophisticated 'play' is listening to music, which causes a cascade of brain regions to become activated, from the auditory cortex to the frontal regions involved in processing musical structure, the mesolimbic system involving the transmission of opioids and the production of dopamine, culminating in activity in the nucleus accumbens. The cerebellum and basal ganglia are active throughout, presumably supporting the processing of rhythm and meter.

Finally, the need for 'work' is rooted in neural mechanism for goal accomplishment, wired into the brain as part of the neurochemical basis for goal representation and reward. Greater effort can lead to greater reward in the form of pleasure, resulting from increased activity of dopamine-transmitting neurons in the nucleus accumbens and the orbito-frontal cortex.

It is along such lines that neuroscience and computational psychology can jointly contribute to explaining why human beings find meaningful what they do, and why those things have meaning for them.

4. The Reckoning

Five global errors infect this story:

i. That a causal explanation is superior to or displaces any other, in particular that it displaces formal, material, and teleological/rational explanation.
ii. That the mind is the brain or that 'you are your brain', and that psychological attributes are attributes of the brain.
iii. That mankind is universally motivated by self-interested hedonic consequentialism.
iv. That the only alternative to Cartesian dualism is neural naturalism.
v. That neuroscience and psychology can shed light on and resolve philosophical questions.

If a building collapses in an earthquake, the efficient cause of the collapse is the occurrence of the earthquake, the material cause may be that it was constructed of inferior concrete that cracks when subjected to such-and-such forces, and the explanation in terms of reasons for action may be that the contractor broke the building regulations for the sake of illicit profit. These may all be correct. If a man flips a light switch, a teleological/rational explanation is that he did so in order to turn on the light, and that he wanted to turn on the light in order to get a book. That is not a causal explanation, since reasons are not causes and explanations in terms of reasons are not a type of causal explanation (see Hacker 2007, chapters 6–7). But there is a physical explanation of the contraction of the muscles in the agent's arm and fingers, but for which he would not have been able to flip the switch, since he would have been paralysed. This, we might say, is a causal explanation of the contraction of muscles and a material explanation of the agent's action of flipping the switch (the notion of 'material explanation' is being stretched here). The explanations are compatible and consistent. The teleological explanation explains why the agent did what he did. The material explanation clarifies what made it possible for the agent to do what he did. So too, in the case of explanations of why someone finds a certain activity enjoyable or pleasant, one explanation may cite the desirability-characteristics of the activity (it is exciting, it is intricate and interesting, it is very amusing or funny, it is absorbing and instructive, it is creative); another may cite neural and pharmacological changes without which an agent can take no pleasure in anything. The latter does not displace the former. Nor does it explain what is enjoyable about the activity.

A human being is not identical with his brain, for no human being is a mere three pounds in weight and seven inches high. The mind is not what the human brain does, since the brain is a material object that is a part of a biological substance, namely the human being, and the mind is neither a substance nor a material part of a substance, since it does not consist of matter. Moreover, what the brain does is primarily to metabolize sugars and oxygen, and transmit minute electrochemical currents. It certainly does not think or reason, perceive or feel, let alone get married, have children, and cure patients. The moot question is not 'What is the mind?', but rather 'What is it to have a mind?' To have a mind is to have an array of intellectual and volitional powers and to exercise them. Human beings have minds, but they are not minds. They would not have minds if they had no brains, but for all that, minds are not brains. However, one might say that but for brains there would be no minds. But one may also say that but for mastery of a developed language embedded in a culture there would be no minds either. Psychological attributes are neither attributes of brains nor attributes of minds, but of human beings. It is not my brain that makes up its mind, since it has none. Nor is it my mind that makes up its mind, since it is one and doesn't have one. It is I who make up my mind, but, of course, I can only do so because I have a well-functioning brain. The reason it is incoherent to ascribe psychological attributes to the brain is that the constitutive grounds for ascription of such predicates to human beings consist in behaviour in the circumstances of life, and *brains do not behave*—they do not chortle with delight, jump with joy, weep with grief, speak with thought or thoughtlessly, they do not form intentions or act in fulfilment of intentions. The brain makes it possible for us to do what we do, but it is not the brain that does it.

To be sure, we sometimes do things for pleasure and we sometimes enjoy ourselves. But the fallacy of psychological hedonism is well known and has been refuted too many times to be repeated (see, for example, Kenny 1963, ch. 6; von Wright 1963, ch. 4; Gosling 1969). It is not true that we do all we do for the sake of pleasure, let alone for the sake of the dopamine or opioids that are released by the brain when we successfully pursue goals. But it may be that if our brain were not functioning normally in respect of its pharmacological dynamic equilibrium, we would be depressed and suffer from 'numbness to value' and motivational paralysis. However, we act for the sake of a wide range of goals and ends: for the sake of justice, for the sake of truth, understanding, and enlightenment, for the sake of God, the Church, the Party, for the sake of the proletariat, the nation, or the *Volk*. We may sacrifice our lives for our friends or for our beliefs—not for a buzz of dopamine (*that* may explain why we like going for a run).

It is an egregious error to suppose that Cartesian dualism and neurological naturalism are the sole alternatives between which we must choose. There are numerous alternatives that philosophers and psychologists have tried out over the centuries, including Aristotelian naturalism, no-ownership naturalism (Hume [1739–1740] 1967, 251–263; *Treatise* I, 4, vi), behaviourism (Watson 1930), double aspect monism (Strawson 1959), and so forth. The alternative that is implicitly advanced in this chapter is pluralist anthropological naturalism, which holds that human beings are a single unitary substance (rather than a combination of two different substances: mind and body) and that there are many different forms of explanation of human behaviour (rather than a single form: causal). There are manifestly too few alternatives in view in neurological naturalism and in computational psychology.

To suppose that empirical and experimental discoveries in cognitive neuroscience and computational psychology can contribute to the elucidation and resolution of philosophical problems involves a profound misunderstanding of philosophy, its nature, and its limits, as well as natural science and its limits. Philosophical questions in what Kant called 'theoretical philosophy' are purely conceptual.[4] In this domain, philosophy is concerned with conceptual elucidation, with disentangling knots we have tied in our understanding, with resolving *aporia*, not with enlarging the sphere of empirical knowledge. Science is concerned with discovery of empirical truth, philosophy (in the domain of cognitive neuroscience and psychology) is concerned with clarification of sense and connective analysis. Science constructs and validates hypotheses, but there is nothing hypothetical in philosophy insofar as it can never be a hypothesis that something makes sense. Science may approximate to empirical truth, but there can be nothing approximate in logico-grammatical assertions, for an approximation to sense is one form or another of nonsense. The idea that science can contribute to the resolution

---

[4] In other domains, such as moral, legal, and political philosophy, the task of philosophy encompasses more than connective analysis, elucidation, and criticism of conceptual confusion.

of logico-grammatical problems is akin to the thought that physics can contribute to the formation and proofs of mathematical theorems. Physics *presupposes* mathematical propositions, and similarly natural science presupposes conceptual ones that delimit the bounds of sense.

In philosophy of psychology and in cognitive neuroscience, philosophical problems arise, among other sources, out of an indefinite variety of conceptual confusions and misunderstandings: of not noting equivocation in argument—as with the use of 'representation' to mean both causal correlate and symbolic representation; or the use of 'information' in the information-theoretic sense and in the common-or-garden sense without noting the difference (as when one part of the brain is said to transmit information to another, thereby imparting knowledge to it); or in supposing neural events to be unconscious, when in fact they are non-conscious; or in the application of predicates beyond their logically licit limits, as when psychological attributes are ascribed to the brain. Similarly, it is a dire conceptual confusion to think that a voluntary action is an action preceded by a volition, which is then compounded by supposing the mythical volition to be a neural event. So too, it is quite wrong to suppose that an act done for a reason must be preceded by reasoning and deliberation, and since there are two distinct neural executive pathways for action, one slow and the other very fast, rational action is far less common than we realize, since much of what we do is done swiftly, without reflection. But for an action to be done for a reason, it suffices that the agent sincerely acknowledge something as his reason *ex post actu* and take responsibility for the action as done for that reason.

Seeing is not a brain process, although brain processes are necessary for one to exercise one's visual powers. It is not the brain that sees, and what we see are not representations in the brain, but objects and events in the environment. The locus of seeing is not six inches behind one's eyes, but where one is when one sees what one sees. None of this invalidates the great neuroscientific discoveries about vision, but only their misconceived interpretation.

Memory is knowledge retained. *What* one remembers may be past, present ('I have a meeting now'), future ('The opera is next month') or timeless ($25 \times 25 = 625$). It is the *acquisition* of the retained knowledge that is in the past, but we commonly do not remember when we acquired what we know. One *can* store knowledge, in notebooks, card files, on film or computers. But one cannot store knowledge in the brain. For knowing something is ability-like, and abilities can be retained and not forgotten, but not stored. What is known can be stored if it is written down, iconically represented in pictures, diagrams, or maps, or encoded in electronic form on a computer. But there is no such thing as storing what is known in the brain. And if there were, how would that help one to say what one knows or to act on the basis of it? For one can read what is written in one's diary, but not one's neural networks.

Decision-making is not a neural selection of action based on emotionally marked neural representations of desirable states of affairs. It is not the brain that decides, it is the human agent. Decision may be based on good reasons and on a deliberate weighing of conflicting reasons. But no decision has ever been taken on the grounds of neural representations of desiderata. For there are no neural representations of desiderata, and if they were, the agent could know nothing of them. Moreover, a multitude of decisions to act or take action are made that have nothing to do with what is desirable and conducive to opioid emission, but rather with what is obligatory or morally necessary (there is nothing desirable about dying on the barricades, but people decide to do so), with what is right or just, what is fair or loyal, and so forth.

Inference and reasoning are not neural processes involving parallel interactions among neural populations, nor step-by-step linguistic procedures. For reasoning and inferring are neither processes nor procedures. *A fortiori* they are not brain processes. Rather to infer a conclusion from a premise or set of premises is to *apprehend* the conclusion *as warranted* by the premise or premises, it is to be able to *justify* the conclusion by reference to what supports it. This neither brains nor computers can do. So neither brains nor computers can reason.[5]

There never was any hope that neuroscience might contribute to the understanding of what a meaningful life is, what it is for something to mean something to a person, what the difference is between objective and subjective meaning, what illusory meaning is and when it may be objective despite resting on false or illusory foundations. These are all conceptual problems that demand conceptual clarification. Neuroscience cannot explain why something lends meaning to a person's life. That is explained by reference to the role of that item in human life in general, or in a given human society at a given time in human history, or in the life of this specific person with his particular autobiography.[6]

References

Aristotle. [fourth century BCE] 2000. *Nicomachean Ethics*, trans. R. Crisp. Cambridge: Cambridge University Press.
Bennett, M. R., and P. M. S. Hacker. 2003. *Philosophical Foundations of Neuroscience*. Oxford: Wiley-Blackwell. 2nd, enlarged edition, 2021.
Crick, F. 1995. *The Astonishing Hypothesis*. London: Touchstone.
Damasio, A. 1996. *Descartes' Error*. London: Papermac.
Edelman, G. M. 1994. *Bright Air, Brilliant Fire: On the Matter of the Mind*. Harmondsworth, UK: Penguin.
Edelman, G. M., and G. Tononi. 2000. *Consciousness: How Matter Becomes Imagination*. London: Allen Lane, Penguin Press.
Frankl, V. [1946] 1984. *Man's Search for Meaning*. New York: Washington Square Press.
Gazzaniga, M. 2011. *Who's in Charge? Free Will and the Science of the Brain*. New York: Harper Collins.
Gosling, J. C. B. 1969. *Pleasure and Desire*. Oxford: Oxford University Press.

---

[5] For considerations of space, I omit consideration of Jamesian accounts of emotion. Those who wish to pursue the matter are recommended to consult Bennett and Hacker (2003, chapter 7); and Hacker (2017, chapter 4).
[6] I am grateful to Parashkev Nachev, Hans Oberdiek, Herman Philipse, Gabriele Taylor, and the editor Iddo Landau for their helpful comments and criticisms of the first draft of this chapter.

Hacker, P. M. S. 2007. *The Categorial Framework: A Study of Human Nature*. Oxford: Blackwell.
Hacker, P. M. S. 2017. *The Passions: A Study of Human Nature*. Oxford: Wiley-Blackwell.
Hacker, P. M. S. 2020. *The Moral Powers: A Study of Human Nature*. Oxford: Wiley-Blackwell.
Hume, D. [1739–1740] 1967. *A Treatise of Human Nature*, ed. L. A. Selby-Bigge. Oxford: Clarendon.
Kandel, E. R. 2007. *In Search of Memory*. New York: Norton.
Kenny, A. J. P. 1963. *Action, Emotion and the Will*. London: Routledge and Kegan Paul.
Koch, C. 2004. *The Quest for Consciousness*. Englewood, CO: Roberts.
Landau, I. 2017. *Finding Meaning in an Imperfect World*. Oxford: Oxford University Press.
Libet, B. 1993. *Neurophysiology of Consciousness*. Boston: Birkhäuser.
Montaigne, M. de. [1580] 1965. *Essays*, trans. D. M. Frame. Stanford, CA: Stanford University Press.
Pater, W. [1885] 1985. *Marius the Epicurean*. Harmondsworth, UK: Penguin.
Strawson, P. F. 1959. *Individuals*. London: Methuen.
Thagard, P. 2010. *The Brain and the Meaning of Life*. Princeton, NJ: Princeton University Press.
Tolstoy, L. [1879] 1971. 'A Confession'. In L. Tolstoy, *A Confession, The Gospel in Brief, and What I Believe*, trans. A. Maude. London: Oxford University Press, pp 15–47.
von Wright, G. H. 1963. *Varieties of Goodness*. London: Routledge and Kegan Paul.
Watson, J. 1930. *Behaviourism*, revised edition. Chicago: University of Chicago Press.
Zeki, S. 2009. *Splendors and Miseries of the Brain*. Oxford: Wiley-Blackwell.

CHAPTER 9

PERSONAL IDENTITY AND MEANING IN LIFE

MARYA SCHECHTMAN

When we talk about meaning in life, the kind of life at issue is typically that of a human person. If the life of a person is the relevant unit of meaning, there should be something about the nature and unity of such a life that makes it suitable to serve as such a unit. This essay explores what that 'something' might be. To begin, I look at a popular way of thinking about personal identity and show how it can be connected in a relatively straightforward way to a common conception of meaning. After this, I consider an objection that has been raised against both this view of personal identity and the conception of the connection between identity and meaning it implies. This suggests a different way of thinking about both personal identity and meaning; I conclude by sketching this approach.

Before beginning, it will be helpful to give a bit more context. The first approach to personal identity I consider is a broad class of accounts that defines identity in terms of a set of core commitments or principles that unify and guide a life. I call this the 'core-self' approach. Very different views fall under this basic rubric. Some see the set of core principles that define identity as chosen; others as given. Some insist that to constitute identity these principles must guide us to purposes that are intrinsically valuable; others place no such restriction. Despite these deep differences, these views have important commonalities. In the first two sections I look at various permutations of the core-self approach to draw these out and consider how the approach as a whole connects personal identity to meaning in life. Although those who defend these views do not usually offer extensive discussion of meaning in life, they do argue that the unity that defines personal identity is also the unity that allows us to have purpose and direction in our lives, which on one very common understanding is at least part of what gives life meaning.

I turn next to the criticism of this picture of identity and its relation to meaning, focusing on work by Galen Strawson. While Strawson's own view is likely that meaning is best found by giving up on the idea of diachronic personal identity altogether, I go in a different direction, using some of Strawson's insights to develop an alternative picture of identity. This alternative can both illuminate the connection between identity and meaning implicit in the core-self approach and gesture toward a different understanding of meaning. This other conception is likely to be controversial, but I hope to show why it is worth further consideration.

1. The Chosen Self

I begin with a first broad category of core-self view, which sees personal identity as constituted by acts of endorsement and commitment. I call this the 'chosen-self' view. Recent influential examples of this approach are found in the work of Harry Frankfurt and Christine Korsgaard. Both understand personhood in terms of agency, and personal identity in terms of a unity of will constituted through decisions and commitments. Their starting point is the observation that humans, like other animals, experience drives and motivations that pull us in many directions. Unlike at least most other animals, however, we are able also to step back from these motivations and consider whether we should, or want to, act upon them. This ability allows us to endorse or repudiate not only individual actions, but also the principles that stand behind them. In other words, we have the capacity to step back and consider what kind of life we want to lead and to commit ourselves to the kinds of actions that make up such a life. The set of principles that has this imprimatur represents the core commitments that constitute the true self.

Frankfurt famously describes this phenomenon in terms of higher-order endorsement of first-order desires. In addition to experiencing desires to do this or that (first-order desires), he says, we also have desires about which first-order desires to have and act upon (see e.g. Frankfurt 1988a, 16–19; 1988b, 66-88). Higher-order endorsement of a first-order desire is, in essence, an endorsement of the principle of action implied by that desire. It means that one is happy to be the kind of person who has such desires and expresses them in action. When I wholeheartedly and without reservation endorse a first-order desire, Frankfurt says, I make it mine. If I wholeheartedly repudiate a first-order desire, on the other hand, it is 'extruded as an outlaw' and becomes external to me (Frankfurt 1988c, 170). If I am weak of will and act on it anyway, *I* am not truly acting, but am being acted through by an alien impulse. His gives the example of an unwilling addict, trying desperately to overcome his addiction. If he nonetheless gives in and takes the drug, he has been overwhelmed by a desire that is external to him, despite its occurring in his psychological history, and so not acting as he truly wishes (e.g. Frankfurt 1988a, 16–19).

Frankfurt thus argues that we create our identities by making wholehearted commitments to some subset of the desires we experience, demarcating those which are truly ours. When someone makes a wholehearted decision to act upon one rather than another of two conflicting desires, 'the decision determines what the person really wants by making the desire on which he decides fully his own. To this extent, the person, in making a decision by which he identifies with a desire, *constitutes himself* (Frankfurt 1988a, 170). He adds that our acts of 'ordering and of rejection—integration and separation' of desires 'create a self out of the raw materials of an inner life' (Frankfurt 1988c, 170). If we fail to make these kinds of choices and commitments, we are not genuinely persons with personal identities but, in Frankfurt's evocative term, 'wantons'.

Korsgaard paints a similar picture. She introduces the idea of 'practical identities' that we may take up (e.g. 'mother', 'philosopher'). These identities, once we have committed to them, have normative force, providing us with reasons for acting. If I have taken up the practical identity 'mother', for instance, I have a reason to care for my children; if I take up the identity of philosopher, I have reasons to write papers and teach. When I act in accordance with the reasons given by my chosen practical identities, I express my true self. When I act on motivations that conflict with these reasons, I am pushed around by drives which are not properly authorized as principles of action, and so fail to do what *I* want to do (Korsgaard 1997, 102–103). Like Frankfurt, Korsgaard sees commitments to practical identities as constituting one's personal identity. As she puts it, '. . . in the relevant sense there is no *you* prior to your choices and actions, because your identity is in a quite literal way *constituted* by your choices and actions' (Korsgaard 2009, 19). On both views, commitments to a practical identity or principle of action must be not only unambivalent, but also diachronically stable if it is to constitute identity. Otherwise the distinction between being moved by a principle I have chosen and being moved by one that acts through me evaporates.

The connection between the picture of personal identity described here and a common understanding of a meaningful life as one involving purposeful activity and direction is easily seen. Having a personal identity as defined here allows us to engage in the kinds of complex, diachronically extended plans, activities, and relationships connected with this sense of meaning. This is so in two ways. Most fundamentally, both philosophers suggest that there is a deep human need to have plans and projects to which we are committed. It is these which give our lives purpose and direction. Korsgaard, for instance, describes a practical identity as 'a description under which you value yourself, a description under which you find your life to be worth living' (Korsgaard 1997, 101). Frankfurt emphasizes the 'importance of the activity of caring as such', which 'serves to connect us actively to our lives in ways which are creative of ourselves and which expose us to distinct possibilities for necessity and freedom' (Frankfurt 1988d, 93). It is because we have commitments that we have reasons to get out of bed in the morning and purposive activities to sustain us over the course of the days and years.

More pragmatically, Korsgaard and Frankfurt both describe how having clear principles of action over time provides the coordination of action necessary to pursue the projects that give life meaning. Without such commitments, and a clear hierarchy among them, our lives are in danger of becoming chaotic. Frankfurt describes how a disunified will interferes with someone's 'effectively pursuing and satisfactorily attaining his goals. . . . However a person starts out to decide or to think, he finds himself getting in his own way' (Frankfurt 1999, 99). A directed life in which we undertake meaningful projects and plans thus requires that we constitute an identity-defining set of commitments and stick to them.

For all their similarities, there is a profound difference between Korsgaard and Frankfurt on the question of whether the projects and principles to which we commit ourselves must be intrinsically valuable if they are to constitute identity or confer meaning. According to Korsgaard, the ultimate normative force of our commitments flows from the fact that honouring them is an expression of our nature as rational and moral agents. This means that any practical identity inconsistent with our fundamental practical identity as an agent, including immoral ones like 'thief' or 'murderer', is incoherent and cannot be part of a well-formed identity (Korsgaard 1997, 251–258). Frankfurt, by contrast, puts no such restriction on which kinds of projects and relationships can constitute identity. What allows a project or commitment to imbue someone's life with purpose, he says, is simply that she *can* commit to or care about it. It does not matter, for these purposes, whether what she cares about is ending world hunger, scoring ever higher on a video game, or running the perfect Ponzi scheme.

This is of course a significant difference. The question of whether the purposes that give life meaning must be objectively valuable is a contested one, and those who have a strong position with respect to that debate may well take it to provide a reason to prefer one of Frankfurt's and Korsgaard's views to the other. For present purposes, however, the points of overlap are more critical, specifically that both see personal identity as constituted by commitment to a coherent and stable set of guiding principles, which coordinate our actions and provide purpose and direction.

2. The Given Self

Not all core-self views see the true self as created by our choices. Another important strain of this approach sees the set of core commitments that constitutes the self as given rather than chosen. I will call these 'given-self' views. According to views of this sort there is a set of traits, values, or pursuits natural to a person, and these represent her true identity. When she expresses these innate features in her actions, she is being herself; if she fails to do so, she is not. Major threats to being oneself on this view are either circumstances that prevent someone from discovering who she really is (e.g. because I am never exposed to music I fail to realize that I was meant to be a musician) or social pressures that make the true self difficult to acknowledge or express (e.g. because intellectual pursuits are ridiculed in my community, I do not consider an academic career). This way of thinking about identity is perhaps even more familiar than the idea that it is constituted by our choices, and also more diffuse.

One familiar conception sees our innate identities as given by God or some other transcendent force. Each of us, on this view, has a destiny we are meant to live out; we are given a purpose on this Earth, which is ours to fulfil. The relation between identity and meaning on this kind of view is straightforward. Following a transcendent purpose is meaningful if anything is. There are, however, also many conceptions of a given identity that do not involve transcendent forces, but instead see the elements that make up the true self as given by genetic or other natural factors. Here the idea is that there are certain deep motivations or proclivities that define who we are deep down, and that it is important to our flourishing that we discover and express these in our lives. This sort of picture, for instance, underlies the idea of a voyage of self-discovery in which we take a break from routine to try to determine what we really wish to do.

The connection to meaning in these cases may be somewhat less straightforward, but in the end is not unlike that seen in views according to which the true self is given by a Divine or transcendent force, and both are of a piece with the connection to meaning in views where the self is constituted through wholehearted choice. On these views, the core self we are given through our natural endowment is a set of principles of action which provide an authentic path through life. The assumption is that this life path will bring satisfaction because when we discover our true selves, we discover what we are genuinely passionate about. The practical identities according to which we value our lives or projects and relationships about which we care are still what make our lives meaningful here; it is just that we discover them rather than choosing them.

With chosen-self views, too, there is a distinction between those who hold that our motivations must be intrinsically valuable for them to be able to constitute a true identity and/or confer meaning on a life and those who do not. Einstein's passion for science, Mozart's for music, or Martin Luther King's for seeking social justice are easily seen as sources of both identity and meaning. It is less clear what to say about someone whose passion is running scams or drinking beer and watching TV. One might, like Frankfurt, dig in and say that if these passions are fulfilling to those who experience them, they make their lives meaningful. This position is not often taken in philosophy. A more common position is that while authenticity is necessary for a meaningful life, it is not sufficient, and that someone must find innate desires which allow for intrinsically-valuable, directed activity to have a meaningful life.

The core-self approach thus includes views on which the core self is chosen or given, requires intrinsic value, or does not. I will not attempt to speak to the strengths and weaknesses of these various versions of the approach. They have been widely debated, and the resolution of these differences is not necessary for the main claim I wish to make here. What is relevant is the broad-strokes picture shared among them. All understand personal identity as a set of stable, consistent, and coherent principles of action that provide guidance for how to live our lives, and insofar as identity provides a consistent path through life and a stable set of purposes, it is connected to meaning.

3. Against Strong Unity

The analysis just given assumes a particular way of thinking about both personal identity and meaning, either of which can be challenged. Here I turn my attention to a challenge that has been raised to the core-self view as an account of both identity and meaning. This challenge leads to an alternative picture of personal identity. After sketching this alternative, I consider its connection to meaning and the implications of this analysis for the connection between the core-self approach to identity and meaning just described.

The challenge on which I focus aims at the assumption shared by all versions of the core-self approach—that living a meaningful life requires having a personal identity in the form of a set of coherent and diachronically stable commitments by which we guide our lives. Objectors suggest that this demand is too strict, and potentially destructive. One example of this kind of worry can be seen in a recent, influential body of work by Galen Strawson. Strawson's immediate target is narrative accounts of identity, but his arguments apply straightforwardly to core-self views. He argues that while some people might experience their lives as highly unified and stable, he and many others do not. His life experience, he says, is disjointed and present oriented. He does not feel any deep connection to, or interest in, the past or future, but simply experiences his present.

He calls those who experience life in this way 'Episodics', in contrast to 'Diachronics', who experience a strong sense of diachronic unity. An Episodic, he says, does not 'figure oneself, considered as a self, as something that was there in the (further) past and will be there in the (further) future' (Strawson 2004, 433) and so does not identify with a stable set of commitments reaching forward, which determine how he should act now. He puts himself forward as an example of a happy and fulfilled Episodic and claims that there is reason to believe that many other figures, living and historical, also fall into this category. Attempts to impose strong coherence and diachronic unity can be deeply harmful, on his view, insofar as they can 'close down important avenues of thought, impoverish our grasp of ethical possibilities, needlessly and wrongly distress those who do not fit their model, and are potentially destructive in psychotherapeutic contexts' (Strawson 2004, 429). He adds that 'truly happy-go-lucky, see-what-comes-along lives are among the best there are, vivid, blessed, profound' (Strawson 2004, 449).

There are two distinct elements of Strawson's argument that are worth separating. The first is the claim that as a matter of fact, not all human lives are stable, directed, diachronic wholes involving coordinated activities, plans, and purposes. The second is that life need not be this way to be meaningful, which is what 'blessed' and 'profound' seem to imply in this context. Those who support core-self views can accept the first claim, but not the second. It is perfectly possible, they can allow, that people fail to unify their lives, but they will then be wantons, their lives shallow and without meaning.

One fundamental disagreement between these positions is thus about what makes a good and, ultimately, a meaningful life. Core-self theorists think of meaning in terms of purpose and direction. To have meaning we need to have reasons to act and something to aim at. Strawson's view suggests that being caught up in plans and purposes can be repressive, and anxiety producing; it can reduce the options available to us and prevent us from being fully present in our own lives. This thought is part of a long and important tradition that has been expressed in different ways in a variety of places throughout history. The dispute between these positions on how to live a meaningful life is complex and intricate. For now, however, I will change the direct focus from Strawson's position on meaning to his position on personal identity, looping back to questions of meaning later.

Strawson does not actually offer an account of personal identity. To the contrary, he suggests that we should stop thinking so much about identity over time and focus more attention on life as it is happening. It is not entirely clear, however, what this amounts to concretely. Defenders of the core-self approach paint a compelling picture of the kind of chaos that ensues if we are driven by whatever impulse we happen to have at the moment. If our impulses are not coordinated either by reflective decision-making or by accessing an innate set of principles which prioritizes them, this does seem a danger. Strawson's response to this worry is to argue that an Episodic life need not be without any kind of coordination. After all, groups of distinct individuals can coordinate activities if they wish. He recognizes, he says, that his present self is part of the human history of Galen Strawson, the 'continuing person and human being' (Strawson 2007, 101). He recognizes also that others see the human life of Galen Strawson as a salient unit and that this has some implications for his present self. It is therefore an 'understatement', he acknowledges, to say that the history of the human person Galen Strawson has a special relevance to his present self (Strawson 2007, 92). The crucial point for him is that recognizing this is not the same as *identifying* with either past or future selves in this human history, or thinking of himself as continuing over time. A person living in the present may decide that what he wants to do now is to continue the work of the revolutionaries who went before him or to work for the future good of humanity without taking himself to be identical to his ancestors or successors. Contributing to ongoing activities does not require diachronic identity.

Strawson's view thus seems to be that we should think of an ongoing person as a collection of distinct experiencing selves, bound together by the fact that they occur in the same human history. This form of unity, on his view, has important implications but is phenomenologically superficial. I find this move puzzling. For one thing, it is not clear how it works with many of the ongoing activities that are taken to give life depth and meaning. The claim that I can be part of the ongoing effort to fight for freedom without being identical to past or future freedom fighters is compelling, but how does this work with friendship or love? What is it to say that I take myself to be part of the ongoing project of being someone's friend or lover even though I do not take myself to be the same individual as the previous individuals in the history of the friendship or affair? And why should I be called upon to take up this relationship simply because I happen to be in a human history in which some previous self was someone's friend or lover? Moreover, to the extent that I do need to coordinate with other selves in my human history to have a meaningful life, the ideal of the happy-go-lucky, come-what-may life seems undermined. Constriction once again rears its ugly head.

To be fair, Strawson's response is far subtler than I have conveyed and deserves more attention than I can give it here. For now, I will just say that for reasons like the preceding, I am not inclined to defend it. I do, however, want to appropriate some of its insights to develop an account of personal identity alternative to that we saw in the core-self approach. Strawson helps to reveal some of the costs of the strong consistency and stability that form the ideal of the core-self view, and to raise real questions about whether they are necessary for meaning. The alternative he ultimately offers is one in which the unity of a person's life amounts to nothing more than the fact that multiple short-term agential selves happen to succeed one another in a single biological life. To many, including me, this relation sounds too weak—or of the wrong sort—to provide the kind of meaning that can attach to the life of a human person.

If the unity offered by the core-self view is too strong and that offered by Strawson too weak, we have reason to consider an intermediate alternative. Finding the middle ground involves, I suggest, a recognition that the unity of a biological human life is not as superficial as it initially sounds and can provide the basis of a form of personal identity that can be connected to meaning in interesting ways. First, we should note that the biological life of a human is not a random, disconnected series of events, but a highly structured developmental process. There is a defined linear progression to the life of a human organism. We start as infants with a typical set of cognitive and physical capacities. If all goes well, we develop into children, adolescents, and then adults. We age, and eventually die. In the process of maturing and aging, humans gain and lose basic behavioural, cognitive, and emotional capacities in a roughly predictable way, making different kinds of activities and pursuits (being an Olympic athlete, for instance) possible at different life stages. A human biological life is replete with developmental benchmarks. These are not always met. Individual lives can and do deviate from the standard path in all kinds of ways. This does not mean, however, that a biological life of this kind is not defined by a broadly predictable trajectory that is the paradigmatic path of this process. A biological life in this sense imposes a structure on the lives of human beings. Being in a particular history is not just a matter of finding oneself in some bounded stretch of space and time; it is occupying a point in an ongoing developmental history.

The unity of a biological life is not, moreover, salient only from a physical point of view, but also has practical significance. We see other humans not just as single biological units over time, but also as ongoing units of interaction, and our practices and institutions are based on the presupposition that a human being is, for practical purposes, a single entity throughout her life. When we decide which children to pick up at school, to whom the honorarium check should be sent or the grade assigned, who has the credentials to practice medicine, and countless other practical questions, we do so by individuating human beings. There are probably excellent evolutionary reasons for us to see and treat our conspecifics as single loci of interaction throughout their biological lives, and our practices and institutions reflect and reinforce this way of seeing things. These practices and institutions are, moreover, indexed to the developmental trajectory of the individuals with whom we interact.

The practical unity of a human history is different from that described in the core-self view. It allows for the dynamics and inconsistencies that are in fact part of most human lives. Rather than separating the drives that occur in a life into 'true self' and 'alien intruder', this notion of unity sees them all as part of one's identity. If someone gleefully harasses female co-workers in his youth but has since come to find this behaviour abhorrent, for instance, core-self theorists might suggest that he has become a different person. It can be useful to frame things this way, but we usually do not let it go at that. While he may indeed have changed, and we may well wish to judge him differently than we would if he had not, we also still tend to think that he should be ashamed of his earlier behaviour, apologize to those he offended, and possibly suffer some consequences. He does not just have the misfortune to be in a human history that includes harassment, nor is he is simply someone else. A similar point applies from a synchronic perspective. If someone is uncharacteristically cruel to her partner while under pressure, it makes sense for her partner to take the circumstances into account and realize that this is not deeply representative of who she is. It is also true, however, that she is the kind of person who will snap under pressure and be cruel to those she loves.

On this more expansive view, contradictory and unstable elements can be as much a part of what makes someone who she is as core principles of action. Knowing that someone is chronically indecisive, for instance, or that my stern and proper grandmother used to travel with the circus, is knowing something important about who she is. What emerges from these considerations is thus a picture of persons as complicated, messy, changeable, and multifaceted beings whose identities are similarly complex and multidimensional. A person's identity, understood this way, is not determined by a consistent, stable subset of her traits or commitments, but by the dynamic whole of her life, with all its twist and turns, conflicts and inconsistencies. The basic sentiment at work here is beautifully expressed by Maya Angelou:

> I do not represent blacks or tall women, or women or Sonomans or Californians or Americans. Or rather I hope I do not because I am all those things. But that is not all that I am. I am all of that and more and less. People often put labels on people so they don't have to deal with the physical fact of those people.... So you don't have to think: does this person long for Christmas? Is he afraid that the Easter bunny will become polluted? ... I refuse that ... I simply refuse to have my life narrowed and proscribed. (quoted in Popova 2014)

Attention to this more expansive sense of self adds a new dimension to our understanding of the connection between personal identity and meaning.

4. Expansive Identity and Meaning

This more expansive conception of personal identity can offer some help in the dispute between the core-self approach and the Strawsonian position on questions of meaning. To begin, we can use this conception of identity to flesh out the worry that the kind of coherent stable commitments described in the core-self view are not only not necessary for a meaningful life, but might interfere with having one. When we think of a person's identity in terms of the whole constellation of events, actions, and traits that make up her human history, we can say, minimally, that if we make sharp distinctions between the true self and alien intruders and focus our attention on trying as far as possible to pursue only the plans and purposes of the true self, we will be suppressing a great deal of what we are or might be, and ignoring many sources of joy and satisfaction that might be available to us. Shutting off exploration and realms of experience truncates our nature, making us unidimensional machines for pursuing set projects and robbing us of the rich complexity that should characterize a human life, giving it depth and nuance.

We must take care not to overstate this objection, which is not entirely charitable to the core-self approach. This approach does not and need not imply that we should commit to a small number of projects and do nothing else with our lives but pursue them. It can allow for many different, and different kinds of, core commitments and values, and so can allow for the true self to be very complex. The central claim is only that a well-formed identity and meaningful life requires our impulses to be vetted, prioritized, and coordinated, and that motivations that undermine what is genuinely important to us (e.g. addictive cravings or destructive fits of anger) must be repudiated. All of this must be recognized, but even so, there remains a kernel of the objection against the core-self understanding of identity that legitimately applies. If nothing else, it shows some obscurity in the view.

The core-self view's emphasis on choosing or finding self-defining commitments and sticking with them makes it difficult to see how the exploration and development that seem critical to a life well lived fit in. It is not that this approach denies the need for some leeway for self-discovery or that change can be part of a meaningful identity. These claims do, however, seem to be in tension with the strong consistency and stability this approach requires for identity. In some ways the heart of the core-self approach is the idea that once the core commitments are settled, they should remain fixed. Reflection on Strawson's complaint reminds us that there is something mythical about the idea of a point in time where we know what we want and can make firm commitments or discoveries that seal our identities and purpose. Life is a process of determining what is important to us or gives our lives meaning. To figure this out, we need a certain amount of latitude for exploration, and this involves relaxing the grip of our current values and commitments so that others may be entertained.

Meaning on this expanded view is thus going to result from a delicate, ongoing negotiation between fixing commitments and exploring, expanding, and recalibrating projects and plans. The exact mix of steadfastness and spontaneity that is optimal for a meaningful life may well differ with individuals and circumstances. Nothing in the core-self approach directly rejects this idea, but accepting it does alter the implicit assumption of what gives depth and meaning to a human life. Original statements of the core-self approach seem to tie meaning very directly to the pursuit of projects that express one's true nature. The picture just given, however, suggests that meaning comes not only from pursuing the projects on which we settle, but also from the experimentation, exploration, and experience that are part of our journey through life. A defender of the core-self approach might say that this just shows that the project of building an identity is a fundamental one, essential to a meaningful life. Fair enough, but only if this allows a certain level of ambivalence, confusion, and drifting as positive parts of this project, and it is difficult to see exactly how this is possible on that approach.

There is, moreover, another, more radical, rethinking of the idea of meaning and its relation to identity suggested by the more expansive view of identity I have described. This one is likely to be more controversial, and certainly requires more explanation and defence than I can offer here. I hope, however, to convey the general idea as a topic worthy of further exploration. In the dispute about identity and meaning between the tradition represented by Strawson and the core-self approach as I have presented it, both remain within a dominant tradition that focuses on the question of what makes someone's life meaningful to them. Meaning in life is connected to a sense of satisfaction or joy that goes somehow beyond the hedonic; it is deeper and involves valuing one's life in a serious way. Disputes are about how to understand 'deeper', 'value', and 'serious'.

Connected to the idea of identity as the whole complex, messy journey of life is another way of thinking about meaning which differs from the one employed so far in many ways. One difference is that it is not most directly about the question of what makes life meaningful from the perspective of the person living it, but focuses more on the question of what makes someone's life meaningful from an external perspective. (I will return briefly to the connection between these perspectives later.) Possibly the more radical departure from the conception of meaning we have been using is that on this alternative view *all* lives are meaningful just in virtue of being the singular events they are. Since most discussions of meaning are aimed at distinguishing meaningful from non-meaningful lives, the idea that every life is meaningful will likely meet some resistance. It might be allowed that every life is important or that every human is deserving of a certain moral status, but this is different, it might be claimed, from saying each is meaningful. I suggest, however, that there is a familiar strain of everyday thought that does suggest this kind of universal meaning of life.

To begin to get a sense of this everyday thought, consider memorials and related efforts to ensure that even very ordinary lives are remembered. The indication is that it matters simply that someone was here. In May 2020, for instance, when the number of US deaths from the COVID-19 pandemic reached 100,000, the *New York Times* devoted their front page to a list of names of some of the victims under the headline 'An Incalculable Loss'. Included after each name was a detail from an obituary. In some cases, this was a core project or impressive accomplishment. In many, however, it was simply a fact about the person, e.g., 'an exuberant laugh', 'known for serenading friends with Tony Bennett songs', 'taught her girls sheepshead and canasta', 'nicknamed "Boxcar Bob" for his luck in shaking dice'. Letters to the editor praised the page for bringing home the true scope of the loss. One said, for instance: 'In humanizing our beloved dead, you have reminded us that each person is precious' (New York Times 2020).

There is a connection between the universal 'preciousness' (a notion I will have to connect to meaning later) of lives, the fact that many of the remembrances in these pages involve seemingly trivial traits, and the expansive view of identity described in the previous section. To unpack this connection, we can begin by asking why the recitation of these details is so poignant. Why should it be so affecting to learn that a person who died had a particular nickname and was lucky at dice, or played a particular card game, or laughed a particular way? What does this tell us beyond the fact that a human being died? One answer to this question is that these small details remind us in a powerful way that the name of the deceased is that of a full-blown person with a complex, multifaceted life and a dense personal history. Because we have people in our lives who sing off-key or have funny nicknames, or teach us card games, when we are given this kind of personal detail, arguably even more than we when we are told of unusual accomplishments or devotion to worthy causes, we are reminded of the individuality and richness of what has been lost. Furthermore, insofar as these sentences lead us to think about all the little details that characterize the people in our lives, they bring home the fact that the individuals who died mattered to those who lost them in the way the people in our lives matter to us. This may evoke a sense of what it would mean to lose those people, and this provides an immediate sense of the enormity of the loss.

So far, it might be argued, all this shows is that these details remind us that the individuals listed among the dead were in loving relationships. There is nothing radical in claiming that this makes their lives either precious or meaningful, since such relationships are quite widely acknowledged to be part of what gives life meaning. To some extent, this rejoinder is legitimate. I do not think, however, that this is the whole of the story. If it turned out that someone died alone, with no family or friends, we would not therefore conclude that the loss was just not that deep or that there is no reason to memorialize them. There might seem to be all the more reason to do so and to try to find some detail that conveys a sense of who they were.

Even so, more must be said to explain why this does not just amount to the claim that all human lives are important and why the language of meaning is appropriate here. To justify this claim we need to think more about the sense in which each life recorded as lost on the *New York Times* page is deemed 'precious'. We have already said that at least partly this is because they are precious *to* someone. What the kinds of details provided suggest, however, is that they were not just precious because of their qualities, but as the particular individual that they were. What we are brought to recognize is that each of these lives is a one-off, irreproducible event, and in that sense the loss is 'incalculable'. If I miss the mother who always made special cookies to cheer me up, or the uncle who would serenade me with Tony Bennett songs, the loss cannot be made good by someone else making me the cookies or singing to me. This might be some comfort (or might cause more pain), but what I am missing is not, or at least not only, the cookies or the songs. These features are part of a history that I have with someone, which I cannot have or continue with anyone else. The profundity of the loss comes from a retrospective appreciation of the life gone as an utterly unique event, not only in its details, but in a more metaphysical, numerical sense.

The suggestion is that it is this which makes every life precious, since each life is irreplaceable in this way. It explains why, for instance, I might be deeply affected by news of the sudden death of a co-worker about whom I have no warm feelings whatsoever. Even if I will not miss his condescension or political tirades, the fact that I will never again interact with someone who was a part of my daily life is a profound fact. This is not a decisive consideration, of course. Some may simply deny that they would feel any deep emotion in such a case. Others might argue that even if they did, it would only be because the co-worker undoubtedly had some redeeming features or because I know that others valued his life and were suffering. Why, though, should we think that the fact that a life of utter depravity and evil is a unique event, for instance, lead us to the conclusion that it is meaningful, or that it should be viewed as a loss when it has ended?

I doubt I can answer this challenge to the satisfaction of those who strongly associate meaning with either purpose or value, but I will conclude by offering two reasons I think it is worth further consideration. First, there is an important and plausible strain of thought suggesting that whatever kinds of evaluative discriminations (e.g. moral, aesthetic) we might want to make with respect to human lives, there is a perspective with respect to which they are all equally significant. Each is a completely singular event, and each is part of the overall tapestry of human history. Here we are in the territory of Donne's famous lines: 'If a clod be washed away by the sea/Europe is the less / As well as if a Promontory were . . . / Each man's death diminishes me / For I am involved in mankind.' While we will like some people better than others, and judge some more talented or morally worthy than others, there is the suggestion that we have missed something if we do not also recognize that there is a deep sense in which all are on a par. This is connected to the sentiment that in knowing or loving someone, we are knowing and loving an entire individual with a unique history, even if there are undoubtedly some parts we like more than others. These features of human life and interaction should not be forgotten.

Even those who have come with me this far, however, may well insist that saying all lives are important is still not enough to show that they are all meaningful, and certainly not that they are all equally meaningful. Admittedly this is not the common understanding of 'meaning', according to which, for instance, a life can gain and lose meaning over time, or someone can despair for the lack of meaning in his life. Nonetheless, there are important connections between the two. I have suggested that each life has meaning insofar as it represents a unique trajectory through space and time. That one's life is meaningful in this way does not mean that one will recognize it as such, and so does not guarantee that one will find one's life meaningful. One route to experiencing one's life as meaningful, however, is to be alive to the fact that each life is meaningful in virtue of its being the singular event that it is, and so that one's own life is meaningful in this way. From the perspective of more standard understandings of meaning, recognizing that one's life matters in the universal sense I describe may be seen as a wake-up call to make it meaningful in the more traditional sense—i.e. 'You have only one life to live; it is a unique event; don't squander it playing video games or being bored, choose or find commitments that will make it meaningful.' But this is not the only way to respond. The tradition that Strawson represents might insist that meaning can come simply from recognizing how profound it is merely to be here. This recognition need not be a call to change our lives, but only to be present in them.

Both traditions are enormously complicated, of course, and the sketch I have offered here needs far more development to be anything like a reason for those committed to a more standard understanding of 'meaning' to concede that that term is aptly applied to what I am describing. I hope, however, to have shown that there are conceptions of identity and elements in the neighbourhood of meaning, at least, that have been less central in the discussion, that these are worthy of exploration, and that questions about identity, meaning, and the relation between them are as multifaced, messy, and intriguing as the lives about which they are asked.[1]

REFERENCES

Frankfurt, H. G. 1988a. 'Freedom of the Will and the Concept of a Person'. In *The Importance of What We Care About*, ed. H. Frankfurt, 11–25. Cambridge: Cambridge University Press.

Frankfurt, H. G. 1988b. 'Identification and Externality'. In *The Importance of What We Care About*, ed. H. Frankfurt, 58–68. Cambridge: Cambridge University Press.

Frankfurt, H. G. 1988c. 'Identification and Wholeheartedness'. In *The Importance of What We Care About*, ed. H. Frankfurt, 159–176. Cambridge: Cambridge University Press.

Frankfurt, H. G. 1988d. 'The Importance of What We Care About'. In *The Importance of What We Care About*, ed. H. Frankfurt, 80–94. Cambridge: Chambridge University Press.

Frankfurt, H. G. 1999. 'The Faintest Passion'. In *Necessity, Volition, and Love*, ed. H. Frankfurt, 95–107. Cambridge: Cambridge University Press.

Korsgaard, C. M. 1997. *The Sources of Normativity*. Cambridge: Cambridge University Press.

Korsgaard, C. M. 2009. *Self-Constitution: Agency, Identity, and Inegrity*. Oxford: Oxford University Press.

New York Times. 2020. *Opinion Letters*. [Online] Available at: nytimes.com/2020/05/24/opinion/letters/coronavirus-100000-deaths.html [accessed 7 August 2020].

Popova, M. 2014. *brainpickings: Maya Angelou on Identity and the Meaning of Life*. [Online] Available at: (https://www.brainpickings.org/2014/05/29/maya-angelou-on-identity-and-the-meaning-of-life/) [Accessed 7 August 2020].

Strawson, G. 2004. 'Against Narrativity'. *Ratio* XVII(4): 428–452.

Strawson, G. 2007. 'Episodic Ethics'. In *Narrative and Understanding Persons*, ed. D. Hutto, 85–116. Cambridge: Cambridge University Press.

---

[1] I offer profound thanks to Iddo Landau for generous and insightful comments on earlier versions of this chapter.

CHAPTER 10

HARD DETERMINISM AND MEANING IN LIFE

DERK PEREBOOM

Scepticism about Free Will

We human beings are situated in a natural world of law-governed causes and effects. Our character and actions are conditioned by causes that we do not control, including our genetic make-up, our upbringing, and the physical environment. In view of such considerations, the seventeenth-century philosopher Spinoza advocates scepticism about free will, arguing that 'in the mind there is no absolute, or free, will, but the mind is determined to will this or that by a cause which is also determined by another, and this again by another, and so to infinity' ([1677] 1985, *Ethics* II, Proposition 48, 483). The reason we don't have free will is that all that happens is causally determined by prior causes, resulting in chains of causes stretching backwards in time. The ultimate deterministic cause of everything that happens is the divine nature. Perhaps surprisingly, Spinoza maintains that the doctrine that we lack free will has good consequences for meaning in life:

> it teaches us... that we must expect and bear calmly both good fortune and bad. For everything that happens follows from God's eternal decree with the same necessity as it follows from the essence of a triangle that its three angles are equal to two right angles. This doctrine contributes to the social life by teaching us to hate no one, to disesteem no one, to mock no one, to be angry at no one, to envy no one. ([1677] 1985, *Ethics* II, Proposition 49, 490)

Understanding that people lack free will counteracts hostile emotions we have toward others, and for this reason can make a significant contribution to human happiness and fulfilment.

However, most of us suppose that our actions are sometimes freely willed. When we choose from among options for action, we typically assume that we do so with free will; in particular, that we could have chosen differently from how we actually did choose. When we are angry with wrongdoers for their immoral actions, we suppose that they could have refrained from acting as they did. There are, however, reasons for believing that these suppositions are false, and that no one has free will, reasons that stem from a number of sources. One such source is invoked by Spinoza: everything that happens, including human action, is causally determined by the divine nature. Another source is the naturalistic perspective that everything that happens, including all human action, is made inevitable by virtue of past physical events in accord with natural laws. Given the prospect that causal determinism of some kind is true, is it reasonable to believe that some of our actions are freely willed nonetheless?

In answering this question, we must keep in mind that due to the complexity of the historical debate about free will, the term 'free will' has a number of distinct senses, and the answer as to whether we have it may depend on which sense is in play. There is currently fairly widespread agreement among participants in the debate that the sense that best serves to draw clear lines of difference is free will as the control in action required for our being morally responsible. More exactly, participants disagree about whether causal determination is compatible with our having the control in action required for being morally responsible for actions in a sense involving desert; specifically, in the *basic desert* sense. On the basic form of desert, an agent who has acted wrongly deserves harm or pain of some sort just because he has acted for morally bad reasons, and someone who has acted rightly deserves benefit or pleasure just because she has acted for morally good reasons. Such desert is basic because these desert claims are fundamental in the sense that they are not justified by further considerations, such as anticipated good consequences of implementing them (Feinberg 1970; Pereboom 2001, xx; 2014, 2).

With the understanding that 'moral responsibility' refers to moral responsibility in this basic desert sense, here are the three traditional positions about free will and causal determinism:

> *hard determinism*: because determinism is true we cannot have the sort of free will required for moral responsibility.
> *(soft determinist) compatibilism*: even though determinism is true, we can and do have the sort of free will required for moral responsibility.
> *libertarianism*: because determinism is false we can have this sort of free will, and we do in fact have it.

Like the hard determinist, I side with the claim that we lack free will defined in this way.[1] But this is not because I'm convinced of the truth of determinism, and that all of

---

[1] Derk Pereboom (1995, 2001, 2014). Historical advocates of scepticism about free will include Spinoza ([1677] 1985); Paul d'Holbach (1770); and Arthur Schopenhauer ([1818] 1961); and in recent decades, Galen Strawson (1986); Bruce Waller (1990, 2011); Saul Smilansky (2000); Daniel Wegner (2002); Gideon

our actions are causally determined by preceding factors beyond our control. Rather, I believe that any sort of indeterminism that has a good chance of being true is also incompatible with free will in the sense just defined. It's often argued that if our actions are not causally determined, they would then be random or chance events, and because we have no control over random or chance events, we can't be morally responsible for them. We'll examine an argument of this sort in what follows. Critics have expressed a number of practical concerns about free will scepticism, that, for example, its rejection of basic desert moral responsibility is too costly, threatening various ways in which our lives can be meaningful. We've already seen that Spinoza disagrees, and in what follows I defend that perspective.

An Argument for Free Will Scepticism

I've argued in detail for my sceptical position about free will (e.g. Pereboom 2001, 2014). In this section I'll present the most recent version of the argument in outline. This argument features challenges to the rival views, compatibilism and libertarianism, in turn. If these challenges are sound, only the sceptical view remains standing.

One way to resist scepticism about free will is to contend that even if all of our actions are causally determined by factors beyond our control, we can still be morally responsible in the basic desert sense for them; this is what compatibilists affirm. Compatibilists often begin by arguing that causal determination is irrelevant to many of the ordinary criteria we use to judge whether people are blameworthy. In legal cases we may want to ascertain that the accused was not compelled by someone else to commit the crime, and that he was rational. But whether causal determinism is true, they argue, is not relevant to whether people are compelled or irrational, and more generally, whether determinism is true is never a consideration in court cases. Compatibilists have set out conditions for moral responsibility, and they maintain that satisfying such compatibilist conditions is sufficient for responsibility. Incompatibilists have objected that even if an agent satisfies these compatibilists conditions, being causally determined by factors beyond her control rules out responsibility. Does this amount to a standoff, or might progress be made in this debate?

I believe the most effective way to argue against the compatibilist option begins with the intuition that if an agent is intentionally causally determined to act by, for example, neuroscientists who manipulate her brain, then she is not morally responsible for that action in the basic desert sense even if she satisfies the compatibilist conditions. The next step in the argument is to point out that there are no differences between such intentionally manipulated agents and their ordinary causally determined counterparts

---

Rosen (2004); Joshua Greene and Jonathan Cohen (2004); Shaun Nichols (2007); Thomas Nadelhoffer (2011); Benjamin Vilhauer (2012); Neil Levy (2011); Gregg Caruso (2012); Per-Erik Milam (2016); and Farah Focquaert (2018).

that are relevant to whether the agent is morally responsible in this sense. The argument concludes that an agent is not responsible in the basic desert sense if she's causally determined to act by factors beyond her control, even if she satisfies the compatibilist conditions (Taylor 1974, 45; Kane 1996, 65–69; Pereboom 1995, 22–26; 2001, 110–120; 2014, 71–103; Mele 2006, 186–194).

In my multiple-case version of this argument, in each of four cases the agent commits a crime, murder, for self-interested reasons. All of the cases are designed so that the action conforms to the proposed compatibilist conditions. For instance, the action meets a criterion advocated by David Hume ([1739] 1978): the agent is not compelled to act by other agents or constrained by other factors such as drugs. The action meets the rationality condition advocated by John Fischer (1994): the agent's desires can be modified by, and some of them arise from, his rational consideration of his reasons, and if he understood that the bad consequences for himself that would result from the crime would be much more severe than they are actually likely to be, he would have refrained from the crime for that reason.

The manipulation cases serve to indicate that it's possible for an agent to be morally non-responsible in the basic desert sense even if the compatibilist conditions are satisfied, and that, as a result, these conditions are insufficient for such moral responsibility, by contrast with what the compatibilist maintains. The argument gains force by setting out three such manipulation cases, each of which is progressively more like a fourth, in which the action is causally determined in an ordinary and natural way. The cases are set up so that there is no difference relevant to basic desert moral responsibility between any two adjacent cases. So if it's agreed that the agent isn't morally responsible in the first case, this feature of the argument will make it difficult to affirm that he is responsible in the final, ordinary case:

> Case 1: A team of neuroscientists possesses the technology and skill to manipulate Professor Plum's neural states remotely. In this particular case, they do so by pressing a button just before he begins to reason about his situation, which they know will result in a neural state that realizes a strongly egoistic reasoning process, which the neuroscientists know will deterministically result in his decision to kill White. Plum would not have killed White had the neuroscientists not intervened, because his reasoning would then not have been sufficiently egoistic to produce the decision to kill.
>
> Case 2: Plum is just like an ordinary human being, except that a team of neuroscientists has programmed him at the beginning of his life so that his reasoning is often but not always egoistic, and at times strongly so, with the intended consequence that in his current circumstances he will be causally determined to engage in the process of deliberation that results in his decision to kill White for egoistic reasons.
>
> Case 3: Plum is an ordinary human being, except that the training practices of his community causally determined the nature of his deliberative reasoning processes so that they are often but not always egoistic. On this occasion, his deliberative

process is exactly as it is in Cases 1 and 2: in his current circumstances he is causally determined to engage in the process of deliberation that results in his decision to kill White for egoistic reasons.

Case 4: All that occurs in our universe is causally determined by virtue of its past states together with the laws of nature. Plum is an ordinary human being, raised in normal circumstances, but his reasoning processes are frequently but not exclusively egoistic, and sometimes strongly so. In the current circumstances he is causally determined to engage in the process of deliberation that results in his decision to kill White, for egoistic reasons.

Case 1 involves intentional manipulation that is local and causally determining, and is the case most likely to elicit a non-responsibility intuition. Case 2 is like Case 1, except that it restricts the deterministic manipulation to the beginning of Plum's life. Case 3 is distinctive in that the deterministic manipulation results from community upbringing. Case 4 is the ordinary deterministic case in which the causal determination of Plum's action is not intentional, but results from the past and the laws. Case 4 is the kind of case about which compatibilists standardly claim that the agent is morally responsible despite being causally determined to act by factors beyond his control.

However, in Case 1, is Plum morally responsible in the basic desert sense for the crime? In this situation it seems clear that Plum is a causally determined victim of the conniving neuroscientists, and thus not responsible. Are there responsibility-relevant differences between Cases 1 and 2 that would justify claiming that he is non-responsible in Case 1 but is responsible Case 2? It was my aim to set out the cases so that it isn't possible to draw a difference relevant to the sort of responsibility at issue between any two adjacent cases. Given this absence of relevant differences, if Plum is not responsible in Case 1, he isn't responsible in Cases 2, 3, and 4 either. I contend that the best explanation for Plum's non-responsibility in each case is that he is causally determined to act by factors beyond his control. Hence the argument's anti-compatibilist conclusion.[2]

Making a case for the sceptical position about free will also requires arguing against the rival incompatibilist position, libertarianism. On libertarian views generally, we do in fact have the ability to freely will actions, and required for an action's being freely willed is that it not be causally determined by factors beyond our control. We'll examine the two most widely endorsed versions of libertarianism, *event-causal libertarianism* and *agent-causal libertarianism*.

In the event-causal libertarian view, actions are caused solely by *events*, conceived as substances having properties at times, such as *Abby wanting at noon today to give Rachel her medicine*, while some type of indeterminacy in the production of actions by such events is the crucial requirement for moral responsibility (e.g. Kane 1996; Ekstrom 2000; Balaguer 2010). This position contrasts with one on which substances, such as particles, stars, and agents, and not just events that feature them, can be causes.

---

[2] Objections to manipulation arguments are discussed in Pereboom (2014, 71–103).

Those who maintain that only events can be causes note that we sometimes speak as if substances are causes, but contend that when we clarify such speech, we see that the event-causal view is right. For instance, imagine that a car drives through a puddle of water and splashes you. We might say; 'The car made you wet!' But more exactly, it's not the car that made you wet, but an event, the car's driving through the puddle at 123 4th Street at 5 p.m. that had this effect. According to *agent-causal libertarianism*, by contrast, free will of the sort required for basic desert moral responsibility is accounted for by agents who, as substances, and not just by virtue of having a place in events, cause decisions without being causally determined to do so. On this view, the causation involved in an agent's making a free choice does not amount to causation among events involving the agent, but is instead fundamentally a case of the agent as a substance causing a choice (e.g. O'Connor 2000, Clarke 2003).

A prominent objection to event-causal libertarianism is that if actions are undetermined in the way this position requires for free will, agents will not have sufficient control in acting to secure moral responsibility. David Hume expresses this concern in his *Treatise of Human Nature* ([1739] 1978, 411–412), where he argues that if an action is not determined by some factor involving the agent, the action will not have the connection with the agent required for her to be morally responsible for it. Here is my way of developing the concern. To be morally responsible (in the basic desert sense) for an action, it's necessary that the agent have a certain degree of control in acting. On the event-causal libertarian picture, agent-involving events don't causally determine the action. Indeed, with the complete causal role of these preceding events in place, it *remains open* whether action occurs. In addition, the role of the agent in the production of the action is *exhausted* by these agent-involving events. Thus nothing about the agent *settles* whether the action occurs. For this reason, the agent lacks the requisite control in acting. Since the agent 'disappears' at the crucial point in the production of the action—at the point at which its occurrence is to be settled—I call this the *disappearing agent argument* (Pereboom 2014, 32–33; 2017).

Agent-causal libertarianism offers a solution to this problem. The agent-causalist maintains that in such an indeterministic situation the agent can in fact settle which of the options for action occurs. The proposal crucially reintroduces the agent itself as a cause, not merely as involved in events, but as fundamentally as a substance-cause. We human agents possess a distinctive causal power—a power for an agent, fundamentally as a substance, to cause a decision without being causally determined to do so, and thereby to settle which option for action actually occurs (e.g. O'Connor 2000; Clarke 2003).

An objection to agent-causal libertarianism is that it cannot be reconciled with our best scientific theories. Suppose that we allow that agents are free in the way specified by agent-causal libertarianism, but that our best science reveals that the physical world is wholly governed by deterministic laws. Given this supposition, the agent-causal libertarians might contend that we agents are non-physical beings. Still, on the route to a bodily action that results from an undetermined agent-caused decision, changes in the physical world—for example, in the agent's brain—result. But it is at this point that we would then expect to encounter divergences from the deterministic laws. This is due to the fact that the alterations in the brain that result from the causally undetermined decision would themselves not be causally determined, and thus would not be governed by deterministic laws. The agent-causal libertarian might respond by proposing that the physical alterations that result from free decisions just happen to dovetail with what can be predicted on the basis of the deterministic laws, and that no event actually occurs that diverges from these laws. However, this proposal would involve coincidences too wild to be credible. Thus it seems that agent-causal libertarianism cannot be reconcile with the physical world's being governed by deterministic laws. I argue that a similar concern arises if the laws of physics are probabilistic and not deterministic (Pereboom 1995, 28–30; 2001, 79–85; 2014, 65–69).

The agent-causal libertarian might now suggest that exercises of agent-causal libertarian freedom do in fact result in divergences from what we would expect given current theories of the physical laws. On this proposal, divergences from the deterministic or probabilistic laws occur whenever we exercise free will, and these divergences are to be found at the interface between the agent and the brain. An objection to this proposal is that we currently have no evidence that such divergences actually occur. Thus it appears that agent-causal libertarianism is not reconcilable with the laws of nature, whether they are deterministic or probabilistic, and we have no evidence that the divergences from the laws that this view would therefore predict in fact are to be found.

In sum, compatibilism falls to the manipulation argument; event-causal libertarianism to the disappearing agent argument; and agent-causal libertarianism is not reconcilable with the laws of nature. Free will scepticism is the view that remains standing. The objections most often raised for this position are practical: Can we live with the verdict that we lack free will? The specific question I will now address is whether this view is reconcilable with meaning in life.

Deliberation, Decision, and Achievement

For life to have meaning, it would seem that our deliberation and decisions about how to act, what course of life to pursue, what projects to engage in, must be efficacious (Sartre [1946] 1956; Landau 2012). If deliberation and decision had no effect, then our conception of ourselves as agents who by deliberation and decision make a difference for our lives would be an illusion. On the supposition of the truth of naturalistic determinism in particular, how do we regard the efficacy of deliberation about what to do and the choice of one of the options being considered? If all of our decisions and actions are causally determined by the past and the laws, factors beyond our control, which option one selects is made inevitable by causal factors that are beyond one's control. The effects of that selection are also inevitable by virtue of such factors. This in turn poses a threat to our sense of achievement, a significant component of meaning in life. Do we ever really achieve anything if our deliberation and decision are an inevitable result of factors beyond our control?

There remains a sense in which how an agent deliberates and chooses makes a difference to the future. Suppose you were scheduled to take a college entrance exam a year ago, and you considered not preparing. But after deliberating—thinking of and weighing reasons for your options—you decided to prepare. Imagine that it was causally determined by the past and the laws that you decided to prepare, and that as a result you did well on the exam, and you were admitted to the school you wanted to attend. It still may be true—and we can suppose it is—that if you hadn't prepared, you wouldn't have done as well, and you wouldn't have been admitted to that school. In this sense your deliberation made a difference to how well you did on the exam and to the subsequent admission. One might contrast this kind of difference-making control with what Eddy Nahmias calls *bypassing*—that 'our rational, conscious mental activity is *bypassed* in the process of our making decisions and coming to act' (Nahmias 2011, 556). As Nahmias points out, causal determination doesn't entail bypassing, because deliberation can make a difference in the way just set out.

Yet, given naturalistic causal determination, there are factors beyond your control—the distant past and the laws of nature—that made it inevitable how you in fact deliberated, the choice that resulted, and the effects it had for your future. This combination of claims may at first appear internally inconsistent, but one must keep in mind that if determinism is true, the difference deliberation can make is limited. Deliberation can indeed make a difference relative to other options one was considering, but given causal determinism, the non-occurrence of the options that weren't selected was still inevitable by virtue of factors beyond one's control. And deliberation can't make a difference to which factors beyond one's control are actual.

Is our sense of achievement undermined by these considerations? Suppose that you aim to succeed in your school or in your profession, and in fact you do well. In such circumstances, we naturally have a sense of achievement, a sense that is a significant component for our sense of meaning in life. But now you come to believe that your success was an inevitable result of the past and the laws. Is your sense of achievement thereby jeopardized? Perhaps it is diminished relative to, say, a libertarian conception on which an agent's undetermined efforts qualify as the ultimate originator of her success. But even supposing causal determination of one's actions by factors beyond one's control, success might still be due to the causal efficacy of one's deliberation and choice, which might yet make the difference between success and failure. The resulting sense of achievement would indeed be diminished, I believe, by comparison to what is on offer on the libertarian conception. But what remains counts as a significant sense of achievement nonetheless.

Relationships and the Reactive Attitudes

A further component of our sense of meaning in life is the fulfilling personal relationships we may enjoy. Love is the core emotion in personal relationships, and one might suppose that love requires free will. So first, is there reason to think that for love to be valuable and provide meaning, the beloved must have free will? One might argue that any valuable kind of love must be deserved by the beloved. Against this, parents typically love their children independently of their having this sort of free will, and we think that such love is highly valuable (Pereboom 1995, 41; 2001, 202–204; 2014, 190). When children are born, parents love them, and whether they have free will is irrelevant. Furthermore, when adults love each other it is often not due to factors that are not freely willed; appearance, intelligence, and affinities with persons or events in one's history all have a significant part. Still, moral action and character are often especially important for occasioning and maintaining love. But it would seem that love would not be threatened if we came to believe that moral character and action do not come about through free will, since they would be loveable whether or not the beloved is thought to deserve praise for them. Love plausibly involves wishing well for the other, taking on aims and projects of the other as one's own, and often a desire to be with the other. Denying that the beloved has the free will required for desert would not appear to threaten any of this (Pereboom 2011, 188–198; 2014, 190–193).

One might argue that for love to be valuable, the loving response itself must be freely willed. If, for example, the loving response were intentionally causally determined through manipulation by another agent, it would have no value. John Milton, in *Paradise Lost* ([1665] 2005, Book III, 101–108), asks if love for God would be valuable if God intentionally causally determined us to love him. In the poem, God provides a negative answer:

> Of true allegiance, constant Faith or Love
> Where only what they needs must do, appeared
> Not what they would? what praise could they receive?
> What pleasure I from such obedience paid
> When Will and Reason (Reason also is choice)
> Useless and vain, of freedom both despoiled
> Made passive both, had served necessity
> Not me.

But even if Milton is right about some such cases, perhaps only the specific character of the causal determination may be objectionable. Suppose Rachel, a specialist in neural stimulation devices, causally determines you to love her by manipulating your brain so that you are oblivious to the ways in which she can be difficult. That would be objectionable. However, imagine instead that you have a self-destructive disposition to love people who are harmful to you, and not to love those who would benefit you, partly because you have a tendency overlook people's valuable characteristics. Suppose Abby slips a drug into your coffee that eliminates this tendency, due to which you are now able to appreciate her valuable characteristics, and as a result you are causally determined to love her. How bad would that be? It would seem that what is unacceptable is not being causally determined to love by another party per se, but rather how one is causally determined, and that there are varieties of such determination that are not objectionable (Pereboom 2014, 192).

One might propose that free will has a key role in *maintaining* love over an extended period. Søren Kierkegaard ([1843] 1971) suggests that marriage ideally involves a commitment that is continuously renewed. Such a commitment involves a decision to devote oneself to the other, and thus, in his view, a marital relationship ideally involves a continuously repeated decision. A relationship with this type of voluntary aspect might in fact be very desirable. However, what might be added by these continuously repeated decisions being freely willed, by contrast with being a voluntary expression of what one deeply cares about? In sum, although one might at first have the sense that love that is freely willed is particularly valuable, it is unclear exactly how such free will might have a desirable role in producing, maintaining, or enhancing love (Pereboom 2001, 203–204; 2014, 190–193).

P. F. Strawson (1962) suggests a different way in which free will and responsibility may be required for meaningful personal relationships. In his view, moral responsibility has its foundation in the reactive attitudes, paradigmatic of which are moral resentment and indignation. In turn, these reactive attitudes and susceptibility to them are required for good personal relationships, given how we are psychologically constituted. According to Strawson, the only alternative is a clinical and cold objectivity of attitude, which would rob personal relationships of their value. But if free will sceptics are right, the rationality of resentment and indignation is jeopardized because they presuppose basic desert moral responsibility, which we lack. Such attitudes are accompanied by the presupposition that targeting the wrongdoer with their expression is deserved, and basically so. Given Strawson's view, free will scepticism would thus threaten good personal relationships and the meaning they confer on our lives (Pereboom 2001, 199–202; 2014, 178–186). Strawson thinks that our commitment to personal relationships rules out taking this threat seriously as a practical matter, and thus we have practical reason to ignore it.

Strawson is right to believe that a thoroughgoing objectivity of attitude of the sort that he envisions would indeed jeopardize our personal relationships. But I think that he is mistaken to hold that such a stance would result if we were to disavow moral resentment and indignation. These attitudes may have a valuable role in personal relationships insofar as they serve to effectively engage others when they act wrongly. However, when we are wronged in our relationships there are other emotions available for such engagement that are not threatened by scepticism about free will. Specifically, moral protest, without anger, can serve this purpose. As I see it, moral protest is a psychological stance, a posture of mind that has certain aims. It is a stance of opposition to an agent for having performed a specific immoral action or a number of immoral actions, or for having a disposition to act immorally. Its function in our moral practice is primarily to engage wrongdoers by communicating opposition to wrongdoing of a general type, together with moral reasons for the agent to refrain from it. Such communication might be confrontational to varying degrees, depending on the circumstances (Pereboom 2021). Moral protest can be supplemented by other attitudes that don't presuppose desert of pain or harm. These emotions include feeling hurt or shocked or disappointed about the wrongs offending agents have done, and moral sadness or sorrow and concern for them (Pereboom 2001; 199–202; 2014, 178–186). I hold out for the possibility that this set of emotions serves to enhance personal relationships relative to the reactive attitudes that Strawson prizes.

At times, moral resentment and indignation are likely to be beyond our power to affect, and thus even supposing that the free will sceptic is committed to doing what is right and rational, she would still be unable to eradicate these attitudes. Shaun Nichols (2007) cites the distinction between narrow-profile emotional responses, which are local or immediate emotional reactions to situations, and wide-profile responses, which are not immediate and can involve rational reflection. Free will sceptics would expect that we will not keep ourselves from some degree of narrow-profile, immediate resentment when we are seriously wronged in our most intimate personal relationships. However, in wide-profile cases, we might well have the ability to diminish, or even eliminate, resentment and indignation, or at least disavow it in the sense of rejecting any force it might be thought to have in justifying harmful reactions to the wrong done.

It's instructive to examine a valued kind of personal relationship in which it is not unusual for us to respond to expressions of disregard and disrespect with attitudes that are personal but not reactive. Very commonly, teenagers go through a period when they have attitudes of disregard and disrespect for parents, expression of which can result in deeply hurt feelings. But often such expressions of disregard and disrespect do not occasion the parents' resentment, but rather their disappointment and sadness (Pereboom 2017). Although these emotions are not reactive attitudes, they are nevertheless manifestations of vulnerability on the part of the parent. Crucially, they are also personal (Shabo 2012), since the teenager's attitudes towards his parents matter to them in their own right, apart from the consequences of these attitudes for their interests. Often parents in such situations are also resentful, but frequently they are not. Thus there are relationships very important to us in which our care for the other's attitudes is personal, but in which many of us are not subject to moral resentment.

Meaning in a Universe without Free Will

How do we conceive of our place in the great scheme of things, supposing that it precludes our having free will, perhaps because causal determinism is true? For many, the foremost source of meaning in life is the plan of the universe, and our role in it is of ultimate significance. The great theistic religions have provided conceptions of this kind, as have modern descendants of orthodox theisms whose conception of the divine is impersonal. A common theme is that such conceptions provide for greater equanimity in our lives through our understanding of the scheme and our place in it. In the theistic religions, the conception typically features divine providential governance of the universe. Whatever happens accords with a comprehensive divine plan that aims at the good, and this provides our lives with meaning.

Such a view is expressed in ancient Stoicism, as well as in Judaism, Christianity, and Islam. Human lives are subject to pain, deprivation, failure, and death, which in turn makes us vulnerable to anger and despair. How do we cope with these difficulties and the suffering they occasion? Accepting a strong notion of divine providence involves the conviction that everything that happens to us, to the last detail, is in accord with God's providential will. Comfort in life may be secured by the belief that even minor harms, let alone horrendous evils, cannot befall us unless God, who is perfectly benevolent, willingly causes or allows them to happen as part of the plan for the good of the universe. Here the ancient Stoic position is representative. God determines everything that happens in accord with the good of the entire universe, although the nature of this good is imperfectly understood on our part. By identifying with this all-encompassing divine plan, we can be reconciled with the world's evils. Equanimity and, more ambitiously, gratitude replace anger and despair as cosmic attitudes within our reach (Inwood 1985; Pereboom 1994; Bobzien 1998; Brennan 2005). The Stoic recommendation is that one should cease to regard the events of one's life solely from one's personal point of view, and instead appraise them by the purposes God has in creating and preserving the universe.

One might object that such identification with divine purposes is too demanding for us. Suppose that one's role in the divine plan involves suffering miserably up to a final end to one's existence. For many theists, the response is to specify that the providential plan not only aims at the good of the whole universe, but also at the good of the individual. As Marilyn Adams proposes, God is good to every person by ensuring each a life in which all suffering contributes to a great good within that very life (Adams 1999, 55). Then it might even be, as Alvin Plantinga (2004) suggests, that God would know that if I were able to make the decision whether to accept the suffering of my life, and knew enough about the divine plan, and had the right affections, I myself would accept that suffering.

Such conceptions of divine providence are seriously challenged by the existence of evil, both moral and natural, that appears not to be in service of any good. If an all-powerful, wholly benevolent, and providential being exists, then that being would have the power and the motivation to prevent all such evil. But there is such evil, so that conception faces a challenge. Responses to the problem of evil are far from decisive, but one might agree that they nevertheless allow for rational hope that a providential God exists (Jackson 2021; Pereboom 2021).

Is a hope of this general sort rational given a perspective that is not traditionally theistic or even atheistic? A conception that we see developed from the mid-eighteenth century onward focuses instead on the role of humanity in the great scheme. Humanity comes to be viewed as a force for inevitable and sustained progress in several dimensions. This theme was advanced by the German Idealists, of which Hegel is representative. Hegel ([1824] 1956) foregrounds a deterministic process of human rational development over the course of history, thereby recapturing the providential aspect of the deterministic scheme by conceiving human development itself as divine.

Hegel's conception of the progress of human history often met with incredulous resistance in the twentieth century. Adorno's retort, 'No universal history leads from savagery to humanitarianism, but there is one leading from the slingshot to the megaton bomb' (Adorno 1970, 312) is a representative reaction. Still, a theme that continued to attract is human progress in history in the long term. This idea was taken up by John Dewey, who advocated a 'common faith', a religious attitude broader than traditional theism. Its core feature is a 'sense of nature as the whole of which we are parts, while it also recognizes that we are parts that are marked by intelligence and purpose, having the capacity to strive by their aid to bring conditions into greater consonance with what is humanly desirable' (Dewey 1934, 25). Dewey's focus is not exclusively on the community of rational beings of which we are members, but on such a community embedded in nature, 'the enveloping world that the imagination feels is a universe' (Dewey 1934, 53). Hope, by contrast with belief, or perhaps even faith, is an appropriate attitude to invoke for humanity's survival in a thriving natural environment. This is partly because we're not assured of this outcome, while it is an open possibility. In addition, hope is apt in contexts in which we are dependent for an outcome on factors beyond our control. As Katie Stockdale (2019, 30) points out, hope reminds us of 'the kinds of creatures we are: we are creatures who, because of the constraints we necessarily and contingently face as agents, must depend on factors external to ourselves for many of our desires to be fulfilled.'

Theodore Parker, American transcendentalist, expresses the idea of continued human progress in its moral dimension in his reflections on the abolition of slavery, using a metaphor that has become familiar:

> We cannot understand the moral Universe. The arc is a long one, and our eyes reach but a little way; we cannot calculate the curve and complete the figure by the experience of sight; but we can divine it by conscience, and we surely know that it bends toward justice. Justice will not fail, though wickedness appears strong, and has on its side the armies and thrones of power, the riches and the glory of the world, and though poor men crouch down in despair. Justice will not fail and perish out from

the world of men, nor will what is really wrong and contrary to God's real law of justice continually endure. (Parker 1853)

In his speeches, Martin Luther King, Jr., also recommended that we envision, quoting Parker, that 'the arc of the moral universe is long, but it bends toward justice'. Parker claims knowledge, but hope is less demanding and more accessible.

What evidence do we have that Parker is right? In the last century humanity faced extremely serious challenges and calamities: two worldwide wars, mass genocide, terrorism, diseases, and epidemics. One might argue that we confronted these challenges with impressive success from the perspective of humanity generally, although not from the point of view of the millions who suffered and the millions who perished. Many of the most oppressive regimes that that century had witnessed have vanished, medical science made tremendous progress, technology advanced spectacularly, and knowledge in many fields saw immense expansion. On balance, were not threats to humanity effectively confronted, and advance achieved? If so, then we may hope that our intelligence, skill, and moral resolve is sufficient for overcoming the challenges humanity will face. And this hope is consistent with causal determinism, and does not depend on our having free will (Pereboom 2021).

REFERENCES

Adams, Marilyn McCord. 1999. *Horrendous Evils and the Goodness of God*. Ithaca, NY: Cornell University Press.
Adorno, Theodor W. 1970. *Negative Dialektik*. Frankfurt am Main: Suhrkamp.
Balaguer, Mark. 2010. *Free Will as an Open Scientific Problem*. Cambridge, MA: MIT Press.
Bobzien, Suzanne. 1998. *Determinism and Freedom in Stoic Philosophy*. Oxford: Oxford University Press.
Brennan, Tad. 2005. *The Stoic Life: Emotions, Duties, and Fate*. Oxford: Oxford University Press.
Caruso, Gregg D. 2012. *Free Will and Consciousness: A Determinist Account of the Illusion of Free Will*. Lanham, MD: Lexington Books.
Clarke, Randolph. 2003. *Libertarian Theories of Free Will*. New York: Oxford University Press.
Dewey, John. 1934. *A Common Faith*. New Haven, CT: Yale University Press.
Ekstrom, Laura W. 2000. *Free Will, A Philosophical Study*. Boulder, CO: Westview.
Feinberg, Joel. 1970. 'Justice and Personal Desert'. In Joel Feinberg, *Doing and Deserving* . Princeton, NJ: Princeton University Press pp 55–94.
Fischer, John Martin. 1994. *The Metaphysics of Free Will*. Oxford: Blackwell.
Focquaert, Farah. 2018. 'Neurobiology and Crime: A Neuro-Ethical Perspective'. *Journal of Criminal Justice* 65. doi:10.1016/j.jcrimjus.2018.01.001.
Greene, Joshua, and Jonathan D. Cohen. 2004. 'For the Law, Neuroscience Changes Nothing and Everything'. *Philosophical Transactions of the Royal Society of London, Series B: Biological Sciences* 359: 1775–1785.
Hegel, G. W. F. [1824] 1956. *The Philosophy of History*, trans. J. Sibree. New York: Dover Publications.
Honderich, Ted. 1988. *A Theory of Determinism*. Oxford: Oxford University Press.

Hume, David. [1739] 1978. *A Treatise of Human Nature*. Oxford: Oxford University Press.
Inwood, Brad. 1985. *Ethics and Human Action in Early Stoicism*. Oxford: Oxford University Press.
Jackson, Elizabeth. 2021. 'Belief, Faith, and Hope: On the Rationality of Long-Term Commitment'. *Mind* 130: 35–57.
Kane, Robert. 1996. *The Significance of Free Will*. New York: Oxford University Press.
Kierkegaard, Søren. [1843] 1971. *Either/Or*, vol. 2, trans. Walter Lowrie. Princeton, NJ: Princeton University Press.
Landau, Iddo. 1992. 'Sartre's Absolute Freedom in Being and Nothingness'. *Philosophy Today* 56(4): 463–473.
Levy, Neil. 2011. *Hard Luck: How Luck Undermines Free Will and Moral Responsibility*. Oxford: Oxford University Press.
Mele, Alfred. 2006. *Free Will and Luck*. New York: Oxford University Press.
Milam, Per-Erik. 2016. 'Reactive Attitudes and Personal Relationships'. *Canadian Journal of Philosophy* 42: 102–122.
Milton, John. [1665] 2005. *Paradise Lost*. New York: W. W. Norton.
Morris, Stephen. 2018. 'The Implications of Rejecting Free Will: An Empirical Analysis'. *Philosophical Psychology* 31(2): 299–321.
Nadelhoffer, Thomas. 2011. 'The Threat of Shrinking Agency and Free Will Disillusionism'. In *Conscious Will and Responsibility*, ed. Lynne Nadel and Walter Sinnott-Armstrong, 173–188. Oxford: Oxford University Press.
Nahmias, Eddy. 2011. 'Intuitions about Free Will, Determinism, and Bypassing'. In *The Oxford Handbook of Free Will*, 2nd ed., ed. Robert Kane, 555–576. New York: Oxford University Press.
Nichols, Shaun. 2007. "After Compatibilism: A Naturalistic Defense of the Reactive Attitudes," *Philosophical Perspectives* 21: 405–428.
O'Connor, Timothy. 2000. *Persons and Causes*. New York: Oxford University Press.
Parker, Theodore. 1853. 'Of Justice and the Conscience'. In In Theodore Parker, *Ten Sermons of Religion by Theodore Parker*. Boston: Crosby, Nichols.
Pereboom, Derk. 1994. 'Stoic Psychotherapy in Descartes and Spinoza'. *Faith and Philosophy* 11: 592–625.
Pereboom, Derk. 1995. 'Determinism *Al Dente*'. *Noûs* 29: 21–45.
Pereboom, Derk. 2001. *Living without Free Will*. Cambridge: Cambridge University Press.
Pereboom, Derk. 2014. *Free Will, Agency, and Meaning in Life*. Oxford: Oxford University Press.
Pereboom, Derk. 2017. 'Responsibility, Agency, and the Disappearing Agent Objection'. In *Le Libre-Arbitre, approches contemporaines*, ed. Jean-Baptiste Guillon, 1–18. Paris: Collège de France.
Pereboom, Derk. 2021. *Wrongdoing and the Moral Emotions*. Oxford: Oxford University Press.
Plantinga, Alvin. 2004. 'Supralapsarianism, or "O Felix Culpa"'. In *Christian Faith and the Problem of Evil*, ed. Peter van Inwagen. Grand Rapids, MI: Eerdmans, pp 1–25.
Rosen, Gideon. 2004. 'Skepticism about Moral Responsibility'. *Philosophical Perspectives* 18 (Ethics): 295–313.
Sartre, Jean-Paul. [1946] 1956. 'Existentialism Is a Humanism'. in *Existentialism from Dostoevsky to Sartre*, ed. Walter Kauffman, 287–311. New York: Meridian Books.
Schopenhauer, Arthur. [1818] 1961. *The World as Will and Idea* (later translated as *The World as Will and Representation*), trans. R. B. Haldane and J. Kemp. Garden City, NY: Doubleday. .
Shabo, Seth. 2012. 'Where Love and Resentment Meet: Strawson's Interpersonal Defense of Compatibilism'. *The Philosophical Review* 121: 95–124.
Smilansky, Saul. 2000. *Free Will and Illusion*. New York: Oxford University Press.

Spinoza. [1677] 1985. 'Ethics'. In *The Collected Works of Spinoza*, ed. and trans. Edwin Curley, Vol. 1. Princeton NJ: Princeton University Press.
Stockdale, Katie. 2019. 'Social and Political Dimensions of Hope'. *The Journal of Social Philosophy* 50: 28–44.
Strawson, Galen. 1986. *Freedom and Belief*. Oxford: Oxford University Press.
Strawson, Peter F. 1962. 'Freedom and Resentment'. *Proceedings of the British Academy* 48: 187–211.
Taylor, Richard. 1974. *Metaphysics*, 4th ed. Englewood Cliffs, NJ: Prentice-Hall.
Vilhauer, Benjamin. 2012. 'Taking Free Will Skepticism Seriously'. *Philosophical Quarterly* 62: 833–852.
Wallace, R. Jay. 1994. *Responsibility and the Moral Sentiments*. Cambridge, MA: Harvard University Press.
Waller, Bruce. 1990. *Freedom without Responsibility*. Philadelphia: Temple University Press.
Waller, Bruce. 2011. *Against Moral Responsibility*. Cambridge, MA: MIT Press.
Wegner, Daniel. 2002. *The Illusion of Conscious Will*. Cambridge, MA: MIT Press.
Wolf, Susan. 1990. *Freedom within Reason*. Oxford: Oxford University Press.

CHAPTER 11

MEANING IN LIFE AND THE NATURE OF TIME

NED MARKOSIAN

1. INTRODUCTION

ACCORDING to Susan Wolf, a person's life is meaningful insofar as it contains love on the part of the agent for objects that are worthy of love, together with actions that are guided by that love (Wolf 2010). Musicians practice their instruments, and play their music, at least partly out of a love for music, and for this reason their hard work and their playing contribute to their lives being meaningful. Similarly with parents, and friends, and even philosophers. On Wolf's view, experiencing love for something that is worthy of love and acting on that love are what makes our lives meaningful.

Thaddeus Metz has a different view. On his account, there are three main things that contribute to a life's having great meaning: moral achievement, intellectual discovery, and aesthetic creation (Metz 2011). And what these three activities have in common is that they all involve an important kind of self-transcendence, whereby the agent transcends some aspect of themself in a substantial way. To oversimplify somewhat, Metz thinks that achieving self-transcendence with respect to the good, the true, and the beautiful is the main thing that makes a life meaningful. Thus, this kind of self-transcendence is the main goal that we should all be aiming for.

An alternative to Wolf's and Metz's views, defended by Ben Bramble, is the idea that what makes one's life meaningful is the simple fact (if it is a fact) that one's life contributes to the world's being better than it otherwise would be (Bramble 2015). Some version of this view was popular among teachers and parents of the kids of my generation, who taught us that what makes our lives meaningful is working to make the world a better place. 'Leave the campsite better than you found it,' as they often said.

I will not here attempt to adjudicate among these different theories (or any of their several plausible rivals) about meaning in life.[1] Instead, I will just note that what these three theories about meaning in life have in common is that they all emphasize the importance of striving for something (even if they disagree about what it is that we ought to be striving for). To the extent that an agent works towards a certain goal, on these theories, that agent's life is meaningful. Thus the theories of Metz, Wolf, and Bramble (as well as many other plausible theories about meaning in life) are all goal-based theories of meaning in life. According to these theories, what makes a life meaningful is working towards a certain goal (or perhaps a certain kind of goal).

None of this will be surprising to anyone who has come across this volume. For anyone who has thought a little bit about meaning in life will have at least taken seriously the idea that working toward some kind of goal is essential to a meaningful life. Perhaps, in the end, you will conclude that this idea is mistaken, and that it is in fact possible to have a perfectly meaningful life without ever working toward any particular goal. But for most of us, reaching that conclusion would require some non-trivial revision of our core beliefs.

Given all of this, here is something that is surprising: There are two main theories about the nature of time that have been defended in the contemporary literature on the metaphysics of time, and on one of them, it is very difficult (maybe even impossible) to make sense of the idea that one ought to be working toward a certain goal, if one hopes to have a meaningful life. In what follows, I will first lay out the two main theories about the nature of time. Then I will show that one of them—The Dynamic Theory of Time—is well-suited to accommodate goal-based views of meaning in life, but that the other—The Static Theory of Time—is not. I will also argue that The Static Theory runs into problems when it comes to accommodating the general phenomenon of having and pursuing goals. Finally, I will consider the possibility that, despite all of this, we should stick with The Static Theory of Time, and revise some of our thinking about whether and in what way our lives can be meaningful.

2. Two Theories about the Nature of Time

It is fair to say that The Static Theory of Time has been the majority view about the nature of time among scientists and analytic philosophers (who tend to follow the lead of scientists) since early in the twentieth century. The guiding thought behind The Static Theory is that time is similar in important ways to space. One main way in which time

---

[1] For an excellent survey of some of the leading theories about what makes a person's life meaningful, see Metz (2013).

is supposed to be like space, on this theory, is that the universe is spread out in four dimensions, which together make up a unified manifold that is appropriately called *spacetime*. This is usually taken to be a consequence of the Special Theory of Relativity. It is also normally thought to be a consequence of Special Relativity that there is no privileged way of orienting the four-dimensional manifold. Some dimensions are said to be 'time-like', but, on this view, there is no single, special dimension that deserves the name 'time'.[2]

A second way in which time is supposed to be like space, on The Static Theory of Time, has to do with the way physical objects are extended in time. On this view, physical objects have *temporal parts*. To get a handle on the idea of a temporal part, think of a film strip showing you as you walk across a room. The film strip is made up of many frames, and each frame shows you at a particular moment of time. Now imagine cutting the frames, and stacking them, one on top of another, in chronological order. Finally, turn the stack sideways, so that the two-dimensional images of you are all right side up. Each image of you in a frame corresponds to a *temporal part* of you, in a specific position, at a particular location in space, at a single moment of time. And what you are, on this view, is the fusion of all of these temporal parts. You are a 'spacetime worm' that curves through the four-dimensional manifold known as *spacetime*. Also, on this view, what it is to have a momentary property at a time is to have a temporal part at that time that has the property in question. So you are sitting right now in virtue of the fact that your current temporal part is sitting.

A third way in which time is supposed to be like space, on The Static Theory, is that no single moment is special. A good way to illustrate this is to imagine taking the filmstrip for the entire universe, and then cutting and stacking the frames. Now you have something—a gigantic block of movie frames—that represents the entire history of the universe. Each frame in this block represents the universe at a moment of time (so the universe has temporal parts, too), and we can see by the way the frames are arranged which ones are earlier than which other ones. But there is no single one of the frames that is privileged. There is no present moment. (Just as no location in space is privileged.)

Here is some terminology that has proven to be useful in stating this aspect of The Static Theory.[3]

A-properties: putative temporal properties such as *being present, being past, being future, being four days future*, etc.
B-relations: temporal relations such as *simultaneous with, earlier than, later than, four days later than*, etc.

---

[2] For the record, I do not think these things really are consequences of Special Relativity. And in fact, quite a few philosophers have resisted arguments for the Static Theory from Special Relativity. See e.g. Emery (2019); Hinchliff (2000); Miller (2004); Markosian (2004, Section 3.9); and Zimmerman (2008, 218–221).
[3] These terms are from Markosian (1993).

On The Static Theory, there are no genuine A-properties, and there are no objective facts about which moments are past, present, or future. (This is why the definition of A-properties contains the word 'putative'—because it is controversial whether there are such things as A-properties. But all parties to the dispute believe in B-relations, which is why the definition of B-relations does not contain 'putative'.) If someone says today, 'My 30th birthday is two years in the future', then, according to The Static Theory, they express the proposition that their birthday is two years later than the time of their utterance. That is, they are talking about B-relations rather than A-properties.

Another way in which time is supposed to be like space, on The Static Theory, has to do with ontology. Everyone agrees that the correct ontology doesn't change from one place to the next. Even if we are in western Massachusetts, we need to include the Brooklyn Bridge in the correct ontology. It's on the list of everything that exists, regardless of where we are as we compile the list. On The Static Theory, it is the same with time: the correct ontology doesn't change from one time to another. So all objects from every region of spacetime are to be included in the one correct ontology.

Here then are six ways in which time is meant to be like space, on The Static Theory of Time.[4] (Note: What I am calling The Static Theory of Time is a natural and popular combination of related theses, but it is not inevitable. It is possible to mix and match.)

The Static Theory of Time

(1) The universe is spread out in four dimensions, which together make up a unified, four-dimensional manifold (appropriately called *spacetime*) in which physical objects are located.
(2) Any physical object that persists through time does so in virtue of having a distinct temporal part for each moment at which it is located.
(3) There are no genuine and irreducible *A-properties*; all talk that appears to be about *A-properties* can be correctly analysed in terms of *B-relations*.
(4) The temporal facts about the world include facts about *B-relations*, but they do not include any facts about *A-properties*.
(5) We do not need to take tense seriously. Propositions have truth values *simpliciter* rather than at times, and so cannot change their truth values over time. Also, we can in principle eliminate verbal tenses like *is*, *was*, and *will be* from an ideal language.
(6) The correct ontology does not change over time, and it always includes objects from every region of spacetime.

---

[4] Some or all of the following components of the Static Theory can be found in Williams (1951); Price (1977); Smart (1966); Lewis (1976); Lewis (1986); Sider (2001); Hawley (2001); and Moss (2012) (as well as many other places).

Static Theorists admit that time *seems* special to us, and even that time seems to pass. But they insist that this is just a subjective feature of how we happen to perceive the world, and not a feature of objective reality that is independent of us.[5]

Let me now turn to The Dynamic Theory of Time. The guiding thought behind The Dynamic Theory is that time is very different from space. One important difference between time and space, on The Dynamic Theory, is that time cannot be added to the dimensions of space to form a unified manifold. Although talking about 'spacetime' is a useful way to codify information about the spread of objects and events in space and time (including information about spatial and temporal locations as well as the laws of nature), it does not follow that space and time actually form a unified manifold in any important sense.[6]

A closely related difference between time and space, on The Dynamic Theory, is that physical objects are not spacetime worms that are extended in time in virtue of having different temporal parts at different times. Instead, each physical object is wholly present at each time at which it is present.[7] It's not a mere *temporal part* of you that is sitting in your chair right now, on this view. It's you.

Another important claim of The Dynamic Theory is that the passage of time is a real, objective, and mind-independent feature of the world, one that makes time very different from the dimensions of space. Opponents of The Dynamic Theory (and sometimes proponents as well) like to characterize the theory using the metaphor of a moving spotlight that slides along the temporal dimension, brightly illuminating just one moment of time, the present, while the future is a kind of foggy region of potential and the past is a shadowy realm of has-beens. This moving spotlight metaphor is an intuitively appealing way to capture The Dynamic Theory, but at the end of the day it is just a metaphor. What the metaphor represents is the essential idea behind The Dynamic Theory, namely, the idea that A-properties like *being future*, *being present*, and *being past* are objective and metaphysically significant properties of times, events, and things. Also, the metaphor of the moving spotlight represents the fact that according to The Dynamic Theory, each time undergoes a somewhat peculiar but inexorable process, sometimes called *temporal becoming*. It goes from being in the distant future to being in the near future, has a brief moment of glory in the present, and then recedes forever further and further into the past.

Despite its being intuitively appealing (especially for Static Theorists, many of whom see it as a caricature of The Dynamic Theory), the moving spotlight metaphor has a major drawback: It encourages us to think of time as a fourth dimension, akin to the dimensions of space. On The Dynamic Theory (as I am conceiving it), this way of thinking—'spatializing time'—is a major no-no. For it is not that there are these four orthogonal dimensions, and one of them—time—has some extra bells and whistles added

---

[5] See e.g. Williams (1951) and Paul (2010).

[6] For a recent argument against the claim that space and time form a unified manifold of orthogonal dimensions, see Markosian (2020b).

[7] For a definition of 'wholly present' see Markosian (1994, 248).

to it. Instead, it is that time is completely different from the dimensions of space—so different, in fact, that it is not even the same kind of dimension. (Just as neither *the moral dimension* nor *the modal dimension* is the same kind of dimension as space. For one cannot stick either of those dimensions onto the three spatial dimensions in order to produce a unified manifold in which physical objects can literally be placed.)

Yet another difference between time and space, on The Dynamic Theory, has to do with ontology. On The Dynamic Theory, the correct ontology does in fact change over time, and it always includes only objects that are present at a given time, never objects that are merely past (like Hypatia) or merely future (like my future grandchildren).

Here, then, is the view.[8] (Note: Like The Static Theory, The Dynamic Theory of Time, as I am formulating it here, is a natural and popular combination of related theses. But it is not inevitable. It is possible to mix and match.)

The Dynamic Theory of Time

(1) Time cannot be added to the dimensions of space to form a unified manifold in which physical objects are located.
(2) Any physical object that persists through time does so in virtue of being wholly present at each moment at which it is present.
(3) There are genuine and irreducible *A-properties*, which cannot be correctly analysed in terms of *B-relations*.
(4) The temporal facts about the world include ever-changing facts involving *A-properties*, including facts about which times are past, which time is present, and which times are future.
(5) We must take tense seriously. Propositions have truth values at times rather than *simpliciter* and can, in principle, change their truth values over time. Also, we cannot eliminate verbal tenses like *is*, *was*, and *will be* from an ideal language.
(6) The correct ontology is liable to change over time, and it is always true that only present objects exist.

Here are some better metaphors for these two theories of time.[9] For The Static Theory, the universe is like a movie that is never shown. The frames are all there, but the movie is just sitting on a shelf, in the dark. Also, instead of being attached end to end, the frames are stacked, one on top of another. Each frame is a temporal slice of the world, and if you look closely you can see the various objects—each of which is a 'spacetime worm'—curving through the four-dimensional continuum that is spacetime. But because the

---

[8] Some or all of the following components of the Dynamic Theory can be found in Prior (1967); Thomson (1983); Markosian (1993, 2004, 2020a); and Sullivan (2012) (not to mention many other places).

[9] The following metaphors for our two theories of time are borrowed from Markosian (2020a).

movie is never shown, no part of it is metaphysically privileged. There is no light shining on any one frame; no frame is special.

For The Dynamic Theory, on the other hand, the universe is like a movie that is being shown in a theatre *right now*. But it's not the frames that are the universe. Instead, it is the image on the screen. There is only one image on the screen, and it keeps changing. That's because reality is one thing that keeps changing. It *was* that way, now it *is* this way. Soon it *will be* some other way. The movie frames in the projection booth are a useful way to represent the different states of the universe at different times—they are like maximal, consistent, tensed propositions. And there is always one of them that is special: the one that corresponds to the image on the screen right now. (But it is important to understand that which frames are in the film, and which one has a light shining through it right now, is determined by the universe, and not the other way around. So this is an important disanalogy between the universe and a movie being shown in a theatre.)

Now that we have our two theories of time before us, we can return to the question of what makes a life meaningful, and the question of whether goal-based theories of meaning in life are consistent with each of our two theories of time.

3. The Dynamic Theory of Time and Meaning in Life

One way to see that The Dynamic Theory of Time is *prima facie* consistent with having a goal such as making the world better is to recall that on that theory, there is one reality, and it keeps changing. Hence it is appropriate to work toward making it—the one reality—change for the better. This can mean taking action to improve things, or it can mean taking action to prevent things from getting worse. And similar remarks will apply to the goals associated with other goal-based theories about what makes a life meaningful. All of this seems to follow from The Dynamic Theory picture of the universe as an enduring and evolving entity. For we can sensibly work to make it evolve in one particular way rather than some other way.

Moreover, there are also available to the Dynamic Theorist very straightforward accounts of what it is to act, and what it is to have an effect. Here the movie metaphors are helpful. On The Dynamic Theory, you are an enduring character in the movie (rather than a spacetime worm curving through a granite-like block of movie frames), and you act by doing things, right up there on the big screen. Hence it is natural to think that the actions you perform now will have many effects in the future. You are a part of the present scene, and what you are doing now will affect what subsequent scenes will look like.

There is a similarly straightforward picture of causation that goes naturally with The Dynamic Theory. On the most naïve version of this picture, an event occurs (a cue ball rolling into an eight ball, for example), resulting in certain forces propagating around, in accordance with the laws of nature. Those forces in turn will result in certain other events happening (the eight ball rolling into the corner pocket, for example), and those other events will be the effects of the first event. All of these events unfold on the big screen, one after another, and although it might be difficult to give a satisfying philosophical analysis of causation, there is nothing puzzling about the intuitive idea that the current events taking place on the screen right now will produce the events that follow them—events that are not occurring yet, but will occur in the future. There are various more sophisticated ways of filling in the details of this naïve picture of causation, but they all involve giving an account of the one reality evolving in accordance with the laws of nature and the rules of causation.[10]

This means that, on this picture, causes literally produce their effects. If we are watching the movie, and one character is currently tidying up a campsite, the resulting state of affairs—the campsite's being tidy—will be a direct result of that character's efforts. In a very straightforward and literal way, the character is making the world better. And when we get to the scene showing the tidy campsite, we will know exactly what caused it to be that way. Similarly, if the current scene includes a character working hard toward the kind of self-enhancement that Metz talks about, then when we arrive at the relevant later scene, in which that character has, say, a better understanding of the true, then that state of affairs will be a direct result of this current one.

This picture of causation also leads to a relatively straightforward account of what it means to have a goal, what it means to work toward your goal, and what it means to hope you succeed. The goal is that the universe should evolve in a certain way (in a good way rather than a bad way, or in an increased-appreciation-for-the-true way rather than some other way). And as an active player in the evolving movie, you get to work toward that goal by trying to shape the evolution of the universe. (It can of course be hard to do this. But at least it is possible, and a reasonable goal to have.) Hoping that you will succeed amounts to hoping that as a result of your efforts, the universe will evolve in the desired way. You are hoping that the universe—the one reality, which keeps changing—will improve as a result of your efforts.

In short, because the world is an enduring thing (that is, one that persists through time by being wholly present at each different time, rather than by having different temporal parts at the different times), because the present moment enjoys a special status, because the future is coming, and because the world evolves as time passes, it is eminently reasonable to try to use your power as a player in the universe to make the world better (or to increase your own self-enhancement, or to act from love for things that are worthy of love), and also eminently reasonable to hope that you will succeed at your preferred goal.

The upshot is that on The Dynamic Theory of Time, goal-based views of what makes life meaningful make perfect sense. There is one reality that keeps changing, so it is natural to think that we ought to try to make it change in a certain way. Making the world

---

[10] For an excellent overview of contemporary theories of causation, see Paul and Hall (2013).

change in some specific way is a goal that it is appropriate to aim for, and once you adopt such an aim, achieving that goal is something that it makes sense to hope for. Moreover, it is worth noting that even if you happen to reject all of the goal-based views of meaning in life, The Dynamic Theory of Time still gives you a natural way to understand the general idea of having a goal and working to succeed at it.

4. The Static Theory of Time and Meaning in Life

Things are very different, however, on The Static Theory of Time. To see why this theory is *prima facie* in tension with a goal such as making the world better, think of the movie metaphor for this theory. And recall that all of the frames in the movie already exist, with none of them being privileged in any way. Hence it is hard to see how you—a spacetime worm that is like a small, thin wire stuck in the middle of a gigantic block of granite—could change anything about any of the later parts of the block. Those other parts are already there—you might as well try to make things better in regions to the east of you, or regions that are earlier than you. All of the other frames that make up the universe, regardless of their specific location in time, are just as real as the current frame containing you. Hence you don't seem to be able to make things better in these other regions of the block, or even to prevent them from being worse than they are. All of this seems to follow directly from The Static Theory's claim that ours is a static world rather than a dynamic and evolving one.

When one tries to spell out the details of what it is to act, and what it is to have an effect, on The Static Theory, things only become worse. For the Static Theorist has to give a not-so-straightforward account of acting, and having an effect. You are a tiny spacetime worm curving through some of the frames in the four-dimensional block that is the universe. So you perform an action in virtue of having a temporal part that performs that action (or perhaps by having a series of temporal parts that perform the temporal parts of the action). And then your action has a certain effect if something in a later frame is causally connected to your action in this frame.

But the idea of causation is very puzzling on this theory! The reason is that the whole of the universe is already there. We have these events over here, and those events over there, and they are all equally real, and all equally unprivileged. This picture of reality is hard to reconcile with the idea that to cause something is to make it happen. How do these events over here make those events over there happen, if they are all already contained in the gigantic block?

It turns out that there are two main accounts of causation in a static universe that are popular among proponents of The Static Theory of Time. The first one is the Counterfactual Dependence Theory of Causation. On this theory, an event, e_1, causes an event, e_2, iff e_1 and e_2 both occur, and if e_1 had not occurred, then e_2 would not have occurred.[11] In short, e_1 causes e_2 iff the nearest world where e_1 doesn't happen is a world where e_2 doesn't happen. Notice that this does not rule out backwards causation, or simultaneous causation. For this account of causation is not based on a picture of the universe as an enduring and evolving thing. Instead, it is based on a picture of the universe as consisting of an enormous block of movie frames (the temporal parts), none of which is more real than any other, and none of which ever has a special property of being present. On the Counterfactual Dependence Theory of Causation, we might say, causation is nothing more than a peculiar, 'otherworldly' relation between the events in one region of spacetime and the events in another.

The second main account of causation in a static universe that is popular among proponents of The Static Theory of Time is based on the thesis known as *Humean Supervenience*. (This account is actually consistent with the Counterfactual Dependence account. For many Static Theorists, this is just the more detailed version of their view about causation.) Humean Supervenience is the thesis that the most fundamental facts about the world—the ones that determine all other facts—are facts about the point-by-point distribution of qualities over all of spacetime.[12] This distribution of qualities is known as 'the Humean mosaic'. Facts about the laws of nature are grounded in these facts about the Humean mosaic. For the laws of nature are just the most basic patterns and generalizations to be found within the mosaic. (The laws generalize and systematize, on this view, but they don't actually *govern*, in the sense of forcing things to happen in a certain way.) And then the facts about causation are in turn grounded by these nomological facts: e_1 causes e_2 iff the Humean mosaic is such that the laws of nature are such that e_2 is a lawful successor of e_1.

So on this picture, all the frames, with all of their contents, are given first. That is the universe. Then there are some derivative facts about the laws of nature. These are generalizations that percolate up from the facts on the ground. And there are some further derivative facts about which events in the four-dimensional spread stand in causal relations to which other events in the four-dimensional spread. But these facts, too, percolate up from the facts on the ground.

It is notable that on this account, whether e_1 is a cause of e_2 depends very much on the entire spread of events throughout all of spacetime, and not just on what happens between e_1 and e_2. There are worlds that are duplicates through the year 2525, only to diverge after that, and are also such that for two events in 2021, e_1 and e_2, e_1 causes e_2 in the first world but not in the second world (due to the general patterns in the universe being different, purely as a result of differences in the frames after 2525).

No doubt there are other possible accounts of causation available to the Static Theorist. But they all share this one main feature: They all involve saying that facts about causal relations between events are grounded in more fundamental facts about the spread of events in all of spacetime. For they all incorporate the Static Theory claims about (a) the

---

[11] This is only a rough characterization of the view. For a more thorough discussion, see Lewis (1973).
[12] This too is a simplification. For a proper discussion of Humean Supervenience, see Lewis (1994).

world being a four-dimensional block, with no privileged present, and (b) all things and all events, from every region of spacetime, being equally real. Another way to say this is that any theory of causation available to the Static Theorist will have to incorporate the Static Theory claim that the universe is a block of movie frames that all exist at once.

All of this in turn means that the Static Theorist has to give a completely unstraightforward account of what it is to have a goal, what it is to work toward your goal, and what it is to hope you succeed. To have a goal is to have the aim that a later state of the universe be a particular way, despite the fact that it already either is that way or not. (So your 'goal' is that a particular later frame in the already existing block should look a certain way—with a tidy campsite, for example.) To work toward a goal is for your current temporal part to perform a certain action in order that a later state of the universe be a certain way—again, despite the fact that it already either is that way or not. (You are working toward the goal of having that later frame, which is already there, contain a tidy campsite.) To hope that you succeed at your goal is to hope that a later state of the universe is a certain way, and also to hope that in the nearest world where your current temporal part does not perform your current action, the corresponding later state of the world is not the relevant way. (You are hoping that a particular later frame looks a certain way, and also hoping that in the nearest world where you do not perform this current action, the relevant later frame looks ... worse.) Or, alternatively, to hope that you succeed at your goal is to hope that a later state of the universe is a certain way, and also to hope that the entire Humean mosaic is such that the combination of the action performed by your current temporal part and the relevant later state of the world fits into one of the most basic patterns to be found in the spread of qualities over all of spacetime. (So you are both hoping that a particular later frame, which already exists and already is whatever way it is, looks a certain way, and also hoping that the rest of the frames in the universe are such that your current temporal part and this particular later frame instantiate a certain general pattern to be found throughout the entirety of the block of frames.)

To hope that your current action will make the world better, then, amounts to either (a) hoping that the nearest world in which you don't perform this current action is less good than the actual world, or else (b) hoping that the entire Humean mosaic is such that your current action and some later, better state of the world fit a basic and universal pattern. Neither of these things, I would submit, is a satisfying or plausible way to cash out the sentence, 'I hope that what I am doing now will make the world a better place'.

The upshot is that on The Static Theory of Time, Bramble's consequentialist account of meaning in life makes little sense. Because the universe is static rather than evolving, the having of goals in general must be understood in a rather complicated and indirect way, and this applies in particular to the goal of making the world better. Moreover, to hope that the world will be made better by your current action is to have a hope that is about much more than what the world will be like at later times. For it is either (a) partly about some other possible worlds, or (b) partly about the patterns to be found in the entire spread of things and events in all of spacetime. Strange!

Note that the strangeness does not go away if the Static Theorist simply gives up the consequentialist account of meaning in life. If we replace *Make the world better* with some other goal (such as *Achieve self-enhancement*) as our answer to the question *What makes a life meaningful?*, the problem will still arise. For the problem is that the whole idea of working toward a goal, and hoping to succeed at accomplishing that goal, can only be understood by the Static Theorist in a strange and convoluted way. This is a general problem for any Static Theorist with goals, but it is especially a problem for a Static Theorist who takes seriously the idea that there is some main goal, or some small number of main goals, that are especially relevant to making our lives meaningful.

This last point is particularly important in the present context. For what we have seen is not only that The Static Theory of Time seems to be incompatible with the consequentialist account of meaning in life. We have also seen that The Static Theory seems to be incompatible with any view according to which there is some goal (or some small number of goals) that all of us should be pursuing, in order to make our lives meaningful. That is, The Static Theory appears to be incompatible with the consequentialist account of meaning in life, and also with each one of its goal-based rivals (including Metz's and Wolf's).

5. Conclusion

I am inclined to think that the correct moral to draw from these considerations is that we should endorse The Dynamic Theory of Time over The Static Theory of Time. But I was already inclined to endorse The Dynamic Theory, and your mileage may vary. For their part, many Static Theorists will want to conclude that the correct moral here is that we must find an alternative to the goal-based theories of what makes a life meaningful. As far as I can tell, however, there are not a great many options along these lines, either in the philosophical literature or in common-sense thought about the topic. So there is work to be done for Static Theorists who want to give a positive account of what makes our lives meaningful.

Another option for the Static Theorist is to accept that some goal-based account of what makes life meaningful (such as Metz's) is correct, but also to accept some nonstandard (and counterintuitive) account of what it is to have a goal and what it is to work toward a goal. One might bite the bullet described earlier, for example, and say (i) that to have Metzian self-enhancement as a goal is just to hope that some already existing, later stage of the universe contains a temporal part of yourself that is better than the current temporal part of yourself in the relevant way; and (ii) that working toward this goal amounts to taking actions that you either (a) hope will be counterfactually related in the appropriate way to those later, enhanced temporal parts of yourself, or else (b) hope will, together with the later, enhanced temporal parts of yourself, fit into a general pattern to be found in the entire block of frames that is the universe. In short, some Static

Theorists may simply want to bite the bullet and accept a non-standard account of the having of goals.

There is a third moral that might be drawn by a Static Theorist (although I do not recommend it). Perhaps the Static Theorist will conclude from the preceding considerations that our lives are in fact meaningless.[13] Perhaps the Static Theorist will say that when we take into account the idea that the universe is a static and eternal block of temporal and spatial parts stretching forever in every direction, the appropriate conclusion to draw is that nothing matters.[14]

REFERENCES

Benatar, David. 2017. *The Human Predicament.* Oxford: Oxford University Press.
Bramble, Ben. 2015. 'Consequentialism about Meaning in Life'. *Utilitas* 27: 445–459.
Emery, Nina. 2019. 'Actualism without Presentism? Not by Way of the Relativity Objection'. *Nous* 53: 963–986.
Hawley, Katherine, 2001. *How Things Persist.* Oxford: Oxford University Press.
Hinchliff, Mark. 2000. 'A Defense of Presentism in a Relativistic Setting'. *Philosophy of Science* 67: S575–S586.
Lewis, David. 1973. 'Causation'. *The Journal of Philosophy* 70: 556–567.
Lewis, Davis. 1976. 'The Paradoxes of Time Travel'. *American Philosophical Quarterly* 13: 145–152.
Lewis, David. 1994. 'Humean Supervenience Debugged'. *Mind* 103: 473–490.
Lewis, David. 1986. *On the Plurality of Worlds.* Oxford: Blackwell.
Markosian, Ned. 1993. 'How Fast Does Time Pass?' *Philosophy and Phenomenological Research* 53: 829–844.
Markosian, Ned. 1994. 'The 3D/4D Controversy and Non-present Objects'. *Philosophical Papers* 23: 243–249.
Markosian, Ned. 2004. 'A Defense of Presentism'. In *Oxford Studies in Metaphysics*, vol. 1, ed. Dean Zimmerman. Oxford: Oxford University Press), pp 47–82.
Markosian, Ned. 2020a. 'The Dynamic Theory of Time and Time Travel to the Past'. *Disputatio* XII: 137–165.
Markosian, Ned. 2020b. 'Sideways Music'. *Analysis* 80: 51–59.
Metz, Thaddeus. 2011. 'The Good, the True and the Beautiful: Towards a Unified Account of Great Meaning in Life'. *Religious Studies* 47: 389–409.

---

[13] After all, many thinkers have already reached this conclusion, for independent reasons; see e.g. Schopenhauer ([1844] 1969); Tartaglia (2016); and, to a lesser degree, Benatar (2017). It is not clear that the arguments presented here will be of any help to traditional 'meaning in life pessimists', however, and it is also not clear that the Static Theorist will want to sign up for the views offered by the traditional pessimists. For the traditional pessimists often give arguments for their view that presuppose something like the Dynamic Theory of Time. There is, for example, the often-heard argument that there can be no meaning to our lives, since the universe is heading inexorably towards its eventual heat death, and there is nothing anyone can do about that.

[14] I am very grateful to David Friedell, Robert Gruber, and (especially) Iddo Landau for helpful feedback on earlier versions of this article.

Metz, Thaddeus. 2013. 'The Meaning of Life'. In *The Stanford Encyclopedia of Philosophy*, ed. Edward N. Zalta. <https://plato.stanford.edu/archives/sum2013/entries/life-meaning/>.

Miller, Kristie. 2004. 'Enduring Special Relativity'. *The Southern Journal of Philosophy* 42: 349–370.

Moss, Sarah. 2012. 'Four-Dimensionalist Theories of Persistence'. *Australasian Journal of Philosophy* 90: 671–686.

Paul, L. A. 2010. 'Temporal Experience'. *The Journal of Philosophy* 107: 333–359.

Paul, L. A., and Ned Hall. 2013. *Causation: A User's Guide*. Oxford: Oxford University Press.

Price, Marjorie. 1977. 'Identity Through Time'. *The Journal of Philosophy* 74: 201–217.

Prior, Arthur N. 1967. *Past, Present and Future*. Oxford: Oxford University Press.

Schopenhauer, Arthur. [1844] 1969. *The World as Will and Representation*. New York: Dover.

Sider, Theodore. 2001. *Four-Dimensionalism*. Oxford: Oxford University Press.

Smart, J. J. C. 1966. 'The River of Time'. In *Essays in Conceptual Analysis*, ed. Antony Flew, 213–227. New York: St. Martin's Press.

Sullivan, Meghan. 2012. 'The Minimal A-Theory'. *Philosophical Studies* 158: 149–174.

Tartaglia, James. 2016. *Philosophy in a Meaningless Life: A System of Nihilism, Consciousness and Reality*. London: Bloomsbury.

Thomson, Judith Jarvis. 1983. 'Parthood and Identity across Time'. *The Journal of Philosophy* 80: 201–220.

Williams, Donald C. 1951. 'The Myth of Passage'. *The Journal of Philosophy* 48: 457–472.

Wolf, Susan. 2010. *Meaning in Life and Why It Matters*. Princeton, NJ: Princeton University Press.

Zimmerman, Dean. 2008. 'The Privileged Present: Defending an "A-Theory" of Time'. In *Contemporary Debates in Metaphysics*, ed. Theodore Sider, Dean Zimmerman, and John Hawthorne, 211–225. Oxford: Blackwell.

PART III
MEANING IN LIFE AND RELIGION

CHAPTER 12

THE MEANING OF LIFE AND TRANSCENDENCE

JOHN COTTINGHAM

1. HUMAN INCOMPLETENESS

THE once off-limits topic of the meaning of life has become something of a philosophical industry. But bringing it within the acceptable limits of today's dominant naturalist and secularist paradigm has led to a characteristic shift of emphasis. Instead of the meaning *of* life, most attention is now focused on meaning *in* life. The result, welcome or unwelcome depending on your perspective, has been a certain lowering of the stakes. For the phrase 'the meaning *of* life' suggests a rather grand holistic perspective—a sense that our life as a whole is to be measured against some overall standard, goal, or purpose. By contrast, asking about meaning *in* life invites us to take a more pragmatic and piecemeal approach, and to look at various activities and pursuits within human life that we may find fulfilling or regard as meaningful. This latter approach typically takes what might be called a radically 'immanentist' perspective: the sources of meaning are to be sought entirely within the sphere of our purely human pursuits and activities. Such immanentism, as Adrian Moore has observed, 'rejects the idea that life needs somehow to be justified, whether by some *telos* towards which everything is striving or by some transcendent structure in terms of which everything makes sense. Nature has no grand design. Nor is there anything transcendent to it' (Moore 2012, 249).

Immanentism so construed is not without problems: the bald denial of a transcendent dimension to human life smacks of dogmatic metaphysics—from what standpoint are we supposed to be able to dismiss the transcendent in this way? But on a methodological (as opposed to metaphysical) level, the immanentist framework may seem to many to make good sense. It is undeniable that certain human pursuits are fulfilling and worthwhile, and give us a sense of meaning and purpose in our lives. So rather than profitless speculation about the ultimate meaning of it all, or the significance of human life against some grand cosmic backdrop, why not simply be content with meaning *in* life, and set about cultivating those entirely sublunary but still valuable ways of living that make our short time here, if not 'ultimately' significant, at least as significant as finite and contingent beings like us can expect? Adopting such 'methodological immanentism', as it might be called, may seem in many practical contexts to offer the best cure for intellectual agonizing about the ultimate meaning of it all: immerse oneself in the particular immanent sources of meaning and forget the grander question.

But the grander question will not go away, and cannot be suppressed by fiat. For any other species on the planet, there is nothing further to be required once its needs and wants have been maximally satisfied. But a human life, even when it is stuffed with maximally meaningful activities, is always open to a further question about its significance. The human being, we might say, is an *essentially incomplete being*. Comfortable and reassuring definitions of what it is to be human, from Aristotle's famous 'rational animal' onwards, cannot disguise the strangeness of our human predicament. Alone of all the creatures we know of, we are not just here, but we are also *aware* of being here, and we are aware that this 'being here' is profoundly problematic.

Our incompleteness has many dimensions. Most prominently, there is the *existential* dimension, famously encapsulated in Heidegger's label for the human being, *Dasein*, or 'being there', and his talk of our being 'thrown' into existence. We are confronted with our existence as something charged with anxiety, a disturbing disclosure of the uncanniness of our seemingly comfortable everyday being in the world (Heidegger [1927] 1967, §67). Second, there is the *cosmological* dimension: that we are here at all, that the universe exists at all, is a profound mystery that we long to fathom, but we know we will never, and can never, solve. Thirdly there is the dimension of *finitude*: we are keenly aware of our limits, our puniness, our mortality, a tiny speck, as Pascal put it, against an infinite backdrop ([1670] 1962, no. 201). This awareness of our finitude is doubly disturbing, for even if (as Descartes for instance argued ([1641] 1973, 45), it implies some inchoate sense of the infinite, the infinite necessarily remains out of reach, something that, by its very nature, cannot be encompassed or grasped by the finite mind. And fourthly and finally, there is the dimension of our *moral inadequacy*. We are all too aware that we are flawed creatures, clouded in our perceptions and weak in will, as Augustine put it ([c. 398] 1911, Bk. VII, Ch. 1; Book VIII, Ch. 5), constantly subject to conflicting desires that we cannot fully reconcile, uncomfortably aware that our lives fall short of the goodness we dimly feel they ought to exemplify.

These troubling manifestations of human incompleteness hardly amount to a knowledge base or set of premises from which one might set out to establish the existence of some ultimate source of our being, or some final end that might bring us the completion we long for. So far from furnishing foundations for knowledge, our human incompleteness seems to bring us to a precipice. We confront the cliff-edge, we cannot avoid edging towards it, but all we are left with is a sense of vertigo. Despite the long history of natural theology that would invoke God as the metaphysical solution to all of this, and despite the undaunted labours of those contemporary philosophers of religion who continue to work on this project, systemic doubts persist, from Kant through to Wittgenstein and beyond, as to whether discursive human knowledge could ever escape the confines of the phenomenal world (Kant [1781–1787] 1965; Wittgenstein [1921] 1961).

Leaving these difficulties aside, there would seem to be something curiously off-key in the idea that the problem of our human incompleteness could be laid to rest by some demonstrative or probabilistic argument establishing the existence of a divine being with such and such properties or powers. For the idea of God as an object of calm rational cognition seems strangely disconnected from the existential human bewilderment and anxiety just outlined. And one might add that it is at odds with the long tradition of spiritual writings insisting that God cannot be grasped by the finite human intellect (as Aquinas puts it, man is directed to God as to an end that 'surpasses the grasp of reason'; [1266–1273] 1911, First Part, Qu. 1, art. 1). Yet perhaps this need not be the end of the story. For it may be that what is beyond our cognitive grasp can nevertheless in a certain sense be an object of longing.

We have spoken of the sense of incompleteness that is inseparable from our humanity. Yet the inescapable corollary of this is a longing for completion, which is bound up with a desire for what Simon May has called 'ontological rootedness' (2014, 7). This is a desire that is so deeply ingrained that we cannot conceive of giving it up. If we ever managed to ignore it, then, as the existentialist theologian Karl Rahner has put it,

> The human being would never face the totality of the world and of him or herself helplessly, silently and anxiously... human beings would remain *mired in the world* and *in* themselves and no longer go through that mysterious process which they *are*. Human beings would have forgotten the totality and its ground, and at the same time, if we can put it this way, they would have forgotten that they had forgotten. What would it be like? We can only say: they would have *ceased to be human beings*. They would have regressed to the level of a clever animal.... (Rahner [1976] 1978, 45–50, emphasis added)

One of the crucial ideas that Rahner brings out here is that of humanity anxiously confronting the *totality of the world*. A similar idea is explored from a different angle in Joseph Pieper's argument that 'fixing the mind's eye on the totality of being' is the essence of the philosophical impulse that defines our humanity ([1948] 1952, 116). Finding some supposed item *in* the world, perhaps a point in the centre of the galaxy or the cosmos which was its putative source, or the exploding cosmic egg from whence it all sprung, would clearly not answer the case at all, nor would it serve to alleviate our anxiety. For the puzzle that confronts us (as Wittgenstein once put it) is not *how* the world is, but *that it is* ([1921] 1976, § 6.44). We find ourselves 'thrown' into the world but we cannot, try as we might, remain wholly and unreflectively engaged in the detailed texture of our lives; we cannot escape being confronted with the mysterious totality of which we are a part, and we cannot cease to raise, at least as a question, the idea of a transcendent source of that totality.

The underlying thought here was articulated perhaps better than any philosopher could do it by means of a famous image introduced by the fourteenth-century mystic Mother Julian of Norwich:

> And God showed me a little thing, the size of a hazelnut, lying on the palm of my hand, round like a ball. I looked at it thoughtfully and wondered, 'What can this be?' And the answer came '*It is all that is made*.' (Julian of Norwich [1373] 1998, 7)

In discussing this passage with an eminent Oxford philosopher, I once remarked that whether one accepted the theistic framework or not, the image of confronting the whole cosmos in this way was one that patently makes sense. He replied drily: 'it patently does *not* make sense'. In a strict and literal interpretation he was I suppose right: the universe is everything there is including us, so we could not see it lying there in front of us. But in another sense, as reflective human beings (and this connects with the point made in our Rahner quotation) we have the special ability that no merely clever animal could have, to see that the universe cannot be a closed system. We can always, at least in our thought, confront it in its entirety. So somewhat analogously to a Gödelian process (reminiscent of Gödel's famous incompleteness theorem, whereby for any set F of sound procedures of mathematical proof we are always able to transcend the methods of F to see the truth of results that are beyond the scope of F; Penrose 2012), we can see that any description of the universe can never be complete; for we can always take one step back from this supposedly finished description and thereby pronounce it incomplete, and so on indefinitely. To put the point another way, even if science were to establish beyond doubt that the entire cosmos is finite, we could still reach beyond those boundaries in our thought and think of something more. Or to put it yet another way, if we think of the universe Spinoza-fashion, as a kind of grand totality, where for every object or *ideatum*, there is a conscious thought or idea, then the total set of *ideata* plus corresponding ideas could never be a complete or closed set. There could always be, as it were, a further thought and its further object. (This may, incidentally, be one route to the Spinozan conclusion that God or nature must be infinite.)

The upshot of these diverse reflections is that we humans, in virtue of our conceptual abilities as reflective and questioning beings, even as we confront or reflect on the cosmos and our own presence in it, are in a certain way brought up against the infinite. This is not a matter of our passively contemplating some object or item of which we have clear and distinct awareness (we have no clear and distinct awareness of the infinite). In a way, it is a matter of *conatus* or striving, rather than cognition or theoretical knowledge. Or to use another Latin term, it has something of the character of what the Romans called *desiderium*—an open-ended longing for something that is beyond our grasp (Cottingham 2019). What is involved is a strange forward reaching of the human mind, a kind of 'desiderative' stretching out towards something we glimpse as out of our final reach, yet in which we somehow participate, insofar as our mental reach can never be finally closed or circumscribed.

2. The Urge for Transcendence

As finite creatures we reach out anxiously towards the infinite, which we know we can never encompass. We might say that our human mode of being is an interrogative one. What we long for is something that will answer this anxious question, that will bring us completion. If we could have an answer, then we might know the meaning of human life. But—and here is the rub—we also know that such an answer is beyond our human capacity to achieve. So there is an inherent instability or tension at the heart of the question of the meaning of life: we long for it, but we know we cannot have it. *We are mired in immanence, yet we yearn for transcendence.*

We seem here to have reached an impasse, or a paradox. Part of the feeling that we have reached a dead-end may be due to our sense that there should be a cognitively accessible answer, but that it is beyond our intellectual powers to reach it. Yet there are other ways of dealing with paradoxes than by intellectual unravelling. Lewis Carroll (1895) recommended the maxim *solvitur ambulando* ('it is solved by walking') as a solution to Zeno's paradox of Achilles and the tortoise, suggesting in effect that action or praxis might serve to deal with a puzzle that defied theoretical or propositional solution. Taking our cue from this, it may perhaps be that, although we cannot reach the transcendent answer we long for, we can find ways of *enacting* our longing for the transcendent, and thus, though we may not be able to *say* what the meaning of life consists in, we may be able to *show* how the puzzle can be addressed.

Many traditional spiritual practices can plausibly be understood as aiming to do precisely this. They do not produce a propositional answer to the puzzle of life's meaning, but they offer a series of formalized procedures and rituals whereby human beings are able to express how they stand in relation to the mystery that confronts them. By enacting their longing for the transcendent, they turn what might have been angry or helpless puzzlement or nihilistic despair into a joyful expression of hope, and thereby find a way of reaching towards the transcendent meaning that is longed for.

As but one very brief and schematic example to illustrate how this might work, consider the following offertory prayer from the Catholic mass:

> Blessed are you, Lord. God of all creation; through your goodness we have this bread to offer, which earth has given and human hands have made. It will become for us the bread of life.

There are of course elaborate theological doctrines presupposed in the liturgy of which this prayer is a part, and for many people the falsity, or unprovenness, of the doctrines may invalidate any possibility of considering such prayers as a route to meaning. But if we leave the doctrinal questions in abeyance for one moment, and simply attend to some of the resonances of the text as it stands, what do we have? First of all, we have an invocation to the mysterious source of 'all creation': in the very way the invocation is phrased we (the participants in the ritual) are acknowledging our finitude—our smallness before the vast totality of the cosmos of which we are a tiny and insignificant part. But next, rather than exploring this intellectually, as if we could fathom it, we instead *do* something: we perform an act of offering. And in this act, the offering of the 'gift' of bread, dependent on all the natural processes that sustain it and us, we both acknowledge our dependency on these processes and express our creative human engagement with them: the bread is something that 'earth has given and human hands have made'. And finally, in offering the bread, we declare that it will become a source of spiritual sustenance.

Even in the enacting of this one small element of the liturgy, the participants are thus weaving their words and actions into a complex web of meaning. They are confronting the infinite, and approaching it in awe, as suppliants, and yet also engaging with it through something very down to earth and human, the making and offering of bread. They are bringing their finitude into confrontation with the infinite, but not in fear or anger or puzzlement, but in the focused calm and tranquillity of a resonant ritual, handed down over many generations, so that they become part of a long succession of human beings who have found this ritual sustaining and empowering.

How is such sustenance possible? Again leaving theology aside, perhaps at the simplest level what is enacted here in the performance of the offering is a certain *harmony or attunement*. The prayer opens with a *blessing*, so that, in the terms discussed earlier, we are reaching out to the transcendent, but now specifically conceived as something which we long for as *good*. And the next phrase of the prayer immediately picks this up—'through your *goodness* we have this bread to offer'. The harmony established here is a harmony between those who long for the good and the object of their longing which they bless as good. So the human confrontation with the infinite is no longer anxious, or fearful, or resentful, or simply baffled, but becomes a loving confrontation, a reaching out in love and blessing to what is trusted as the source of all goodness.

At this point it seems only fair to allow the sceptic a voice. Is not all this a doomed attempt to try to manufacture meaning where none exists? We shall return to this worry in the following section, but for the present it may help to draw a comparison with other less theologically charged spiritual practices and enactments. When two people lovingly give and receive rings in a wedding ceremony to express their love and commitment to each other, it would be absurd, or at least inept, to say that they are attempting to manufacture meaning where none exists. For their enactment is, precisely, a performance that, insofar as it *expresses* their love, carries an ineradicable charge of significance. To be sure, the giving and receiving of rings could be described in purely secular terms, whereas it might be objected that in the case of the offering of gifts at the altar, there must, if the practice is to be meaningful, be a supernatural presence, subtraction of which would strip the ritual of its meaning. Yet putting the matter in these terms involves a certain distortion. For the ritual in question remains an act of love and trust and thus carries an ineradicable charge of meaning, irrespective of the validity or otherwise of the underlying theology.

Am I saying that religious rituals are self-validating? I should prefer to put it slightly differently. Such rituals function as *vehicles for the longing for the transcendent that is an inherent part of our human makeup.* And insofar as they enact that longing, they express the faith and hope that there is, after all, a meaning to human life as a whole, a meaning that arises from our ability to orient ourselves, or attune ourselves, to the source of meaning and goodness which we long for. Nothing in the ritual, to be sure, can guarantee that there is indeed such a transcendent source; and nothing, to be sure, compels us in logic to adopt the path of spiritual praxis (let alone to do so in the specific form described in this liturgical example). But if we resolve to turn our back on any such path, we will, in the absence of some alternative vehicle for expressing the longing in question, be shutting down something in our nature that is not easily silenced. We will have to fall back on purely immanent sources of meaning, which may of course bring great satisfactions in their wake, but which will leave part of our nature unprovided for. And the life of a creature who longs for transcendence but is mired in immanence cannot be a fully meaningful one.

3. Transcendence, Teleology, and the Good

The conclusions reached so far might seem on further scrutiny to boil down to very thin gruel. If there can be no sound cognitive route to 'a transcendent structure in term of which everything makes sense' (in Adrian Moore's phrase quoted in our opening paragraph), we seem to be left with nothing more than a mere desire or longing for there to be such a structure. So pointing to the fact that there are forms of spiritual praxis that enact our longing for such a structure would seem to show not that there *is* an overall meaning to human life, but merely that we would *like* there to be one.

Such a deflationary reading of the argument is possible, but it leaves out of account certain striking features of our human desire for transcendence. We are dealing not with ordinary appetitive desire, the drive to pursue and possess some object that is plainly in view, but (in the terminology introduced earlier) with a *desiderative* longing, a pervasive, deep, and open-ended yearning for something that beckons us forward but is beyond our grasp. And crucially, the desire in question does not simply relate to something we may happen to want (as some people might for a time want to collect postage stamps, but then turn their attention to porcelain), but constitutes (as suggested in our earlier quotation from Karl Rahner) an indelible part of what it is to be human. Our longing for the transcendent is in a certain sense indispensable: it is not something we can with integrity give up, while still retaining the anxious, questing spirit that is the signature of our humanity.

But could not one address the human urge for transcendence in a lower key or more down-to-earth fashion, by interpreting it not as directed to something that could provide the key to life's meaning, but merely as the desire to make our lives as a whole more valuable and worthwhile? Along these lines, Clifford Williams (2020, chapter 4) has offered various interpretations of what he calls 'the urge to transcend oneself', such as the urge to do good things for other people instead of focusing only on one's own good (we could call this 'altruistic transcendence'). Or alternatively, he suggests it could be construed as the urge to do something that is big and important, such as participating in an innovative and momentous project, or to identify with something 'larger' than oneself (we could call this 'bigger picture' transcendence). These various notions perhaps capture something of the meaning of 'to transcend'—to cross or go beyond certain boundaries, in particular the narrow boundaries of the ego, or the individual agent, and to reach for something wider and grander. But neither of these notions captures the existential and cosmological dimensions of the human desire for transcendence; neither of them captures the sense in which these deep human longings are insatiable and indispensable. It is not just that there is a perpetual restless inquisitiveness in our human makeup—an evolutionary trait one might well expect to prove an advantage in the struggle for survival. More than that, we know that however many of our wants and goals were secured, we would still be puzzled, anxious, reaching for a completion that forever eludes us.

But even if the idea of transcending oneself by doing things for others or for a worthy cause does not capture the deeper character of the human urge for transcendence, there seems to be something right about connecting the urge for transcendence with the moral domain. In our earlier discussion of the example of the offertory prayer, it emerged that a crucial element in the alignment of the worshipper with the object of longing was the conception of that object as *blessed* and *good*. And this in turn links with one of the four dimensions of human incompleteness outlined in the first part of our discussion, namely our *moral incompleteness*. This is perhaps a somewhat unfashionable notion in our modern culture, where self-help manuals often stress the importance of self-esteem and discourage wallowing in guilt. No doubt there is something valuable in such advice, but we do not have to be obsessively self-deprecating in order to be all too aware of our inevitably many human failings. To be human is to be uncomfortably conscious that our lives fall short of the goodness we dimly feel they ought to exemplify. Consistently with this, we may say that part of our yearning for transcendence is a yearning to align ourselves with the good, so as to bring our lives closer to how they should be.

The idea of a basic orientation to the good being present in the human psyche is widespread in the theistic tradition, not least in Thomas Aquinas. Aquinas is of course as aware as anyone else that people often seek bad things, and indeed might well have agreed with Hobbes's view that people often label 'good' whatever object they happen to want to pursue: ('Whatsoever is the object of any man's appetite or desire, that it is which he for his part calleth good'; Hobbes [1651] 1965, chapter 6.) But in Aquinas's view, someone who eagerly pursues an evil end (for example bullying another human being or taking delight in their distress) will nevertheless retain, in spite of him- or herself, some residual pull in the opposite direction. As Eleonore Stump has underlined in several of her recent writings, Aquinas is committed to the idea of an objective standard of goodness that, at least in its rudiments, no human being can be indifferent to. And a striking conclusion follows from this, namely that 'no one can be wholehearted in evil'. For 'a person who lacks one or another degree of integration in goodness will hide some part of his mind from himself [and will be] alienated from some of his own desires' (Stump 2018, 126).

Stump's interpretation of Aquinas may serve as a pointer to a certain way of understanding human incompleteness. In the theistic picture, the conception of the human being is a strongly *teleological* one: we have a destination that is laid down for us by a supremely benevolent and just creator, so that there is something we are meant to be, or a way we are meant to be. We are, as it were, *configured towards the good*, so that our fulfilment is only possible when we strive towards it. But because of human finitude and weakness, our vision of that good is necessarily imperfect, and our resolution to pursue it is weak. Often we choose the bad, or the lesser good. Yet something in our nature, if the theist is right, ensures that such bad choices necessarily produce a psychic dissonance. The yearning for what is truly and objectively good cannot be wholly damped down, however much we try; and this, for the theist, will be part of the diagnosis of that sense of queasiness, the dread, the Angst, of which the existentialists speak so eloquently (Kierkegaard [1843] 2006). We may set our heart on all sorts of bad objectives, and, if we please, take our cue from Hobbes and label them 'good'. But the inevitable result will be self-alienation, a double-mindedness manifest in the fact that these objectives are at war with the better good that at some level we continue to long for.

Assuming one accepts the psychological validity of the ideas of alienation and double-mindedness just sketched, why, one might ask, could one not rest content with an entirely naturalistic or humanistic account of what is going on? Internal moral conflict or confusion may produce a sense of restlessness, or incompleteness, a feeling of something missing. So much is clear. But why bring in a transcendent dimension?

Part of the answer to this is suggested by the teleological conception of our human nature referred to a moment ago. To think of human nature as teleologically configured is, at the minimal level, to recognize that our lives are structured in terms of goals and purposes. Alasdair MacIntyre, one of the most systematic defenders of this kind of Aristotelian approach, insists that human agents, 'as participants in the form of life that is distinctively human... can only be understood, they can only understand themselves, teleologically' (2016, 237). But the Aristotelian conception is not simply the idea that we pursue certain ends. There is deeply engrained in the Aristotelian and many subsequent accounts an intrinsic connection between the notion of a *telos*, and the idea of the good. Charles Taylor brings this out powerfully in his *Sources of the Self*, where he stresses that to make sense of our lives, and indeed to have an identity at all, 'we need an orientation to the good'; we need to have some sense of our lives as moving towards moral growth and maturity. It follows from this, on Taylor's view, that our lives have a *narrative* shape: as I develop, and learn from my failings and mistakes, there is always a story to be told about how I have become what I now am, and where my current journey towards improvement will take me. Just as my sense of where I am in physical space depends on how I got here and where I am going next, so it is, Taylor argues, with 'my orientation in moral space' (1989, pt. 1, ch. 2, sec. 3).

This brings us to the nub of the argument. Teleology, selfhood, narrativity, the idea of the self as fundamentally configured towards the good—this cluster of concepts seems inevitably to point us towards transcendence. The reason is simple: on a purely naturalistic or humanistic conception of human nature, the mere facts of evolution and biology cannot possibly furnish the idea of a way we are meant to be, a good we are meant to achieve. For the naturalist, the idea of life as an open-ended journey towards moral improvement can only be understood simply in terms of the drives, inclinations, and conflicting desires we happen to have. And there is nothing in this assorted ragbag of propensities that marks out as normative a given *telos* for human life. The *telos*, the goal we are meant to strive for, has to be set, determined by or derived from something that transcends the confused catalogue of biological and historical facts concerning what human beings amount to.

What is more, the *telos* in question also has to transcend the *cultural* facts—the facts of our 'second nature', as John McDowell called what we have acquired by social acculturation. For since it is patently the case that cultures can degrade as well as improve, can take the wrong path and resist moral improvement, it follows that the direction of a given culture cannot in and of itself be the furnisher of authentic teleology. McDowell attempts to counter this by presupposing a strong moral objectivism: what acculturation does, according to his formulation, is to 'bring into view' normative reasons that are, as he puts it, 'there in any case' (1994, 82–83). But this very way of putting it necessarily invokes the reality of objective normative requirements that transcend the facts of culture. Does this take us all the way to Transcendence with a capital T, or to what the theist calls God? Perhaps not all the way—few arguments in philosophy are watertight in this sense—but it does suggest that without theism, or failing that, perhaps some Platonic spiritual realm, the idea of a moral teleology, the conception of the self that I am meant to be, is left hanging in the void.

It is time to draw the threads together. If the argument of this chapter has been on the right lines, our human incompleteness leaves us with a longing for transcendence that cannot be assuaged by an immanent framework of goals and goods, however meaningful we may find them. We retain a longing for a transcendent framework that might disclose the meaning of our lives as a whole and thereby bring us fulfilment and completion. But to access that transcendent framework, to gain a clear grasp of it, is beyond the reach of our human cognitive capacities. As Aquinas remarked, 'the cause of that at which we wonder is hidden from us' ([1265–1266] 2012, Qu. 6, art. 2); and yet our very wonder bears witness to the *desiderium sciendi*, our presently unrequited longing to know ([1266–1273] 1911, Ia IIae, Qu. 32, art. 8; cf. Pieper 1952, 129–130). Where cognition gives out, we have to proceed not cognitively but *desideratively*, by enacting our longing for the transcendent and thereby striving to bring our lives into harmony with what we long for. Such harmony presupposes that we can overcome double-mindedness by seeking to align ourselves by reference to an objective way we are meant to be, a good that is laid down not by our conflicting collection of desires and inclinations, but by an objective teleological framework that holds the key to our fulfilment. For human beings, who are acutely aware of their incompleteness, and who can only understand themselves teleologically, the meaning of life must consist in the determination to reach forward and seek to align themselves with the transcendent good for which they long.

REFERENCES

Aquinas, T. [1266–1273] 1911. *Summa theologiae*. Trans. Fathers of the English Dominican Province. London: Burns, Oates and Washbourne.

Aquinas, T. [1265–1266] 2012. *The Power of God* [*Quaestiones disputatae de potentia Dei*]. Trans. R. Regan. Oxford: Oxford University Press.

Augustine of Hippo. [c. 398] 1912. *Confessions* [*Confessiones*]. Transl. W. Watts. Cambridge, MA: Harvard University Press.

Carroll, L. 1895. 'What the Tortoise Said to Achilles'. *Mind* 104: 691–693.

Cottingham, J. 2019. 'From Desire to Encounter: The Human Quest for the Infinite'. *Religious Studies* 55: 375–388.

Descartes, R. [1641] 1973. *Meditations* [*Meditationes de prima philosophia*], ed. C. Adam and P. Tannery, *Œuvres de Descartes*, vol. VII. Paris: Vrin/CNRS. Transl. *The Philosophical Writings of Descartes*, ed. J. Cottingham, R. Stoothoff and D. Murdoch, vol. II. Cambridge: Cambridge University Press, 1985.

Heidegger, M. [1927] 1967. *Sein und Zeit*. 11th ed. Tübingen: Niemeyer. Transl. *Being and Time*, ed. J. Macquarrie and E. Robinson. New York: Harper and Row, 1962.

Hobbes, T. [1651] 1965. *Leviathan*. Cleveland, OH: Meridian.

Julian of Norwich. [1373] 1998. *The Revelations of Divine Love*, ed. E. Spearing. London: Penguin.

Kant, I. [1781–1787] 1965. *Critique of Pure Reason* [*Kritik der reinen Vernunft*]. Transl. N. Kemp Smith. New York: St. Martin's Press.

Kierkegaard, S. [1843] 2006. *Fear and Trembling* [*Frygt og Bæven*]. Cambridge: Cambridge University Press.

MacIntyre, A. 2016. *Ethics in the Conflicts of Modernity*. Cambridge: Cambridge University Press.

May, S. 2014. *Love: A History*. New Haven, CT: Yale University Press.

McDowell, J. 1994. *Mind and World*. Cambridge MA: Harvard University Press.

Moore, A. 2012. *The Evolution of Modern Metaphysics: Making Sense of Things*. Cambridge: Cambridge University Press.

Pascal, B. [1670] 1962. *Pensées*, ed. L. Lafuma. Paris: Seuil. Transl. A. Krailsheimer. Harmondsworth, UK: Penguin, 1972.

Penrose, R. 2012. 'Kurt Gödel's Groundbreaking Work'. Interview with C. Carlini, at https://simplycharly.com, accessed 15 June 2020.

Pieper, J. [1948] 1952. *Leisure the Basis of Culture* [*Muße und Kult*], and *The Philosophical Act* [*Was heißt Philosophieren?*]. San Francisco, CA: Ignatius Press.

Rahner, K. [1976] 1978. *Foundations of Christian Faith* [*Grundkurs des Glaubens*]. London: Darton, Longman and Todd.

Stump, E. 2018. *Atonement*. Oxford: Oxford University Press.

Taylor, C. 1989. *Sources of the Self*. Cambridge: Cambridge University Press.

Williams, C. 2020. *Religion and the Meaning of Life*. Cambridge: Cambridge University Press.

Wittgenstein, L. [1921] 1961. *Tractatus Logico-Philosophicus*, transl. D. Pears and B. McGuinness. London: Routledge & Kegan Paul.

CHAPTER 13

ATHEISM AND MEANING IN LIFE

ERIK J. WIELENBERG

1. Introduction

In ancient Greek mythology, Sisyphus is condemned by the gods to push a large boulder to the top of a steep hill. However, the boulder is enchanted so that it rolls away from Sisyphus and back down the hill just before he reaches the top. Sisyphus must then return to the bottom of the hill and start all over again. This process repeats itself forever.

Sisyphus's endless punishment is often invoked as a vivid image of an activity that is entirely devoid of meaning. Pushing the stone up the hill is difficult and Sisyphus never attains his goal of getting the boulder to the top of the hill, so his existence is one of continual frustration, devoid of enjoyment or attainment of one's goals. Furthermore, his endless labours seem to have no consequences beyond themselves and hence seem pointless and worthless.

How might the case of Sisyphus be modified to bring some meaning into Sisyphus's life? That question immediately raises another: What does it mean for a life to be meaningful?[1] I suspect that trying to pin down precisely *the* standard or typical meaning of 'meaningful' when applied to a life is a futile task (see e.g. Cottingham 2002, 3–10; Mawson 2019, 5–24). I agree with Landau's suggestion that the claim that a life is meaningful (or meaningless) is typically a claim about value (2017, 12), but there are various types of value that a life can have or fail to have. Accordingly, I think the most sensible procedure when thinking about meaningful lives is to distinguish some of the main kinds of meaning that a life can have.

---

[1] The use to which I put the case of Sisyphus here is modelled on the approach taken by Taylor (2000, 322–323).

Some have thought that without God and an afterlife, all human lives are like Sisyphus's in that they are devoid of meaning. Judaism, Christianity, and Islam share a commitment to the reality of an omnipotent, omniscient, morally perfect God who created and sustains the universe. Let us suppose for the sake of argument that no such being exists. Suppose further that there are no non-physicals souls, there is no afterlife, reincarnation never occurs, and that each human being's death marks the permanent end of his or her actions and experiences. I think that human lives can be meaningful even given these assumptions. To defend the possibility of meaningful lives in a godless universe, I will draw on my discussion of different types of meaning and explain how human lives can have these types of meaning in a godless universe. Following that, I will directly criticize some arguments for the claim that without God and an afterlife, all human lives are meaningless.

2. Varieties and Sources of Meaning

One way that a person's life can be meaningful is by being good for that person—that is, by possessing what philosophers sometimes call *well-being* or *prudential value* (see e.g. Bradley 2015, 1–8; Fletcher 2016, 1–4). The value of a person's life for her is enhanced when she engages in intrinsically good activities or has intrinsically good experiences and the intrinsic goodness of these activities or experiences is not outweighed or defeated (in Chisholm's sense; see Chisholm 1968) by evils in her life. If a person's life is good for her overall, then her life has *intrinsic meaning*. Intrinsic meaning obviously comes in degrees—two lives might both be intrinsically meaningful yet one might be more intrinsically meaningful than the other.

Which activities or experiences are intrinsically good? Attempting to provide a comprehensive list is obviously futile, so instead I'll try to identify some central examples. Many thinkers have identified *love* as an important source of meaning in human life. Spending quality time with those one cares for and who care for one in return is an intrinsically valuable activity. Part of what makes Sisyphus's existence so bleak is that he is entirely alone. Suppose that Sisyphus had a partner in punishment—that Sisyphus and a close friend were condemned to try to push the boulder to the top of the hill together. That would create the possibility for some intrinsic meaning in Sisyphus's life. Indeed, the shared suffering of Sisyphus and his friend would create the opportunity for increased closeness as they could form what Sebastian Junger calls a 'brotherhood of pain', in which shared adversity and suffering promotes egalitarianism, altruism, and willingness to sacrifice for the good of the group (2016, 54–55).

Haidt proposes that, along with love, an important element of a meaningful life is *flow* (2006, 219–26). Haidt characterizes flow this way:

> [T]he state of total immersion in a task that is challenging yet closely matched to one's abilities. . . . There's a clear challenge that fully engages your attention; you have

the skills to meet the challenge; and you get immediate feedback about how you are doing at each step.... You get flash after flash of positive feeling with each turn negotiated, each high note correctly sung, or each brushstroke that falls into the right place. (2006, 95)

Pushing a heavy stone up a steep hill is not only difficult and tiring; it is also *boring*. As Frankfurt (2004) notes, '[b]oredom is a serious matter.... Any substantial increase in the extent to which we are bored threatens the very continuation of our conscious mental life' (53–54). The gods might have shown mercy and given Sisyphus a more stimulating task—one that varies and increases in difficulty as time goes on and that provides flashes of positive feeling along the way. Indeed, Csikszentmihalyi, who originally introduced the concept of flow into psychology, discusses some real-life cases of prisoners who found ways of introducing flow into their lives to stave off the boredom of their imprisonment (2008, 90–92).[2]

Giving Sisyphus companionship and flow would prevent his existence from being entirely meaningless, but such a life would nevertheless still lack an important type of meaning if it had no consequences beyond itself. Another type of meaning a life might have is suggested by Smuts's defence of the *good cause account* of the meaning of life, according to which '[o]ne's life is meaningful to the extent that it promotes the good' (2012, 1). Smuts appeals to the case of George Bailey in Frank Capra's film *It's a Wonderful Life* to motivate his account. Although George didn't realize it, some of his actions greatly improved the lives of people around him.

Let's say that a life has *extrinsic meaning* to the extent that it produces good consequences. The good consequences produced by a life may not necessarily make that life better for the one living it, which implies that extrinsic meaning is distinct from intrinsic meaning. Taylor (2000) considers a version of the Sisyphus scenario in which Sisyphus is able to get the boulder to the top of the hill and then uses multiple boulders to create a beautiful and enduring temple (322–323). In this version of the scenario, Sisyphus's life would have extrinsic meaning.[3]

Many who write on meaning in life emphasize the importance of *identifying with or working towards something larger than oneself.* As Landau points out, such claims are most plausible when construed as suggesting that a person can make her life meaningful by working towards something of *value* beyond herself (2017, 11). Sisyphus's construction of a beautiful and enduring temple is an example of this idea; the temple's beauty makes it valuable. Another version of this basic idea is suggested by Singer (1995, 219–235), who

---

[2] Although I focus here on the intrinsic value of flow, I do not mean to suggest that flow is only intrinsically valuable—it may have valuable consequences as well. A prominent theme in Csikszentmihalyi (2008) is that flow can be a means to personal growth.

[3] Taylor's view seems to be that Sisyphus's creation of a beautiful temple would not bring real meaning to his life because after creating the temple Sisyphus would be faced with 'infinite boredom' (2000, 331). However, Taylor does not distinguish different types of meaning as I have here; furthermore, even if Sisyphus's *post-temple-creation* life is boring and meaningless, that does not entail that the period of his life during which he was building the temple is meaningless.

argues that a particularly effective way of attaining a meaningful life is to live what he calls 'the ethical life', the essence of which lies in devoting oneself to the reduction of unnecessary suffering. Reducing evil can be construed as a way of promoting the good, so by effectively reducing unnecessary suffering, one can give one's life extrinsic meaning. Suppose that each time Sisyphus gets his boulder almost to the top of the hill, he relieves the needless suffering of another person. Even if Sisyphus were entirely unaware of this effect, the extrinsic meaning of his life would grow with each trip up the hill.

Frankl ([1959] 2006), drawing on his own experiences as a concentration camp prisoner during World War II, argues that one route to meaning in life lies in *responding to unavoidable suffering* in a certain way: '[E]ven the helpless victim of a hopeless situation, facing a fate he cannot change, may rise above himself, may grow beyond himself, and by doing so change himself' (146). Responding to unavoidable suffering in the right way can result in personal growth, for example in the form of moral or intellectual development, thereby giving one's life extrinsic meaning.

Another source of extrinsic meaning is suggested by Confucianism. In Confucian thought, the highest good is *harmony* (Li 2006, 588). This harmony encompasses both interpersonal social harmony and intrapersonal psychological harmony (Angle 2009, 65–66). Li suggests that precisely because there is no God in the Confucian universe 'there is no order or natural law from God' and hence 'the world has to generate an order of its own' (2006, 594). Responsibility for creating and sustaining such order falls to human beings, and doing so is an important source of meaning in human life. Furthermore, intellectual and moral self-improvement—crucial to internal harmony—are lifelong projects, for even the wisest human being has something to learn from the most foolish (Klancer 2012, 668) and 'Confucius maintains that even someone with the highest virtue of humanity is [morally] fallible' (Sim 2007, 209; see also Angle 2009, 85). Being part of a well-ordered family and society brings intrinsic meaning to one's life, and helping to sustain well-ordered selves, families, and societies gives one's life extrinsic meaning. As Hang explains, '[f]or a Confucian, the meaning of life can be realized ... through ... the commitment of oneself to the welfare of the family, community and society, as well as the influence of his moral and cultural realms over the world' (2011, 443).

The sketches of intrinsic and extrinsic meaning offered to this point mesh nicely with some prominent accounts of the meaningfulness of life.[4] Wolf (2010) proposes that 'meaning arises from loving objects worthy of love and engaging with them in positive ways ... meaning arises when subjective attraction meets objective attractiveness' (8–9; see also Frankfurt 2004). This conception of meaning incorporates both intrinsic and extrinsic meaning: Wolf's 'subjective attraction' seems to be pleasant or enjoyable and so enhances the value of a person's life for her, while the 'objective attractiveness' component requires the production of something of value (Wolf 2010, 107).[5] While Wolf

---

[4] The distinction between intrinsic and extrinsic meaning corresponds roughly with Quinn's (2008) distinction between axiological and teleological meaning.

[5] For an interesting elaboration of the objective aspect of Wolf's view based on 'narrative values', see May (2015, 61–104).

holds that a life has meaning only if both the subjective and objective aspects are present, I suggest that it's more sensible to distinguish intrinsic and extrinsic meaning and hold that a life may have one type of meaning without the other, but that both types are present when one attains a meaningful life as envisaged by Wolf. On Wolf's view, one's life is devoid of meaning of any kind if one is not subjectively attracted to the worthy activities of one's life, but that position seems to have some counterintuitive implications. It implies, for example, that a person who volunteers to be bored so that others do not suffer boredom (Metz 2014, 183) or a tortured artist who creates great art despite deeply resenting the artistic process, 'finding it a terrible, life-denying calling' (Hamilton 2018, 59) does not do anything meaningful. It seems more plausible to hold that the lives of such persons have a significant degree of extrinsic meaning while possessing little or no intrinsic meaning.

Metz (2014) develops a sophisticated theory according to which a person's life is meaningful to the extent that the person living it 'employs her reason and in ways that positively orient rationality towards fundamental conditions of human existence' (222). Fundamental conditions of human existence are those conditions of human life that are responsible for the obtaining of many of the other conditions of human life (Metz 2014, 226). Metz applies this basic idea to three domains—the good, the true, and the beautiful. With respect to the good, Metz says that human agency is responsible for many of the other conditions of human life and hence '[t]he more intensely one supports people's decision-making, the more meaning that will accrue to one's life; such is a plausible explanation of the moral achievements of [Nelson] Mandela and Mother Teresa' (2011, 402). With respect to the true, Metz offers as examples the discovery of foundational theories in biology and physics by Darwin and Einstein. And with respect to the beautiful, Metz suggests that '[a] compelling artwork . . . is about those facets of human experience responsible for much else about the human experience . . . topics such as morality, war, death, love, family, and the like' (2014, 230). Metz's account thus identifies meaning in life with a specific type of extrinsic meaning—though, on his theory, valuable moral, intellectual, and aesthetic accomplishments enhance the meaning of a person's life only if they are produced in the right way (see Metz 2014, 235).[6]

3. Meaningful Life in a Godless Universe

The discussion so far suggests that, on the face of it, a person's life can have a significant amount of both intrinsic and extrinsic meaning even if there is no God or afterlife. Companionship, flow, reducing avoidable suffering, personal growth through suffering, commitment to valuable causes and projects larger than oneself (like reducing

---

[6] For an interesting critique of the views of Wolf and Metz, see Matheson (2018).

unnecessary suffering or attaining personal and social harmony), and positively orienting one's rationality toward fundamental conditions in human life are all plausible sources of meaning, and all seem to be things that can exist without God or an afterlife.

Zuckerman's (2008) interviews with non-religious Danes and Swedes suggest that ordinary non-religious people see many of the things discussed so far as sources of meaning in life. When asked about the meaning of life, Zuckerman's subjects cited things like spending time with their families (70), doing something good for other people (71), or completing challenging projects, such as writing an English-Swedish-Yiddish dictionary (72). Zuckerman reports: 'Many people I talked with cited the raising of children as the thing that makes life meaningful. Others talked about hobbies, such as elk hunting' (72). To a significant degree, the responses of Zuckerman's interviewees correspond with Freud's famous identification of love and work as two important sources of meaning in life (Erikson 1963, 265).[7]

Denmark and Sweden are highly secularized nations—indeed, they are among the most secular civilizations in human history. Interestingly, even if atheism is true, being religious in a religious nation can contribute to the meaning of one's life. That is because a prominent social effect of organized religion is that it binds people together into communities (see Wilson 2002; Wade 2009; and Graham and Haidt 2010), thereby promoting the sort of personal relationships that enhance the intrinsic meaning of life. Attaining meaning in life can be more challenging for non-religious people living in highly religious nations, such as the United States. For people in that situation, it can be difficult to find secular organizations that have the same power to bind people together. However, some such organizations do exist (see Ozment 2016, 125–165). One example is the Societies for Ethical Culture, which began in 1876 and are based on the idea that 'people create meaningful lives by striving to live more ethically and treat others with inherent worth and dignity' (Ozment 2016, 144).

It is also worth noting that even without God and an afterlife, the meaningfulness of one's life does not end with one's death, and indeed the extrinsic meaningfulness of one's life can grow after death. As Audi (2005) points out, institutions and ideals can live much longer than individual human beings (354).[8] Audi writes: 'One can found institutions, endow them with programs, and give them ideals; all of these can carry one's memory forward' (2005, 354). Plato and Aristotle have been dead for centuries, yet the extrinsic meaning of their lives continues to grow thanks to the efforts of scholars, teachers, and students who keep their ideas alive. For a contemporary example, consider the case of Pat Tillman, well-known in the United States as a professional football player who decided shortly after the terrorist attacks of September 11, 2001, to put his career in the National Football League (NFL) on hold in order to serve in the US military. Tillman was killed in a friendly-fire incident in Afghanistan in 2004.

---

[7] For a defence of work as the highest form of meaning in life, see Levy (2005). Note that 'work' here is meant not in the sense of work done merely to acquire money but rather work 'in the sense of free productive activity' (Singer 2000, 33–35).

[8] Audi actually says that such things can last *forever* (in a godless universe), which is an overstatement.

In a journal entry about his 2002 decision to turn down a three-year, $3.6 million contract and leave the NFL, Tillman wrote that in light of the 9/11 attacks and subsequent events, his football career seemed 'shallow and insignificant' and that the path he had been following was 'no longer important' (Krakauer 2009, 138). According to Jon Krakauer, Tillman 'was agnostic, perhaps even an atheist' but believed 'in the transcendent importance of continually striving to better oneself—intellectually, morally, and physically' (2009, 116). While serving in Iraq Tillman wrote in his journal that he was confident that 'nothing' awaited him after death (2009, 314) and he requested that no chaplain or minister officiate at any memorial services held for him in the event of his death (2009, 315).[9] One of the consequences of Tillman's life and death was the creation of the Pat Tillman Foundation which, among other things, provides competitive scholarships for military veterans and spouses.[10] Tillman's life seems to have contained much intrinsic meaning and its extrinsic meaning continues to grow—even if there is no God or an afterlife.

What, then, may be said on behalf of the view that without God and an afterlife, no human lives have intrinsic or extrinsic meaning? In the next section I critically examine some of the main arguments for such a view.

4. Arguments That All Human Lives Are Meaningless without God or an Afterlife

According to *the final outcome argument*, if every human life culminates in death and death is the permanent end of conscious experience, and if the ultimate fate of the physical universe is static, lifeless heat-death, then every human life is entirely devoid of meaning. Craig (1994; see also 2013) declares:

> If there is no God, then man and the universe are doomed. . . . The contributions of the scientist to the advance of human knowledge, the researches of the doctor to alleviate pain and suffering, the efforts of the diplomat to secure peace in the world . . . all these come to nothing. In the end they don't make one bit of difference. . . . And because our lives are ultimately meaningless, the activities we fill our lives with are also meaningless. (1994, 58–59)[11]

---

[9] That request was not honoured.
[10] See pattillmanfoundation.org.
[11] This also seems to be the gist of Meursault's rant toward the end of *The Stranger* (Camus 1989, 120–122).

Think of a person's life as a series of events. Say that a life has *ultimate meaning* only if it makes a difference in the nature of the final outcome. Without God, goes the argument, no life makes a difference in the final outcome—all lives, and indeed the universe itself—end in the same way, regardless of what anyone does. Thus, all lives lack ultimate meaning. The crucial inference in the final outcome argument is from (i) without God or an afterlife, all human lives lack *ultimate* meaning to (ii) without God or an afterlife, all human lives lack *all* meaning.

But that is a non sequitur (see Wielenberg 2005, 29–30; 2014, 47–48; Landau 2017, 37). From the fact that an activity makes no difference to the nature of the final outcome, it simply does not follow that the activity lacks intrinsic or extrinsic meaning. The bad inference that the final outcome argument depends on is similar to reasoning that because all films end with credits, no film is better or worse than any other.

A second argument is the *absence of purpose* argument. Without God, each human life, as well as the human race as a whole, not to mention the universe itself, lacks an ultimate, divinely-given goal or purpose toward which it does, or at least should, lead. Craig says, 'if God does not exist . . . life is utterly without reason' (2013, 163). Although Craig does not claim that the lack of an ultimate purpose for human life implies that human lives are meaningless, in the present context it's worth noting that the absence of ultimate purpose for human life does not render all human lives meaningless.

Imagine two intrinsically identical roses. The two roses have the same number of petals, the same exquisite rose-colour, the same perfect proportions, and so on. The only difference between them lies in how they came to be. The first rose is the culmination of the lifelong dream of a meticulous rose-grower who picked the perfect location to plant the rose and carefully tended and protected it as it grew. The second rose sprouted from a pile of cow manure, into which a staggering drunk on his way home from the bar accidentally dropped one of the rose seeds his wife had asked him to purchase earlier that day. The first rose came into existence through a carefully conceived and executed plan; the second arose by dumb luck. The first rose has an ultimate purpose—it exists for a reason (in the teleological sense), whereas the second rose does not. Yet the two roses are equally beautiful and equally valuable; their origins are irrelevant to the intrinsic value that they carry within themselves. Additionally, both roses can bring the same admiration and joy to those who experience their beauty, so both roses can generate extrinsic goods despite their very different origins. Similarly, the fact that a given human life has no ultimate purpose and is a happy accident that exists for no (teleological) reason does not imply that it lacks intrinsic or extrinsic meaning.

Another argument is suggested by Tolstoy's famous remarks on his famous existential crisis. Tolstoy wonders 'What meaning has my finite existence in this infinite world?' (2008, 13) and asserts that religious faith 'gives to the finite existence of man the sense of the infinite' (2008, 14). In response to the question 'What real result will there be from my life?', faith answers: 'Eternal torment or eternal bliss' (2008, 14). If there is a God and an afterlife, then the stakes of our earthly lives are high indeed—infinitely high, in fact.[12] This view of things is nicely expressed by C. S. Lewis this way:

> There are no ordinary people. You have never talked to a mere mortal. Nations, cultures, arts, civilizations—these are mortal, and their life is to ours as the life of a gnat. But it is immortals whom we joke with, work with, marry, snub and exploit—immortal horrors or everlasting splendors. (Lewis 2001, 46).

In comparison with the infinite, anything finite can seem like nothing. Pascal expresses this idea thusly: 'When I consider the short span of my life absorbed into the preceding and subsequent eternity... the small space which I fill and even can see, swallowed up in the infinite immensity of spaces of which I know nothing and which knows nothing of me, I am terrified' ([1670] 1995, 16).

Such remarks suggest *the no infinity argument*, according to which a life that does not have infinite significance or meaning has no meaning at all. Without God or an afterlife, no human life has infinite meaning and hence no human life has any meaning at all. This argument is reminiscent of the final outcome argument discussed earlier. An important difference between the two arguments is that as far as the final outcome argument goes, a life could have finite meaning (by making a difference to how things turn out in the end), whereas the no infinity argument rejects that as a possibility.

This argument depends on a flawed version of what Landau calls 'perfectionism'. Landau writes that '[w]hat marks perfectionists is that they fail to see the worth that inheres also in the nonperfect' (2017, 35). The maxim that if a life lacks infinite significance then it lacks any significance at all is a flawed version of perfectionism that simply overlooks the reality of finite significance. The maxim is no more plausible than the absurd maxim of Ricky Bobby in the film *Talladega Nights*: 'If you ain't first, you're last.' As Audi (2005) points out, '[f]inite values can still be great' (354).

A final argument is based on the claim that without God, nothing has any value whatsoever. In making the case for the possibility of meaning in life in a godless universe, I have helped myself to the claim that in a godless universe certain things are valuable, and objectively so. But according to the *no value without God* argument, objective morality requires a theistic foundation. Craig is an advocate of this argument; he declares that '[i]n a universe without God, good and evil do not exist—there is only the bare valueless fact of existence' (1994, 61).

Whether this argument stands or falls depends on a highly controversial question, namely: What is the correct meta-ethical theory? If the correct meta-ethical theory is a God-based theory that implies that objective values *must* have a theistic foundation, then the no value without God argument succeeds; otherwise it fails. Craig defends a version of divine command theory according to which God is the ultimate standard of good and evil and finite things are valuable only in virtue of resembling God in a certain

---

[12] For an interesting alternative reading of Tolstoy's 'Confession', see Perrett (1985).

way (see e.g. Craig 2009). That sort of theory has been developed in great depth by Adams (1999). Of course, there are a great many alternatives to that sort of theory, many of which, if correct, allow for the existence of objective values in a godless universe. On some theories, moral properties are entirely reducible to natural properties (e.g. Brink 1989; Foot 2001). Another prominent approach has it that moral properties are distinct from natural properties but are entirely dependent or supervenient upon such properties (in a way that doesn't require God); that approach has seen a resurgence in contemporary philosophy (e.g. Moore 1903; Huemer 2005; Enoch 2011; and Parfit 2011, 263–620). Furthermore, it's worth noting that properly defending the no value without God argument requires making the case not only that objective value in fact depends on God but that objective values *cannot* exist without God. The claim that objective value in fact depends on God does not by itself imply that without God there is no objective value (see Mawson 2018, 77–78). Adams holds that the objective value of finite things in fact depends on God, but he also says this: 'If there is no God . . . then my theory is false, but . . . some other theory of the nature of the good may be true' (1999, 46; see also Baggett and Walls 2011, 98–99).

A full discussion of these meta-ethical issues is beyond the scope of this chapter, but it is worth noting that the plausibility of the view that some things distinct from God have intrinsic worth seems to count against any theistic view according to which nothing can have value without God, since on the latter view things distinct from God could only possess extrinsic value, value possessed in virtue of being related to God in some way (see Wielenberg 2014, 83–84; Davison 2018, 42).[13] In any case, defenders of the no value without God argument face the challenging task of showing that no non-theistic meta-ethical account of objective value is plausible. I think the prospects of accomplishing that task are dim.

Overall, then, I do not think that the claim that without God or an afterlife no human lives are meaningful is plausible. What is plausible is *moderate supernaturalism*, according to which the existence of God and an afterlife allows human lives to have *more* meaning than they could otherwise. But as far as I can see, there is little to commend the more radical view that atheism implies meaninglessness.

5. Conclusion

In the introduction to this chapter, I invited the reader to suppose for the sake of argument that there is no God, there are no non-physical souls, there is no afterlife, reincarnation never occurs, and that each human being's death marks the permanent end of his

---

[13] This is a consequence of the fact that *intrinsic* value is the value a thing has in and of itself, independently of how it is related to anything else, whereas *extrinsic* value is the value a thing has in virtue of how it is related to other things. So, if human love, for example, has intrinsic value, that value is not grounded in human love's resemblance to divine love.

or her actions and experiences. In fact, I think that the available evidence suggests that each of these claims is true. I hope in this chapter to have made some progress in showing that these truths do not imply that all human lives are meaningless and to have identified some important sources of meaning in life in a godless universe. As Cottingham points out, in a godless universe, luck (i.e. factors beyond one's control) plays a significant role in the extent of meaning in one's life such that, as he puts it:

> [T]he lucky ones on whom fortune smiles will be able to look back at the end of their lives and pronounce them meaningful, while those who are, by birth, or upbringing, or ill-health, or lack of resources, or accident, unable to pursue worthwhile goals, or prevented from reaching them, will just have to lump it. (2002, 69)

According to Cottingham, such a view is 'psychologically indigestible' and 'ethically repugnant' (2002, 69). Psychologically indigestible? On the contrary, it's a reality faced by millions of human beings through history and today. Ethically repugnant? Yes, but that's obviously no reason to think that it's not true. As Detective Somerset says at the end of the film *Se7en*: 'Ernest Hemingway once wrote: "The world is a fine place and worth fighting for." I agree with the second part.' I would add that in that fight there is much meaning to be found—God or no God.[14]

References

Adams, Robert. 1999. *Finite and Infinite Goods*. Oxford: Oxford University Press.
Angle, Stephen C. 2009. *Sagehood: The Contemporary Significance of Neo-Confucian Philosophy*. Oxford: Oxford University Press.
Audi, Robert. 2005. 'Intrinsic Value and Meaningful Life'. *Philosophical Papers* 34(3): 331–355.
Baggett, David, and Jerry L. Walls. 2011. *Good God: The Theistic Foundations of Morality*. Oxford: Oxford University Press.
Bradley, Ben. 2015. *Well-Being*. Malden, MA: Polity Press.
Brink, David. 1989. *Moral Realism and the Foundations of Ethics*. Cambridge: Cambridge University Press.
Camus, Albert. 1989. *The Stranger*, trans. M. Ward. New York: Vintage Books.
Chisholm, Roderick. 1968. 'The Defeat of Good and Evil'. *Proceedings and Addresses of the American Philosophical Association* 42(21): 21–38.
Cottingham, John. 2002. *On the Meaning of Life*. New York: Routledge.
Craig, William Lane. 1994. *Reasonable Faith*, rev. ed. Wheaton, IL: Crossway Books.
Craig, William Lane. 2009. 'The Most Gruesome of Guests'. In *Is Goodness without God Good Enough?*, ed. N. L. King and R. K. Garcia, 167–188. Lanham, MD: Rowman and Littlefield).
Craig, William Lane. 2013. 'The Absurdity of Life without God'. In *Exploring the Meaning of Life: An Anthology and Guide*, ed. J. Seachris, 153–172. Walden, MA: Wiley-Blackwell.

---

[14] I am grateful to Tim Mawson and Iddo Landau for helpful comments on earlier versions of this chapter.

Csikszentmihalyi, Mihaly. 2008. *Flow: The Psychology of Optimal Experience*. New York: HarperCollins.
Davison, Scott. 2018. 'God and Intrinsic Value'. In *Does God Matter? Essays on the Axiological Consequences of Theism*, ed. K. Kraay, 39–45. New York: Routledge.
Enoch, David. 2011. *Taking Morality Seriously*. Oxford: Oxford University Press.
Erikson, E. H. 1963. *Childhood and Society*, 2nd ed. New York: Norton.
Fletcher, Guy. 2016. *The Philosophy of Well-Being: An Introduction*. New York: Routledge.
Foot, Philippa. 2001. *Natural Goods*. Oxford: Oxford University Press.
Frankl, Viktor E. [1959] 2006. *Man's Search for Meaning*. Boston, MA: Beacon Press.
Frankfurt, Harry G. 2004. *The Reasons of Love*. Princeton, NJ: Princeton University Press.
Graham, Jesse, and Jonathan Haidt. 2010. 'Beyond Beliefs: Religions Bind Individuals into Moral Communities'. *Personality and Social Psychology Review* 14(1): 140–150.
Haidt, Jonathan. 2006. *The Happiness Hypothesis: Finding Modern Truth in Ancient Wisdom*. New York: Basic Books.
Hamilton, Christopher. 2018. 'Frail Worms of the Earth: Philosophical Reflections on the Meaning of Life'. *Religious Studies* 54: 55–71.
Hang, Lin. 2011. 'Traditional Confucianism and Its Contemporary Relevance'. *Asian Philosophy* 21(4): 437–445.
Huemer, Michael. 2005. *Ethical Intuitionism*. New York: Palgrave-Macmillan.
Junger, Sebastian. 2016. *Tribe: On Homecoming and Belonging*. New York: Hachette Book Group.
Klancer, Catherine Hudak. 2012. 'How Opposites (Should) Attract: Humility as a Virtue for the Strong'. *The Heythrop Journal* 53: 662–677.
Krakauer, Jon. 2009. *Where Men Win Glory: The Odyssey of Pat Tillman*. New York: Anchor Books.
Landau, Iddo. 2017. *Finding Meaning in an Imperfect World*. Oxford: Oxford University Press.
Levy, Neil. 2005. 'Downshifting and Meaning in Life'. *Ratio* (new series) 18(2): 176–189.
Lewis, C. S. 2001. 'The Weight of Glory'. In C. S. Lewis, *The Weight of Glory and Other Addresses*, 25–46. New York: HarperCollins.
Li, Chenyang. 2006. 'The Confucian Ideal of Harmony'. *Philosophy East & West* 56(4): 583–603.
Matheson, David. 2018. 'Creativity and Meaning in Life'. *Ratio* (new series) 31(1): 73–87.
Mawson, T. J. 2018. 'An Agreeable Answer to a Pro-Theism/Anti-Theism Question'. In *Does God Matter? Essays on the Axiological Consequences of Theism*, ed. K. Kraay, 70–92. New York: Routledge.
Mawson, T. J. 2019. *Monotheism and the Meaning of Life*. Cambridge: Cambridge University Press.
May, Todd. 2015. *A Significant Life: Human Meaning in a Silent Universe*. Chicago: University of Chicago Press.
Metz, Thaddeus. 2011. 'The Good, the True, and the Beautiful: Toward a Unified Account of Great Meaning in Life'. *Religious Studies* 47: 389–409.
Metz, Thaddeus. 2014. *Meaning in Life*. Oxford: Oxford University Press.
Moore, George Edward. 1903. *Principia Ethica*. Cambridge: Cambridge University Press.
Ozment, Katherine. 2016. *Grace without God: The Search for Meaning, Purpose, and Belonging in a Secular Age*. New York: HarperCollins.
Parfit, Derek. 2011. *On What Matters*, Vol. II. Oxford: Oxford University Press.
Pascal, Blaise. [1670] 1995. *Pensées*, trans. H. Levi. Oxford: Oxford University Press.
Perrett, Roy W. 1985. 'Tolstoy, Death and the Meaning of Life'. *Philosophy* 60(232): 231–245.

Quinn, Philip L. 2008. 'The Meaning of Life According to Christianity'. In *The Meaning of Life: A Reader*, ed. E. D. Klemke and Steven M. Cahn, 35–41. Oxford: Oxford University Press.

Seachris, Joshua. 2013. 'Introduction'. In *Exploring the Meaning of Life: An Anthology and Guide*, ed. J. Seachris, 1–17. New York: Wiley-Blackwell.

Sim, May. 2007. *Remastering Morals with Aristotle and Confucius*. Cambridge: Cambridge University Press.

Singer, Peter. 1995. *How Are We to Live? Ethics in an Age of Self-Interest*. Amherst, NY: Prometheus Books.

Singer, Peter. 2000. *Marx: A Very Short Introduction*. Oxford: Oxford University Press.

Smuts, Aaron. 2012. 'It's a Wonderful Life: Pottersville and the Meaning of Life'. *Film and Philosophy* 16(1): 15–33.

Taylor, Richard. 2000. *Good and Evil*. Amherst, NY: Prometheus Books.

Tolstoy, Leo. 2008. 'My Confession'. In *The Meaning of Life: A Reader*, ed. E. D. Klemke and Steven M. Cahn, 7–16. Oxford: Oxford University Press.

Wade, Nichols. 2009. *The Faith Instinct: How Religion Evolved and Why It Endures*. New York: Penguin.

Wielenberg, Erik J. 2005. *Value and Virtue in a Godless Universe*. Cambridge: Cambridge University Press.

Wielenberg, Erik J. 2014. *Robust Ethics: The Metaphysics and Epistemology of Godless Normative Realism*. Oxford: Oxford University Press.

Wilson, David Sloan. 2002. *Darwin's Cathedral: Evolution, Religion, and the Nature of Society*. Chicago: University of Chicago Press.

Wolf, Susan. 2010. *Meaning in Life and Why It Matters*. Princeton, NJ: Princeton University Press.

Zuckerman, Phil. 2008. *Society without God: What the Least Religious Nations Can Tell Us about Contentment*. New York: New York University Press.

CHAPTER 14

THEISM AND MEANING IN LIFE

T. J. MAWSON

THE meaning-of-life question on which the contemporary literature in the analytic tradition centres may be put like this: 'What is it that constitutes meaning in an individual's life?' The literature characteristically supposes its task to be to give a correct account of this property, which I shall call 'meaningfulness', and construes meaningfulness as a single gradient value that individuals' lives may have. On my own view, meaningfulness is not in fact just one feature of individuals' lives, but several; some of them are valuable whilst some of them are not. In this chapter, I aim to guide us in looking at how the God of Theism affects (or would affect, were He to exist) one of the sorts of meaningfulness that our individual lives may have, one which I shall call 'significance' and describe as the chapter goes on.[1] And I shall concentrate on the valuable sort of significance.

With that aim in mind, allow me to invite you to consider two worlds, both of which—I shall be assuming—are logically possible. Each of these worlds is as close as possible to the other in what properties it has, given that in Atheism World, as we shall call it, there is no God of the sort believed in by the adherents of the monotheistic religions of Judaism, Christianity, and Islam (nor anything at all similar), and in Theism World, as we shall call it, there is such a God. And each of these worlds is as close to the actual world in its properties as it can be in consistency with that. Atheism World then is the world that most atheists reading this believe to be the actual world: there's this—physical—universe, with us in it; after our deaths, we cease to exist, never to live again. Theism World is the world most theists reading this believe to be the actual world: as well as this, physical, universe, with us leading our lives within it, there's a God; and,

---

[1] I argue for the 'polyvalence' view, as I call it, of the question 'What is the meaning of life?' and of meaningfulness in a number of places. My most sustained and detailed argument for it is given in my (2016). I also discuss how God affects other meanings in my (2019).

after our lives here, we shall go on to a heavenly afterlife with Him.[2] The question I shall be addressing requires us then to compare the significance of our lives in Atheism World with that which they have in Theism World.

A thought which is commonplace outside professional philosophical circles goes as follows: if we're in Atheism World, then our lives—as *ante-mortem* lives alone, for that is the only lives we have—fail to have significance in anything but a very small-scale and fleeting way. If, by contrast, we're in Theism World, then our lives—as *ante-mortem* plus infinite *post-mortem* lives—have much greater significance, indeed possibly even infinite significance. However commonplace in the wider community, such a thought is subject to some suspicion interior to professional philosophical circles. Is this commonplace thought right? In this chapter, I shall argue that it is right (on certain assumptions).

First, I wish to introduce a distinction between two types of significance: 'subjective significance' and 'objective significance', as I shall call them.

Williams has a thought-experiment which makes the distinction nicely (Williams 1986, 182–183). Henry, according to this thought-experiment, is someone who cares greatly about adding a last 'missing' stamp to his stamp collection. We might say that it matters a lot *to* Henry that he obtains this last stamp; it is significant and important *to* him. But nevertheless, we might say that it does not matter much *for* him or *for* the world more broadly. That is, if he adds this stamp to his collection, that perhaps adds some objective value to the world, but still, common sense would suggest, this addition to the objective value of reality is not a significant addition. I shall call this more objective sort of significance, naturally enough, 'objective significance' and talk about it more in a moment. In contrast with that, then, I shall call this other sort of significance 'subjective significance.' Subjective significance is a matter of how much, as a matter of fact, something is cared about; saying that adding the last missing stamp is subjectively significant to Henry is simply another way of saying that Henry cares a great deal about it. With regards to subjective significance, it immediately looks rather easy to make the case for us having more significance in Theism World than we do in Atheism World.

In Atheism World, one is significant to those who love one, but of course one eventually dies and the people who loved one die too. It may be that some who come after one's death and did not know one personally will nevertheless care about one's existence, e.g. through reading a chapter one once wrote for a book and caring about the fact that one wrote it—perhaps wishing that it had not been written; one can, after all, be significant to people for bad reasons as well as good.[3] But let's continue to concentrate on 'the good case'. It may be that, for those of us who have children (who in turn have children and

---

[2] Note, I shall be assuming that in Theism World we *all* go to Heaven. I discuss how things would play out were one to alter this assumption in my (2016, 134ff). Space considerations do not permit me to go into it here.

[3] Whilst it doesn't affect the issues in this chapter, negative significance does have implications. So, for example, I would say that Adolf Hitler was more significant than my paternal grandfather (a man who spent his working life in a clerical job in a confectionary company), but Hitler's life was of far less objective value than my paternal grandfather's; indeed Hitler's life was plausibly of negative value. That being so, it is in fact implausible that objective significance is simply a matter of being 'significantly good';

so on onwards to the necessary extent), one of our distant descendants cares about our existence, if only as he or she appreciates it to be a necessary condition of his or her own. But however far these sorts of connections might be stretched, in the Heat Death of the universe, if not in fact long before, they will come to an end; in Atheism World we shall, in the end, lose our significance to all people.

In Theism World, by contrast, we have a lot more subjective significance than that. First, and entirely sufficient to make the case, we have—added to whatever subjective significance we have in Atheism World—our significance to God, a being who has the capacity to care infinitely about each of us and, being perfectly loving, does indeed do so.[4] Secondly, in that those humans who have loved us will not be lost to death, but rather too will resurrect with their love for us magnified yet further, we will continue to have the subjective significance of our lives that is generated by the love of humans towards us; we will have it at a higher intensity and—if Heaven is best construed as an everlasting temporal span (rather than an atemporal realm)—we will have it for a potentially infinite duration. Admittedly, there are issues e.g. about whether or not, even *post-resurrection* and thus post-perfect-sanctification, humans are the sorts of beings who are capable of loving other creatures only a finite amount (either atemporally, if Heaven is atemporal, or at any one time, if Heaven is temporal) and about whether or not the afterlife should be construed as atemporal or temporal in the first place. All of these issues bear further consideration, some of which I shall give them later in this chapter. But, for now, we may observe that, however these issues fall out, the contrast between Theism World and Atheism World is a stark one, between finitude and infinitude. In Atheism World, we are significant to certain humans to a finite extent and for a finite period and that's that; in Theism World, we are infinitely significant to God and we are significant to all humans in Heaven. The case is made, for subjective significance.

Could it be argued that this addition of subjective significance in itself affects the objective value of our lives? Of course, it does so 'extrinsically', as we might say; it adds due to its causal powers—it is precisely because God loves us that He provides for us a *post-mortem* and eternal/everlasting afterlife with Him in Heaven. And this afterlife adds the value of these *post*-mortem lives to whatever value our *ante-mortem* lives have in both Theism World and Atheism World. But does it do so, as we might say, 'intrinsically'? Does one's life go better for one if someone cares about one *simply in virtue of their caring about one*? To control for the extrinsic factors, we do best to consider a case where someone is cared about but that care doesn't make any (other?) causal contribution to the quality of their lives.

---

this is an additional reason for us to doubt the idea that the scale of significance always recalibrates by reference to the 'top scorer(s)', as I shall put it in the main text, when it comes to objective value.

[4] If God is atemporal, then this is infinitely from His eternal perspective; if God is temporal, then this is a love of infinite intensity had for us over His never-ending time. Waghorn raises with me a potential down-side to this given that God may perhaps care infinitely about our bad actions, giving them an infinite negative significance. In the chapter, I thus focus exclusively on His care for *us*, not for our actions. Even if He hates the sin, He loves the sinner.

We get close to seeing such a case in the film *The Truman Show*. The main character in this film, Truman, has, since his birth, been in a 'reality' TV show, entirely unbeknownst to himself. As the creator and curator of this show, Christof, explains in a wonderful God-like speech towards the end of the film, millions of viewers care deeply about the ins and outs of Truman's everyday life. He gives this speech to Truman himself when Truman, after having realised his true situation, is contemplating walking through a door which will mean him leaving the set of the TV show, the implication being never to return. Does the fact that Truman is, as Christof then tells him, the star of a television show that gives hope and inspiration to millions reveal to Truman something about his TV-life which in itself makes that TV-life objectively better than it would have been had Christof had to concede that Truman was playing merely a 'bit' part in a show that had very limited emotional investment from any of those very few people who watched it? I think it does. Those who know the film may have conflicting intuitions, but that— I would say—is because there is so much else objectively bad about Truman's TV-life. Christof is right in thinking that the points he makes in his speech are points in favour of Truman staying in the TV show; he's just wrong in supposing—as he seems to suppose—that there aren't weighty considerations on the other side of the scales. To see this, suppose that Truman is told by Christof that he *has* to stay in *a* TV show—the door through which he is thinking of walking merely leads to another (and itself inescapable) TV set. Truman's only choice is between moving from the TV show in which he is cared about and provides joy and inspiration to millions and one in which he is cared about by nobody. After Truman has made his choice, his memory of having made it will be erased and he will again be unaware of his true condition. It seems to me that, controlling for other variables, it would be rationally self-interested for Truman to choose to stay. So, I incline to conclude that being cared about in itself adds value to the life of the person cared about. I also have some intuitions that this value-adding increases with the amount of care; being cared about to no extent by anyone is worse than being cared about a small amount by a small number, which is in turn worse than being cared about to a large extent by a large number. Still, such value judgements are controversial. It also seems clear to me that, whatever objective value is added to a life by its being cared about, it cannot ever outweigh certain other disvalues. Even if Christof had been able to say (truly) that Truman's role in his current TV show gave hope and inspiration to an *infinite* number of people, Truman would—on balance—have been rationally self-interested to leave for the real world. Or so it seems to me; again, others would disagree.[5] Thus whilst our being cared about an infinite amount by God may in and of itself add some objective value to our lives in Theism World (relative to that which they have in Atheism World), it would be dangerous to rely upon this addition alone to make the case that our lives are more objectively significant in Theism World (than they are in Atheism World). Another reason for caution is that, as we shall see in a moment, objective significance is

---

[5] And much depends of course on the character of the real world which he would be entering. In the film, the love of his life is waiting for him there.

plausibly a relative measure and, even if an infinite addition of subjective significance to our lives by God's love for us pushes us up the absolute scale of objective value in the direction of the top end (where objective significance may be taken to lie), it may not push us far enough in relative terms. But to see quite what is being suggested here and appreciate its plausibility, we must turn to a consideration of how best we should understand objective significance.

With that aim now in mind, I shall look at the work of a couple of philosophers, both of whom would call into question the commonplace thought that we have more objective significance in Theism World than we do in Atheism World—Bernard Williams again and Guy Kahane. I shall use their work to form an understanding of objective significance on which the commonplace thought emerges vindicated, to an extent.

In his famous essay, 'A Free Man's Worship' (Russell 1953, 50–59), Russell expounds the view that, given our small and transitory lives here on earth, we must despair of judging ourselves significant. After having described this essay as one in which Russell 'went on about' the ephemeral nature of human existence 'in a style of self-pitying and at the same time self-glorifying rhetoric', Williams says of people who take a Russellian line in this context that they involve themselves in a 'muddle'. 'It is a muddle between thinking that our activities fail some test of cosmic significance, and (as contrasted with that) recognising that there is no such test. If there is no such thing as the cosmic point of view, if the idea of absolute importance in the scheme of things is an illusion, a relic of a world not yet thoroughly disenchanted, then there is no other point of view except ours in which our activities have or lack a significance' (Williams 2006, 137). If we are—as Williams supposes—in Atheism World, the standard for significance is one of our own intersubjective creation (roughly, that is significant which is taken to be so by us) and we meet the standard which we thus create. On the other hand, if we had been in Theism World, the standard of significance would have been, Williams elsewhere in this paper tacitly concedes, one that God would have created but then we would have met that standard. The bottom line then is that, either way, there is no cause for worry about our significance. Either there is a God, in which case He creates the standard for significance and we meet it; or there's not, in which case we create and meet our own standard.[6]

Of course Williams's happy 'fork' cannot be deployed by someone still attached to a view of values such as that from which Williams himself is disenchanted, one in which—even absent God—there are some supra-human standards of value and significance. If one thinks that there are such standards in Atheism World, it is—at least initially—an open question whether or not we satisfactorily measure up to them if that is indeed where we are. And such a view of values and standards has enchanted many writing in contemporary philosophy. So, Kahane—like Williams—thinks that we are in fact in Atheism World, but—unlike Williams—he thinks that there is nevertheless, as he puts it, an "objective" standard of value (i.e. one which is independent of anything we

---

[6] This seems to me Williams's position in this paper, anyway; elsewhere, he says things that do not easily mesh with it.

humans might happen to think or feel about it, one which remains the same across logical space as the measure of value in Atheism World and Theism World). We humans—collectively and individually—affect reality in such a way as to affect its overall value by reference to this standard—affect it, one must hope, positively. But at least initially it is an open question whether or not we do so in any way that is significant. The mere fact that the intersubjective standard of significance we set up may well be met by us does not vouchsafe *true* significance for us. In calibrating our scale of significance as we have, we humans may have been rather too myopic, rather as children taking as significant that which adults can see from their larger perspective is not really significant at all. According to Kahane, we may affect value, but not *significantly* affect it.

Kahane tells us that '[f]or something to be significant it needs to possess (or at least bring about) some value [by reference to this objective standard]'; *but not just any amount of value, however negligible, will do.* According to Kahane, for a life to be significant, it needs to possess or bring about value that is '*important* . . . it needs to possess, or bring about, enough value to make a difference' (Kahane 2014, 749). The intrinsic value of something cannot be changed by its surroundings. But its significance can' (Kahane 2014, 750). 'We can think of the relation between value and significance as parallel to that between having an absolute size and being large or small. If one is a certain size, then one just is that size. But how large or small one is depends on the comparison class: atoms, ants, rhinoceroses, quasars. . . . And to know our comparative size to everything else is to know something we wouldn't know just by knowing our absolute size' (Kahane 2014, 765).

Bringing all of this together, Kahane is thus willing to entertain as a live possibility that, despite any overall positive contribution to value that humanity might make, we might nevertheless be insignificant given what else of positive value is around in the universe. In the end though, Kahane concludes—tentatively—on a more positive note: if we humans are in fact the most valuable beings in the universe, then we possess great significance, for nothing is more valuable than us—us collectively, that is. As Kahane points out, individual humans may fail the test of significance even whilst humanity as a whole succeeds by reference to it; indeed, most individuals do fail. So, on Kahane's understanding, if we are in Atheism World and there are not in fact other superior civilisations on different planets and the like, we have great significance collectively, even though only a few 'world historical' individuals have it individually. Of course, given the Drake Equation and plausible fillings-out of its variables' values, it is—one might argue—highly likely that ours is a universe in which there are many superior extraterrestrial civilisations (superior to any which humanity will achieve) and so one might conclude that Kahane's tentative sounding of a positive note about our having significance is, in the end, unwarranted. His argument, when buttressed by such considerations, leads to the conclusion that we are almost certainly neither collectively nor individually significant in Atheism World.[7] Supposing such a view is right, surely then, things are better

---

[7] The Drake Equation is a way of mathematicising our understanding of the probability of extraterrestrial life. Wielenberg points out that one might throw so-called Great Filter considerations in

for us with regards to the prospect of our having significance if we are in fact in Theism World. Perhaps surprisingly, Kahane argues they are not.

The 'problem', as it were, is that in Theism World there is, of course, a God who is, of course, supremely valuable, so much so as to dwarf into insignificance any significance humanity collectively might otherwise have had or any of us as individuals might have managed to achieve. 'If God exists, then trivially we couldn't be the most valuable entities in the universe [by which Kahane means reality *per se*, not simply the space-time manifold which on Theism is but a proper part of reality], indeed we would be of absurdly negligible value compared to His perfect goodness' (Kahane 2014, 761). Thus Kahane's argument has what may be a surprising conclusion. 'The vastness and indifference of the universe present no challenge to our significance. But the existence of a perfect supreme being of infinite value certainly does' (Kahane 2014, 761).

Despite their differences, we can see a similarity here between Williams and Kahane, one which is pertinent to answering the question we now have before us, viz. 'How does our (objective) significance vary between Atheism World and Theism World?' Or rather, it is pertinent to seeing some controversial assumptions that I must make if I am to answer it.

In their own ways, both show us that it would be controversial to assume that there is a standard of significance that stays fixed across logical space so as to be the cogent measure in both Atheism World and Theism World. According to both Williams and Kahane, the standard for significance is precisely not the same in Atheism World and in Theism World. For Kahane, the standard is not fixed across all worlds in which Atheism is true—it recalibrates itself, as it were, relative to what in each world is the most valuable individual.[8] For Williams, the problem goes deeper; there is not even—as Kahane would allow—a measure of objective value that is robust enough across logical space so that both our contributions to value in Atheism World and Theism World may be assessed by reference to its absolute measure; rather, it too, whilst present in Theism World, drops out in Atheism World.

I cannot afford to open up too many topics in this context, so allow me to accept as a premise at this stage that Williams is wrong and Kahane is right about the fact that there is a standard of value robust enough to obtain over Theism World and Atheism

---

the way of this point. Perhaps climate change, weapons technology, or some combination of such things reduces sufficiently the chances of these extraterrestrials getting far beyond us in value.

[8] Kahane points out to me in correspondence that his view is that the standard of significance is not a matter determined in each world merely by the score of *the* top-scorer, but also by how many top-scorers there are. Different views are available here, depending on the relative weightings one gives to, say, the amount by which the top-scorer surpasses the lower-scorers (or perhaps the lowest-scorer; or perhaps some average scorer?); how many top-scorers there are (and whether to be a top-scorer one must match exactly in value other top-scorers or whether something more approximate will suffice); and perhaps other factors. These epicycles would complicate, but not fundamentally affect, the issues to which this chapter addresses itself. So, although they are of interest in their own right and worthy of further exploration, I shall proceed in the main text by only considering the simplest view—the view that the top-scorer determines the standard, though sometimes I shall talk of the top-scoring species.

World and, further, allow me to assume that humanity is making a (net) positive contribution to value by reference to this standard, and so are each of us.[9] It seems to me that Kahane is also right to think that significance is a relativistic notion, rather than an absolutist one. And so it is indeed true that it is—at least initially—an open question whether or not, even given the controversial assumptions to which I have helped myself, humanity is significant, let alone whether or not all of us are significant as individuals. However, it seems to me that Kahane errs elsewhere in his analogy with size and in what Theism entails, meaning that we may conclude that our lives are more objectively significant in Theism World than they are in Atheism World and infinitely so. The commonplace thought, as I called it at the start of this chapter, emerges vindicated (albeit only on certain assumptions, about one of which I shall express some diffidence). Or so I shall now argue.

Recall that for Kahane, significance (of the objective sort which we are now considering) may be seen as analogous to size. I think this is a useful insight and I shall expand upon it.

First, something either has a size or it does not; it either occupies space or it does not. A mouse has a size; so too does an elephant; but a point particle (by hypothesis) does not. Analogously then, something either has objective value or it does not. We are assuming that humanity generally, and each of us as individuals, does have positive value. As well as this absolutist sense, whereby something has a size just if it's on the scale (occupies space to a non-zero extent), there's also a relativistic sense; we might call it size as a matter of being size*able*, whereby something is sizeable only if it is large in comparison to some comparator or class of comparators (other things in a suitable comparison class). 'Big' or 'large' are, I take it, synonyms of 'sizeable.' When it comes to sizeableness then, as sizeableness is a relativistic, rather than an absolutist, measure, so much depends on one's choice of comparators. Thus, in the context of comparing animals, one would perhaps most naturally say that a mouse is not sizeable whereas an elephant is sizeable. In comparing both with the planet Jupiter, one would say that neither is sizeable. Something similar, it will be recalled, is claimed by Kahane of significance. And that seems right.[10] A particular move may be significant in the context of a particular game of chess (compared to other moves in the game), but the game of chess itself may be insignificant (it being played merely to pass the time) in the context of a person's life as a whole (compared to other things that happen in this person's life). And so on. This draws to our attention then the need to think a bit more about what comparators are the right ones for such judgements, or if the notion of 'right' is itself misplaced here.

---

[9] That is, I am ignoring potentially problematic cases such as Hitler.

[10] In fact, as already mentioned, I think that significance as a notion does not mean only significantly good, whereas sizeable does mean only significantly large. Things can be significant through being significantly bad. The Planck length is a significant length, even though a very small one—perhaps the smallest. Though this would complicate the discussion, it wouldn't fundamentally affect it, so I am, it will be recalled, leaving such issues aside.

Kahane, it will be recalled, suggests that the *only right* comparator in the case of value is whatever is of most value. But that, I shall suggest, is stipulative.

In being asked to compare the size of a mouse with that of an elephant—'Is a mouse sizeable compared to an elephant?'—or being asked to compare a mouse within the context of a group of animals of which it is a member—asked a question such as 'Is a mouse sizeable for a mammal?'—then the 'compared to an elephant' or the 'for a mammal' clause does, it seems to me, determine a single right comparator, viz. the things that make up the class of elephants and class of mammals, respectively. But it would seem odd (to me) to suggest that when a question is posed as to how sizeable something is and yet such a clause is not introduced (either explicitly or implicitly, by context), there is, even then, one and only one suitable comparator or comparison class. When being asked simply, 'Is an elephant sizeable (large, or big)?', one might, it seems to me, most naturally respond, 'Relative to what? Relative to extant land animals, yes. Relative to Jupiter, no.' Some of these choices—comparing an animal with Jupiter, say—seem at least strained and I shall say more about that in a moment. But certainly, one would protest if someone maintained that an elephant *cannot* be sizeable as the *only* acceptable comparator is the largest space-time manifold and, of course, relative to that, an elephant is tiny. Analogously, and *pace* Kahane then, it seems to me that we should maintain that one cannot conclude that the scale of significance recalibrates as we move over logical space relative to whatever is of most absolute value. If we are in Atheism World and there are extraterrestrial civilisations more valuable than anything humanity will achieve, that does not straightforwardly entail that we are not significant, for it is not that the 'top-scorers' in value automatically define significance for everything else; the top-scorers may not be the only permissible comparators or even permissible comparators at all. Similarly, if we are in Theism World, then arguably (we'll return to this in a moment) nothing has much value compared with God, but again, even so, humanity might be significant compared to all other biological species on Earth; Bobby Moore might be significant as a footballer; I might be significant within my family; and so on. These are suitable comparators and they may even be argued to be the *only* suitable comparators. Why the only ones? Well, common linguistic intuitions would seem to license them and (arguably) only them. One might see this move as representing a Williams-esque view of significance reinserted into a Kahane-esque view of value. Even if (against Williams but with Kahane), humanity may be judged in both Atheism World and Theism World by the same—objective—standards of value, nevertheless (with Williams and against Kahane) it's up to us what comparators we choose when thinking about significance and we do in fact choose in a way that makes us significant. So, is a Williams-esque response, such as this, enough to alleviate all worries that we might have about our significance? After all, on it, it seems, we may—indeed would—say that the least strained comparators for individual humans are those who make up the class of humans per se and humans as such are thus trivially significant; and some of us as individuals—at least the world-historical individuals, as I have been putting it—are significant for humans. I think something along the lines of this Williams-esque response may indeed allow us to arrive at our 'commonplace', as I called it, conclusion, albeit that there are a few more bumps in the road ahead. Let's look at the bumps and how we might flatten them out.

Here's one bump. If we do assume objectivism, we do not need to confine ourselves to intra-species judgements of significance; we can rank species of things by reference to their value and thus form a judgement of the relative significance of species. Of course the correct ranking of species will be a matter of controversy. But, on objectivism, there will be a correct ranking, even if there are overlaps[11] and even if it is one that is to an extent indeterminate. And so it may be that, given the correct ranking, we should say that even if certain world-historical humans are significant for humans and humans as a class are significant for humans, each individual human and humans as a class are *not* significant relative to other comparator species, higher up the ranking, just as elephants are sizeable relative to the class of extant land animals, but no elephants (and, more generally, no land animals at all) are sizeable relative to planets. And one might go on to insist that *true* significance is best understood using the 'top-scoring' species as the relevant comparison class. But whilst one *might* go on to insist that, a natural Williams-esque question to raise of someone who does go on to insist on it is 'Why?' Why call that 'true' significance and—by implication—the significance which one retains when allowed to use other comparison classes 'false' significance? Indeed, if one is to accord one sort of significance the honorific 'true', it seems that we might be well advised to make a Williams-esque appeal to common linguistic intuitions, which surely would suggest that appealing to the top scorers by way of comparators generates an irrelevance if such a comparison seems too strained, as in some cases it certainly does.

There seems to me to be much in this, and I don't have space here to do more than sketch an overview. It seems to me plausible that comparing an elephant with Jupiter is strained because, in such a case, we are choosing as a comparator something from a class to which the thing we are comparing it with does not fundamentally belong; elephants aren't planets. Thus the fact that—relative to Jupiter—an elephant is not sizeable *is* an irrelevance to judging the elephant's 'true sizeability', insofar as we may form and stabilise this notion. Judging of something's true significance, insofar as we may form and stabilise this notion, requires that we not use 'strained' comparators, and a comparator is strained if it belongs to a different class from the object in question.[12] Of course I paint with a broad brush at this stage: there are many big philosophical issues here. After

---

[11] I have in mind the possibility that it may be that—say—the most valuable poet is more valuable than the least valuable philosopher, even if, as a class, philosophers are (on average then) more valuable than poets.

[12] Other intuitions are available here. Waghorn, for example, thinks that these common linguistic intuitions are germane only to common linguistic situations; when we shift location to a philosophical conversation, it becomes permissible to use the most valuable lives any humans could (in a broad metaphysical sense) lead as the relevant comparators. And I should report that, perhaps unsurprisingly, Kahane does not think that the point about strained comparators being inadmissible is persuasive in this context. As will be seen, I myself am somewhat ambivalent about it, thinking that in the end it at best blocks us from using the honorific 'true' of the sort of significance that I thence go on to talk of as 'ultimate significance'.

all, the elephant and the planet *do* both belong to the class of 'spatio-temporal objects that have been used as examples in this chapter'. But still and leaving it at the level of common sense, we would say that Jupiter and an elephant are not the same *fundamental* type of thing; one's a planet and the other is an animal. Much more could be said (and arguably needs to be said [e.g. about the crucial notion of fundamental types]) to make this robust enough to be relied on to do the necessary work, but supposing that it can be made robust enough, it could be argued that it still won't suffice to secure our significance for the following reason.

The class of *people as such* seems to common sense to be one that includes all and only things of a certain fundamental type (in a way that the class of spatio-temporal objects that have been used as examples in this chapter does not group together all and only things of the same fundamental type), and we humans are people. People per se then, it could be argued, is a suitable comparison class for judging of the significance of people such as humans—humanity generally and as individuals. If that is so; if we are in Atheism World; and if there are actually extraterrestrial civilisations much more valuable than ours, then, even if Winston Churchill is significant for a human and humans collectively are significant for humans, still, neither he nor humans collectively are significant *for people*. And if we are in Theism World, there is similarly a person of such value as to dwarf whatever value any of us (individually or indeed collectively) might have—God. If only these extraterrestrials and God hadn't been persons, then recalibrating by reference to them could have been argued to be too 'strained' a recalibration to be relevant, for we are fundamentally persons and thus only persons are suitable comparators in assessing our true significance. Thus it could have been argued that our true significance was secure. However, these extraterrestrials and God *are* persons, so this move won't secure us our true significance. Or at least it won't without some adjustments to its details. But these adjustments may be made—it's only a matter of how ad hoc they will end up seeming.

First, as there is this linguistic pull towards not granting that this sort of significance should be accorded the honorific label 'true' and, by implication, other sorts the pejorative 'false', let us bypass that issue by referring to this sort of significance as 'ultimate significance' from now on. Now let's look to making the adjustments.

Not all theists have thought of God as a person, but even amongst those who have, it is a commonplace to observe that He's a very different sort of person from the sort of people we are. On the account which I myself have argued for, God is best thought of as an atemporal person, and atemporal persons are very different indeed from temporal ones. On almost all accounts, God is best thought of as necessary, rather than contingent.[13] And there are many other great metaphysical differences between the Creator and all creatures. These differences could be argued to be enough to make a difference here—a difference when it comes to determining our ultimate significance; even if extraterrestrial lives may be suitable comparators for us, God—in virtue of His

---

[13] See my (2018).

atemporality, necessity, and/or other metaphysical differences—is not a suitable comparator. Let's allow ourselves to suppose for a moment that the comparison of created persons with the uncreated one *is* too strained to be permissible in this context. How then would the argument play out?

Given that in Theism World we have an afterlife the quality of which is superior to any that we achieve prior to death, our lives (as *ante-mortem* plus *post-mortem* lives) obviously have more value than our lives (as *ante-mortem* lives alone) in Atheism World. For reasons which I have given elsewhere, I think it best if we suppose that the heavenly afterlife which awaits us in Theism World is one that will be temporal.[14] On this assumption, the amount of value that is added to our lives in Theism World (relative to that which they have in Atheism World) will always be a potential infinity, rather than an actual infinity; that is, it will always be finite. Nevertheless, if we allow ourselves, in our discussion of our relative states in Atheism World and Theism World, to assume a vantage-point similar to that of the atemporal God[15], we may say that the objective value of our lives is infinite in Theism World and finite in Atheism World. Thus, we are amongst the top-scorers for created (temporal, contingent, and so forth) people. It is not, *pace* Kahane, that in Theism World there is a being of such great value as to dwarf our value into insignificance; rather, there is a being who by His loving care and actions raises us to such an extent that we are—from the point of view of eternity—of infinite value. And He does not Himself dwarf us into insignificance, as He is not a permissible comparator.

Now, it must be admitted that there are what one might call 'orders of infinity' issues too, even potentially amongst temporal beings. So, suppose God creates two everlasting (in the forwards direction) beings, the first of whom has, over any finite period, only half as much value as the second. Even though, from the point of view of eternity, each has infinite value, there is obviously a sense in which they are not equal; there is no time at which the first has more than half the value of the second. Perhaps, it might be suggested, the extraterrestrials, whose superior civilisations are worrying for the prospect of our ultimate significance in Atheism World and Theism World alike, are like the second of these sorts of being and we are like the first. If so, then *they*, not us, could be argued to be the top-scorers amongst permissible comparators (creatures) and we could thus be argued to be thereby relegated out of ultimate significance once more. However, for reasons that must remain off-stage here, I think that an 'equality assumption', as I have elsewhere called it, about Heaven can be argued for on independent grounds, meaning that in Theism World all created persons—humans and extraterrestrials—are 'levelled-up' to the same order of infinity in the afterlife.[16] Thus there is only one

---

[14] See my (2005, chapter 5).

[15] If God is atemporal, then He occupies a point of view from which He sees all our lives in their infinitely extended (and thus infinitely valuable) entirety and thus sees them all as worthy of infinite love, which of course He can and does direct towards them. Thus God's infinite love for us (which it will be recalled secures us our infinite subjective significance in Theism World) is not disproportionate to our status as He (and possibly He alone) can see it.

[16] See, for example, my 2021.

person[17], relative to whom we certainly would be insignificant in an orders-of-infinity way; and so, only on the further assumption that this person—God—is a sufficiently different type of person from created persons (or is no person at all) can we think of ourselves as being—alongside, no doubt, certain extraterrestrials, but not 'pipped' for top-place amongst created persons by them—truly (or as we are now putting it, 'ultimately') significant. These assumptions haven't been argued for to any great extent here. But, on these assumptions, the commonplace thought with which we started emerges fully vindicated; we have more objective, as well as subjective, significance in Theism World than we do in Atheism World.

Allow me to sum up.

We have assumed that we have positive objective value in both Atheism World and Theism World. We have seen that we have finite subjective significance in Atheism World and infinite subjective significance in Theism World. The infinite subjective significance which we have in Theism World in itself plausibly adds to our value there (relative to that which we have in Atheism World), but not enough to secure us objective significance, for objective significance is a 'relativistic' value. We have seen that we do not plausibly (on the assumption that various fillings-out of the Drake Equation's variables are plausible[18]) have objective significance in Atheism World as (on these fillings-out) it's close-to-a-certainty that there are extraterrestrials whose objective value far surpasses ours; they more-than-pip-us to be top-scorers and, given that they are created persons (that is, beings of the same fundamental type as ourselves, temporal, contingent, and so forth), it is hard to object to using them as suitable comparators when determining our 'true significance', as we may understand the term. Of course, we may understand the term 'true significance' differently; we remain significant 'for human persons', 'for an Earthly species', and so on; and there is at least some intuitive pull in favour of thinking of these types of significance as equally good (possibly even better) contenders for being true significance, or—perhaps better put—there's reason to think that true significance is a notion without a stable conceptualisation. Still, if we suppose that true significance can be made to make sense in the manner sketched (we call it 'ultimate significance', so as to bypass the intuitions spoken of), it follows that, if we are in Theism World, then, on the assumption of Universalism and the equality assumption about the afterlife, we humans, alongside all these extraterrestrials, are 'levelled up' to infinite value (of the same order) through our collective infinite afterlives; from the point of view of eternity, we are *all* amongst the top-scorers for created (temporal, contingent, etc.) persons, and thus, as long as created persons are the right comparators for determining our ultimate significance, we are all ultimately significant. So, the commonplace view, as I called it at the start of this chapter, emerges fully vindicated.

Let me close by stressing again that the commonplace view emerges fully vindicated only on certain assumptions—assumptions which may seem somewhat ad hoc in the

---

[17] I am ignoring the doctrine of the Trinity and the possibility of angels.
[18] Again, I am assuming that Great Filter solutions to the Fermi Paradox do not kill off all extraterrestrial civilisations prior to their far surpassing anything humanity will ever achieve.

context of this chapter, where their justification has been more gestured towards than provided, and about one of which I have myself expressed some diffidence. Still, I wonder if a believer is likely to be worried by this somewhat-qualified and somewhat-cautious conclusion. I believe it has been shown that in Theism World our lives have infinite objective value and infinite subjective significance, whereas in Atheism World they have finite objective value and finite subjective significance. If I'm right in that, then the fact that it has proved impossible to show that our lives have what we settled on calling 'ultimate' objective significance in Theism World whilst not in Atheism World (without relying on controversial assumptions) is unlikely to disappoint. But that of course is a psychological, not a philosophical, speculation.[19]

References

Kahane, G. 2014. 'Our Cosmic Insignificance'. Nous 48(4): 745–772
Mawson, T. J. 2005. *Belief in God*. Oxford: Oxford University Press.
Mawson, T. J. 2016. *God and the Meanings of Life*. London: Bloomsbury.
Mawson, T. J. 2018. *The Divine Attributes*. Cambridge: Cambridge University Press.
Mawson, T. J. 2019. *Monotheism and the Meaning of Life*. Cambridge: Cambridge University Press.
Mawson, T. J. 2021 'Why Heaven Doesn't Make Earth Absolutely Meaningless, Just Relatively'. *Religious Studies* 57(4): 732–751.
Russell, B. 1953. 'A Free Man's Worship'. In B. Russell, *Mysticism and Logic*, 50–59. London: Penguin.
Williams, B. 1986. *Ethics and the Limits of Philosophy*. Cambridge: Cambridge University Press.
Williams, B. 2006. 'The Human Prejudice'. In *Philosophy as a Humanistic Discipline*, ed. A. Moore. Princeton, NJ: Princeton University Press. 135–154.

---

[19] I am grateful to Stewart Goetz, Guy Kahane, Iddo Landau, Ben Page, Nick Waghorn, and Erik Wielenberg for their comments on an earlier draft of this chapter.

CHAPTER 15

MYSTICISM, RITUAL, AND THE MEANING OF LIFE

GUY BENNETT-HUNTER

Mysticism and the Meaning of Life

CONTEMPORARY philosophical debate about the meaning of life often involves discussion of religion, especially the relative merits of theism and atheism. While some writers in the field appeal to the purposes of a transcendent God to explain life's meaning in supernatural terms, others insist that it is incumbent upon human beings to explain the meaning of life in wholly naturalistic terms. Thaddeus Metz (2013, 78) summarizes the distinction: 'Supernaturalism is the general view that one's existence is significant just insofar as one has some kind of relationship with a spiritual realm', while naturalism 'is the broad perspective that meaning in life can be a function of living in a purely physical world as known by science'. For Metz (2013, 80), the most plausible version of supernaturalism is 'purpose theory': 'the view that one's life is meaningful just insofar as one fulfils a purpose that God has assigned to one'.

However, Metz (2013, 137, italics his) opposes such views because he thinks that supernaturalist theories of life's meaning share and are motivated by the implausible perfection thesis: 'the claim that *meaning in one's life requires engaging with a maximally conceivable value*'. He objects that many undeniably meaningful lives and actions appear to confer meaning even in the absence of a perfect or supernatural condition. He also argues that the perfection thesis and supernaturalism in general are incoherent because they entail the following inconsistent claims: '(1+) I know "If meaning exists, then perfection (and a spiritual realm) exists" is true; (2+) I know meaning exists; (3+) I do not know whether perfection (a [sic] spiritual realm) exists' (Metz 2013, 145). His own solution to these problems is to reject the perfection thesis and supernaturalism.

But Metz agrees with Landau (2017, chapter 18) that while religion is neither necessary nor sufficient to confer meaning on life, it may still be compatible with such meaning and make a significant contribution to it. As Metz (2013, 159, italics his) puts it, 'an attractive conception of life's meaning need not be grounded *solely* on the natural [. . . W]hat matters in life *could be* something in addition to mere matter, and if a spiritual (or non-natural) realm were to exist, then it probably would be.' However, Landau (2017, 253) points out that the contrast introduced by religions between a perfect supernatural realm and the imperfect human one importantly allows for welcome 'nonperfectionist' elements to religious explanations of life's meaning: 'You do not have to be a religious Einstein in order to reach a satisfactory religious status, be blessed, saved, loved by God, or enter heaven.'

Other writers, like David Benatar (2017), advance more thoroughgoing criticism of (theistic) supernaturalist explanations of life's meaning that, from a 'cosmic' or unlimited perspective, would derive it solely from divine purposes. For example, the idea that the meaning of life is to love God and serve him raises the immediate question why a maximally great being would require or want love from his creatures—a question that in turn raises the possibility of the supreme narcissism of such a being (Benatar 2017, 38). The main objection here is that the obscurity of what the divine purposes (if any) actually are reduces the account of meaning provided by appeal to them to mere 'handwaving' (Benatar 2017, 37). In Benatar's (2017, 38) slick *précis*: 'The account [of life's meaning] is as mysterious as the ways in which the Lord is often said to move.'

Some philosophers, more insistent on religion's central role in conferring meaning on life, have given ground to naturalism but have introduced the distinction between cognition and understanding to prevent evaluative and emotional spheres of human experience (especially religious ones) from being reductively subsumed under baldly naturalistic explanation, either by science or by the kind of philosophy whose methods consist in the 'specious *mimicry* of scientific procedures' (Cottingham 2009, 240, italics his). For example, Fiona Ellis (2018) advocates 'expansive naturalism', which exceeds the narrow, cognitive limits of scientific naturalism, leaving room for religious understanding. Agreeing with Cottingham (2018), Ellis argues that a major feature of the religious way of understanding the world, which protects it from being reduced to the bald naturalism of an explanatory hypothesis, is precisely the element of mystery that Benatar pithily dismisses. Unfortunately, the concept of 'mystery' as invoked by Ellis and Cottingham remains undefined, and an explanation of how it can coherently be said to be 'revealed and lived at the level of moral action and spiritual practice' is painfully absent from their work (Ellis 2018, 58). Left in these vague terms, the appeal to divine mystery as a way of articulating the meaning of life remains decidedly vulnerable to Benatar's deflating charge of 'hand-waving'.

It is into this debate about naturalism versus supernaturalism, which lies at the heart of the contemporary scholarship on the meaning of life, that the philosophical study of mysticism is able to inject some much-needed nuance, providing a clearer and more sophisticated picture of what the appeal to 'mystery', or ineffability, might amount to. For we shall see that mysticism is inassimilable to the binary categories of theism and atheism. Founded on the concept of ineffability, the mystical perspective (which may be expressed in either religious or secular terms) invokes a transcendent reality on which the meaning of life depends, but nothing supernatural, in principle separable from the quotidian fabric of human life itself. The relational account of meaning that I endorse here allows for the mystical perspective to cultivate a sense of the meaning *of* life and thereby, no less, a sense of meaning *in* life. That perspective thus provides an alternative way of looking at these intimately related questions of life's meaning which transcends both naturalist and supernaturalist approaches.

This chapter adopts an existential phenomenological perspective on mysticism, and there is another major debate in the literature to which this particular methodology can make a more implicit, though equally essential, contribution: that between subjectivism, objectivism, and hybridism. As Metz (2013, 164, italics his) describes the division, subjectivists who follow Sartre hold 'the view that lives are meaningful solely by obtaining what the field calls objects of "propositional attitudes", mental states such as wants, emotions, goals, and the like that are *about* states of affairs'. By contrast, objectivists like Peter Singer hold that 'certain states of affairs in the physical world are meaningful "in themselves", apart from being the object of propositional attitudes' (Metz 2013, 165). Other thinkers adopt a hybrid view incorporating both subjectivist and objectivist elements (Politi 2019). 'Among those who believe that a significant existence can be had in a purely physical world', Metz (2013, 164) writes, 'the most salient division concerns the extent to which, and the respects in which, the human mind constitutes it'.

The question at issue here is whether meaning is a 'thick' concept, as Cottingham thinks. For Cottingham (2003, 20–21), meaning is inescapably evaluative in nature but not reducible to purely arbitrary personal preference. It is conceived as a kind of value grounded in objective features of the world in virtue of which something is judged to be meaningful. A meaningful life, therefore, is to be commended in virtue of its relevant specific features. Metz (2016, 1252, 1255; cf. Bennett-Hunter 2016) agrees, responding to my own 'strictly relational' view of meaning with the 'weaker view', that 'that [relational] dimension might be a supplement to some meaning that is intrinsic'. Existential phenomenological reflection on mysticism not only provides a fresh perspective on the division between naturalism and supernaturalism, but also provides good reason to question the basis of the sharp division between objectivism and subjectivism. We shall see that for the phenomenologists meaning is not best construed as a thick concept but something more like *the thickness of concepts*, the condition for the carving up of experienced reality into subjects, which apply concepts, and objects, to which concepts are applied. Rather than viewing the available options as exhausted by objectivism, subjectivism, or a hybrid of the two, the present chapter uses the phenomenological approach to transcend all these distinctions and provide a quite different perspective on the topic.

The reconciliation of opposites and the dissolution of dualisms are abiding themes in much mystical and existentialist writing, and it is perhaps the tendency for such reconciliation that makes the phenomenological study of mysticism so relevant to the contemporary debates about the meaning of life.

Ineffability and Mysticism

I define 'mysticism' as the kind of experience, religious or non-religious, in which ineffability plays a central role. The concept of ineffability has been part of almost every philosophical discussion of mysticism since the early 1900s, when William James (1958, 292–293) seminally identified ineffability as one of the five 'marks' of mystical experience. The concept of ineffability, as I delineate it, evokes what in principle resists conceptual grasp and literal linguistic articulation. I endorse an argument put forward by David E. Cooper (2002, 2005) to the effect that the only way to terminate the regression regarding meaning that results from the search for *ultimate* meaning is by appeal to this concept of ineffability. In other words, I think there are good reasons to affirm the ineffability of ultimate reality. Cooper (2003, 2005) defines meaning as a relation of appropriateness that something has to a context broader than itself, ultimately a relation of appropriateness to human Life.[1] It is only by appeal to the concept of ineffability, his argument concludes, that the meaning of life as a whole can be explained. Here follows a brief summary of the argument.

If the meanings of things, the concepts and values with which we invest them, must be explained in terms of their contribution to human concerns, practices, and projects—and therefore ultimately in terms of their relation of appropriateness to the human perspective (the world of human life to which those practices and concerns themselves contribute)—how can life itself and as a whole be said to have meaning? The answer is: only by placing it in a relation of appropriateness to what is beyond itself, independent of the human contribution, and ultimately real. This 'beyond' cannot, without circularity, be invested with any of the concepts and meanings that constitute life—which it is invoked to explain—therefore it must be ineffable.

An important implication is the rejection of supernaturalism: the concept of ineffability cannot coherently be held to refer to a transcendent object or realm, like a cosmos or a god—or indeed to any object whatsoever. The common explication of the concept of ineffability in terms of some object is incoherent because it implies a familiar paradox. We must be able to say enough about a putatively ineffable object to secure reference to it, identifying it as that to which the ineffability applies (see Bennett-Hunter 2015). But if we can say even this much about an object (as we must of any putatively ineffable object), that object cannot be ineffable by definition. On this dismissive view, all ineffability claims appear to be self-refuting. But Cooper's argument implies, to similar effect, that it is impossible, without circularity, to invest the ineffable with any of the concepts, meanings, and values with which life itself (and its constituents) are invested, whose meaning is already in question. From the philosophical perspective adopted by phenomenology and (neo-) pragmatism, the concept of existence must be included among

---

[1] Cooper's capitalization is intended to indicate that the term is not being used in a purely biological sense.

these. As the contemporary pragmatist philosopher Sami Pihlström (1996, 123) puts it, 'Words like "object" and "exists" are used in different ways in different contexts (or language-games). No usage is "forced" by the world.' And as Leszek Kołakowski (1975, 65) reads Husserl's phenomenology, ' "Existence" itself is a certain "sense" of an object. Consequently it would be absurd [. . .] to say that an object "exists" independently of the meaning of the word "to exist"—independently of the act of constitution performed by the consciousness.' Similarly, Silvia Jonas (2016), in her recent study of the metaphysics of ineffability, has thoroughly dismissed 'objects' (alongside 'properties', 'propositions', and 'content') as plausible candidates for the relevant, non-trivial kind of ineffability in which she, too, is interested.

Jonas suggests that the metaphysics of ineffability be understood, not in terms of objects but 'Self-acquaintance', an experience in which the 'object' turns out to be nothing other than the 'subject': our primitive point of view on the world, for which there are any objects at all. Perhaps for this reason, towards the end of her book, Jonas begins to use the terms 'experience of ineffability' and 'ineffable experience' interchangeably. If the 'subject' becomes the 'object' of an experience which for that very reason confounds the subject–object split, it will in that case seem quite natural to say that an ineffable experience amounts to an experience of ineffability and vice versa. Read in this way, Jonas's metaphysical work supports my own existential phenomenological view that mystical experience dissolves the distinction between subject and object, a view that clearly undermines the debate between subjectivism, objectivism, and hybridism about the meaning of life.

While the subject–object distinction is necessary and useful for everyday purposes, it breaks down at the deeper levels at which the question of life's meaning is addressed. With John Dewey (Dewey and Bentley 1949, 276–278), I think it most instructive to view that split as a useful distinction that can be transcended, rather than an inescapably problematizing dichotomy. For phenomenologists interested in what transcends, and can therefore explain the meaning of, human life (like Karl Jaspers and Gabriel Marcel), experiences of ineffability shipwreck the subject–object split. Marcel distinguishes between a 'problem', which can be dissolved by rational thought (the kind of thought inescapably conditioned by the subject–object distinction), and a 'mystery', which eludes such objectification. He defines a mystery as 'a problem which encroaches upon its own data' (Marcel 1948, 8). And the ineffable dimension of reality that Jaspers calls 'Transcendence or God' is strictly interdependent with human existence. There is no existence without Transcendence. Human existence is realized only in the presence of Transcendence, and Transcendence is, as it were, created in the same moment that it is revealed to us. Jaspers (1967, 71) summarizes this dissolution of the *Subjekt–Objekt-Spaltung*, which (in harmony with Dewey) should be translated as 'split' or 'cleavage' rather than 'dichotomy':

> The encompassing that we are confronts the encompassing that is Being itself: the one encompassing encompasses the other. The being that we are is encompassed by encompassing Being, and Being is encompassed by the encompassing that we are.

If the meaning of the concept of ineffability does not lie in securing reference to a supposedly ineffable determinate object but rather in the dissolution of the subject–object split, then the antinomy apparently implied by ineffability claims is also dissolved (Bennett-Hunter 2015, 492–493). So with the important qualification that I do not have in mind the experience of a determinate 'ineffable object' or a supernatural realm of such objects (an idea which has been repeatedly shown to be incoherent to the point of paradox), I want to go further into the nature of that experience of ineffability which I am calling 'mysticism'.

Mysticism, Religious and Non-Religious

Mysticism is immediately associated with religious or spiritual experience, and many religious thinkers have predicated their approach on the concept of ineffability (Kenny 2006, 443). This 'apophatic' or 'negative' approach to theology has deep roots in Christian neo-Platonism as well as branches that extend far out to the fringes of orthodoxy. Two of the most influential practitioners, Pseudo-Dionysius the Areopagite (fl. c. 650–c. 725 CE) and Meister Eckhart (1260–1328), lived under the influence of neo-Platonism in doctrinally formative historical periods, and both were regarded as heretical at some point in Christian history—in Eckhart's case, during his own lifetime. Kołakowski (1988, 49) suggests that pseudo-Dionysius's writings were allowed to become as influential as they were only because the author was for centuries mistaken 'for whom he pretended to be—the first Bishop of Athens converted by St Paul (Acts, 17.54)'. The distinctive, controversial claim made by both apophatic writers is that the word 'God' does not refer to a being—a claim that has been echoed by twentieth-century and contemporary theologians writing in the shadow of Heidegger's (1969) critique of ontotheology, including Paul Tillich (1968, vol. 1, 227, 262–263, 301), Simone Weil (see Williams 2007), John Macquarrie (1984, 186), and Vito Mancuso (see Simuţ 2016). Religious mysticism falls into Henri Bergson's (1935, 171) category of 'dynamic', as opposed to 'static', religion: the kind to which 'verbal expression is immaterial', 'an elevation of the soul that can dispense with speech'. But religious mystics like pseudo-Dionysius and Eckhart have notably tended not to dispense with *writing*, and we may view their works as necessarily imperfect testimonies to the experience of ineffability.

However, given that mystical experience is not a matter of comprehending or perceiving some (divine) object, neither can mysticism be confined to religion, some forms of which do insist on such supernatural claims. An impressionistic literary portrait of secular mysticism has been provided by the Austrian writer (also Richard Strauss's librettist) Hugo von Hofmannsthal (2005), in his 1902 prose work *The Lord Chandos Letter*. The author of the fictional letter is a writer, Philipp, Lord Chandos, explaining that his total break in literary activity has been occasioned by an acquired inability to capture experienced reality in words. 'I lived at that time in a kind of continuous inebriation and saw all of existence as one great unity' (Hofmannsthal 2005, 120). His experience of the world has become characterized by a reconciliation of opposites: the mental and the physical, 'the courtly and bestial, art and barbarism, solitude and society', no longer seem distinct from one another (Hofmannsthal 2005, 120). The author therefore finds himself in the disturbing position of being unable to articulate his experience in (prosaic) language, which depends on the opposition between subject and object: 'the abstract words which the tongue must enlist [. . .] disintegrated in my mouth like [mouldy] mushrooms' (Hofmannsthal 2005, 121). Lord Chandos explains that the experience is not a religious one and is incapable of being subsumed under supernaturalistic theological explanations, but the author is clear that the possibility of religious *interpretation* of the experience retains for him an allegorical meaning:

> For me the mysteries of faith have boiled down to a grand allegory which stands over the fields of my life like a shining rainbow, at a constant remove, always ready to recede in case I think of running up and wrapping myself in the hem of its cloak. (Hofmannsthal 2005, 120–121)

Lord Chandos finds that anything at all, a 'watering can, a harrow left in a field, a dog in the sun, a shabby churchyard, a cripple, a small farmhouse—any of these can become the vessel of my revelation' (Hofmannsthal 2005, 123). Any 'confluence of trivialities' has the potential to carry within it 'a presence of the infinite', to the point where the author wishes—but remains unable—'to bring out words, knowing that any words I found would vanquish those cherubim, in which I do not believe' (Hofmannsthal 2005, 124). The author experiences a plenitude of meaning in his life. Everything seems to mean something, the world is saturated with meaning, and his own body seems to consist entirely of meaningful, coded messages (Hofmannsthal 2005, 125). The author participates in a dissolution of the distinction between subject and object, experiencing his embodied self as inseparable from the ineffable reality that he tries vainly to describe:

> I can no more express in rational language what made up this harmony permeating me and the entire world, or how it made itself perceptible to me, than I can describe with any precision the inner movements of my intestines or the engorgement of my veins. (Hofmannsthal 2005, 125)

In this non-religious mystical state, in which Lord Chandos experiences the ineffability of the whole of experienced reality, including himself, he feels a keen need for a new kind of language that transcends bald naturalism, 'a language in which mute things speak to me' (Hofmannsthal 2005, 127–128).

If Cooper (2002) is right to argue that the meaning of life as a whole can only be coherently explained in terms of the concept of ineffability, then a sense of meaning in life will be apprehensible pre-eminently in experiences of ineffability—in mysticism, as elaborated in this section so far. This being the case, the need for Hofmannsthal's language in which mute things speak to us becomes a particularly urgent one. But we may also note that the main point of the text is surely to demonstrate that this need has already been met by the non-prosaic, literary language in which the fictional letter's secular mysticism is itself written.

Given the central concept of intentionality, however, the very possibility of mysticism remains in question, even from a phenomenological point of view. Since Brentano and Husserl, it has been noted, in Brentano's (1995, 68) words, that '[e]very mental phenomenon is characterized by [. . .] the [. . .] reference to a content, direction toward an object'. Mystical experience, as I am defining it, is a mental phenomenon ultimately directed towards the ineffable, which is no determinate object at all. How, therefore, is mysticism possible? Hofmannsthal's text suggests that experiences of ineffability are mediated by the more or less mundane furniture of the world even as they transcend it; nothing is in principle unable to become transparent to the ineffable, not even one's own finger:

> Once I saw through a magnifying glass that an area of skin on my little finger looked like an open field with furrows and hollows. [. . .] Everything came to pieces, the pieces broke into more pieces, and nothing could be encompassed by one idea. Isolated words swam about me; they turned into eyes that stared at me and into which I had to stare back, dizzying whirlpools which spun around and around and led into the void. (Hofmannsthal 2005, 122)

This passage in particular exemplifies what Cooper (2002, 322) more prosaically calls the 'double-exposures' that are involved in the experience of ineffability. There is, firstly, the experience

> of 'seeing through' something—a tree, say—to the network of relations, the 'relational totality of significance', on which that depends, whilst also 'seeing' that whole 'gathered', 'con-centrated' in the tree. Then, second, [. . .] the experience of seeing things as ordinary particulars, while also 'seeing through' the world as a whole, a sense of which is cultivated in the first experience, to [the ineffable].

So, in rationally defending the non-rational possibility of mysticism, the task ahead of us is not to demonstrate the possibility of a special, 'non-intentional' kind of experience. Rather, it is to show in greater detail how intentional experience as a whole, directed toward the mundane objects that comprise the meaningful fabric of the human world, can manifest ineffability. In other words, how can the ineffable, which transcends the subject–object distinction, be manifest in human experience, which, given its intentionality, seems at least to an extent conditioned by that distinction? And how could such experience be expressed?

This question has a familiar answer in a major strand of twentieth-century and contemporary theology, which takes the post-Heideggerian critique of ontotheology as its point of departure. If we are to think of the word 'God' as evoking what explains the existence and/or meaning of everything that exists, the ineffable Ground and Source of Being itself, we may not also think of 'God' as referring to one of the things that exists—a thought that would introduce circular reasoning into theological explanation. How, then, are religious experience and expression possible? Post-Heideggerian theologians like Paul Tillich affirm that it is incorrect to interpret the meaning of the word 'God' in terms of objects. Repeating the apophatic claims of earlier neo-Platonic thinkers, Tillich (1968, vol. 1, 227) writes, for example, that 'God does not exist. He is being-itself beyond essence and existence. Therefore, to argue that God exists is to deny him.' But Tillich and others persist in using the literally inaccurate, supernaturalistic language of theism, which has been used to evoke the divine for centuries, defending its continued use by appeal to symbolic theories of religious experience and expression. I have criticized such theories elsewhere (Bennett-Hunter 2014, 67–75) and remain unconvinced that they are robust enough to bridge the gulf between the realm of rational thought and everyday experience, where the subject–object distinction holds sway, and the dimension of ineffability, where, as a condition of entry, that distinction must be transcended.

A better philosophical explication of the general possibility of mysticism can be provided by a suitably modified version of Karl Jaspers's philosophical theory of ciphers of Transcendence—a neo-Jaspersian theory of ciphers.[2] This theory makes it possible to view mystical experience (whether religious or secular) as attunement to a kind of cipher language. In Hofmannsthal's terms, this attunement involves listening for a new kind of language that exceeds bald naturalism: the kind of language in which mute things speak to us.

Mysticism and Ciphers of the Ineffable

The main problem with symbolic theories of religious experience and expression is that symbols are defined as objects that symbolically represent other objects, even if the latter are imaginary and do not exist outside the symbolic representation. Symbols operate like road signs indicating nearby destinations. But the concept of ineffability requires

---

[2] In the following section, which draws on Jaspers's philosophical work, I modify his theory of ciphers, as discussed in detail elsewhere (Bennett-Hunter 2014, 95–104). In essence, I have a less thoroughgoing view than Jaspers of the utility of the subject–object distinction. Invoking again the central phenomenological concept of intentionality, Jaspers (1967, 94) makes the strong claim that if we are not in the subject–object split we are unconscious. From an existential phenomenological (as opposed to a transcendental phenomenological) perspective, this view of consciousness appears unduly restricted. In my view (as I argue in my book), Jaspers's more thoroughgoing commitment to the validity of the subject–object distinction ultimately compromises the structural integrity of his tripartite system as a whole. If we *must* speak of ourselves as "unconscious" when we are not in the subject–object split, then it is necessary to add that this is not a pre-conscious state but a post-conscious one, which can come about only when the ladder of rational thought has been ascended and kicked away (Bennett-Hunter 2014, 121).

us to transcend the subject–object distinction: it does not refer to any determinate, representable object. It is therefore incumbent upon the defender of religious symbols to explain how a symbol (which is something objective, located unambiguously within the subject–object distinction) can represent, or otherwise manifest, a transcendent reality unconditioned by that distinction—a logically impossible task. What we need instead are what Karl Jaspers calls 'ciphers'. Unlike symbols, ciphers have an importantly ambiguous relationship to the subject–object distinction. Ciphers arise out of the subject–object distinction (and can be experienced) but they remain ambiguous. They are not assimilable to the subject–object distinction's binary terms but remain open to the ineffable and therefore indecipherable. It is by means of this cardinal ambiguity that ciphers can embody the ineffable dimension of reality that Jaspers calls 'Transcendence or God', which outruns that distinction, thus enabling us to transcend it.

Ciphers embody the ineffable in the only way that it can be embodied. They are not statements about it or representations of it. Jaspers provides two metaphors to help us better understand how ciphers function: one of language, the other of physiognomy. Ciphers are the language of Transcendence (not Transcendence itself). This metaphor stresses the fact that ciphers and Transcendence are not to be identified. It is not that a cipher *is* Transcendence, any more than the phonemes of a language *are* what a sentence of that language means. But Transcendence needs ciphers to be realized, in just the way that linguistic meaning needs concrete phonemes. Unlike symbols and spoken languages, however, the cipher language remains indecipherable; it is untranslatable. What a cipher embodies does not exist outside it and is not independently accessible. For example, when T. S. Eliot says in *The Waste Land*, 'I will show you fear in a handful of dust', only the most pedantic reader would try to translate the poetry into prose, insisting that Eliot made a category error because a handful of dust cannot literally contain fear. When we read this phrase as a cipher of the ineffable, we see that the poetic language evokes what is already there, embodied in the sonority, the emotional and cultural resonance, of the poetry itself.

Deploying a complementary physiognomic metaphor, Jaspers describes how a person's involuntary gestures express something of his or her being. Similarly with ciphers, Jaspers (1969, vol. 3, 125) writes, 'all things seem to express a being [. . .] we experience this physiognomy of all existence'. Whereas human physiognomy arguably expresses something accessible in other ways (for example, through empirical psychology), Transcendence is accessible only in and through its cipher physiognomy. This view of existence is not a process of drawing inferences from signs; rather its 'knowledge' is 'all in the viewing' (Jaspers 1969, vol. 3, 134).

Pace Jaspers (who was a physician as well as a philosopher), human physiognomy is arguably just the same, a similarity which actually sharpens the point of his metaphor. For example, what an angry gesture expresses is not located in some separate mental shrine *beyond* the angry person's body. Rather, the anger is inescapably bound up with, and realised through, the body and its gestures. The phenomenologists Maurice Merleau-Ponty (2004, 83) and Hans-Georg Gadamer both argue, in Gadamer's (1986, 79) words, that 'what a gesture expresses is "there" in the gesture itself [. . . it] reveals no inner meaning behind itself'. Either way, the point of Jaspers's comparison remains clear: ciphers are significations without there being any determinate object signified. As Jaspers (1959, 42) puts it, 'Signification is itself only a metaphor for being-a-cipher'.[3] So although best understood as a kind of language, the cipher language cannot be deciphered or translated into other terms. While it is always possible to state in other terms, what a symbolic signification 'really means', ciphers can be experienced (or 'read') but they remain indecipherable. Ciphers make the ineffable accessible to us the only way it can be, but they do not reveal it the way it 'really is'. Since the ineffable is not purely objective, but transcends the subject–object distinction, there is no such way.

So ciphers have a distinctive ambiguity with regard to the subject–object split. Like languages, they are cultural phenomena that are both created and appropriated by us. Without us, there would be no ciphers. Yet ciphers must be appropriated from cultural and intellectual traditions that are older and greater than we are. In the terms of the subject–object distinction, ciphers are subjective and objective at once (Jaspers 1969a, 93–94). It is through this unique ambiguity (lacked by symbols) that ciphers can embody the ineffable, which outruns the subject–object distinction, eluding our cognitive and literal linguistic grasp.

As Hofmannstahl's literary portrait shows (in harmony with naturalism), a cipher can be literally anything, even something quite mundane: a work of art, a religious myth, a ritual performance, a guttering candle, even one's own finger. Even something previously taken to be a determinate object can be read as a cipher. However, a cipher is not merely a determinate intentional object but a point of focus for experience that effects the two double-exposures described by Cooper which, together, evoke the ineffable. A cipher can have a religious or secular cultural meaning, or both. When experienced as such, ciphers allow us to transcend bald naturalism by making themselves, and the referential totality of the human world along with them, transparent to the ineffable. In this way, the experience of ciphers—which comprises what I am calling mystical experience—may cultivate an otherwise elusive sense of life's meaning which can be reduced neither to bald naturalism nor supernaturalism, theism nor atheism.

It is worth stressing an important implication of this theory, recognized by Jaspers himself: that there can be no exclusive, exhaustive, or final, authoritative system of ciphers, even though a system of thought (whether religious or secular) can be read as a cipher-language among a near-infinity of others. Underscoring ciphers' ambiguity with respect to the subject–object split, Jaspers (1969 vol. 3, 131, italics his) makes the point in both subjective and objective terms:

> *From where I stand*, the cipher remains permanently ambiguous—which means, speaking from the standpoint of Transcendence, that Transcendence *has other ways yet to convey itself.*

---

[3] For the sake of consistency, I have changed the idiosyncratic spelling 'cypher' used in this English translation.

If a religious system is read as a cipher of ineffability, what is most important is not the culturally specific concrete forms of the tradition in question but the way these are understood (or 'read') philosophically. Philosophy becomes the essential prolegomenon to theology from the Jaspersian point of view. No determinate meaning, whether religious or non-religious, should be debarred from being regarded as a valid imagining or evocation of the ineffable. Discussing the theological implications of his theory, Jaspers (1967, 340) described the metamorphosis that the reading of religious systems as cipher-languages would effect:

> Dogmas, sacraments, rituals would be melted down, so to speak—not destroyed, but given other forms of conscious realization. [. . .] Not the substance, but the appearance in consciousness would change. Philosophy and theology would be on the road to reunification.

In order for religious experience to be melted down, in the fire of philosophical thought, into cipher-reading, the 'poison' of exclusive, dogmatic claims on the ineffable must be removed (Jaspers 1967, 340). In the next section, I try to make some progress towards this philosophical melting down of religious experience by examining the possibility of reading rituals in general as ciphers of ineffability.

Rituals as Ciphers of Ineffability

Alongside ineffability, transience and passivity appear as two of William James's other marks of mystical experience. James (1958, 293–294) noted that mystical states cannot be sustained for long and that, while they may be 'facilitated' by voluntary actions, the mystic does not typically feel responsible for, or in control of, her experience. On the neo-Jaspersian theory set out earlier, mystical experience may be understood to be mediated by ciphers. But the transience and passivity of such experience raise the question what, if anything, human beings can do to cultivate a sense of life's meaning in themselves and communicate that sense to others. In this final section, in an attempt to answer this question, I discuss the possibility of reading ritual performances as ciphers of ineffability.

In its religious mode, mysticism correlates with Bergson's (1935, 171) category of 'dynamic religion', as opposed to the more supernaturalistic 'static religion', which is correlated instead with 'the incantations of magic [. . .] aimed, if not at compelling the will of the gods and above all of the spirits, at least capturing their goodwill'. Therefore, in bringing out its relevance to mysticism, ritual must be sharply distinguished from magic, as it is by Wittgenstein and others. In *Remarks on Frazer's* Golden Bough, Wittgenstein argues thoroughly against the supposed dependence of ritual on (usually mistaken) beliefs. This logical independence of practice from theory explains why showing someone an error in their beliefs remains insufficient to convince that person to change or abandon the ritual practices apparently founded on those beliefs. As Wittgenstein (1979, 12e) illustrates, 'towards morning, when the sun is about to rise, people celebrate rites of the coming of the day, but not at night, for then they simply burn lamps'. The American philosopher Susanne Langer (1957, 158) takes the same approach, suggesting that the supposedly magic effect for which a ritual might appear to aim is not the desired causal result of the ritual but rather its completion or consummation. She considers the example of a rain dance, interpreting it not as a practical mistake but a ritual in which the appearance (or not) of rain plays an integral part:

> No savage tries to induce a snowstorm in midsummer, nor prays for the ripening of fruits entirely out of season, as he certainly would if he considered his dance and prayer the physical causes of such events. He dances *with* the rain, he invites the elements to do their part. (Langer 1957, 158)

The failure of rain to come would indicate that the rite is not ineffective but unconsummated. The import of the ritual is an expression of the reciprocal relationship between human beings and the natural world, and the ritual's supposed causal power to produce rain is only one metaphorical way of apprehending and expressing this import. So Langer reverses the standard formulation that ritual has its origin in magic, arguing instead that the roots of magic are in religion. Magic's typical form—the practical use of certain means of expression to bring about a desired effect—is, for Langer (1957, 155), 'the empty shell of a religious act'.

Similarly for Wittgenstein (1979, 4e), the essence of ritual is captured in an act like kissing the picture of an absent loved one. The idea that the beloved is somehow causally affected by the kiss is irrelevant to the meaning of the act, properly understood. If this mistaken idea were to contaminate the understanding of the action's meaning, the act itself would degenerate into magic, as its full meaning became entirely replaced by one metaphorical way of understanding that meaning. As Wittgenstein (1980, 8e) puts it elsewhere, 'ritual is permissible only to the extent that it is as genuine as a kiss'. Rightly viewed, then, a ritual is not a magical attempt to bring about mystical experience, or to manipulate or control the (divine) object that is regarded as the ultimate cause of such experience. If my earlier remarks on ineffability are correct, then there can be no such object anyway.

I suggest instead that rituals be read along neo-Jaspersian lines as ciphers of ineffability which embody the ineffable in the only way that it can be embodied. Thus, rituals exemplify the many religious and non-religious means by which we may cultivate a sense of the meaningfulness of life. I have explored the suggestive analogies and overlaps between ritual and the arts at length elsewhere (Bennett-Hunter 2014, chapter 6). The main point to repeat here is that both works of art and rituals, both of which incorporate linguistic as well as non-linguistic practices, may be read as ciphers of the ineffable—embodying a transcendent meaning that can be embodied only thus and in no other way. In both the aesthetic and the religious sphere, there is a transubstantiation: *what* is presented (*not re*presented) is inseparable from the *way* in which it is presented. On this point, I am drawing on a long line of European thinking about the arts, which extends from the French poets Mallarmé and Valéry, through the phenomenologists Gadamer (1986, 67) and Merleau-Ponty (2004) to Wittgenstein and George Steiner (1989, 1996), with his notion of 'real presences'. In relation to the visual arts, Merleau-Ponty (2004, 96–97) affirms that 'form and content—what is said and the way in which it is said—cannot exist separately from one another'. Wittgenstein (2001, §523) also argues for the logical inseparability of the meaning of an artwork from the specific formal characteristics, the lines and colours, of the work itself. For Wittgenstein (1980, 70e), it follows that the only effective way to communicate the meaning of a work of art is performative. While one cannot literally state it, one can *show* the meaning by the *way* in which one reads out the lines of poetry, or plays, hums, or whistles the musical phrase.

As distinct from magic, then, rituals should be understood in the same, broadly aesthetic way: as phenomena that may be read as ciphers of ineffability, embodying the ineffable in the only way that it can be embodied. Read as a cipher, a ritual may thereby cultivate mystical experience, allowing its participants to transcend the subject–object distinction. Importantly, unlike other, more transient ciphers (the ones read by Hofmannstahl's Lord Chandos, for example), rituals can mitigate the typical transience and passivity of mystical experience. Ritual performances—which often incorporate gestures, works of art, architecture, music, and pieces of poetic language—are ciphers which can be repeated and performed at will, both expressing and cultivating a community's shared experience of the ineffable in a way that inculcates over time an otherwise elusive sense of life's meaning.

I have stressed the parallels and suggestive analogies that exist between aesthetic and ritual modes of meaning. As with 'great' art, like the Greek temple according to Heidegger (1993, 168), which 'first gives to things their look and to [women and] men their outlook on themselves', rituals not only reflect but also help to found, modify, and hone the wider cultural worlds that produce them. As Julian Young (2001, 57) observes, this originative function is a precondition for life's meaning. But unlike most works of art, rituals also have a distinctive temporal role within religious and cultural traditions as they unfold across time. For example, the Eucharistic ritual can be seen both to memorialize and make 'really present' past ciphers: the bread broken and wine poured out by Christ at the Last Supper. Even for the Gospel writers, this repeated act had already taken on a mystical and almost ritualistic significance; Jesus is recognized after his Resurrection only when he repeats the act of breaking the bread (Luke 24:30–31).

Rituals can also be read as realizing in the present imagined or hoped-for future ciphers. An appendix to one of the Dead Sea Scrolls, *The Rule of the Congregation* (1QS[a]), was produced by the Qumran community, an isolated sect of Jews often identified with the Essenes. This document provides evidence that the members of this sect believed in the imminent arrival of a new age ushered in by a banquet presided over by two messiahs, one priestly and one political. The text indicates that the sect's members proleptically performed this messianic banquet in a ritual meal, which Schiffman (1989, 67) calls a 'preenactment'. By behaving ritually as though the anticipated *eschaton* had already arrived, the Qumran community realized it in the present through their proleptic ritual performance.

Read as ciphers, rituals like the Eucharist and the Qumran community's messianic banquet are not understood as magical attempts to bring about mystical experience, to manipulate or control ultimate reality, supernaturalistically construed. Nor do they manifest a baldly naturalistic answer to the question of life's meaning. Rather, these rituals re-enact past moments of mystical experience and proleptically enact hoped-for future ones. They attenuate the transience and passivity of mystical experience, not by means of magical causation but by means of their *meaningfulness* and their temporal elasticity. As the early Heidegger (1962, 425, italics his) says, 'Dasein *stretches along between* birth and death', and rituals mirror this meaningful stretching of Dasein. Rituals impart meaningful structure to the shape of their participants' lives by marking significant points by rites of passage (birth by baptism, copulation by marriage, death by burial) and the mundane, repeating rhythms of eating and sleeping by regular practices like morning and evening prayers and grace before meals. It is by mirroring and structuring life in these theatrical ways that rituals are especially suited to being read as ciphers of the ineffable, allowing those who participate in them to apprehend the evanescent, ineffable meaning of life itself.[4]

References

Benatar, David. 2017. *The Human Predicament: A Candid Guide to Life's Biggest Questions*. New York: Oxford University Press.
Bennett-Hunter, Guy. 2014. *Ineffability and Religious Experience*. Oxford: Routledge.
Bennett-Hunter, Guy. 2015. 'Divine Ineffability'. *Philosophy Compass* 10(7): 489–500.
Bennett-Hunter, Guy. 2016. 'Ineffability: Reply to Professors Metz and Cooper'. *Philosophia* 44(4): 1267–1287.
Bergson, Henri. 1935. *The Two Sources of Morality and Religion*, trans. R. Ashley Audra, Cloudesley Brereton, and W. Horsfall Carter. London: Macmillan.
Brentano, Franz. 1995. *Psychology from an Empirical Standpoint*, ed. Oskar Kraus, trans. Antos C. Rancurello, D. B. Terrel, and Linda L. McAlister, 2nd ed. London: Routledge.
Cooper, David E. 2002. *The Measure of Things: Humanism, Humility, and Mystery*. Oxford: Clarendon.
Cooper, David E. 2003. *Meaning*. Chesham: Acumen.
Cooper, David E. 2005. 'Life and Meaning'. *Ratio* 18: 125–137.
Cottingham, John. 2003. *On the Meaning of Life*. Oxford: Routledge.
Cottingham, John. 2005. *The Spiritual Dimension: Religion, Philosophy and Human Value*. Cambridge: Cambridge University Press.
Cottingham, John. 2006. 'What Difference Does it Make?: The Nature and Significance of Theistic Belief'. *Ratio* 19: 401–420.

---

[4] I am grateful to Professors David E. Cooper and Iddo Landau for their helpful comments on earlier versions of this essay.

Cottingham, John. 2009. 'What Is Humane Philosophy and Why Is It at Risk?' *Royal Institute of Philosophy Supplement* 65: 233–255.
Cottingham, John. 2018. 'Transcending Science: Humane Models of Religious Understanding'. In *New Models of Religious Understanding*, ed. Fiona Ellis, 22–41. Oxford: Oxford University Press.
Dewey, John, and Arthur F. Bentley. 1949. *The Knowing and the Known*. Boston: Beacon Press.
Ellis, Fiona. 2018. 'Religious Understanding, Naturalism, and Theory'. In *New Models of Religious Understanding*, ed. Fiona Ellis, 42–58. Oxford: Oxford University Press.
Gadamer, Hans-Georg. 1986. *The Relevance of the Beautiful and Other Essays*, ed. Robert Bernasconi, trans. Nicholas Walker. Cambridge: Cambridge University Press.
Heidegger, Martin. 1962. *Being and Time*, trans. John Macquarrie and Edward Robinson. New York: Harper & Row.
Heidegger, Martin. 1969. *Identity and Difference*, trans. Joan Stambaugh. New York: Harper & Row.
Heidegger, Martin. 1993. 'The Origin of the Work of Art'. In *Basic Writings*, ed. David Farrell Krell, 2nd ed., 143–206. London: Routledge.
Hofmannsthal, Hugo von. 2005. 'A Letter [1902]'. In *The Lord Chandos Letter: And Other Writings*, ed. and trans. Joel Rotenberg, 117–128. New York: New York Review of Books.
James, William. 1958. *The Varieties of Religious Experience*. New York: Mentor.
Jaspers, Karl. 1959. *Truth and Symbol: From* Von der Wahrheit, trans. Jean T. Wilde, William Kluback, and William Kimmel. London: Vision.
Jaspers, Karl. 1967. *Philosophical Faith and Revelation*, trans. E. B. Ashton. London: Collins.
Jaspers, Karl. 1969. *Philosophy*, trans. E. B. Ashton, 3 vols. Chicago: University of Chicago Press.
Jaspers Karl. 1969a. *Philosophy Is for Everyman: A Short Course in Philosophical Thinking*, trans. R. F. C. Hull and Grete Wels. London: Hutchinson.
Jonas, Silvia. 2016. *Ineffability and Its Metaphysics: The Unspeakable in Art, Religion, and Philosophy*. New York: Palgrave Macmillan.
Kenny, Anthony. 2006. 'Worshipping an Unknown God'. *Ratio* 19: 441–453.
Kołakowski, Leszek. 1975. *Husserl and the Search for Certitude*. London: Yale University Press.
Kolakowksi, Leszek. 1988. *Metaphysical Horror*. Oxford: Blackwell.
Landau, Iddo. 2017. *Finding Meaning in an Imperfect World*. Oxford: Oxford University Press.
Langer, Susanne K. 1957. *Philosophy in a New Key: A Study in the Symbolism of Reason, Rite and Art*, 3rd ed. Cambridge, MA: Harvard University Press.
Macquarrie, John. 1984. *In Search of Deity: An Essay in Dialectical Theism; The Gifford Lectures Delivered at the University of St Andrews in Session 1983–4*. London: SCM.
Marcel, Gabriel. 1948. 'On the Ontological Mystery'. In G. Marcel, *The Philosophy of Existence*, 1–13, trans. Manya Harari. London: Harvill Press.
Merleau-Ponty, Maurice. 2004. *The World of Perception*, trans. Oliver Davies. London: Routledge.
Metz, Thaddeus. 2013. *Meaning in Life*. Oxford: Oxford University Press.
Metz, Thaddeus. 2016. 'Is Life's Meaning Unthinkable?: Guy Bennett-Hunter on the Ineffable'. *Philosophia* 44(4): 1247–1256.
Pihlström, Sami. 1996. *Structuring the World: The Issue of Realism and the Nature of Ontological Problems in Classical and Contemporary Pragmatism*. Acta Philosophica Fennica, vol. 59. Helsinki: The Philosophical Society of Finland.

Politi, Vincenzo. 2019. 'Would My Life *Still* be Meaningful?': Intersubjectivism and Changing Meaning in Life'. *Human Affairs: Postdisciplinary Humanities & Social Sciences Quarterly* 29(4): 462–469.

Schiffmann, Lawrence. 1989. *The Eschatological Community of the Dead Sea Scrolls: A Study of the Rule of the Congregation*. Atlanta, GA: Scholars Press.

Simuț, Corneliu C. 2016. 'Vito Mancuso in English: Presenting the Thought of a Contemporary Radical Catholic Theologian and Philosopher to the English-Speaking World'. *Expository Times* 128(1): 20–29.

Steiner, George. 1989. *Real Presences*. London: Faber.

Steiner, George. 1996. 'Real Presences'. In G. Steiner, *No Passion Spent: Essays 1978–1996*, 20–39. London: Faber.

Tillich, Paul. 1968. *Systematic Theology*, 3 vols. Welwyn: James Nisbet.

Williams, Rowan, 2007. 'Simone Weil and the Necessary Non-Existence of God'. In R. Williams, *Wrestling with Angels: Conversations in Modern Theology*, 203–227. London: SCM.

Wittgenstein, Ludwig. 1979. *Remarks on Frazer's Golden Bough*, ed. Rush Rhees, trans. A. C. Miles. Retford: Brynmill.

Wittgenstein, Ludwig. 1980. *Culture and Value*, trans. Peter Winch. Oxford: Blackwell.

Wittgenstein, Ludwig. 2001. *Philosophical Investigations*, trans. G. E. M. Anscombe, 3rd ed. Oxford: Blackwell.

Young, Julian. 2001. *Heidegger's Philosophy of Art*. Cambridge: Cambridge University Press.

PART IV

ETHICS AND MEANING IN LIFE

CHAPTER 16

MEANING AND MORALITY

TODD MAY

In seeking to understand the relationship between morality and the meaningfulness of life, two questions immediately arise. First, what is the meaningfulness of life? Second, what is moral?

At the outset, then, our reflections threaten to become not just difficult, but paralyzed. How are we even to approach the questions that comprise our task, much less the task itself? To embark on a direct approach—answering each question and then discussing their relationship—would seem hopelessly complicated. Perhaps we should take a different tack.

1. Relationships between the Realms of Meaning and Morality

Here's one way to start. We can divide views of life's meaningfulness into two types: subjective and objective. (For ease of presentation, we'll use the term 'meaningfulness' to cover both 'meaning in life' and 'meaning of life,' although the view presented here will tilt toward the former.) Then we could do the same for morality. From there we could ask about the relationships among the four possible categories: subjective meaningfulness and subjective morality, subjective meaningfulness and objective morality, etc. This division begs a number of questions, such as whether there are categories outside of these two, for instance culturally grounded meaningfulness or morality. We will need to lay these aside as variations on these distinctions. All we ask of this division is that it allows us to gain a broad grip on the question we're trying to address.

However, we can make the task easier if we eliminate one of the categories: subjective morality. This would allow us to divide the number of categories in half: the relationship of subjective meaningfulness to objective morality and objective meaningfulness to objective morality.

But what would justify such an elimination at the outset? Let me offer two reasons, one regarding morality itself and the other the relationship between meaningfulness and morality. First, a subjective morality—that is, a morality in which right and wrong are up to individuals to decide—seems to be hardly a morality at all. It is a moral relativism on steroids, one in which what is right for me has no bearing on the moral rightness or wrongness of what anyone else believes or does. I don't believe that any type of moral relativism is in the end compelling; however, to argue for that would be beyond the scope of this discussion.[1] What I take to be entirely implausible, however, is the idea of morality that is up to each individual to decide, at least on any conception of morality that would preserve the meaning of the term.

However, even if we were to allow for the possibility of a subjective morality, we would not be able to advance beyond the discussion of the relationship of a subjective view of meaningfulness with objective morality, and the latter is a much more plausible possibility. In order to see this we will need to turn to the latter task; so let's do that now.

What would be the relationship between a meaningfulness of life that is subjectively given and an objective morality? In other words, if the meaningfulness of my life is up to me and yet there is an objective character to moral rightness and wrongness (or whatever other terms one wants to use to capture morality), what might their relationship be? Here the answer can be straightforward. In this case the relationship would be not just contingent, but arbitrary. That is to say, whatever overlap or interaction there would be between a subjective meaningfulness and an objective morality would arise because the meaningfulness decided upon by the subject would just happen to overlap with the requirements (duties, obligations, recommendations, etc.) of the objective morality. Because the meaningfulness of my life is up to me, I could decide to have it overlap with aspects of morality, or not overlap with any at all.

To see this, let's take an example. Richard Taylor, in the final chapter of his book *Good and Evil: A New Direction*, after rejecting an objective view of meaningfulness, argues for a subjective view. His point of entry into the discussion is Sisyphus, a figure famously discussed by Albert Camus in regard to meaningless in life in *The Myth of Sisyphus*. Taylor, though, imagines another possible life for Sisyphus, one in which he pushes the rock up the mountain continuously but, Taylor (1970, 259) says, 'Let us suppose that the gods, while condemning Sisyphus to the fate just described, at the same time, as an afterthought, waxed perversely merciful by implanting in him a strange and irrational impulse; namely, a compulsive impulse to roll stones. . . . [Sisyphus] has but one obsession, which is to roll stones, and it is an obsession that is only for the moment appeased by his rolling them—he no sooner gets a stone rolled to the top of the hill than he is restless to roll up another'.

From an objective viewpoint, Taylor argues, Sisyphus's life is just as meaningless as it was before this impulse was implanted in him. The only difference is that he has become

---

[1] A very good discussion of this issues is presented in Michelle Moody-Adams (Adams 2002), *Fieldwork in Familiar Places: Morality, Culture, and Philosophy*.

attached to what he is doing. Taylor then broadens this picture into a view of our place in the universe. From a cosmic standpoint, our lives mean nothing. We appear, we do our bit, and then we die. There is no objective point to our living. 'Each man's life thus resembles one of Sisyphus' climbs to the summit of his hill, and each day of it one of his steps; the difference is that whereas Sisyphus himself returns to push the stone up again, we leave this to our children' (Taylor 1970, 263).

Can anything give meaning to our lives, then? Taylor argues that if we turn from the objective standpoint of the universe to our own living, then we can infuse those lives with meaning. Meaning, in short, is subjective, not objective. It comes with the living itself. 'What counts is that you should be able to begin a new task, a new castle, a new bubble. It counts only because it is there to be done and you have the will to do it'. That, he argues, has a certain grace, a grace that lights up life from within, rather than having it conferred from without. 'The meaning of life is from within us, it is not bestowed from without, and it far exceeds in both its beauty and permanence any heaven of which men have ever dreamed or yearned for' (Taylor 1970, 268).

This subjective meaning, we can see, is not something we discover or come to understand. It is something we decide upon and create in our own living. We grant our lives meaning in the attitude we take toward them through an act of our own will. However, if we can orient our will one way, so can we orient it another. As Taylor's example of Sisyphus shows, if a certain desire is implanted in him his life becomes meaningful; absent that desire, it is simply endless drudgery. Meaningfulness is a product of the decision to take a certain attitude toward our lives; it is a product of our will. And if we can will one attitude, presumably we can take another. Thus the subjective viewpoint opens out on to the contingency of meaningfulness. And if the meaningfulness of my life is contingent on my decisions, then its relationship with (objective) morality is contingent as well.

One might argue here that Taylor's view, though subjective, is not contingent. While he finds meaningfulness in one's subjective relation to life, that meaningfulness can only appear in one place, in a particular type of willing: the willing that seeks 'to begin a new task, a new castle, a new bubble'. To be sure, Taylor does not say that one can make just any decision about what will make life meaningful. However, once he places the decision about the meaningfulness of life within the subject living it, it seems difficult to avoid the slide to a wider, more decisionistic, view. Moreover, even within the confines of his view, the relationship of meaning to morality remains contingent. Whether one is acting morally or not will, on this view, depend on the relation of the new task, the new castle, or the new bubble to morality.[2]

Once we see this contingency of the relationship of subjective meaningfulness to objective morality, we can immediately see that the same would apply to the less plausible

---

[2] It is probably worth noting in passing that Taylor's view of morality is also grounded in subjective desire rather than objective goodness. However, his approach to morality can be seen as relying on the idea that, given that we have desires, some ways of being are indeed morally better than others. That idea in turn issues out into a virtue-ethical framework for his morality.

possibilities of either subjective or objective meaningfulness with subjective morality. If moral rightness or wrongness is up to me, then whatever relationship that has to what makes life meaningful would either be up to me as well (in the case of subjective meaningfulness) or contingently related to a meaningful life (in the case of objective meaningfulness). There would be little more to say about those relationships than about the possibility just discussed.

This leaves us with one more relationship: that of objective meaningfulness with objective morality. At the outset, it would seem that the situation is similar to that of subjective meaningfulness with objective morality. Would the relationship be entirely contingent? Even if there are objective characteristics to a meaningful life and to a moral one, wouldn't the distinction between them be one in which there might just happen or not happen to be overlap?

There would, of course, be one exception to this: if a meaningful life were simply a moral one. If an objectively moral life were the only kind of meaningful one, then the two would necessarily coincide. However, what if there are distinct criteria for meaningfulness and morality? Then wouldn't the relationship be entirely contingent?

Contingent, yes, but not arbitrary. And here is where the interesting aspects of their relationship can arise. To see it, let's look first at a general picture before turning to specific examples. If both meaningfulness and morality are objective, then it is possible that what we ought to do from a moral standpoint clashes with what would make our lives meaningful (or more meaningful). This introduces a tension into our lives. Should we follow moral precepts, should we, as is sometimes said, 'do what's right', or instead should we allow ourselves to do what would make our lives more meaningful? Of course, for those who think that morality always trumps other reasons, the answer is clear. But let's lay that aside for the moment so that we can linger with the tension between the two normative realms.

Now those who hold a position that meaningfulness is subjective might argue that the same tension can hold between subjective meaningfulness and objective morality. Could it not be the case that the meaning I posit for my own life clashes with what objective morality requires? And if so, what would be the difference between that and the tension between objective meaningfulness and (objective) morality?

In order to make that case, the subjectivist view would have to jettison any decisionism associated with the view. That is, rather than grounding the subjective meaningfulness in what I happen to decide would be meaningful, the view would need to ground it in a meaningfulness that grips me, a meaningfulness that I find myself committed to, rather than deciding to commit to. The reason for this is that if meaningfulness is grounded simply in a decision, then it is always possible for me to decide otherwise. And if it's possible for me to decide otherwise, then the lived *tension* between the subjective meaningfulness and objective morality begins to dissipate. To the extent to which I can easily abandon my conception of meaningfulness, it does not grab hold of me to the point where it can cause a deep tension with what morality demands of me.

There is at least some support for the idea that a subjective view of meaning can grip me in this way. As Harry Frankfurt has argued in 'The Importance of What We Care

About,' what is important to me can arise from my finding myself caring about it rather than the other way around. 'It certainly cannot be assumed that what a person cares about is generally under his immediate voluntary control' (Frankfurt 1998, 85). Caring, in turn, creates importance, at least subjective importance. '[I]f there is something that a person does care about, then it follows that it is important to him. This is not because caring somehow involves an infallible judgment concerning the importance of its object. Rather, it is because caring about something *makes* that thing important to the person who cares about it' (Frankfurt 1998, 92).

Caring, then, and the meaningfulness (or importance) that results from it, need not be a result of a decision. It can happen to me, as love often does. It offers subjective importance to a person as a result not of reasons that lead to a decision, nor even of any decision without reasons, but simply because I am gripped by a caring that I did not choose but that makes itself felt in me and in doing so lends meaningfulness to my life.[3]

If this is right, then could there not be the same tension between a subjective view of meaningfulness and morality as there is between an objective view and morality? To be clear, we should recognize at the outset that that tension, if it exists, would be lived rather than theoretical or philosophical. That is to say, it would not be a tension that arises from the clash of two objective standards. It might be experienced as a tension, but not one that is grounded in something deeper than one's own commitments. But even within a lived tension, there is a difference between the lived tension of subjective meaningfulness and the way objective meaningfulness would be lived. To see it, though, we need to address a complication.

For the subjective meaningfulness view to be full-blooded, the person living it needs to recognize it *as subjective*. If she fails to do so, she may be living a life whose subjective meaningfulness is experienced as objective, and in that case the lived tension between meaningfulness and morality would be experienced in the same way as someone who, in the case where meaningfulness is objective, recognized it as objective and yet in tension with morality. Alternatively, once she recognizes her view as subjective, the tension between her commitment to meaningfulness and her recognition of what morality demands does not have the same lived quality as that between someone whose commitment (or falsely believed commitment) to an objective view of meaningfulness would have. The lived tension would be something along the lines of, 'I know it's just me, but what I find meaningful isn't in tune with what morality is requiring of me', rather than, 'What would make my life more meaningful isn't in tune with what morality is requiring of me'. The former, while not decisionistic, is closer to the decisionism discussed earlier than the latter would be. We might say that it locates a *dislocation* here between what one finds meaningful and what morality asks, rather than a proper *tension* between them, since the two realms (subjective meaningfulness and objective morality) exist in distinct

---

[3] Frankfurt (1998, 87) makes it clear that such being gripped does not render one entirely passive with regard to such caring. She may ratify the caring itself. 'He accedes to it because he is *unwilling* to oppose it and because, furthermore, his unwillingness is *itself* something which he is unwilling to alter.'

realms rather than operating on the same plane—that of objectivity. They operate at cross purposes, rather than coming into direct conflict.

(We should note as well that things can be the other way around. That is, a person who lives objective meaningfulness but falsely considers it to be subjective would be in much the same position as someone who correctly believes her meaningfulness is subjectively grounded.)

2. Objective Meaningfulness and Morality—Two Views

So far we have been treating matters in a general and abstract way. Where we have arrived is at a recognition that if there is to be a tension between meaningfulness and morality, that tension appears most sharply when both are objective. This is true both theoretically or philosophically—where the tension is between two objectively grounded standards—and, though under certain conditions to a lesser extent, phenomenologically—where the tension between the two normative realms is experienced or lived. To see this possible tension in play, let's turn to a couple of examples of an objectively grounded view of meaningfulness.

The first example is from Susan Wolf's influential *Meaning in Life and Why It Matters*. Wolf's view, it should be noted at the outset, is not solely grounded in an objective standpoint. Her motto, in fact, is that 'meaning arises when subjective attraction meets objective attractiveness' (Wolf 2010, 9). It is a hybrid view, arguing that meaning in life does not emerge simply through subjective considerations nor through objective conditions, but rather through their intersection. On the subjective side, a meaningful life is one in which is person is taken up by what one is doing. '[A] person's life can be meaningful only if she is gripped, excited interested, engaged, or as I earlier put it if she loves something—as opposed to being bored by or alienated from most of what she does' (Wolf 2010, 9).

However, subjective fulfilment is not enough. 'Even a person who is so engaged, however, will not live a meaningful life if the objects or activities with which she is so occupied are worthless' (Wolf 2010, 9). This is why her view is hybrid. Meaningfulness lies at the intersection of subjective engagement and objective worthwhileness.

Our focus here is on the objective side. While it is true that for Wolf there is no meaningfulness without subjective conditions being fulfilled, there must a set of objective conditions as well in order for it to emerge. What might these objective conditions be? Wolf offers some examples of objective attractiveness, examples that she is at pains to distinguish from moral considerations or from considerations of pure self-concern. 'When I visit my brother in the hospital, or help my friend move, or stay up all night sewing my daughter a Halloween costume, I act neither for egoistic reasons nor for moral ones... I act neither out of self-interest nor out of duty or any other impersonal or impartial reason. Rather, I act out of love' (Wolf 2010, 4). These examples are interpersonal ones, but meaning can arise from other activities as well; she offers the writing of philosophy or learning to play a musical instrument as examples of objectively meaningful activities that do not meet a specifically moral standard.

We should note (a point we will return to) that Wolf's view presupposes a certain view of what moral considerations consist in. For her, they are a matter of impersonally drawn duties towards others. This view, of course, contrasts at points with a more virtue-ethical approach, particularly that defended by Aristotle. For the moment, however, what is important is the distinction between the meaningful and the moral that she draws in her approach.

We might ask here, beyond the examples she provides, whether there is a more general account she offers of objective meaningfulness. The short answer is that there is not. This is by design. 'To the question, "Who's to say which projects are independently valuable and which are not?" my answer is, "No one in particular." Neither I, nor any group of professional ethicists or academicians—nor, for that matter, any other group I can think of—have any special expertise that makes their judgment particularly reliable' (Wolf 2010, 39). Instead, she sees the answer to that question as one that arises from general reflective considerations, open to everyone to consider. There need not be a particular philosophical account, one that discovers what is common to all activities having objective worth, what underlying theme they express. There can be a diversity of activities with no thematic unity that have objective attractiveness.

In a moment we will consider a broad thematic approach to objective worthiness, but before that, we need to ask about the relationship between meaning and morality in Wolf's view. While it is clear the two are not the same, are they necessarily in conflict? Might they be in conflict at points? How should we understand their relationship?

Wolf tells us that

> [m]orality, at least as I understand it, is chiefly concerned with integrating into our practical outlook the fact that we are each one person (or perhaps one subject) in a community of others equal to ourselves.... But there is another perspective, possibly even more external, in which the demands and interests of morality are not absolute. Viewed from the perspective of our place in the universe, as opposed to our place in the human or sentient community, a person's obedience to moral constraints may itself seem to be only one consideration among others. (Wolf 2010, 59)

Here Wolf lays out a view that is central to her general philosophical view, one that is encapsulated in the title to her recent book of essays, *The Variety of Values*.

For Wolf, moral considerations—considerations arising from the fact that each of us is only one among others—are not necessarily overriding in the way some philosophers have thought. Value comes in different forms. Moral values are among them, but don't necessarily occupy a privileged space. Values such as meaningfulness, depending on the circumstances, can be just as compelling as those arising from moral reflection. Wolf offers an eloquent example of this in her essay 'Morality and Partiality'. 'Consider', she asks us, 'the case of a woman whose son has committed a crime and who must decide whether to hide him from the police. He will suffer gravely should he be caught, but unless he is caught, another innocent man will be wrongly convicted for the crime and imprisoned' (Wolf 2015, 39). This case, she argues, is best seen not solely through the lens of moral considerations—what does she owe to her son versus what does she owe to the police or society? This does not capture the character of her difficulty. (Moreover, it probably runs afoul of Bernard Williams's famous 'one thought too many' test.)

Rather, she says, 'To describe the woman's conflict as one *between* morality and the bonds of love seems to me to capture or preserve the split, almost schizophrenic reaction I think we ought to have to her dilemma', and concludes that '*she* had reached a point where the issue of moral approval had ceased to matter' (Wolf 2015, 59).

What Wolf offers is an account of meaningfulness that is distinct from that of morality, that can conflict with morality, but that does not *necessarily* conflict with morality. To be sure, the criteria for meaningfulness and for morality are, in her eyes, distinct. The former is a matter of subjective engagement in activities that are objectively worthwhile, while the latter is action stemming from the recognition that one is 'only one person (or perhaps one subject) in a community of persons equal to ourselves'. However, activities that are meaningful can be morally permissible as well. Think here of the examples Wolf describes of visiting her brother in the hospital or sewing a Halloween costume for her daughter. These activities, in contrast to the woman hiding her son from the police, do not conflict with any moral demands.

In fact, there can be situations where the actions stemming from meaning and those required by morality converge, when 'reasons of love' (a phrase Wolf borrows from Frankfurt) lead one to do something that would emerge from considerations of oneself as only one among others in a community of equals. Imagine, for example, in a case we in the United States unfortunately are faced with, a person who sees on television an immigrant child being held in a cage, separated from his parents, after the family has crossed the border and asked for asylum. This image becomes seared in the viewer's mind, not only as an instance of cruelty, but also in her sympathy for the child. She decides that she's going to do something to help that child, or if not her, then another child in the same circumstances. (There were many such children to choose from, and as I write these lines there still are.) So she donates money to an organization that represents immigrants in a suit against the government, or she writes her Congress members to demand that this treatment be stopped, or, more determined, she goes to the border to protest the caging of children.

These actions can be performed out of something that might be called 'reasons of love', even if she does not know the child personally. To see this, we can contrast this with the person who knows that this practice is taking place, has not seen images that would stir her, but thinks to herself, 'This is unfair; I would not want to be treated this way, and so I am obliged to do something to stop others' being treated this way'. That would be a moral consideration on Wolf's view, one that might lead to the same action from a different motivation, corresponding to criteria of morality rather than meaningfulness.

Wolf's view, as we have seen, is catholic in what she considers to be objective worthiness. She is hesitant to circumscribe or offer criteria for what would be objectively worthwhile, thinking that it is not the task of any particular group of people or specialists, largely because the realm of the objectively worthwhile likely crosses a number of different normative boundaries. However, let us consider a specific proposal for what might be an account of objective worthwhileness. In my book *A Significant Life*, I have offered such a proposal. It is not meant to be exhaustive, and so is not in conflict with the sanctions Wolf has placed on such accounts. Rather, it is meant to offer *one* way of thinking of objective worthiness that would capture an important arena of what we often think (although not as reflectively as the account delineates) as meaningful.[4]

I am sympathetic to Wolf's overall account that 'meaning arises when subjective attraction meets objective attractiveness'. My proposal is that a way to think of objective attractiveness is in terms of what I call 'narrative values' (May 2015). A narrative value is not a story; it is not a full-blooded narrative. Rather, it is a value (a positive value as opposed to a disvalue) that could be seen as a theme of a person's life, or at least a sufficiently large segment of it. Adventurousness is such a value. Some people spend a good part of their lives getting wide of themselves, putting themselves in potentially vulnerable situations where they can challenge themselves in new activities that might allow them to experience their lives in new ways. Explorers, rock climbers, travellers who seek out remote areas: these are examples of lives that exhibit the value of adventurousness. However, adventurousness is only one of many narrative values that a life can exhibit or express. Spirituality, intensity, curiosity, spontaneousness, and loyalty: all of these and others are narrative values that can stand as candidates for objective worthwhileness in a life.

To be clear, a single life does not have to express only one of these values. They are not mutually exclusive. A person's life trajectory could be one of both adventurousness and spirituality, for example, a life that sees her adventurousness as expressive of a gratitude to the universe or some theological being for offering so many ways of casting oneself out into the world.

One might ask here why we should consider these life themes as conferring objective worthwhileness. What is the justification for narrative values as criteria for judging a life to be meaningful? And here, I would have to say, in a Wittgensteinian vein, that my spade is largely turned. We just do think of these themes as life values, if not necessarily in those particular terms. Many if not most of us would like to see our lives as exhibiting one or another narrative value, and we admire people whose lives do. Even if I am not a

---

[4] A distinct but related way of thinking about meaningfulness in life is Thaddeus Metz's influential 'fundamentality theory' he offers in *Meaning in Life*, a view which argues that a 'person's life is more meaningful, the more that she, without violating certain moral constraints against degrading sacrifice, employs her reason and in ways that either positively orient rationality towards fundamental conditions of human existence, or negatively orient it towards what threatens them, such that the worse parts of her life cause better parts towards its end by a process that makes for a compelling and ideally original life-story; in addition, the meaning in a human person's life is reduced, the more it is negatively oriented towards fundamental conditions of human existence or exhibits narrative disvalue' (Metz 2013, 235).

spontaneous person or a very spiritual person, I can admire the spontaneity or spirituality that I see in another. Moreover, such admiration is deeper when I see it not as a one-off but as a theme that has characterized a person's life or a large part of it.

If we accept that one way to think of objective worthwhileness is through narrative values, our next question would be about the relationship between narrative values and morality. Here we should linger for a moment over a particular moral—or at least ethical (a point we will return to in a moment)—view that might seem close to that of narrative values: virtue ethics. Instead of thinking of narrative values as a realm of meaningfulness distinct from morality, can we not think of them instead as an expansion of Aristotelean values, a 'friendly amendment' to the idea that the good life is one that is lived in accordance with particular personal virtues?[5]

The idea would be this. Aristotle was interested in the question of how one should live rather than, with the moderns, how one should act. He thought that a proper life for human beings involved the cultivation and expression of certain personal virtues like courage, temperance, magnanimity, and so on. We can think of these virtues as themes that would characterize the trajectory of a life. Rather than, with the moderns, asking about whether particular actions are morally right or wrong (or permissible, etc.), Aristotle focused on what makes a good life overall. Could not the same be said for the narrative values? Don't they also characterize a good life, a proper human life, adding to the themes that Aristotle or others would propose rather than forming a separate category?

There is a difficulty in responding to this question, one that involves a larger question: What is the point of morality? For Wolf, as we have seen, it is largely a guide to our interpersonal relations, one that asks us to see ourselves as one among others. This would be an example of modern morality, one in which it is our attitude and behaviour towards others that are central to the moral realm. In contrast, an Aristotelean view asks about the conditions for the good life, a life well lived as a human being. This distinction is often drawn by using the term *morality* for what Wolf is interested in and the term *ethics* for a more Aristotelean or virtue-ethical view.

For Aristotle, of course, this life was one in accord with the cosmos. For him, everything had a telos, a goal, and the point of the *Nichomachean Ethics* is to discover and unfold what that telos is for human beings. In our more secular age, this grounding of ethical action is likely to be less compelling (unless it is grounded in a theological rather than cosmological framework). Nevertheless, might one still say that a virtue-ethical view seeks to answer the question of what a (or the) good life is for human beings, and that narrative values can be seen as elements of a good life, providing an objective worthiness to a life in much the same way other virtues would?

This is an intriguing suggestion, but one that I want to resist in favour of a more modern moral approach. There are two reasons for this. First, I think it's important to preserve the idea of obligation that attends to a more modern approach to morality.

---

[5] I owe this suggestion to my colleague Chris Grau, who brought it up in conversation.

That is, a principle or recommendation that is one we would consider moral has a certain *ought* to it that does not attach to narrative values. Now it is easy to go wrong here, so I don't want to overstate the power of that ought. It is not that we ought, all things considered, to do what a moral *ought* recommends, if for no other reason than that one *ought* might be outweighed by another one. It could also be the case, as we have seen with Wolf, that a moral *ought* might also be overridden, or at least challenged, by something that is not an *ought* at all, like love. But even if we hold to the latter view, we still attach the idea of the *ought* to what we are calling moral obligations or recommendations.

This *ought*, I believe, is grounded in the idea that morality is a matter of guiding our relationships with others. Because of this, it might seem that I'm arguing in a circle, taking for granted the modern moral view rather than arguing for it. One might respond here that an Aristotelean view is focused on the goodness of a life rather than on our relationships with others. However, my claim is that there is a distinction worth preserving, one that is captured in modern moral thought, between what might be considered a good life in the virtue-ethical sense and how we should conceive our relationships with others. If that distinction is compelling, then there is also a distinction between the moral realm and that of narrative (or other meaning) values.

Related to this is another reason to preserve the distinction between narrative values and morality. The argument just presented has to do with the *ought* in my relationships with other people. However, in relationship to myself, in the conduct of my own life, I think the *ought* is out of place. That is, I do not see that we have obligations to ourselves. I recognize that this is an area of some controversy, and will not wade into it in a sustained way. This is also, admittedly, a very modern view, bound up with notions of privacy and even questions of democracy that are outside the scope of this discussion. For those who believe we have obligations to ourselves, this will not be compelling. However, my own view is that when it comes to morality, our relationship to ourselves is an arena that is off limits to morality. If this is right, then while we might admit that there are ways in which living in accordance with one or another narrative value might make a life better—and thus offer an objective worthiness to a life—that is a distinct question from whether one has a reason that might be grounded in an *ought* to do so.

If we embrace the idea that narrative values occupy a realm distinct from morality, then the question can arise of the relationship between the two. Does the realm of narrative values necessarily conflict with morality, or is that relation contingent?[6]

We can dismiss immediately the idea of necessary conflict. There is nothing within the realm of narrative values, nothing among the themes of adventurousness, spirituality, intensity, etc., that would lead to a necessary conflict with the obligations that morality asks of us. (Might there be a particular narrative value that would necessarily

---

[6] To say that the realm of narrative values is distinct from the realm of morality does not preclude the possibility that there is a value that can serve both narratively and morally, particularly if one's morality tilts towards the virtue ethical. It might be, for instance, that courageousness might lend meaning to a life as well as being a morally valuable character trait. However, even so, the fact that it lends meaning to a life in a narrative sense is distinct from the moral implications it would have.

conflict with morality? Since this concept of narrative values is a recent one, I can't say for sure that this is impossible; however, I can't think of a life theme that we would call a narrative value that would be in necessary conflict with morality.) However, the fact that there is no necessary conflict would not allow us immediately to conclude that narrative values exist in the moral realm of, say, the permitted. That will depend on how those values are incorporated into a life.

To see this, let's take a contrasting pair of examples in regard to adventurousness. In the first example, our adventurous person is a traveller. She seeks ever new environments, often putting herself at risk by going into unfamiliar surroundings and seeking to navigate through them. She's not careless; she doesn't just show up without any research into where she's going. But she's willing to trek in rain forests, cross deserts, go into war zones, each of which gives her a new experience but will be accompanied by unavoidable danger. She is single and does not have anyone who counts on her providing for them, and so the risks she takes are entirely on her own behalf. To be sure, she worries her parents a bit, but they understand that this is who she must be and they accept it.

By contrast, our second adventurer's life is morally more precarious. While he is not reckless either—he researches his journeys and does not take unnecessary risks—he has a family he neglects to take into account. His spouse does not agree with his taking these adventures; he or she feels abandoned when he does. Moreover, each adventure requires leaving his job, which puts the family in a precarious financial situation. For him, these are the unavoidable aspects of his being adventurous.[7] To be adventurous in this life requires these sacrifices, not only by himself but by those around him as well. He wishes it were otherwise, but is willing to live with the fact that it is not. The needs and desires of others are just not that pressing on him.

How do things stand morally with regard to these two people? Let's imagine ourselves as friends of both. In the first case, with the woman, we are likely to admire her adventurousness. Speaking for myself, this admiration is mixed with a bit of envy (though not going so far as jealousy). She exhibits a courage and a free-spiritedness that contrasts with the hankering after security that characterizes most of our lives. How many of us, after all, don't worry at moments about the degree to which we are living what Thoreau famously called 'lives of quiet desperation'? This woman seems free of that worry, throwing herself out upon the world with an admirable abandon.

The second case is not quite so clean. Even as a friend, he is hard to admire, and yet hard completely to condemn. Perhaps he is wrong to engage in his adventurous behaviour; his callousness in regard to his family's needs and feelings may tilt us toward that judgement. But even if we do, we cannot entirely dismiss the worth of what he is doing. It is not as though he is forsaking his family to satisfy a drug addiction or to lavish money on people with whom he is having affairs. A life of adventure has value—narrative value, I would call it. And so towards this man we might feel something more like

---

[7] Readers here will be reminded of Bernard Williams's (1982) Paul Gauguin in his essay 'Moral Luck'.

ambivalence, even if that ambivalence would lead us to a particular judgement in the end. (Moreover, we could further complicate the normative picture here if we added certain details, for instance that his adventurousness is rooted in a restlessness that his spouse knew was an important aspect of who he was even before they were married.)[8]

The relationship between narrative values and morality, then, is a complicated one, one that resists assessment based solely on the value itself. Instead, it must be assessed within the life that expresses or exhibits that value; even then the assessment might not be a simple one, and at times our ultimate judgement about the person herself even less so. This latter point should not be surprising in light of our discussion of Wolf's view about 'the variety of values'. Consider, for instance, how difficult it would be to come to an ultimate normative judgment of the mother who hides her son, even though the moral judgment is a straightforward one.

3. Conclusion

In reflecting on the relationship between meaningfulness and morality, we have seen several possibilities. If we take morality to be objective and meaningfulness to be subjective, there are a couple of possibilities. At the level of lived subjectiveness, that is, a subjective view of meaningfulness that is recognized as such by the person, the relationship can be either contingent and decisionist—where a person can decide what meaning they would like their lives to have and therefore what relation meaning is to morality—or, with Frankfurt's possibility, contingent but not decisionistic. Alternatively, if the relationship is not one that is recognized, i.e. if the person mistakenly thinks that the meaningfulness of her life is objective, then the relationship will be lived as contingent and not decisionistic, but in contrast to the Frankfurt case, any conflict between meaningfulness and morality will be lived as objective rather than personal.

However, at the philosophical level, the relationship between subjective meaningfulness and objective morality remains a conflict between what one is personally committed to, either through decision or not, and what morality requires. This is in contrast to the relationship between an objective meaningfulness and objective morality. There, as with the former relationship, the relationship is contingent; however, it is contingent in a different way. The contingency is not between personal commitments and moral requirements, but rather between two (or more) sets of objective standards. To understand the relationships in that case—as we have seen with our two examples of Wolf's view and my view of narrative values—requires delving not only into the relationship

---

[8] The question might arise of whether a person can violate morality deeply enough that it would withdraw meaningfulness from his or her life. In *A Significant Life*, I argue that the relation of meaningfulness and morality is asymmetric in the sense that a more moral life does not necessarily add meaningfulness, but that a deeply immoral life does necessarily withdraw meaningfulness (May 2015, chapter 4).

of values of meaning with morality, but also into the role that values of meaning play in the person's life itself. It is a matter, as it were, of triangulating objective values of meaningfulness, objective moral values, and a person's life. In contrast, in the relationship between subjective meaningfulness and objective values, the contrast is more directly between that meaningfulness as lived or understood by the person and objective moral values.

This discussion has focused on a particular, although central, aspect of the relationship between meaning and morality. There are other important issues that might be addressed, such as the question of whether a more meaningful life would make one more likely to be a moral person. I have left this issue aside, not only for reasons of space, but also because it seems to me more a psychological question than a philosophical one. What I hope to have accomplished here is to offer a broad framework, undoubtedly not the only possible framework, from within which further questions about the relationship between meaningfulness and morality might be asked and reflected upon.

References

Frankfurt, Harry. 1998. 'The Importance of What We Care About'. In H. Frankfurt, *The Importance of What We Care About*, 80–94. Cambridge: Cambridge University Press.
May, Todd. 2015. *A Significant Life: Human Meaning in a Silent Universe*. Chicago: University of Chicago Press.
Metz, Thaddeus. 2013. *Meaning in Life*. Oxford: Oxford University Press.
Moody-Adams, Michelle. 2002. *Fieldwork in Familiar Places: Morality, Culture, and Philosophy*. Cambridge, MA: Harvard University Press.
Taylor, Richard. 1970. *Good and Evil: A New Direction*. London: Macmillan.
Williams, Bernard. 1982. 'Moral Luck'. In B. Williams, *Moral Luck*, 20–39. Cambridge: Cambridge University Press.
Wolf, Susan. 2010. *Meaning in Life and Why It Matters*. Princeton, NJ: Princeton University Press.
Wolf, Susan. 2015. 'Morality and Partiality'. In S. Wolf, *The Variety of Values: Essays on Morality, Meaning, and Love*, 31–46. Oxford: Oxford University Press.

CHAPTER 17

MEANING AND ANTI-MEANING IN LIFE

SVEN NYHOLM AND STEPHEN M. CAMPBELL

In ordinary thinking, there are only two ways to categorize lives or activities in terms of meaning: they can be *meaningful* to a greater or lesser extent, or they can be *meaningless*. This naturally gives the impression that meaning is some positive value attached to certain actions or ways of living, and that meaningless activities simply lack this value, whereas meaningful ones have it to some extent. This chapter will complicate this simple picture by suggesting that meaning has an opposite—a negative counterpart that we may call 'anti-meaning'—and that perhaps we should view some activities and lives as being *anti-meaningful*.

To get a sense of the intuitive idea, it is helpful to look at some concrete examples. Consider the case of the Swedish teenager and climate activist Greta Thunberg. In 2018, she began skipping school on Fridays in order to stand outside of the Swedish parliament holding a 'School Strike for Climate' sign. At first she was alone, but within a year this student-activist had 'succeeded in creating a global attitudinal shift', influencing hundreds of thousands of young people to take part in climate activism (Alter et al. 2019). Because of her significant contributions to this worthy cause, Thunberg was named *TIME Magazine*'s 2019 'Person of the Year', and has been nominated for the Nobel Peace Prize. Contrast this with the case of former US president Donald Trump, who repeatedly dismissed global warming as a 'hoax' (De La Garza 2019). Trump rolled back numerous previously instated environmental rules and regulations, and also formally withdrew the United States—one of the world's leading carbon-emitters—from the 2015 Paris Agreement on climate change mitigation (Popovich et al. 2020; Friedman and Sengupta 2021). Thunberg's activities appear to be positively impacting the world in a way that renders her undertaking quite meaningful. In contrast, Trump's climate-related activities had a profoundly negative impact and might be thought of, not simply as meaningless, but as being the opposite of meaningful. They seem anti-meaningful.

The overarching aim of this chapter is to shed light on two main questions: (1) What is anti-meaning? and (2) Is anti-meaning an illuminating or otherwise useful concept for philosophical theorizing or practical thinking about living in the modern world? After reviewing the modest literature that exists on the topic of anti-meaning, we present two formal interpretations of the anti-meaning concept and then discuss different substantive conceptions of what anti-meaning might be. Turning to the second question, we discuss some reasons why one might be sceptical about the idea of anti-meaning, focusing on an argument presented by Christopher Woodard. Then we make the case for adopting the concept of anti-meaning on at least one of the two formal interpretations. As we will discuss, which interpretation is favoured will depend to some extent on how we view philosophical ethics: whether its primary purpose is to articulate and spell out implications of common-sense thinking, or whether ethics should also try to construct new 'thinking tools' that can enrich and build upon common-sense thinking.[1]

1. Anti-Meaning: A Brief Literature Review

Suppose you have a job that you find boring, performing tasks that are repetitive and not very challenging. You don't think the company you work for makes any particularly valuable contribution to society, and you also feel replaceable in the role you play within the company. This might be a case where you find your job to be meaningless and are led to seek out more meaningful work options. This example illustrates a distinction people commonly make in thinking about how they spend their time and the options that are open to them: the distinction between things that are meaningful in a positive sense and things that are meaningless by lacking any positive meaning.

But some philosophers have suggested that it is not enough to merely distinguish between what is meaningful and what lacks meaning. They have found it useful to invoke the idea of anti-meaning. Thaddeus Metz (2002, 806; 2012, 444; 2013, 64, 73–74), for example, argues that while some things to which we can devote our time and efforts matter in a positive sense that can help to make our lives and actions meaningful, there may be other things that are so negative in nature that they 'anti-matter'. They have a negative impact on how meaningful our lives and actions are.[2] To draw out our views on this matter, Metz asks readers to contemplate the following:

---

[1] We get the expression 'thinking tools' from Daniel Dennett (2013). We are also inspired by Alexis Burgess and David Plunkett's (2013a–b) idea of 'conceptual ethics' here—the idea that one branch of ethics should concern itself with what concepts we should or should not use.

[2] Just how controversial the idea of anti-meaning (or anti-matter) is may depend on what we take the relevant bearers of meaning and anti-meaning to be. It may be easier to get people to agree that actions can be the opposite of meaningful than it is to get people to agree that whole lives can be the opposite of meaningful. In between these two ideas, there is also the possibility that portions or 'chunks' of lives can be the opposite of meaningful. Our own view is that, at least in theory, it is possible for whole lives to be anti-meaningful. But even if only actions or parts of lives can be anti-meaningful, that would still be an important fact that is worth articulating and investigating.

> Consider a life composed of actions such as killing one's spouse for the insurance money or blowing up the Sphinx for fun. Does this life merely lack meaning or does it contain antimatter? Is it more akin to an impoverished life, one that lacks money, or to an unhappy life, one that contains misery? (Metz 2002, 806–807)

Metz expects us to think that such a life is more like the second of the two options: it is more like an unhappy life that contains misery than a life lacking in wealth.

Similarly, Iddo Landau (2011, 317) discusses the importance of ethics and moral considerations for meaning. According to Landau, if some activity is immoral, this not only means that it lacks positive meaning. It may be the 'inverse' of meaningful. Take, as an example, Adolf Hitler's role in the mass murder of millions of people and other crimes against humanity. Landau writes:

> Hitler's life is not merely meaningless, a life in which meaning is absent, but instead a life in which the converse of meaning is present. To use an arithmetic analogy, the meaningfulness of lives such as Hitler had should not be evaluated at around zero or even as simply zero, but in negative numbers. The scale of meaning of life should be conceived as stretching into that negative sphere as well. (Landau 2011, 317)

Aaron Smuts (2013) understands positive meaning in life to derive from whether our life is devoted to a 'good cause', and he thinks that this also leaves open the possibility that a life can have what he calls 'negative meaning'. To illustrate his point, Smuts also points to Hitler's life as one having 'a high degree of negative meaning' and being 'the opposite of meaningful' (Smuts 2013, 23).

Ingmar Persson and Julian Savulescu (2019, 229) use the phrase 'bad meaning' to refer to a similar idea. They suggest that, in general, we should understand the meaning in a person's life in terms of what the person intentionally does and what effects the person intentionally produces. If the effects of a person's intentional actions are good, this gives good meaning to the person's life. In contrast, if what a person intentionally does has negative consequences, this gives bad meaning to the person's life.[3]

Campbell and Nyholm (2015) offer the first article-length discussion of the concept of anti-meaning and why it may have significance for our lives. In that essay, we identified four popular theories of meaning in life and examined what the opposite of meaning would be on each theory. (In the next section, we will summarize the main findings of that investigation.) We then argued that the prospect of living lives that are anti-meaningful in certain respects is applicable not only to extreme figures like Donald Trump, but also to ordinary, morally decent people. Our claim was based on the fact that, as

---

[3] It is worth asking whether non-intentional actions (e.g. things we do accidentally or unknowingly) might also have negative meaning. It is also interesting to reflect on whether other people's actions could make our lives or aspects of our lives the opposite of meaningful. For example, if we spend much time and effort parenting a child, and that child turns out to be a terrorist through no fault of our own, would our child's evil actions make our own lives the opposite of meaningful? We will not explore these questions in this chapter, though they certainly deserve attention.

citizens of the modern world, it is very hard not to participate in activities that, in some fashion, adversely impact present or future people (Campbell and Nyholm 2015, 705–706; cf. Lichtenberg 2010, 2014). This is not to say that ordinary people's lives are always or even typically anti-meaningful on the whole. Rather, the point is that various aspects of participating in modern society can serve to counteract, if not undermine, the meaningfulness of our lives.

Lastly, Marcello Di Paola (2018, 27, 128) highlights some of the ways our modern lifestyles have a 'sinister meaning'. As Di Paola points out, there is a certain loss of agency and responsibility dissolution that occurs when we participate in modern practices where our individual contributions do not have much of a negative effect (on climate change, the global distribution of wealth and resources, and so on), but where our individual contributions combine to cause incredibly bad consequences. There is little that individuals can do to change anything about this, and yet we know that we are part of the problem. Although it can seem wrong to classify these individual contributions as immoral, they do seem to have some sort of negative value—and the concept of anti-meaning is one concept that seems to apply quite naturally.

2. Two Formal Interpretations of Anti-Meaning

Let us now consider in more detail how we should understand the notion of anti-meaning. We will start with something more technical and formal in this section, and then move on to the substance of anti-meaning in the next section.

We can start by noticing that there are two distinct ways to understand the idea of anti-meaning. To illustrate the difference, imagine two different kinds of card game. In both games, the goal is to achieve the highest score possible, which players do by acquiring black cards (which yield positive points) and avoiding red cards (yielding negative points). In the first game, it is possible to have an overall negative score by holding more red cards than black ones. In the second game, it is not possible to have a negative score; the worst possible score is zero. Red cards only have the function of 'cancelling' or 'defeating' black cards. Hence, two players can end the game with the very same score of zero despite the fact that one player accrued far more red than black cards than the other.

Analogously, anti-meaning can be conceived in one of two ways. On what we will call the *counterforce model*, meaning and anti-meaning are similar but diametrically opposed forces that move us, respectively, in the direction of a meaningful life or an anti-meaningful life. If the meaningful elements of a life outweigh or in some other way defeat the anti-meaningful ones, a person will have an overall meaningful life. If anti-meaning dominates, it will be an anti-meaningful life. On this view, meaninglessness is essentially a score of zero on the meaning/anti-meaning scale and results from either (1) having no meaning or anti-meaning at all in one's life or (2) having roughly equal amounts of meaning and anti-meaning that balance each other out. So, this is a conception of meaning in life on which there is a bipolar scale with both a positive and negative side (cf. Metz 2002, 806). Like the first game described earlier, it is possible to end up with a negative score with respect to meaning.

In contrast, we could conceive of a life's meaning on a monopolar scale and still recognize a role for anti-meaning. On what we will dub the *defeater model*, anti-meaning only has the function of cancelling out or defeating meaning. There is no such thing as an 'anti-meaningful life' or activity on this view; a life can only be meaningful (to a greater or lesser extent) or meaningless. On this model, there are, in theory, three ways to end up with a meaningless life: (1) having neither meaning nor anti-meaning in one's life, (2) having roughly equal amounts of meaning and anti-meaning, or (3) having an amount of anti-meaning greater than the amount of meaning. Thus, meaninglessness—the analogue of a zero score in the second game described earlier—is the worst one can do when it comes to meaning.

To our knowledge, the preceding distinction has not yet been explicitly made in the literature on anti-meaning. Based on textual clues, most everyone who has discussed anti-meaning in the literature (including us) appears to have had the counterforce model in mind. But the defeater model of anti-meaning is also worth considering since, as we shall discuss in section 5, it fits nicely with, and helps to account for, many of our everyday judgements about meaning. We will argue that those who are unwilling to adopt the more revisionist counterforce model of anti-meaning should at least be willing to acknowledge the existence of anti-meaning on the more conservative defeater model.[4]

3. Substantive Theories of Anti-Meaning

To this point, we have discussed anti-meaning at a very abstract and theoretical level. But what is anti-meaning exactly? Our favoured strategy for getting deeper insight into anti-meaning is to first examine different competing theories of meaning. Taking different positive conceptions of meaning as a starting point, one can then ask what the

---

[4] There is a further complication that we have been setting aside for simplicity's sake: namely, the possibility that some anti-meaningful things would have a negative value that cannot be offset or compensated for by any amount of positively meaningful things. To invoke the Hitler example again: if a person conducts themselves like Hitler and manages to have the devastating influence he had, this might function as a trump card that makes it impossible to score meaningfulness points by performing positively meaningful actions. We assume that most people do not engage in behaviours that are so bad that the meaningfulness in their lives is cancelled out. But we are open to the possibility that this could happen. On the positive side, in contrast, it seems less plausible that there could be so much positive meaning in one's life such that no amount of anti-meaningful activity could bring down the meaningfulness of the person's life to the level of meaninglessness or anti-meaning. If so, there might be an interesting asymmetry between meaning and anti-meaning here.

polar opposite of meaning, understood in these different ways, would be (Campbell and Nyholm 2015, 696–704).

In the philosophical literature on meaning in life, most scholars appear to accept that meaning in life is either a purely subjective matter (that ultimately depends on our own attitudes towards what we do), a more objective matter (dependent on the value of what we do, irrespective of our attitudes about these things), or some combination of subjective and objective elements. Accordingly, three general types of theories of meaning have been the most widely discussed: subjectivist theories, objectivist theories, and 'hybrid' theories.[5]

Subjectivist theories of meaning come in different forms. On some subjectivist ways of thinking about meaning, whether our lives are meaningful depends on whether we have certain positive affective attitudes towards our lives (e.g. Taylor 1970). On other subjectivist theories, it might instead depend on whether we make certain positive judgements about our lives and activities, or on whether we achieve our freely chosen aims (e.g. Hooker 2008; Luper 2014). Of course, there can also be mixed forms of subjectivist theory, where meaningfulness requires some combination of affective attitudes and more cognitive judgements about ourselves and our lives.

Objectivist theories understand the test of whether our lives and activities are meaningful to be a matter of the value associated with them. One type of theory says that having many good and valuable things and/or making a positive contribution to the world contribute to a life's meaningfulness (e.g. Smuts 2013; Bramble 2015). Stated in such abstract normative terms, such a theory leaves it open what exactly is good and what counts as making a positive contribution. Objectivist theories can be made more substantive or concrete by also staking a claim on what sorts of activities are good and worthwhile contributions—e.g. activities that help other people, foster knowledge, create beauty, promote love and friendship, fight injustice, and so on.

A third kind of theory incorporates elements of subjectivist and objectivist theories into what is often called the hybrid theory of meaning. This theory has been popularized by Susan Wolf. In Wolf's oft-quoted formulation, meaning arises when 'subjective attraction meets objective attractiveness' (Wolf 2010, 26) According to this point of view, if somebody does much good (helps other people, creates valuable art, cures diseases, saves the climate, or whatever else) but at the same time is alienated from what they

---

[5] As Metz 2019 notes, theories of meaning usually are about the lives and actions of human persons and the value of their actions and choices. However, there are other (less widely discussed) theories that deviate from the standard ways of understanding meaning in life. For example, some theories do not view meaning as particularly related to value, and some theories do not see this as a value specifically related to human agency. See, for example, theories of meaning discussed in Mawson (2010, 2019); Repp (2018); Seachris (2019); and Thomas (2018, 2019). Such non-standard theories might be hard to combine with the notion of anti-meaning; in other words, if we accept some such non-standard theory, perhaps the idea of anti-meaning will not make sense anymore. Be that as it may, we follow Metz (2019) in thinking that philosophical theories of meaning should stick fairly close to the standard sorts of assumptions about meaning in life on which subjectivist, objectivist, and hybrid theories all tend to agree.

are doing, this would not be a truly meaningful life. The person also needs to be engaged by and invested in what they are doing and have a subjective sense of its value and importance.

These three types of theories of meaning suggest different views about what anti-meaning is (Campbell and Nyholm 2015, 696–704). If meaning is a matter of positive attitudes about one's activities or life as a whole, then the polar opposite would be having negative affective attitudes and/or negative judgements about one's life and activities. For example, if you really hate your job, a subjectivist view of anti-meaning might imply that your job is anti-meaningful.[6] If one instead understands meaning in life to be a matter of doing good or having positive values instantiated in one's life, then anti-meaning will involve having bad or disvaluable elements in one's life. Doing things that harm others, spread ignorance, pollute the environment, or undermine democracy and justice are all plausible examples of things that are the opposite of meaningful.

The hardest theory to analyse in terms of what it implies about anti-meaning is the hybrid theory. Does it need to be the case that one both has a negative attitude about what one is doing and is doing something bad in order for one's activities to be anti-meaningful? Or is it enough that there is some sort of mismatch so that, for example, we either have negative attitudes about good things we are doing or have positive attitudes about bad features of our lives? One way to proceed is for the hybrid theorist to make a theoretical choice about what they understand the opposite of meaning to be, which will have implications for the nature of meaning as well. Another way of going is to simply recognize different kinds of anti-meaning on the hybrid theory: anti-meaning involving both negative attitude and bad actions, and anti-meaning involving some sort of mismatch between one's attitudes and the value or disvalue in one's life.[7]

4. A Challenge to the Idea of Anti-Meaning

Before turning to the positive case for recognizing the concept of anti-meaning, it is instructive to consider some reasons why one might be resistant to the idea. In an interesting discussion about how meaningfulness relates to other key values in life, Christopher Woodard (2017, 72–73) makes a clearly stated case for why we should reject the notion of anti-meaning.

Woodard's challenge begins with the observation that the notion of anti-meaning is, as he puts it, 'self-consciously revisionary' (2017, 73). As he notes, many philosophers

---

[6] For more on meaningfulness (or threats to meaningfulness) and work, see Danaher (2019, chapter 3); and Smids, Nyholm, and Berkers (2020).
[7] We discuss the different theoretical options open to hybrid theorists in greater detail in Campbell and Nyholm (2015, 700–703).

think that philosophical ethics should be in the business of articulating ideas that are already part of common sense. And anti-meaning does not seem to be a part of common sense. Accordingly, there is some theoretical cost to adopting the notion of anti-meaning inasmuch as it is a philosopher's invention that deviates from our ordinary thinking about meaning.

Even so, Woodard allows that there still might be grounds for adopting a revisionary concept if it offers theoretical advantages that concepts taken from common sense are not able to provide. However, he is sceptical about the prospects for the notion of anti-meaning to provide sufficient benefit to justify adopting it. Contemplating Metz's example of 'blowing up the Sphinx for fun' as an anti-meaningful activity, Woodard claims that there is no reason to go beyond already existing concepts such as moral wrongness or badness to describe what is negative about that imagined course of action. Unless the notion of anti-meaning can be shown to yield some advantages that we cannot secure otherwise, we should dismiss the idea of anti-meaning. Or so Woodard argues.

As we interpret it, Woodard's challenge to the concept of anti-meaning boils down to the following argument:

(1) If a concept is revisionist, then we should adopt it if and only if the costs of adopting that concept are outweighed by clear benefits.
(2) The concept of anti-meaning is revisionist.
(3) The costs of adopting this concept are not outweighed by any clear benefits.
(4) Therefore, we should not adopt the concept of anti-meaning.

In the remainder of this chapter, we will draw on the preceding argument to frame our discussion of why we should recognize the concept of anti-meaning on at least one of the two formal interpretations of anti-meaning discussed earlier.

5. THE CASE FOR RECOGNIZING ANTI-MEANING

We now wish to confront Woodard's challenge and defend the need to recognize the concept of anti-meaning on some interpretation. Focusing first on the defeater model, we will make the case that this conception of anti-meaning arguably *is* a part of common-sense thinking, even if people have failed to recognize this. Hence, on this interpretation of anti-meaning, premise 2 of Woodard's challenge is false: the concept of anti-meaning so conceived is not revisionist. If the concept is already embedded in our common-sense thinking, the issue is not whether we should *adopt* the concept, but instead whether we should explicitly *acknowledge* the existence of a concept that we already employ. This is one way of 'recognizing' the concept of anti-meaning. Next, we will turn our attention to the counterforce model. Although this model has at least some foothold in common-sense intuitions, we grant that there is a much stronger case for regarding this notion of anti-meaning as revisionist. Even so, we will offer a preliminary case that premise 3 in Woodard's argument is false when applied to this conception of anti-meaning: arguably, the benefits of adopting this revisionist notion do outweigh the costs. If so, this would yield the conclusion that we should recognize this concept of anti-meaning in the sense of adopting it.

5.1. The Defeater Model

A key part of Woodard's challenge lies in his assumption that anti-meaning is a revisionist concept—a departure from our ordinary, common-sense ways of thinking about meaning in life. At first glance, this seems plausible. After all, the fact that we are forced to coin some strange new term ('anti-meaning', 'antimatter', 'negative meaning', etc.) to talk about the opposite of meaning makes it very tempting to conclude that it must be a strange new idea. If anti-meaning is part of ordinary thinking, why don't we already have a name for it? While we do not pretend to have an answer to that question, we wish to argue that there is good reason to believe that anti-meaning on the defeater model is an essential, though non-obvious, part of our everyday thinking.

To illustrate this, imagine that you could perform some action that would greatly improve the lives of ten other people (and would thereby bring you a sense of fulfilment) and would have a neutral impact on a thousand other people, neither harming nor benefiting them. Most people will happily grant that this would be a meaningful action. This should hold true whether they subscribe to an objectivist theory, subjectivist theory, or hybrid theory.

Contrast this with an action that resembles the first in that it too would greatly improve the lives of ten people and yield just as much of a feeling of fulfilment. However, this second action would also render a thousand other people much worse off, a fact that would provide you with no sense of meaning or fulfilment and, when focusing upon it, would actually cause you much distress and dissatisfaction. We take it that virtually no one would judge this second action to be meaningful. But what could account for this difference of judgement?

If common-sense thinking only acknowledges the idea of meaning and its absence, we should expect people to judge the two actions to be on a par and equally meaningful. After all, by stipulation they have the very same amount of meaning: both involve finding fulfilment in bestowing a great benefit on a fixed number of individuals. No one thinks that harming others or experiencing dissatisfaction with one's activities is constitutive of meaning in life, and therefore the presence of these features should be beside the point in assessing whether or not an action is meaningful.

Our asymmetrical judgements about these cases are best explained by the fact that the concept of anti-meaning, understood along the lines of the defeater model, is implicitly embedded in our ordinary thinking about meaning in life. It neatly explains why we make asymmetrical judgements about the two preceding actions. Although they contain identical meaningful elements, they differ dramatically in the amount of anti-meaning that they involve. It is because the second action contains so much anti-meaning that no one would dare think the action is a meaningful one. The anti-meaningful elements—the harm done to hundreds of people and/or the negative feelings toward the effect—more than suffice to cancel out or defeat the meaningful elements. Thus, it seems that, in ordinary thinking, we perform a kind of aggregation of the meaning and anti-meaning in an activity or life in order to arrive at an assessment of its overall meaningfulness or lack thereof.

We can appreciate the same point by focusing on a real-life case. Suppose—as is not implausible—that Hitler managed to perform some actions in his life that had good and beneficial consequences and that this fact brought him a sense of fulfilment. Even granting this fact, no sensible person will think that Hitler's life was thereby positively meaningful. But if his life contained a significant amount of meaningful activity, why shouldn't we deem his life meaningful? The obvious answer is that Hitler was personally responsible for some of modern history's worst atrocities and that his contribution to these tremendous evils overrides or offsets any meaning that might have been present in his life. Hence, the defeater interpretation of anti-meaning allows us to avoid the conclusion that Hitler's life was a meaningful one.

In sum, there is good reason to think our common-sense thinking about the meaningfulness of lives and activities makes active use of the notion of anti-meaning on the defeater model. Thus, anti-meaning (at least on this understanding) is not a revisionist concept after all. With regard to the defeater model of anti-meaning, premise 2 of Woodard's argument is false.

5.2. The Counterforce Model

Most, if not all, of the theorists who have entertained the idea of anti-meaning appear to have had the counterforce model in mind. Unlike the defeater model on which the worst kind of lives are meaningless, the counterforce model allows for the possibility that an activity or life can be substantially anti-meaningful. On this view, it is possible to be in the negatives with respect to meaning.

While we ultimately grant that this is a revisionist idea, it is worthwhile to highlight the fact that it has a partial foothold in our common-sense judgements about meaning. Consider again the case of Hitler, a popular example with authors who have wanted to motivate this understanding of anti-meaning (Landau 2011; Smuts 2013). As these authors point out, the statement 'Hitler's life was meaningless' seems not quite right. It is tempting to think that Hitler's life was not merely lacking in meaning but was somehow much, much worse than that. The proposal that his life was characterized by 'negative meaning' or anti-meaning provides one natural way of articulating how Hitler's life was worse than meaningless.

That said, even if some of our common-sense intuitions gesture in the direction of the counterforce model of anti-meaning, we grant that it does not seem to be a part of most people's thinking about meaning in life. First, people do not typically try to articulate the idea that something is worse than meaningless, despite the fact that a great many activities would qualify as anti-meaningful on the counterforce model. Second, the counterforce model would seem to imply that meaningless lives should be a fairly rare occurrence. Recall that there are two ways for a life to be meaningless on this view: either it involves no meaning or anti-meaning, or it involves roughly equal amounts of meaning and anti-meaning. It is extremely rare for an entire life to be meaningless in the first way; most people manage to do at least *some* things that are meaningful and/or anti-meaningful. And we suspect that it will be somewhat rare for a life to be meaningless in the second way. More often than not, there will not be a neat balance between the meaning and anti-meaning in individuals' lives. So, the rarity of actual meaninglessness is one striking implication of this model.[8] Since many people are inclined to think that many lives are meaningless, this yields further evidence that the counterforce model is a deviation from our everyday understanding of what meaning is and, thus, adopting this concept would be a revision. Accordingly, we think premise 2 of Woodard's argument is plausible when it comes to the counterforce model. Even so, we wish to question premise 3 of Woodard's argument by highlighting various advantages to be had by adopting this concept.

A first advantage of adopting this stronger conception of anti-meaning has already been hinted at. When confronted with activities or lives that seem to be filled with the outright opposite of what would be meaningful, it feels somehow wrong to label it as 'meaningless'. Return to one of the cases with which we began: the climate-endangering actions and policies of Donald Trump. When a person with so much influence takes actions that threaten humanity's future on this planet, it can seem too weak and simply not forceful enough to say that these climate-change-denying and climate-endangering actions cancel any meaningful things that Trump might have done. Indeed, it does not feel accurate to say that, overall, his actions while in office were meaningless. We seem to need a new notion to fully express the nature of such actions. The notion of being anti-meaningful in the sense of going into the negatives with respect to meaning seems to capture this.

Woodard implies that we can remedy this feeling by adding further descriptors from our stock of ordinary concepts. For instance, we might simply point out that Trump's actions are both meaningless and immoral. However, that solution does not address our sense that the label 'meaningless' does not quite fit. Being able to deem Trump's activity *anti-meaningful*—not meaningless—strikes us as a more satisfying solution. It extends the weaker conception of anti-meaning that is arguably already part of everyday thinking about meaning in life.

---

[8] Admittedly, the force of this point depends on how 'rough equality' is interpreted. If precise equality of meaningful and anti-meaningful elements were required for a life to qualify as meaningless, then the counterforce model would imply that meaningless lives are extremely rare since presumably such equality very rarely occurs in our world. However, the rarity of meaningless activities and lives will decrease as the degree of divergence allowed by 'rough equality' increases.

A second advantage of the counterforce model of anti-meaning is that it avoids a misleading feature of the defeater model. The defeater model lumps a wide range of actions and lives into the category of the meaningless, and it might seem to imply that all meaningless lives and activities are essentially 'in the same boat' with respect to meaning, given that each has a score of zero. This, in turn, might give the false impression that if any two individuals who have been living meaningless lives begin to engage in similar kinds and amounts of substantially meaningful activity, the result is that their lives will end up with same level of overall meaningfulness. Yet, even on the defeater model, that is not so, as we will now explain.

Consider the case of someone who commits a single murder and, upon release from prison, hopes to make amends by actively serving others. In many cases of this sort, it seems quite possible that, with enough time and good deeds, the person can achieve a life that is overall meaningful, taking into account the person's crime and their activities after prison. Contrast that with the case of Adolf Hitler, who was responsible for crimes against humanity on a massive scale. Presumably, a great many lifetimes' worth of good deeds would not suffice to generate enough meaning to counterbalance all of the anti-meaning in Hitler's life.

So, when we attend to meaningless lives and activities on the defeater model, the amount of anti-meaning in a life matters. It would take far less meaningful activity to get the reformed murderer to the point of leading a meaningful life than it would take for Hitler, who had vast amounts of anti-meaning 'on reserve' and ready to cancel out any newly acquired meaning. Thus, on the defeater model of anti-meaning, two individuals with meaningless lives can be in an importantly different situation. If one person has far more anti-meaning, they are—in one important sense—much further away from being able to live a meaningful life. One clear advantage of the counterforce model of meaning is that it makes this important difference apparent and thereby brings to light something that is obscured by the defeater model. Rather than treating Hitler and the reformed murderer as falling into the same category of leading meaningless lives, the counterforce model treats anti-meaningfulness as a matter of degree and explicitly captures the vast distance between the two lives.

Yet another advantage of adopting the counterforce model is that it speaks to the concerns that anyone ought to have if they care about meaning. If we are motivated to lead lives or engage in activities that are positively meaningful, it would seem that we should—out of rational consistency—also be motivated to avoid activities and lifestyles that are the complete opposite of meaningful. This is satisfied, to an extent, by the defeater model of anti-meaning, which we have suggested is embedded in ordinary thinking about meaning. However, it seems arbitrary to care about anti-meaning only to the point where there is enough of it to cancel out all of a life's meaning. To illustrate, suppose that benefiting others adds to a life's overall meaningfulness, whereas harming others detracts from it. If a certain amount of harming others is so negative that it serves to undermine all of the meaning in one's life, then surely harming in excess of that is even more worrisome. It would be quite odd, if not irrational, for a meaning-seeking person who is distressed by the thought of harming ten people (where this would suffice to cancel out all of the meaning in her life) to be indifferent between harming ten or fifty people.[9] The defeater model of anti-meaning does not track levels of anti-meaning once the threshold of meaninglessness is met. The counterforce model does. For that reason, it is a more useful concept for those who care about the amount of anti-meaning in their lives, even in cases where the anti-meaning exceeds the meaning.

A final, more practical advantage of the counterforce model is that it has special relevance to situations that face most of us in the modern world. When our powerful technologies and modern ways of living together pose a threat to the future of human existence and the future prospects of many other species as well, it is not enough to ask if what we are doing is positively meaningful or whether it is lacking in meaning. We should also—if we are concerned with living meaningful lives—start asking ourselves if we are participating in modern lifestyles and ways of living together that are the opposite of meaningful. For these kinds of normative questions that we are now facing as a global community, we need new ethical concepts to augment our current stock of ethical and philosophical concepts. And anti-meaning—understood along the lines of the counterforce model—is one such concept. With its symmetrical treatment of meaning and anti-meaning, the counterforce model facilitates taking anti-meaning as seriously as we take meaning.

We have now highlighted four considerations that favour adopting the counterforce model of anti-meaning. For those of us who care about living meaningful lives and engaging in meaningful activities, the introduction of the concept of anti-meaning in the stronger sense associated with the counterforce model is a useful conceptual innovation. This provides us with some grounds for thinking that the benefits of this model do outweigh the costs.

6. Concluding Reflections

Our inclination is to think that ethical theorists have two important roles to play. On the one hand, they should attempt to clearly articulate concepts and ideas from common sense. Here the goal is to discover, illuminate, and clarify what is already there. On the other hand, philosophers also have a more disruptive role to play. They should assess our everyday concepts and views in terms of their internal consistency and their ability to

---

[9] Of course, this is a somewhat contrived example. For one thing, if one is the kind of person who will intentionally harm ten people, one might not be too concerned with how meaningful one's life is. But it could also happen that one has unintentionally harmed either ten or fifty people, and that one might have done so for some insignificant reason, which might be thought to make one's behaviour the opposite of meaningful. For example, if one is carrying an infectious virus and one gets on public transport to go and do something insignificant, then one's trip might seem the opposite of meaningful if one ends up spreading the virus to ten people. But it might seem even more anti-meaningful if one accidentally spreads that virus to fifty people in this way. If one cares about meaning, it would be odd to be indifferent between these two imagined scenarios.

withstand critical reflection, which may call for the destruction of commonly held ideas and views. In some cases, philosophers should also seek to revise, construct, create, and innovate—proposing new or modified concepts, distinctions, and positions that people can use to make better sense of our world and think critically about themselves and the lives they lead. In this chapter, we have played both of these roles to some extent.

At first glance, the idea of anti-meaning appears to have no place in how we ordinarily think about the meaning in our lives. As Woodard (2017, 73) put it, it looks 'self-consciously revisionary'. Yet, we have sought to show that, on one interpretation, the idea of anti-meaning does not lead to any counterintuitive conclusions. Indeed, the defeater model actually helps us make sense of our everyday judgements about meaning—to the point that we believe it is an essential but largely unrecognized part of our common understanding of meaning in life. If nothing else, everyone should acknowledge the existence of anti-meaning in this weaker and more conservative sense.

The counterforce model of anti-meaning, however, is a noteworthy departure from everyday thinking about meaning in life. Like Woodard, we share the opinion that ethical theory should not veer so far from common sense that it completely loses touch with how ordinary people think about ethics. If ethical theorizing leads to highly counterintuitive conclusions, as certain extreme forms of utilitarianism can, then it makes sense to appeal to common sense and ask whether we might have gone wrong somewhere. At the same time, we also agree with Woodard that conceptual innovations are sometimes justified when they yield enough benefits. We have offered some grounds for thinking that the revisionary counterforce interpretation of anti-meaning has several benefits. Ultimately, it might make good sense for us to begin to view some activities and lives as worse than meaningless.[10]

References

Alter, Charlotte, Suyin Haynes, and Justin Worland. 2019. 'Time 2019 Person of the Year—Greta Thunberg'. *TIME*, https://time.com/person-of-the-year-2019-greta-thunberg/ (accessed on 10 May 2020).
Bramble, Ben. 2015. 'Consequentialism about Meaning in Life'. *Utilitas* 27(4): 445–459
Burgess, Alexis, and David Plunkett. 2013a. 'Conceptual Ethics I'. *Philosophy Compass* 8(12): 1091–1101.
Burgess, Alexis, and David Plunkett. 2013b. 'Conceptual Ethics II'. *Philosophy Compass* 8(12): 1102–1110.
Campbell, Stephen M., and Sven Nyholm. 2015. 'Anti-Meaning and Why It Matters'. *The Journal of the American Philosophical Association* 1(4): 694–711.
Danaher, John. 2019. *Automation and Utopia: Human Flourishing in a World without Work*. Cambridge, MA: Harvard University Press
De La Garza, Alejandro. 2019. 'President Trump Reviews Climate Change Denial Days after Defense Department Releases Daunting Report on Its Effects'. *TIME*, https://time.com/5508259/trump-climate-change-defense-department/ (accessed on 10 May 2020).

---

[10] Many thanks to Iddo Landau and Marcello Di Paola for their very helpful feedback.

Dennett, Daniel. 2013. *Intuition Pumps and Other Tools for Thinking*. New York: W.W. Norton.
Di Paola, Marcello. 2018. *Ethics and the Built Environment: Gardens of the Anthropocene*. Berlin: Springer.
Friedman, Lisa and Somini Sengupta. 2021. 'The U.S. Left the Paris Climate Pact. Allies and Rivals Are Pressing Ahead.' *New York Times*, https://www.nytimes.com/2020/11/04/climate/paris-agreement-us-election.html (Accessed on 8 December 2021).
Hooker, B. 2008. 'The Meaning of Life: Subjectivism, Objectivism, and Divine Support'. In *The Moral Life: Essays in Honour of John Cottingham*, ed. N. Athanassoulis and S. Vice, 184–200. New York: Palgrave Macmillan.
Landau, Iddo. 2011. 'Immorality and the Meaning of Life'. *Journal of Value Inquiry* 45: 309–137.
Lichtenberg, Judith. 2010. 'Negative Duties, Positive Duties, and "New Harms"'. *Ethics* 120: 557–578.
Lichtenberg, Judith. 2014. *Distant Strangers: Ethics, Psychology, and Global Poverty*. Cambridge: Cambridge University Press.
Luper, Steven. 2014. 'Life's Meaning'. In *Cambridge Companion to Life and Death*, ed. Steven Luper, 198–214. Cambridge: Cambridge University Press.
Mawson, T. J. 2010. 'Sources of Dissatisfaction with Answers to the Question of the Meaning of Life'. *European Journal for Philosophy of Religion* 2: 19–41.
Mawson, T. J. 2019. *Monotheism and the Meaning of Life*. Cambridge: Cambridge University Press.
Metz, Thaddeus. 2002. 'Recent Work on the Meaning of Life'. *Ethics* 112(4): 781–814.
Metz, Thaddeus. 2012. 'The Meaningful and the Worthwhile: Clarifying the Relationships'. *Philosophical Forum* 43: 435–448.
Metz, Thaddeus. 2013. *Meaning in Life*. Oxford: Oxford University Press.
Metz, Thaddeus. 2019. 'Recent Work on the Meaning of "Life's Meaning": Should We Change the Philosophical Discourse?' *Human Affairs* 29: 404–414.
Persson, Ingmar, and Julian Savulescu. 2019. 'The Meaning of Life, Equality and Eternity'. *Journal of Ethics* 23(2): 223–238.
Popovich, Nadja, Livia Albeck-Ripka, and Kendra Pierre-Louis. 2020. 'The Trump Administration Is Reversing Nearly 100 Environmental Rules: Here's the Full List'. *New York Times*, https://www.nytimes.com/interactive/2020/climate/trump-environment-rollbacks.html (accessed on 10 May 2020).
Repp, Charles. 2018. 'Life Meaning and Sign Meaning'. *Philosophical Papers* 47: 403–427.
Seachris, Joshua. 2019. 'From the Meaning Triad to Meaning Holism: Unifying Life's Meaning'. *Human Affairs* 29(4): 363–378.
Smids, Jilles, Sven Nyholm, and Hannah Berkers. 2020. 'Robots in the Workplace: A Threat to—or Opportunity for—Meaningful Work'. *Philosophy & Technology* 33(3): 503–522.
Smuts, Aaron. 2013. 'The Good Cause Account of the Meaning of Life'. *Southern Journal of Philosophy* 51: 536–562.
Taylor, Richard. 1970. *Good and Evil*. New York: Macmillan.
Thomas, J. L. 2018. 'Can Only Human Lives Be Meaningful?' *Philosophical Papers* 47: 265–297.
Thomas, J. L. 2019. 'Meaningfulness as Sensefulness'. *Philosophia* 47: 1555–1577.
Wolf, Susan. 2010. *Meaning in Life and Why It Matters*. Princeton, NJ: Princeton University Press.
Woodard, Christopher. 2017. 'What Good Is Meaning in Life?' *De Ethica* 4(3): 67–79.

CHAPTER 18

FORGIVENESS AND MEANING IN LIFE

LUCY ALLAIS

In contrast to revenge, which is the natural, automatic reaction to transgression and which because of the irreversibility of the action process can be expected and even calculated, the act of forgiving can never be predicted; it is the only reaction that acts in an unexpected way and thus retains, though being a reaction, something of the original character of action. Forgiving, in other words, is the only reaction which does not merely re-act but acts anew and unexpectedly, unconditioned by the act which provoked it and therefore freeing from its consequences both the one who forgives and the one who is forgiven.

—Hannah Arendt (1958, 241)

[W]e are not to suppose that we are required, or permitted, as philosophers, to regard ourselves, as human beings, as detached from the attitudes which, as scientists, we study with detachment.

—P. F. Strawson (1962, 26–27)

1. Introduction

This chapter argues that forgiveness, as a release from blame of a highly distinctive kind, plays an essential role in meaningful human lives. When done well, forgiveness is a response which takes wrongdoing seriously but also enables both the victim and the wrongdoer to get beyond it, making it an essential feature of relationships between flawed moral agents—which is to say between all humans. At its best, it provides a way we can actively move forward with each other (and with ourselves, allowing the significance of self-forgiveness) without seeing each other as forever fixed by our worst choices, but without giving up on standards that have been offended against. It is something we sometimes desperately desire from those we have wronged and something people find meaning in both giving and receiving.

There are at least two main ways philosophers approach the idea of 'meaning' in relation to 'the meaning of life'; forgiveness is significant in relation to both. One approach understands meaning as a value, distinct from moral and aesthetic value, as well as from happiness, that lives can have more or less of, and that depends on the presence in a life of various goods or things of value that contribute meaning, such as self-transcendence, friendship (Railton 1984), creativity, loving things worth loving (Wolf 2010), responding well to suffering, redemptive patterns of growth (Velleman 2015, 141–173), and the realization of human excellence (Bond 1983, chapters 15–16). These are things that contribute to our experiencing our lives as fulfilling and worthwhile, and do not seem to be reducible to happiness or to doing what morality requires (see Wolf 2010, 2, for discussion). They are things that a life can have more or less of, making particular lives more or less meaningful, in this sense. Philosophical discussion of this approach refers to it as meaning *in* life (see Metz 2013; Wolf 2010). Most philosophical accounts of this see friendships and other relationships as primary goods that contribute meaning, and when people reflect on their lives, it is frequently loving relationships that are a source of meaning. If forgiveness is essential for relationships, it follows straightforwardly that it is a necessary condition of a central component of meaning. Further, as I outline in the following, thinking about what forgiveness is and how it works gives us insight into features of the human condition and how relationships and growth contribute meaning to our lives.

A different way of thinking about the meaning *of* life is in terms of existential questions about whether any human lives have significance, or a point, at all—whether our lives, as such, matter. Doubt that there is meaning in this existential sense arises from measuring our lives on a cosmic scale, in relation to which they seem insignificant. This approach is not contrastive between particular lives but rather concerns human life as such. I argue that through the notion of what P. F. Strawson (1962) calls the participant view, which much writing on forgiveness takes as a starting point, philosophical writing on forgiveness reveals relationships to provide a point of intersection between thinking about meaning *in* life and the meaning *of* life.

Strawson's participant view is the non-detached view of human lives situated in relationships with each other; he opposes it to what he calls the objective view. The participant view is characterized in terms of our proneness to affective responses, such as resentment and forgiveness, which disclose and express our recognition of other persons as persons—co-participants who have value, of whom we have expectations, and whose attitudes toward us we care about. A crucial part of Strawson's account is that while the personal values disclosed in participant responses do not show up from the perspective of the objective view (or, similarly, Thomas Nagel's (1989) view from nowhere, or the point of view of the universe), this does not affect their significance from the participant view, which Strawson argues to be neither susceptible to nor requiring of external justification. Further, the participant view is not something we need to be or can be argued into from the objective view, and the values in it are not undermined or made less real by their not showing up in the objective view. The fact that we can (at least to some extent) think from the objective view does not thereby replace, exclude, or dissolve the participant view and the values that appear in it. So to find participant meaning and value does not require (impossibly) showing how we can get to participant value from the view from nowhere, but rather appreciating the reality of the participant view. Our exploration of the role of forgiveness in relationships will therefore be both an investigation of its role in meaning in life, and also an account of it as embedded in a point of view which we can neither avoid nor argue ourselves into, from which our lives and actions simply are recognized as meaningful and value-laden.

In addition to the distinction between meaning in life and the meaning of life, philosophers writing on the meaning of life have disagreed whether meaning is contributed by goods that are actually (objectively) valuable, or goods that are subjectively experienced as meaningful by the person whose life they are in, and therefore depend for their meaningfulness on the attitude toward them of the individual. (See Nagel 1989; Metz 2007; and Wolf 2010 for discussion.) On the one hand, it seems implausible that lives are made meaningful by things which are not actually valuable and worthwhile. On the other hand, it is hard to see something as contributing meaning if the person whose life it is in is alienated, bored, or left feeling empty, rather than engaged, gripped, and absorbed (Wolf 2010, 8–10). Susan Wolf thus proposes an account that involves both components cohering: something actually valuable that is experienced as such by the individual whose life it is in. This approach seems appropriate for understanding the contribution made by forgiveness, which cuts across a distinction between objective and subjective. On the one hand, forgiveness can be objectively necessary for people in relationships to move forward with each other, as well as for moral growth, and it involves an actual change. It is the actual change that is meaningful both to those who forgive and those who want to be forgiven. But, on the other hand, its role is rooted in how we *feel* about each other, and our particular caring about others' caring about us: blamers typically want those they blame to understand their concerns. And it is these (blaming) feelings with respect to which the person who wants forgiveness desires a change.

There is debate about whether forgiveness must be earned, through apologies, remorse and amends (see, for example, Allais 2013; Garrard and McNaughton 2002; Milam 2018a; Warmke 2016; Fricker 2021; Griswold 2007). Those who hold that it must be earned argue that in the absence of this, forgiveness fails to take wrongdoing sufficiently seriously, which is a moral and rational mistake. In contrast, others argue that forgiveness is essentially something gifted, that goes beyond what we can earn or show that we deserve. On both accounts, forgiveness contributes to meaningful relationships. However, I will argue that understanding forgiveness as gifted gives an account on which it is both riskier and more powerful. Further, this account can contribute to thinking about the meaning of life through the ways it reveals and responds to fundamental features of the human condition: what persons are and what actions are, and how we form our moral selves in interaction with others, and, in particular, in response to hurt and suffering to others caused by our flawed choices.

Before starting (in section 2) to look at the role of blame and forgiveness in our lives and relationships, and then (in section 3) to look at how this contributes to meaning, I emphasize one more feature of forgiveness that is central to understanding its role in meaning in life, and this is the fact that it is a response to *wrongdoing*. It follows from this that its contribution to living meaningful lives is a matter of its role in relationships between imperfect people—people who let each other down, disrespect, disregard, mistreat, hurt, and wrong each other.[1] Rather than seeking value in perfection, it is situated in an approach which finds value in constructive approaches to imperfections and flaws (see Landau 2017 for a critique of perfectionism). It is therefore part of the project of making sense in the face of suffering and unhappiness—and suffering of a highly specific kind: that caused by the carelessness, callousness, disregard, or other ill will of one person for another.

2. Forgiveness and Blame

Almost all accounts of forgiveness take it to involve a release from blame, and its contribution to meaningful relationships and moral growth consists in this. Understanding its role in these central parts of meaning in life therefore first requires understanding the significance and role of blame in our lives. Anger and resentment are often thought of as negative feelings, and some hold that our lives would be better without them. An extreme version of this view is defended by Martha Nussbaum, who understands anger as a morally and metaphysically confused and indefensible response. She sees anger as expressing a morally wrong desire for the wrongdoer to suffer—as payback, to assuage the pain of the wrong, or in the pursuit of rectifying an imaginary metaphysical balance in which the wrongdoer needs to be lowered (Nussbaum 2016, 15, 24, 25). Similarly, she understands guilt as the wrongdoer's rationally and morally inappropriate desire for themselves to suffer, again reflecting, she thinks, a mistaken belief that this suffering will make things better (Nussbaum 2016, 130–131). Her critique of anger and guilt does not, however, mean that she thinks favourably of forgiveness, because, together with most authors writing on forgiveness, she sees it as a response to blaming emotions that are taken to be warranted, a starting point she rejects. Thus she considers forgiveness to be problematically implicated in the backward-focused, (in her view) intrusive logic of anger and guilt, and argues that we would be better off just thinking about future welfare, and confining the negative feelings we have about wrongdoing to grief (Nussbaum 2016, 47–48). On this view, both 'negative' emotions like blame and guilt, and also forgiveness

---

[1] At least with respect to secular forgiveness.

as a release from these, lead us away from moral growth and harm relationships and so detract from worthwhile and meaningful lives.

In contrast, those philosophers who think forgiveness has a role to play in our relationships and lives typically also think that blame (and guilt) can be warranted and can play positive, meaning-enhancing roles. It is argued that blame can protest wrongdoing, can be a way the wronged person stands up for themselves, can be a defense of self-respect, and can play an essential communicative role in moral growth and shared understanding which is necessary for meaningful relationships (see Hieronymi 2001; Hampton 1988; Fricker 2021; 2014). On Miranda Fricker's account of communicative blame, appropriate blame aims to get a wrongdoer 'to see or fully acknowledge the moral significance of what they have done or failed to do' (Fricker 2014, 9) and 'to see things from the wronged party's point of view, thereby enlarging her perception and altering her reasons' (Fricker 2014, 13; see also McKenna 2018). Understood in this way, when blame is appropriate and well communicated, it aims at promoting greater alignment between the moral understandings of the blamer and the blamee. Communicative blame, on this account, can be an important, positive, and arguably necessary part of 'the interpersonal normative energy that perpetually regenerates and develops shared moral consciousness' (Fricker 2014, 3). In discussions of moral responsibility, this view of blame is understood in terms of the idea of its role in developing or *scaffolding* moral agency (see McGeer n.d.; Fricker 2014; McGeer 2012).[2] Victoria McGeer points out that human agency is a social phenomenon which requires social feedback, and that this is particularly true of the skills needed for understanding and complying with mutually shared and interpreted norms (McGeer n.d., 25). Blame can play a role in this. Consider what it would be for flawed, complex, insecure, agents, who have defences and emotional patterns of interpreting the world they do not fully understand (i.e. human beings), to stay good and to grow (or even to stay sane) in the absence of mutual recognition and accountability to shared norms. Trying to envisage relationships without this suggests to me something more like the 'parallel play' toddlers engage in.

A central part of what is distinctive about forgiveness is that it is situated in a logic which sees blame as warranted—otherwise there is nothing to forgive. This is something forgiveness has in common with such responses to wrongdoing as punishment, mercy, and some forms of reconciliation, responses which require no change in seeing blame as warranted. In this respect, forgiveness can be distinguished from justifying, excusing, and accepting, all of which involve a changing understanding of what happened such that it no longer warrants blame. I could be angry with you for something you did, but then learn more about the specific circumstances and understand better how things looked from your point of view, such that I cease to think there is anything to forgive. I could come to see that, while prima facie a wrong, in fact in the circumstances what you did was the best thing to do (it was justified), or that it was not really your fault (you

---

[2] McGeer argues that 'our attitudes and practices of holding responsible play a critical role in developing and sustaining our capacity to recognize and respond to moral reasons' (n.d., 27).

have an excuse), or that the obstacles you were facing were so great that no ordinary human could have been expected to overcome them. In all these cases, blame is given up because it is no longer seen to be warranted. Forgiveness, like justifying, excusing, and accepting, somehow lifts blame, but unlike these responses it does this *without* changing the forgiver's assessment of the wrong. Like punishment, mercy, and some forms of reconciliation, forgiveness maintains a judgement of wrongdoing, but unlike these responses it involves a unique release from blame in which the wrongdoing is no longer seen as held to the wrongdoer's account.

Justifying, excusing, and accepting all play important roles in human lives and relationships; we don't always know what another person's life and situation involve, we should not be too quick to blame and condemn, and we should be willing to reconsider our blaming judgements. But the saying that 'to understand all is to forgive all' involves a wildly optimistic view of human agency, according to which no one ever really acts out of cruelty, malice, disregard, thoughtlessness, cowardice, insensitivity, impatience, selfishness, carelessness, vanity, jealousy, callousness, arrogance, or other such bad willing. The brutality of much of human history and the upsets and mistreatment involved in almost all relationships make this view completely implausible. Sometimes we wrong each other in ways which are not excusable or justifiable, and to the extent that we think these wrongs shouldn't just be accepted or condoned, blame is warranted. What makes forgiveness puzzling is that it seems to involve a shift in attitude toward the wrongdoer in which the action is no longer 'held against' them but where this is not because the wronged one has changed their view of the wrongness of the action. Something else has changed, and characterizing this change is a large part of what philosophers working on forgiveness are concerned with.

In the literature on forgiveness there is debate about whether the release from blame that constitutes forgiveness is fundamentally an emotional change (a ceasing to have blame-feeling; see Russell 2016; Allais 2008; Emerick 2017; Warmke 2011 for discussion), a matter of no longer expressing blame, a speech act (an act of saying 'I forgive you', whereby someone is forgiven; Warmke 2016; Pettigrove 2012), a process, a commitment (undertaking to feel or act towards someone in a non-blaming way), or a waiving of obligations, where the forgiver makes it the case that the wrongdoer no longer owes apologies and/or recompense, by their declaring it to be so (see Bennett 2018; Nelkin 2013; Twambly 1976; Warmke 2011; Watkins 2005). These need not be in tension with each other, and pluralist or varied accounts are possible. In what follows I will focus on a change in blame-feeling (forgiveness as a change of heart), which is the dominant account in the literature, but this is compatible with the other changes described here also playing a role.

A further debate is whether forgiveness primarily requires that the wrongdoer has done something to deserve or earn it (sometimes referred to as conditional forgiveness) or whether it can be granted independent of apologies and remorse, so could be something fundamentally gifted and unearned (sometimes referred to as unconditional forgiveness). (For discussion see Allais 2008, 2013, forthcoming; Garrard and McNaughton 2002; Fricker 2021; Milam 2018a, 2018b.) Some of those who think forgiveness requires apologies and remorse hold that in the absence of a change that shows blame to be no longer warranted, forgiveness would be a rational or moral mistake (Griswold 2007; Milam 2018a, 2018b). On these accounts, the wrongdoer earns forgiveness by taking steps to demonstrate that blame is no longer warranted. Others hold, more strongly, that in the absence of the right reasons, ceasing to have blame feeling doesn't even count as forgiveness, and is simply some other kind of giving up of blame, perhaps indistinguishable from justifying, accepting, and condoning (Griswold 2007; Milam 2018a, 2018b may have this view). On Charles Griswold's demanding account, the conditions necessary for forgiveness include that the wrongdoer acknowledges responsibility for the act, repudiates the act, experiences and expresses regret, commits to becoming the kind of person who does not act in the wrong way they acted before and demonstrates this through word and action, showing that they understand, from the injured person's perspective, the damage done by the action (Griswold 2007, 49–50). Forgiveness, on this view, turns out to be *like* justifying, excusing, condoning, and accepting in that it too only gives up blame that is not warranted; the difference is that in this case it is further action by the wrongdoer which alters judgements about their overall blameworthiness, rather than a change in assessment of whether the initial blame was warranted.

In contrast to the idea that forgiveness must be earned, some argue that forgiveness can sometimes be gifted, or more strongly, that there is something essentially gifted about forgiveness, in that it (almost always) goes beyond what the wrongdoer is able to demonstrate that they have earned or deserve (for example, Allais 2013, 2021; Garrard and McNaughton 2002). While giving up blame that is no longer warranted is of course important, some (including me) argue that purely conditional accounts of forgiveness sell short the powerful role it can play in contributing and revealing meaning. Forgiveness has been thought of as something potentially transformative, as well as something with respect to which the wronged person often has a lot of discretion. These aspects of forgiveness seem lost if it is nothing more than a required recognition that someone has done what they needed to do—a matter of working out what way of evaluating the wrongdoer is most supported by the combination of their initial action and their subsequent responses to this. I will argue that while both earned and gifted forgiveness play important roles in relationships, gifted forgiveness plays a distinctive role, and that making sense of this is revealing of significant features of the human condition.

3. Forgiveness and Meaning in Life

Earned forgiveness is clearly important for relationships and therefore for meaning in life. As Fricker argues, once blame has achieved the goal of recognition and moral alignment, there could be no purpose served by continuing to demand what has already been achieved, and there are many ways in which this would be destructive (Fricker 2021). And the recognition that the lifting of blame has been earned can enable repair of relationships. Forgiveness, on this account, is part of an interactive, interdependent process involving blame, apologies, amends, and acknowledgement of apologies and amends; it builds on the moral scaffolding communicative blame can provide, enabling blame to come to an end, so that people can move forward together. At its best, this process can increase closeness and understanding. Although appropriate blame and forgiveness are responses that are only at issue when something has gone wrong, if done well they can involve positive meaning-making as part of building a shared moral understanding, mutual recognition, caring about each other, and helping each other grow in a context of mutual vulnerability and dependency.[3]

Recognizing steps a wrongdoer has taken to earn the lifting of blame is a phenomenon in our relationships that is both important and not particularly philosophically puzzling. Gifted forgiveness, in contrast, is puzzling, since understanding it requires making moral and rational sense of giving up blame that is in some sense still fitting or justified. I will argue that it is precisely in taking seriously the features that seem to make it puzzling that its power and significance are to be found. Making sense of this requires detailed attention to the content of blame-feeling, for which P. F. Strawson's (1962) notion of reactive attitudes is very helpful. In Strawson's famous account, which plays a dominant role in most writing about forgiveness, reactive attitudes are affective responses to persons' actions which express our seeing them as responsible agents—seeing their actions as flowing from their willing. These attitudes are affective: they essentially involve feeling. These feelings are understood as having complex content, which includes understanding an action not just in terms of what happened (for example, that you stepped on my hand), but in terms of what the person was intending, thinking, and feeling, or more broadly, what they willed (you stepped on my hand with malice, or as an accident in the process of saving a life). Further, these responses assess what was willed in the light of a legitimate demand for a minimum amount of goodwill, and see the agent's attitude to this demand as reflecting on them (see Smith 2013). Finally, it is part of the content of these attitudes that they have communicative force. Darwall expresses this by saying that they come with an implicit RSVP (Darwall 2006; see also McGeer 2012, 2013; Smith 2013; Macnamara 2013b, 2013a). This does not mean that these attitudes are always in fact communicated, but rather that it is part of the content of blame, for example, that the blamer seeks recognition and acknowledgement. On this account, a blaming reactive attitude is a complex affective (feeling) attitude which involves a painful presentation of someone as having done something which you were entitled to expect them not to have done and which showed insufficient regard for you, sees this as reflecting badly on them, and (implicitly) calls for recognition and acknowledgement of this.[4]

It is important here that the painful feelings involved in blaming reactive attitudes need not (contra Nussbaum) be understood as vindictiveness, and to the extent that

---

[3] Of course, there are many ways blame can go wrong and can harm relationships, and this may also be true of forgiveness.
[4] The desire for acknowledgement might be centrally for acknowledgement from the wrongdoer, but could include from the community or others. See Smith (2013).

they involve suffering or a desire for suffering this is not extrinsic from their presentation of the wrongdoing and our caring about it. These emotions are an intrinsically painful way of caring about someone's having disregarded you in their willing, and wanting them to grasp this and care about it. Strawson's starting point in introducing reactive attitudes is to emphasize 'how much we actually mind, *how much it matters to us*, whether the actions of other people—and particularly of some other people—reflect attitudes towards us of goodwill, affection, or esteem on the one hand, or contempt, indifference, or malevolence on the other' (Strawson 1962, 5). How other persons regard us matters to us, and we care about their caring about our regard for them: our mattering to them matters to us. In this way, both 'positive' reactive attitudes like gratitude and 'negative' ones like resentment are in fact part of our recognition and caring about each other, and our recognition of (non-detached) value.[5] On this account, blame and forgiveness are embedded in a view from which actions matter and have significance not just because they cause harm or good, but because they express our choices and our responses to value. As Hannah Arendt says, action and speech constitute a 'disclosure of who somebody is' (Arendt 1958). In addition to the idea that we *disclose* ourselves through our actions, I would add that we *form* ourselves through our choices, and this is an ongoing process. Being an agent with a will who responds to reasons is being in an ongoing process of making oneself and revealing the self we are making. Part of seeing someone as a person is seeing their actions as reflecting on their willing and therefore on what I will call their moral person, something continually formed by them through their choices.[6] We have no way of knowing another person's moral person other than through what their actions reveal about their willing: it is not only reasonable to take their choices and responses to value as expressed in their actions as reflecting on them, it is all we have to go on. This is part of the context in which blaming reactive attitudes have a role: they are part of how we take each other seriously as responsible agents, and how we form ourselves and grow morally in interaction with others.

Critics of gifted forgiveness argue that it would fail to condemn wrongdoing. But blaming reactive attitudes, as we have seen, contain much more than judgements about the wrongness of the action: they include a view of the wrongness of the action as reflecting on the wrongdoer, together with a call for acknowledgement of the wrongness of the action from the wrongdoer. This is not yet enough to show that gifted forgiveness can make moral and rational sense, because our evaluative-affective views of persons also have aptness conditions, and we wouldn't want forgiveness to be characterized by an essentially unrealistic or unwarranted way of seeing persons. We have seen that reactive attitudes see agency and actions from a participant view in which we understand actions as flowing from the willing of persons. While this might make it seem that the rational thing to do is to evaluate a person in the light of the totality of their choices,

---

[5] Similarly, grief, as a way of attending to the loss of value, is part of our valuing people.

[6] This is a simplification, as not all the choices that our willing reflects on are moral. Further, it is no part of this view that persons form themselves *ex nihilo*; the point is simply that to the extent that we have freedom, we form ourselves (out of material we with which we find ourselves).

in my view this misses a fundamental feature of persons which I take to be central to making sense of forgiveness and explaining its role in creating meaning in relationships: what I will call the openness of persons. The openness of persons is the idea that the agents we evaluate in our reactive attitudes are, intrinsically, works in progress, rather than fixed products concerning whom there is a fact of the matter about the ongoing value of their willing. I suggest that this allows space for them to genuinely be better than their wrong action indicates their being. In my view, when we forgive someone we see them in this more positive way, and thus do not hold the wrongdoing against them; this is the key release from blame that forgiveness involves. Forgiveness thus involves something like hopefulness in its interpretation of the other's willing. The openness of persons makes sense of how it is possible to view someone's willing as better than their actions indicate, and it is in this hopeful openness that forgiveness is so significant in meaningful relationships. Philosophical analyses of despair and emptiness take these to be centrally characterized by a lack of hopeful openness and possibility in the way the future is seen (see Ratcliffe 2013; Steinbock 2007); this forecloses opportunity for anything to make a difference, making it hard to see anything as mattering. Forgiveness sees hopeful openness in a specific location, one of central importance to us: the willing towards us of other persons.

Arendt says that forgiveness, uniquely, offers the possibility of redemption from 'the predicament of irreversibility' (1958, 237). She says that '[w]ithout being forgiven, released from the consequences of what we have done, our capacity to act would, as it were, be confined to one single deed from which we could never recover; we would remain the victims of its consequences forever' (1958, 237). While this dramatic claim may sound exaggerated, I think it captures something of significance that forgiveness reveals about the human condition and the nature of action: our actions cannot be undone; they stand. Our moral persons are formed and disclosed through the choices we make and the ways we respond to value in our actions, and our moral persons are not something over and above this. Given this, one could see the point in thinking that each of our acts is something that can be held to our total account, no matter what we have done to distance ourselves from it. Think back to Griswold's highly demanding set of conditions for forgiveness. These conditions rightly recognize that showing that an act no longer reflects on you is not easy. Coming to see that what you did was wrong is not the same as being different, and wanting to be different is not the same as being different.[7] Being sorry does not show that an act does not reflect on you. Apologizing expresses your recognition of the wrongness of what you did, but it does not change what you did and it does not show that you are now different.[8] Similarly, making amends, where this is possible, does not change the fact that you were willing to do the thing that you did,

---

[7] As Kant says: 'if improvement were a matter of mere wishing, every human being would be good' ([1793] 1998, 71).

[8] And we have surely all experienced (or given) apologies which are in fact an attempt to prematurely shelve what was done, through the wrongdoer's claiming the distancing of themself from it which apologizing expresses, and wanting it to be thereby dealt with.

and does not prove that it does not still (in at least some small way) reflect on you. This, I take it, is why Griswold adds the condition of committing to becoming the kind of person who no longer acts in the wrong way, and demonstrating this through words and actions. Griswold, in my view, is one of the few among those who want forgiveness to be earned who really takes seriously just how much would need to be done to demonstrate this. But the task of demonstrating that forgiveness is what we are owed might be more demanding than even Griswold's account recognizes. It may not be possible to show that the wronged person isn't entitled to keep the wrongdoing in mind in their overall accounting and judging you as a person. Yes, they may say, you get it now, but still, *you* were prepared to do *that* to *me*; why shouldn't I simply keep this in mind in my tracking of your willing as we move forward? This need not involve disproportionate blame, but simply a careful moral book-keeping in which the wrong stands, in whatever small or large way is warranted. One could accept an apology, stop dwelling on a wrong, and agree to move forward with someone while still holding it as reflecting on them (possibly in some small way), and in this sense holding it against them. In my view, this is often reasonable: (at least in many cases) we don't have to forgive. There may even, sometimes, be moral value in the ongoing protest constituted by not forgiving; this possibility is bound up with idea of forgiveness as gifted.

Earned forgiveness (a response to the wrongdoer's demonstration that blame is no longer warranted) would be something that fits in a practice of moral book-keeping. While moral book-keeping has a role in our mutual accountability practices, in my view, the most significant contribution of gifted forgiveness is in transcending it. Rather than being merely a required recognition of what a person has earned, gifted forgiveness sees a wrongdoer in an open, hopeful, more positive way than her wrong action warrants, where this is something which (at least often) goes beyond the evidence. That participant attitudes see persons as free and therefore allow an openness in which our affective evaluations of them can go beyond the evidence is a point commonly made by philosophers writing about trust. For example, McGeer says that substantial trust '(1) involves making or maintaining judgments about others, or about what our behavior should be towards them, that go beyond what the evidence supports; and (2) it renounces the very process of weighing whatever evidence there is in a cool, disengaged, and purportedly objective way' (McGeer 2008, 240).[9] It seems to me that this is also true of forgiveness, and that this allows it to play the radical role that Arendt attributes to it.

On an understanding of forgiveness as gifted, the reasons that apologies and amends provide are not best understood as shifting the preponderance of evidence pertaining to the overall assessment of the wrongdoer, but rather as the wrongdoer expressing reorientation of themselves towards better values. The forgiver accepts this expression and believes in the reorientation. This account allows that while apologies and making amends can provide reasons for forgiveness,[10] they (at least often) do not mandate it,

---

[9] There are of course similar questions with the rationality of this attitude.

[10] And makes sense of why apologies and amends are standard grounds for forgiveness: they are how the wrongdoer rejects the self disclosed by her previous action.

and it is possible to accept an apology, reconcile with someone, and still hold the action against them. So even in the case where the wrongdoer has provided the reasons constituted by apologies and amends, there is still (at least in many cases) something gifted in the wronged person's ceasing to hold the action against the wrongdoer. This is because the action always stands (irreversibly) as something the wrongdoer chose to do, and we are entitled to keep this in our view of them. However, we are not obliged to do so; the openness of persons means that it is always possible that their orientation to value no longer includes the problematic willing expressed in the wrongdoing. At the same time as making sense of apologies and remorse as standard kinds of reasons for forgiveness, this account allows that forgiving can occur without conditions having been met. In loving, trusting relationships that contain confidence about the other's goodwill, partners might frequently and easily respond to a mere apology (much less than would be required to demonstrate that the wrongdoing doesn't reflect on the wrongdoer), or even a gesture, or even say there is no need to apologize, because they are so easily able to get themselves to see the other in the optimistic, open, hopeful view that interprets the wrongdoer in the light of better willing than the wrong demonstrates.

Being forgiven can be meaningful and can be something people deeply desire, but one might wonder why, if the act is irreversible, some other person's attitude towards it should matter so much. How can a change in the forgiver's feelings have the seemingly magical effect of releasing us from the irreversibility of the action? This change does not somehow metaphysically absolve the act or change the wrongdoer. Yet, in my view, this change—the release constituted by how the forgiver feels—is crucial for our moral agency. The affective views others have towards us are not mere epiphenomenological add-ons, but are part of the context in which our actions have significance, what it is to see each other as persons and to care about each other's agency. Here it is helpful to return to McGeer's interpretation of reactive attitudes as an essential part of socially scaffolding moral agency, through our interactive concern with each other's willing and each other's responding to normative requirements. She argues that the hopeful, going-beyond-the-evidence attitude towards another's will expressed by trusting plays a crucial role in scaffolding our moral agency; the same seems to me true of forgiveness. McGeer argues that knowing that someone is willing and able to go beyond belief based on evidence because of their hope of what you might yet achieve can have a galvanizing effect, and that this can be empowering through helping someone reconnect with a sense of their own agential abilities (McGeer 2008, 252–253).

The gifted openness with which another views us when they forgive can be helpful for moral progress because it can help us avoid the pitfalls of despair and leniency, both of which undermine growth. Taking seriously what our wrongdoing says about ourselves can lead to despair, which undermines engaging with moral progress, or to bad faith, where we give up trying to be better because we decide that this is how we inevitably are. The thought might be something like: 'there is nothing I can do to make it the case that I didn't do this thing, and this shows who I am—what I am capable of'. A tempting but problematic way of avoiding this despair is leniency with ourselves—for example, mistaking an apology and a desire to be different with already being the better person the apology indicates we think we should be. This can be an obstacle to actually doing the work of orienting ourselves to better willing, and it can show insufficient regard for the concerns of those we have wronged. We need to take the wrong and what it says about us sufficiently seriously without this leading us to give up hope of being better. When someone we care about forgives us and communicates this, they generously see us in a hopeful, open way in which the wrongdoing is not taken to reflect on us. This can help us hold on to being oriented to being this better way, allowing us to take the wrongdoing seriously while having a hopeful view of ourselves as not forever stained by this action.[11] Our caring about getting this from those we have wronged and the force it can play in our lives are testament to the interpersonal scaffolding of moral agency: the significance of others' views of our agency in our continuing development and forming of ourselves.

On this account, part of what is so special and powerful about forgiveness in meaningful relationships and moral growth is how it sees people as able to make a fresh start. Arendt argues that this possibility is in fact needed for meaningful free agency. She says that

> trespassing is an everyday occurrence which is in the very nature of action's constant establishment of new relationships within a web of relations, and it needs forgiving, dismissing, in order to make it possible for life to go on by constantly releasing men from what they have done.... Only through this constant mutual release from what they do can men remain free agents, only by constant willingness to change their minds and start again can they be trusted with so great a power as that to begin something anew. (Arendt 1958, 240)

As I understand Arendt's view of the irreversibility of action, the wrongdoer cannot make it the case that not having the act held against them is what they are due or what they deserve; their action stands. But the wronged person can release them from the act, in no longer seeing them in a way that holds it to them. This release involves an openness of view in which the wrongdoer is seen in the light of better willing than their wrongdoing indicated. In a puzzling phrase (in this chapter's opening quotation) Arendt says that this retains 'something of the original character of action'. The original character of action is freedom, but our choices can reasonably be taken as reflecting and forming ourselves, and therefore creating—conditioning—the selves who now act.[12] Earned forgiveness is conditioned by the actions the wrongdoer has taken to earn it. In seeing a person in a way which frees them from being tied to a particular past action, gifted

---

[11] Wanting forgiveness can be a desire for such leniency, and expressions of forgiveness may have the unfortunate effect of supporting this: the account presented here allows that there can be problems and harms associated with forgiving.

[12] Of course there are also lots of other contextual, historical, social, biological, and other factors which condition ourselves; the claim is simply that *to the extent* that we have freedom there are actions through which we are responsible for how we make ourselves, given the materials we are working with.

forgiveness creates anew a view of the person as free to be something better, despite what they have done, to act in a way that goes beyond the conditioning of their past choices.

While, arguably, forgiveness can be inappropriate or premature, it is on the whole a response that takes wrongdoing seriously. This is because it is a release from blame that is seen as warranted—otherwise there is nothing to forgive. It is thus, as we have seen, implicated in the judgements made by warranted blame, as well as interactions involving the communication of blame, the giving and receiving of apologies. Like blame, it is essentially embedded in interactions and relationships with others about whom we care, and about whose views of us we care, and in which feedback from others is part of how we form ourselves and help each other stay on track. Blaming and forgiving find meaning in reciprocal vulnerability, caring, and interaction between flawed individuals making themselves together. Here, something worthwhile comes out of responding well to what has gone wrong, enabling shared growth and understanding that would not occur between more perfect agents who never hurt each other.

In addition to these ways in which forgiveness is essential for meaning in life, it is situated in a participant view which, I have suggested, provides a point of intersection between philosophical discussion of meaning *in* life and of the meaning *of* life. Reactive attitudes recognize persons as persons, as acting freely, as having value, and react to the way someone has acted in relation to a legitimate demand for a minimal amount of goodwill. They thus express our seeing persons as having value and significance, and our caring about each other and about each other's attitudes. On Strawson's account, this participant view on human agency is not the only way we can look at the world, and we can also take what he calls an 'objective' view, which we can understand here in terms of the point of view of the universe or the 'view from nowhere' (Nagel 1989). The latter view, especially on secular versions on it, can make our lives seem so insignificant as to undermine the possibility of their having meaning. However, while the participant view is not something one could be argued into from the objective view, at the same time, it is not something we can give up for long. It would be a mistake to look for a kind of non-detached value from a detached perspective, from which it cannot show up, and then conclude that it does not exist. Forgiveness is situated in a point of view on human action which we can't be argued into, but also can't avoid, from which we simply do see human lives and choices as significant, and further, from which we can take seriously human flaws, mistakes, and wrongs while being open to real fresh starts.[13]

References

Allais, Lucy. 2008. 'Wiping the Slate Clean: The Heart of Forgiveness'. *Philosophy & Public Affairs* 36(1): 33–68.

---

[13] I am grateful to a research fellowship at the Stellenbosch Institute for Advanced Studies in 2020, during which the work for this paper was completed. For helpful comments on earlier versions of this paper, thanks to Iddo Landau, Thaddeus Metz, Saul Smilansky and Abe Stoll.

Allais, Lucy. 2013. 'Elective Forgiveness'. *The International Journal of Philosophical Studies* 21(5): 637–653.
Allais, Lucy. 2021 'The Priority of Gifted Forgiveness: A Response to Fricker'. *The Australasian Philosophical Review* 3(3): 261–271.
Arendt, Hannah. 1958. *The Human Condition*. Chicago: University of Chicago Press.
Bennett, Christopher. 2018. 'The Alteration Thesis: Forgiveness as a Normative Power'. *Philosophy and Public Affairs*. 46(2): 207–233.
Bond, E. J. 1983. *Reason and Value*. Cambridge: Cambridge University Press.
Darwall, Stephen. 2006. *The Second Person Standpoint*. Cambridge, MA, and London: Harvard University Press.
Emerick, Barrett. 2017. 'Forgiveness and Reconciliation'. In *The Moral Psychology of Forgiveness*, ed. Kathryn Norlock. London: Rowman & Littlefield. 117–134.
Fricker, Miranda. 2014. 'What's the Point of Blame? A Paradigm Based Explanation'. *Nous* 50(1): 165–183.
Fricker, Miranda. 2021. 'Forgiveness—An Ordered Pluralism'. *Australasian Philosophical Review* 3(3): 241–260.
Garrard, Eve, and David McNaughton. 2002. 'In Defence of Unconditional Forgiveness'. *Proceedings of the Aristotelian Society* 103(1): 39–60.
Griswold, Charles. 2007. *Forgiveness: A Philosophical Exploration*. New York: Cambridge University Press.
Hampton, Jean. 1988. 'Forgiveness and Mercy'. In *Forgiveness and Mercy*, by Jeffrie G. Murphy and Jean Hampton. Cambridge: Cambridge University Press. 35–87.
Hieronymi, Pamela. 2001. 'Articulating and Uncompromising Forgiveness'. *Philosophy and Phenomenological Research* 62(3): 529–555.
Kant, Immanuel. [1793] 1998. 'Religion within the Boundaries of Mere Reason'. In *Religion within the Boundaries of Mere Reason and Other Writings*, ed. Allen W. Wood and George Di Giovanni, trans. George Di Giovanni, 31–191. Cambridge: Cambridge University Press.
Landau, Iddo. 2017. *Finding Meaning in an Imperfect World*. New York: Oxford University Press.
Macnamara, Coleen. 2013a. 'Reactive Attitudes as Communicative Entities.' *Philosophy and Phenomenological Research* 90(3): 546–569.
Macnamara, Coleen. 2013b. '"Screw You!" & "Thank You"'. *Philosophical Studies* 165: 893–914.
McGeer, Victoria. 2008. 'Trust, Hope and Empowerment'. *Australasian Journal of Philosophy* 86(2): 237–254.
McGeer, Victoria. 2012. 'Co-Reactive Attitudes and the Making of Moral Community'. In *Emotions, Imagination and Moral Reasoning*, ed. C MacKenzie and R. Langdon, 299–326. New York: Psychology Press.
McGeer, Victoria. 2013. 'Civilizing Blame'. In *Blame: Its Nature and Norms*, ed. D. Justin Coates and Neal A. Tognazzini, 162–188. New York: Oxford University Press.
McGeer, Victoria. n.d. 'Scaffolding Agency'. Unpublished manuscript.
McKenna, Michael. 2018. *Conversation and Responsibility*. Reprint ed. Oxford: Oxford University Press.
Metz, Thaddeus. 2007. 'The Meaning of Life', Stanford Encyclopedia of Philosophy. https://plato.stanford.edu/entries/life-meaning/#Nihi.
Metz, Thaddeus. 2013. *Meaning in Life: An Analytic Study*. Oxford: Oxford University Press.
Milam, Per. 2018a. 'Against Elective Forgiveness'. *Ethical Theory and Moral Practice* 21: 569–584.
Milam, Per. 2018b. 'Reasons to Forgive'. *Analysis* 79(2): 242–251.)
Nagel, Thomas. 1989. *The View from Nowhere*. New York: Oxford University Press.

Nelkin, Dana. 2013. 'Freedom and Forgiveness'. In *Free Will and Moral Responsibility*, ed. Ishtiyaque Haji and Justin Caouette. Newcastle upon Tyne: Cambridge Scholars Press. 165–188.

Nussbaum, Martha C. 2016. *Anger and Forgiveness*. Oxford: Oxford University Press.

Pettigrove, Glen. 2012. *Forgiveness and Love*. Oxford: Oxford University Press.

Railton, Peter. 1984. 'Alienation, Consequentialism and the Demands of Morality'. In *Consequentialism and Its Critics*, ed. Samuel Scheffler, 93–133. New York: Oxford University Press.

Ratcliffe, Matthew. 2013. 'What Is It to Lose Hope?' *Phenomenology and the Cognitive Sciences* 12(4): 597–614.

Russell, Luke. 2016. 'Forgiving While Punishing'. *Australasian Journal of Philosophy* 94(4): 704–718.

Smith, Angela. 2013. 'Moral Blame and Moral Protest'. In *Blame: Its Nature and Norms*, ed. D. Justin Coates and Neal A. Tognazzini, 27–48. New York: Oxford University Press.

Steinbock, Anthony J. 2007. 'The Phenomenology of Despair'. *International Journal of Philosophical Studies* 15(3): 435–451.

Strawson, P. F. 1962. 'Freedom and Resentment'. *Proceedings of the British Academy* 48: 1–25.

Twambly, P. 1976. 'Mercy and Forgiveness'. *Analysis* 36: 84–90.

Velleman, J. David. 2015. 'Front Matter'. In J. D. Velleman, *Beyond Price: Essays on Birth and Death*, 1st ed., [i]–[iv]. Cambridge, UK: Open Book.

Warmke, Brandon. 2011. 'Is Forgiveness the Deliberate Refusal to Punish?' *Journal of Moral Philosophy* 8(4): 613–620.

Warmke, Brandon. 2016. 'The Normative Significance of Forgiveness'. *Australasian Journal of Philosophy* 94(4): 687–703.

Watkins, Jeremy. 2005. 'Forgiveness and Its Place in Ethics'. *Theoria* 71(1): 59–77.

Wolf, Susan. 2010. *Meaning in Life and Why It Matters*. Princeton, NJ: Princeton University Press.

CHAPTER 19

BETWEEN SISYPHUS'S ROCK AND A WARM AND FUZZY PLACE

Procreative Ethics and the Meaning of Life

RIVKA WEINBERG

No one needs to exist.[1] Yet, here we all are. Every generation creates another generation of people, floundering about in our meaningless universe. Yet creating and raising children are widely claimed to be among life's most meaningful activities (Ferracioli 2018; Solomon, Greenberg, and Pyszczynski 2015; and Velleman 2005a, among many others). You can see the problem: Creating children can be deeply and uniquely meaningful but, by creating children, we condemn another generation to lives that are meaningless. What does that imply about the morality of procreation? Why does the meaningful give rise to the meaningless?

The answers require us to distinguish between different kinds of meaning, because procreation is a source of one, or maybe two, kinds of meaning, but nothing can help us with the third kind. I suggest that there are three basic kinds of meaning, and six characteristics that meaning can sometimes have within a kind of meaning.[2] The kinds of meaning are: Everyday, Cosmic, and Ultimate. These kinds of meaning may include six characteristics of meaning: significance, value, explanation, impact,[3] purpose, and point.

Everyday meaning refers to the value and significance of our everyday lives, including values such as beauty, morality, love, and truth; and the significance of engagement with

---

[1] As I have argued elsewhere, existence is value neutral and possessed by everyone at some point. See Weinberg (2008, 2013, and 2015).

[2] This is my conclusion from surveying the meaning landscape. It is, of course, possible that there are some other dimensions or aspects of meaning that have eluded me.

[3] I thank Joey Gruman for noting this characteristic of meaning.

them. It includes the purpose (i.e. the reason for which something is done) and point (i.e. justifying valued end) of much of our meaningful, everyday lives, which aim at these valued ends. It includes the impact we have on others and on the world around us, as well as the explanation of some of our meaningful activities and pursuits. Cosmic meaning refers to our meaningful role in the cosmos: to the significance and value of our niche in the cosmos, to the explanation of our role in the cosmos, our impact on the cosmos, and the purposes or point of the cosmos and our place in it. Ultimate meaning refers to the point of leading and living a life *at all*.[4] Why bother with the project, effort, or enterprise of life? What is the valued end of leading, running, and living a human life? Ultimate meaning is the end-regarding justifying reason, the valued end, or the point of leading a life at all.[5] (Unlike Everyday and Cosmic meaning, in my view, Ultimate meaning has only one of the six potential characteristics of meaning: it is confined to point.)

I will argue that having children can be a deep source of Everyday meaning, and perhaps Cosmic meaning as well. But nothing can provide us with Ultimate meaning. That is the sense in which having children can be (Everyday and Cosmically) meaningful, yet may still leave us with the sense that we are condemning another generation to (Ultimate) meaninglessness. In this chapter, I will analyse the ways in which procreation is meaningful to us, and the implications this may have for procreative ethics. As I've argued elsewhere, life is a risk (Weinberg 2015). As with other risks, we justify imposing it on our children due to our interest in procreation and the effect of the procreative risk on the children we will have. In other words, we consider how important having children is to us, as well as how the risk of life is likely to play out in the lives of the children onto whom it is imposed. This is consistent with how we justify risk imposition, generally: we consider the interests of both the risk-imposer and the risk-imposee (Weinberg 2015, 2021a).[6] An important aspect of parental interest in procreation is the ways in which procreation is a route to meaning in life. So the ways in which and the extent to which this is the case is of moral importance because the stronger the parental interest

---

[4] I explain Ultimate meaning in detail and argue that we cannot possibly have or achieve Ultimate meaning in Weinberg 2021b.

[5] Here's a little chart, for those who like charts, to represent the kinds and characteristics of value. We can imagine filling in the blanks with a verdict on whether a characteristic and kind of value is accessible or possible for us.

	EVERYDAY	COSMIC	ULTIMATE
Value			
Significance			
Impact			
Explanation			
Purpose			
Point			

[6] However, there are unique aspects of procreation that make the standard model of risk permissibility incompletely applicable to procreation—see Weinberg, 2021a.

in procreating, the more justified we are in having children. But, if the risk of life is likely to ripen into overwhelming and terrible harms, then we will have a hard time justifying procreation, even if it is so meaningful to people alive already. So we must also consider whether the ways in which life may be meaningless may be so terrible for people as to make creating them morally problematic or even wrong.

That is what I will explore here. I will discuss procreative meaning as it pertains to the three kinds and six possible characteristics of meaning (which I take to cover all the meaning bases). I will use the terms 'procreation' and 'having children' quite sloppily, to refer to both creating and raising children, even though these are separable activities. Where they come apart, I will note which aspects of meaning can or cannot apply to the separate acts of procreating and raising children. I will then consider the implications of procreative meaning for procreative ethics.

I. Everyday Meaning

Everyday meaning is the ordinary, everyday kind of meaning that we have in our everyday lives. It runs deep, it runs wide, and it pervades most lives. That's lucky, because, as we will see, it's the only kind of meaning we can be somewhat sure of. Having children is a sure route to several characteristics of Everyday meaning (Brighouse and Swift 2014; Smilansky 1995). The parent-child relationship is a highly valuable and unique love relationship; a true case of the warm fuzzies. As Ferracioli (2018) has pointed out, parental love is uniquely deep, robust, and resilient. It often includes steep sacrifices rarely seen in other loving relationships, and often proves enduring in the face of challenges of distance, time, and offence. We love our children from far away, be they dead or alive, and even when they are not particularly nice to us.

Procreation is therefore extremely significant; it is often a defining meaningful feature of a person's life, life story, and life trajectory. If something bad happens to one's child or to one's relationship with one's child, it is almost never a 'who cares?'. It is significant to you; you care. The parent-child relationship is deeply and uniquely valuable such that it renders almost anything about it significant. It is nearly impossible not to care about your children, so your life includes some significance from the moment of your child's conception. Your child is significant to you, and your role as the parent is significant as well as impactful. It is hard to overstate the impact a parent has on her child, even while the child is still developing in utero.[7]

Children anchor you to the world, connecting you to humanity's past and future. For some, children provide a sense of immortality and the comfort of being remembered

---

[7] A developing child is deeply impacted by its uterine environment, including whether it is nourished, maintained, stressed, etc. I take this as obvious: just as any organism is impacted by its environment, a developing fetus is as well.

after you die (at least for a while) (Solomon, Greenberg, and Pyszczynski 2015).[8] By procreating, you become part of the chain of human history, linking one generation to the next. Thus, the fate of the world gains significance to you. It is harder to stand apart, aloof, indifferent about the world. By procreating, you have committed to the world, invested in its future. Political stability, long-term peace or war, the health of the planet—it all matters so much more to you because it will affect your children, and their children, etc. In these ways, children make you deeply vulnerable to the world, to nature, and to other people. Everything matters.[9] The value, significance, and impact of so much of your life is amplified by procreating. Having children makes life deeper and fuller; better, worse, happier, and sadder—in other words, much more meaningful.[10]

Procreating can also provide people with a purpose: to raise their child well, to nourish the parent-child relationship for the duration of their lifetimes. That can serve as a purpose, the reason for which so much of your life's work is done. And because the value of your child and your relationship with your child is so high and unique, your child can serve as the valued end, or the point, of much that you do for and with your child. Thus, there is a point to playing with your child: you stack blocks with her, even though the activity itself can be mind-numbingly boring and meaningless on its own for an adult, because you value your child and your relationship with her. So there's a point to stacking blocks with her, and an explanation for many of your everyday activities.

Procreativity can explain a good deal of your life. It expresses your nature as a biological being, as an animal that reproduces, as part of the physical world and, in so doing, may help clarify what it can mean for you to be a biological human organism. Procreativity explains many of your aims and acts. We all do many things that are explained by the fact that we are parents (e.g. we love our children, we care for them, we work for them, we sacrifice for them, etc.). Procreating can thus render a good deal of human activity fairly intelligible, which is not always easy to do.

Even if one does not personally procreate, as Scheffler (2012) has argued, human procreation in general can be an important source of meaning in our lives, as we can see by imagining the doomsday prophesy, in which we know that everyone will die thirty days after our own death. The tragedy of this future, he argues, shows us that our values make most sense in the context of a collective afterlife (i.e. in which others live on after we ourselves die).

Creating versus Raising: Both creating and raising a child can be a source of Everyday meaning. If one raises but does not create one's child, as is the case in adoption, the parent-child relationship can be characterized by much of the same everyday meanings

---

[8] They argue that empirical evidence shows that having children helps people cope with mortality because a part of us is thought to live on through our children.

[9] Though, as Daniel Groll pointed out to me, some things matter less to people once they become parents since their children take up so much mattering that there is less energy and emotion left to care about things that don't concern their children.

[10] *Ceteris paribus*, of course. I am not claiming that a life with children is *always* more meaningful than a childless life.

as biological procreation, though likely not all. For example, adoption does not express your nature as a biological animal that reproduces, but it does express your nature as a biological animal that cares for its young, and it does produce a uniquely valuable parent-child relationship. If one creates but does not raise one's child, depending on the level of parental involvement, that too can be meaningful in the everyday sense of it being something significant, valuable, and impactful but rarely meaningful in the sense of providing explanatory meaning or everyday purpose or point to your everyday activities since your everyday activities in this sort of case are not explained by or aimed at your child or your relationship with your child.

II. Cosmic Meaning

As noted earlier, Cosmic meaning refers to our meaningful role in the cosmos. As rational, intelligent, moral agents, people may have a valuable role to play in the cosmos because our characteristics are valuable and, at least in our corner of the universe, quite rare (see Korsgaard 2006). Having children is therefore taken by some to be a way to contribute to cosmic value (Smilansky 1995) and can similarly be seen as an explanation of what we are doing here in our corner of the cosmos: perpetuating a special kind of value. Some argue the opposite—that people are uniquely awful and should not be perpetuated because we add negative value to the cosmos (see Benatar 2015), but I find that conclusion unrealistically focused on the small percentage of villainous people. Procreation allows us to play a valuable and significant role in the cosmos, and provides us with one way to have cosmic impact: we create more of this cosmic specialness and leave our children to continue to play this role in the cosmos. Because the universe is vast, this impact might be quite small indeed, and some may find it insignificant or meaningless, but it can also seem more important if we are indeed as rare as we seem to be in our discernible corner of the universe.

Whether there is any cosmic point or purpose and whether or how procreation participates in that is unknown, at best. If there is a cosmic purpose or point, it is certainly not obvious. Though it is also not obvious that this particular lack of meaning should bother us very much.

Insofar as we have non-cosmic points in our lives (such as those provided by our Everyday meaningful pursuits), it is not clear that the fact that these points aren't cosmic should bother us, and if there was a cosmic point but that didn't serve to provide our own lives with a point (be it Everyday or Ultimate), it is not clear why or how that would serve as much of a comfort to us.[11] My view is that our lives are indeed ultimately pointless and no amount of Cosmic meaning can change that (see section III, Ultimate Meaning).

---

[11] Nozick (1981), for example, notes that finding out that we served the cosmic purpose of being tasty food for beings higher up than us in the cosmic food chain would give our lives some cosmic significance, but not of the kind to make our lives Cosmically meaningful to us.

Some use the term *sub species aeternitatis*, or 'the perspective of the universe',[12] as a way of referring to Cosmic meaning. However, I find that a confusing concept because the universe is non-agential and doesn't seem to have much of a point of view. Moreover, it is unclear why we should care about that point of view, even if there was one. Perhaps, however, the so-called perspective of the universe is a descendant or a naturalistic variant of the view that Cosmic meaning is spiritual or godly. Some think there is cosmic spiritual meaning in the context of a religious cosmic order or purpose. On that view, having children could be seen as a way of participating in or perpetuating that supernatural cosmic order (if having children is part of how that order or purpose is supposed to work). Religion is supernatural. Not being wise to magic, I have no access to supernatural realms, if they exist. I guess I cannot rule out the possibility of this sort of cosmic purpose but, as I will explain in section III, I don't think that could provide us with Ultimate meaning. As such, I don't think that procreation provides us with a cosmic point to our lives, though it can provide other sorts of Cosmic meaning (in terms of value, significance, explanation, and impact, as explained earlier).

Creating versus Raising: Both creating and raising a child can be ways of achieving Cosmic meaning insofar as both creating and raising a child are ways of contributing value to the cosmos. (This differs from Everyday meaning in that the meaning provided by procreativity is not confined to our everyday lives, though it will overlap with it.) Because the uniquely valuable moral, artistic, and rational qualities of people are likely a combination of natural and social factors, both creating and raising children can be important to this sort of meaning.

III. Ultimate Meaning

Ultimate meaning refers to the point of leading and living a life *at all*. What is the valued end of the meta-project, effort, or enterprise of leading or running your life? Ultimate meaning is the end-regarding justifying reason, the valued end, or the point of running a life at all. I have argued elsewhere (2021b) that we cannot have this kind of meaning, and that presents a human tragedy. I won't repeat the argument in detail here, but I will very briefly state some of the central points so that we can consider how it may apply to the procreative ethics and the meaning of life.

We live our lives in several ways. We have our everyday lives, which include much of what we care about and value, and the ways in which we pursue or embody those values. But we also do this other thing: we have a human agential life that we run or lead, as a sort of project, effort, or enterprise of its own (Brännmark 2003; Nagel 1987; and Velleman 2005b). Points, or valued ends, lie outside the efforts or enterprises towards

---

[12] Both Nagel (1986 and 1987) and Benatar (2017) discuss meaning from a cosmic, universal perspective.

which they are aimed: e.g. you visit your grandma because you value her and you value loving relationships—the visit itself is not the point of the visit; you fight for justice because you value justice—the fight is not its own point; you study because you value truth—the study itself is not the point of the study. In all of these pointful pursuits, the point or valued end does not consist in the pursuits themselves, even if the values aimed at or grounded by such pursuits, such as love or truth, are valuable for their own sake. (The project or pursuit itself doesn't tell you why you're doing it; the pursuit itself doesn't tell you what the purpose or point of all that effort is.) Because our life encompasses its entirety, including all of the everyday values in it, there is nothing that can serve as the point or valued end of leading it because nothing lies outside of it to serve as a valued end for it.

The point of enterprises, pursuits, or efforts, like all points, are the valued ends that those enterprises or pursuits aim at or are grounded by. Those ends are separate from the pursuits or efforts themselves, even if they are attained while engaging in them. But, since your life includes its entirety, including all the values in it (be those values objective, subjective, natural, or supernatural), there is nothing that can serve as a point for bothering to lead a life at all. We can see that by imagining justice achieved: then what?[13] Sisyphus's rock does not roll back down: then what (Levy 2005)? You're hanging out with god blissfully in the afterlife, then what? What is the point of the rest of your life/afterlife?

Because our lives include their entirety, including their possible afterlife portion and including the values that guide our everyday activities, projects, and pursuits, the effort or enterprise of leading and living our lives cannot have a point. Thus, Ultimate meaning is metaphysically impossible due to the nature of points, or valued ends (i.e. that they are separate from the projects, pursuits, and efforts towards which they're aimed) and the nature of human life (i.e. that it includes its entirety).[14]

Although my diagnosis of the cause of the problem of Ultimate meaning is different from the explanations given by other philosophers, several philosophers have noted this problem, so it is not that controversial a problem to acknowledge. Nagel, for example, says: 'The problem is that although there are justifications and explanations for most of the things, big and small, that we do within life, none of these explanations explain the point of your life as a whole' (Nagel 1987, 95). Nozick seems aware of the problem as well, saying: 'Once you come to feel your existence lacks purpose, there is little you can do' (Nozick 1981, 588). Thus, if you are not persuaded by my explanation of the etiology or nature of the problem of Ultimate meaning, you can still recognize the problem itself, which is that we *lead* our lives, we *run* them, agentially, as an effort, enterprise, or

---

[13] You might wonder about seemingly inexhaustible values we can aim at, such as love. But I am sceptical of inexhaustible values. I think there can be too much love and it could feel smothering or, at some point, annoying, overwhelming, or just *too much*. There is even a phenomenon of seeing something so cute, you can't stand it and want to obliterate it (Hamilton 2018).

[14] Ultimate meaning is metaphysically rather than conceptually impossible. I thank Thaddeus Metz for urging me to clarify this point.

project of its own. And, although we can find justifying reasons, in the form of valued ends, or points, for many of the things we do and enterprises we run within our lives, we don't have those sorts of reasons—*points*—for the agential effort or enterprise of leading and living our lives. So that leaves us with a lot of pointless effort since running one's life takes a lot of work and often includes much suffering. The value within, i.e., Everyday meaning, may suffice for some to make leading a life worthwhile despite the lack of Ultimate Meaning, but it still will not give the leading of one's life a point, a valued end of its own. Having and/or raising children can't give us this kind of point because nothing can. Boo hoo (I mean it!). When we create new people, we know that they too will lead lives that are pointless—Ultimately meaningless—in this way.

IV. Implications for Procreative Ethics

Procreating is a source of deep and unique Everyday meaning, and perhaps a source of Cosmic meaning as well (as we noted earlier). That strengthens our moral case for procreating insofar as it gives prospective procreators a very strong interest to go ahead and force another person to live: namely, that procreating is likely to be an Everyday and possibly Cosmic meaning boon for procreators. Yet we know that our future child will not have Ultimate meaning (because no one can) and that, at least in my view, is contrary to our future child's interests. Putting forth sustained and significant effort, as we do in the leading of our lives, without a point or end-regarding justifying reason for that effort is disappointing at best and potentially demoralizing. If the effort or enterprise of leading and living, or running, our lives could have a point, we would want it to. It would be nice if there was a point to the hard, wearying, and long-term agential effort we put into leading our lives in their entirety. Thus, issues regarding the meaning of life present us with a procreative ethics conflict: Does the fact that our children's lives will lack Ultimate meaning outweigh or override the fact that procreating is a deep and unique way to achieve and enjoy Everyday and perhaps Cosmic meaning, or does this work the other way round?

Before I address that question, I will address two issues that could render the question practically, if not philosophically, moot. The first is the possibility of adoption as an alternative to procreation. If we could achieve much of the meaning we get out of procreating by adopting instead, we can incur the meaning gains without imposing procreative risks on anyone since adoption does not create new people. The second is the Ponzi scheme problem. Some have argued that even if we can achieve meaning by procreating and our children can proceed to do the same thing, because humans, like all species, will eventually fade out of existence, this amounts to a procreative Ponzi scheme of sorts, and is therefore morally suspect (Benatar 2015; Reddit u/BeastBeef 2019 and u/(deleted) 2019).

Adoption: The Procreative Panacea!

When discussing adoption, it is hard for me to appreciate the philosophical attention devoted to discussing whether adoption as an alternative to biological procreation provides us with reasons or obligations to adopt rather than procreate biologically (even though I'm participating in it right now!) (Friedrich 2013; Rulli 2016a and 2016b; Rieder 2015; Betzler and Löschke 2016; Peterson 2002; Ferracioli 2018; De Wispelaere and Weinstock 2015; among others). First, obviously, not everyone can adopt. *Someone* will have to create the children to be adopted, so the adoption solution to procreative ethics is quite limited, at best.

Second, it is simply not the case that there are numerous children available for adoption. So there is quite the pie-in-the-sky quality to these discussions. Since single parenthood, unmarried parenthood, and abortion have become more socially accepted in many parts of the world, the number of children relinquished for adoption has dropped precipitously, and the demand far exceeds the supply (Bitler and Zavodny 2002; Miller and Coyl 2000; *The Economist* 2017).[15] International adoptions have proven to be rife with corruption, human trafficking, and with children who were not knowingly and/or voluntarily relinquished by their birth parents for adoption, causing some countries to restrict or cancel these programs (Goodwin 2010; Smolin 2006; Wang 2019; and Westerman 2018). Thus, adoption is hardly a procreative ethics panacea. As intended, it is a post-fact solution to children born to parents unable or unwilling to raise them. But even then, it is not clearly always the best solution or the best way to help those children and their parents. If we gave the biological parents the money that is used to arrange for the adoption of their children instead of using that money to arrange the adoptions, many of those parents would likely be delighted to have been rendered financially able to raise their children. Moreover, adoption comes at the cost of significant suffering, as it is usually emotionally difficult to relinquish a child for adoption (Aloi 2009; Memarnia et al. 2015; and Jones 2016), and many (though certainly not all) adoptees struggle with feelings of rejection, alienation, and loss (Nickman and Rosenfeld 2005; Velleman 2005a; and MacLeod 2017). It is also worth noting that since the demand for babies relinquished for adoption far exceeds the supply, by choosing to adopt rather than procreate biologically, you may be making it harder for infertile or gay people to find babies available for adoption.

Finally, there is the matter of biological connection. While some argue that biological connection is nonexistent, mythical, fanciful, or of minimal importance (Silver 2001 and Haslanger 2009),[16] it seems a stretch to me to think that it amounts to nothing of value or nothing meaningful. Parent-child relationships, as argued, can be a source of Everyday and perhaps even Cosmic meaning. Biology is one sort of parent-child

---

[15] Increased availability of contraception may also be a factor contributing to fewer children placed for adoption.

[16] For arguments explaining the value of biological ties or biological procreation, see Ferracioli (2018) and Velleman (2005a).

relationship that people can have with each other, and the sense of continuity and familiarity many feel for their close biological relatives, or when they discover new relatives, or long-lost relatives, attests to the meaning that biological relationships can provide (Groll, 2021 and Velleman 2005a). The fact that people are primates who, like many other species of primates, tend to live in and favour kin groups makes it plausible to think that there is often a natural biological human bond, as does the fact that we are evolved to care about the survival of our kin. I certainly don't think that all biological relationships are always valuable to all people. Any kind of relationship can be soured in nearly infinite ways. However, the fact that people are formed and influenced by a combination of nature and nurture makes it likely that both natural and 'nurtural' bonds are usually meaningful (i.e. significant, valuable) to people. And I also think that the fact that so many people seem so interested in their DNA, their genealogy, and in finding biological relatives shows that it is common for people to find biological connections valuable, as does the lengths people often go to have biological children. For all of these reasons, I think it unreasonable to insist that adoption poses no loss to those who wish to procreate biologically. It may be a loss that people should or even must incur, under certain circumstances, but it is not something that comes at no cost.[17]

Of course, adoption often works out quite well, to the benefit of all parties to it, and many times even better for parents and children than many biological procreative arrangements. And, as argued, it allows for most of the Everyday meaning that people get from procreativity. But it is not the way out of our procreative ethical problems. For anyone to enjoy the Everyday and Cosmic meaning that procreation can provide, someone will have to procreate biologically (at least so far—perhaps technology might prove otherwise). Moreover, adoption is expensive, exclusionary, beset with moral problems of its own, involves the loss of biological connection and, in any case, is only realistic for a miniscule fraction of the population. So it is not a way for us to reap procreative meaning benefits for adults without imposing any meaning risks on our future children. We will have to face the conflict.

The Procreative Ponzi Scheme?

Some have argued that procreating as a way of achieving Everyday or Cosmic meaning is morally suspect because, as with all Ponzi schemes, the last generation of 'investors' or, in the procreative case, of humans, will be left without a return on their investment. As Benatar (2015, 129–130) argues:

> Continued procreation in order to save existing people from harm is a giant procreative Ponzi scheme. Each generation has to procreate to save itself from the fate of the final generation, thereby creating a new generation that must procreate in order to

---

[17] I discuss some of these sorts of circumstances in Weinberg (2015).

spare itself the same fate. Like all Ponzi schemes, it cannot end well. . . . As a species, we can tread the perilous waters of purposelessness by procreating only so long. The final people's problems of purpose will be no different whether the final people are the current generation or some distant future one.

This is an intriguing argument, but its factual basis seems rather hazy. Even if it is accurate to describe each generation as 'borrowing' meaning from the next by creating the next generation, it is a 'scheme' we were all born into—it's not as if someone cooked it up as an alternative to honest procreative dealing. Unlike most Ponzi schemes, it is also not the case that most, on this view, stand to lose; it would just be the last few generations.[18] Moreover, it is no moral crime so long as this sort of borrowing or creating of meaning is also available to the next generation. Sure, it seems unrealistic to expect that, unlike almost all known species, humans will go on in perpetuity without ever succumbing to extinction. But, deciding that we are all morally obligated, on pain of being immoral Ponzi scheme operators, to do our best to go extinct now in order to save some future generation from that sort of crisis of existential meaning is ridiculously speculative. We have no idea how long it will take for humans to go extinct and how that extinction process might occur. Therefore, we also have no idea whether forcing extinction now will spare future generations greater extinction suffering or, instead, cause vast suffering to current generations for no important reason. Maybe humans will painlessly evolve into another species, going extinct in an extremely slow and barely noticeable fashion over thousands of years. Maybe humans will colonize other areas of the universe and persist long after the earth's sun burns out. Maybe a nuclear war will take us all out tomorrow. Because we know so little about the ways in which human extinction may occur, it is not a reason sufficiently grounded in fact to demand the steep sacrifice in meaning that a current moral procreative ban would incur.

However, if each generation condemns the next to ultimate pointlessness, as I believe it does, we must consider whether the gains in Everyday or Cosmic meaning, which we may reap by procreating, are enough to justify putting the next generation in the same position.

How Tragic Is Our Lack of Ultimate Meaning?

One might wonder why I am making that big a deal over our lack of Ultimate meaning. Where is the harm in lacking Ultimate meaning? If a good deal of what our everyday lives are about is meaningful, who cares if life itself—the life we lead as a project, effort,

---

[18] I thank Iddo Landau for pointing this out. Landau also suggests that another difference between the procreative Ponzi scheme and the standard Ponzi scheme is that, in the procreative case, even the last few generations can enjoy some kinds and characteristics of meaning. So they get some 'profit', so to speak. However, Scheffler (2012) challenges this possibility by arguing that an impending human extinction would erode or erase much of what is meaningful to us.

or enterprise of its own—happens not to have a point? 'Why isn't Everyday meaning enough?'[19] That is a fair question and it seems clear that, to many people, Everyday meaning is the most important kind of meaning.

If my conception of a flourishing life includes loving your children, playing the banjo, being a good friend and a clear teacher, what sense does it make to ask me what the point of having this sort of life is? The point is the Everyday meaning, the living of this meaningful life. And that's legitimate: Everyday meaning counts. Without it, everyday life might well be unbearable. But I argue that you're not just loving your children, playing the banjo, being a good friend, and competently doing your productive and worthwhile job. You are also putting effort and agency into the meta-project, which is the running of your life as an effort or project of its own; conducting the enterprise of living, *leading* a life. So, to the question, how else do we live our lives but in this everyday sense? In the ultimate sense, I'd say (and, in fact, have said). It makes sense for us to want that effort, project, and enterprise to have a point of its own. (Just as we want all the rest of our efforts, projects, or enterprises to have a point.) But it can't.

As persons, we live an agential life that we shape, lead, and run as its own project. This, I argue, is part of what Velleman (2005b) means when he argues that we have a narrative identity, that we want our lives to makes sense as a whole story. It is also part of what Brännmark (2003) means when he argues that the fact that we *lead* lives is crucial to our sense of meaning. Just as one can wonder why Everyday meaning is not enough, I wonder the opposite: Who cares if your everyday activities and pursuits have meaning if the whole fraught business of your life is pointless? If leading a life is pointless, why bother with all the everyday activity that goes into that effort? Thus, one way to put the harm of lacking Ultimate meaning is that you now are putting forth the effort of leading your life as an enterprise of its own, which is part of living and leading a human agential life, with a frustrating lack of end-justifying reasons, valued ends—a *point*—for that effort.

I can see the legitimacy of both perspectives. Of course, nearly all of us would prefer to have Everyday meaning *and* Ultimate meaning. But which of the two is more critical is hard to determine. Yet that is the conflict we have to assess in the procreative case (as noted earlier): we must consider whether the lack of Ultimate meaning our children will have to bear outweighs or overrides the interest that prospective parents have in procreating, which includes the ways in which procreativity is a deep and unique way (available to us and our progeny) of attaining Everyday and perhaps Cosmic meaning.

Although almost everyone puts effort into running their lives, not everyone does so with the same degree of effort, aimed at achieving some kind of overall coherence and purpose.[20] It seems plausible that people who are most conscious of putting lots of effort into running or leading their lives are most acutely disturbed by the fact that we cannot have Ultimate meaning because it makes that effort itself seem rather

---

[19] I thank Thaddeus Metz and Daniel Groll for pressing me on this question. My answer here is the same as the one I provide in Weinberg, 2021b.
[20] This point is one I made originally in Weinberg 2021b.

pointless. It also seems plausible that those of us who are more goal-oriented rather than live-in-the-moment types would find Ultimate meaning more important than Everyday meaning. In other words, some run or lead their lives more consciously, and with greater priority over other everyday life pursuits, than others. The more you consciously aim at something, the more disturbing it may be to discover that you cannot possibly accomplish what you thought you were setting out to accomplish. Those who treat life like it's the journey rather than the destination that matters are likely more focused on Everyday meaning than those of us who find a dreary, dangerous, and difficult journey without a destination disturbingly pointless. Some, perhaps the laziest and happy-go-luckiest among us, may even feel relieved to discover that there is no Ultimate meaning because that can remove the onus of pursuing it, leaving one more carefree to enjoy the pleasures of everyday life.[21] Finally, it seems plausible that those of us for whom life is more of an effort than a joy find Ultimate meaning more important because we put a great deal of effort into leading our burdensome lives and, without a point to it, that effort can feel draining, exhausting, and even alienating (because the connection between the effort and the point is missing). But if you think of life as fun, carefree, and delightful, then it would make sense for you to care less about whether it is Ultimately meaningful. It doesn't have to be so meaningful if it has another reason for you to bother with it: the fun! (How could I forget how much fun life is?)

Then there is the matter of Cosmic meaning. If we set aside the spiritual or supernatural aspect that some believe exists cosmically,[22] we are left with the fact that procreating can provide people with a valuable, significant, and impactful cosmic role. To me, this is neither here nor there. It is not clear to me why we should find our role in the cosmos any more important or significant than our roles in our everyday lives. If our role in the cosmos could provide us with Ultimate meaning, that would be a game-changer and solve much of our meaning problems. It would be quite the party trick! But, as argued, that is not possible because Ultimate meaning is impossible due to the nature of points, or valued ends (i.e. that they are separate from the activities and efforts towards which they're aimed), and the nature of human life (i.e. that it includes its entirety). While Cosmic meaning may be available to people, the kind of value it offers, i.e., significance, value, and impact, does not seem different enough from Everyday meaning as to make much of a difference to our consideration of the implications that issues of meaning have for procreative ethics.

When considering whether it is fair for us to impose the risks of life on future people, we must consider as well the meaning risks of life. While Everyday meaning, and some forms of Cosmic meaning, are often achievable, Ultimate meaning is not. Therefore, when we consider procreative benefits and burdens, we now need to include the known burden of the frustrating lack of Ultimate meaning, which is a burden every person will bear (though it is likely that it will weigh more heavily on some than on others). Other

---

[21] As with so many of the optimistic points in my work, I owe this one to Saul Smilansky.
[22] Again, I set that aside because I have no access to supernatural information.

than to say, unhelpfully, that both Everyday and Ultimate meaning seem incredibly important, which of the two kinds of meaning is more important is not something I will attempt to settle here. That remains an area open for further research. What I hope to have done here is to have made the issues of meaning relevant to procreative ethics clear and salient.[23]

REFERENCES

Aloi, J. A. 2009. 'Nursing the Disenfranchised: Women Who Have Relinquished an Infant for Adoption'. *Psychiatric and Mental Health Nursing* 16: 27–23.

Betzler, Monika, and Jörg Löschke. 2016. 'New Developments in Family Ethics: An Introduction'. *Journal of Moral Philosophy* 13: 641–651.

Benatar, David. 2015. In David Benatar and David Wasserman, *Is It Wrong to Reproduce?*, Chapter 4. Oxford: Oxford University Press.

Benatar, David, 2017. *The Human Predicament*. Oxford: Oxford University Press.

Bitler, M., and M. Zavodny. 2002. 'Did Abortion Legalization Reduce the Number of Unwanted Children? Evidence From Adoptions'. *Perspectives on Sexual and Reproductive Health* 34: 25–33.

Brännmark, Johan. 2003. 'Leading Lives: On Happiness and Narrative Meaning'. *Philosophical Papers* 32: 321–343.

Brighouse, Harry, and Adam Swift. 2014. *Family Values: The Ethics of Parent-Child Relationships*. Princeton, NJ: Princeton University Press.

De Wispelaere, Jurgen, and Daniel Weinstock. 2015. 'Privileging Adoption over Sexual Reproduction? A State-Centered Perspective'. In *Permissible Progeny: The Morality of Procreation and Parenting*, ed. Sarah Hannan, Samantha Brennan, and Richard Vernon. Oxford: Oxford University Press. 208–226.

Ferracioli, Laura. 2018. 'Procreative-Parenting, Love's Reasons and the Demands of Morality'. *The Philosophical Quarterly* 68: 77–96.

Friedrich, Daniel. 2013. 'A Duty to Adopt?' *Journal of Applied Philosophy* 30: 25–39.

Goodwin, Michele, 2010. 'International Adoption—A Market in Babies?' *New York Times*, April 12. https://parenting.blogs.nytimes.com/2010/04/12/questioning-international-adoptions/

Groll, Daniel. 2021. *The Need to Know*. Oxford: Oxford University Press.

Hamilton, John. 2018. 'When Cute Is Too Much, the Brain Can Get Aggressive'. *National Public Radio, Morning Edition*, December 31. https://www.npr.org/sections/health-shots/2018/12/31/679832549/when-too-cute-is-too-much-the-brain-can-get-aggressive

Haslanger, Sally. 2009. 'Family, Ancestry and Self: What Is the Moral Significance of Biological Ties'. *Adoption and Culture* 2: 91–122.

Jones, Merry Bloch. 2016. *Birthmothers: Women Who Have Relinquished Babies for Adoption Tell Their Stories*. Open Road Distribution.

Korsgaard, Christine. 2006. 'Morality and the Distinctiveness of Human Action'. In *Primates and the Philosophers: How Morality Evolved*, ed. Frans De Waal. Princeton, NJ: Princeton University Press. 98–119.

---

[23] Many thanks to Yuval Avnur, David Boonin, Daniel Groll, Joey Gruman, Iddo Landau, Thaddeus Metz, Paul Hurley, Dion Scott-Kakures, and Saul Smilansky for helpful comments and discussion.

Levy, Neil. 2005. 'Downshifting and Meaning in Life'. *Ratio* 18: 176–189.
MacLeod, Jean. 2017. 'Connecting With Our Children: 7 Core Issues in Adoption'. *Rainbow Kids: Adoption and Child Welfare Advocacy*, February 22, https://www.rainbowkids.com/adoption-stories/connecting-with-our-children-7-core-issues-in-adoption-1909.
Memarnia, Nina, Lizetter Nolte, Claire Norris, et al. 2015. '"It Felt Like It Was Night All the Time": Listening to the Experiences of Birth Mothers Whose Children Have Been Taken into Care or Adopted'. *Adoption and Fostering* 39: 303–317.
Miller, Brent C., and Diana D. Coyl. 2000. 'Adolescent Pregnancy and Childbearing in Relation to Infant Adoption in the United States'. *Adoption Quarterly* 4: 3–25.
Nagel, Thomas. 1986. *The View from Nowhere*. Oxford: Oxford University Press.
Nagel, Thomas, 1987. *What Does It All Mean? A Very Short Introduction to Philosophy*. Oxford: Oxford University Press.
Nickman, S. L., and A. Rosenfeld, et al. 2005. 'Children in Adoptive Families: Overview and Update'. *Journal of the American Academy of Child and Adolescent Psychiatry* 44: 987–995.
Nozick, Robert. 1981. *Philosophical Explanations*. Cambridge, MA: Harvard University Press.
Petersen, Thomas Sobirk. 2002. 'The Claim from Adoption'. *Bioethics* 16: 353–375.
Rieder, Travis. 2015. 'Procreation, Adoption, and the Contours of Obligation'. *Journal of Applied Philosophy* 32: 293–309.
Rulli, Tina. 2016a. 'We Should Adopt'. *The Philosopher's Magazine* 75: 83–88.
Rulli, Tina. 2016b. 'Preferring a Genetically-Related Child?' *Journal of Moral Philosophy* 13: 669–698.
Scheffler, Samuel. 2012. *Death and the Afterlife*. Oxford: Oxford University Press.
Silver, Lee M. 2001. 'Confused Meanings of Life, Genes and Parents'. *Studies in History and Philosophy of Biological and Biomedical Sciences* 32C: 647–661.
Solomon, Sheldon, Jeff Greenberg, and Tom Pyszczynski. 2015. *The Worm at the Core: On the Role of Death in Life*. New York: Random House.
Smilansky, Saul. 1995. 'Is There a Moral Obligation to Have Children?' *Journal of Applied Philosophy* 12: 41–53.
Smolin, David M. 2006. 'Child Laundering: How the Intercountry Adoption System Legitimizes and Incentivizes the Practices of Buying, Trafficking, Kidnaping, and Stealing Children'. *Wayne Law Review* 52: 113–200.
The Economist. 2017. 'Adoptions in America are Declining'. June https://www.economist.com/united-states/2017/06/24/adoptions-in-america-are-declining.
BeastBeef. 2019. 'Having Kids Is the Original Pyramid Scheme'. *Reddit*.
NA. 2019. 'Having Kids to Give Life Meaning Creates More Lives That Need Meaning. It's a Ponzi Scheme'. *Reddit*.
NA. 2019. 'Notice How Family Trees and Ponzi Schemes Look Exactly Alike?' *Reddit*.
Velleman, David, 2005a. 'Family History'. *Philosophical Papers* 34: 357–378.
Velleman, David, 2005b. 'The Self as Narrator'. In *Autonomy and the Challenges to Liberalism*, ed. John Christman and Joel Anderson, 56–73. Cambridge: Cambridge University Press.
Wang, Nafu, and Lynn Zhang. 2019. *One Child Nation* (documentary film).
Westerman, Ashley. 2018. 'Why International Adoption Cases in the U.S. Have Plummeted'. *National Public Radio*, June. https://www.npr.org/2018/06/25/623114766/why-international-adoption-cases-in-the-u-s-have-plummeted
Weinberg, Rivka. 2008. 'Identifying and Dissolving the Non-Identity Problem'. *Philosophical Studies* 137: 3–1.

Weinberg, Rivka. 2013. 'Existence: Who Needs It? The Non-Identity Problem and Merely Possible People'. *Bioethics* 27: 471–484.

Weinberg, Rivka. 2015. *The Risk of a Lifetime: How, When, and Why Procreation May Be Permissible*. Oxford: Oxford University Press.

Weinberg, Rivka. 2021a, 'Risk, Responsibility, and Procreative Asymmetries'. In *The Oxford Handbook of Intergenerational Ethics*, ed. Stephen Gardiner. Oxford: Oxford University Press.10.1093/oxfordhb/9780190881931.013.37

Weinberg, Rivka. 2021b. 'Ultimate Meaning: We Don't Have It, We Can't Get It, and We Should Be Very, Very Sad'. *Journal of Controversial Ideas*, 1: 4–24.

CHAPTER 20

NATURE, ANIMALS, AND MEANING IN LIFE

KATIE MCSHANE

Many people want their lives, experiences, or activities to be meaningful, but there are philosophical debates about what meaning in life consists in. Some writers on the topic take a narrow view: they view meaning in life as a matter of belonging to a social group (Haidt 2010, 97–100), making a lasting difference in the world (Nagel 1986, 11), or fulfilling one's divine purpose (Craig 2000, 44–46, 50–53). The tendency in contemporary philosophy, however, has been to take a broader view. Susan Wolf and Iddo Landau, for example, understand meaning in life to be a matter of engaging with a wide range of worthy things. Wolf (2010, 26, 30) describes it as interacting with a 'worthy object of love' in positive ways; Landau (2017, 15) describes it as living a life 'in which there is a sufficient number of aspects of sufficient value'.

One reason for preferring a broader view is that the sources of meaning in people's lives—the things that make their lives meaningful—seem to be quite varied. Some people find meaning in participating in social groups, but hermits can live meaningful lives too. Some people might believe that their lives will make a lasting difference in the world, but others find meaning in impermanent features of their lives: relationships with friends and family, for example. Some people find meaning in fulfilling what they believe to be their divine purpose, but atheists find meaning in their lives absent any belief in divine purpose. None of these people seem to be making a mistake about whether their lives include meaning. These sources of meaning appear, at least *prima facie*, legitimate.[1]

In spite of the tendency towards broader views in the contemporary literature, discussions of meaning in life have still tended to be human-centred. This is true in two ways. First, examples of sources of meaning in life often focus on the contributions that

---

[1] Regarding the atheists' view, I thus disagree with Craig (2000). See Metz (2013, 83–85) for what I take to be a persuasive criticism of Craig's position.

we humans make to other human lives, communities, and endeavours. Second, the presence of meaning in our lives and the importance that we attach to it is often understood to be a uniquely human feature, one that sets us apart from other species. The aim of this chapter is to interrogate these forms of human-centredness and ask what we might learn about meaning in life from giving them up. In the first section I will explore briefly the many ways in which nature[2] can be a source of meaning for people. In the second section, I will raise the question of whether cognitively sophisticated, emotionally complex, social, non-human animals[3] can lead meaningful lives according to different theories of meaning in life. In this chapter, I will argue that by avoiding human-centredness in our thinking about meaning in life, we can get a fuller and more accurate picture of the sources of meaning in human life and the ways in which animal lives might also be meaningful.

1. Nature as a Source of Meaning in Human Lives

There are of course many ways in which non-human nature enables people to lead meaningful lives: by providing them with the materials and conditions that are necessary for leading lives at all (food, water, shelter) and by providing them with resources that they rely on in performing meaningful activities. However, nature can also be a direct source of meaning in human lives. The natural world can be an important part of what people regard as 'home', i.e. a connection to place that can ground their sense of who they are, where they came from, or where they belong. The communities that people find meaning from participating in and contributing to can be natural as well as human communities. Parts of nature can be nurtured and protected by people, producing a kind of meaning that resembles that which some people find in caring for young children. Parts of nature can likewise play the role of friends or elders, keeping a person company or being a source of wisdom. Even in cases where parts of nature do not play such roles in a person's social life, they can still be among the cherished, admired, loved, or respected things in that life. Finally, nature can provide human lives with meaning in that it can provide a sense of purpose, of being 'part of something larger than oneself', in the sense of having a role to play in a broader ongoing narrative: being part of natural cycles, processes, and history.

Most views of meaning in life do not rule out the natural world as a possible source of meaning in human lives, and I am not claiming here that nature is a source of meaning

---

[2] I use the term 'nature' hereafter rather than 'non-human nature' to refer to the non-human, non-artificial parts of the world: plants, non-human animals, ecosystems, etc. The term 'nature' has been subject to many legitimate criticisms in environmental ethics. See e.g. Vogel (2015).

[3] For the sake of parsimony, hereafter I will refer to non-human animals simply as 'animals'.

for everyone. However, taking these cases seriously as important and common sources of meaning for people might well affect the intuitions about meaning in life that lie behind much philosophical theorizing on the topic. Seeing human relationships with animals, plants, ecological communities, and natural cycles as important sources of meaning might make theorists less likely to adopt understandings of meaning according to which it must come from our rational choices or intentional actions (rather than the ecological relationships or kinships not produced by choices/intentions), or our cultural achievements (e.g. scientific discoveries, artistic creations, or beneficence toward other humans). It might make theorists more likely to regard the ways that we relate to the world as organisms, or as animals, as legitimate sources of meaning, as opposed to thinking that meaning must be related to our 'rational nature'.[4]

Thus far I have merely argued that parts of the non-human world should be seen as important sources of meaning within human lives. However, there is a further question we might ask about the natural world: Could non-human lives be meaningful in their own right? That is to say, might the natural world be not just a source of meaning for humans, but a locus of meaning, meaning that exists in non-human lives independent of humans and our concerns? If so, there might be important ethical implications of this fact: if it matters that humans be able to live meaningful lives, it might also matter that animals be able to live meaningful lives. In the next section I will discuss these issues, focussing on those animals that seem antecedently most likely to be capable of meaningful lives: social animals such as gorillas, wolves, and elephants that are cognitively sophisticated and emotionally complex.

2. Meaningful Lives of Animals?

Are humans the only creatures capable of living meaningful lives? Perhaps surprisingly, on many understandings of what meaning in life is, the answer is no. Many cognitively sophisticated, emotionally complex, and social animals meet the requirements set forth by these views for having meaning in their lives.

Before considering this matter further, three caveats are in order. First, is important to distinguish two different questions from one another:

(1) Do (or can) some animals lead meaningful lives, have meaningful experiences, or engage in meaningful activities?
(2) Do (or can) some animals care or have beliefs about whether their lives, experiences, or activities are meaningful?

---

[4] See e.g. Metz (2019) for a critical discussion of the focus on choice or intention; see Metz (2013, 219–239) for claims about the importance of our rational (as opposed to animal) nature.

Here I will focus on question (1), setting aside question (2) except as necessary to answer question (1). Second, research about animal minds is still in its infancy, and it is complicated by widespread philosophical disagreement about how to understand some of its core concepts (such as 'consciousness'). There are also methodological disagreements among researchers concerning how much and what kind of evidence would be needed in order to justify the attribution of humanlike subjective states or abilities to animals. Here I will focus on claims about the lives and abilities of cognitively sophisticated, emotionally complex, social animals, and I will focus on those claims that are grounded in science. However, few such claims are uncontroversial, and those I rely on here are no exception. Third, in order to understand whether animals are capable of leading meaningful lives, having meaningful experiences, and engaging in meaningful activities, we will need to look more closely at the details of different theories of meaning. There is no room here to consider every important theory of meaning, and many well-regarded views will be left out. I will, however, consider views within each of the three main categories in the literature on meaning in life: subjectivism, objectivism, and hybridism.[5]

2.1. Subjectivism

Subjectivist views hold that whether meaning is present in a life, experience, or activity is fully determined by the subjective attitudes that are or would be taken towards or within that life, experience, or activity (Metz 2013, 164–165).[6] To apply this view to animals, we first need to know: Which subjective attitudes determine meaning? Different versions of subjectivism answer this question in different ways. A. J. Ayer (1990, 226; see also Smart 1999, 16), for example, identifies the meaning of a person's life with its purpose, and claims that its purpose is 'constituted by the ends to which [the person], consciously or unconsciously, devotes himself'. E. D. Klemke (2000, 196) claims that sources of meaning in human lives are things that 'provide us with some of our most heightened moments of joy and value'. Harry Frankfurt (2002, 250) claims that 'devoting oneself to what one loves suffices to make one's life meaningful'. On these views, any animals that devote themselves to ends, feel joy, or devote themselves to what they love are capable of having meaning in their lives. Are there animals that can do these things?

The literature on animal psychology suggests that on most ordinary uses of the terms 'ends', 'joy', 'devote', and 'love', the answer is yes. Here are just a few examples: the hunting behaviour of wolves cannot be reasonably explained without appeal to their adoption of ends. They clearly have the end of getting food in mind, and they adjust their

---

[5] For reasons of space, I omit here a discussion of supernaturalism. Whether a supernaturalist view will allow for animal lives to be meaningful depends on what relationship between the supernatural and animals one's theology posits, and what relationship is required for meaning. For an overview and critique of supernaturalist theories, see Metz (2013, 77–160).

[6] The term 'attitudes' here is used broadly to include affective, conative, and cognitive states.

behaviour in different circumstances to achieve this end. They also seem to weigh the value of achieving this end against the importance of other ends when making decisions about where and how far to travel for food, whether and how to attack prey in a particular situation, and so on (Mech et al. 2015, 1–9). Wolves and elephants appear to feel joy, most notably when being reunited with members of their pack. The intensity, frequency, and persistence of play behaviour over the lifetime of many animals is also difficult to explain without appealing to the fact that they experience joy in it (Bekoff 2000, 865; Masson and McCarthy 1995, 111–132). Elephants are famous for their loving devotion to one another; they make enormous sacrifices to help injured members of their pack and display grief over the death of a pack member, evidence of a kind of loving devotion that one also sees in humans (Bates et al. 2008b). The evidence for the presence of these states in animals is not merely anecdotal or observational: neurobiological, physiological, and evolutionary data suggest that these mental states are not unique to humans (Bekoff 2000).

Of course, one might object that even if animals can pursue ends, feel joy, and devote themselves to things they love, they cannot do it to the degree or in the way that produces meaning. At least in the cases of ends or sources of joy, some further qualifications do seem warranted. I pursue many ends (getting the laundry done, raising happy and decent children, keeping my books arranged alphabetically on my bookshelf), not all of which seem to qualify as sources of meaning in my life. I likewise find joy in small things (hummingbirds, the smell of a freshly sharpened pencil) that—at least considered alone—should probably not be counted as sources of meaning in my life. (Loving devotion does not seem to have the same problem; people do not seem to take this attitude towards minor things.) Some subjectivists have proposed further qualifications so as to include only the right kind of subjective attitudes as determinants of meaning. William James (1977, 656), for example, argues that meaning is only present when the relevant subjective states are accompanied by an ideal of how to live, which he understands as something that must be 'intellectually conceived' and 'novel'. While animals do seem to have higher-order purposes and deeper sources of joy, it is not clear that they have ideals of the kind James describes. Such ideals, at least as 'intellectually conceived', seem as though they might require a specific kind of conscious metacognition: a conscious awareness of general facts about how one does or might live. There is not clear evidence that any animals have this ability.[7]

The cost of restricting the class of subjective states that confer meaning, of course, is that fewer people will turn out to have such states. Requiring, as James does, that a person's subjective states be accompanied by a novel, intellectually conceived ideal of how to live rules out many human lives as meaningful. If a person lives a life full of projects she works to advance and relationships she cares about, and these projects and relationships make her life a joyful and fulfilling one, it's not clear we should say that her

---

[7] Research about animal metacognition is ongoing, however. For discussion, see Smith (2009) and Kornell (2009).

life is without meaning because she never took up, as an intellectual matter, the question of how to live. Many people do not reflect on such questions, sometimes because they consider it useless to do so, other times because it never occurs to them to ask questions at this level of generality. A Jamesian might respond that such people could still possess the relevant ideal implicitly, or subconsciously. If the ideal needn't be conscious but merely operative in one's life, however, it's not clear why elephants wouldn't also count as having it.[8]

The final type of subjective view to consider is the narrative view.[9] On a narrative view, meaning in one's life is determined by the narrative that makes sense of that life (Kauppinen 2012; Wong 2008). Whether or not animals can have meaning in their lives thus depends on whether there can be narratives that make sense of their lives. Wai-hung Wong (2008, 131) argues that 'lower animals' cannot have meaning in their lives, since biographies require autobiographies, and autobiographies require self-awareness. Of course, if biographies did not require autobiographies—if there could be a meaning-making story about one's life that was not constructed by oneself—then there would be room for meaning in animal lives even if they do not have the ability to write that story. Indeed, from 'Seabiscuit' to 'Hachi', the film industry seems to provide ample evidence that biographies of animals are possible even in the absence of autobiographies.[10] If one needn't be the author of the narrative that makes sense of one's life, then many animals would be able to meet this requirement for meaning in life.

Even if narratives do require a first-person narrator, however, at least some cognitively sophisticated, emotionally complex, social animals may well be capable of the necessary degree of autobiographical self-understanding, a possibility that Wong seems to leave open by ruling out only 'lower animals'. Animals who are long-lived and have good memories, such as elephants, or those who have complex and temporally extended social interactions, such as gorillas, may well have a sense of who they are in the context of their social group (their social identity), and how they got this way. Animals that stay with and raise their young for long periods of time, such as orangutans, might need such an ability in order to keep track of the development of their young, and their relationship with their young, over time. Animals that transmit knowledge or skill through teaching might similarly need to keep track of what has been taught and what has been

---

[8] In this section, I omit discussion of intersubjectivism of the kind argued for by Stephen Darwall (1983, 164–166). Darwall claims that for something to be a meaningful aspect of one's life, one must see it as having intersubjective worth, i.e. value as seen from the intersubjective standpoint (a perspective available to all members of a valuing community) that rests on an 'intersubjective agreement of preferences' when fully appreciated from that standpoint. This is a much more difficult standard for non-human animals to meet. Their ability to do so would depend on whether they have cognitive access to an intersubjective standpoint and whether they can regard things as having value from that standpoint.

[9] Narrative views are difficult to categorize as subjective, objective, or hybrid, but all seem to require a subjective element: the subjectivity needed for constructing a narrative. Depending on the other elements that are seen as required for narrative, however, particular narrative views might be better thought of as intersubjective or hybrid. See Wong (2008, 136) for discussion.

[10] See also Hauskeller (2019, 13), discussing Strawson (2004) and Kauppinen (2012).

learned. All of these may be understandings of the world and one's place in it that arguably rise to the level of narrative, which fundamentally concerns using facts about past events to determine the significance of present events, imposing a kind of coherence that makes sense of one's history and affects one's understanding of the present and future (Kauppinen 2012; Velleman 1991).

One might object that these abilities of animals are too rudimentary to produce narratives of the kind that confer meaning on life. The meaning in a person's life, one might argue, concerns that person's views about what she stands for as a person, how she contributes to the world, what she does that is worth doing. However, we must be careful of making the requirements for meaningful narrative too stringent. As with earlier views, the higher we set the bar for meaning in life, the fewer people are likely to reach it. Some people never reflect on the preceding questions, though they undoubtedly stand for things, contribute to the world, and do many things worth doing. Some people have a number of short stories about their lives, but never form them into a coherent overall narrative. And some people argue that coherence itself is overrated: that it invites fictionalizing, or that it overlooks the value of fractured or inconsistent aspects of one's identity (Anzaldúa 1987; Strawson 2004).

2.2. Objectivism

Objectivist views hold that whether or not meaning is present in a life, experience, or activity is fully determined by mind-independent facts about that life, experience, or activity. There are different views about what these mind-independent facts consist in. I will consider two such views here: consequentialism and perfectionism.

2.2.1. *Consequentialism*

On a consequentialist view, whether a life (or experience or activity therein) is meaningful depends on its effect on the world, i.e. on the consequences that it produces. Kurt Baier (1997, 58) has a view of this type, claiming that the meaning of a person's life is a matter of either the value of their life ('the good they have done to others') or the significance of their life ('the impact, whether for good or evil, which they have or are generally known to have made on others'). Kai Nielsen (1981, 157) makes a similar claim, saying that lives can be meaningful in virtue of containing 'things that are worthwhile doing, having or experiencing, things that bring joy, understanding, exhilaration or contentment to ourselves or others'. On this type of view, for animal lives to be meaningful, they only need to be able to produce the aforementioned consequences in the world. Perhaps for this reason, those who have argued for the inclusion of animal lives as bearers of meaning have often favoured a consequentialist standard. Duncan Purves and Nicolas Delon (2018), for example, argue that animal lives can be meaningful because through their intentional action, they produce good consequences. Aaron Smuts (2013) and Joshua Thomas (2018) argue that causing good consequences, even in the absence of intentional action, is sufficient for meaning, with the result that animals can easily count as living meaningful lives.[11] A consequentialist standard for meaningfulness, because it considers animals primarily as causes of good consequences, is one that animals often have little difficulty meeting.

2.2.2. *Perfectionism*

On a perfectionist view, meaning in life is a matter of the perfection of one's nature, i.e. of developing the excellences that are relevant to the kind of thing one is.[12] Thaddeus Metz (2013, 212–215) discusses two such accounts: one from Quentin Q. Smith (1997), and one from Thomas Hurka (1993). (Metz argues that while the latter is sometimes treated as a theory of well-being, it is best understood as a theory of meaning in life.)[13] Perfectionism has mostly been discussed in the context of human beings, and thus is accompanied by a view of human nature. Meaning in human lives is understood as the development ('perfection') of those capacities or aspects of humans that are central to human nature (Hurka 1993, 3–4). Following Aristotle, perfectionists often regard the ability to reason as central to human nature, and thus they have claimed that the development of reasoning abilities is central to meaning in life (Aristotle 2000, I.7; Hurka 1993, 39). For this view to be applied to animals, animals must have a nature that can be perfected. If one does follow Aristotle, animals do have a nature, though one that is different from humans. On Aristotle's view, perception is central to the nature of lower animals, and locomotion is central to the nature of higher animals. As Hauskeller (2019, 22) points out, this means that animals can lead meaningful lives, though these lives won't be meaningful in the way that human lives are meaningful.

One might argue against this view, claiming that while animals have a *well-being* in virtue of having excellences relevant to their natures, meaning is something more than that: it is distinctive of the way that human lives can be perfected; it attaches to the perfection of humans' rational nature, a nature that is not shared with other animals. To make this argument work—to use it to exclude animal lives as meaningful—it must be true that humans' rational nature is not shared with other animals.

Do animals have a rational nature? The answer to this question depends on what we mean by 'rational nature'; 'reasoning' is a term used to describe a wide range of abilities. Scientific understandings of animal psychology have advanced considerably since Aristotle, and it is perhaps not surprising that abilities that fall into the categories of both practical reason (reasoning about what to do) and theoretical reason (reasoning about the way the world is) can be found outside of the human domain (Hurley and Nudds

---

[11] See Metz (2019) for a critical discussion of these positions. See also Milburn (2017) for a non-consequentialist approach to meaning in animal lives, and Bramble (2015) for a recent defense of a consequentialist approach to meaning in life that is not focused on animals.

[12] I discuss perfectionism here as a form of objectivism that is independent from other forms of objectivism. However, there are views about meaning in life that combine it with other forms of objectivism (Hurka 1993), with consequentialism (Metz (2013), with deontology, or even with subjectivism (e.g. Hauskeller 2019).

[13] Hurka (1993, 17–18) explicitly rejects the description of it as a theory of well-being. He describes it as an account of 'the good human life', rather than an account of well-being.

2006). In rejecting the claim that animals have a rational nature, Hurka (1993, 39) argues that distinctively human rationality is a matter of forming 'sophisticated beliefs and intentions, ones whose contents stretch across persons and times and that are arranged in complex hierarchies'; having 'explanatory beliefs' rather than merely 'isolated perceptual beliefs'; being able to 'grasp generalizations that apply across objects and times and [being able to] use them to explain diverse phenomena'; being able to 'envisage patterns of action that stretch through time or include other agents and [being able to] perform particular acts as a means to them'; and 'constructing hierarchies of ends, [in order to] engage in intelligent tool use and have complex interactions with others'. Animals, he claims, do not have these abilities.

While there is not room here to work through all of the cognitive abilities of animals and the evidence for them, some examples may suffice to cast doubt on Hurka's generalizations. Elephants seem to have sophisticated beliefs and intentions that are hierarchical and stretch across time and other creatures. They have complex ecological and topographical understandings of their environments, and they pursue different strategies for obtaining water, for example, in different circumstances. They adjust their strategies in light of new obstacles or difficulties (Byrne and Bates 2009). Wolves make complex calculations of costs and benefits in deciding where, when, and what to hunt, depending on their need for food, their environmental circumstances, the health of their pack, and the type of prey they are likely to find in different places at different times. Wolf pups learn general hunting strategies by watching older members of their pack hunt, strategies that they then apply to the particular circumstances they find themselves in once they are grown (Mech et al. 2015). These are clearly patterns of action that stretch through time and include other wolves. Chimpanzees, elephants, and New Caledonian crows use tools, teach their young how to use tools, and even develop new tools in order to solve new problems that they face (Bates et al. 2008a; McGrew 2010; Weir et al. 2002). Social animals generally manage complex social relationships both within their own group and with other groups. Elephants and chimpanzees are well-known for mourning their dead, sometimes falling into such a depression that they simply lie down and allow themselves to die (Goodall 2000). Some animals do seem to be motivated to act by moral considerations; they feel many of the same 'moral emotions' (empathy, compassion, spite, sense of fairness) as humans (Bekoff 2000; Rowlands and Monsó 2017).

Metz (2019) denies that animals can have meaning in their lives, not by appeal to broad types of cognition as Hurka does, but by describing goods that give meaning to human lives and by claiming that these goods are not present in animal lives. In criticizing those who argue that meaning can exist in animal lives, he says,

> Animals (or at least a very large majority of them) cannot, among a wide array of other things: love, where that involves a concept of another's self distinct from one's own; get an education; discover fundamental truths about themselves or their environment; compose poetry; appreciate music; tell jokes; do what it takes to become an Olympic athlete; avoid a repetitive existence; redeem bad parts of their

lives by making good come from them; strive to have their lives end on a high note. (Metz 2019, 407)

At least in the case of cognitively sophisticated, emotionally complex, social animals, this seems to get animals quite wrong. Some animals do have a concept of others—including those they love—as distinct from themselves; many are capable of learning; some have a sophisticated understanding of the causal structure of their physical environment; some seem to have an aesthetic sense; some play together (including games that involve pretence) and spend time with one another just because they enjoy doing so; many work to develop their physical skills, even if doing so won't gain them admission to the Olympics; many go to great lengths to avoid dullness and repetition, and they get depressed when they are unable to do so; some have long memories about past conflicts and act to make peace with former enemies—or in some cases, to exact revenge on them; some seem to understand death and find comfort in staying with a dying group member or in having their group members stay with them as they die (Bekoff 2007, 3, 70–77; Burn 2017; Kuczaj and Horback 2013; Masson and McCarthy 1995, 64–90; Watanabe 2013; Wemelsfelder 2005). This isn't exactly writing poetry or training for the Olympics, but then again, many humans can't do those things either. Of course the hedge in Metz's description matters. What he actually says is, 'Animals (or at least a large majority of them) cannot. . . .' However, the hedge turns out not to make a difference to Metz's final analysis. His conclusion is about animals, not about 'a large majority of them'. He says, 'if one wants to describe the lives of animals as "meaningful," I submit it should be deemed a sort that is not continuous with that conceptually ascribed to us' (Metz 2019, 407).[14]

On Metz's own positive theory of meaning in life, it is more straightforward to see how animal lives are excluded as meaningful. Since he considers it a conceptual fact about meaning in life that it is about, among other things, 'transcending one's animal nature' (2013, 34), and since his own view is that meaning requires use of our reason, where reason is defined as those capacities of ours that we do not share with any animals ('even higher ones such as chimpanzees'; 2013, 223), animal lives are ruled out as meaningful by definition. His view is thus not subject to empirical falsification in the way that Hurka's view is: if an animal can do it, on his view it doesn't count as reason. However, Metz also defends his view against the charge of being an 'overly intellectual theory' by pointing out that he understands 'rational nature' (a 'cognate term' of 'reason', on his view) 'to signify not merely cognition and intentional action, but also any "judgement-sensitive attitude"' (2013, 222–223; citing Scanlon 1998, 18–22). As the literature on animal

---

[14] Metz also claims that animal lives cannot have meaning because while we do normally act to make human lives meaningful for the sake of the humans in question, we do not do so for animals. This is a strange criterion by which to judge which lives can be meaningful; it threatens to render humans who are despised by others incapable of meaningful lives. Nevertheless, the claim about animals is false. Not only do we see this in the way that people care for their companion animals, but also in the approach to animal welfare taken by professionals. The Positive Animal Welfare approach and the commitment to cognitive enrichment for captive animals are two examples of this.

psychology makes clear, however, many animals do have judgement-sensitive attitudes, even if they do not have metacognitive beliefs about those attitudes (Rowlands and Monsó 2017). Metz's 'fundamentality theory' of meaning further requires that a person's reason be used in ways that 'orient rationality toward fundamental conditions of human existence' (2013, 235), conditions he summarizes as 'the true, the good, and the beautiful' (2013, 5). Animals are unlikely to orient their cognitive abilities towards the fundamental conditions of *human* existence, though it is unclear why they should. Their cognitive abilities do seem to be devoted to the fundamental conditions of their own existence: raising their young, caring for their elders, keeping the pack together, getting food, keeping safe from predators.[15] Moreover, unlike humans, animals are rarely distracted from these matters. While Metz defines rationality so as to prevent animals' cognitive abilities from counting as instances of rationality, accepting his definition in the current context would amount to assuming rather than proving that animals don't have what it takes to lead meaningful lives. To say this, of course, is not yet to answer the question of what ought to count as orienting their cognition toward the fundamental conditions of their own existence in the way required for meaning in life. As with earlier views, the higher our standards for doing so, the more likely animals are to be excluded from the possibility of leading meaningful lives, but the more people we will exclude from this possibility as well.

2.3. Hybrid Views

A hybrid view of meaning in life is one that contains both a subjective condition and an objective condition. The idea is that meaning in life comes from engaging in a certain way with something of value in the world, typically something outside of oneself. Joe Mintoff (2008, 67–70), for example, argues that meaning comes from a subjective attachment (ideally: knowing) to some objectively 'transcendent' thing (i.e. something not 'arbitrary, insignificant or impermanent'). John Kekes (1986) argues that meaning in life comes from the subjective will deeming significant some object that is objectively appropriate. On both of these views, taking the right kind of subjective attitude towards something is not enough to confer meaning; the object must also be one that has the right kind of objective worth.

The best-known contemporary hybrid view is probably that of Susan Wolf. Wolf distinguishes meaning in life from both well-being and moral goodness. Meaning, on her view, generates 'reasons of love', which are distinct from both reasons of self-interest and moral reasons. She defines meaning in life as a matter of 'loving something (or a number of things) worthy of love, and being able to engage with it (or them) in some

---

[15] Metz (2013, 239) briefly considers a view according to which meaning in human lives can come from orienting our rationality toward the fundamental conditions of animal life, but he does not pursue the idea further.

positive way' (Wolf 2010, 26). As she describes it, 'meaning in life arises when subjective attraction meets objective attractiveness'. On this view, the subjective condition for meaning is the 'subjective attraction' part. Wolf (2010, 9) says, 'a person's life can be meaningful only if she cares fairly deeply about some thing or things . . . as opposed to being bored by or alienated from most or all that she does'; she later describes the subjective condition as a matter of feeling fulfilment (Wolf 2010, 24). The objective condition is the 'objective attractiveness' part: the good in question must be worthy in the sense that it 'contributes to or connects with something the value of which has its source in something outside the subject' (2010, 20). Finally, these two conditions need to be 'suitably linked' (2010, 20): what makes the object worthy of love must be part of what one cares about in engaging with it (2010, 21).

On Wolf's view, whether animals can have meaning in their lives depends on whether they can satisfy the subjective condition and do so in a way that is 'suitably linked' to the objective condition. (The objective condition is not difficult to meet; many animals' projects and attachments take as their objects things that are worthy of love. Even if one thinks that only humans and their welfare are worthy of love, one can find many animals who care for humans and act to improve human welfare.) Wolf argues that fulfilment, the subjective condition, must consist of more than just pleasure; one must additionally 'find [the object that is meaningful] such as to be characterizable in terms that would portray it as (objectively) good' (2010, 24). Notice that this isn't a requirement that one *characterize* the object in these terms, nor that one have a *belief* that it is characterizable as such, but rather that one find it such as to be characterizable in these terms. Much depends on how we are to understand 'find' and 'such as to be characterizable'. If an alpha wolf decides to move the pack into new territory, a risky move that will probably involve suffering but will ensure the survival of the pack, one might say that the wolf finds the pack's survival to be a good thing. This seems to be a case of the wolf finding the pack's survival such as to be characterizable in certain terms ('a good thing'; 'worth ensuring') that would portray it as objectively valuable. How different is this from an unreflective person who cares for her children, and sees this as worth doing, but never asks whether it is (or could be characterized as) objectively good? Wolf does want to allow that people who never think about whether their lives are meaningful or whether their projects are objectively good can still have meaningful lives (2010, 31), and she describes the feeling of being connected to something of independent value as not requiring a desire for our lives to be so connected, and as coming from our 'social nature' (2010, 29). This suggests an understanding of the subjective condition that cognitively sophisticated, emotionally complex, social animals might be able to meet. That said, if finding something such as to be characterizable in a certain way means (or includes) thinking of it as characterizable-in-these-terms, then perhaps creatures without the concept of characterizability could not find things 'such as to be characterizable' in one way or another. On that view, however, any humans who do not possess the concept of characterizability would also not be able to have meaning in their lives.

3. Discussion

Three general aspects of the views of meaning discussed here are worth noting. First, in many cases we see that more restrictive views of meaning—those that require, for example, that what is meaningful involve the use of certain forms of reasoning or be accompanied by an intellectually conceived ideal—rule out the possibility of meaning in animal lives, but also rule it out in many human lives. Such views have the consequence that unreflective humans do not lead meaningful lives and that goods that aren't objects of reflection (directly or indirectly) are not sources of meaning.

Second, we might worry that there is also a substantive bias in these views. Perhaps non-coincidentally, they leave us with a view of meaning in life that privileges goods and abilities that philosophers tend to care most about: reasoning, reflection, and a kind of engagement with the world that connects us up with fundamental facts about the good, the true, and the beautiful. (Mintoff [2008, 76–77] is particularly explicit about this judgement: he claims that the best way to a meaningful life is to live a life of 'cultivated leisure', exemplified by a life of philosophical contemplation.) On a view that privileges reason in this way, a mother nursing her child is not a meaningful experience for the mother but rather a mere pleasure until it engages with her reasoning. The same can be said for other 'mere pleasures': a gastronome tasting a superlative meal, a long-separated couple embracing, a child feeling comfort in his parents' arms. On such views, the feelings in these experiences alone are not enough to make them meaningful; they must be taken up rationally in some way in order to be sources of meaning. Of course, there is much to be said about how we should understand the relationship between the cognitive and the affective or conative aspects of our experiences; there is not room for a full analysis of this issue here. But for some theorists about meaning in life, a kind of rational element is required for something to count as a source of meaning. One might worry that this over-intellectualizes our understanding of meaning in life.[16]

Related to this is a third aspect worth noting. Some views openly aim to distinguish humans from other animals and locate meaning in distinctively human capabilities. Metz and Hurka are the most explicit about this strategy, claiming not only that animals do not have meaning in their lives, but also that meaning in human lives comes from our 'rational nature' rather than our 'animal nature'. Calling those parts of ourselves that don't involve reasoning our 'animal nature', however, invites a kind of careless identification between *our* 'animal nature' and the nature of actual animals: as if animals were not rational, but merely motivated by an attraction to pleasure and an aversion to pain; as if they were feelers but not thinkers, bodies but not minds. This, of course, gets animals quite wrong. Distinguishing our 'animal nature' from our 'rational nature' and identifying meaning in life with the latter also have a further cost: this renders

---

[16] Metz (2013, 193) criticizes Hurka's view for being overly narrow in this way, though I argue in the following that his own view suffers from the same type of problem.

unintelligible people who find great meaning in what they have in common with other creatures in the world rather than in what distinguishes them from those creatures. A feeling of kinship with other forms of life, a sense of continuity with the natural world rather than transcendence over it, is what many people find to be one of the deepest sources of meaning in their lives.

There are two general lessons we might take away from this survey. First, in thinking about whether animal lives can be meaningful, it is important to look carefully at what animal lives are actually like, rather than relying on vague or outdated notions of humans as distinctively rational. Second, in thinking about meaning in life, we should think about the full range of sources of meaning in a wide variety of lives: not just making scientific a discovery or creating a great work of art, but also nursing an infant, tending a garden, watching the spring arrive after a long winter, getting to play a role—however small—in the peculiar story of life on earth.[17]

Challenging human-centredness can allow us to take a broader perspective on what is, and could be, meaningful in one's life and in the lives of others. As I have argued here, sources of meaning are not limited to human beings, and thinking about our relations with the broader natural world might allow broader understanding of the sources of meaning in life. Moreover, our thinking about meaning in life should not presuppose that all meaning must be meaning-to-humans. Depending on how we understand what meaning in life is, ours might not be the only lives that can be meaningful.[18]

References

Anzaldúa, Gloria. 1987. *Borderlands: The New Mestiza = La Frontera*. San Francisco: Aunt Lute Books.
Aristotle. 2000. *Nicomachean Ethics*, trans. Roger Crisp. Cambridge: Cambridge University Press.
Ayer, A. J. 1990. *The Meaning of Life*. New York: Scribner's.
Baier, Kurt. 1997. *Problems of Life and Death: A Humanist Perspective*. Amherst, NY: Prometheus Books.
Bates, Lucy A., Joyce H. Poole, and Richard W. Byrne. 2008a. 'Elephant Cognition'. *Current Biology* 18(13): R544–R46.
Bates, Lucy A., et al. 2008b. 'Do Elephants Show Empathy?' *Journal of Consciousness Studies* 15 (10–11): 204–225.

---

[17] This, I take it, is the lesson of the contemporary moves toward broader accounts of meaning in life. If meaning in life were thought of as something achieved only by the Da Vincis and Mother Teresas of the world, it would be difficult to explain why so many ordinary people seek meaning in their lives and think of their activities, experiences, and lives as meaningful, even in cases where they know that their lives will almost surely not contain any such great accomplishments. It would be wiser for philosophers to take such views about meaning seriously and incorporate them into the reflective equilibrium used for theory choice than to write them off as cases of widespread delusion.

[18] I wish to thank two anonymous reviewers for their critical commentary on earlier versions of this chapter and Iddo Landau for his careful and helpful comments throughout the editorial process.

Bekoff, Marc. 2000. 'Animal Emotions: Exploring Passionate Natures'. *BioScience* 50(10): 861–870.
Bekoff, Marc. 2007. *The Emotional Lives of Animals*. Novato, CA: New World Library.
Bramble, Ben. 2015. 'Consequentialism about Meaning in Life'. *Utilitas* 27(4): 445–459.
Burn, Charlotte C. 2017. 'Bestial Boredom: A Biological Perspective on Animal Boredom and Suggestions for Its Scientific Investigation'. *Animal Behaviour* 130: 141–151.
Byrne, Richard W., and Lucy A. Bates. 2009. 'Elephant Cognition in Primate Perspective'. *Comparative Cognition & Behavior Reviews* 4: 65–79.
Craig, William Lane. 2000. 'The Absurdity of Life without God'. In *The Meaning of Life*, ed. E. D. Klemke, 40–56. Oxford: Oxford University Press.
Darwall, Stephen. 1983. *Impartial Reason*. Ithaca, NY: Cornell University Press.
Frankfurt, Harry. 2002 'Reply to Susan Wolf'. In *Coutours of Agency: Essays on Themes from Harry Frankfurt*, eds. Sarah Buss and Lee Overton, 245–252. Cambridge, MA: MIT Press.
Goodall, Jane. 2000. 'A Sorrow beyond Tears'. In *The Smile of a Dolphin: Remarkable Accounts of Animal Emotions*, ed. Marc Bekoff, 140. New York: Discovery Books,.
Haidt, Jonathan. 2010. 'Finding Meaning in Vital Engagement and Good Hives'. In *Meaning in Life and Why it Matters*, ed. Susan Wolf, 92–101. Princeton, NJ: Princeton University Press.
Hauskeller, Michael. 2019. 'Living like a Dog'. *Between the Species* 23(1): 1–29.
Hurka, Thomas. 1993. *Perfectionism*. Oxford: Oxford University Press.
Hurley, Susan, and Matthew Nudds. 2006. 'The Questions of Animal Rationality: Theory and Evidence'. In *Rational Animals?*, ed. Susan Hurley and Matthew Nudds, 1–83. Oxford: Oxford University Press.
James, William. 1977. 'What Makes a Life Significant'. In *The Writings of William James: A Comprehensive Edition*, ed. John J. McDermott, 645–660. Chicago: University of Chicago Press.
Kauppinen, Antti. 2012. 'Meaningfulness and Time'. *Philosophy and Phenomenological Research* 84(2): 345–377.
Kekes, John. 1986. 'The Informed Will and the Meaning of Life'. *Philosophy and Phenomenological Research* 47(1): 75–90.
Klemke, E. D. 2000. 'Living without Appeal: An Affirmative Philosophy of Life'. In *The Meaning of Life*, ed. E.D. Klemke, 2nd ed., 186–197. Oxford: Oxford University Press.
Kornell, Nate. 2009. 'Metacognition in Humans and Animals'. *Current Directions in Psychological Science* 18(1): 11–15.
Kuczaj, Stan A., II, and Kristina M. Horback. 2013. 'Play and Emotion'. In *Emotions of Animals and Humans: Comparative Perspectives* ed. Shigeru Watanabe and Stan Kuczaj, 87–112. Tokyo: Springer.
Landau, Iddo. 2017. *Finding Meaning in an Imperfect World*. Oxford: Oxford University Press.
Masson, Jeffrey Moussaieff, and Susan McCarthy. 1995. *When Elephants Weep: The Emotional Lives of Animals*. New York: Delacorte Press.
McGrew, William C. 2010 'Chimpanzee Technology'. *Science* 328(5978): 579–580.
Mech, David L., Douglas W. Smith, and Daniel R. MacNulty. 2015. *Wolves on the Hunt: The Behavior of Wolves Hunting Prey*. Chicago: University of Chicago Press.
Metz, Thaddeus. 2013. *Meaning in Life: An Analytic Study*. Oxford: Oxford University Press.
Metz, Thaddeus. 2019. 'Recent Work on the Meaning of 'Life's Meaning': Should We Change the Philosophical Discourse?' *Human Affairs* 29(4): 404–414.
Milburn, Josh. 2017. 'Robert Nozick on Nonhuman Animals: Rights, Value and the Meaning of Life'. In *Ethical and Political Approaches to Nonhuman Animal Issues*, ed. Andrew Woodhall and Gabriel Garmendia da Trindade, 97–120. Cham: Palgrave Macmillan.

Mintoff, Joe. 2008. 'Transcending Absurdity'. *Ratio* 21(1): 64–84.
Nagel, Thomas. 1986. *The View from Nowhere*. Oxford: Oxford University Press.
Nielsen, Kai. 1981. 'Death and the Meaning of Life'. In *The Meaning of Life*, ed. E. D. Klemke, 2nd ed, 153–159. Oxford: Oxford University Press.
Purves, Duncan, and Nicolas Delon. 2018. 'Meaning in the Lives of Humans and Other Animals'. *Philosophical Studies* 175(2): 317–338.
Rowlands, Marc, and Susana Monsó. 2017. 'Animals as Reflexive Thinkers: The Aponoian Paradigm'. In *Oxford Handbook of Animal Studies*, ed. Linda Kalof, 319–344. New York: Oxford University Press.
Scanlon, T. M. 1998. *What We Owe to Each Other*. Cambridge, MA: Belknap Press.
Smart, J. J. C. 1999. 'Meaning and Purpose'. *Philosophy Now* 24: 16.
Smith, J. David. 2009. 'The Study of Animal Metacognition'. *Trends in Cognitive Sciences* 13(9): 389–396.
Smith, Quentin. 1997. *Ethical and Religious Thought in Analytic Philosophy of Language*. New Haven, CT: Yale University Press.
Smuts, Aaron. 2013. 'The Good Cause Account of the Meaning of Life'. *Southern Journal of Philosophy* 51(4): 536–562.
Strawson, Galen. 2004. 'Against Narrativity'. *Ratio* 17(4): 428–452.
Thomas, Joshua Lewis. 2018. 'Can Only Human Lives Be Meaningful?' *Philosophical Papers* 47(2): 265–297.
Velleman, J. David. 1991. 'Well-Being and Time'. *Pacific Philosophical Quarterly* 72(1): 48–77.
Vogel, Steven. 2015. *Thinking like a Mall*. Cambridge, MA: MIT Press.
Watanabe, Shigeru. 2013. 'Animal Aesthetics from the Perspective of Comparative Cognition'. In *Emotions of Animals and Humans: Comparative Perspectives*, ed. Shigeru Watanabe and Stan Kuczaj, 129–162. Tokyo: Springer.
Weir, Alex A. S., Jackie Chappell, and Alex Kacelnik. 2002. 'Shaping of Hooks in New Caledonian Crows'. *Science* 297(9): 981.
Wemelsfelder, Francoise. 2005. 'Animal Boredom: Understanding the Tedium of Confined Lives'. In *Mental Health and Well-Being in Animals*, ed. Franklin D. McMillan, 79–91. Oxford: Blackwell.
Wolf, Susan. 2010. *Meaning in Life and Why It Matters*. Princeton, NJ: Princeton University Press.
Wong, Wai-hung. 2008. 'Meaningfulness and Identities'. *Ethical Theory and Moral Practice* 11(2): 123–148.

PART V

PHILOSOPHICAL PSYCHOLOGY AND MEANING IN LIFE

CHAPTER 21

THE EXPERIENCE OF MEANING

ANTTI KAUPPINEN

WHETHER our lives are meaningful or meaningless, we certainly sometimes *experience* them as being one or the other. Such experiences can take many different forms. Indeed, one of the questions I will address in this chapter is whether there is a unity to all the experiences that people are apt to describe in the language of meaning. And if there are different experiences of meaning, are some more important for philosophical purposes than others?

Let me start with a passage from a classic work of literature, Ivan Turgenev's 1862 novel *Fathers and Sons*. The speakers are the young widow Odintsova, and the nihilist student Bazarov, who is in love with her and is goading her to reveal her secrets. Here's how one of their discussions goes, beginning with Odintsova's frank confession:

> 'I am unhappy because... I have no desires, no passion for life. You look at me incredulously; you think that's said by an 'aristocrat', who is all in lace, and sitting in a velvet armchair. I don't conceal the fact: I love what you call comfort, and at the same time I have little desire to live. Explain that contradiction as best you can. [...]' Bazarov shook his head. 'You are in good health, independent, rich; what more would you have? What do you want?' 'What do I want', echoed Odintsova, and she sighed, 'I am very tired, I am old, I feel as if I have had a very long life. Yes, I am old', she added, softly drawing the ends of her lace over her bare arms. [...] Behind me I have already so many memories: my life in Petersburg, wealth, then poverty, then my father's death, marriage, then the inevitable tour in due order.... So many memories, and nothing to remember, and before me, before me—a long, long road, and no goal.... I have no wish to go on.' (chapter 17)[1]

---

[1] The quotations are all from Constance Garnett's translation, online at http://www.gutenberg.org/files/30723/30723-h/30723-h.htm.

Although it's never explicitly stated, it's quite clear in the novel that Countess Odintsova's problem is that she finds her life meaningless at the advanced age of twenty-nine. All her life, she has done what she was supposed to do, but the things she has done do not add up to anything—there's 'memories, but nothing to remember'. And looking ahead, there's no purpose to her activities, 'no goal'. As she goes on to say, she might find satisfaction if she could interest herself strongly in something, but she just can't. What's more, it's not just her own life that feels empty to her—sometimes when she comes out of her fragrant bath, she 'fall[s] to musing on the nothingness of life, the sorrow, the labour, the malice of it...' (chapter 16). In brief, she's disoriented, bored, demotivated, and perhaps on the verge of existential anxiety. And since like most people, she is hungry for meaning, she can't be happy, in spite of being in a comfortable position to enjoy any pleasure that money, status, and beauty can buy (Kauppinen 2013). For her to experience her life as meaningful, many things would have to change. As we'll see, it's becoming a kind of consensus view in psychology and philosophy that for the fullest kind of experience, she would need to feel that her choices make sense over time, that her actions have a larger purpose beyond the present, and that her existence matters beyond herself, at least to someone who matters to her.

1. Three Kinds of Experience of Meaning

While philosophers have understandably focused on the question of what it *is* and what it *takes* for our lives to be meaningful, the *experience* of meaning has been thematized in psychology in particular. It should therefore be fruitful to begin by looking at the different accounts in psychology.

While it is common for psychologists to say that they study meaningfulness or meaning in life or personal meaning, it is more accurate to describe their work as investigating the impact of various things on people's experience or sense of meaning, as well as correlations between the experience of meaning and other things. In recent years, psychologists working on these issues have made several attempts to clarify the object of their research. A tripartite classification of experiences of meaning has emerged in this literature. Here are some representative summaries:

> We define MIL [meaning in life] as the extent to which one's life is experienced as making sense, as being directed and motivated by valued goals, and as mattering in the world. (George and Park 2016, 206)
>
> Lives may be experienced as meaningful when they are felt to have significance beyond the trivial or momentary, to have purpose, or to have a coherence that transcends chaos. (King at al. 2006, 180)
>
> [W]e thus define meaning in life as emerging from the web of connections, interpretations, aspirations, and evaluations that make our experiences

comprehensible, direct our efforts toward desired futures, and provide a sense that
our lives matter and are worthwhile. (Martela and Steger 2016, 538)

These definitions are naturally read as saying that there are three components to a unified experience of meaning. But it is also clear that these experiences can and do come apart, as Frank Martela and Michael Steger (2016), in particular, rightly emphasize—you can find your life intelligible without finding it significant, for example. Perhaps we can say that no one *fully* experiences their life as being meaningful without all of them. (I'll come back to this later.)

The three main varieties that psychologists have focused on, then, are experiences of (1) *making sense*, or *intelligibility*, or *coherence*, which have to do with finding patterns and connections; (2) *purpose*, or orientation towards goals felt to be valuable; and (3) *significance* or *mattering*, or making a positive difference in the world. Psychologists recognize that these experiences have cognitive, motivational, and affective elements (Reker and Wong 2012, 435), but don't agree on what these elements are. I will next make my own proposal concerning what is involved in these different kinds of experience, drawing on philosophy as well as psychology.

2. Making Sense, Purpose and Resonance, and Significance

Making Sense

Many kinds of things can make sense or can fail to do so. Sentences, utterances, and gestures can be meaningful, and random strings of numbers meaningless. There might be distinctive experiences associated with meaning in this sense—think of the moment when it dawns on you what the perfectly grammatical English sentence 'Fish fish fish fish fish' says, or the bafflement that precedes the correct parsing—but they are not experiences of meaning in life, contrary to what psychologists sometimes suggest.[2] No one can seriously claim that you can't find *your life* meaningless as long as you get what people mean by what they say.

We might also say that an inane plot twist in a movie, or a young, healthy person suddenly dying of a stroke, doesn't make sense, or that going to a fancy restaurant to celebrate a victory does. In such cases, there is an expected *pattern* or a cultural script into which the events and actions either fit or don't. When things fit into an expected pattern, we can give a kind of an *explanation* for why things are as they are: she went into the restaurant to celebrate, because when people succeed in something important,

---

[2] For very broad uses of meaning-talk, see Baumeister (1991) and Thomas (2019).

they typically want to enjoy the good things in life and share the joy with friends. When psychologists talk about 'meaning-making', they often mean finding (real or imagined) patterns in our environment. For example, Steven Heine, Travis Proulx, and Kathleen Vohs say that people are 'meaning-makers, driven to make connections, find signals in noise, identify patterns, and establish associations in places where they may not inherently exist' (2006, 89).

However, there are two major reasons why we should distinguish sense-making in general from experiences of meaning in life. First, while some have found that even experiencing coherent rather than discordant perceptual stimuli is linked to increased sense of meaning in life, as measured by self-report (Heintzelman and King 2014), the connection is merely *causal*. Just as with symbols, I can find my environment intelligible without *thereby* finding *my own life* meaningful. For example, if I'm sitting on the couch watching a reality show on the TV, I certainly get the meaning of what is shown and said, and find my own activity intelligible as the sort of thing people in my culture are expected to engage in to relax, but none of this amounts to experiencing my own life as meaningful. To be sure, if my world doesn't make any sense to me, it's unlikely that my life will, but they are still two different things.

Second, it is arguably possible for me to find even my own life *intelligible* in the sense of fitting with expectations or forming recognizable patterns without yet experiencing it as meaningful in any way. Maybe it seems to me that the various things that make it up are related to each other, as might be expected in the light of my aims and cultural context. The things I do fit together nicely—they're mutually supportive and coherent, and my life isn't fragmented or incoherent (George and Park 2016). Perhaps, as Joshua Seachris (2009) and Helena de Bres (2018) have argued, I have come to see my life in this way by way of forming the right kind of self-narrative, by 'selecting, distilling, ordering, and unifying' my life's events in a story I tell myself and others, drawing on local conventions (de Bres 2018, 557; cf. Rosati 2013). Still, however, what I have done might not make sense to me. Countess Odintsova is not the only person who has done what she was supposed to do, and yet fail to see the *point* of it.

The problem with the thin sort of intelligibility linked to patterns and expectations is that not just any sort of explanation will do to make the *right kind* of sense. For example, if I don't value learning or whatever instrumental benefits college may offer, it *doesn't* make sense for me to go to college, even if it is perfectly *intelligible* to me and everyone else why someone like me—with my social background and high school grades, etc.—would go to college. For my life to properly make sense to me, I must regard my activities as contributing to or realizing something I consider *desirable* or worthwhile, as Elizabeth Anscombe (1957, 70 ff.) emphasized. Philosophers of action talk here about a *rationalizing explanation*, which is a source of a distinctive kind of understanding.[3] For example, it makes sense for me to go to college if I regard learning as valuable for its own

---

[3] See e.g. Davidson (1963) and O'Brien (2019).

sake, and it makes sense for me to study at the library, given that I'm a student. There is something that *justifies* and doesn't merely causally explain what I do. When the justification takes the form of showing later actions as worthwhile in the light of earlier ones (or vice versa), it merits being called a *narrative justification*. This is important to emphasize, since it makes clear why even meaning-in-life-as-sense-making is not the same kind of thing as intelligibility in general.[4]

What if my life doesn't make sense to me? The opposite of meaning as intelligibility is *disorientation*—I don't know what my life is about, or why I do what I do. I can't answer the question 'Why am I doing this/have done these things?' to my own satisfaction. Since much of what we do makes sense in the light of cultural frameworks, major changes in cultural circumstances can bring about large-scale disorientation. Consider here Jonathan Lear's (2008) description of what happened to the members of Crow nation, who were nomadic hunters and warriors until 'the buffalo went away' and they were forced to live on a reservation in the late nineteenth century. As a result, the framework of meanings in the light of which people's aspirations and individual actions made sense collapsed.[5] Where one once had to be either a warrior or a coward, neither was now a live option—one could neither be a success nor a failure by the traditional yardsticks. It's no wonder if the surviving Crow experienced a sense of meaninglessness. They were at a loss about how to proceed in a way that would be a sensible continuation of what they had done before—they struggled to find a narrative justification. On an individual level, the loss of a loved one may cause similar disorientation—suddenly, it no longer makes sense for me to go on as before, since the person for whose sake I did things is no longer there.

Purpose and Resonance

When psychologists talk about having *purpose* in life, they mean something like 'a sense of core goals, direction in life, and enthusiasm regarding the future' (George and Park 2013, 371). When we feel like our lives have purpose (or, sometimes, *a* purpose), we feel like there is some goal in the light of which we have reason to go on and do what serves the realization of that goal. The thought is something like 'I am here to X, and I'm going to X'. Clearly, the aims that give rise to this kind of feeling are at a high level in the hierarchy of our aims—they are ends to which many other things we do are means, like taking care of a youth sports team or guarding a border. This is

---

[4] When Martela and Steger (2016, 536) describe intelligibility as 'descriptive' and 'value-neutral', they overlook this difference between the kind of intelligibility involved in our lives making sense to us and the intelligibility of predictable patterns.

[5] As Lear puts it, in earlier times '[e]very meal was in effect the cooking-of-a-meal-so-that-those-who-ate-it-would-be-healthy-to-hunt-and-fight. At a certain point, though, hunting and fighting have become impossible. Indeed, they cease to be intelligible acts' (2006, 40).

unquestionably an experience of meaning in life in the sense that philosophers, too, are interested in.

Sense of purpose is most clearly manifest in motivation, in feeling energetic and optimistic in pursuit of our goals, in feelings of flow, and in the belief that our aims give reasons for actions that serve them. As Susan Wolf puts it, we are 'gripped, excited, interested, and engaged' (2010, 9). Cheshire Calhoun (2018) highlights the experience of what I'll call *resonance* that seems to be closely related to purpose, but nevertheless distinct. She emphasizes that we spend a lot of time doing things that we feel we *have to* do or do for the sake of doing something rather than nothing (2018, 15ff.). This includes activities that we find purposeful, if we'd rather skip them. In what I call the *resonance* sense, we experience our activities as meaningful only when we do things that we regard as worthwhile to include in our lives *for their own sake*. Calhoun emphasizes that they need not be life-shaping projects or commitments, but simply ways of spending time we regard ourselves as having personal reason to engage in for their own sake—what resonates with us may be watching a movie or carving a statue of a god. We might say that such activities are from our personal perspective purposeful in a *self-justifying* way, not in terms of a future goal.

In addition to these feelings that are linked to specific aims and values we have, there is also a much deeper kind of feeling that is also plausibly related to finding life purposeful. It is what Matthew Ratcliffe (2013) calls radical hope, a species of what he labels 'existential feeling'. Such feelings, often vague and unnamed, are not directed towards particular objects but towards kinds of *possibilities* that matter to us, and thus shape how the world appears to us. So when I have the attitude of radical hope, I experience it as possible to do *something* that matters, independently of the particular purposes I now happen to have. Using a different language for what is likely the same phenomenon, Calhoun talks about *taking a globally motivating interest* in one's future, which is manifest in having *basal hope* (2018, 52).

One reason to focus on existential feelings in this context is that they play an important role in relevant experiences of meaninglessness. This is manifest in at least some cases of depression. As Ratcliffe describes it, for the depressed person, the horizon of possibilities surrounding objects and activities changes: 'What is lacking from the world of depression is not simply the anticipation and/or experience of pleasure, but a sense that there could be *meaningful* change, change of a kind that matters' (Ratcliffe 2014, 66, emphasis in the original). It's not just that one thinks one will fail in one's aspirations, but that there's no point in aspiring to anything, since one's sense of the possibility of a better future has shrunk or vanished. This is, of course, an extreme case. One might lack a sense of purpose with respect to a particular area or aim—for example, going to school might seem pointless to someone who at the same time is excited about playing in a band. Experiences of meaninglessness would then be localized. A different sort of local experience of *boredom* may result when one does something *only* as a means to an end, even a valued end, or only because one has to kill time for one reason or another, rather than as a way of engaging positively with what resonates with one (Calhoun 2018, 136–144).

Significance

Experiences of *significance* have traditionally been central to philosophical accounts of meaning in (or 'of') life. As the term is used in this context, significance refers to making a positive difference beyond one's own life. Sometimes this is put in terms of 'connecting to something larger', but as many have observed, what is at issue is rather a sense of contributing to some *value* beyond ourselves (Nozick 1981, 611; Wolf 2010, Martela 2017).[6] And not just any value, either—when we think of our lives as significant, we think of ourselves as promoting or realizing some value that is both *final* (that is, not valuable merely as a means to something else) and *objective* (that is, not just something we happen to value, but which anyone has reason to value). It is also common to think that significance requires the value to be *lasting* beyond the individual moment or even life. What's more, for me to feel that *my* life is significant, I must also think that it matters that *I* am doing it, and not someone else. This explains why *creative* achievements tend to generate experiences of significance—after all, insofar as what I do is creative, there's something unique and irreplaceable to my contribution.[7]

Further, I don't get a sense of significance if I bring something good about by accident or without particular effort. For example, if I lose control of my car and end up killing a dictator, thus improving millions of lives, it's not something that gives me comfort if I worry about the point of my existence. Thus, a sense of significance is also associated with acting purposefully and with the non-trivial exercise of our capacities. And finally, we don't find our activities as personally meaningful if we are *alienated* from what we do—if our heart isn't in it, however valuable the outcome may be. So I must feel I can be who I really am while doing something that has value. This is one reason why close personal relationships are typically so important to the experience of meaning. When I open up to another person and feel that they cherish what we do together and value me as the unique person I am, I feel that I really matter to someone whom I think really matters. This is a way to make a contribution to value beyond the self, even if it isn't world-historical significance. Perhaps we could sum up these observations by saying that experienced significance involves thinking that our authentic self is expressed by actions that non-accidentally promote or realize something of value beyond our own good.

What is it to *experience* my life or activities as being significant beyond my own good? I believe that it is not in the first instance to *believe* that one is making a positive difference. Indeed, we might even believe that our lives are significant without *experiencing* that they are. That's because the experience consists in the first instance of emotions

---

[6] Or, perhaps, beyond our *animal* self, as Thaddeus Metz (2013, 29) has it—maybe displaying extraordinary integrity, say, is enough to warrant a sense of significance.

[7] On creative achievements, see Kauppinen (forthcoming). The creativity in question need not be artistic, of course—it could be a new way of delivering breech babies, for example. Also, it may be worth emphasizing that evidently experiences of significance can also result from non-creative grunt work that someone just has to do, as long as we think it is genuinely worth doing.

that construe our activities as contributing to objective value. They include feelings of *fulfilment* and *pride*. Feelings of fulfilment and gratification seem to be associated especially with meaningful relationships, in which we find our worth affirmed by people who matter to us. Pride, more specifically *agential* pride in contrast to merely associative pride, has to do with what we regard as praiseworthy achievements.[8] The thought involved in this kind of pride is that what we've done or are doing meets or exceeds some demanding standards for something of objective value in virtue of exercising our capacities, so that we are praiseworthy for what we've done (and not merely lucky to have brought about something good) (Kauppinen 2017). In having such feelings when we contemplate our lives as a whole or its defining moments, then, we affectively construe our lives as having meaning in the sense of significance.

What about experiences of lacking significance? As with purpose, it's useful to distinguish here between local and global experiences. In the local case, you feel that what you actually do doesn't contribute to anything of objective value or doesn't matter to anyone who matters, either because you fail to realize your goals, or you think that your goals themselves are not worthwhile. This is consistent with thinking that there are other activities that would be significant, and that other people are doing significant things. In the latter case, the feeling involved in the experience could be agential shame or other feelings of failure—you're the one wasting their life while others do great things. In the global case, in contrast, the experience is a kind of existential feeling involving the thought that it's not even *possible* for your activities to contribute to objective value or even to the good of someone who genuinely matters, because there *is* no such thing or person. This is the kind of *Angst* or dread or generalized sense of futility that is a staple of what we sometimes call existential crises. You think of the vastness of space and time and the barely noticeable role that you play in the general scheme of things—from the perspective of the universe as a whole, what difference would it make if you had never existed? And what's more, it's not just you who are mortal, but also everyone you care about, so all your actions will soon enough vanish without a trace.

What these thoughts of cosmic or historical insignificance do is best understood in terms of their impact on the value of our activities: whatever we do, we can't bring about anything whose value would be important enough in the grand scheme of things to justify our existence. A shortcut to the same conclusion is embracing value nihilism, the thought that nothing is objectively valuable, which often seems to go together with the thought that there is no divine or supernatural order in which we have a place. Conversely, if we think we can achieve something of sufficient objective or at least intersubjective value in spite of our finitude, existential Angst is reduced—indeed, according

---

[8] Psychologists like Jessica Tracy and Richard Robins (2007) further distinguish between what they call 'hubristic' pride, which involves the thought that the cause of the achievement is something stable and uncontrollable within us, like some innate ability, and 'authentic' pride, which involves the thought that it is something specific that is under direct voluntary control, such as effort.

to the Terror Management Theory in psychology, it is to avoid such experiences that we construct and subscribe to cultural worldviews such as religions that promise us a place at the centre of the grand view of things (Greenberg and Arndt 2012).

3. Is There a Unity to Experiences of Meaning?

Table 21.1 summarizes my proposal of what the three distinct kinds of experience of meaning in life amount to.

These experiences can and frequently do come apart. Yet it is also easy enough to see links between them. The first thing to emphasize is that all of these experiences have to do with *agency*. Experiences of meaning in life result from how we view the past, present, and future exercises of our own agency. In this respect, they contrast with, say, pleasure, with respect to which we may be purely passive. Second, they all involve some sort of *positive evaluation* of our activity. When our activities make sense to us, we regard our investment as somehow justified in the light of our personal narrative. When they're purposeful, they serve a major end we have. And when we see them as significant, they make something beyond our lives better.

Third, I've tried to describe some of the central emotions and moods involved in these experiences, and it's clear that they are distinct from each other. Still, since affective states plausibly have several components, what I've said leaves it possible that 'though distinct in some ways, experiences of coherence, purpose, and significance may share the same feeling state', as Samantha Heintzelman and Laura King put it (2014, 162). The question of whether there is such a *quale* is very difficult to settle, as we might expect,

Table 21.1 Experiences of Meaning and Meaninglessness

Experience Type	Dimension: Sense-Making: Contribution to a Subjectively Desirable Pattern	Purpose and Resonance: Contribution to Aims	Significance: Contribution to Value beyond the Self
Experience of meaning	Belief in or feeling of narrative justification or rationalizing explanation	Enthusiastic future- or present-oriented motivation and seeing aims as source of reasons against the background of basal hope	Feelings of fulfilment and pride, beliefs about objective or intersubjective value of efforts
Experience of meaninglessness	Disorientation	Demotivation, boredom, depression	Angst, feelings of failure

given that there's no agreement even on whether there is a single sensation common to all pleasurable experiences (Feldman 2004; Bramble 2013). In any case, experiences of meaning involve *positive feelings*. It is therefore unsurprising that rating well on one or another self-report scale of meaning in life is linked with high levels of life satisfaction, positive affect and physical health, and low levels of depression, among other things (for a summary, see Steger 2018).

One of the key questions that the plurality of experiences of meaning raises is how they are related to each other and whether some are more fundamental than others. My suggestion is that there is indeed a kind of hierarchy among them, at least insofar as we're rational. Roughly, the picture is as follows. When we are immersed in our ordinary activities, they *make sense* to us by default. What we do fits together with other things we do and have done, and is justified by this connection. But occasionally we take a step back from this immersion, perhaps because something goes wrong or we can't fit everything together. We're then led to ask about the bigger *purpose* of what we do—how they relate to what we aspire to in our lives. As Will Crescioni and Roy Baumeister put it, the sort of 'existentially meaningful life stories' in the light of which our lives make sense 'depict actions and decisions as following from important, stable values and contributing to the fulfillment of one or more crucial goals' (2013, 3). There seems to be a kind of negative dependence of sense-making on purpose: if we don't see our activities as serving some larger purpose, once the issue has been thematized for us, they don't make sense to us.

The same sort of dialectic then repeats itself on a higher level. Normally, even if we're led to ask about larger purposes, once we are clear on how what we do serves a purpose or resonates in itself with our values, we experience our lives as meaningful. But it is also possible that our purposes turn out to conflict, or doubts about them are raised in some other way. Then we take a further step back and reflect on those purposes themselves. Are they really worth the investment we're making in them? Is there sufficient value in bringing them about, either for the world in general or for someone who matters to us? Do they express who we really are? Again, if we answer in the negative, the feelings echo down the chain: if I experience what I do as having insufficient significance, I'm demotivated or depressed, and consequently it ceases to make sense to me.

According to this picture, then, there is a sense in which experiences of significance are the most fundamental kind of experience of meaning. This is good news for philosophers, who have traditionally focused precisely on questions related to significance. If there is anything like *the* experience of meaning, it is the experience of the significance of our existence, in the light of which our particular projects appear as purposeful (and the activities we're engaged in resonate with us), and our lives make sense. Yet in another way, we can also say that experiences of sense-making are most fundamental, since they are part and parcel of our everyday activities, while feelings of significance tend to arise only on special occasions. We could hardly experience our lives as significant if we didn't also think that they make sense. So in different ways, both philosophers and psychologists have been getting their priorities right.

4. Conclusion

In this chapter, I have been drawing on philosophical and psychological literature to categorize and characterize three different kinds of experience of meaning in life: sense-making, purpose and resonance, and significance. They appear to be unified by focus on agency, positive evaluation, and positive affect. Their mutual dependence comes to light when we disengage from our ordinary immersion in activity, step by step.

The last question I want to broach concerns the implications of the *variety* of experiences of meaning for philosophical questions about meaning in life. One straightforward way in which the two might be connected is provided by the idea that for a life to *be* meaningful is for experiences of meaning to be *fitting* towards it (Kauppinen 2012). If we accept this idea, and also accept that there are *many* kinds of experience of meaning, it follows that our lives can be said to be meaningful in different ways—that is, when they *really* make sense, have a purpose or resonate with us, or have significance. This offers a possible way of reconciling competing views on what makes life meaningful. When Helena de Bres (2018) and Joshua Thomas (2019) say it is intelligibility that makes life meaningful, and Cheshire Calhoun (2018) says that it's activity we value for its own sake, and Susan Wolf (2010) and Thaddeus Metz (2013) say that it is something like subjective engagement with objective value or positive orientation of rationality towards the fundamental conditions of human existence, they could *all* be right about meaning, albeit in different senses. The remaining question, then, would be whether one of these ways of being meaningful is the most fundamental. This question can't be settled here, though given that it is significance that is called into question in paradigmatic existential crises and concerns, there's at least some reason to think that it is the philosophically most basic issue.[9]

References

Anscombe, Elizabeth. 1957. *Intention*. Oxford: Basil Blackwell.
Baumeister, Roy. 1991. *Meanings of Life*. New York: Guilford Press.
Bramble, Ben. 2013. 'The Distinctive Feeling Theory of Pleasure'. *Philosophical Studies* 162(2): 201–217.
Calhoun, Cheshire. 2018. *Doing Valuable Time: The Present, the Future, and Meaningful Living*. New York: Oxford University Press.
Crescioni, Will, and Roy Baumeister. 2012. 'The Four Needs for Meaning, the Value Gap, and How (and Whether) Society Can Fill the Void'. In *The Experience of Meaning in Life: Classical Perspectives, Emerging Themes, and Controversies*, ed. Joshua Hicks and Clay Routledge, 3–16. Dordrecht: Springer.

---

[9] I'm grateful to Frank Martela for help in navigating the psychological literature and Lilian O'Brien for comments on an earlier draft.

Davidson, Donald. 1963. 'Actions, Reasons, and Causes'. *Journal of Philosophy* 60(23): 685–700.
de Bres, Helena. 2018. 'Narrative and Meaning in Life'. *Journal of Moral Philosophy* 15(5): 545–571.
Feldman, Fred. 2004. *Pleasure and the Good Life: Concerning the Nature, Varieties, and Plausibility of Hedonism*. Oxford: Clarendon Press.
George, Login, and Crystal Park. 2013. 'Are Meaning and Purpose Distinct? An Examination of Correlates and Predictors'. *Journal of Positive Psychology* 8: 365–375.
George, Login, and Crystal Park. 2016. 'Meaning in Life as Comprehension, Purpose, and Mattering: Toward Integration and New Research Questions'. *Review of General Psychology* 20(3): 205–220.
Greenberg, Jeff, and Jamie Arndt. 2012. 'Terror Management Theory'. In *Handbook of Theories of Social Psychology*, ed. P. M. Van Lange, A. W. Kruglanski and E. Higgins, Vol. 1, 398–415. Thousand Oaks, CA: Sage.
Heine, Steven, Travis Proulx, and Kathleen Vohs. 2006. 'The Meaning Maintenance Model: On the Coherence of Social Motivations'. *Personality and Social Psychology Review* 10(2): 88–110.
Heintzelman, Samantha, and Laura King. 2014. '(The Feeling of) Meaning-as-Information'. *Personality and Social Psychology Review* 18(2): 153–167.
Kauppinen, Antti. 2012. 'Meaningfulness and Time'. *Philosophy and Phenomenological Research* 84(2): 345–377.
Kauppinen, Antti. 2013. Meaning and Happiness. *Philosophical Topics* 41(1): 161–185.
Kauppinen, Antti. 2017. 'Pride, Achievement, and Purpose'. In *The Moral Psychology of Pride*, ed. Emma Gordon and Adam Carter, 169–189. Lanham, MD: Rowman & Littlefield.
Kauppinen, Antti. Forthcoming. 'Creativity, Spontaneity, and Merit'. In *Art and Philosophy*, ed. Alex King and Christy Mac Uidhir. Oxford: Oxford University Press.
King, L. A., J. A., Hicks, J. L., Krull, and A. K. Del Gaiso. 2006. 'Positive Affect and the Experience of Meaning in Life'. *Journal of Personality and Social Psychology* 90: 179–196.
Lear, Jonathan 2006. *Radical Hope: Ethics in the Face of Cultural Devastation*. Cambridge, MA: Harvard University Press.
Martela, Frank 2017. 'Meaningfulness as Contribution'. *Southern Journal of Philosophy* 55(2): 232–256.
Martela, Frank, and Michael Steger. 2016. 'The Three Meanings of Meaning in Life: Distinguishing Coherence, Purpose, and Significance'. *Journal of Positive Psychology* 11(5): 531–545.
Metz, Thaddeus. 2013. *Meaning in Life: An Analytic Study*. Oxford: Oxford University Press.
Nozick, Robert. 1981. *Philosophical Explanations*. Cambridge, MA: Harvard University Press.
O'Brien, Lilian. 2019. 'Action Explanation and Its Presuppositions'. *Canadian Journal of Philosophy* 49(1):123–146.
Ratcliffe, Matthew. 2013. 'What Is It to Lose Hope?' *Phenomenology and the Cognitive Sciences* 12(4): 597–614.
Ratcliffe, Matthew. 2014. *Experiences of Depression: A Study in Phenomenology*. Oxford: Oxford University Press.
Reker, G. T., and P. T. P. Wong. 2012. 'Personal Meaning in Life and Psychosocial Adaptation in the Later Years'. In *The Human Quest for Meaning: Theories, Research, and Applications*, ed. P. T. P. Wong, 433–456. New York: Routledge.
Rosati, Connie. 2013. 'The Story of a Life'. *Social Philosophy and Policy* 30(1–2): 21–50.
Seachris, Joshua. 2009. 'The Meaning of Life as Narrative: A New Proposal for Interpreting Philosophy's "Primary" Question'. *Philo* 12(1): 5–23.

Steger, Michael. 2018. 'Meaning and Well-Being'. In *Handbook of Well-Being*, ed. E. Diener, S. Oishi, and L. Tay. Salt Lake City, UT: DEF. DOI: nobascholar.com

Thomas, Joshua. 2019. 'Meaningfulness as Sensefulness'. *Philosophia* 47(5):1555–1577.

Tracy, Jessica, and Richard Robins. 2007. 'The Psychological Structure of Pride: A Tale of Two Facets'. *Journal of Personality and Social Psychology* 94: 516–530.

Wolf, Susan. 2010. *Meaning in Life and Why It Matters*. Princeton, NJ: Princeton University Press.

CHAPTER 22

DESIRE AND MEANING IN LIFE

Towards a Theory

NOMY ARPALY

1. INTRODUCTION

ONE theory that some young, beginning philosophy students, in their unearned world-weariness, find very attractive is called 'psychological hedonism'. This is the view that when we act, we always aim—either in a smart or in a stupid way—at maximizing pleasure for ourselves and minimizing our displeasure, a goal that I will refer to as 'improving one's Pleasure Balance'.

Conclusive arguments against psychological hedonism already exist,[1] and it is not my aim to add to them or summarize them. Instead, let us focus on the things people want *besides* a good Pleasure Balance. When talking to my students about hedonism, discussion soon turns to heroic altruistic acts, but I do my best to point out that non-hedonistic motivation occurs elsewhere as well. In addition to desiring the wellbeing of others, people also intrinsically want the victory of their sports teams, to fit in or to stick out, to please their parents or to enrage them, to break a Guinness record by building the world's biggest ball of twine, the demise of their enemies, and countless other things, and often they are willing to let their Pleasure Balance get worse for the sake of obtaining these things.

Here are three cases of this kind:

(1) *Endurance*. Joseba is an excellent endurance athlete. He spends much of his time training for ultra-marathons and so experiences severe pain quite often. His

---

[1] The most famous one is in Nozick (1974, 43).

passion is costly in a variety of other ways as well. He wins a race every few years, but his sport does not make him a millionaire or give him mainstream fame, and many people think he is 'crazy'. Still, Joseba is devoted to ultra-marathons. Finishing the races successfully, the occasional win, and the knowledge of what he can do are *worth* every moment of pain to him.

(2) *Parenthood.* Phirose is aware of the studies indicating that parents who are taking care of children do not tend to be any happier than people who do not have children. In fact, parents appear to experience, during the years in which they raise their children, more moments of misery and drudgery and fewer moments of pleasure than people in similar circumstances who do not have children. Phirose's intuition, based on his experience, aligns with the studies: 'Why am I not surprised?', he thinks, reviewing his years of child-rearing. Still, he says, if he were given another life, he would have children again, because for him the rewards of parenthood have been *worth* the displeasure (one should note that while good parenthood involves a lot of altruism, the choice to have children is, typically, not itself altruistic).

(3) *The Long Wait.* Marcia's favorite baseball team, the Boston Red Sox, went through decades in which it did not win the World Series. Still, Marcia had watched nearly all games, enduring endless mood swings and various forms of cruel heartbreak as a result. Her friends who do not care about baseball told her to try to stop being a fan as it had obviously done her more harm than good. Her friends who follow other teams teased her relentlessly. Then one day, finally, the team wins the Series. 'It was all *worth* it!', Marcia declares sincerely, 'now I can die in peace'. She does not change her judgement after the following baseball seasons turn out to be painful emotional roller coasters as well.

My introductory-level ethics students, charmed as they are by psychological hedonism, are quick to try to explain away these cases by pointing out that Joseba enjoys winning, Phirose does not deny that parenthood has its joys, and Marcia eventually experiences happiness made sweeter by the anguished wait. Hedonism, after all, does not deny that one can choose to endure some displeasure for the sake of a better Pleasure Balance, usually in the future. One might, for example, dislike exercising but exercise for the sake of the joys that being healthy to an old age can provide, as the agent predicts that they would outweigh the pain. Perhaps being an endurance athlete, raising children, and being the loyal fan of a team with mixed fortunes all involve moments, days, weeks, or months of incredible pleasure that simply *outweigh* the many years spent in displeasure. This, however, is implausible, and anyone taking on a grueling pursuit or encouraging an emotionally costly attachment in herself for the sake of this supposed ecstasy is bound to be bitterly disappointed long before accumulating Joseba's, Phirose's, or Marcia's rich experience with the respective things they are engaged with. Our brains only allow us a certain amount of pleasure in each moment, and it makes no biological sense to talk about a pleasure so intense that mere months of it somehow improve the agent's Pleasure Balance despite years of displeasure.

However, there do seem to be things that can make even a long stretch of disproportional displeasure, or downright suffering, *worthwhile* for a person. I think finding meaning in life is finding things that are *worth it* for you, in the same way that being an endurance athlete is 'worth it' for Joseba, being a parent is 'worth it' for Phirose, and being a Red Sox fan is 'worth it' for Marcia.

2. A Theory Sketched

My goal in this chapter is to sketch a way in which a thing being worthwhile for a person in this manner—and thus contributing to the meaningfulness of the person's life to that person—can be explained in terms of the person's desires. My sketch will have to draw, to some extent, on a theory of desire developed by Timothy Schroder (2004) and also summed up in a less technical way in Schroder's and my book *In Praise of Desire* (2014). There is of course no room in the chapter to argue for that theory. I'll have to do with showing how, given some tenets of our view of what desire is—hopefully not the *most* controversial ones—one can explain the idea of meaning in life in terms of desires and objects of desire. The resulting view, it will seem, has some things in common with theories, such as Harry Frankfurt's, that anchor meaning in life in what one cares about or loves, and some who would object to my view might still accept some versions of the claims I make here provided that they are put in terms of *caring* rather than of desiring (see Frankfurt 1982, 2004).[2] I, however, subscribe to the neo-Humean view that caring about something just is intrinsically desiring it, or, in some cases, intrinsically desiring its wellbeing.

Here, then, is the view I want to sketch. One desires a good Pleasure Balance, but there are things for which one has strong intrinsic desires such that one intrinsically desires them even at the price of making one's pleasure balance significantly worse. Things that a person desires this way, when they are present in her life, contribute meaning to her life, in the sense that they make her life more meaningful *to her*. A person's life is meaningful to that person to the extent that things are present in it, the presence of which increases the net satisfaction of her intrinsic desires even under conditions when it results in a significantly worse Pleasure Balance.

When saying that the objects of intrinsic desires can give your life meaning I mean to exclude one group of them—roughly, those that mice possess as much as humans. By saying that intrinsic desires which humans share with mice do not make their objects the sort of things that contribute meaning to an agent's life I mean to exclude our intrinsic desires, if such they be, for things like air, correct body temperature, the right amount of sugar in the blood, the right amount of water, and so on. These desires belong

---

[2] Frankfurt does seem to relate meaning to desire, in a more roundabout way that passes through the concept of caring.

with an older part of the brain which is not distinctly human, making their exclusion almost an Aristotelian move.

Some clarifications are in order.

Assumptions about Desire. When I speak of desires, I do not speak of urges, longings, or what philosophers call 'occurrent desires'. I speak of desires of the sort that one can have without experiencing them, as when one is fast asleep or overcome by an irrelevant emotion. If I tell you, for example, that Tim intrinsically desires his father's wellbeing, or simply that Tim wants his father to be happy, you would not provide a refutation of what I say by pointing out that Tim is asleep. Tim wants his father's wellbeing even when he, Tim, is asleep, and even when his fear of missing a flight is all he can think of—in fact, it might be that, even as it is the fear of missing the flight that he vividly thinks about, his desire for his father's wellbeing is much stronger than whatever desire or desires motivate him to catch the plane.

When I speak of intrinsic desires, I speak of desires that are not derivative. One could want money only as a means to buy books, in which case one has an *instrumental* desire for money. One could want to avoid the flu in a way that is non-instrumental, but is still *derivative* from one's intrinsic desire to be healthy in general—what Schroeder and I have called a *realizer desire*. An intrinsic desire is a different matter.

Desires are not the same as dispositions to act, though they cause dispositions to act. Most importantly for our present purposes, some dispositions to act are not desires. A case that Schroeder and I use is the case in which Travis is disposed to turn left when he drives through a certain intersection. Travis is so disposed because normally he uses the intersection to go to work, and to get to work he needs to turn left. However, due to the force of habit, Travis turns left in that intersection even on the few occasions in which he knows he ought to turn right, seeing that his destination is not his workplace. Imagine an occasion in which Travis, yet again, complicates his life by turning left instead of right. We can imagine him muttering a curse under his breath as soon as he realizes what he has done. Travis, on such an occasion, did not *desire* to turn left. His disposition to do so is not a desire to do so (Arpaly and Schroeder 2014, 83).

Relatedly, one cannot always assume that a person's action reveals what they most desire to do. Imagine, for example, a teenager who finds himself unable to talk to the peers he most desires to talk to—the more physically attractive ones, say. When approaching them, the very strength of his desire makes him tongue-tied. As a result, the teenager ends up spending his socializing time talking with the people with whom he second-most desires to talk. We don't always act on our strongest desires, and the best way to look at desires is not as some sort of decision-theory-style revealed preferences.

Incredulous Stare. Even with these clarifications in place, one is still bound to ask: How can meaning in life be a matter of desire satisfaction? It seems that a classical occasion for doubting the meaning in one's life would be an occasion in which one obtained or received what one has always wanted and something is still missing. Perhaps, let us imagine, David has always wanted to be rich, and wanted it much more than he wanted anything else. He wanted it intrinsically, not just as a means to some other thing that it would help him obtain. David becomes rich, and after a while, he notices that something is missing, and he is bitterly disappointed. Despite having, it seems, all he wanted, he does not feel satisfied with his life, and he begins, for the first time, to question its meaning to him. It seems like a reasonable thing for him to do. How would a desire-based theory of meaning in life explain it?

It would say that in ordinary life, an agent who behaves like David only seems to be a person who got all he wanted. Instead, a real-life David would be a person who faces the fact that he does not have some things that he intrinsically wants. Though it is natural to say that being rich was all David ever wanted, it is also natural to say that being rich turned out *not* to be *all* he wanted—or, in some possible variations of the story, simply that being rich turned not to be *what he wanted*. On one variation the case can take, the life of a rich person is not what David took it to be, and therefore not what he wanted. Perhaps, for example, he imagined that wealth will bring with it freedom from worry, but found that, at least in his case, this is not the way it works. On another variation, David might not have been mistaken about what it is like to be rich, but he nonetheless made a mistake about *himself*: he believed that all he wanted was to be rich, or that he wanted it so badly that no other desire really counted, but of course, being human, he had always wanted other things, like loving relationships, which he failed to pursue due to his error. Now that he is rich, the absence of these other things he intrinsically desires makes itself known through his mood. A third possibility is that David made a more concrete type of error about what he wanted, or at least what he wanted intrinsically. He did not, in fact, want intrinsically to be rich, or did not want it as much as he thought. He has always wanted something else—say, the respect of his sneering childhood neighbours, or of people resembling them—which he thought could be gained by becoming rich. Now that being rich does not give him that, he does not quite understand why he is disappointed—didn't he want to be rich? I will say more in section 4 about ways in which a person can 'miss out' on meaning in life due to these kinds of errors.

Awareness. When I say that the things that increase intrinsic desire satisfaction need to be 'present in the person's life' in order for her life to be meaningful to her, I mean to imply that she needs to be aware of them. Imagine that Urunima intrinsically desires social justice. Social progress made during her lifetime but of which she is not aware does not contribute meaning to her life. This is true even if, unbeknownst to her, she contributes to the progress. Perhaps a talented writer is secretly chronicling Urunima's life who is interested, among other things, in the injustices she suffers. The writer publishes a fictionalized account of her life and some features of her character catch the interest of readers, some of whom are moved to agitate against structural sexism, with some success. Urunima, however, has no idea: perhaps she had died in the meantime. In such a case, the story might make Urunima's life more meaningful to the world, her country, or the revolution. One can even say that it makes Urunima's life meaningful 'on her own terms', but it does not make it any more meaningful *to her*.

Opacity. While the subject needs to be aware of the things that make her life meaningful to her, she does not need to know *that* these things make her life meaningful to her. A 'forbidden' passionate same-sex relationship can contribute meaning to Gilbert's life even if Gilbert believes that same-sex relationships are not only wrong but, of necessity, shallow and meaningless. Conversely, a person might be of the opinion that her life is meaningful to her but be wrong. Perhaps she does things that she correctly believes are valuable but which leave her cold, having too little to do with her desires ('How can my life be meaningless if I work at a charity?' she might wonder). A related truth is that a person can have plenty of meaning in her life who does not particularly wish for meaning in her life.

It should not seem strange that a person can have a meaningful life even if she applies a false theory of meaning to her life. A person who risks strong public disapproval can be brave even though she mistakenly believes that bravery necessarily involves risking bodily harm. A person who sees that being a philosopher would be better for him in the long run than being a lawyer can be prudent even if he mistakenly believes that prudent people always go for the more lucrative option, and similarly a person's life being meaningful or meaningless to her does not hang on her favored theory of meaning in life.

The Role of Displeasure. I do not mean to say that a meaningful life has to involve suffering, or a bad Pleasure Balance, as a matter of definition. One can in principle be so lucky that the satisfaction of one's strong intrinsic desires, the ones that outweigh the desire for a good Pleasure Balance, always improves one's Pleasure Balance or leaves it the same, and such a person can have meaning in her life. It is also not necessary for the intrinsic desires in question to be such as to *always* outweigh the desire for a good Pleasure Balance—one needs to be ready to incur a significantly worse one, but one does not need to be ready to incur an extremely bad one. In other words, one need not be willing to die or be tortured for the sake of something in order for it to contribute meaning to one's life, though one needs to be willing to suffer for it.

Irrationality. A thing that contributes meaning to the life of an agent is a thing which the agent desires intrinsically even on (some) occasions in which having it results in a significantly worse Pleasure Balance. Such cases need to be distinguished from cases in which an agent acts so as to worsen her Pleasure Balance not because she wants something more than she does a good Pleasure Balance, but because of simple ignorance or because of such forms of irrationality as hyperbolic discounting (i.e. underestimating displeasures and other harms that are going to take place in the future), self-deception, blind habit (as with Travis), or failures of self-control (as might happen when a person who is somewhat drunk literally can't hide her opinion of Michael Jackson to save her job, even though, drunk or not, she wants the job more than she wants to express her opinion of Michael Jackson). Without being able to read an agent's mind, it can be very hard to tell if a person who buys a beautiful suit knowing that she might have to skimp on meals during the coming weeks is someone who is irrational in one of these ways or someone who, with no illusions, really does want good clothes to the point of being ready to go through a hard time rather than completely forgo them.

'Higher' Pleasures? I am unable to trace where I have read that pleasure cannot contribute meaning to a life as people on their deathbeds do not reminisce about 'donuts' and 'hot baths'. One must avoid such an impoverished vision of pleasure. It seems likely that Casanova and the Marquis de Sade found their adventures worth reminiscing upon. It might seem as if, on my view, there is no room for something like the monkfish

in savoury vanilla sauce that I had eight years ago in the Basque Country to contribute meaning to my life. This, however, would be wrong. A good Pleasure *Balance* does not in itself contribute meaning to a life, but a *particular pleasurable experience*, for which one is willing to compromise one's overall Pleasure Balance, can contribute meaning to a life, and that includes some experiences of sensual pleasure.

You might ask how that is possible, seeing that mice, and not only humans, have desires for food and for sex. However, contra Aristotle and Mill, humans have gastronomical and sexual desires they do not share with other animals. Food can be an aesthetic experience or, alternately, a Proustian fountain of memories from one's old home. While mice can have sex, they cannot fall in love, nor can they experience the thrill of, say, casting aside social conventions. Quintessentially human pleasurable experiences can become the stuff of memories—and also a component of a life that makes considerable suffering *worthwhile* ('ah, what I won't give to have that experience again').

The Relationship between Pleasure and Desire Satisfaction. In many circumstances, getting something that we intrinsically desire results in pleasure. If Marcia desires that the Red Sox win, she will normally feel pleasure when she believes they just won and displeasure when she believes they just lost. A paradigmatic fan, she does want glory for the Red Sox intrinsically. It would not do to say that she wants Red Sox victories *because* they give her pleasure, as this would be reversing the causal order: Red Sox victories cause Marcia pleasure only *because* she intrinsically wants the Red Sox to win. Those who lack that desire do not find Red Sox victories pleasurable. However, if Marcia is a typical human, she would develop, on top of her desire for the glory of the Red Sox, a desire for the pleasure that she experiences when they win, or, at least, an aversion to the displeasure she experiences when they lose. Thus, she might want the Red Sox to win next week both due to her intrinsic desire for the glory of the Red Sox *and* due to her desire not to be miserable.

Such second layers of motivation easily spring into existence on the countless occasions where getting what one intrinsically wants is pleasing, or losing it is displeasing. If Hande intrinsically desires the right and the good, she will do right things and promote the good for their own sake. Under many circumstances, that would mean that she would feel at least some pleasure at successfully promoting the good or doing right. Under these circumstances, she might easily develop a second layer of motivation, as when she finds that it cheers her up, when mildly depressed, to volunteer for a cause, because promoting the right and the good causes her pleasure. In such a case she would be doing her good works both for the sake of the right and the good themselves *and* for the pleasure that doing right and promoting the good gives her. This is one thing that can easily give my beginning students the impression that we only ever do good for the sake of the warm fuzzy feeling we get from it.

But if all of this is true, how come there can be cases where increasing your net intrinsic desire satisfaction actually worsens your Pleasure Balance?

The answer is that not every satisfaction of an intrinsic desire brings pleasure with it. For example, the object of your desire might fail to give you pleasure if you are used to it. A friend of mine who travels to poor countries informs me that when he comes back to the so-called first world, he derives great pleasure from using running water. I, too, desire to be comfortable, but I never go for very long without running water, and so having it is unlikely to cause me much pleasure. For another example, desire satisfaction can fail to give you pleasure because, in a particular case, the fact that one's desire has been satisfied is hard to grasp vividly. A person who desires money might feel great pleasure at the sight of a check in her mailbox, but fail to feel much pleasure upon finding a loan at a 3.4% interest rate instead of 3.5%, even though the latter find means a much larger financial gain for her.

Neo-Aristotelians suggest that a good person often enjoys doing what is right, and if the good person is, as I have argued elsewhere, a person who desires the right and the good, then it seems reasonable. However, even if Hande desires the right, or desires to do the right, there will be plenty of cases in which doing the right will fail to please her. She might, for example, be as used to telling the truth as I am to having running water, so that no pleasure comes to her when she tells a person a painful truth that she morally ought to tell. Furthermore, the crying face of the recipient of that truth can be vivid in her mind in a way that the long-term good that she *might* be doing him is not vivid at all. Thus the knowledge that she is doing right, as she wanted, is not enough to make the interaction *pleasant* for her. In the cases of Joseba, Phirose, and Marcia, it stands to reason that knowing that one might win a race, as one wants, knowing that one might raise a child to be a happy person, as one wants, and knowing that the Red Sox are likely to win sometimes in one's lifetime, as one wants, are not enough to make the relevant slogging periods pleasant.

'*Projects?*' On some views of meaning in life, the clearest representative of which would be Antti Kauppinen (2012, 2013), one only finds meaning in life through successful 'projects' in the sense of intentional, extended courses of action in which goals are set and achieved. This is wrong. The Red Sox winning the World Series is a wish come true for Marcia, a desire satisfied, but it is not, strictly speaking, a goal achievement or the culmination of a project for her.

Personal relationships such as friendship and romance contribute meaning to life, and while they have some project-like components, they are not projects in the sense cited previously. Compare the sentence 'I am working on my dissertation' with the sentence 'we are working on our relationship'. Listen for connotation. If one is working on one's dissertation, things are as they should be. If one is working on one's relationship, it's generally a sign that something the has gone wrong. Dissertations are projects, and the natural thing to do with a project is work on it. While all is well with a loving relationship you do not think of the relationship as a project, and much of the meaning the relationship brings to your life hangs on things that sneak up on you as you make other plans, and so cannot be shoehorned into such terms as 'meeting relationship goals'.[3]

---

[3] Kauppinen (2013) presents a project-like model of relationships. Kauppinen (2012) does not, but seems to see the role of relationships in a meaningful life as indirect and auxiliary to that of projects.

Unendorsed and Alien-Feeling Desires. I have mentioned before that a same-sex passion can contribute meaning to the life of someone who disapproves of same-sex passions. Similar things are true about art made when one believes one should be a businessperson, time spent with one's children when one believes one should be helping starving kids in Africa instead, anger at social injustice in a woman who thinks good girls should never get angry, and in general things of which one disapproves. This can be true even if one feels alienated from one's unendorsed desires and actions.[4]

Wellbeing. There is, famously, a view of wellbeing that makes it out to be overall desire satisfaction, a view many consider problematic.[5] One need not to be committed to such a view of wellbeing in order to accept my view of the meaningful life. On any reasonable theory of wellbeing or happiness, a meaningful life need not be a happy life or a life of wellbeing. On common-sensical grounds, I take it that some meaningful lives are simply too filled with suffering to be considered lives of wellbeing. There are agents whose meaningful lives included sacrificing their wellbeing, sometimes in dramatic ways such as being tortured or imprisoned for their causes. There are also people like Ludwig Wittgenstein, who, after what appears to have been a life of relentless, severe depression, claimed once to have had a wonderful life, but of whom it is hard to believe that he meant to say that his life was a life of wellbeing (presumably, he believed that his genius, the most important thing in his world by far, made it all *worthwhile*).

3. THE QUESTION OF OBJECTIVE VALUE

But is it enough for a meaningful life for one to have things in one's life that one desires in a certain way? Shouldn't these things also be objectively valuable? Countless philosophers agree that part of what gives lives meanings consists of 'attachments' or 'attractions' or some other desire-like attitudes, but maintain, as Susan Wolf (2010) puts it, that for a life to have meaning, 'subjective attraction' has to meet 'objective attractiveness'.

Not all things that people say give meaning to their lives have that intuitive flavor. Consider the case of Marcia. Let us grant that baseball is an objectively valuable pursuit. The victory of any particular sports team is still not an objectively valuable thing and what the fan desires deeply is success for a particular team, a desire that, whatever its beginnings, has become intrinsic. One might protest that the victory of a team can be valuable in various ways: perhaps it helps the economy of a city that needs the

---

[4] Schroeder and Arpaly (1999) argue that feeling alienated from a desire or an action is not a metaphysically significant feeling, but simply a reaction to the fact that the relevant desire or action does not fit in well with an agent's visceral self-image, as when a person might feel alienated from the new white hairs on his head, that are nonetheless his.

[5] For a good critique of the view, see Darwall (2004).

help, perhaps the team has morally superior hiring practices for which it deserves to be rewarded, and so on. However, being a fan is not about desiring a better economic situation for your town or a victory for morality. It is not even about desiring to support the sport in general by supporting a team that one takes to be the best. It's about desiring your team to win.

But the philosopher who takes objective value to be a necessary component of things that contribute meaning to a life may point out that there are seemingly clear cases in which a life seems meaningless exactly because it is lacks engagement with objectively valuable things. Wolf give various examples, such as that of a person who does nothing in her life but keep a goldfish (2010, 16, 23). Even if the goldfish keeper is 'fulfilled' by her project of goldfish keeping, Wolf says, she still has a meaningless life. Another example mentioned in this context is Rawls's example of the grass counter—an intelligent man who devotes his time to counting the blades of grass at Harvard's lawns (Rawls 1971, 432). The life of the grass counter also sounds meaningless.[6] How does one explain the sense that these two lives are meaningless? Wolf's answer is simple: because keeping goldfish and counting grass are not objectively valuable. A person sympathetic to Wolf might ask me: Don't examples like the Wolf's goldfish lover and Rawls's grass counter show, at the very least, that the intrinsic desires that contribute meaning to a life need to be intrinsic desires for objectively valuable things? If I am to defend the view proposed here, I need an alternative explanation for the sense we have that such lives are not worthwhile—not even for the agents.[7]

First, let me agree that the life of a (very) *broadly normal adult human* cannot be meaningful to her if it is devoted to the keeping of a single, ordinary goldfish or to the counting of blades of grass. Accordingly, no broadly normal adult human has intrinsic desires such that a goldfish-devoted life or a life counting grass would result in a high overall level of desire satisfaction for him. That is true in that no such human has a powerful intrinsic desire to keep a goldfish or to count grass, and importantly, it is also true in that such a human will have many strong intrinsic desires the frustration of which is guaranteed by a goldfish-devoted or a grass-counting life. Broadly normal adult humans seem to intrinsically desire at least some form of relating to other humans—friendship, romance, parenting, other family relationships, group membership, play, or even simply doing work that other humans find interesting—and all these forms of human relating would be absent from the life of a devoted goldfish keeper or grass counter. Broadly normal adult humans seem to desire tasks in their lives that challenge their intellectual capacities at least to a degree (and if such desires are not satisfied, the result is deep boredom). They are averse to extreme monotony (that is, they intrinsically desire its absence). The goldfish keeper and the grass

---

[6] There are many cases of supposedly meaningless pursuit in the relevant literature—see, for examples, maintaining a precise number of hairs on one's head (Taylor 1992, 36).

[7] My arguments regarding Wolf's goldfish example appeared in a different form in Arpaly (2010).

counter, if they are broadly normal adult humans, do not experience such intellectual challenges—it's too easy to keep a goldfish, it's too easy to count, and both pursuits seem extremely monotonous.

What about humans who are not adults, or who are neurologically unusual? Imagine a five-year-old child, or a person who is disabled to the point of having only the cognitive abilities of such a child. Such a person who learns to raise her own goldfish can probably thereby add a significant measure of meaning to her life. It is easy to imagine her gaining a sense of purpose that is absent in peers who spend their days on nothing but passive entertainment. She *is* challenging her intellectual abilities, she does not find greeting the fish every day monotonous, and far from isolating herself from human company, she might avail herself of more meaningful relating, as she can show other people the pretty fish, connect with adults who help her with fish care, and so on.

Bertrand Russell makes a similar point in his self-help book *The Conquest of Happiness*, in which he discusses his gardener, seemingly a person of fairly low cognitive abilities, who seems to derive energizing, enjoyable challenges from the tricky task of outwitting the rabbits that threaten the garden. Russell chides the reader not to think of himself as too superior a creature to derive a sense of purpose this way, because after all, a rabbit is much bigger than a yellow fever bacillus and yet great people have seen it as a worthwhile challenge to outwit the yellow fever bacillus (Russell 2013, 133). Imagine a neurologically *very* unusual person for whom counting grass is something they deeply desire to do and not too disruptive of the other intrinsic desires they have. Perhaps they do not mind monotony at all, or perhaps they are built in such a way as not to find grass-counting monotonous. I do not know if such a person exists, but there exist equally unusual brains with unusual disabilities, unusual abilities, and unusual combinations of abilities and disabilities. Compare her, with her quest to know how many grass blades there are at Harvard, to the respected academics who devote a lot of their lives to finding out how many prime numbers there are. The number of prime numbers is, to you and me, a more interesting question than the number of blades of grass anywhere, but the word 'interesting' designates a relational property, not the kind of absolute value that Wolf seems to talk about. I see no reason to deny the possibility that someone who is *not* a broadly normal adult human can derive meaning from engaging in pursuing knowledge that is interesting to her (even if that knowledge does not have much worth *for others*).

Having heard all that, a friend of mine said: 'Forget the goldfish and the grass counter, what about my relatives who do nothing but stare vacantly at their TVs? Surely there is something that they are missing'. I agree that this *can* be the case. Desires are not revealed preferences, and a person who, without being forced, spends all her time watching television while drinking beer is not necessarily a person whose sole intrinsic desire, or strongest one by far, is to watch television while drinking beer, or a person whose combined intrinsic desires are best satisfied by this lifestyle. In the next section I would like to discuss the ways in which, given an intrinsic desire-based view of meaning in life, a broadly normal adult human who is relatively free to choose how to live can find herself living without much meaning.

4. How to Miss Out on Meaning

Suppose, then, that meaning in life can be had simply through having things that one strongly and intrinsically desires—apart from a good Pleasure Balance and things that mice desire too. Does that make it easy for one to have a meaningful life? Not as much as it might seem. Some of us might have an easier time than others, but finding meaning in life can be tricky.

There are various sources of difficulty in finding meaning in life. An obvious one is *difficulty getting what one desires*. Such difficulty can often be the result of simple, and sometimes tragic, bad luck.

How dependent is meaning on luck? Do I wish to imply, for example, that a scientist who fails to meet his overarching goal of finding a cure for a major illness has had a largely meaningless life, or at least that her project has contributed no meaning to her life? That would depend on the specific content of the desire or desires that led to this goal. If the scientist is motivated by a desire to be useful or contribute to human knowledge, she might find some meaning in her project having been, to some degree, useful or knowledge-promoting—at least through showing her and other scientists looking for the cure which direction not to take. If she is motivated by a desire to be the first to find the cure, or simply to become famous, she might find that her project failed to provide her with meaning. These various desires can be hard to tell apart—even in oneself.

In addition to simple cases of bad luck—cases that involve the world not 'cooperating' with an agent—there are cases in which a person has the bad luck to have particularly strong desires that are unusually hard or simply impossible for him to satisfy. For example, a person might have a strong desire for immortality, or for being universally liked, or for his narcissistic mother to love him in a way that a narcissist cannot. Desires cannot give a person meaning in life if they cannot be satisfied, which makes it impossible for their objects to be present in a person's life. Related problems involve having two or more strong desires that cannot be satisfied together.

So you can have difficulty getting what you desire, due to bad luck with the world or desires that are hard or impossible to satisfy. A different sort of problem with getting meaning in life would be *ignorance of one's intrinsic desires*. Recall David, who believed that all he wanted was to be rich and became disappointed with his life when he became rich. There are many other scenarios one can come up with in which a person does not, in a way, know what she wants.

Ignorance about what one intrinsically wants is much easier to come by than philosophers make it seem. Consider another example, also adapted from a real-life case. Claire, a young and relatively privileged person, having taken too many economics classes, believes that humans are all selfish. Claire believes that since she is human, she, too, is completely selfish. One day, as she drives her car, she notices a child running into the road. To avoid hitting the child, she swerves into a tree. Afterwards, she realizes that she does, after all, desire things other than her own wellbeing—and always had.

There is no need for a psychoanalysis-style explanation for Claire's ignorance of her unselfish intrinsic desires. We can imagine that Claire, reasonably enough, is glad to realize that she had been mistaken: it is not the case that she knew she was unselfish but wanted to suppress or forget that fact. She was simply mistaken.

How can a person be ignorant of something so important about herself? If one accepts the view Timothy Schroeder and I defend, it is not that hard to explain. Desire itself, we say, is not an experience (though an urge or a craving can be). Recall that if you desire the wellbeing of your father, you desire the wellbeing of your father even when you are fast asleep and have no experiences at all. Since desire itself is not an experience, our knowledge of our desires is essentially inferential. You 'automatically' conclude that you desire the wellbeing of your father from other things: the tense displeasure you experience when you think your father might be sick, the pleasure you experience when he sounds like he's doing well, the easy time you have recalling to mind what things your father likes or dislikes, and so on. If our knowledge of our desires is inferential, it stands to reason that one will sometimes make a flawed inference—or simply be misled by very complex evidence to reasonably infer things that are not the case. Here are just a few of the ways in which this can happen, illustrated by examples:

(1) Bad theories about humans in general—as in the previous case of Claire, where the belief that we are all selfish is applied by an individual to herself.
(2) Generalizations that make sense given the evidence available to one. Khalil is asexual, but as a young person, he has never heard of asexuality and neither has anyone in his immediate environment. As he grows up, following his observation of people around him, he reasonably assumes that everyone has sexual desires and is thus inclined, for example, to interpret some warm feelings he has towards others as sexual desires, to suspect that his sexual desires are somehow repressed, etc.
(3) Taking something for granted (being jaded to it) and thus not noticing that one desires it: Janice does not realize how much she desires to do philosophy until she is thrown into an environment where she has no opportunity to do it.
(4) Being hardened to the absence of something, and thus not noticing that one desires it: Silvester falls unexpectedly into a romantic relationship. As he experiences intense happiness, he realizes that after decades of living without romance, he got so used to its absence from his life that he came to assume he no longer wanted it. He was wrong.
(5) Mistaking a desire for another one that has similar symptoms: Tonya feels pleasurably excited at the thought of being invited to activities involving the popular girls at her high school and so concludes that she wants to participate in these activities. However, she does not: she only wants to be *invited*, which in turn bespeaks an intrinsic desire for approval.
(6) Having an out-of-date self-image: it is rather common to have a visceral image of oneself that does not take into account changes that have been creeping up on one. This is true when it comes to one's hair turning grey, and it can also be

true about desires. Debopriya used to be very keen on excitement. Looking for places to go on vacation, he still looks for exciting possibilities. However, like many people as they get older, Debopriya does not desire excitement as much as he used to, and his ideal vacation would be a quiet one on a beach.

(7) Desiring something 'symbolically': Zhu thinks he really wants to keep all of his mementos from his days playing *Dungeons and Dragons* as a young man. After he loses them, he doesn't miss them at all. What he really wants is to have friendships in his life despite being a busy middle-aged person.

(8) Doing *what 'one does'*: John buys a new car every three years because he assumes 'one' needs a car every three years. In truth, John does not like or care about cars, nor does he even have a desire to keep up with the Joneses that would be frustrated if he bought a car every six years instead, or bought gently used cars. He simply never questions that *one buys a new car* every three years. He intrinsically desires to travel the world, and would have been able to do so if he didn't spend money on new cars.

This is by no means a complete list of ways to be mistaken about one's intrinsic desires—and so, potentially, about what kind of thing might contribute meaning to one's life. Thus, in an unexpected place, we find something to say in favour of the (somewhat!) examined life. Perhaps if John, instead of spending all his free time vacantly staring at his TV, occasionally asked himself what he 'really' wanted, he would have travelled the world instead of buying those needless cars?

Some Remaining Questions

A question worth discussing is whether an immoral life can be worthwhile for an agent, and whether any meaning can be gained from immoral actions or from experiences available only to people of bad character. Harry Frankfurt, to whose view of meaning I have most kinship, argues controversially that yes, it is possible for Hitler to have had a meaningful life[8]. There were a lot of wrong things with Hitler's life, but we must choose our condemnations carefully. I sympathize with Frankfurt's view, but will not presume to solve the controversy here, nor suggest ways in which a view similar to mine or Frankfurt's can accommodate a strong contrary intuition.

A cluster of important questions concern wellbeing. What is the precise relationship between meaning in a life and wellbeing, on the view presented here? Relatedly, a meaningful life need not be happy, but a lack of meaning in life seems to be distressing for at least some people. How does this work? Can there be, at least for some people, a happy meaningless life?

---

[8] See especially his reply to Susan Wolf (Frankfurt 2002).

In addition to those, there are questions that Schroeder and I discuss elsewhere (2013) and concern the nature of desire and the relationship between it and pleasure and displeasure. If a desire is not a disposition to act and not a revealed preference, what is it? What is the relationship between desires and other states that affect action? For a full version of the theory sketched here, we might need to know these things.

The topic of unusual human motivation—the kind that exists, for example, in mental disorders—needs more discussion. Some special questions concern phenomena such as addiction.[9]

Despite these loose ends, I hope you found reading this worthwhile.

References

Arpaly, Nomy, and Timothy Schroeder. 2014. *In Praise of Desire*. New York: Oxford University Press.
Arpaly, Nomy. 2010. 'Response to Susan Wolf'. In *Meaning in Life and Why It Matters*, ed. S. Wolf, 85–91. Princeton, NJ: Princeton University Press.
Darwall, Stephen. 2004. *Welfare and Rational Care*. Princeton, NJ: Princeton University Press.
Frankfurt, Harry. 1982. 'The Importance of What We Care About'. *Synthese* 53: 257–272.
Frankfurt, Harry. 2002. 'Reply to Susan Wolf'. In *The Contours of Agency: Essays on Themes from Harry Frankfurt*, ed. S. Buss and L. Overton, 242–252. Cambridge, MA: MIT Press.
Frankfurt, Harry. 2004. *The Reasons of Love*. Princeton, NJ: Princeton University Press.
Kauppinen, Antti. 2012. 'Meaningfulness and Time'. *Philosophy and Phenomenological Research* 84(2): 345–377
Kauppinen, Antti. 2013. 'Meaning and Happiness'. *Philosophical Topics* 41(1): 161–185.
Nozick, Robert. 1974. *Anarchy, State and Utopia*. Cambridge, MA: Harvard University Press.
Rawls, John. 1971. *A Theory of Justice*. Cambridge, MA: Harvard University Press.
Russell, Bertrand. 2013. *The Conquest of Happiness*. New York: Norton Press.
Schroeder, Timothy. 2004. *The Three Faces of Desire*. New York: Oxford University Press.
Schroeder, Timothy, and Nomy Arpaly. 1999. 'Alienation and Externality'. *Canadian Journal of Philosophy* 29(3): 371–387.
Taylor, Charles. 1992. *The Ethics of Authenticity*. Cambridge, MA: Harvard University Press.
Wolf, Susan. 2010. *Meaning in Life and Why It Matters*. Princeton, NJ: Princeton University Press.

---

[9] For an attempted solution to the problems posed by addiction for desire-based moral psychology, see Arpaly and Schroder (2014, chapter 11).

CHAPTER 23

LOVE AND MEANING IN LIFE

ALAN H. GOLDMAN

Introduction

EVERYONE agrees that love, or being in love, adds meaning to one's life. Those who are in love find their lives to be more meaningful than they were before. No one who deeply loves another person, or even passionately loves what she is doing or pursuing during a period of her life, thinks to question whether her life seems meaningful to her at that time. In the case of romantic love, perhaps the connection with meaning holds only when the love is reciprocated and does not lead quickly to disappointment. If we can accept that love contributes to meaning in life as an uncontroversial premise, it will make a good test for accounts of the nature of love and of meaning in life.

To apply this test, we must try out accounts of love and meaning and see whether the connection that follows strikes us as right. The accounts I will defend here easily pass this test. The concept of love will be the less controversial and original, at least in regard to the aspect of love that I take to connect it most closely to the creation of meaning. The account of meaning to be defended here, by contrast, differs from those most prominent among philosophers, but will show in greater detail how being in love facilitates a person's finding his life meaningful. I will take romantic love to be our paradigm, since most people think first of that type, especially when they speak of being in love. We will see, nevertheless, that love of things or activities can play a similar role in creating meaning within life. I will also focus on the first-person perspective, our question being what makes a person's life seem meaningful to her and how love contributes to that impression.

Love

Romantic love can be analysed as a combination of sexual desire plus the aspects that constitute non-sexual or Platonic love, e.g. love for children, siblings, or friends. The two can be combined despite the facts that they can clearly exist independently and that in themselves they are quite different. Love in itself is mainly other-regarding, mainly concerned for the welfare of the loved one, while sexual desire is mainly self-regarding, aimed at the pleasure that physical contact with the sexual object brings. Love tends to be relatively exclusive and intentionally long term, relatively exclusive because loving a person involves valuing her above virtually all others, and because we have only a limited supply of emotional energy such as that involved in the total commitment to the loved one. We can love more than one person, but not a great many, while we can have fleeting sexual desires for countless others over a lifetime, sexual desire in itself having nothing to do with long-term commitment.

Despite these differences, the physical and emotional intimacy involved in sex and love respectively explains why the two make a natural combination in romantic love, why sexual activity can lead to feelings of love and then can naturally express those feelings, and why partners in love can prefer sexual exclusivity or resent its violation. Romantic love tends to focus sexual desire on the loved one, while the sex it includes makes for the most complete union, physical and mental or spiritual, between two people.

According to psychologists and laypersons alike, romantic love is an emotion. To assess this categorization, we may first characterize emotions generally and then see whether love fits this description. The predominant concept of emotion is what philosophers call a cluster concept. Psychologists do not use that term, but their characterizations of emotions fit that mould. A cluster concept has multiple criteria for application, none of which is necessary or sufficient. All apply in paradigm instances, but objects instantiating less than all criterial properties can also count as instances, albeit less than paradigmatic. In the case of emotions, the criterial properties include sensations, cognitive evaluations, compelled attention, behavioural dispositions, and physical symptoms (Frijda 2008; Gross 2008; Bates et al. 2008; Stein et al. 2008; Niedenthal 2008; Clore and Ortony 2008; Frederickson and Cohn 2008). These properties are conceptually linked or constitutive of the emotions that instantiate them, but this does not prevent them from causally interacting—the evaluative judgements, for example, causing the sensations and physical symptoms.

Thus, to take a prime example of a basic emotion, fear involves queasy sensations, a judgement that a situation is dangerous, a disposition to flee, increased heartbeat, sweating, and release of adrenaline. One might also fear, say, a snake or spider that one knows not to be dangerous, but, lacking in evaluative judgement, this will not be a paradigm case and can be judged to be irrational. Fear can be occurrent or dispositional, the sensations, for example, occurring only in the presence of the snake one fears or when vividly thinking of it. Basic emotions, when triggered, involve set responses initiated without deliberation or reflection, and therein lies their adaptive value. Better to flee immediately than to stop and think about it. Other emotions, such as jealousy or pride, are more cognitively elaborated and less fixed in their behavioural responses, or they can combine basic emotions, as contempt can be analysed as anger plus disgust.

Romantic love instantiates all the types of properties that constitute emotions. The sensations include feelings of attraction in the presence of the loved one and yearning in her absence; the evaluative judgement involves an idealization of certain of the loved one's properties; the behavioural dispositions include sustained efforts to be with the loved one, to have sex, to share long-term projects and many experiences, to reveal intimacies, to bestow preferential caring attention or contribute to her welfare; the physical symptoms in the presence of the loved one include 'flushing face, widening eyes' (Brogaard 2019, 459), increased heartbeat, and in the brain, the release of adrenaline, oxytocin, and dopamine (Brogaard 2019, 468–469). Other types of love lack some of these features of the paradigm romantic type. Platonic love lacks the sexual dispositions and sensations; a young child's love for a parent lacks the disposition to altruistic intentions. As mentioned, romantic love might be most closely connected to meaning, but love of one's work, for example, or indeed any love that involves long-term commitment, can generate meaning in life, as will be made clear later.

As with other emotions, love is not completely under our voluntary control: it is triggered passively and sometimes overwhelmingly and immediately (love at first sight) (Naar 2017), especially when the sexual aspect is prominent and triggers other aspects. We can do things to indirectly affect or break up loving relationships, but falling in love is not something we can simply choose to do. Love responds to certain properties of its object unreflectively and without deliberation, although the properties to which it responds are not as fixed as they are in the case of more basic emotions. As are other emotions, love is most likely biologically programmed, and not only in its sexual aspect if children survive better in family units, and families involve commitment. But while probably biologically programmed, it is socially directed into forms acceptable to different societies, typically marriage.

Some differences from basic emotions have led some philosophers to deny that love is an emotion (Pismenny and Prinz 2017). Fear responds to danger; anger to having been wronged. Love might be said to respond to the property of being lovable, but this property reduces to others such as kindness and beauty, and, as noted, the loved one is often idealized as having lovable properties that others do not perceive. Others may not be lacking in failing to see the properties that one sees in one's loved ones. True love survives changes in those properties that initially triggered it, and love is long term and mainly dispositional, as opposed to anger and fear, which typically are short-lived.

But these features of love are in fact found even in basic emotions, albeit not in paradigm instances. As noted, one can fear objects one knows to be harmless, and a fearful person is disposed to fear various things that others don't, although he does not always feel fear. Likewise, we are not always elated in the presence of the loved one or yearning in her absence, but we tend to be. Fear of harmless things is irrational: while emotions can respond to reasons such as danger, they do not always do so and may arise without justifying reasons. Love fits this mould: while it might respond to such properties as kindness, beauty, or brilliance, there are often other triggering causes that do not seem to serve as justifying reasons. Love may then be characterized as irrational, but so are other emotions sometimes.[1] Others might not respond to properties that one finds lovable, but then a calm person might not respond to what makes one angry, or a brave person to what one fears.

The properties in another person that trigger love for her are general, but the love is then directed at a particular person. Once it exists, one does not trade that person for another with the same properties, even if the second person should be, for example, more beautiful or brilliant. It can be questioned whether a person who constantly seeks to 'trade up' is really in love. In normal cases, the relationship itself with the loved one provides a reason to continue it, although the emotion arose prior to that relationship. From the first-person perspective, one wants to be loved for the wonderful properties one has, but wants that love to continue when one loses those properties, such as physical beauty (Jollimore 2019, 64).

Thus, as with other emotions, the relation of love to reasons is complex and sometimes puzzling. Love often responds initially to reasons, but it can arise without justification in the loved one's properties and can survive the loss of those properties that aroused it (Zangwill 2013). It can even survive a change from a positive or idealized evaluative judgement to a negative judgement. Those properties that trigger love might justify some of its features—wanting to be with the loved one in the case of great intellect or sense of humour, or to have sex in the case of physical beauty—but they won't justify other features, such as wanting to preferentially benefit the loved one in those situations in which one is required to be impartial (Bagley 2019).

As with other emotions, the evaluative judgement involved in love is most often implicit. It reflects the reasons that give rise to it, but it does not arise through reflection on those reasons or deliberation. The emotion of love might seem unique in creating reasons as well as reflecting them (Frankfurt 2004, 37). Love creates a reason to prefer the loved one over others who objectively are no more lacking in value. One has reason to be especially concerned about the welfare of those whom one loves, and love itself provides the reason for this special concern.

But is this so unique among emotions? Fear can create a reason to avoid objects one fears, for example snakes, spiders, or mice, even when they are not harmful, and the fear itself is irrational. Perhaps unlike fear, love can arise without reasons without being irrational. One needs no reason to love one's children, but such love is not irrational. It might be said again that the relationship itself creates the reason for love in this case. But in other cases, such as that of future spouses, love creates the reason to have a relationship, having arisen before the relationship exists.

---

[1] A perfect capturing of this feature of love is the 1960s song, 'Do You Love Me, Now That I Can Dance?'

Whom or what we love helps to define our identities, who we are (Ebels-Duggan 2019). I am a husband, father, philosopher, tennis player, and opera enthusiast, and presumably these all refer to people or activities and things I love. Love is again most prominent among emotions in this regard, but not entirely unique. I can also be defined to a lesser extent by what I most fear, by what makes me most angry or jealous, by what I have contempt for, and so on. If I am generally a fearful or angry person, that is certainly part of my personality, who I am. Character is judged in all these ways, largely by one's emotional make-up, whom and what I love being central in this self-definition.

Having classified love as an emotion and specified its components, we can focus more narrowly on those components and which of them might be connected to meaning in life. What distinguishes love from other emotions is not so much its sensations, physical symptoms, or evaluative judgement, which can signal almost any desire and the reward of its satisfaction, or almost any positive emotion. What distinguishes the emotion of love is mainly the behavioural dispositions that are captured by the notion of long-term commitment, essentially wanting or being disposed to share one's life. The sort of commitment involved in love exists nowhere else. One can be committed to a person, action, or long-term cause out of a sense of duty, but that is not the all-in desire to commit that love entails.

This loving commitment to share one's life or personal narrative is nearly unconditional—nearly, because it might be recognized to lapse only if the loved one acts beyond the moral pale (Delaney 1996, 352). Such commitment must also be qualified by the recognition that one cannot commit or promise to love long term if love is an emotion, as I have argued it is, since emotions are mostly beyond our control. We cannot commit or promise to do what is beyond our control. And indeed, as noted, love or continuing to love is mostly beyond our control. But the point is not that the lover commits to love, but that while in love he commits to sharing his life long term. And this commitment, like the preferential concern that is part of love, implies the relative exclusivity of love, since one cannot share one's life in all its intimate aspects with many other people.

The intention or disposition to share one's life with a person one loves implies sharing the loved one's interests as well. Some of these interests will be shared only in the sense that one wants them satisfied in the loved one; others will be more deeply shared in that her interests are truly also one's own. These two senses of sharing interests and projects explain how identities are partly merged in love, while at the same time remaining separate (Nozick 1989, 70–71; Westlund 2008, 573). Lovers maintain some of their own interests while sharing in their satisfaction or frustration.

However else we characterize love, it is uncontroversial that it involves this intention or disposition to share one's life in many or all its intimate aspects, and to do so long term. As is usual, Shakespeare in Sonnet 116 expresses this central aspect best:

> Love is not love which alters when it alteration finds . . . O, No! It is an ever fixed mark, that looks on tempests and is never shaken. . . . Love's not Time's fool, though rosy lips and cheeks within his bending sickle's compass come; Love alters not with his brief hours and weeks, but bears it out even to the edge of doom.

As Shakespeare eloquently explains, a lover who constantly flits from one romance to another does not really love (Bovens 2019, 266). And this long-term commitment is not only what most clearly distinguishes love from other emotions that might be short-lived; it is also what connects it most closely to meaning in life. Brief sexual encounters, for example, are not very meaningful unless connected to longer love stories or other extended narratives.

The same holds true of love in the broader sense in which we can love things or activities (although not romantically). If one loves one's work or career, one is again committed to it long term. If one loves one's country, one identifies with its ideals and interests and wants to be part, however small, of its ongoing narrative or history. To love anything is, as Harry Frankfurt points out, to care deeply about it, and through such caring we 'provide ourselves with volitional continuity' (Frankfurt 2004, 17; Singer 1994, 9).

'Long term', however, may be relative to the object of love. I can love the music of Mahler while recognizing that eventually I might tire of listening to it. I can love playing baseball while recognizing that I will at some point in the not-too-distant future be too old to play. But a fleeting interest, even if intense, is not love. If the attraction turns out to be short-lived, one might well say, 'I thought I loved *x*, but it was only a brief infatuation'. Brief love, like weak love, is not really love. Love spawns shared long-term interests and projects, and these, I will claim, create meaning in one's life.

Meaning

It remains mainly to explain how this central feature of love, its long-term commitment to the loved one or thing, generates meaning in life. But before doing so, we must explore different conceptions of meaning in life offered by philosophers to see which connect it plausibly to love. Initially I emphasize that we are speaking of meaning *in* life, not the older notion of meaning *of* life, a distinction important in recent discussions. The older concept conceived of all human lives having meaning in relation to God's plan for them, or, in its secular version, in relation to some overarching historical myth. Loss of faith in such grand eschatological schemes renders this concept archaic, although in seeing meaning in terms of broader narrative frameworks into which each life fits, it provides a clue into the type of meaning we are after. It is important to explicate the subject, rather than change it.

While contemporary discussions are correct in seeking the meaning internal to a life instead of imposed from without, they are often guilty of changing the subject rather than capturing any ordinary sense of meaning. The most popular one shared by Susan Wolf (1997), Stephen Darwall (2002), and John Cottingham (2003), among others, defines meaning in life as engagement with objectively valuable projects. I say this changes the subject because 'value' and 'meaning' are distinct concepts, not inter-definable, although, as we shall see, they are more indirectly related. These philosophers note that subjective commitment is not sufficient for meaning—being committed to watching TV soaps endlessly does not make for a meaningful life—and so they add objective value to the equation. But their notions of objective value seem to reflect only what they happen to value.[2]

More to our main point, this conception ill fits any connection between love and meaning. While we do value our loved ones above all others, as our earlier discussion made clear, we do not love particular people because we believe they or their lives are objectively valuable, or objectively more valuable than the lives of others. If all people's lives are equally valuable from an objective point of view, and if we love based on objective value, we would have to love all people equally (Soble 2008, 161). But of course we don't, and, as argued earlier, we could not, given preference for loved ones and limited emotional resources. And if we have a notion of a valuable life according to which one life is more valuable than another, e.g. Mother Teresa's life has more value than a pimp's or drug dealer's, we still do not fall in love based on such considerations. I love my wife and not Mother Teresa, no matter how much I see her life as a paradigm of value. Thus romantic love does not connect in any way I can see with this concept of meaning in life based on the notion of objective value. And the same is true of things or activities we love: I love tennis but not soccer, although I would not claim that the one is objectively more valuable than the other.

Unless directed at objective value, subjective commitment does not suffice to make life meaningful on this view, and yet life does seem meaningful to a person in love. A defender of the view can say that love or a loving relationship is itself objectively valuable (Jenkins 2019, 73–74), but once more we do not fall in love because we think it objectively valuable to do so, and such value, which according to believers attaches to the countless things they happen to value, is not what explains the way that love distinctively contributes to meaning. It does matter to what commitment is directed, but objective value is not the required target.[3]

There is a secondary sense of meaning in which it equates with importance. This is the sense in which we say, 'his endorsement meant a lot to me', i.e. it was very important to me. Once more it is true that our loved ones and the things we love are very important to us, more important than anything else. They mean a lot to us. But again, this is not the sense in which love makes our own lives seem meaningful to us. In fact, importance fails to distinguish meaningful lives from those that lack meaning from the first-person point of view. We perhaps consider some people's lives to be more important than others—Shakespeare, Einstein, Mozart, or major political figures in history—but few of us lead such important lives in terms of their long-term effects on the lives of many others. By contrast, from the first-person point of view, virtually all of us think of our lives as important, even those leading lives of dull repetition or near chaos, or without

---

[2] Susan Wolf (2014) includes epistemology, poetry, and Olympic athletics, but not pig farming or corporate law.
[3] I have written a book (2018) largely attacking the notion of objective value, but will not repeat those arguments here.

loving relationships. Thus, once more this sense of meaning fails to capture meaning in life or its connection to love. Nor is it the primary sense of meaning.

That primary sense and its paradigm bearers are the meanings that attach to words in a language. The dual sources of such meaning are the relations to the referents of the words and relations to other words in sentences and inferential patterns. Lives and portions of lives that make them meaningful do not have referents, and so the relevant linguistic clues to meaning more generally, which includes meaning in life, are the meanings of such terms as logical connectives (and, or . . .), which are exhausted by their relations to other terms and the inference patterns they allow. Words have meaning when they cohere in sentences. Sentences are intelligible when they cohere in more extended discourse, when they follow from previous sentences and lead to later ones, and when their utterances make sense as actions within broader intentions or plans.

Elements in artworks, musical tones or painted patches, have a similar type of meaning in the broader contexts of the artworks. Musical tones combine into chords and melodic phrases, which in turn combine into harmonic progressions and themes, and ultimately into movements. The thematic and harmonic elements at the third level refer back to earlier appearances and point the listener ahead ultimately to the final cadence. The meanings of these elements lie in their roles in these broader musical developments, and the listener understands a piece when she can follow these progressions, when she hears repetitions and variations as such and anticipates the resolutions of the harmonic tensions. Once more meaning here, as in the case of linguistic elements, lies in the relations of the musical elements to each other and their broader context, as these are grasped by the experienced listener.

Finally, we have another sort of aesthetic meaning that is closest to what creates meaning in life, the meanings of fictional events in novels. Such events have meaning in terms of their roles in the narrative structures of the novels, foreshadowing future developments or tying up earlier dramatic and aesthetic loose ends. When someone in the middle of a mystery novel tells the detective that she wants to meet him in order to convey information that will solve his case, the experienced reader knows that this means that she will not stay alive long enough to meet the detective. The meaning of the event of contacting the detective is transparent in the same way that a modulation to the dominant key is transparent to a seasoned listener to tonal music, transparent in what it foreshadows based on what it developed from.

Fiction, of course, is different from real life. The norms that govern the development of fictional narratives are aesthetic, requiring total coherence, variation, dramatic rhythm, thematic elaboration, and so on. Ideally, all events in a novel acquire their meanings in obedience to these aesthetic norms, and all of them are meaningful as they occur or in retrospect. Life, as many point out, is far messier. Not all the things that happen to us, or even all we intend, fit intelligible narratives. Much of it is simply forgotten. But the meaning of events in our lives still consists in narrative intelligibility—our ability to incorporate them into personal stories.

Some of these meanings derive from causal relations: the riots at Columbia University in 1968 meant that my qualifying exams were delayed. This again matches an ordinary sense of meaning: smoke means fire; clouds mean rain; a rash means fever will ensue. Causes mean their effects; effects mean their causes; and effects of common causes mean each other. But events in narratives have a deeper kind of connectivity too. Typical narratives aim at certain outcomes. They are unified by aims fulfilled or frustrated. Understanding them as they are read or lived involves anticipating these outcomes, having inferred the past and present intentions that guide them and foreseeing the factors that might affect their future developments. That is, they are understood not only in causal terms, but teleologically, affording them greater intelligibility or deeper meaning than mere causal sequences possess. Novels or plays in which plots lead nowhere, such as *Waiting for Godot*, are parasitic on these more typical narratives in which events aim at unambiguous closure. Part of the point of the former variants lies in the frustration of expectations based on the typical narrative conventions of the latter.

This account of meaning in life is confirmed by our intuitions regarding its opposite, a meaningless existence. Once again, Shakespeare expresses it perfectly in Macbeth's most famous speech: 'Tomorrow, and tomorrow, and tomorrow creeps in this petty pace from day to day, to the last syllable of recorded time.... Life's ... a tale told by an idiot, full of sound and fury, signifying nothing.' There are two ways indicated here in which life can be meaningless. The opening lines refer to endless repetition with no progress toward a desired (or dreaded) outcome. The closing lines portray total chaos, random events again without intelligible progression toward an end, literally lack of narrative intelligibility.

Macbeth, of course, is wrong about events in the play: all lead inexorably to his downfall, and hence possess clear meaning, albeit negative, for the reader. But in the heat of the battlefield Macbeth himself cannot discern this meaning: to him all was repetitive, chaotic, meaningless. In more prosaic contemporary terms, we have again on the one hand the life of the compulsive repetitive TV watcher or shopper, and on the other hand the life of one who flits from one fleeting interest to another without fulfilling or even cumulatively pursuing any. Neither life is capable of generating intelligible narratives. Both lives lack meaning.

To return to the positive account of meaning and the way that meaning in life matches the most ordinary sense of meaning, just as words cohere in sentences, which again gain in intelligibility as parts of more extended discourse, so movements combine into intentional actions, which in turn become intelligible as parts of more extended plans or projects. The deepest meanings accrue to elements, especially pivotal events, in the most extended and coherent narratives. The most meaningful events are those which play pivotal roles in such real-life narratives: births, deaths, marriages, initiations, culminations, or achievements.

Personal narratives can derive from outside sources, from what happens to us and how we react, but the most sustainable ones are largely self-created, reflecting the central values of the agent that she is willing to pursue through substantial obstacles. Thus, value does enter indirectly into meaning in life—not objective value that exists independently of our desires and motives, but those values that define our distinct personal identities and underlie our personal central projects and relationships. Those values direct our commitments and pursuits, sustaining the courses of actions and interactions captured in our personal narratives in terms of which our lives, or the events in them, acquire their meanings.

The view of meaning in life outlined here resembles others that also unpack the notion in narrative terms. It will clarify matters to indicate differences from some of the most prominent and recent of those other views. The three philosophers I will mention all see meaning in life in narrative terms, but they all combine narrative intelligibility with value, aligning themselves in part with earlier mentioned philosophers whose views I dismissed. As I have argued, value and meaning (in any sense other than importance) are simply distinct concepts.

According to Wai-hung Wong (2008), one's life is meaningful if the various identities with which one identifies (e.g. father, philosopher) are valued by oneself and others. These identities make up the content of one's complete and accurate biography. The latter is where the notion of narrative enters the account, but for Wong, to ask if one's life is meaningful is still to ask whether it is worthwhile or valuable. To his credit, this is not an appeal to objective value, but again to one's identities being valued by oneself and others.

Helena de Bres (2018) asks whether the relations among events in one's life that make the life narratable constitute meaning, or whether it is the actual telling of one's story to oneself and others that confers meaning. She argues that it is the latter, largely on the ground that causal relations themselves among events are not valuable. By contrast, telling one's story gives one insight or understanding, which is valuable in itself, and telling one's story to others allows for a sense of community when one's narrative conforms to certain conventional structures that are shared by the life stories of others. This sense of community is again of great value to individuals.

I have held that it is relations among events themselves that confer meaning, not only causal relations, but forward-looking orientations toward a final outcome or resolution of dramatic tensions and conflicts. My position is not as far from de Bres's as it might seem, however. She holds that the life stories told must be true if they are to make lives meaningful, which implies that only actual relations count. I hold that, since meaning is a three-term relation—something means something else to someone—a subject must grasp these relations for them to be meaningful. But this grasp need not consist or result in the actual telling of a story. While de Bres is herself an author, most of us do not tell life stories to ourselves or others, although our lives can be meaningful.

The grasp of meaningful events in our lives consists largely in projecting past connections into the future, building upon those prior events in forming intentions for future actions. This account of grasping the meanings of events in our lives does differ from de Bres's. But the biggest difference between us is again her insistence that meaning in life must have positive value. I pointed to the negative valued meaning of events in Macbeth's life, exemplifying throughout the coherent theme of the terrible cost of unbridled ambition.

Antti Kauppinen (2013) contrasts with de Bres in holding, as I do, that it is the narratability of events in lives, not their actual narration, that confers meaning. But the equation of value and meaning is even more central in his account. For him, meaningful lives make appropriate feelings of pride, fulfilment, hope, and admiration. A meaningful life consists in 'identity shaping engagement in challenging projects that build on the past in successful pursuit of something objectively valuable' (Kauppinen 2013, 162). Such projects must develop in a positive direction, such that meaning in life is a component of happiness.

Once more, this account excludes meaningful but negatively valenced lives such as that of Macbeth, narratives that progress inexorably downward, in which all events are intensely meaningful in pointing to a tragic end. And it also excludes happy people who prefer to live in the present and do not seek meaning in Kauppinen's sense. For all I know, an anti-narrativist such as Galen Strawson, who prefers not to think of his life in narrative terms or to dwell on the past in forming intentions for the future, might be very happy indeed.

Meaning is not only distinct from both value and happiness, it can derive from both comedic and tragic narratability. If one's life can fit a perfectly coherent narrative in which all events relate to others as antecedents or consequents in this possible narrative, then it is a meaningful life, one filled with meaningful events, whether or not its subject values herself as the protagonist of the story and her life as a happy and fulfilled one. As we shall see next, loving relationships, as well as protracted love affairs, can afford meaning in life in either of these directions.

Love and Meaning in Life

It is not hard now to see how love contributes to meaning in life, given our prior characterizations of both. The central feature, we noted, that distinguishes love from other emotions is its behavioural-dispositional component, the long-term commitment to share one's life with the loved one, or, for love of things, a commitment to pursue the work and activities that one loves—careers, hobbies, etc. We noted as well that the deepest meanings of events in one's life derive from their incorporation into the most extended personal narratives that relate the events to many others that contribute in various ways to the happy or sad endings of these stories. The commitments involved in love generate the most extended and coherent narratives of our lives, and hence create the deepest meanings of our lived events.

In the case of romantic love, the fact that these life narratives are shared contributes to their sustainability. First, one's commitment to pursue certain values is confirmed when commitment to those values is shared. Values and what ensues from them are more easily and confidently pursued through obstacles when endorsed by others. And shared commitments are more likely to be directed to activities that are themselves meaningful, as opposed to seemingly senseless or merely boringly repetitive activities. We noted earlier with believers in objective value that the objects of our commitments matter for meaning in life. But we see now that appeal to objective value is superfluous here: love, in producing shared commitments, mostly excludes commitment to simple repetitive activities or to jumping aimlessly from one infatuation to another. And appeal to narrative itself takes care of the rest: simple repetitive or chaotic activities do not produce extended narratives.

Second, sharing in itself is of great value to those linked by romantic love. The interests of the person one loves tend to become one's own interests precisely because of the desire or disposition to share one's life (Singer 1994, 29). This desire to share whatever the loved one is pursuing once more contributes to the sustainability over the long haul of joint projects. And when the romantic relationship culminates in marriage and children, raising them automatically becomes prominent among one's long-term projects, spawning many more extended narratives.

Our love interests, both romantic and non-romantic, are therefore the primary source of our extended personal narratives. And these narratives, we have seen, are the sources of the meaning of events in our lives, events that make up meaningful lives. I have argued against Kauppinen that projects that are sources for these narratives need not progress cumulatively toward success or happiness in order for key events that determine their outcomes to be meaningful. But just as sharing projects and relationships facilitates the sustained pursuit of them, so does the prospect of success as one increasingly approaches it. Success is important for both persistence before it is realized and retention in memory after the fact. Relationships themselves are projects to be sustained and improved upon (ask any married couple). Successful romantic relationships that culminate in marriage or lifelong commitments and shared aims, interests, and activities that fit coherent narratives do therefore typically progress.

But, as Shakespeare tells us in *A Midsummer's Night's Dream*, 'the course of true love never did run smooth'. The typical romantic narratives therefore involve many bumps along the road that help to sustain their interest as stories. The usual structure of such narratives is instantiated in the genre of romantic comedy and often mirrored in real life. As one recent examiner of the tradition writes: 'the pattern of romantic narratives [is] the overcoming of obstacles that stand in the way of true love' (Shumway 2003, 12). More specifically, we find in fictional romantic narratives variants of the following plot structure: initial attraction, conflicts, development in actions that prolong or aim to resolve the conflicts, climax, denouement.

In the tradition of fictional variants, the conflicts and obstacles often derive from parents, often as representatives of an upper social class, when their children want to marry out of love for members of a lower class. Less often they derive from social stereotyping by the future lovers themselves that must be overcome through their interactions. Whether their perceptions of each other are initially negative or over-idealized, by the end they are able to see each other as they are and to ground their love in more realistic self-knowledge and knowledge of their partner. In real life, the obstacles to successful romantic relationships might be different, but the basic structure of these fictional narratives is often partly mirrored in the stories of real couples, which in part explains the lasting popularity of the fictional genre.

Since this is not a chapter on literature and meaning in life, allow me to just name a few instantiations of this plot structure across the centuries and different genres dating back to Shakespeare. By Shakespeare himself, *All's Well That Ends Well* and *A Midsummer's Night's Dream*; in early English novels, *Tom Jones* and *Pride and Prejudice*; in opera, *Marriage of Figaro*, *Don Pasquale*, and *L'Elisir d'Amore*; in film, *Lady Eve* and *Crazy Rich Asians*. Countless other romantic comedies with similar plots could be named.

In fiction, all narrated events are intended to be meaningful. That this plot structure is so widely instantiated across centuries and genres indicates its functionality in fulfilling that aim. More to the point here, it is evidence of the close connection between love and meaning in life as described earlier. And, as I noted, the long enduring popularity of romantic comedy attests to its resonance with real audiences. Of course, as also noted, real life is messier than fiction, which caters to people's fantasies as much as to their real experiences. But the quote from Lysander in *A Midsummer's Night's Dream* applies to real people, many of whom are protagonists in their own romantic comedies.

In my personal experience, both I and my son broke up with our future wives before reuniting and deciding on marriage. For those of us living in long-term successful marriages, the love narrative barely begins where romantic comedies typically end. For others, the model of love narratives is not the traditional romantic comedy, but relationship movies such as *Annie Hall* or *500 Days of Summer*, in which romances ultimately fail. But whether the endings are happy or sad, when the narratives are extended and unified by the shared commitments of the lovers, love generates the broadest and deepest meanings of events in our lives. It is therefore the primary source of most meaningful lives.

References

Bagley, B. 2019. '(The Varieties of) Love in Contemporary Anglophone Philosophy'. In *Routledge Handbook of Love in Philosophy*, ed. A. M. Martin, 453–464. New York: Routledge.

Bates, J. E., J. A. Goodnight, and J. E. Fite. 2008. 'Temperament and Emotion'. In *Handbook of Emotions*, ed. M. Lewis, J. M. Haviland-Jones, and L. F. Barrett, 485–496. New York: Guilford.

Bovens, L. 2019. 'What Is This Thing Called Love?' In *Routledge Handbook of Love in Philosophy*, ed. A. M. Martin, 264–274. New York: Routledge.

Brogaard, B. 2019. 'Love in Contemporary Psychology and Neuroscience'. In *Routledge Handbook of Love in Philosophy*, ed. A. M. Martin, 465–478. New York: Routledge.

Cavell, S. 1981. *Pursuits of Happiness*. Cambridge, MA: Harvard University Press.

Clore, G. L., and A. Ortony. 2008. 'How Cognition Shapes Affect into Emotion'. In *Handbook of Emotions*, ed. M. Lewis, J. M. Haviland-Jones, and L. F. Barrett, 628–642. New York: Guilford.

Cottingham, J. 2003. *On the Meaning of Life*. London: Routledge.

Darwall, S. 2002. *Welfare and Rational Care*. Princeton, NJ: Princeton University Press.

De Bres, H. 2018. 'Narrative and Meaning in Life'. *Journal of Moral Philosophy* 15: 545–571.

Delaney, N. 1996. 'Romantic Love and Loving Commitment'. *American Philosophical Quarterly* 33: 339–356.

Ebels-Duggan, K. 2019. 'Love and Agency'. In *Routledge Handbook of Love in Philosophy*, ed. A. M. Martin, 300–312. New York: Routledge.

Frankfurt, H. G. 2004. *The Reasons of Love*. Princeton, NJ: Princeton University Press.
Fredrickson, B. L., and M. A. Cohn. 2008. 'Positive Emotions'. In *Handbook of Emotions*, ed. M. Lewis, J. M. Haviland-Jones, and L. F. Barrett, 777–796. New York: Guilford.
Frijda, N. 2008. 'The Psychologists' Point of View'. In *Handbook of Emotions*, ed. M. Lewis, J. M. Haviland-Jones, and L. F. Barrett, 68–87. New York: Guilford.
Gross, J. J. 2008. 'Emotion Regulation'. In *Handbook of Emotions*, ed. M. Lewis, J. M. Haviland-Jones, and L. F. Barrett, 497–512. New York: Guilford.
Jenkins, C. S. I. 2019. 'All Hearts in Love Use Their Own Tongues'. In *Routledge Handbook of Love in Philosophy*, ed. A. M. Martin, 72–82. New York: Routledge.
Jollimore, T. 2019. 'Love, Romance, and Sex'. In *Routledge Handbook of Love in Philosophy*, ed. A. M. Martin, 61–71. New York: Routledge.
Kauppinen, A. 2013. 'Meaning and Happiness'. *Philosophical Topics* 41: 161–185.
Naar, H. 2017. 'Subject-Relative Reasons for Love'. *Ratio* 30: 197–214.
Niedenthal, P. M. 2008. 'Emotion Concepts'. In *Handbook of Emotions*, ed. M. Lewis, J. M. Haviland-Jones, and L. F. Barrett, 587–600. New York: Guilford.
Nozick, R. 1989. *The Examined Life*. New York: Touchstone.
Pismenny, A., and J. Prinz. 2017. 'Is Love an Emotion?' In *Oxford Handbook of Philosophy of Love*, ed. C. Grau and A. Smuts. Oxford: Oxford University Press.
Shumway, D. R. 2003. *Modern Love*. New York: New York University Press.
Singer, I. 1994. *The Pursuit of Love*. Baltimore, MD: Johns Hopkins University Press.
Soble, A. 2008. *Philosophy of Sex and Love*. St. Paul, MN: Paragon House.
Stein, N. L., M. W. Hernandez, and T. Trabasso. 2008. 'Advances in Modeling Emotion and Thought'. In *Handbook of Emotions*, ed. M. Lewis, J. M. Haviland-Jones, and L. F. Barrett, 574–586. New York: Guilford.
Westlund, A. C. 2008. 'The Reunion of Marriage'. *The Monist* 91: 558–577.
Wolf, S. 1997. 'Happiness and Meaning: Two Aspects of the Good Life'. *Social Philosophy and Policy* 14: 207–225.
Wolf, S. 2014. 'Susan Wolf on Meaning in Life'. In *Philosophy Bites Again*, ed. D. Edmunds and N. Warburton, 265–272. Oxford: Oxford University Press.
Wong, W-h. 2008. 'Meaningfulness and Identities'. *Ethical Theory and Moral Practice* 11: 123–148.
Zangwill, N. 2013. 'Love: Gloriously Amoral and Arational'. *Philosophical Explorations* 16: 298–314.

CHAPTER 24

MEANING IN LIFE AND PHONINESS

IDDO LANDAU

MANY people complain that phoniness causes, or contributes to causing, life to be insufficiently meaningful. They say that they are phony, or others are phony, or society and culture are phony, or everything is phony, in a way that ruins, or at least diminishes, life's meaning. This complaint is more common among young people, but it appears at all ages, and also has many literary expressions. For example, in Tolstoy's *The Death of Ivan Ilych*, a major factor in the meaninglessness of Ivan's life before he becomes terminally ill is that he is a phony. When he realizes that he is dying, as an important part of redeeming himself from the meaninglessness of his earlier life, Ivan ceases to be a phony and rejects the phoniness of his family, friends, and doctors (Tolstoy 1960, 106–108, 137–138, 141–142, 148, 152–153). In Camus's *The Fall*, a crucial reason for Jean-Baptiste Clamence's decision to leave his life as a well-respected Parisian lawyer for a life of squalor in Amsterdam bars is his feeling that in his previous life he was a phony (1956, 47–48, 55–56, 60–61, 70–71, 84–90, 133–134). In Hemingway's 'The Snows of Kilimanjaro', Harry, in the few hours he has remaining until he dies, contemplates what he has not achieved in his life and comes to believe that phoniness is one of the factors that have led him to live a less meaningful life than he otherwise could have (2003, 8–11, 23). In Robert Yates's *Revolutionary Road*, a major reason for April Wheeler's feeling that her life is meaningless and for her decision to opt for a suicidal self-administered abortion is what she takes to be the inescapable phoniness that she senses in her life, her marriage, her husband, and their friends. She sees her suicidal abortion as 'something absolutely honest, something true', which, in her view, like all other honest and true things, 'turned out to be a thing that had to be done alone' (1961, 311). However, to the best of my knowledge, the nature of the relation between phoniness and life's meaninglessness has never been analysed. This chapter aims to explore this relation, suggesting that the relation is more complex and ambivalent than some of those who see phoniness as undermining life's meaning, and who therefore occasionally vigorously fight against phoniness, believe it to be.

1. What Typifies Phoniness

When one is being phony, one misrepresents reality in a way that one consciously or unconsciously takes to serve one's interests, understood widely as including one's interest in being liked and in enhancing one's positive self-image and public image. For example, when people are being phony, they may misrepresent themselves as kinder or cleverer than they actually are. They may also misrepresent themselves as less kind or clever than they are in order to appear 'tough' or to be socially accepted in a certain group. People are phony both in order to gain rewards and in order to avoid penalties (such as personal and social rejection). They can be phony both in showing positive attitudes, such as happiness or kindness, and in showing negative attitudes, such as anger or hatred (for example toward individuals, political leaders, or views that one feels that one is 'supposed' to hate; cf. Crisp and Cowton 1994, 344). It is possible to be phony while uttering true sentences if they imply wrong facts (for example, when what one says implies that one is an expert in a certain field). Phoniness need not be verbal: enthusiastic body language or friendly expressions such as smiles can also be phony. But people can also be phony in refraining from any positive or negative, verbal or physical, expression, as when one's silence indicates that one does not disagree with a view. The term 'phoniness' is derogatory; when we attribute phoniness to people, we are criticizing them. People do not want to be typified as phony, and if they are thus typified, they often try either to correct us or to change their behaviour.

Phoniness comes in degrees. A person's phoniness increases with (1) the percentage of time that person is phony; (2) the number of issues that person is phony about; (3) the difference between what that person represents and reality (for example, indicating that one loves a great deal more than one actually does is phonier than indicating that one loves only just slightly more than one actually does); and (4) the importance of the issues that person is phony about (for example, phoniness about one's deep moral beliefs makes one phonier than does phoniness about an unfunny joke). Phoniness has many possible bearers, but in this chapter I focus on the phoniness of individual people and only to a lesser degree on the phoniness of expressions, attitudes, relationships, organizations, societies, and cultures.

Phoniness may, but does not need to, involve self-deception, and one can be phony without being aware of it.[1] For example, in Salinger's *The Catcher in the Rye*, the young undergraduate Carl Luce, who often replies to questions with an 'obviously' or a 'certainly', explains that he prefers Chinese girlfriends because he 'simply happen[s] to find Eastern philosophy more satisfactory than Western' (1958, 152). If we questioned Mr.

---

[1] In discussions of hypocrisy, Statman (1997) argues that it often involves significant degrees of self-deception, while McKinnon (1991, 322–324) takes hypocrisy to always be consciously willed, and Crisp and Cowton (1994, 343–344) hold that it can but need not involve self-deception and be consciously willed. Alicke, Gordon, and Rose (2013, 674, 681–682) see this as an unresolved question and discuss laypersons' views on the topic.

Luce, we might discover that he in fact knows very little, if anything, about Western philosophies, Eastern philosophies, or the advantages of the latter over the former, and that he is saying what he does (or repeating what he has heard) because he senses that this will make him appear to be a sophisticated intellectual. Yet he may be completely unaware of all this and may be surprised when we suggest it. It is easier to remain unaware of a low degree of phoniness, but people can also be unaware of their quite high degrees of phoniness. It is unclear whether conscious phoniness should be considered to be worse than unwitting phoniness (if phoniness is bad—see section 5). On the one hand, knowing that one is phony yet continuing to be so seems more blameworthy than being phony without realizing it. On the other hand, unawareness of oneself, especially when the phoniness is of a high degree, is also unappealing. Unwitting phoniness should be distinguished, however, from simply making a mistake. In both cases, one misrepresents reality without being aware that one is doing so, but in the former one does so in a way that serves one's interests, often also ignoring readily available information. Although mistakes and unwitting phoniness differ, distinguishing between them in individual cases is often difficult, also because there are cases in which people's misrepresentations of reality are partly phony and partly mistaken.

Being phony should also be distinguished from other neighbouring notions such as lying, deceiving, cheating, pretending, being hypocritical, and being dishonest. The distinction is often not sharp, and there are many situations and behaviours that could accurately be described both with phoniness and with some of these other terms. Hence, much of what I will say in this chapter about phoniness and meaning in life also holds for these other notions and meaning in life. Yet there are differences in emphasis and connotation. First, the phrases 'lying', 'deceiving', 'cheating', 'pretending', 'being dishonest', and even 'being hypocritical' connote misrepresentation of reality in more conscious, deliberate, and serious ways than does phoniness, which may describe misrepresentations of reality that are lighter, less self-aware, and more automatic.[2] Second, the preceding notions tend to be more verbal than phoniness, which involves body language more often than the other concepts do. Third, these other notions seem to be more limited in time than phoniness, often referring to specific behaviours or events rather than to a condition, character trait, or attitude (hypocrisy, however, does seem somewhat similar to phoniness in this respect). Fourth, phoniness may be seen as more intimately related to a lack of self-confidence, an urge to please others, and submission to peer pressure than are lying, deceiving, etc. Fifth, since phoniness tends to be less conscious or deliberate than the other notions (including hypocrisy), it is more difficult to monitor and avoid than the others. Sixth, being harder to monitor, phoniness is also more prevalent than are the other behaviours. And finally, phoniness is generally treated as a less serious moral offence than the others are. Our main criticism of phoniness is not a *moral* one, because we do not see it as predominantly an attempt to take advantage of or harm

---

[2] For example, failing to mention that one hasn't read a book that was briefly mentioned in a conversation that then quickly moved on, thus allowing the impression that one has read it, can be a case of phoniness rather than of hypocrisy.

others (unlike lying, deceiving, cheating, pretending, being dishonest, or even being hypocritical), but often rather as an attempt to be liked (or not to be disliked) by others. We see phoniness primarily as something that suggests weakness rather than nastiness (this also holds for the literary examples of phoniness presented earlier). Nevertheless, some people, while feeling moral contempt towards liars, cheaters, pretenders, or hypocrites, feel a sharper non-moral contempt towards phonies, perhaps since the latter are seen as more moved by lack of self-confidence, an urge to please others, and submission to peer pressure. Curiously, some people seem to despise the urge to please others, lack of self-confidence, etc., more than they despise lying or deceiving. Related to this, it is hard to find people who are proud of being phony, while some are proud of their ability to lie, deceive, pretend, or even be hypocritical.

Phoniness also differs from bullshitting. Frankfurt claims that 'the essence of bullshit . . . is that it is *phony*' (2005, 47; emphasis in the original). But while, according to Frankfurt (2005, 33–34), bullshitters are indifferent to truth, phonies need not be so. Phonies may care about the truth, wish that their claims or insinuations expressed the truth, and feel bad about being phony, yet not have sufficient power or confidence to refrain from phoniness. Furthermore, Frankfurt presents bullshitting as intentional (2005, 41, n.5) and verbal, while phoniness need not be so.

Phoniness is also similar to inauthenticity in that both convey a misrepresentation of reality, and in both cases one can be unaware of one's own condition. But here, too, there are differences. 'Inauthenticity' is often used to describe an incongruence between the supposed 'kernel' of a person and how that person behaves and expresses herself.[3] Let us suppose that such a kernel exists (which I doubt) and even that we are able to clearly identify its nature. Under this interpretation of authenticity, inauthentic people need not be phony. For example, a feminist theorist might consider a woman who consciously adopts the traditional role of catering to her husband's needs while ignoring her own to be inauthentic but not phony. And just as inauthentic people need not be phony, phony people need not be inauthentic. For instance, if someone's hypothetical 'kernel' is taken to have to do with a will to be liked by others, there may well be circumstances in which acting phonily (so as to make others like one) would be authentic for that person.

Phoniness differs from politeness in that the latter doesn't misrepresent things but only communicates them in a pleasant, respectful way that often follows conventions. Although what is said politely might not be literally true (as in 'Nice to meet you', said to someone one does not yet know), the message is meant to be clear to both sender and recipient. Phoniness, however, involves misrepresentation. Thus, one can be polite without being phony. One can also be phony without being polite (for example, phonily assuming an impolite manner in order to appear more 'masculine').[4]

---

[3] There are other uses of 'authenticity' and 'inauthenticity', such as those of Heidegger and Sartre, that are heavily laden with philosophical theory. I do not have the space to discuss them here.

[4] For an elaborate discussion of the difference between politeness and hypocrisy, see McKinnon (1991, 324).

Phoniness should also be distinguished from self-deception. While people who deceive themselves are not aware that they are doing so, people who are phony may or may not be conscious of their phoniness. While in self-deception one misrepresents oneself to oneself, in phoniness one often also misrepresents oneself to others. And while phoniness involves self-interestedness, self-deception need not involve self-interestedness (see e.g. the impostor syndrome example later in the chapter). Being phony is quite close to being insincere, but insincerity, too, carries connotations of somewhat stronger awareness and intent than does phoniness, and seems to be more verbal and more related to specific behaviours or issues than to a condition or an attitude. 'Being false' is probably closer than all of the preceding notions to being phony.

Some may disagree on the specifics of the characteristics that I take to be more typical of phoniness than of the other notions, but for the purposes of this chapter the precise distinction between phoniness and these other notions is not very important. Much of what I will say in the following about meaning in life and phoniness also holds true for meaning in life and the neighbouring notions, and if readers prefer to think about meaning in life in connection with those notions, I have no objection. I focus here on phoniness since—perhaps because it is more difficult to avoid and more widespread than the other notions are, as well as because it often arouses harsher non-moral contempt—many tend to treat phoniness with special hostility and to see it as especially undermining life's meaning. Moreover, as will be discussed in section 4, phoniness is also more likely than the other notions to be seen as existing where in fact it does not.

2. How Phoniness Can Undermine Life's Meaning

There are several ways in which phoniness can undermine meaning. To see life as meaningful is to see it as having a sufficient number of aspects of sufficient value (see, e.g., Wolf 1997, 208–213; Metz 2001, 138; Cottingham 2003, 31; Brogaard and Smith 2005, 443; Landau 2017, 6–16). But to the extent that we ascribe disvalue to falseness, phoniness—which inserts falseness into our lives—undermines value and meaning in life. Furthermore, it conceals aspects of low value in people's lives, thus allowing them to remain unimproved; due to phoniness, people do not make efforts to maintain or achieve higher degrees of meaning. Phoniness can also lead those aware of its presence in their lives to feel that it is not *they* who are befriended, loved, or appreciated by others, but rather their façade. Thus, even when they are accomplished or in relationships, phonies sometimes feel that it is not *they* who are living their lives but someone else. Since it is their façade, rather than they themselves, who are in relationships they also sometimes feel alienated, lonely, excluded, and unappreciated; moreover, they fear that once they cease to be phony, they will be rebuffed. Put differently, while phoniness sometimes allows people to attain credit, positions, and relationships that they would otherwise not have had, at the same time it diminishes the genuineness of what is attained and, hence, also value and meaning in life. In some cases, less 'impressive' but more genuine achievements or relationships would have contributed more to life's meaning.

Another way in which phoniness undermines meaning has to do with its association with qualities such as weakness, lack of confidence, lack of character, or a tendency to ingratiate oneself with others. Such qualities are taken by many people who see themselves as phony to be humiliating for themselves and, thus, to diminish meaning.

I have focused thus far on cases in which people feel that they themselves are phony. But phoniness can also diminish meaning when it is attributed to others, rather than to oneself. Other people's phoniness can lead to deception that disrupts trust and smooth social functioning, weakens our sense of security, and decreases the ability to know reality and, hence, to find our way in the world. Taking others to be phony also undermines our ability to develop a rich and satisfying love or friendship with them, which is also an important potential source of meaning in life for many people; this undermining then leads to feelings of loneliness and alienation.[5] Others' (real or attributed) phoniness may also lead to an excessively cynical attitude that undercuts the capacity to see things as valuable and, thus, perceive life as meaningful. Phoniness can also decrease meaning when it is attributed to a society or a culture at large. Many people derive meaning from their identification with a society to which they belong and of which they are proud. But if they perceive many aspects of the society as phony, their inclination to see the accomplishments, achievements, and cultural heroes of that society as valuable and as related to themselves is weakened, thus diminishing their ability to gain meaning in life. This also holds true, of course, for other organizations or communities, such as one's church, social movement, political party, or profession.

Subjectivism and objectivism about meaning in life can be understood in more than one way (Landau 2020), but according to common understandings of the terms, phoniness can be seen as undermining life's meaning under both. As shown earlier, many of the ways in which phoniness undermines life's meaning have to do with views and feelings, which is what subjectivism about meaning in life focuses on (e.g. Ayer 1990, 189–96; Trisel 2002, 79). Conscious phoniness is likely to diminish meaning under subjectivism to a greater extent the stronger the phoniness is, the more one is aware of it, the more one conceives it as a wrong, and the more impact it has on other aspects of the subjective sphere (e.g. in creating feelings of alienation, loneliness, and lack of self-worth). But unwitting phoniness, too, can undermine life's meaning under subjectivism. It does so when it leads to lower achievements (of which one is aware) in the objective sphere, or to cases (of which one is aware) in which people distance themselves from one.

Objectivism about meaning in life (e.g. Smuts 2013; Bramble 2015) is often taken to focus on external actions and achievements and, as mentioned previously, phoniness can undermine meaning by allowing actions or achievements of lower objective value to appear to be of higher objective value, so that higher value is not aimed for or attained.

---

[5] This is vividly portrayed in Salinger's *The Catcher in the Rye* (1958).

Further, in some cases, the subjective results of phoniness, such as feelings of loneliness and depression, may lead people to give up on actions and achievements that might have increased objective value in their lives.

For hybridists about life's meaning, such as Wolf (2010, 13–33) and May (2015, 50–59), phoniness would diminish life's meaning when undermining either subjective attraction or objective attractiveness, or both. It is unclear whether phoniness undermines life's meaning under hybridism more than it does under subjectivism or under objectivism. On the one hand, there seem to be more cases of mere subjective attraction, and more cases of mere objective attractiveness, than cases of (fitting) subjective attraction to objective attractiveness, and thus more 'opportunities' for phoniness to disrupt meaning under subjectivism and under objectivism than under hybridism. On the other hand, since under hybridism phoniness can undermine meaning when undermining either its subjective or its objective aspects or both, it seems that meaning under hybridism is the most vulnerable to phoniness.

3. Reactions to Phoniness

There are several typical reactions to phoniness among those who identify it in themselves or in others and take it to undermine life's meaning. Some lose hope, treating it as inescapable. They seem to think that their own or others' phoniness is incurable and therefore take life, or central aspects of it, to be meaningless, believing there is not much they can do about it.

A second reaction is self-seclusion. Some hold that because everyone and everything around them are so phony, or because they themselves tend to fall into phoniness whenever they interact with others, their only hope of avoiding phoniness is to distance themselves from society. They therefore seclude themselves.[6] In some cases, they do not distance themselves from society completely, but only from certain aspects of it, such as from those that require a lot of human interaction or from functions that require self-promotion or adjustment to other people's preferences, such as working in sales or trying to rise in the ranks of hierarchical organizations. They interact with their social environment only on some limited level (usually strictly professional or formal), keep to themselves psychologically, and refrain from 'playing the game'. Some people try to distance themselves from society not alone but together with like-minded others, in a small community or a commune.

A third strategy, perhaps more common among younger people, is to try to fight phoniness by being unconventional, being destructive, and expressing oneself in a blunt or rude manner. Many people are phony because they are adapting to peer pressure and

---

[6] A literary expression of this can be found in Tolstoy's *Father Sergei*, in which the protagonist tries for some years to avoid others' (and his own) phoniness by choosing to live alone in a cave (Tolstoy 2003). See also the quote from Yates's *Revolutionary Road* at the beginning of this paper.

conventions, because they want to be liked, or because they wish to rise in the ranks of various organizations. Thus, behaving unconventionally, destructively, or rudely may safeguard a person from becoming phony. Ironically, however, in certain subgroups it is unconventionality itself that becomes the peer-pressured convention. Those who think of themselves as unconventional can be very conventional in following the subgroup's internal conventions, which differ only from the more common conventions of the wider society. Likewise, one's destructiveness can be a way of constructively rising in the social ranks of one's subgroup. More generally, people can easily adopt non-phony mannerisms in a phony way, and can fight their own and others' phoniness phonily.

Yet a fourth strategy is to seek intensive and strong experiences that, by completely dominating one's attention for a while, disallow phoniness. This may be one source of some people's intuition that war, danger, pain, and, again, destructiveness (or romanticized representations thereof) can sometimes augment rather than undermine life's meaning. Perhaps this is also one of the sources of the interest in other intense experiences, such as mystical enlightenment and sex (or, again, romanticized representations of them), as enhancing meaning in life.

A fifth, and perhaps more realistic and less radical, way of trying to cope with phoniness is to educate oneself to be less phony. Although phoniness is often a strong and deeply ingrained habit that is difficult to monitor, it is not entirely undetectable or incorrigible. Attention and training can help. Although such efforts affect only one's own phoniness, rather than the phoniness of others or of society, having an effect on oneself is already an important change.

And a sixth way of coping with phoniness—again, in my view, more realistic and constructive than some others, although it is not commonly employed—involves considering whether one's standards are not too high or even unrealistic. Phoniness is often used to cover a gap between one's standards, on the one hand, and one's behaviours and feelings, on the other. Of course, when behaviours and feelings can be improved to match plausible standards, they should. But if they cannot, and the standards are too high and unattainable, another way of coping with the gap, instead of disguising it by phoniness, is to endorse more plausible standards, recognizing that people can be good and worthy even if they are not tremendously knowledgeable, confident, clever, popular, moral, successful, etc. This also holds for overly high standards for humility and lack of ego. Probably influenced by Christian discussions (e.g., Matthew 6:1–5), some favourite targets of those who criticize both themselves and others for phoniness are concealed pride, pursuit of social esteem, and self-interestedness. But standards that demand the *complete* elimination of these urges are, for most people, unrealistic. The urges are strong and prove resilient to efforts to eradicate them, just reappearing with a different content (for example, trying to eradicate one's pride sometimes leads to pride for trying to eradicate one's pride or to pride in being humble). Furthermore, when related to positive ends, and not excessively strong, these urges are legitimate and can even be helpful, as they can help to motivate the achievement of much that is good in life. Lowering overly high standards for humility and lack of ego by accepting as legitimate, and being open about, some degrees of pride, pursuit of social esteem, and self-interestedness may considerably diminish phoniness.

Phoniness and meaninglessness are related in being founded on the same basic structure or source, namely a sensed gap between standards and reality (see Camus 2000, 33–34, 51 for a discussion of this structure as constituting the absurd). The feeling that the reality of one's life falls short of one's standards, that is, that one is insufficient, leads both to efforts to disguise it by phoniness and to seeing one's life as meaningless. In Landau (2017, 31–63, 267–273), I call for lowering implausibly high standards as a central way of coping with life's meaninglessness. Doing so also makes it possible to cope better with phoniness.

4. Misidentifying the Prevalence or Degree of Phoniness

Some people react to phoniness more strongly than necessary because they take their own or others' lives, or society or culture at large, to be phonier than they really are and, hence, also more meaningless than they really are. It is easy to be mistaken about the prevalence and degree of phoniness. One source of mistakes is wrong views about what the putatively phony expressions refer to. For example, we may wrongly interpret as phony an enthusiastic evaluation of an artwork or a scholarly achievement because we incorrectly undervalue that artwork or achievement.

Another source of mistakes in ascribing phoniness is the misinterpretation of verbal and nonverbal expressions. People may incorrectly attribute phoniness to themselves when they misperceive how they have represented themselves to others. For example, a person might believe that he has represented himself as being very smart when in fact he has only represented himself as being moderately smart. When ascribing phoniness to other people, too, we may wrongly interpret what is, in fact (for example), a display of moderate love to be a display of strong love, and thus phony. Such inaccurate attributions of phoniness are especially likely to occur with members of cultures or subcultures with which we are unfamiliar. For example, the first time that I went to North America, I took the casual utterances of service workers, such as 'How are you today, sir?' to be phony once I had gathered that they were not really interested in a real answer. It took me some time to understand that they were just saying 'hello' in a lengthier, more polite way. Expressions should not be understood literally, but according to their real meaning in the culture in which they are presented. What has been said here of cultures is true also of subcultures. For example, youngsters sometimes take older people to be phony when the youngsters interpret literally the verbal and nonverbal expressions of mere politeness that older people sometimes use, such as 'Glad to meet you' and smiles. Thus, those who interact with members of other cultures or subcultures should be especially aware of the likelihood of misinterpreting gestures by members of other cultures, or even the whole cultures themselves, as phony.

Yet another source of incorrect attributions of phoniness is the misinterpretation of internal states. When we attribute phoniness, we take an external event, such as the display of a high degree of interest, to misrepresent an internal state, such as a low degree of interest. But since other people's internal states are hidden from us, it is easy to misconceive them. For example, people to whom we ascribe a phony expression of interest may in fact be as interested as they represent themselves to be. Those who are convinced that what all people really want all the time is just 'money, sex, and power' will wrongly see all expressions of compassion, intellectual curiosity, love, friendship, moral sensitivity, religious sentiment, etc., as phony. Since people are not fully transparent even to themselves, they may also be mistaken about their own internal states and wrongly ascribe phoniness to themselves. For example, a person may think that she has represented herself as more courageous, more knowledgeable, or smarter than she really is, when in fact she is indeed very courageous, knowledgeable, or smart. This may well happen when people are afflicted, for example, with what has come to be called 'impostor syndrome' (Clance and Imes 1978), that is, the conviction held by many gifted and successful people that they are significantly less talented or capable than they are commonly taken to be, so that the position and reputation they have achieved are undeserved. For example, academics who suffer from this syndrome may think that they achieved their academic status only because they were lucky, polite, or knew how to make a good impression on others, rather than because of their real competence or the genuinely high quality of their work.[7]

What has been said here of those afflicted with impostor syndrome also holds for all others with unjustly deprecating views of themselves, such as those who are overly modest, insufficiently confident, or somewhat depressed. Even people who have achieved very much can have wrong, harshly self-deprecating views of their contributions or abilities. Montaigne, for example, writes: 'if only talking to oneself did not look mad, no day would go by without my being heard growling to myself, against myself, "you silly shit!"' (2003, 264; *Essays* I, 38).[8] Likewise, Wittgenstein (1998, 16–17) complains that he never contributed any original idea to philosophy; in his view, he merely reproduced what others had already said, only adding clarification and comparison. Other common emotional tendencies, such as survivor guilt (see e.g. Niederland 1981; Williams 1988), in which, after having taken part in events in which others were harmed, people wrongly experience guilt even if they have done nothing wrong, can also unnecessarily lead people to consider themselves phony. Although they are, in fact,

---

[7] In earlier stages of research, impostor syndrome was thought to be more prevalent among women than among men. However, some of the recent research on the syndrome does not identify such differences. See e.g. Badawy et al. (2018, 157, 161); Patzak, Kollmayer, and Schober (2017, 2–3).

[8] However, he also emphasizes that this self-contempt is only one of several conflicting emotions, and adds 'yet I do not intend that [the self-contempt] to be a definition of me' (2003, 264).

guilty of nothing, they consider themselves not only guilty but also phony, since they behave as if they were not guilty.

Wrong attributions of phoniness can also result from misconceptions of people's ambivalence. Many people emotionally react to much in their lives in a number of different ways at the same time, some of the reactions conflicting with each other—broadcasting, so to speak, on several channels even if only one of them appears on the screen. This may lead some people to believe, once they realize that they or others also have other, even if slighter, reactions that they have not conveyed, that they are phony not to have conveyed them all. (Sometimes they also wrongly suppose that the reactions not conveyed must be the 'true' ones, and that those that are conveyed must be false.) But it is implausible and unrealistic to demand of oneself or others to represent all of one's reactions. In order to function successfully, people often have to follow only their main reaction or reactions. Failing to express or act upon the others should not be considered phoniness.

Some take their own and others' lives to be phonier than they really are because they are oversensitive to phoniness and insufficiently sensitive to non-phoniness; they take notice only of the events in which they and others have been phony, while completely overlooking all the many events in which they and others have not been phony. Further, for some, even a few cases of slight phoniness are sufficient to contaminate a person as a phony (although they would not hold, for example, that a person who occasionally makes a stupid mistake is an idiot).[9] For them, distinctions in the prevalence and intensity of phoniness are irrelevant. Some also adopt the 'suspected therefore guilty' or the 'guilty till proven innocent' principles regarding their own and others' phoniness, so that in any case of doubt whether phoniness has or has not occurred, they judge that it has. In order to corroborate their view, those who see phoniness as extremely pervasive and radical sometimes emphasize that phoniness presents itself as non-phoniness and, thus, may well pass unnoticed. Sometimes they also present cases in which people who had hidden their phoniness were exposed as phony. Such cases suggest that phoniness may be more common than meets the eye, but not that it is as common or pervasive as some take it to be.

But since people may well be mistaken about the extent and degree of others' and their own phoniness, it is wise, before embarking on crusades against it, to examine whether one is correctly identifying the phoniness that one aims to combat. Such an examination may save people from unnecessarily seeing life as highly phony and meaningless, as well as from distancing themselves from society or culture, opting for rudeness and unconventionality, or engaging in other types of unnecessary effort to diminish theirs or others' supposed phoniness.

---

[9] Salinger (1958) portrays Holden Caulfield as often doing this.

5. Does Phoniness Always Undermine Meaning?

In the previous section, I focused on cases in which negative reactions to phoniness are misplaced since the phoniness does not in fact exist to the degree or in the way in which it is believed to do. But some negative reactions to phoniness are unnecessary even when phoniness and meaninglessness *are* identified correctly. Even when we correctly identify the extent of phoniness in a meaningless life, we may still be mistaken on whether the phoniness *makes* that life meaningless. A life can be both meaningless and phony without being meaningless *because* it is phony. It may well be meaningless for other reasons, such as one's loneliness, one's failure to achieve important goals in life, or one's inability to be satisfied with whatever one has achieved. In such cases, focusing wrongly on phoniness as the source of the meaninglessness in one's life and combating the phoniness instead of the real sources of the meaninglessness will be unhelpful. Moreover, in some cases not only does phoniness not lead to meaninglessness but, in fact, the opposite occurs: it is meaninglessness that leads to phoniness. Some of those whose lives are meaningless due to sources of meaninglessness other than phoniness behave in a phony manner in order to conceal this meaninglessness from themselves or from others. In the latter cases, too, combating phoniness in order to diminish meaninglessness will be unhelpful.

There are also cases in which combating phoniness is counterproductive because phoniness, in fact, enhances, rather than undermines, life's meaning. Many discussions of hypocrisy present examples of hypocritical behaviours that have positive results from the moral point of view. Thus Feder Kittay (1982, 277) describes a sexist employer who hires a well-qualified woman in order to impress some women with his 'open-mindedness'. Alicke, Gordon, and Rose (2013, 685) present an example of a racist football team owner who hires talented African-American players. Shklar (1984, 78) points out that pretended virtue may curtail corruption. Although these behaviours do not seem to enhance the agents' meaning in life, they may well enhance other people's meaning in life. And I would take many cases in which one improves one's life in the domains of the good, the true, and the beautiful (see Metz 2013, 222–239) while phonily concealing that one is partly motivated by pride or by interest in social esteem to also enhance one's meaning in life (cf. Landau 2017, 179–184).

Another way in which phoniness sometimes enhances or, at least, protects meaning has to do with what Feder Kittay (1982, 287–289; see also McKinnon 1991, 325) calls *victim hypocrisy*, that is, the hypocrisy that victims endorse in order to alleviate their oppression or even plainly to survive. For those for whom the non-phony, assertive, or confrontational alternative is psychologically, economically, socially, or politically too costly or even impossible, phoniness—if it is not excessively high—can be a helpful and at times necessary way of protecting meaningful aspects of life.

Likewise, in some cases, a certain degree of phoniness allows people to work together efficiently as a team and, thus, attain important goals (such as medical breakthroughs) that can enhance life's meaning both for themselves and for others. It may also be that friendship and love—very important ingredients of life's meaning—cannot survive without at least some small degrees of phoniness. People who are completely un-phony may be quite lonely and perhaps also a little depressed, since they may find it difficult to cooperate with others professionally or personally.

Another category in which phoniness can enhance meaning is that of 'fake it till you make it'. These are cases in which the way to reach a certain state of mind is initially to fake it. When this happens, one's happiness, sympathy, compassion, love, courage, etc., are feigned at the beginning (sometimes unwittingly), but as things proceed, they become sincere. The initial phoniness disappears not because one's representation of oneself has changed to match one's inner reality but, rather, because one's inner reality has changed to match the representation. Of course, it is problematic if the phony condition continues forever, or even for too long.[10] And there might sometimes be other, better ways of changing inner reality. But if there are none, or they are not easily available, and one does in fact change for the better within a reasonable period of time, such phoniness could be seen as enhancing meaning.

6. Conclusion

I have explained in this chapter how phoniness can undermine various types of meaning in life, and have pointed at several ways of coping with phoniness. But I have also argued that we can be wrong about the existence and degree of phoniness in our own and in others' lives and about the degree to which phoniness undermines meaning. Moreover, there are cases in which phoniness even enhances meaning. Under some circumstances, phoniness promotes more meaning in life than would the truth that phoniness conceals. More generally, there are circumstances in which untruth enhances life's meaning while truth undermines it. However, an important difference between untruth and truth in this context is that untruth sometimes has *instrumental* value for promoting meaning in life. True knowledge of some things, on the other hand, can have both *instrumental* value for promoting meaning and, as Metz (2013, 229–230) points out, *intrinsic* value as part of what constitutes meaning in life.

Hence, cases of phoniness, and their impact on meaning, should be distinguished from each other. Those who try, in order to protect or enhance meaning, to rid themselves and their environment of any phoniness, sometimes scathingly, may be using a medicine that exacerbates the sickness they are trying to cure. In many cases, the correct

---

[10] Hence the 'till' in the idiom 'fake it *till* you make it' seems problematic. 'Fake it to make it if doing so is helpful' would be preferable.

attitude toward phoniness and phonies should be more compassionate, understanding, and empathetic than the attitude that many people show. It is good to remember that the charge of phoniness can also be a way of bullying weaker people who use phoniness in order to survive in a difficult world. (One can contest phoniness phonily.) Many should also be more understanding, empathetic, and compassionate towards the phoniness they identify in themselves.[11]

Distinguishing between the cases where phoniness, all in all, undermines meaning and those where, all in all, it enhances it (as well as those where the impact of phoniness is neutral or not important enough to deal with) is not always easy. But it seems that low degrees of phoniness are often the ones that enhance meaning or are harmless, while high degrees of phoniness are more likely to be those that, overall, undermine meaning. Yet, in some cases, especially for people who are psychologically, socially, or economically weak, even higher degrees of phoniness may enhance meaning. Many cases of phoniness simultaneously undermine meaning in some ways while enhancing it in other ways. Much depends, of course, on context and on the details of the short- and long-term impact of the phony behaviours on meaning.

This partly rehabilitative discussion of phoniness should not be mistaken, however, for a suggestion that we should always accept phoniness. I agree that, especially in the present marketing- and achievement-oriented culture, phoniness often appears to an overly high degree that in many cases abrades meaning.[12] Many are not aware of the excessive phoniness in their lives and of the negative impact that this has on their lives' meaning. Many also miss how, because phoniness is hard to monitor and can become habitual, it can easily permeate from one sphere of life (e.g. the economic) into others (e.g. the personal). Thus, while criticizing the simplistic view that phoniness always undermines meaning and should always be shunned, I am not endorsing the inverse simplistic view. I am calling, rather, for a more precise and nuanced understanding of the relation between phoniness and meaning that would lead to accepting some forms and degrees of phoniness while rejecting others.[13]

---

[11] For example, I find Jean-Baptiste Clamence's self-flagellation for his phoniness in Camus's *The Fall* (1956) to be unnecessary, and his move to Amsterdam, in order to rid his life of its phoniness, to have considerably diminished meaning in his life. Clamence's phoniness had much to do with the fact that he was not very self-confident and that he very much wanted others to like and think well of him. But these are not such terrible traits.

[12] Note that unlike sources of meaninglessness such as acts of cruelty, loss of dear ones, or betrayal of one's cause, which can diminish meaning sharply over a short period of time, phoniness *abrades* meaning, grinding it down slowly and continuously. Thus, it can sometimes be difficult to notice the harmful impact it can have on life's meaning. In this quality, phoniness is similar to sources of meaninglessness such as laziness or conceitedness.

[13] Earlier drafts of this paper were read at *The First International Conference on Philosophy and Meaning in Life*, Hokkaido University, Sapporo, Japan (20–21 August 2018) and at the *Meaning in Life and Meaning of Life International Workshop*, University of Graz, Austria (17–19 June 2019). I am grateful to the participants at these meetings for their helpful comments. I am also very grateful to Dorothy Bauhoff, Marie Deer, Peter Hacker, Samuel Lebens, Ariel Meirav, Saul Smilansky, Daniel Statman, and Michele L. Waldinger for their helpful comments on earlier drafts of this paper.

References

Alicke, M., E. Gordon, and D. Rose. 2013. 'Hypocrisy: What Counts?' *Philosophical Psychology* 26(5): 673–701.
Ayer, A. J. 1990. 'The Meaning of Life.' In A. J. Ayer, *The Meaning of Life and Other Essays*, 178–197. London: Weidenfeld and Nicolson.
Badawy, R. L., B. A. Gazdag, J. R. Bentley, and R. L. Brouer. 2018. 'Are All Impostors Created Equal? Exploring Gender Differences in the Impostor Phenomenon-Performance Link.' *Personality and Individual Differences* 131: 156–163.
Bramble, B. 2015. 'Consequentialism about Meaning in Life.' *Utilitas* 27(4): 445–459.
Brogaard, B., and B. Smith. 2005. 'On Luck, Responsibility and the Meaning of Life.' *Philosophical Papers* 34(3): 443–458.
Camus, A. 1956. *The Fall*, trans. J. O'Brien. New York: Knopf.
Camus, A. 2000. *The Myth of Sisyphus*, trans. J. O'Brien. London: Penguin.
Clance, P. R., and S. A. Imes. 1978. 'The Impostor Phenomenon in High Achieving Women: Dynamics and Therapeutic Intervention.' *Psychotherapy Theory, Research, and Practice* 15(3): 241–247.
Cottingham, J. 2003. *On the Meaning of Life*. London: Routledge.
Crisp, R., and C. Cowton. 1994. 'Hypocrisy and Moral Seriousness.' *American Philosophical Quarterly* 31(4): 343–349.
Feder Kittay, E. 1982. 'On Hypocrisy.' *Metaphilosophy* 13: 277–289.
Frankfurt, H. G. 2005. *On Bullshit*. Princeton, NJ: Princeton University Press.
Hemingway, E. 2003. 'The Snows of Kilimanjaro.' In E. Hemingway, *The Snows of Kilimanjaro and Other Stories*, 3–28. New York: Scribner.
Landau, I. 2017. *Finding Meaning in an Imperfect World*. New York: Oxford University Press.
Landau, I. 2021. 'Externalism, Internalism, and Meaningful Lives.' *Ratio* 34(2): 137–146.
May, T. 2015. *A Significant Life*. Chicago: University of Chicago Press.
McKinnon, C. 1991. 'Hypocrisy, With a Note on Integrity.' *American Philosophical Quarterly* 28(4): 321–330.
Metz, T. 2001. 'The Concept of a Meaningful Life.' *American Philosophical Quarterly* 38(2): 137–153.
Metz, T. 2013. *Meaning in Life*. Oxford: Oxford University Press.
Montaigne, Michel de. 2003. *The Complete Essays*, trans. M. A. Screech. London: Penguin.
Niederland, W. G. 1981. 'The Survivor Syndrome: Further Observations and Dimensions.' *Journal of the American Psychoanalytic Association* 29(2): 413–425.
Patzak, A., M. Kollmayer, and B. Schober. 2017. 'Buffering Impostor Feelings with Kindness.' *Frontiers in Psychology* 8: 1–10.
Salinger, J. D. 1958. *The Catcher in the Rye*. Harmondsworth, UK: Penguin.
Shklar, J. M. 1984. *Ordinary Vices*. Cambridge, MA: Belknap Press.
Smuts, A. 2013. 'The Good Cause Account of the Meaning of Life.' *Southern Journal of Philosophy* 51(4): 536–562.
Statman, D. 1997. 'Hypocrisy and Self-Deception.' *Philosophical Psychology* 10: 57–75.
Tolstoy, L. 1960. 'The Death of Ivan Ilych,' trans. A. Maude. In L. Tolstoy, *The Death of Ivan Ilych and Other Stories*, 95–156. New York: Signet.
Tolstoy, L. 2003. 'Father Sergei.' In L. Tolstoy, *The Devil and Other Stories*, trans. L. Maude and A. Maude, rev. R. F. Gustafson, 237–279. Oxford: Oxford University Press.
Trisel, B. A. 2002. 'Futility and the Meaning of Life Debate.' *Sorites* 14: 70–84.

Williams, T. 1988. 'Diagnosis and Treatment of Survivor Guilt'. In *Human Adaptation to Extreme Stress*, 319–336, ed. J. P. Wilson, Z. Harel, and B. Kahana. Boston: Springer.

Wittgenstein, L. 1998. *Culture and Value: A Selection from the Posthumous Remains*, trans. P. Winch, rev. ed. A. Pichler. Oxford: Blackwell.

Wolf, S. 1997. 'Happiness and Meaning: Two Aspects of the Good Life'. *Social Philosophy and Policy* 14(1): 227–225.

Wolf, S. 2010. *Meaning in Life and Why It Matters*. Princeton, NJ: Princeton University Press.

Yates, R. 1961. *Revolutionary Road*. Boston: Little, Brown.

CHAPTER 25

GRATITUDE AND MEANING IN LIFE

TONY MANELA

1. Introduction

MANY people find it obvious that gratitude is necessary for meaning in life. Many also find it obvious that the relationship between gratitude and meaningfulness is a positive one: the more gratitude in our lives, the more meaningful our lives are. The truth about the relationship between gratitude and meaning in life, however, is more complicated. This is in part because we use gratitude terms to refer to two distinct attitudes. One is the attitude we reference when we speak of gratitude *to* someone. The other is the attitude we reference when we talk of gratitude *that* something is the case. The purpose of this chapter is to discuss the variety of ways these two attitudes influence meaning in life. It will discuss ways that they, in their ideal forms, can enhance and threaten meaningfulness, and how their pathological relatives, like ingratitude and overgratitude, can further undermine meaning in life.

2. Preliminaries

To set the stage for this discussion, I will begin with a few preliminary remarks about meaning in life and a few preliminary remarks about gratitude.

2.1. Theories of Meaning in Life

This chapter is intended to help philosophers incorporate insights about gratitude into their understanding of meaning in life. Unfortunately, though, given space constraints, I will not be able to discuss how gratitude is relevant to every theory of meaning in life. I will remain silent on nihilistic or pessimistic theories of meaning in life, and I will also remain silent on supernaturalist theories of meaning in life.[1] This chapter, in other words, will focus exclusively on optimistic, naturalist theories of meaning in life. I would like this chapter to be useful to as many philosophers as possible working within that tradition. So, in this chapter, rather than presupposing a particular narrow theory of meaning in life, I will presuppose a vague, inclusive and pluralistic view of meaning in life—a view in which most philosophers working in the naturalist tradition will recognize elements of theories they find plausible. Meaning in life, I will take it, is a kind of value in life, which has subjective and objective dimensions, and tends to give a life coherence, organize it around a purpose, and/or give it significance. It tends to be enhanced by things like pleasure, subjective feelings of satisfaction, objectively worthwhile achievements, creative projects, morally upstanding or heroic conduct, being part of noble causes larger than oneself, and deep and healthy social and romantic relationships. It also tends to be enhanced when the subjective elements line up with the objective ones (e.g. when one subjectively enjoys working toward an objectively worthwhile achievement), and a person's life tends to be more meaningful the wider and more long-lasting the positive effects of her actions are. I will also take it that certain things can detract from a life's overall meaningfulness, or count as negative meaning or anti-meaning in a life. These things include committing severely immoral acts, as well as contributing to evil or nefarious causes or projects.

2.2. Gratitude

In order to see how gratitude influences meaning in life, it is important to distinguish two concepts that we use gratitude terms to refer to. Sometimes, we use gratitude terms to describe a two-place relation between a person and something (e.g., a state of affairs) he finds valuable. We do this when we say things like, 'Yardley is grateful *that* it did not rain on his wedding day'. We also do this when we describe an attitude a person has toward good things that were not given to him by anyone, as in, 'Yardley is grateful *for* sunny days like today', or 'Yardley is grateful *for* his children' (when uttered about, e.g., a non-theist). Sometimes, though, we use gratitude terms to describe a *three*-place relation, as in, 'Yardley is grateful *to* Rachel for saving him'. In cases like this, gratitude terms are used to describe an attitude that a beneficiary, Y, has regarding a benefactor, R, as a result of something, ϕ, that R did. This use of gratitude terms, unlike the two-place relation use, always involves the preposition *to*.

---

[1] Gratitude will play a large role in such theories, of course, since having an appropriate relationship to supernatural entities like God will almost certainly involve gratitude to such entities. But what exactly gratitude to such entities is, and how it fits into a supernaturalist account of meaningfulness, would perhaps be best dealt with by theologians in particular religious traditions.

Perhaps surprisingly, the attitude described by the two-place relation use of gratitude terms and the one described by the three-place relation use of gratitude terms are distinct attitudes (Manela 2016a; 2019a, §1; R. Roberts and Telech 2019, 1). Though they often occur together, neither one logically or conceptually implies the presence of the other. It is possible, for a given Y, R, and ϕ, for Y to be grateful *to* R *for* ϕ-ing but not grateful *for* R or grateful *that* R ϕ-ed, and vice versa (Manela 2016a, 281–283; 2020, 3249–3254). Some philosophers have noted that the attitude expressed by the two-place use of gratitude terms (gratitude *that* and gratitude *for* [but not to]) is essentially a kind of *appreciation* (Gulliford, Morgan, and Kristjánsson 2013, 299; Manela 2016a, 289–290; R. Roberts and Telech 2019, 1). To be grateful that it did not rain on my wedding day is just to appreciate that it did not rain on my wedding day. To be grateful for sunny days like today is just to appreciate sunny days like today. In this chapter, I will use the term 'appreciation' to refer to the attitude expressed by the two-place use of gratitude terms. The attitude expressed by the three-place use of gratitude terms (Y's gratitude *to* R *for* ϕ-ing), which always involves the preposition *to*, is sometimes called targeted gratitude (McAleer 2012, 55) or prepositional gratitude (Manela 2016a, 281). In this chapter, the terms 'gratitude' and 'grateful', when not preceded by any specifying term, will refer to prepositional gratitude.

One difference between prepositional gratitude and appreciation has to do with the circumstances that call for each attitude. As I noted earlier, appreciation is the fitting response to good things—things one finds valuable for oneself. Prepositional gratitude, on the other hand, is the fitting response, in a beneficiary, to ϕ-ing that is at least in part done out of *benevolence* for that beneficiary (Berger 1975, 299; R. C. Roberts 2004, 62; Manela 2016a, 284; McConnell 2019, 36). By *benevolence* here I mean, roughly, a desire to benefit someone for that person's own sake, and not merely as a means to some other end. Paradigm examples of gratitude-warranting benevolence include giving a beneficiary a gift he appreciates, when this gift-giving behaviour is ultimately motivated primarily by the thought of the recipient's happily enjoying the gift. Examples of gratitude-worthy benevolence also include successful helping behaviours motivated primarily by sympathy, empathy, or compassion for the beneficiary. Sometimes, people can act benevolently towards us in ways we do not find valuable for ourselves, or in ways that we do not welcome or enjoy, and those are cases when we can be grateful *to* someone for acting a certain way but not grateful *that* they did (Manela 2016a, 282–283; 2020, 3249–3254). And sometimes, people can benefit us in important ways without benevolently intending to do so, and those are cases when we can be grateful *that* someone acted as they did without being grateful *to* them for so acting.

Appreciation and prepositional gratitude are distinguished not just in when they are called for, but also in how they are constituted. Appreciation has both a cognitive component and an affective component, which are each necessary and jointly sufficient for a person to count as appreciative. More specifically, to appreciate something is (1) to recognize it as valuable or good for oneself, and (2) to welcome it, enjoy it, or be glad that it is in one's life (Manela 2020, 3248). So to appreciate one's children, or be grateful *for* one's children, is to recognize how valuable they are and to welcome their presence in one's life. To appreciate, or be grateful *that*, the weather was pleasant on one's wedding day is to recognize how valuable that state of affairs was and to have welcomed it. If either one of these components is missing, then a person might be glad, or aware that something is valuable, but he will not be *grateful for* that thing, or *grateful that* something is the case.[2]

Prepositional gratitude, as the called-for response to a benevolent act, is a different attitude. Part of being grateful *to* someone is recognizing that an act of benevolence has occurred (Berger 1975, 302; Walker 1980–1981; Manela 2019b, 299). A grateful beneficiary should also remember the particular act of benevolence for which he is grateful. Any beneficiary who fails to recognize an act of benevolence or quickly forgets that it occurred would fail to be a grateful beneficiary. But prepositional gratitude involves more than just recognition and remembering. It also involves the motivation to express thanks to a benefactor (Berger 1975, 42; Swinburne 1989, 65, 67; McConnell 1993, 57; Manela 2019b, 301–303).[3] A beneficiary who felt no urge to thank his benefactor would seem to fall short of gratitude, even if he recognized and remembered an act of benevolence. Beyond recognition and expression, a grateful beneficiary should also have certain feelings regarding the beneficiary. Specifically, part of being grateful is bearing a special sort of goodwill toward a benefactor—a desire or hope that she fare well, and a tendency to be sad when she is not doing well (Walker 1980–1981, 50–51; Fitzgerald 1998, 120; Manela 2016a, 283; 2016b, 136). Related to this, a prepositionally grateful beneficiary should also be motivated to do certain things that will benefit, help, or please his benefactor (Camenisch 1981; McConnell 1993, 48–51; Manela 2016a,

---

[2] Some might suspect that there is a third necessary condition for appreciation: in addition to recognizing something as valuable and welcoming it, one must also *not* feel entitled to it or take it for granted. This possibility is suggested by examples like the following: imagine a person born into a well-off family in a privileged segment of society, who works hard and finds himself wealthy as an adult. Such a person might recognize his wealth as valuable and welcome the fact that he's wealthy, but he might not feel grateful for his wealth because he attributes it entirely to his own efforts. He believes that such efforts were sufficient on their own to bring about his wealth, and so he feels entitled to his wealth; he takes for granted that given his hard work, he could expect to be wealthy. Such a person seems to meet the two conditions I listed earlier, but he seems to fall short of being grateful for his wealth, because of his strong belief that his wealth resulted entirely from his own efforts. This might suggest that feelings of entitlement or taking something for granted can disqualify one from being properly appreciative, or *grateful for*. And that would imply that not feeling entitled, or taking something for granted, is a third necessary condition for being *grateful for*.

A little reflection shows, though, that this third condition is actually implied by my first condition. Part of accurately recognizing something's value is understanding how rare it is—how hard it is to come by. The person in the example in the previous paragraph fails to recognize the role that chance played in his winding up wealthy—the role played by his luck in being born into a privileged segment of society. He thus overestimates a person's chances of being wealthy, and underestimates the value of his being wealthy, and that explains why he falls short of fully appreciating his wealth, or being grateful for it. I am grateful to both Jason D'Cruz and to Iddo Landau for each independently raising this concern.

[3] There are virtually no philosophers who argue against this point, though Roslyn Weiss (1985, 496–497) believed that the requirement to thank was a social rather than a moral requirement associated with gratitude.

283–284; 2019b, 300–301).[4] Part of being grateful to someone who does you a favour, for instance, is being willing to do them a similar favour in the future if they ever need it, and to do it for their sake. If someone benevolently rescues you at great risk to themselves, then insofar as you are grateful, you should be prepared to risk a similar amount to rescue or help them in the future, should they need rescuing. If someone benevolently gives you a gift they want you to enjoy, then insofar as you are grateful to them, you should keep an eye out for and be willing to buy them a similar gift, should the opportunity arise (Wellman 1999, 287). In the meantime, you should take care not to lose their gift or damage it. And you should be motivated to try to enjoy the gift as your benefactor hoped you would (Camenisch 1981, 10). A grateful beneficiary will recognize that his benefactor gave the gift benevolently, and he will see his benefactor's benevolence as an invitation from his benefactor to enjoy the gift—an invitation his benefactor would be pleased to see him accept. A beneficiary need not have an ongoing relationship with a benefactor in order to act gratefully towards them. In fact, beneficiaries can act gratefully even towards *inaccessible benefactors*: benefactors who are anonymous or deceased. Imagine an anonymous or now-deceased benefactor had benevolently given you the tuition money you needed to attend the college of your dreams. Even though you cannot present such a benefactor with a similar gift in the future, your gratitude might take the form of 'paying it forward' (Walker 1980–1981, 50; Card 1988, 120; McConnell 1993, 72–79). Paying for someone else's college in the future might be a fitting way to manifest your gratitude insofar as you think such an act would please your benefactor. It can sometimes be difficult to think of ways to benefit inaccessible benefactors, like anonymous or deceased benefactors, and there could be several fitting ways to do that—of which paying it forward and trying to enjoy a benefit are just two. However, any beneficiary who recognizes an act of benevolence but feels no desire to please or help a benefactor when an opportunity presents itself falls short of gratitude. To sum up: prepositional gratitude consists of four elements, each of which is required for a beneficiary to count as grateful. These elements are (1) recognition that an act of benevolence occurred, (2) motivation to express thanks to the benefactor, (3) an enhanced tendency to wish the benefactor well to a certain extent in the future (that is, a beneficiary's tendency to be happy when he learns his benefactor is flourishing and sad or upset when he learns his benefactor is suffering), and (4) an enhanced willingness or motivation to advance or protect the benefactor's interests (e.g. a motivation to please, benefit, protect, or refrain from harming the benefactor in certain ways) in the future, should an opportunity arise.

In the next two sections of this chapter, I will discuss ways that reflection on each of these concepts can shed light on meaning in life. I will begin with a discussion of prepositional gratitude.

---

[4] Those who dispute this point include Roslyn Weiss (1985, 492) and Patrick Fitzgerald (1998, 120). For arguments against those philosophers on this point, see Manela (2016a, 283).

3. Prepositional Gratitude and Meaning in Life

Prepositional gratitude can enhance meaning in life in a variety of positive ways. For instance, part of prepositional gratitude is recognizing that someone else has goodwill toward us, and the experience of that recognition can be a positive one. It can boost our self-esteem or self-respect when we realize someone else found us important enough to be worthy of their help, kindness, thought, or time (Berger 1975, 302). Sometimes, when people show us benevolence, they also reveal that they trust us to help them in similar ways if they are ever in trouble (Camenisch 1981, 15, 19; Card 1988, 120); and knowing we are trusted in such ways can make our life more meaningful, in that it can reveal how we are connected to others, that we are important for something beyond ourselves, and that we have a purpose.

Grateful feelings and behaviours can also contribute to the meaningfulness of a life. A beneficiary who feels prepositional gratitude will wish his benefactor well and will be motivated to help her in the future—to reciprocate a favour, or buy her a thank-you gift. And he will wish her well and want to help her for her own sake—not as a means to making anyone else better off. Gratitude to someone is thus a kind of altruistic care for that person. And insofar as meaning in life is enhanced by caring for and helping others (Landau 2017, 218), gratitude enhances meaning in life.

These features lead gratitude to play an essential role in the formation of deep social relationships. Typically, when a benefactor performs an act of benevolence, the beneficiary takes this as a signal that the benefactor finds him worthy of being trusted to take the benefactor's interests into account in the future. The benefactor also thereby invites the beneficiary to reciprocate these behaviours and the feelings these behaviours convey (Camenisch 1981, 16–18). A properly grateful beneficiary accepts this invitation, welcoming the opportunity to look out for and benefit his benefactor, and waits patiently and contentedly for the chance to do so. In the meantime, the grateful beneficiary is also content to get to know the benefactor, spend time and increase contact with her. When the grateful beneficiary finally does a return favour or gives a return gift to the benefactor, that favour or gift might lead the original benefactor to feel gratitude for the return-benefit, and that will make her even more likely to show more goodwill in the future. The result, in many cases, is a virtuous circle of goodwill or care, spiralling upward and outward and ultimately blossoming into a friendship (R. C. Roberts 2004, 67–68; Camenisch 1981, 12).

To be sure, there is more to any deep social relationship than mutual benevolence. But it seems plausible that mutual benevolence and gratitude are essential to any such relationship. Indeed, it is difficult to imagine any healthy deep relationship forming without many rounds of benevolence and gratitude. It thus might be fair to say that gratitude is necessary for deep personal relationships to form, and partly constitutive of them once they do. We might say that benevolence and gratitude are the parents of deep personal relationships. And such relationships facilitate a meaningful life in a number of ways. For instance, it is plausible that such relationships are intrinsically meaningful, and add meaning to a life directly. Beyond that, such relationships can help teach us how to value meaningful things outside ourselves, insofar as such relationships are often the first and most long-standing commitments we have to things outside our own welfare. And these relationships can be essential in helping us achieve goals or advance projects that make our lives meaningful (Kauppinen 2012, 363).

We must be careful, though, not to overstate the connection between relationships and gratitude. Some might be tempted to go beyond the claims that gratitude is necessary for friendship and constitutive of caring relationships, and endorse a stronger claim: that the *point* of gratitude is to establish such relationships, or that gratitude essentially *aims* to establish such relationships. To endorse such a claim, though, might cause us to overlook gratitude and benevolence in important circumstances. We should not forget that one can be benevolent and grateful to people one does not like or want to spend time with or get to know better. And, of course, we can be benevolent and grateful to people we are incapable of having relationships with. We can be grateful to deceased benefactors, faraway benefactors, and anonymous benefactors. And in the case of gratitude to these varieties of inaccessible benefactors, even when gratitude does not lead to deep relationships like friendship or romantic love, it can still bring meaning to our lives in a variety of ways.

One of these ways comes from the fact that grateful beneficiaries will attend to their benefactors' wishes for how a gift or favour will be put to use. A grateful beneficiary who receives a mixtape should be inclined to give it a listen. A grateful beneficiary who receives a book should have some motivation to try to read it. A grateful beneficiary who has his college tuition paid for should be inclined to take his studies seriously. Respecting use conditions on gifts, and our benefactors' wishes more generally, can thus open us up to experiences and values that we might not have experienced or adopted otherwise.

Perhaps the most significant way that gratitude to inaccessible benefactors might contribute to meaning in life is through paying it forward. A beneficiary who had his college tuition paid for by an anonymous benefactor might anonymously help pay the tuition of a younger stranger one day in the future. A philosopher whose mentor is now deceased might show gratitude to her for her mentorship by mentoring his own students with a level of care and compassion similar to hers (McConnell 1993, 76). In paying forward the benevolence of inaccessible benefactors, beneficiaries can find a great deal of meaning. Paying it forward can lead them to form and reinforce potentially deep relationships, like a philosopher does when he pays forward his mentor's kindness in mentoring his own students. But paying it forward can bring meaning to the life of a grateful beneficiary even when it doesn't lead to new deep relationships. In some cases, paying it forward to strangers can enhance or strengthen a community. If I receive especially supportive and constructive feedback on a journal submission from an anonymous reviewer, I might send a note of thanks to that reviewer through the journal's editors. But I might also take their kindness as an invitation to be a little more compassionate, supportive, and constructive than usual the next time I write an anonymous review. When I do that, I might come to see my identity, as a scholar of philosophy, as salient in a way I didn't before. This illustrates how gratitude to an anonymous benefactor, expressed by paying it forward to an anonymous person in the future, can serve to strengthen one's sense of membership in a community, make more salient one's place in a community, and tighten that community. And insofar as seeing ourselves as part of, and enhancing, something bigger than ourselves brings meaning to a life, gratitude to inaccessible benefactors can bring meaning to a life.

Paying it forward can have an impact not just on one's community at present, but on future people as well. Imagine someone gifts me a book that profoundly changes me, and I am grateful to them for doing so. One day decades later, I decide, out of gratitude, to pay it forward, and I gift a copy of that book to someone else. In doing so, I play an important role in transmitting something valuable out into my community and, potentially, down the generations of people within it. The same happens when I pay forward any benevolent gift or favour that enhanced my life in some way—a gift or favour that opened my eyes to a new experience or introduced me to some value. And if the gift or favour I pay forward inspires my beneficiary not only to enjoy that value, but also to share it with others, who share it with others in turn, and so on, then I have become an essential link in a chain of benevolence, gratitude, and value-sharing that could touch many lives over decades or even centuries. This possibility shows how paying it forward can bring deep meaning to a life. Paying it forward can be a way I fit into, or play an important and significant role in, something valuable that is much larger and more long-lived than myself. Those philosophers who believe that a life tends to be more meaningful insofar as it connects to valuable things outside itself (such as, perhaps, Robert Nozick 1981, 610) should recognize paying it forward as a manifestation of gratitude that can enhance the meaning of a life in this way.

So prepositional gratitude can enhance meaning in life in various ways. It can allow us to see ourselves as important, worthy of help and care and trust. It can motivate us to care for others. In those ways, it can sow the seeds of friendships and romantic relationships. And even when it doesn't lead to relationships, as in the case of gratitude to inaccessible benefactors, it can still bring meaning to our lives. Gratitude can motivate us to accept our benefactors' invitations to find value in the gifts and favours they present us with. And it can motivate us to pay their kindness forward to others. That can help define and secure our places in communities and thereby help us build and contribute to those communities—both in the present and over time.

But reflections on gratitude can also highlight certain pitfalls for those of us interested in leading meaningful lives. For instance, it is often thought that being grateful is a pleasant experience, and that the feelings associated with gratitude are always positive feelings. But while this may be true of appreciation, it is not always true of prepositional gratitude. This is because prepositional gratitude involves an affective disposition of goodwill toward one's benefactor: an affective tendency to wish her well, which means a tendency to be pleased when things go well for her and a tendency to be sad or upset when things go poorly for her. So if we are grateful to someone, and then something bad happens to her, that will give us, as grateful beneficiaries, negative (painful) feelings of gratitude—feelings that are phenomenologically similar to those of grief or sadness (Manela 2016b, 134–136). And if we are very grateful to a benefactor, and something terrible happens to her, we could be left with deep, long-lasting grief-like feelings. These feelings could be compounded by feelings similar to survivor guilt if our benefactor suffers in the process of helping us. And this is especially true if our benefactor was a great hero, who sacrificed profoundly to save us from dire circumstances we were responsible for getting ourselves into in the first place. So, like the feelings associated with love, friendship, and other kinds of care, feelings of gratitude can be a two-edged sword—and they do not always make a beneficiary's life more pleasant.

Gratitude can also be a liability for a meaningful life because of the action tendencies that arise in the grateful beneficiary. Part of being grateful is being motivated to do certain things that would save, help, please, or otherwise benefit a benefactor. Indeed, a grateful beneficiary should be *committed* to doing some of these things—like saving a benefactor if she needs rescuing. And a grateful beneficiary should be committed to keeping an eye out, and paying attention, to the desires and welfare of his benefactor, to make sure he does not miss an opportunity to help her. A grateful beneficiary should be more sensitive to requests from his benefactor than to those of strangers. Now, the more people we are grateful to, the more such commitments we find ourselves with. And the more commitments we have to the welfare of others, the less time and the fewer resources we have to pursue our other commitments—like the activities, projects, and deep personal relationships that tend to make our lives meaningful. In the extreme case, a person who owes too much gratitude might be left with no time or resources to pursue his own projects. Such a person would be robbed of autonomy, and (perhaps) a chance at a meaningful life. It was worries similar to this that led Kant (1981, 118–119) to argue that we should avoid accepting favours, when we can.

Now, our commitments to doing good things for benefactors are not mere personal commitments, like a commitment to learn French or to run a marathon. Commitments of gratitude are not commitments we can simply pick up or lay down at will. We find ourselves with them pretty much whenever someone does us a benevolent favour. Relatedly, commitments of gratitude are *moral commitments*. When we fail to live up to them, we become fair targets of moral condemnation. People who fail to live up to commitments of gratitude are ingrates, guilty of ingratitude. Commitments of gratitude are commitments we *owe to our benefactors*, in the sense that our benefactors can feel especially disappointed in us, aggrieved, slighted, or wronged when we fail in those commitments (Manela 2015, 163–165). And sometimes, the commitments we have to do good things for benefactors rise to the level of strict, weighty moral obligations. Imagine that one night you fall off a bridge into a lake, and a passer-by, out of benevolence, risks great harm to herself in order to save you from drowning. You thank her, and you go your separate ways. Years go by, and you dedicate your life to growing a business. One day, as you are about to open a new retail location, you realize that doing so will destroy the business of a nearby competitor—and this competitor, you discover, turns out to be your long-lost benefactor. In light of your benefactor's past benevolence, it would be wrong for you to open the retail location anyway. To do so would be a violation of a rather weighty moral obligation: an obligation of gratitude.

So gratitude can set boundaries within the space of what we can do in our lives, and crossing these boundaries can be morally dangerous. Crossing them can leave us in the territory of ingratitude, and ingratitude can be a severe moral failing. Owing gratitude, then, can put us at risk of grave vice and immorality. And immorality that's serious enough can constitute anti-meaning (Campbell and Nyholm 2015, 708), or the converse of the sort of value that makes a life meaningful. This isn't to say that we should lament having to be grateful, or that gratitude is on balance a negative force when it comes to meaning in life. On the contrary, it seems plausible that the blessings of gratitude typically outweigh gratitude's liabilities. And it would be a mistake, as a beneficiary, to always fixate on the risk of immorality every time someone does us a favour. But it would also be a mistake to fail to realize that gratitude is a morally serious matter, that obligations of gratitude can sometimes be hard to live up to, and that ingratitude can be a serious moral failing. Being grateful, or at least owing gratitude, opens up new pitfalls on the road to a meaningful life.

Not all of these pitfalls arise from the risk of ingratitude. Some of them arise, perhaps surprisingly, from the risk of *overgratitude*: having more of a grateful response than a situation calls for (Manela 2019b, 308–310). Overgratitude occurs when a beneficiary, in response to an act of benevolence, sees more benevolence in the act than the benefactor likely had, or thanks a benefactor more profusely than she deserves, or has more affective goodwill and more of a desire to return a favour than the benefactor's benevolence calls for. Overgratitude can detract from meaning in life in a variety of ways. Sometimes, when an overgrateful person perceives more benevolence toward himself than is really there, that can lead him to the arrogant belief that he is more important to people around him than he really is. That can lead to an overinflated sense of his importance in the world. And insofar as a meaningful life requires an accurate picture of one's role in the broader scheme of things, and insofar as a vice like arrogance can undermine meaning in life, overgratitude can be a liability for meaningfulness.

Overgratitude is perhaps most dangerous when it looms so large, relative to one's other moral commitments, that it eclipses or overwhelms those other commitments. A habitual overgrate who receives a small favour from a morally corrupt benefactor might find himself over-motivated to do good things for her, to help her out when she needs a favour. If the favour she calls in is one that requires her beneficiary to do something unjust or cruel, then the more overgrateful he is, the more likely he is to do the unjust or cruel thing. Indeed, a recent empirical study by Zhu et al. (2020) has suggested that the more grateful a beneficiary is, the more likely he is to engage in morally corrupt behaviour. Overgrates who habitually experience the pull of gratitude more strongly than the pull of other virtues might also be more likely to fall into friendships with morally corrupt benefactors. They might be more likely to form tight bonds of loyalty with such benefactors and become locked into their social networks. They may feel the pull of gratitude, and the relationships it gives birth to, so strongly that even when they see evidence that their benefactors and their social networks are morally corrupt, they cannot pull away. In this way, overgratitude could fuel tribalism and nationalism, and could draw overgrates into factions, tribes, or causes that no decent person should be a part of. And this of course has crucial ramifications for meaning in life. If overgratitude can lead us to do unjust and cruel things, and doing unjust and cruel things leads to anti-meaning, or negative meaning value, then overgratitude is a liability for living a meaningful life. And if overgratitude can lead us to join and support evil organizations and causes, and supporting such causes brings anti-meaning to a life, then that is another way overgratitude could be a liability for living a meaningful life. The solution to these concerns is to learn and teach others how to properly balance gratitude against the pull of other virtues. We should strive, and teach others, not just to avoid ingratitude, but to beware of overgratitude as well.

4. Appreciation and Meaning in Life

In what remains of this chapter, I would like to discuss some ways in which appreciation can have an impact on meaning in life. Appreciation can bring meaning to a life in several ways—and some of these are described elegantly by Iddo Landau's discussion of *recognizing*. Recognizing, for Landau, occurs when we go beyond believing that our lives contain meaning-conferring value, and actually *feel* the meaning-conferring value in our lives. It happens when we overcome a 'numbness to value' and thus come to sense 'the worthy aspects of the world more acutely' (Landau 2017, 230–231). There may be more to recognizing than just appreciation—i.e., gratitude *that* and gratitude *for* (but not to). Recognizing may also involve sensing the worthy aspects of one's own achievements more acutely. In those cases, recognizing is less about gratitude and more about pride. But insofar as appreciation is a kind of recognizing, or a form that recognizing can take, Landau's remarks about how recognizing impacts meaning will also apply to appreciating.

Appreciating, as a form of recognizing, can help deliver meaning to a life. As Landau points out, recognizing value—which can happen when we enjoy or welcome things we find valuable—sometimes increases our optimism and our energy, which in turn can motivate us to go out and engage in meaning-conferring achievements (Landau 2017, 245). Appreciating, as a form of recognizing, can also indicate the absence of certain attitudes that might threaten meaning in a life. Unhealthy, rebellious nonconformism, dark pessimism, and cynicism each often manifest as an absence of appreciation. And someone might deliberately grind away their capacity for appreciation in order to send to others the troublingly elitist signal that they have exceptionally high standards—that they are not easily pleased by the valuable things that please the average person (Landau 2017, 197).

Appreciation, as a form of recognizing, may also constitute meaning in a life. Appreciating occurs when one emotionally connects with the things one judges to be valuable in one's life. It is the opposite of being detached or alienated from the things we see as valuable in our lives. Now, getting enjoyment out of the objectively valuable things in our lives is the essence of certain so-called hybrid views of meaning in life, according to which 'meaning arises when subjective attraction meets objective attractiveness' (Wolf 1997, 211). Every instance of appreciating objectively valuable things in a person's life could thus be seen as a site where objective attractiveness meets subjective attraction. And generally, the more such sites we have in our lives, the more meaningful our lives are.

That means it is important for us to be able to find or build such sites wherever and whenever we can. And fortunately, that skill—the skill of being appreciative—is one we can cultivate. As Landau notes, we can deliberately work to become more sensitive to meaning-conferring value in our lives, just as we can work to make ourselves more sensitive to beauty in our lives (Landau 2017, 242–243). We can develop the habit of appreciating through exercises like gratitude journaling, through which we fall into the routine of attending to, reflecting upon, and writing about valuable things, big and small, in our lives each day. This can put us in the habit of noticing valuable things, which in turn can put us in the habit of taking the time and space to enjoy, absorb, consume, and be nourished by those valuable things. Gratitude journals can also serve as a record to help us remember such things (Landau 2017, 238–239). When we flip back through past gratitude journal entries, we can remind ourselves of and continue to derive enjoyment from valuable things that entered our lives a long time ago.

Gratitude journals are often used to focus our attention on valuable things in our lives and then increase our enjoyment of and emotional connection to those things. This, I believe, is how Landau understands the process of recognizing more generally: start with things in our lives we know are valuable, and then work to increase our enjoyment of or emotional connection to them. But there is another way to promote recognizing and appreciation. Rather than starting with what we know is valuable and then working to connect with it, we could start with elements in our life that bring us enjoyment and then work to see those things as valuable. For instance, a person who finds great pleasure in playing golf might do well to learn more about the sport—take a course on the philosophy of sport, or the history of golf, say—and thereby come to see and understand more deeply the value that sport brings to her life. In that way, she can take a site where there is already subjective attraction and excavate that site until she discovers objective value there as well.

Once we take these steps to bring appreciation of valuable things into our lives, it would be wise to protect that appreciation by watching out for and working through factors that can diminish our sensitivity to value. These factors include positive ones, like passionate love, which can distract us from enjoying the other valuable things in our lives. They also include darker factors, like anger, sadness, and pain, which, if not managed properly, can lead to numbness (Landau 2017, 233). This last point highlights an important reminder for those who might be tempted to think that appreciation is always easy to achieve and maintain. Under certain circumstances, cultivating appreciation can be easy. It is easy to be grateful for one's children when they are happy and healthy, because positive emotions like enjoyment arise naturally in us in those cases. It can be much harder to be grateful for one's children—grateful that one had such great children—in the immediate aftermath of their unexpected deaths. It's not that in such times, one finds one's children less valuable. On the contrary, it's that in such moments, the value one saw in one's children, who are now suddenly gone, threatens to make any positive emotion impossible. People do nonetheless survive the sudden deaths of beloved children, and many such survivors make it to a point where they can again look with joy on the memories they had with their children. But preparing oneself for such a possibility without pre-emptively numbing oneself to the love of one's children, and working through the deaths of one's children if that possibility occurs, are among the most difficult things a person can do.

My discussion of appreciation has highlighted several ways that achieving just the right amount of appreciation can be important for a meaningful life. It has also highlighted several ways we can fail to be properly appreciative. We can fail to recognize the full value in the valuable things in our lives, and we can fail to emotionally embrace the valuable things in our lives to the extent we should. These are two ways in which one could be *sub-appreciative*: ways in which one's cognitive and affective responses could fall short of what they should be. There are perhaps other kinds of failure to be properly appreciative that might negatively impact meaning in life, and I will close out this section with a discussion of two of these.

One possible kind of pathological appreciation might occur when a person appreciates, or is grateful for, something that it is wrong to value. We could imagine, for instance, a white supremacist who sees value in being a member of the white race and welcomes the fact that she is.[5] Such a person might say she feels grateful for being a member of the white race. And she may very well be. But appreciating something that is wrong to value would seem to detract from meaning in life. Indeed, it would seem to constitute anti-meaning, or negative value. And this isn't just because seeing value in something we ought not to value constitutes anti-meaning in life. *Appreciating* such a value may be even worse than just seeing value in it. That is because when we appreciate such values, we connect with them and enjoy them in a way that might make them harder for us to reject down the line. We might call this pathological kind of appreciation—appreciating something we should not value—*dys-appreciation*.

Another sort of pathological failure of appreciation might occur when a person responds to something valuable in his life by judging it to be more valuable than it really is, and/or welcoming it more than he should. Imagine a member of an oppressed social group who learns her government just passed certain political reforms that reduce (but do not eliminate) oppression against her social group. Insofar as such a person appreciates those reforms too much—values them more highly than she should, or is happier about them than she should be—that might sap her motivation to continue to work for a fully just and equal society. If she appreciates such half-measures too much, the positive emotions she feels might eclipse or wash out the feelings of indignation she

---

[5] This example was suggested to me by Iddo Landau.

should still feel about lingering injustice and oppression. Those feelings of indignation might be essential for her to connect with others in her community and to motivate her to continue the struggle for justice and equality—and those are sources of meaning in a life that *over-appreciation* might threaten. The moral of the story to be drawn from over-appreciation and dys-appreciation is this: appreciation is not something to be blindly maximized in the life of someone looking for meaning. A meaningful life is one in which appreciation, like prepositional gratitude, needs to be cultivated carefully and thoughtfully, in response to the right things, and to the right degree.[6]

5. Conclusion

In this chapter, I have highlighted ways that prepositional gratitude and appreciation can be relevant to meaning in life. Each of those attitudes can play positive roles in enhancing meaning in life: they can indicate that one has a meaningful life, they can help bring about meaning in life, and they can partly constitute meaning in life as well. But reflection on prepositional gratitude and appreciation also reveals pitfalls to watch out for in the quest for a meaningful life. Being underappreciative can drain a life of meaning, and over-appreciation and dys-appreciation can undermine meaning in life too—as can ingratitude and overgratitude. These concerns highlight the importance of working to understand gratitude and appreciation as deeply as possible. The better we understand those attitudes, the more surefooted we can be as we work to balance them against grief, love, friendship, loyalty, justice, and the other attitudes, virtues, values, and commitments that populate a meaningful life.

Bibliography

Berger, Fred. 1975. 'Gratitude'. *Ethics* 85(4): 298–309.
Camenisch, Paul F. 1981. 'Gift and Gratitude in Ethics'. *The Journal of Religious Ethics* 9(1): 1–34.
Campbell, Stephen M., and Sven Nyholm. 2015. 'Anti-Meaning and Why It Matters'. *Journal of the American Philosophical Association* 1(4): 694–711.
Card, Claudia. 1988. 'Gratitude and Obligation'. *American Philosophical Quarterly* 25(2): 115–127.
Fitzgerald, Patrick. 1998. 'Gratitude and Justice'. *Ethics* 109(1): 119–153.
Gulliford, Liz, Blaire Morgan, and Kristján Kristjánsson. 2013. 'Recent Work on the Concept of Gratitude in Philosophy and Psychology'. *Journal of Value Inquiry* 47: 285–317.
Kant, Immanuel. 1981. *Lectures on Ethics*, trans. Louis Infield. Cambridge: Hackett.
Kauppinen, Antti. 2012. 'Meaningfulness and Time'. *Philosophy and Phenomenological Research* 82: 345–377.
Landau, Iddo. 2017. *Finding Meaning in an Imperfect World*. New York: Oxford University Press.

---

[6] I am grateful to Iddo Landau for pressing me to make this point.

Manela, Tony. 2015. 'Obligations of Gratitude and Correlative Rights'. In *Oxford Studies in Normative Ethics*, ed. Mark Timmons, 151–170. Oxford: Oxford University Press.

Manela, Tony. 2016a. 'Gratitude and Appreciation'. *American Philosophical Quarterly* 53(3): 281–294.

Manela, Tony. 2016b. 'Negative Feelings of Gratitude'. *Journal of Value Inquiry* 50(1): 129–140.

Manela, Tony. 2019a. 'Gratitude'. In *Stanford Encyclopedia of Philosophy*, ed. Edward N. Zalta <https://plato.stanford.edu/archives/win2020/entries/gratitude/>.

Manela, Tony. 2019b. 'The Virtue of Gratitude and Its Associated Vices'. In *The Moral Psychology of Gratitude*, ed. Robert Roberts and Daniel Telech, 296–316. New York: Rowman & Littlefield.

Manela, Tony. 2020. 'Does Gratitude to R for φ-ing Imply Gratitude That R φ-ed?' *Philosophical Studies* 177: 3245–3263.

McAleer, Sean. 2012. 'Propositional Gratitude'. *American Philosophical Quarterly* 49(1): 55–66.

McConnell, Terrance. 1993. *Gratitude*. Philadelphia: Temple University Press.

McConnell, Terrance. 2019. 'Acting from Gratitude'. In *The Moral Psychology of Gratitude*, ed. Robert Roberts and Daniel Telech, 35–55. New York: Rowman & Littlefield.

Nozick, Robert. 1981. *Philosophical Explanations*. Cambridge, MA: Harvard University Press.

Roberts, Robert C. 2004. 'The Blessings of Gratitude'. In *The Psychology of Gratitude*, ed. Robert A. Emmons and Michael E. McCullough, 58–78. Oxford: Oxford University Press.

Roberts, Robert, and Daniel Telech. 2019. 'Introduction'. In *The Moral Psychology of Gratitude*, ed. Robert Roberts and Daniel Telech, 1–12. New York: Rowman & Littlefield.

Swinburne, Richard. 1989. *Responsibility and Atonement*. Oxford: Clarendon Press.

Walker, A. D. M. 1980–1981. 'Gratefulness and Gratitude'. *Proceedings of the Aristotelian Society* 81: 39–55.

Weiss, Roslyn. 1985. 'The Moral and Social Dimensions of Gratitude'. *The Journal of Southern Philosophy* XXIII(4): 491–501.

Wellman, Christopher Heath. 1999. 'Gratitude as a Virtue'. *Pacific Philosophical Quarterly* 80: 284–300.

Wolf, Susan. 1997. 'Happiness and Meaning: Two Aspects of the Good Life'. *Social Philosophy and Policy* 14: 207–225.

Zhu, Ruida, Zhenhua Xu, Honghong Tang, Huagen Wang, Sihui Zhang, Zhiqi Zhang, Xiaoqin Mai, and Chao Liu. 2020. 'The Dark Side of Gratitude: Gratitude Could Lead to Moral Violation.' *Journal of Experimental Social Psychology* 91: 104048, https://doi.org/10.1016/j.jesp.2020.104048.

CHAPTER 26

PSYCHOLOGICAL APPROACHES TO LIFE'S MEANING

ROY F. BAUMEISTER

QUESTIONS about life's meaning engage multiple disciplines across the social sciences and humanities. The topic has long been regarded as a philosophical issue, but psychologists have studied it increasingly it over the past half century. This chapter covers psychological contributions and perspectives. My impression is that philosophical approaches have superior conceptual rigor and careful analysis. In contrast, the contributions of psychology lie in bottom-up data collection of general or typical cases, often based on average and composite patterns. Psychology also benefits by using experimental manipulations designed to establish causality, as well as sophisticated measurement of stable dispositions. A comprehensive treatment of the problem would benefit by incorporating both, albeit in different ways.

One notable change over the past two decades has been that psychological researchers who study life's meaning have switched prepositions. In both popular culture and traditional scholarly discourse, the topic was the 'meaning *of* life'. These days, however, researchers favour 'meaning *in* life', which carries less grandiose aspirations. The meaning of life is a singular noun, suggesting that there is a single answer, ideally for everyone, though perhaps different people's lives could have different singular meanings. In contrast, studying meaning *in* life allows that there may not be any singular meaning for everyone or even for a particular individual. The quest to find a single meaning of life may be quixotic, which is discouraging to those who collect data. But there is plenty of meaning scattered throughout individual lives, so the prospects for successful research are better. Martela (2020, 92, and elsewhere) has also suggested that the notion of a meaning *of* life implies some objective truth, whereas meaning *in* life is essentially subjective—thus again cutting the problem down to a more manageable size.

Psychological research on life's meaning is thus heavily subjectivist. Psychologists themselves may be agnostic as to whether there is an objective meaning to life, either individually or collectively. But when they collect data, they rely on the research participant's own subjective evaluation of how meaningful his or her life is. Unlike, say, perceptual judgements, or problem-solving performance, or tests of memory for experimental stimuli, there is no objective basis for saying that someone's rating of the meaningfulness of his or her life is wrong. It is possible to furnish a brief description of someone's life and have other people rate its meaningfulness. But even this is hard to do with actual lives, as any description will inevitably omit a great deal of information that could alter the rating.

In theory, mistakes in both directions are eminently possible. Laboratory rats presumably do not have any sense that their lives are meaningful, but people might well say that lab rats who were killed in the process of developing a vaccine (such as in the recent COVID pandemic) had highly meaningful lives. Conversely, people may live and die with a passionate sense of meaning even if they were mainly pursuing a lost cause, such as if the life is spent trying to promote a scientific theory that is eventually shown to be entirely wrong, or it is devoted to killing unbelievers in the name of promoting a false religious system.

What Is Meaning? Definitional Issues

Conceptual precision is one of the specialties of academic philosophy, while psychology's conceptual schemes have long been primitive and flawed. In part this reflects methodological focus. Philosophers perform carefully thoughtful analysis of borderline cases, while psychologists can cheerfully use fuzzy sets because they focus on the main, paradigmatic case and use empirical tools to show how its causal processes unfold. It is therefore with humble trepidation, mindful of risk of ultracrepidarianism, that I seek to explicate the nature of meaning and related concepts. In my defence, it is obligatory for authors to define their key concepts, if not aiming for perfection, at least to furnish a working basis for interpreting data.

In psychological research, meaning is used in two different ways, as articulated in an integrative article by the editors of a journal special issue on the psychology of meaning (Baumeister and Landau, 2018). Indeed, some languages use different words for the two ways (e.g., German *Sinn* and *Bedeutung*). One is denotative meaning, such as what a sentence means. The other is existential meaning, as in meanings of life. The two overlap, but they do produce somewhat separate research programs. Those who study denotative meaning consider issues such as metaphor (e.g., Landau 2018). Researchers studying life's meaning often examine causes and predictors of why people find their lives more or less meaningful.

My focus here is on the second (existential) meaning of meaning, associated with issues of life's meaning. Researchers on existential meaning focus on causes and consequences of people's self-assessment of the relative degree of meaning in their lives. This chapter will seek to explicate what is involved in a meaningful life, but it includes having a coherent narrative, usually featuring individual choice and action, in service of some valuable purpose.

The phrase 'making meaning' is popular among psychology researchers on meaning but presumably would give philosophers pause, as it implies that something new is created that did not exist previously. The editors of the 2018 special issue on psychology of meaning agreed in advance that if contributing authors used the phrase 'making meaning' it would be permitted, but authors would be prompted to explain exactly in what sense something new was created. Tellingly, most authors responded to this editorial injunction by deleting the phrase from their manuscripts. The sole exception was by Park and George (2018). Park has developed a theory about meaning making, dating back to the 1990s. Park and George explained that it was a matter of making a mental connection, even if others had made it previously, so even though it was not new to the world, it was new to that particular person. We allowed that, but we note that it seemingly concedes the point that the 'making' is purely subjective. The question of whether meaning can be made thus remains open, though true creation of new meaning remains without empirical or conceptual support. Perhaps highly creative works of art, or perhaps the transition from mere possibility to historical reality, could qualify as genuine creation of meaning. This is one issue in which psychologists could benefit from philosophical input and guidance.

Operationally, many psychologists rely on questionnaire measurement of life's meaning. The Meaning in Life questionnaire (Steger et al. 2006) is currently popular, and it has the advantage of having two subscales: one measures presence of meaning in life, while the other measures the quest for meaning. Another popular measurement tool is the Purpose in Life Test (Crumbaugh and Maholick 1964). Various other ad hoc measures have been used, particularly in large surveys that require brevity across multiple measures (see Heintzelman and King 2014 for review). Notably, all these measures rely on self-reports. There is a woeful lack of objective measures of meaning in life. And it is fair to question how much one can learn about the meaning of life from how ordinary people (mostly undergraduate students) rate their own lives' meaningfulness on a series of five-point scales. This is not to dismiss those data, but merely to raise a question. In my view, the best methods collect more information than simple ratings.

Monkeys in Tuxedos?

Suppose we do accept the validity of students' (and online paid samples') ratings of how meaningful their lives are. What happens when one pushes things a bit farther to see what they think makes their lives meaningful, and what correlates with those ratings, or even what causes them to go up or down? Scholars hoping to find that meaning in life evokes grand, supra-human themes may be disappointed by the answers. In particular, family and other close social relationships routinely top the list of sources of meaning.

The problem is, this is low-level stuff. Plenty of animals have family bonds and feelings. Humans might therefore just be animals, doing their animal thing and festooning it with meaning to pretend it's something grander. This is not unlike the perennially popular practice of dressing up monkeys or chimpanzees in tuxedos and evening gowns. They may be cute, amusing, and picturesque, but the illusion lacks substance. The apes don't get the point, and they remain just apes. They look like they're ready for the opera, but of course no ape or chimp has ever written an opera, or sung in one, or of its own free will attended one. Yet to humans it is soothing if not downright pleasing to see them thus, to fantasize and pretend that they are more than they are. How much of research participants' ratings of life's meaningfulness is like that?

Thus, one broad question is how much of the meaningfulness of people's lives (especially in psychological data, but also out in the world) boils down to basic animal functions and concerns, dressed up with fancy-foofy meanings. Love, sex, competition for status, aggression—humans have all these animal patterns and imbue them with meaning. Natural selection has installed motivations in all animals to do things that increase survival and reproduction, such as eating and having sex and nurturing offspring. Humans may report that such activities are highly meaningful to them, but the animals do the same things without much use of meaning. This raises the suspicion that much of the meaty part of human meaning in life is doing the basic animal things. Humans merely dress up these basic animal functions with superimposed, seemingly more advanced meaningfulness.

To be sure, there are some sources of meaning that do not reduce to putting tuxedos on monkeys. No species except humankind has religion, and many people cite their religious beliefs as an important source of meaning. In today's secular society, many suggest that politics has come to substitute for religion, and this would possibly explain the zeal with which politically correct Twitter mobs seek out and destroy unbelievers. Artistic creation is another potent source of meaning in life for some, and it too is pretty much limited to humankind. (Birds may make songs, and so forth, but the deliberate creation of an enduring new work of beauty is absent, as is having a group recognition of the value and nature of art.)

In any case, the scrupulous thinker must be watchful for how much of everyman's data on life's meaning is really just monkeys in tuxedos.

Causes, Sources, and Correlates of Meaning in Life

People find meaning in many places. An attempt to specify a single meaning or purpose of life that applies to all people is likely to be either starkly reductionistic (e.g. to survive and reproduce) or hopelessly vague (e.g. to do God's will), and as such it will inevitably fail to account for the extraordinary diversity of human activities, values, and strivings.

Where People Find Meaning

Indeed, the diversity of sources of meaning led me to conclude that the topic should be organized around the questions rather than the answers (Baumeister 1991). That is, people have several basic kinds of needs for meaning, and they can satisfy these needs in a great many different ways. The motivation is thus to have some answer, not any particular answer, to the several questions about life's meaning, purpose, and value. Indeed, one of the stunning findings from 1970s research was that nearly all accident and trauma victims ask 'Why me?' and some find answers—and in terms of psychological outcomes, no particular answer was better than any other. What mattered empirically was the difference between having some meaningful answer and not having any (Bulman and Wortman 1977). The data on the benefits of religion likewise indicate clearly that having strong religious faith produces palpable and diverse benefits, including longer life—but apart from some fringe exceptions, any religion is as beneficial as any other.

Nevertheless, some of the obviously common sources of meaning are family and love, work, and religion. Family and love are obvious and may be little more than dressing monkeys up in tuxedos. Work is a more complicated source of meaning, however. Many people find their work meaningful, while others do not. Graeber (2013, 2018) ranted about 'bullshit jobs', performed by people who readily acknowledge that their job ideally should not even exist and that it contributes little or nothing to society.

Many researchers and writers (e.g. Barnett 2012) have followed Bellah et al.'s (1985) distinction among three attitudes toward work: job, career, calling. The job attitude treats work purely as a means to an end (typically money), with little reference to the future or higher values. These workers find little meaning other than the money they get, which may be important, such as for supporting a family. In contrast, the career approach to work is concerned with accumulating status and recognition, such as by garnering promotions and awards. The career mentality is again extrinsic, in that the work's content is largely irrelevant, but people perform it for the rewards. It is somewhat more meaningful than the job mentality, because the career does build across time and is seen as having purpose and value, as well as bolstering self-worth if the person performs well.

The third view, work as a calling, is highly meaningful. Such individuals regard the work as valuable for its own sake. The term was perhaps first used for missionaries and priests, but also applies to many scientists, physicians, artists/musicians/dancers, political activists, teachers, and more. (Admittedly, today most of those people have careerist attitudes also.)

Religion may seem to provide meaning in life by answering deep existential questions, and that is indeed one source. But my conclusion was that religiosity often boils down to social connections as well (Baumeister 1991). For example, new converts to religious cults decide whether to remain in or leave the cult based less on doctrinal and metaphysical subtleties than on whether they make friends in the cult (Robbins 1988). Thus, even some meaningfulness of religion might be a tuxedo, even if most is not.

Causes of Meaningfulness

No doubt the philosophical reader will be sharply alert as to whether psychologists 'merely' provide correlates of self-rated meaningfulness, as opposed to demonstrating causal processes. Correlational findings are more common, but there are some experimental studies with random assignment, which are the best test of causal relationships among all methods in the social sciences. Recent work has turned to experimental manipulations of relevant factors followed by measurement of self-reported meaning in life. For example, being socially rejected and ostracized has been shown to reduce meaningfulness (Williams 2001, 2007). Even brief laboratory-administered rejection experiences cause people to rate their lives as less meaningful (Stillman et al. 2009). These are administered by random assignment, so whether the person is ostracized or not is no reflection on anything about the person. This enables the differences among people to even out. Every person is slightly unique, but random assignment yields two groups that should be on average about the same on everything except the experimental treatment.

A particularly impressive research program on causes of self-rated meaningfulness by Heintzelman and King (e.g. 2014) showed that rather simple things affect meaning, even within a brief time frame. (The effects are presumably also transient. Otherwise it would probably not be ethical to do the experiments. The point is to show the causal relationship, and one can infer that if small fleeting manipulations produce very temporary changes in meaningfulness, then out in the world, big ongoing experiences, like being in love or being the target of ongoing discrimination, will produce more substantial and lasting impact.)

Experiments that manipulate people into positive moods and feelings cause participants to rate their lives as more meaningful, as compared to neutral-mood controls. Habits and routines also seem positively related to meaning. Heintzelman and King (2019) showed that people felt their lives were more meaningful when they engaged in more routine activities, and Heintzelman and King (2015) showed that inculcating a habit (regarding how to solve puzzles) led to higher feelings of meaning in life.

Perhaps most remarkably, perceiving order in the environment (thus stability again) increases meaning (Heintzelman, Trent, and King 2013). In a deceptively simple manipulation, participants viewed a series of 16 images of trees in different seasons. For the control group, the images were in random sequence. For the experimental group, they were presented in seasonal sequence (spring, summer, fall, winter, repeated 3 more times). Afterward, students rated how meaningful their lives were. Those who had seen the seasons in proper sequence rated themselves higher on meaningfulness than those who had seen the random sequence. These days, while social psychology is busy torturing and discrediting itself with an overblown 'replication crisis', it is worth adding that my laboratory has borrowed their procedure and found significant results with it. It works.

The finding that looking briefly at tree pictures in random versus seasonal sequence can produce significant differences in self-rated meaningfulness of life gives pause. Clearly we are not dealing with changes to a carefully thought-out personal philosophy. Indeed, further work by the same group showed that ratings of life's meaning—and especially high ratings—are linked to automatic, intuitive styles of thinking rather than deliberate, rational analysis (Heintzelman and King 2016). Indeed, one of their studies used the Cognitive Reflection Test, which requires use of careful reasoning to get the right answer instead of an intuitively appealing wrong answer. People who rated their lives as low in meaning before the test performed better on the test (i.e. used more deliberate reasoning). People who put more faith in intuition likewise rated their lives as more meaningful than others. All of this suggests that the generally high levels of self-rated meaningfulness in life are linked to automatic, intuitive, and emotional processes, rather than deep thought.

Correlates of Finding One's Life Meaningful

Showing consequences of meaning in life is difficult, but there are many correlates, and some of these likely involve being a causal consequence. (Proper experimental studies in which meaningfulness is the independent variable are difficult, given the ethical and practical problems with convincing research participants, even temporarily, that their lives are meaningless.) Heintzelman and King (2014) summarized multiple things that correlate with self-rated meaning. People who regard their lives as more meaningful have higher quality of life, including superior physical health, and these effects increase with advanced age. They have fewer psychological disorders and less suicidal ideation. They cope better with stress and adjust to their jobs better.

Regarding one's life as meaningful makes one attractive to others (Stillman, Lambert, et al. 2011). Participants watched videotaped interactions. Afterwards, they reported more interest in being friends with the videotaped persons who (unbeknownst to the observers) had rated their lives higher in meaning. People who regard their lives as more meaningful are more likable than others, even if their meaningfulness is never explicitly mentioned. To be sure, it is far from clear that the meaningfulness causes the likability—though the effect remained significant after controlling for some of the possible confounds, such as self-esteem, extraversion, agreeableness, and even happiness.

The Meaning in Life Questionnaire has two subscales, one focusing on presence of meaning, the other on search for meaning. The initial studies to validate the measure found that these were essentially unrelated, with a correlation of -.07 (Steger, Frazier, Oishi, and Kaler 2006). A review of subsequent studies found that the correlation varies across samples, ranging from about .40 to -.40 (Steger et al. 2018). That range also suggests that the grand average is again close to zero. When people use the scale to rate the meaningfulness of someone else's life, there are occasionally some high positive numbers. This apparently reflects a common assumption that people who are searching for meaning are finding it. But self-ratings do not confirm that optimistic assessment.

Searching for meaning and having it in one's life seem subjectively independent and unrelated.

The review by Steger et al. (2018) also reported that self-rated presence of meaning correlates positively with various good things, including life satisfaction, positive emotions, trait agreeableness, extraversion, and intrinsic religiosity. Meanwhile, search for meaning correlates positively with depression, trait neuroticism, and various negative emotions. One possible take-away message is that it is better to have meaning than to be searching for it!

Motivations for Meaning

Is the human mind motivated to use meaning? If so, in what ways, and are these motives innate or acquired? Most relevant to the present discussion are widespread assertions that people are motivated to find their lives meaningful (e.g. Heintzelman and King 2014).

If we accept that people want meaningful lives, what does that involve? Frankl (1959) pioneered the psychology of life's meaning. His analysis focused on purpose: Present actions and events draw meaning by connection to goals and other elements of the future. Recent work has confirmed that meaning connects powerfully across time. People rate their own thoughts that combine past, present, and future as more meaningful than their thoughts that invoke only one of those three (Baumeister et al. 2020). In general, all subsequent theories have agreed with Frankl that purpose provides meaning in life.

Purpose is one of four needs for meaning proposed by Baumeister (1991). Value was perhaps implicit in Frankl's analysis, assuming that not every purpose is equally useful as a source of meaning. A meaningful life requires purpose with a positive value. More broadly, though, as need for meaning, value includes having criteria to know right from wrong, good from bad. Moreover, the need for value includes having a way to construe the self and its actions as (mostly or fundamentally) good.

The other two needs in Baumeister's (1991) scheme were efficacy and self-worth. Having goals and values is arguably not enough to make life meaningful, unless one can also do something to reach those valued goals (efficacy). Last, people seek self-worth, often in the crude form of having some way of regarding themselves as better than other people. Self-worth may come from the successfully efficacious pursuit of valued goals.

Recent work has emphasized three needs as postulated by George and Park (2016). These are purpose, mattering, and comprehension. For me, then, the question is how to update my thinking in light of this newer model. How do we integrate the purpose-value-efficacy-self-worth quartet into the purpose-mattering-comprehension trio? George and Park emphasize that the purposes must be valued, so both value and purposiveness are implicated. Mattering is the sense that one's life has value and significance in the world, thus in a sense it combines value and efficacy (though it is possible that some lives could be seen as having value without accomplishing anything).

Comprehension is defined in terms of coherence and understanding: One's life makes sense and the parts fit together. One's life makes sense to oneself. Coherence presumably means that the different parts and events are consistent and have thematic unity, including narrative integration across time. This seems the most important advance over my earlier thinking. One's life should fit together into a coherent unity. Some meaningful concept or story has to make sense by combining past, present, and future.

The Meaning Maintenance Model proposes that people are motivated to sustain a given quantity of meaning (Heine, Proulx, and Vohs 2006). When some important meaning is taken away or even threatened, they compensate by finding more meaning elsewhere. My own investigation concluded that loss of meaning does not so much make people search for new sources of meaning, as replacement—instead, they seem to double down on the sources of meaning they have, investing them with more importance (Baumeister 1991).

Meaning and Incompleteness

The medieval writing of lives comprised mainly biographies of saints, and there was little concern with factual accuracy (e.g. Altick 1965; Weintraub 1978). The purpose of biography was to inspire the reader to live a better Christian life, by following the magnificent example of the saint. Many different saints' lives contained the same miracle stories. In the early modern period, however, biographers began to feel an obligation to get the facts correct. This is also when novels first appeared and became popular. My suspicion is that this reflects the hunger for a good, coherent story of a highly meaningful life. Objective reality was generally not quite satisfying, so people began to prefer reading false stories (novels) rather than true biographies.

The culprit is the pervasive incompleteness of actual life. I invite the reader to reflect on your own life. Could not the story have been improved if a few things had gone differently? Were there not some false starts, other things to regret?

My broader hypothesis, which awaits testing with data, is that the more meaningful the life is, the more incomplete it is. High meaning comes from involvement in many different ongoing undertakings and relationships. These are rich with choice points, alternative strategies, unexpected outcomes, and multiple meanings. The major long ones (both undertakings and relationships) lead in unexpected directions, rarely turning out exactly as initially sought and expected.

This is rooted in the basic nature of denotative meaning. Meaning identifies what is by contrasting it with what is not (e.g. high rather than low). Applying meaning to life therefore invokes alternative possibilities. The more meaningful, the more alternative possibilities. If the life has been an unbroken series of successes and triumphs, the alternatives would be mostly failures and are therefore forgettable, but hardly anyone's life fits that description. And other alternative possibilities (the career path not chosen, the romance not pursued) might have been better or worse or the same but still remain unfulfilled.

Meaning and Happiness

Sigmund Freud (1969, 13) observed, albeit without providing data, that the common person's understanding of the purpose of life was to become and remain happy. Deep thinkers are dismayed by such a simple notion (as Freud presumably intended), especially given that dumb animals can seem pretty happy without meaning. Equating happiness with meaningfulness could be another case of monkeys in tuxedos: humans resemble other animals in mainly striving to feel good, and humans glorify their simple animal drive by pretending it invokes grand existential reverberations. Nevertheless, there is more to meaning than happiness.

Self-ratings of meaningfulness and happiness are positively correlated, and indeed the overlap approaches half the variance. Still, one can tease them apart by focusing on the differences. Crudely put, a researcher can see what correlates with happiness while controlling for meaning, and vice versa. Some colleagues and I attempted this a few years ago, given the luxury of some large data sets that contained self-ratings of meaning in life, happiness, and abundant other factors (Baumeister, Vohs, Aaker, and Garbinsky 2013). This work was exploratory, though convergence with subsequent, replicating work has been good. Five main dimensions differentiated happiness from meaning in life.

First, happiness (but not meaning) is tied to getting what you want. Goal satisfaction, good health, frequent good feelings and infrequent bad ones, and having enough money were significantly related to (higher) happiness but irrelevant to meaning. To some extent, this helpfully addresses the monkey tuxedo problem. Feeling good based on satisfying desires is mainly about happiness rather than meaning.

Second, happiness is largely about the present, but meaning is more about the future—or, more precisely, about integrating across time. Frequently thinking about the future was linked to lower happiness but higher meaning. A subsequent thought-sampling study found that the most meaningful thoughts combined past, present, and future, while thoughts that lacked a time dimension were on average the least meaningful (Baumeister, Hoffman, Reiss, Summerville, and Vohs 2020). That study also replicated the point that happiness peaked with focus on the here and now: happiness was highest and meaning was lowest when the mind was focused on the present. Focus on the future was the opposite (high meaning but lower happiness, though focus on the past was the lowest for happiness, by far).

Third, belongingness was strongly linked to both happiness and meaning overall, but the patterns differed. Happiness came from spending time with friends, while meaning was linked to spending time with loved ones. Regarding oneself as 'a giver' meant lower happiness and higher meaning, while rating oneself 'a taker' showed the opposite. For parents only, taking care of children boosted meaning while trending toward lowering happiness. This fits a common conclusion among researchers, which is that much meaning in life comes from contributing to others' lives.

Fourth, involvement in various challenging activities bolstered meaning but often at the cost of lower happiness. Having had more negative events in one's life, having more stress, reflecting on struggles and challenges, and spending more time worrying all correlated in opposite directions: with higher meaningfulness but lower happiness. Apparently, the simple and uncluttered life on the sidelines is best for happiness but reduces meaning, while striving and struggling are best for meaning but costly to happiness.

Fifth and last, doing things to express the self was associated with meaning but generally not with happiness (see also MacGregor and Little 1998). More broadly, higher concern with issues of personal identity was linked toward more meaningful life—but not with more happiness (if anything, the opposite).

One can pull these together into composite portraits of life with either happiness or meaning but not both. The happy but low-meaning life is marked by carefree existence, easily getting what one wants and needs, without much stress or worry. It pays little heed to past and future, enjoying the present and avoiding difficult and stressful involvements. In contrast, the meaningful but unhappy life (one thinks of missionaries, terrorists, crusading reformers) is heavily involved in challenging activities, with the inevitable defeats and stresses that those bring, also devoted to helping other people. Much time in such a life is spent thinking deeply and about past and future.

Concluding Remarks

Psychology aspires to use the scientific method to study human nature, and the viability and success of this aspiration vary across topics. Meaning in life is one of the more difficult ones. Nevertheless, psychologists do turn up interesting and important facts and findings. How far these generalize to other cultures and historical periods is debatable. Martela (2020) notes that any discussion of life's meaning as a problem dates back only a couple centuries in Western civilization. If human civilization has existed for 150,000 years, the first 140,000 were all dominated by hunter-gatherer societies, who seem not to have struggled with meanings of life, even while they struggled to map the basic universe of meaning into a language and to create a shared body of knowledge about the environment.

It is my hope that philosophy can learn from psychology. Conversely, psychology could benefit much from continued input from philosophers. If I may close with an editorial comment, philosophy seems frequently misplaced among the humanities and properly belongs with the social sciences. Its relation to social science is not unlike the relation of mathematics to the natural sciences: sharpening a potent conceptual basis for collecting and interpreting data. This is acutely needed in psychology's studies of meaning. I hope the meaningful dialogue between our disciplines may increase!

References

Altick, R. 1965. *Lives and Letters: A History of Literary Biography in England and America*. New York: Knopf.

Barnett, B. 2012, April 25. 'Make Your Job More Meaningful'. *Harvard Business Review Blog*. https://hbr.org/2012/04/make-your-job-more-meaningful.

Baumeister, R. F. 1991. *Meanings of Life*. New York: Guilford Press.

Baumeister, R. F. 1994. 'The Crystallization of Discontent in the Process of Major Life Change'. In *Can Personality Change?*, ed. T. F. Heatherton and J. L. Weinberger, 281–297. Washington, DC: American Psychological Association.

Baumeister, R. F., W. Hofmann, A. Summerville, P. Reiss, and K. D. Vohs. 2020. 'Everyday Thoughts in Time: Experience Sampling Studies of Mental Time Travel'. *Personality and Social Psychology Bulletin* 46: 1631–1648.

Baumeister, R. F., and M. J. Landau. 2018. 'Finding the Meaning of Meaning: Emerging Insights on Four Grand Questions'. *Review of General Psychology* 22: 1–10.

Baumeister, R. F., K. D. Vohs, J. L. Aaker, and E. N. Garbinsky. 2013. 'Some Key Differences between a Happy Life and a Meaningful Life'. *Journal of Positive Psychology* 8: 505–551.

Bellah, R. N., R. Madsen, W. M. Sullivan, A. Swidler, and S. M. Tipton. 1985. *Habits of the Heart: Individualism and Commitment in American Life*. Berkeley: University of California Press.

Bulman, R. J., and C. B. Wortman. 1977. 'Attributions of Blame and Coping in the Real World: Severe Accident Victims React to Their Lot'. *Journal of Personality and Social Psychology* 35: 351–363.

Crumbaugh, J. C., and L. T. Maholick. 1964. 'An Experimental Study in Existentialism: The Psychometric Approach to Frankl's Concept of Noogenic Neurosis'. *Journal of Clinical Psychology* 20: 200–207.

Frankl, V. E. [1959] 1976. *Man's Search for Meaning*. New York: Pocket.

Freud, S. 1969. *Civilization and Its Discontents*, trans. J. Riviere, rev. and ed. J. Strachey. London: Hogarth Press.

George, L. S., and C. L. Park. 2016. 'Meaning in Life as Comprehension, Purpose, and Mattering: Toward Integration and New Research Questions'. *Review of General Psychology* 20: 205–220.

Graeber, D. 2013. 'On the Phenomenon of Bullshit Jobs: A Work Rant'. *Strike!*, Issue 3: 1–5.

Graeber, D. 2018. *Bullshit Jobs: A Theory*. London: Penguin.

Heine, S. J., T. Proulx, and K. D. Vohs. 2006. 'The Meaning Maintenance Model: On the Coherence of Social Motivations'. *Personality and Social Psychology Review* 10: 88–110.

Heintzelman, S., and L. A. King. 2014. '(The Feeling of) Meaning-as-Information'. *Personality and Social Psychology Review* 18: 153–167.

Heintzelman, S. J., and L. A. King. 2015, February. 'Mundane Contributors to Meaning in Life'. Presented at the annual conference of the Society for Personality and Social Psychology.

Heintzelman, S. J., and L. A. King. 2016. 'Meaning in Life and Intuition'. *Journal of Personality and Social Psychology* 110: 477–492.

Heintzelman, S. J., and L. A. King. 2019. 'Routines and Meaning in Life'. *Personality and Social Psychology Bulletin* 45: 688–699.

Heintzelman, S. J., J. Trent, and L. A. King. 2013. 'Encounters with Objective Coherence and the Experience of Meaning in Life'. *Psychological Science* 24: 991–998.

Landau, M. 2018. 'Using Metaphor to Find Meaning in Life'. *Review of General Psychology* 22: 62–72.

MacGregor, I., and B. R. Little. 1998. 'Personal Projects, Happiness, and Meaning: On Doing Well and Being Yourself'. *Journal of Personality and Social Psychology* 74: 494–512.

Martela, F. 2020. *A Wonderful Life: Insights on Finding a Meaningful Existence*. New York: Harper Design.

Park, C., and L. S. George. 2018. 'Lab- and Field-Based Approaches to Meaning Threats and Restoration: Convergences and Divergences'. *Review of General Psychology* 22: 73–84.

Robbins, T. 1988. *Cults, Converts, and Charisma: The Sociology of New Religious Movements*. London: Sage.

Steger, M. F., P. Frazier, S. Oishi, and M. Kaler. 2006. 'The Meaning in Life Questionnaire: Assessing the Presence of and Search for Meaning in Life'. *Journal of Counseling Psychology* 53: 80–93.

Steger, M. F., J. L. Morse, M. B. O'Donnell, T. A. Dao, and R. Borgschutle. 2018. *Seeking and Finding Meaning: A Review of Research on the Presence of Meaning and Search for Meaning Subscales of the Meaning in Life Questionnaire*. Unpublished manuscript, Colorado State University.

Stillman, T. F., R. F. Baumeister, N. M. Lambert, A. W. Crescioni, C. N. DeWall, and F. D. Fincham. 2009. 'Alone and without Purpose: Life Loses Meaning Following Social Exclusion'. *Journal of Experimental Social Psychology* 45: 686–694.

Stillman, T. F., N. M. Lambert, F. D. Fincham, and R. F. Baumeister. 2011. 'Meaning as Magnetic Force: Evidence That Meaning in Life Promotes Interpersonal Appeal'. *Social Psychological and Personality Science* 2: 13–20.

Vallacher, R. R., and D. M. Wegner. 1985. *A Theory of Action Identification*. Hillsdale, NJ: Erlbaum.

Vallacher, R. R., and D. M. Wegner. 1987. 'What Do People Think They're Doing: Action Identification and Human Behavior'. *Psychological Review* 94: 3–15.

Weintraub, K. J. 1978. *The Value of the Individual: Self and Circumstance in Autobiography*. Chicago: University of Chicago Press.

Williams, K. D. 2001. *Ostracism: The Power of Silence*. New York: Guilford.

Williams, K. D. 2007. 'Ostracism'. *Annual Review of Psychology* 58: 425–452.

PART VI
LIVING MEANINGFULLY: CHALLENGES AND PROSPECTS

CHAPTER 27

PESSIMISM, OPTIMISM, AND MEANING IN LIFE

DAVID BENATAR

We are born, we live, and we die. All this happens in a miniscule fraction of cosmic time on a planet that is but a speck in the universe (or perhaps multiverse). It is thus unsurprising that many people ask whether life has meaning. Although the question itself may seem pessimistic, there are many people who think that the correct answer is an affirmative one. These are the optimists about life's meaning. The pessimists are those who think that life lacks meaning.

This brief and simple summary masks many details and some complexity, which now need to be probed. Three questions need to be engaged. First, what are we asking when we ask whether life has meaning? Second, what constitutes optimism or pessimism about life's meaning? Third, how optimistic or pessimistic should we be about life's meaning?

WHAT ARE WE ASKING WHEN WE ASK WHETHER LIFE HAS MEANING?

There are those who think that it is fundamentally confused to ask what life's meaning is. They think that it is a nonsensical question or, in other words, that it is meaningless to ask whether life has meaning. Life, they think, is not the sort of thing that can have a meaning. Words and signs, they say, can have meanings, but life (itself rather than the word that designates it) cannot have meaning.

This seems far too literal an interpretation of the perennial question. When people ask whether life has meaning, they are asking something like whether it has a significant point, purpose, or impact, or whether instead it is all an exercise in futility. That seems like an entirely sensical question. This is not to deny that there are disagreements about precisely how to interpret the question. For example, having a purpose and having an impact are not exactly the same. However, we do not need to resolve these disagreements in order to understand that the kind of question (with a suitable number of disjunctions to cover the main options) is a coherent question.

Even with this recognition, the question requires further clarification. First, not every point or purpose is a positive one. Hitler or Stalin, for example, had lives filled with purpose. Nor were their endeavours futile, in the sense of failing to achieve any of their goals. Are such lives meaningful?

If one answers this question negatively, then we need to stipulate that for a life to be meaningful, its purpose or point must have positive value. Alternatively, if one answers the question positively, then one must acknowledge that not every meaning a life can have is one we should (positively) value. Although it is not clear that we *must* opt for the first of these answers, it may often simplify the discussion to do so. One does not then need to keep stipulating a positive meaning, as the positive value will be implicit. That said, optimists and pessimists (and others) sometimes disagree about whether some purpose or point is positive or negative. Thus, what optimists may count as meaning, pessimists might deny to be so, if they disagree that the relevant purpose or point is positive.

Even with this clarification, we need to distinguish between different questions we might be asking when we ask whether life has meaning. One distinction is between asking whether life in general has meaning, and asking whether an individual life has meaning. Sometimes this difference is encapsulated in the distinction between 'the meaning *of* life' and 'meaning *in* life'. However, it seems more helpful to capture the difference in a distinction between 'meaning of life' and 'meaning of *a* life'.

This distinction can be further refined. When one asks whether 'life in general' has meaning, one could be referring to all life, or to all life of a certain kind—such as all *human* life. Few people worry whether *all* life has meaning. For example, very few people, if any, worry whether the lives of cows or chickens—and, *a fortiori*, mosquitoes or fungi—have meaning. There are two likely (and mutually compatible) explanations for this. First, humans typically have no stake in the meaning of these other lives. (Exceptions might be made for companion animals.) Second, there is a widespread belief in human exceptionalism. Humans tend to think that humans stand apart from all other life forms and are special.

Many people *do* worry whether human life has meaning—a worry that may well be exacerbated by some striking similarities human life has with other life. Humans are not exempt from striving, suffering, and death. These similarities to non-human animals are discomforting and threaten the belief in human exceptionalism. Arguably, even more people are concerned about whether their *own* life has meaning. Each of us is most invested in the question at that level of specification.

There is a second distinction to be drawn between different questions about the meaning of life (or *a* life). One might ask whether life (or a life) was created for some significant purpose. Is there a reason why human life, or a particular human life, came to be? Alternatively, one might ask whether life has successfully been put to some significant purpose irrespective of whether it was brought into existence for that purpose. In other words, can life (or a life) be made meaningful? The first is a purpose endowed by whomever brings (the) life into being, whereas the second is a purpose generated by the being (or species) whose life it is.

These two distinctions—between the meaning of life and the meaning of a life, and between the purpose for which (a) life was created and the purpose to which it is put—cut across one another, yielding four possible questions (Table 27.1).

Not all of these questions are equally important because not all are equally central to most people's concerns when they wonder about life's meaning. Arguably, the third question is of the least interest. If it has *any* interest at all, this is likely derivative from a positive answer to the first question. In other words, if one believes that humanity was created for some important purpose, one might worry whether the species is acting in a way that fulfils that purpose. If, by contrast, one thinks that humanity was not created for any purpose, then the third question does not seem to arouse any interest. It seems clear that humans, in all their diversity, do not agree on—and could not coordinate to fulfil—a common purpose. Even if they could, this would have neither the personal interest of the fourth question nor the 'authority' of a positive answer to the first question.

The second question is also not of widespread interest, at least if the purpose of one's parents is sufficient for an affirmative answer. After all, worries about the meaning of a life are not typically thought to depend on what, if any, purpose one's parents had in bringing one into existence. It's not the case that those whose conception was an 'accident' are left with existential crises while those who were intentionally brought into existence have their existential worries eliminated by the knowledge that their parents created them for some or other purpose—such as providing those parents with the pleasure of having offspring, or perpetuating their culture, or looking after them in their dotage. Even if those were reasons why one was created, they do not seem to address the existential worry.

Table 27.1 Distinguishing Questions About Life and Meaning

	Meaning of Life = (Human) life in general	Meaning of *a* Life = Individual lives
Created for a purpose?	1. Was human life created for a significant purpose?	2. Was my (or your) life created for a significant purpose?
Put to some purpose?	3. Is humanity put to some significant purpose?	4. Is my (or your) life put to some significant purpose?

The second question holds more interest for those who take the relevant purpose to be that of God rather than their parents (perhaps because they think that any purpose of their parents would be insufficiently significant). Then the question is whether a particular person's life—such as mine or yours—was created for a divinely ordained purpose.[1]

However, the more common existential questions are the first and fourth questions. A positive answer to the first question is possible only if the human species were created—presumably by God. Those who believe this may or may not believe that it has implications for the fourth question. They could believe that God's purpose for humanity carries over to individual humans. Alternatively, they might believe that even if humanity as a whole serves God's purpose, it does not follow that each individual's life does too. One possible explanation for this is that individuals may not be living in a way that fulfils the divinely ordained purpose.

Atheists must answer the first question negatively. (An evolutionary *explanation* of how humans came to be is not the same as attributing a *purpose* to the existence of humanity.) Some atheists might still regret the absence of a positive answer to the first question. Whether or not they do, they could provide a positive answer to the fourth question. In other words, they can think that individuals can put their lives to some worthwhile purpose.

Although it is common to speak of *the* mean*ing* of life, we should not preclude the possibility that life (or a life) can have more than one meaning—more than one purpose or point. For this reason, it is better to ask whether life *has* meaning than to ask what *the* meaning of life is. Moreover, lives that have meaning may have more or less of it. This is because meaning is a matter of degree. Lives that are not meaningless (in the literal sense of being entirely devoid of any meaning) may not be meaning*ful* in the literal sense of being full of meaning (whatever that might mean). Instead, they might be meaningful in the sense of having *some* or perhaps *sufficient* meaning. Optimists and pessimists might disagree on how much meaning is sufficient.

There are different perspectives from which we can judge whether life has or lacks meaning (Benatar 2017, 21–23). These perspectives might be said to pick out different *kinds* of meaning (or meaninglessness). The most important distinction here is between meaning from a cosmic perspective and meaning from an earthly perspective. The latter is not a single perspective, but rather a category of perspectives of different breadths.

The broadest of these is the perspective of all humanity. Some lives, but relatively few, have meaning from the perspective of all humanity. These are the lives of those who have made some valuable contribution to humanity. Among those who come to

---

[1] An affirmative answer to this question, which presumes that responsibility for one's coming into existence does not lie entirely with one's parents, will require some mechanism for dividing responsibility for one's existence between God and one's parents. Barring virgin births, presumably responsibility for bringing one into existence cannot lie entirely with God. God gets to veto or endorse attempts to procreate, and could impose or withhold procreative outcomes where people have sex even without attempting to procreate. However, God does not create new individual humans without some human agency playing a role.

mind are Edward Jenner (pioneer of the smallpox vaccine), Ignaz Semmelweiss (whose hand-washing proposals in obstetric clinics radically reduced the incidence of puerperal fever), and Charles Darwin (whose theory of evolution revolutionized our understanding of biology, with its consequent impact on, among other areas, modern medicine). The impact they had on the lives of others is often not noticed and the beneficiaries of their impact may be completely unaware of them, but it remains the case that they had the positive impact they did have.

A narrower terrestrial perspective is that of specific human groupings—in other words, not all of humanity, but of some component group of humanity. These groups, in turn, may be larger or smaller. They might be nations, associations, communities, or families, for example. The life of a prime minister of Tuvalu, the small Polynesian sovereign state, may not matter from the perspective of humanity, but it may well matter from a Tuvaluan perspective. The life of a president of the African Chess Confederation could matter from the perspective of that chess community, even if it does not matter from the perspective of humanity. You or I matter from the perspective of our families, even if we do not matter nationally or from the perspective of humanity.

The narrowest terrestrial perspective is that of a single person. If one matters to at least one person, then one matters from this individual perspective. (There may be some debate about whether that individual could be oneself. Could a Friday-less Robinson Crusoe who is never found have a meaningful life? It seems unlikely. However, such cases are of little practical interest because almost everybody matters to at least one *other* person.)

One final important distinction is between perceived (or subjective) meaning and actual (or objective) meaning. A subjectively meaningful life is one that feels meaningful. An objectively meaningful life is one that actually meets some (non-subjective) standard of meaningfulness. If one accepts this distinction, then it is possible for a life to feel meaningful but not be meaningful, or to feel meaningless but to have meaning. However, the distinction is not uncontroversial. There are those who think that the objective criterion for a meaningful life is its feeling meaningful.[2] This seems too optimistic. While it is entirely plausible to think that one cannot be mistaken about whether one's life *feels* meaningful, it is hard to believe that the feeling is all it takes for life to be meaningful. Goals are not worthwhile just because people think that they are. Nor is it the case that one is achieving one's goals just because one thinks that one is achieving them.

What Constitutes Optimism and Pessimism about Life's Meaning?

The terms 'optimism' and 'pessimism' are in no less need of clarification than questions about whether life has meaning. Both 'optimism' and 'pessimism' carry connotations.

---

[2] One prominent example is Richard Taylor (2000, 319–334).

In general, the connotations of the former are better than those of the latter. There are at least two reasons for this. First, the denotations of the words carry over into attitudes towards them. Optimism is so easily associated with what is positive, and pessimism with what is negative. Second, there is a widespread human bias towards optimism, as a result of which optimists are lauded while pessimists are either condemned or at least pitied. Yet there are some confident and committed pessimists for whom the valence of the connotations runs in the reverse direction. For them, Ambrose Bierce's tongue-in-cheek description of optimism as 'an intellectual disorder' is resonant, as is his definition of pessimism as a 'philosophy forced upon the convictions of the observer by the disheartening prevalence of the optimist with his scarecrow hope and his unsightly smile' (Bierce 1993, 88, 93).

It is helpful to distinguish two questions about life's meaning on which optimists and pessimists might disagree. The first question is whether life has meaning of a certain kind—cosmic meaning, for example. There might be disagreement about this, with the optimist answering affirmatively, and the pessimist negatively. The second question is whether the absence of meaning of some kind is bad. Those who believe that it is bad are pessimists about this matter. By contrast, those who believe that it is not bad are the optimists.

What of those who think that the *presence* of some kinds of meaning would be bad? This may sound like a strange view to hold (if we stipulate meaning to be positive). However, there are those who think that not just any kind of (positive) meaning would be a good thing. Robert Nozick, for example, has plausibly suggested that it would not be good if the purpose of humanity were to serve as food for intergalactic travellers (Nozick 1981, 586). If that were our purpose, we might be making a positive difference, but it would hardly be the kind of purpose we would find ennobling. Should those who think that the presence of such meaning would be bad be called pessimists? That would be an odd usage of the word 'pessimism', but that is only because the bad meaning is thought to be a *counterfactual* rather than real. If being food for intergalactic travellers were indeed thought to be our purpose, then the view that this is bad would appropriately be labelled 'pessimistic'. The optimists would be those who were in denial about our purportedly true purpose.

This is not because we should regard pessimists as realists, and optimists as deluded. Instead, it is because we should apply the term 'optimism' to any view that depicts some element of life's purported actual meaning as positive. 'Pessimism' should refer to any view that depicts some element of life's purported actual meaning as negative (either in the sense that it is not actually meaning because, contrary to the views of others, it is not positive, or in the sense that while it is positive, it is not ennobling). In other words, whether a view counts as optimistic or as pessimistic depends on whether some claim about the actual situation is said to be respectively good or bad (or, in at least some situations, better or worse than the relevant alternative).

Thus, for example, those who believe that God exists and endows human life with meaning are optimists about meaning (whether or not God actually exists). Those who believe that God does not exist and that our lives are thereby deprived of valuable meaning are pessimists. However, those who believe that God does not exist but that we can get all the meaning we need without God are optimists about meaning.

This approach to understanding 'optimism' and 'pessimism' is better than one that privileges either of the views as more accurate, or that understands both as deviations from an accurate view. If 'optimism' means 'too positive a view' or pessimism means 'too negative a view' then we are precluded from using one or both of those labels to describe an *accurately* positive or a negative view about life's meaning. That gives 'optimism' and 'pessimism' more content than they need to have, and renders expressions such as 'too optimistic' as tautologous. We should not have to decide first whether a view about life's meaning is accurate before we decide whether it counts as optimistic or as pessimistic. The labels 'optimistic' and 'pessimistic' should apply irrespective of whether the views to which they apply are true or false. It is a further question whether they are *too* optimistic or pessimistic.

As this locution suggests, both optimism and pessimism are a matter of degree. One can be either optimistic or pessimistic to varying degrees. Thus, the question is not merely whether one should be optimistic or pessimistic about some matter, such as life's meaning, but also *how* optimistic or pessimistic one should be.

The expected and reasonable upshot of these various thoughts is that sometimes optimism (to some or other degree) and sometimes (some amount of) pessimism will be correct. This, in turn, implies that we should be optimists about some matters and pessimists about others. More specifically, we should be optimists or pessimists to some degree when that level of optimism or pessimism is warranted. How often and when we should be optimistic or pessimistic depends on how often each view is apt. There is no reason to think that each must be true as often as the other. With regard to life's meaning, I shall argue, some but only limited optimism is warranted. We should be optimistic that some kinds of meaning are possible, but pessimistic about the existence of other kinds of meaning.

How Optimistic or Pessimistic Should We Be about Life's Meaning?

It should be clear that there are very good grounds for being optimistic about a life having meaning from the narrower perspectives, but that the grounds for optimism diminish the broader the perspective. Almost all lives will have meaning from the perspective of one other person. It is a very rare person whose life matters to *nobody*. Most people's lives also matter to some kind of grouping—most especially a family, but typically also some broader human community, such as their friends, co-workers, and clients. What you do and what happens to you matters to some others. Almost everybody has some (positive) impact on others. It is relatively rare, however, for a life to have meaning from the perspective of all humanity.

Thus, almost all lives have meaning from some or other terrestrial perspective, even if most lives have meaning from only the more limited terrestrial perspectives. This is not to say that all concern—perhaps pessimism—that people have about an absence or dearth of terrestrial meaning is misplaced. First, some people may be concerned that their lives have meaning only from one of the more limited terrestrial perspectives, and may want to make their lives meaningful from a broader earthly perspective. Second, even from a given terrestrial perspective, they might be concerned that their lives are insufficiently meaningful. Perhaps what they do matters to their family, but they want to make an even more meaningful contribution at that level. There are sometimes things that can be done to address such a (perceived) shortfall of meaning. Very often, however, the kind or degree of meaning that is desired cannot be achieved. Thus, while there is some room for optimism about terrestrial meaning, there is also plenty of scope for pessimism about this kind of meaning.

Matters are worse when it comes to cosmic meaning. Absent some kinds of theistic view, to be discussed shortly, it is very difficult to see how either human life as a whole or any individual life could (currently) have meaning from that perspective. It is possible to imagine a scenario in which human lives could have such meaning. If, for example, there were sentient life pervading the universe, and things that we did here on earth had a positive impact on these lives, then our lives would have at least some cosmic meaning—parallel to the degree of terrestrial meaning that a relatively small number of humans currently have from the perspective of humanity. However, we have no reason to believe that this is currently the case. Even if there is sentient life elsewhere, we have no reason to think that we are having any—let alone, a positive—impact on that life.

Optimists respond in one of two ways to the problem of cosmic meaning(lessness). One response is to claim that there is a God who endows our lives with cosmic meaning. This is theistic optimism. Another response is to deny that God exists, but also either to deny that our lives therefore lack cosmic meaning, or to accept that although they lack such meaning, it is not bad that they do. These are forms of atheistic optimism. Consider theistic optimism first.

Theistic Optimism

It is not difficult to see why many theists think that God gives cosmic meaning to our lives. If God is the creator of the entire cosmos, including us, then God likely created us with a specific purpose within the universe. This provides a comforting answer to the question 'Why do we exist?'. If we were created for some purpose, then we can put our lives to that purpose. We can live in such a way as to fulfil God's purpose.

If we, and the way we live, matter to the ultimate being that (according to the theistic view) God is, we have ultimate meaning. If we are loved by and matter to a cosmic being then we have cosmic meaning, for the same reason that if we are loved by and matter to our family then we have familial meaning. It is hard to imagine a more important *form* of mattering than mattering to God. (This does not preclude the possibility that there can be varying degrees of mattering to God, and thus that some beings matter more than others to God. Indeed, most theists think that humans matter more to God than do non-human animals.)

Not everybody accepts that God is an attractive source of meaning. Unsurprisingly, given the optimism bias, those who think that divinely bestowed meaning is not meaning worth wanting tend to be those—atheists—who deny that God is the source of any meaning (because he does not exist). In other words, those who think that God's existence would contribute positively to the meaning of our lives are generally those who think that God exists, while whose who think that God's existence would not contribute or would even detract from the meaning of our lives tend to be those who think that God does not exist. There are some exceptions—most commonly pessimistic atheists who think that God would, or at least could, be a source of valuable meaning if he existed even though, regrettably on this view, he does not.[3]

One reason why some people think that God would detract from the meaning of our lives is that if we existed to fulfil his purposes, then instead of each of us being the author of his own purpose and life, we would be relegated to being servants to God's purpose. Jean-Paul Sartre, for example, declares: 'Man is nothing else but that which he makes of himself'. This, he says, is why humans have 'dignity', but stones and tables do not (Sartre 1948, 28). The implication seems to be that if a person were fashioned by God rather than by himself or herself, then he or she would lack dignity and would be bound to serve God's purposes rather than his or her own.

This sort of view strikes many pessimists about cosmic meaning as a bad case of sour grapes. One believes that one cannot have cosmic meaning, and thus one proclaims that it is better that one does not have it. One denies any need for cosmic meaning because that, allegedly, enables a self-fashioned terrestrial meaning.

However, that sacrifice seems unnecessary. There is no reason why, on a theistic view, humans could not have at least significant scope to put their lives to purposes of their own. The divine purpose might constrain the range of purposes to which a human may put his or her life, but that is hardly a disadvantage. Anybody who thinks that meaning must be positive to be worth pursuing or having, will recognize that there are constraints. An omnibenevolent God would only impose appropriate constraints and would presumably recognize that individual variation in aptitude and interest would necessitate a range of positive purposes open to different people. Thus, the theistic view does not preclude an appropriate measure of purposive self-authorship. Yet it adds to the terrestrial meaning some cosmic meaning. Because one's terrestrial purposes matter to God, they also have some degree of cosmic meaning.

Optimistic atheists might offer other reasons for thinking that meaning arising from God would not (necessarily) be good. One possibility is that God may not have a sufficiently ennobling purpose for us—as would be the case if our purpose were to serve

---

[3] It is also logically possible, though rare, for a theist to think that it would have been better for the meaningfulness of our lives if there were no God.

as food for intergalactic travellers. However, the convenient feature of the theistic position is that it has an all-purpose response to such challenges. Any meaning derived from an omnibenevolent, omniscient, omnipotent being would be meaning that, all things considered, would be worth having. Such a God would not have assigned us a de-meaning purpose.

The real problem is that it is *too* convenient. The suggestion that there is such a God, whose existence would solve all these problems, as well as many other others, is too good to be true. In other words, the bigger problem is not that God, if he existed, could alleviate some of our existential yearnings. Instead, the problem is that it is unlikely that there is a God.

This is not the place to defend *that* claim. (It would be far too optimistic to think that something as controversial as the existence of God could be settled, *en passant*, in a short essay on a different, albeit connected topic.) However, it should be easy to see why theism itself can be understood as an optimistic view. The claim that there is an omnipotent, omniscient, and omnibenevolent God has to be reconciled with colossal amounts of suffering and death that quite clearly exist. One need think no further than the billions of animals that are consumed, often alive, by other animals, every day. Atheism faces no such challenge. Nor does the atheist have any difficulty in explaining all the pleasure in the world, because there are compelling naturalistic accounts of these.

The 'too good to be true' argument stands in stark contrast to a curious argument *for* theism. This is the argument that atheism is too bad to be true. In the context of life's meaning, William Lane Craig is a prominent exponent of this view (2000, 40–56). He argues that without God (and immortality), our lives lack ultimate purpose and are absurd. He says that it is impossible for atheists to 'live consistently and happily within such a world view' (Craig 2000, 47). According to him, accepting the absurdity of life is practically inconsistent with living happily, and thinking that life could have meaning without God is inconsistent.

There is an equivocation in this argument—more specifically in the meaning of 'meaning'. Recognizing that life has no 'ultimate' or 'cosmic' meaning (perhaps because God does not exist) does not entail that it can have no terrestrial meaning. There is no inconsistency in denying cosmic meaning but acknowledging terrestrial meaning. It may still be utterly awful that life has no meaning beyond the terrestrial realm. However, that is no reason to think it is false. The horror of something is no bar to its being true.

Atheistic Optimism

Optimism is not the preserve of theists (Benatar 2008, 19–22). Atheists can be just as optimistic, even though their optimistic faith does not include a deity.

Some atheistic views suggest that our lives do indeed have cosmic meaning. Iddo Landau offers an argument of this kind. He distinguishes between (1) perspectives and (2) standards for meaningfulness, and argues that we can view a life from an expansive perspective without having to judge its meaningfulness by the standard of how extensive an impact it has (2017, 95). Thus, some (hypothetical or actual) observer elsewhere in the universe may view some act of kindness that you perform and recognize that it matters to its beneficiaries. Its impact may be local, but its value can be recognized even from a cosmic perspective.

This is *too* optimistic. If, using a very powerful telescope from outer space, I observe your kind deed, I may recognize from afar that it matters to the person or people affected. However, it would be implausible to say that just because it is being viewed from elsewhere in the cosmos it therefore has cosmic meaning. Its local meaning may be recognized by an observer anywhere in the cosmos, but that is different from saying that it has cosmic meaning. If it *did* have cosmic meaning, we would be unable to differentiate meaning from different perspectives. Playground squabbles would be incidents of international—and cosmic—significance!

Guy Kahane offers a conditional argument that human life might have cosmic significance. He suggests that *if* humans are the only intelligent life in the universe, then we possess the most value there is, and thus have immense cosmic significance (2014, 745–772). One problem with this suggestion is that it requires a slip from the claim that humans have value to the claim that they are cosmically significant. Even if there is *some* sense in which the existence of intelligent life on earth is cosmically significant, this is not the kind of significance about which people are wondering when they fear that human life has no cosmic meaning. That fear is not the dread that there may actually be intelligent life elsewhere in the universe. If anything, something close to the opposite would be the case. If there were at least conscious if not sapient life elsewhere in the universe, then there might be some remote chance of our lives having meaning from the perspective of those lives.

Another optimistic response to the lack of cosmic meaning is to discount the importance of the cosmic perspective. 'Discount' is ambiguous between 'count less' and 'do not count at all'. Discounting the cosmic perspective in the second sense is even more optimistic than discounting it in the first sense. If the absence of cosmic meaning only counted less, then there would still be some grounds for regret about its absence. By contrast, if the absence of cosmic meaning is not counted at all, then the absence of cosmic meaning provides *no* grounds for regret.

Thomas Nagel advances an argument that discounts cosmic meaning in the more optimistic way. He says that if it is true that 'nothing we do now will matter in a million years ... then by the same token, nothing that will be the case in a million years matters now' (1979, 11). This seems to imply that we should not worry at all about the long-term insignificance of our actions and lives. That is overly optimistic. Professor Nagel is correct that just because our actions and lives do not have long-term significance, this does not imply that they have no shorter-term significance. However, this, in turn, does not imply that the absence of longer-term meaning provides no grounds for regret.

Professor Nagel also asks: 'would not a life that is absurd if it lasts seventy years be infinitely absurd if it lasted through eternity?' (1979, 12). Although this is a rhetorical question aimed at blocking the inference people make from the brevity of our lives to their insignificance, there is actually an answer to the question. The answer depends on the kind of absurdity (or meaninglessness) one has in mind. If a life is terrestrially absurd, then it would indeed be infinitely absurd if it lasted for eternity. However, a life that is terrestrially meaningful can be cosmically meaningless in part because it is so ephemeral. If one accepts that most lives have some terrestrial meaning but no cosmic meaning, then it is a mistake to think that our ephemerality makes no difference to our (cosmic) absurdity.

An even more common optimistic response to our cosmic meaninglessness is simply to ignore it. A number of philosophers do this.[4] Their discussions about life's meaning are focused entirely on terrestrial meaning, but without explicitly noting that they are speaking only about terrestrial meaning. Unsurprisingly, they reach the conclusion that most lives have (such) meaning and that it is at least partially within our power to enhance this meaning. By conveniently ignoring the cosmic meaning, they leave us with an unduly rosy picture about life's meaning. It is unduly rosy because it tells only part of the truth, namely the happy part—that terrestrial meaning is possible. The bad news is glossed over.

Another optimistic strategy acknowledges the absence of cosmic meaning but denies that having such meaning would be good. Although those offering such an argument would resist describing it as a 'sour grapes' argument, such a description is appropriate if it would be better if our lives had cosmic meaning in addition to terrestrial meaning. The 'sour grapes' argument is a more general version of the optimistic atheistic argument, considered earlier, that it is better that God does not bestow any meaning on our lives. Whereas that earlier argument concluded that *divinely* bestowed cosmic meaning is not worth wanting, the general sour grapes argument concludes that no cosmic meaning is worth wanting.

One possible explanation for this is that it is not worth wanting the unattainable. If one cannot have something, moderating one's desires so that one no longer wants it will result in less dissatisfaction. That, of course, is exactly what the sour grapes phenomenon is. While there may very well be benefits to this, it would be a mistake to infer that it would not be better if one *did* have what one could not have—cosmic meaning, in this case. In other words, there is a difference between whether wanting the unattainable makes one less happy and whether it would be good if the unattainable were in fact attained. Even if the former is true, the latter may be too.

Another way of defending the sour grapes argument is to claim that the desire for cosmic meaning is indicative of a defect in the person with such a desire. It has been suggested that such a desire is narcissistic or megalomaniacal (Kahane 2014, 763–764). Such accusations fail to demonstrate that cosmic meaning would not be good. If the accusations are justified, they might show only that one should not estimate oneself worthy of or entitled to such a good. But *are* the accusations justified? Why is it narcissistic or megalomaniacal to want cosmic meaning but not narcissistic to want terrestrial meaning (of varying degrees)?

---

[4] For example, Peter Singer (1995) and Thaddeus Metz (2013).

It seems that cosmic meaning would be valuable for extensions of the very reasons that terrestrial meaning is valuable. If it is said to be narcissistic to desire only unattainable meaning, then this accusation really is merely sour grapes. If it is not the unattainability of cosmic meaning but its expansiveness that renders the desire for it narcissistic, then the question is why the bar for narcissism must be set precisely at this level. Why is it not also narcissistic to want the more expansive kinds of terrestrial meaning? And if the latter desire *is* also narcissistic, then it is narcissistic to want to make the sort of difference that Edward Jenner and Jonas Salk made. Although there is a difference between *wanting* to make such a difference and *making* such a difference, the latter often results from the former. It would be both imprudent and unfair to judge people who want to have an extensive positive impact as narcissists. One can want to make such a difference without being infatuated with oneself.

Conclusion

Neither optimism *qua* optimism, nor pessimism *qua* pessimism, has anything to recommend it. In other words, we should adopt a view not because it is optimistic or because it is pessimistic, but rather because it is an accurate view. Sometimes the most accurate view will be a congenial one. On other occasions, it will be disagreeable. Optimism is warranted in the former cases and pessimism in the latter.

When it comes to life's meaning, there is some scope for optimism, but more for pessimism. Almost all (if not all) lives have at least some terrestrial meaning. That is the good news. The bad news is that the meaning most lives have is significantly limited. While meaning from the narrower terrestrial perspectives is common, it becomes much rarer as one adopts broader terrestrial perspectives. Even those lives that have some meaning from the perspective of all humanity have only limited amounts of such meaning. Edward Jenner and Jonas Salk, for example, each made an important difference to humanity, but only a small difference relative to the aggregation of the achievements of all those who have made comparable contributions.

Moreover, unless we are in the grip of extremely wishful thinking, we are forced to acknowledge that none of our lives has *any* cosmic significance. The situation could, in principle, be different, but we do not have good reason for thinking that it actually is. The glass of life's meaning is neither half full nor half empty. It contains some dribblings, the bulk of which are squeezed with great effort. If meaning is good, then we should be sorry that our lives do not contain much more of it.[5]

---

[5] I am grateful to Iddo Landau for helpful comments on the first draft of this chapter.

REFERENCES

Benatar, David. 2008. 'The Optimism Delusion'. *Think* 16: 19–22.
Benatar, David. 2017. *The Human Predicament*. New York: Oxford University Press.
Bierce, Ambrose. 1993. *The Devil's Dictionary*. New York: Dover.
Craig, William Lane. 2000. 'The Absurdity of Life without God'. In *The Meaning of Life*, ed. E. D. Klemke, 2nd ed., 40–56. New York: Oxford University Press.
Kahane, Guy. 2014. 'Our Cosmic Insignificance'. *Nous* 48: 745–772.
Landau, Iddo. 2017. *Finding Meaning in an Imperfect World*. New York: Oxford University Press.
Metz, Thaddeus. 2013. *Meaning in Life*. Oxford: Oxford University Press.
Nagel, Thomas. 1979. 'The Absurd'. In T. Nagel, *Mortal Questions*, 11–23. Cambridge: Cambridge University Press.
Nozick, Robert. 1981. *Philosophical Explanations*. Cambridge, MA: Belknap Press.
Sartre, Jean-Paul. 1948. *Existentialism and Humanism*, trans. Philip Mairet. London: Eyre Methuen.
Singer, Peter. 1995. *How Are We to Live?* Amherst, NY: Prometheus Books.
Taylor, Richard. 2000. 'The Meaning of Life'. In R. Taylor, *Good and Evil*, 319–334. Amherst, NY: Prometheus.

CHAPTER 28

THE RATIONALITY OF SUICIDE AND THE MEANINGFULNESS OF LIFE

MICHAEL CHOLBI

THE sense that one's life is meaningful seems to confer a high level of resiliency and perseverance on human beings. As Viktor Frankl (1992, 87–88) observed, even the hardships associated with life in a Nazi concentration camp become more survivable for those able to develop and retain a sense of their lives as meaningful. One recent meta-review of literature concerning meaning in life and suicide (Costanza, Prelati, and Pompili 2019) found that experiencing one's life as meaningful serves as a reliable 'protective factor' against suicidal thinking, suicide attempts, and death via suicide. Correlations between meaningfulness in life and lowered tendencies for suicide appear remarkably widespread, having been identified in children and adolescents (Schnell, Gertsner, and Krampe 2018, Tan et al. 2018); elderly adults (Heisel and Flett 2016; Heisel, Neufeld, and Flett 2016), and military personnel, including those with depression or post-traumatic stress disorder (Bryan et al. 2013; Sinclair, Bryan, and Bryan 2016). And in general, the sense that one's life is meaningful appears to have the powerful capacity to bolster individuals' ability to persist in the face of adversity that might otherwise contribute to suicide risk (Kleiman and Beaver 2013; Khan et al. 2018). Conversely, the mental pain closely associated with suicide seems to be negatively correlated with subjects' sense of whether their life is meaningful (Orbach, Mikulincer, and Sirota 2003).

Philosophers interested in the meaning of life are likely to view these empirical findings as suggestive, but will press two critical issues. First, this research often leaves unclear exactly what conception of meaningfulness is at play here. As Martela and Steger (2016) observe, this empirical literature measures meaningfulness in life in different ways, sometimes as a matter of a life being *coherent*, that is, its making sense to the person whose life it is by exhibiting a larger pattern or narrative; as its having *purpose*, a set of goals or an overall direction; or as *significance*, as one the subject values, finds worthwhile, or endorses. This imprecision is evident in the questionnaires commonly deployed in this research. One prominent instrument either leaves it to the test subjects to determine what meaningfulness is, simply asking them to agree or disagree with statements such as 'I understand my life's meaning' or 'I am searching for meaning in my life', or invokes coherence ('I have a good sense of what makes my life meaningful') or purpose ('my life has a clear sense of purpose') (Steger et al. 2006). To a philosophical eye, these features of a life may be positively interrelated (a coherent life may be more likely to be purposeful or significant, etc.) and each has a claim to at least being an ingredient in a meaningful life. But it less clear that any of these are what *renders* life meaningful, and they are clearly distinct. A person's life may make sense to them but lack purpose, or may not be a life they endorse or find worthwhile (Metz 2019, 408–409). A person's life may be worthwhile in their own eyes but lack the pattern or narrative needed to lend it coherence, etc. For philosophers interested in the meaning of life, this conceptual untidiness will be frustrating but unsurprising. After all, philosophical disagreement persists about what just meaning in life, meaningfulness, etc., *are*.

Second, this research appears to show that meaningfulness is, as a matter of fact, a *motivating* reason with respect to suicidal choice and action—that it plays a psychological role in how actual agents deliberate about whether to end their lives. But philosophers (and other reflective individuals) will want to know whether, and how, the meaningfulness of a person's life bears on her *justificatory* or normative reasons for continuing her life and, conversely, for hastening her death. In other words, does meaningfulness provide compelling rational grounds for ending (or continuing) one's life?

This chapter takes up the mantle of investigating the relationship between suicidal decision and meaningfulness in life, with an eye to ascertaining how the latter might provide justificatory reasons relevant to the former. If, as seems likely, suicidal thought or action is diminished by a sense of one's life being meaningful, and vice versa, then what notions of suicidal thought or action *and* of life's meaningfulness best make rational sense of this relation? Answering this question satisfactorily will require an exercise in seeking conceptual equilibrium, identifying those notions of suicidal thought or action and of life's meaningfulness that most convincingly vindicate the apparent rational relation between these.

My objective is to demonstrate that meaningfulness provides reasons relevant to suicide that either cannot be reduced to the reasons of well-being that philosophers have typically used to analyse suicide decisions, or at least forms a distinct class of reasons within those that contribute to well-being. Most centrally, the decision to engage in suicide can be understood as a choice related to life's meaningfulness insofar as an individual can see no *point* in living through her anticipated future. The absence of current or anticipated meaningfulness can thus provide reasons to divest from one's future lifespan by shortening one's life, while the presence or expectation of meaningfulness can provide reasons to invest in one's future lifespan by continuing to live.

My discussion begins (in section 1) with a brief interrogation of how Albert Camus, one of the few philosophers to investigate the relationship between suicide and life's meaningfulness, understood their relation. I conclude that Camus's understanding errs insofar as his nihilism rests on an inflated conception of what is required to render a human life meaningful and implausibly implies that suicide, as a response to life's ostensible meaninglessness, is equally rational throughout the changing temporal circumstances of a human life. Section 2 renders more precise the ordinary conception of suicide as choosing to die, arguing that suicide is an act wherein a person alters the timing of her death, but from a prudential perspective, also evaluatively divests from her own future. In section 3, I advance a conception of meaningfulness of life, heavily indebted to Cheshire Calhoun (2018), in which meaningfulness is a function of whether a person finds her future worth investing her agency in. Section 4 unifies the findings of sections 2 and 3, proposing that choices regarding suicide are sometimes oriented around meaningfulness, where meaningfulness is measured by an individual's reasons for investing in her future. Section 5 argues that considerations of meaning form a discrete class of reasons relevant to the rationality of suicide that may stand apart from familiar considerations of well-being.

To forestall one crucial confusion: in considering whether meaningfulness bears on suicide's rationality, I set aside the vital question of the *morality* of suicide (Cholbi 2011, 39–69). Suicide is subject to multiple evaluative norms, and suicide that meets conditions of rationality does not necessarily meet the conditions of moral permissibility, or vice versa. Thus, whether suicide is rational does not exhaust the factors relevant to whether it ought to be pursued.

1. Camus on Suicide and Meaningfulness

Camus famously remarked that suicide is the only 'truly serious philosophical problem' (1955, 3). For Camus, the prospect of suicide becomes acute once we appreciate that life is essentially and unavoidably absurd, i.e. that human existence is meaningless at its core. No value, purpose, or endeavour, according to Camus, can lend our lives meaning, and the fact that we eventually die only makes a further mockery of all human efforts to live meaningfully. Our hope of leading meaningful lives is thus as futile as Sisyphus's endless struggle to push his rock to the top of the mountain. Every attempt to find meaning for our existence rolls back at us, so to speak. Although Camus saw suicide as one possible response to the undeniable absurdity of our existence, he ultimately rejects suicide in favour of rebelling in the face of absurdity, thereby affirming our freedom. Suicide, in Camus's eyes, represents a capitulation to, rather than a triumph over, the universe's meaninglessness and indifference.

Camus deserves credit as one of the few philosophers to explicitly investigate the relation between suicide and meaningfulness in life.[1] Nevertheless, there are reasons

---

[1] The relation has been explored more extensively in connection with assisted dying. See Little (1999); Varelius (2013 and 2016).

to think that Camus himself gets their relation wrong. As he saw it, suicide acquires its practical gravity as a consequence of philosophical nihilism. For nihilists such as Camus, our lives are *necessarily* meaningless because there is nothing that answers to *the* meaning of life, no fact written into the nature of the universe or ordained by God to confer meaning upon *a* life, i.e. upon the life of any given individual. Perhaps Camus was correct on that score: From a wider cosmic or external perspective, a perspective outside our day-to-day experiences, his nihilism seems plausible because there are no transcendent facts about the universe to lend our lives the seriousness or gravity requisite for them to seem meaningful (Nagel 1986, 214). After all, an individual human life is but one of billions of such lives, a small and transient blip within the multibillion year history of the universe, and so when we 'zoom out' from our individual lives, they will invariably seem minute and insignificant (Fischer 2020, 16).

But one might reject Camus's nihilism because he subscribed to an overinflated understanding of what a meaningful human life requires. Specifically, his nihilism may reflect a kind of vanity, assuming our human lives can only be meaningful insofar as they are indispensable to the world's history. Perhaps lives can instead be meaningful, especially from within the internal perspectives of those whose lives they are, even if their meaningfulness disappears when viewed from a larger third-personal or timeless perspective (Bradley 2015, 416–417). It may, in other words, suffice for our lives to be meaningful that we be the right kind of protagonist within our own lives, even if it is impossible for us to be central to the story of the world as a whole.

Thus, we may reasonably doubt that our meaning-based reasons concerning suicide rest on anything like Camus-style nihilism. His position also has counterintuitive implications regarding judgements of meaningfulness in life and the reasons that bear on suicidal decision. For nihilists, the meaninglessness of our lives is a necessary truth, unrelated to the particular circumstances of individual lives. But this seems unlikely. Sisyphus's life may well be meaningless in Camus's terms, but it is difficult to swallow that (say) Nelson Mandela's life was *equally* meaningless, and all the more, that Mandela had reasons of the same kind or magnitude for suicide that Sisyphus has. Furthermore, Camus's nihilism implies that meaningfulness is invariant across our lifespans. After all, young Sisyphus pushing his rock up a hill is engaged in no less futile an endeavour than old Sisyphus; well-rested Sisyphus pushing his rock up a hill is engaged in no less futile an endeavour than weary Sisyphus; etc. But this too strikes me as an unlikely implication. Most actual human lives seem to oscillate in their meaningfulness or the prospects for meaningfulness, with meaningfulness rising or falling in response to various contingencies (our relationships, health, etc.). Nihilism seems to overlook how, because meaningfulness varies across and within lives, the question of whether facts about meaningfulness can matter to the justification of suicide will only be salient at *certain* points during the lives of *some* human beings.

Camus's understanding of the relation between suicide and meaningfulness thus seems questionable both in terms of the nature of the reasons that meaningfulness bears vis-à-vis suicide and their ubiquity. The reasons that meaningfulness provides are not cosmic and timeless, but local, personal, and temporally specific. But before filling in these reasons, we must work from the other side of the relation, clarifying the nature of suicidal decision.

2. Suicide, the Time of Death, and Time's Prudential Significance

Suicide is standardly defined as intentional self-killing, i.e. intentionally choosing one's own death (Cholbi 2011, 20–34; Hill 2011).[2] This definition is apt to mislead, however. If we possessed what philosophers have called *medical immortality*, suicide would amount to a choice to die. For medical immortals cannot die from aging, disease, or deterioration. But they can die from external causes (falling off a cliff or being mauled by a wild animal) or as a consequence of human agency, including their own (Fischer 2020, 95). For inherently mortal creatures like ourselves, though, death itself is *not* chosen. We will die, and the clock is ticking on our lives the moment ovum and sperm meet. Suicide does not therefore introduce death into the human condition. Rather, suicide is a choice to alter the *timing* of one's biological death, to wit, to knowingly act with the aim that one die earlier in time rather than later. Hence, just as saving a person's life prolongs it, suicide represents an attempt at foreshortening one's biological biography, hastening death and thus forgoing some quantum of lifespan that one could otherwise have expected to have. Note that the stretch of lived time a person forgoes need not be very extensive (a person with advanced stage cancer may engage in suicide and thereby forgo only a day, or even hours, of life). Nor need the stretch of lived time a person forgoes be imminent in time. Imagine that there exists a toxin whose ingestion invariably leads to a medical condition known to reduce lifespan, such as multiple sclerosis. A young adult who ingested such a toxin, aware of its tendency to reduce lifespan, is engaging in suicide inasmuch as she acts with the aim of reducing her lifespan, even though her actual death may not occur until much later.

These metaphysical claims are, I hope, uncontroversial. But time matters to our understanding of suicide not merely definitionally. Time also plays a distinctive part in prudential decision-making, one that (it turns out) will help illuminate how considerations of meaningfulness bear on the rationality of suicide.

Our lifespans are measured in time, and for mortal creatures like us, time (like most every other good) is finite. But time—and I have in mind here *lived* time, or time as we

---

[2] Though for a recent dissenting view, see Dowie (2020). There is also the further complication that, if human beings enjoy an afterlife or if our personhood depends on our occupying a certain social role rather than on the continued existence of our subjective consciousness, then acts of self-killing end our biological lives but do not cause us to die, i.e. to no longer exist (Schechtman 2014, 110–118, 147–150; Stokes 2019, 768–769).

consciously experience it—occupies a special place among the resources we draw upon in trying to live good lives (Brown 1970).

For one, time has a special sort of value because we expend it in the course of every other pursuit. A two-week holiday costs money, plus two weeks of time. Getting a university education costs money and energy, as well as several years of time. So we are constantly expending time in the pursuit of other goods. Indeed, to commit to some pursuit is necessarily to commit some quantum of one's time to it. This makes time and the expenditure thereof relevant to all of our choices; for we must consider not only the wisdom of a given option in its own right, but also whether the time needed to successfully pursue an option is wisely spent thereby. The economics of time thus sits in a uniquely foundational place in our practical rationality, a penumbral 'balance sheet' that lurks in the background of all our choices and actions.

Furthermore, the human capacities for memory, imagination, etc., ensure that we know of these facts about time as a distinctive kind of resource. We are aware of ourselves as having personal pasts, and orient our intentions and choices toward a personal future. We can regret how we have spent durations of time now past, for instance, or look forward to future uses of our time. We live, then, in awareness of time's distinctive importance. In contrast, to the extent that non-human animals can be viewed as agents, their comparatively limited awareness of time, along with their presumed ignorance of the inevitability of their own deaths, ensures a kind of obliviousness to time unavailable to us human agents. Our experience of ourselves as agents is therefore greatly shaped by the temporal scarcity characteristic of human life and our knowledge thereof.

Of course, we *experience* different spans of time differently. For instance, our experience of time varies in pace: time flies when we are having fun, and seems to pass oh-so-slowly when we are bored or listless. But we must not confuse our first-personal sense of time's passage, whose pace can vary, with the passage of time, whose pace does not. Time itself passes steadily and unrelentingly, indifferent to our concerns. Can we nonetheless therefore hope for more time? In a sense, yes. We speak of medical treatments 'buying' a patient time, and we sometimes compensate others for their time in order that we may use our time differently, as when we hire another person to perform a task for us. Still, our relationship to time differs from our relationship to other scarce goods. Again, we expend our time at a constant rate. In extending or shortening our lifespans, we do not create or destroy time, in the way that we might create or destroy wealth, relationships, or other goods. For time is not a commodity in the ordinary sense; it cannot be manufactured, preserved, banked, or improved upon. At most, then, we can decide to try to be *present* for more or less time. This is why the question of suicide is so momentous: for mortal beings, ending one's life is final, a choice to relinquish one's remaining time that cannot be revisited.

These considerations underscore that the choice to engage in suicide is not simply a choice to change the timing of one's own death. From a prudential point of view, suicidal choice *concerns* time. Under the ordinary conditions of human life, we are evaluatively invested in our futures. We look forward to the future as the time when various pleasures may occur, commitments may be pursued, projects may be realized, and so forth. To end one's life prematurely, on the other hand, is to decide that one lacks sufficient reasons to be present for some future span of time. That future span of time is not a resource one wishes to exploit in the pursuit of one's other concerns. Just as every reason to continue living is a reason to expend some future time, any reason not to continue living is, *inter alia*, a reason not to expend some future time.

Thus, suicide represents not only a change in the timing of one's death. It also represents the relinquishing of a resource—time, or one's future—that, if one's suicide is rational at least, one has judged it is not worth trying to benefit from. Suicide is therefore an act of *temporal divestment*, an act wherein a person opts to forgo biological existence and in so doing gives evidence of having determined that her future time lacks sufficient value to warrant her continuing to live to be present for it.

Pivoting, then, to address meaningfulness explicitly: if suicide represents a temporal divestment, then whatever considerations speak in favour of maintaining one's investment in the future or divesting from it could be among the reasons for (or against) suicide. And if those considerations in turn are considerations pertaining to life's meaningfulness, then in at least some cases, the decision to engage in, or to forgo, suicide will be a decision concerning the meaningfulness of one's life. Let us now consider a recent account of meaning in life that appears to vindicate these claims.

3. Life's Meaning and the Expenditure of Time

Cheshire Calhoun (2018, 46) has recently proposed that one's life is meaningful to the extent that one's time is expended on 'ends that, in your best judgment, you take yourself to have reason to value for their own sake and thus to expend your life's time on'. How we expend our time, according to Calhoun, thus determines how meaningful our lives are. She observes that our time expenditures vary with respect to their relationship to those ends we pursue for their own sake. Some time expenditures bear essentially no relationship to such ends. For instance, some of our time is spent conforming to various norms (moral or legal, norms of etiquette, etc.). Other parcels of time are devoted to what Calhoun calls 'filler spending', i.e. 'what we do while waiting, or when we're too tired or ill or unmotivated to do much of anything else' (2018, 15). Filler-time expenditures amount to passing the time, in a literal sense: in the absence of some more valuable activity being available to engage in, we doodle, scour social media, bend and unbend paper clips, etc. What Calhoun terms 'entailed' time expenditures are those concerned with doing those activities that are instrumental to those ends we value for our own sake (commuting to a job, for instance).

But most centrally for Calhoun, 'primary' time expenditures are dedicated to those ends and activities we find worth pursuing for their own sakes, those ends and activities that constitute our 'normative outlook'. Calhoun does not seem to think that the other three categories of time expenditure are value*less:* norm expenditures matter inasmuch as it matters that we be morally decent, law abiding, or polite. Filler expenditures can be amusing and help us endure stretches of time that would otherwise be pure tedium. And entailed expenditures help us realize the pursuit of what is valuable for its own sake. But Calhoun associates meaningfulness in particular with primary time expenditures: the meaningfulness of one's life, on her view, is measured by the amount of one's time dedicated to those ends one finds valuable for one's own sake (Calhoun 2018, 18).

A thorough examination of Calhoun's view of life's meaningfulness cannot be undertaken here, and I do not necessarily intend to endorse every detail of her view. My purpose here is not to systematically evaluate rival conceptions of meaningfulness in life, but to identify how meaningfulness in life relates to suicidal decision-making. Let us now consider how a Calhoun-like view of meaningfulness fares on that score.

4. Suicide and Reasons of Meaningfulness

Calhoun emphasizes that her understanding of meaningfulness, unlike most all others, reflects the centrality of time to living a meaningful life. The question of meaning, she argues, cannot be 'entirely a question of how valuable one's projects are'. Some projects, while valuable enough to contribute a great deal to the meaningfulness of a person's life, are highly time-consuming. Others may contribute only marginally to a life's meaningfulness but involve more modest time expenditures. As noted earlier, selecting among such projects must therefore take into account the necessity of budgeting time, for without attention to the relevant magnitudes of time expenditure, a person may invest her time badly and end up with a faulty prioritization among possible projects. Thus, because our pursuit of meaning occurs within a 'finite life', we will, according to Calhoun, need to evaluate projects not only in their own right but in light of the claims such projects make on our time, a resource that (again) has a foundational role in human agency (2018, 39).

Suicide, we have noted, is a decision wherein an individual opts to shorten her biological future via death. Such a decision amounts to divesting oneself from one's future, renouncing or forgoing a resource—time—that has a fundamental role in human personhood or agency. In Calhoun-like terms, a person who rationally opts for suicide on grounds of meaninglessness has concluded that there is not sufficient value in one's present or future time to merit committing to living through additional time, to manage that time, etc. Such a person is not deciding to invest her time *badly*; she has instead lost whatever grounds she might once have had for investing *at all*. She cannot find a rational basis for expecting that her future will accommodate those primary time expenditures (again, those expenditures of time immersed in ends or activities a person values for their own sake) that accord her life meaning. Such a conclusion is compatible with an agent finding other kinds of value in her future expenditures of time. She may well imagine that her future will involve filled time, dedicated merely to passing time that cannot be expended other ways, or to time whose expenditure allows us to fulfil moral or social norms. What the suicidal person driven by meaninglessness cannot do is muster sufficient hope to think that her future time is worth being present for. As Calhoun writes (2018, 1),

> as evaluators who also live through time, we have to decide not just what we value but also how committed we are to our future containing that value, and thus how much time we are willing to invest in pursuing our aims in the face of obstacles and setbacks that push the realization of our aims into a remoter future. Moreover, one of our aims as temporal evaluators is to spend time with what we value.

In the case of rational suicide motivated by meaninglessness, an individual has concluded, with good reason, that the answer to how much time she is willing to invest in pursuing her aims in the face of obstacles and setbacks, etc., is none—or at least, *no more*. She has lost what Calhoun calls 'basal hopefulness', the hope not for 'this or that particular future occurrence, but a more basic, globally motivating interest in the future' (2018, 52).

Calhoun's account of meaningfulness draws upon rich and underappreciated interconnections between temporality, agency, and selfhood. We are future-oriented agents because the future anchors our desires, goals, and plans; while the past and present no doubt shape what ends we value for their own sake, the future is 'where', so to speak, the choices and actions we undertake will bear fruit with respect to those ends. Under ordinary circumstances, we imaginatively project ourselves into futures in which we expect to retain those attitudes toward ends wherein we value them for their own sake (Calhoun 2018, 49). In the case of rational suicide motivated by meaninglessness, no such projection appears rationally well-founded. What Calhoun calls the future's 'content'—not 'the way the future will actually turn out' but 'the future as we imagine, anticipate, predict, assume, or sense it will be'—does not, from that standpoint, warrant one's investment.

Fortunately, for most human agents for most all of their lives, the future 'stretches out ahead' as a valued resource 'in which to do things'. But for all agents, future time is also a 'burden, as we will have to decide what to do with the immediate, mediate, and long-range parts of that lifetime' (Calhoun 2018, 8). When rationally motivated by meaninglessness, suicide, I propose, rests on the warranted judgment that one's future time has become irremediably or overarchingly burdensome. For the characteristic activity of agency, to wit, deliberation, cannot instantiate its purpose in a future world inhospitable to its worthwhile or effective exercise. A rationally suicidal individual may thus find reason to divest from her future so as to divest from that agency, and in divesting from that agency she divests from the continued existence of her biological self. In deciding not to use future time on oneself, an agent in effect decides not to use herself up (2018, 21). Her suicide is a final act of deliberation wherein she welcomes rather than spurns the death that will invariably lead to the destruction of that self and her agency. Note that her suicide may or may not preserve whatever meaningfulness her life *had*. Suicide is a choice concerning the timing of one's death, and judgements about that matter are independent of whether one's *life* is or has been meaningful (or good, desirable, etc.) on balance. Indeed, suicide may be rational even if a person's life has been meaningful as a whole, or irrational because a person stands to live a more meaningful life by continuing to exist even when her life is itself *not* meaningful (Benatar 2017, 190–194). For suicide's rationality, so far as considerations of meaningfulness go, flows from the belief, at least when justified, that no further meaningfulness is to be had by living further.

How might a person come to view her future as so disenchanted as to merit her divestment from it by means of suicide? To lead lives as agents, Calhoun argues, we must be able to take interest in a future in which 'exercising our agential capacities makes sense', and their making sense depends on what she calls 'background frames of agency' (2018, 52–53) that sustain our interest in exercising our agency to shape our futures. One background frame is the belief that *our* choices and actions can be instrumentally effective in attaining those ends we care about for their own sake. To learn that one's ends cannot be attained, that one's ends will increasingly be attained through the exercise of agency not one's own, that the solution as to how to attain some end is not forthcoming, or that one's efforts to implement one's plans will not realize one's ends can be profoundly demoralizing, inducing the kind of helplessness, hopelessness, or haplessness associated with suicidal thinking (Lester 1998). Another background frame Calhoun identifies is confidence that we will not succumb to 'disastrous misfortune or indecent harm' (2018, 66). To know that one's entire civilization is under threat (Scheffler 2013, 18–23) or that one's future will be suffused with pain so grotesque as to hamper any deliberation about or attention to one's ends (Velleman 1999, 618) undermines the viability of exercising one's agency in the pursuit of one's ends. But the most central of these background frames is simply finding ends worth pursuing for their own sake. The inability to identify any such ends need not occur out of frustration or disillusionment. Indeed, it may occur because all the ends one values have largely been realized, as seems to be the case for those who desire suicide because they are 'tired of life' or believe their lives are 'complete' (van Wijngaarden, Goossensen, and Leget 2018).

An intimate connection may thus exist between suicidal choice and action, on the one hand, and meaningfulness in life, on the other. In this section, I have focused on how reasons related to meaningfulness, understood as Calhoun does in terms of having grounds for investing oneself and one's agency in the future, may provide for reasons *for* suicide. But as we saw in section 1, the relation in question also holds when individuals find their lives to be meaningful, with meaningfulness serving to mitigate or protect against suicidal risks rooted in other causes. My analysis readily accommodates this conclusion: suicide is less rational to the extent that an agent correctly views her future as a time worth investing herself and her agency in. And of course, as meaning-seeking creatures, human beings are remarkably resilient and resourceful in finding ends in which to invest one's future time and agency and thereby keeping suicidal ideation at bay. As Frankl emphasizes, even in the midst of horrific suffering, some individuals manage to identify and engage with future goals, however modest, that foster a sense of their lives as meaningful (Frankl 1992, 79–82, 116–117).

5. Well-being and Reasons of Meaningfulness

In this final substantive section, I will clarify how reasons of meaningfulness bear on suicidal decision, with special attention to how such reasons relate to reasons rooted in well-being.

As I have depicted it, meaningfulness is not a 'ground level' input in the rational appraisal of suicide. That one's future is not worth investing in is a *conclusion* reached by considering one's ends, the desirability of a future oriented toward their pursuit, one's hopes for success in attaining them, etc. Meaningfulness thus functions as a *summative*, second-order reason for or against suicide: for in deciding whether to engage in suicide, a person is deciding whether her future self is worth investing in, a decision that in turn rests on more basic judgements about whether her future time expenditures can be oriented around those ends she finds intrinsically worthwhile.

Philosophers have typically analysed the rationality of suicide in terms of well-being or happiness, in terms of whether a person's prematurely ending her life would make for a better or worse life on balance (Graber 1981; Pabst Battin 1996, 115; Cholbi 2011, 90–97). Of course, if we treat the notion of 'well-being' broadly enough so as to encompass every fact that makes one's life go well, then it may well be trivially true that reasons of meaningfulness pertaining to suicidal decision are in fact reasons of well-being. And indeed, many of the facts that inform suicidal decision oriented around meaningfulness will also be among the facts that inform suicidal decision oriented around well-being. Most centrally, pursuing and realizing those ends we value for their own sake tends to make our lives better, to contribute positively to well-being. Hence, meaningfulness—understood in terms of whether one can envision a future worth investing oneself and one's agency in—may turn out to be one among many factors that contribute to well-being, and in deliberating about suicide in terms of meaningfulness, an individual is deliberating with a focus on one among several ingredients of well-being.

However, some philosophers have thought that meaningfulness is a distinct value from well-being inasmuch as a meaningful life need not be happy, or vice versa (Metz 2013, 5; Wolf 2010, 3). I offer no refutation of the thesis that well-being incorporates meaningfulness, but the relation that I suggest holds between suicidal decision and meaningfulness speaks against it.

For one, a person's future may be good for her in various ways without being meaningful in the way I have sketched. A person may have grounds to expect her future to be filled with a large number of pleasant or amusing experiences whose acquisition does not involve any exercise of her agency (for instance, the diminishment of discomfort that occurs as our food is digested). Her future time is valuable to her as a resource that makes possible greater well-being, but if none of those facts that make it valuable is an end that engages her agency, she may well find suicide more compelling because that future, however amiable, lacks meaningfulness. Conversely, a person's future could be filled with suffering that, if endured, would make her life worse overall as measured by well-being, but allow her to attain ends she judges are worth investing her time and agency in. A person with a painful terminal illness may strive to continue living in order to achieve extant ends that confer meaningfulness on her life (atoning for past wrongs, for instance). In other cases, undergoing suffering may be a necessary means to achieve ends that confer meaningfulness. (Imagine a Marie Curie–like figure, who knowingly exposes herself to life-threatening substances in the course of pursuing scientific or medical breakthroughs.) Self-sacrifice offers a still more extreme example: in a classic 'lifeboat scenario', an altruistic person may choose to sacrifice their life, thereby placing a limit of the overall well-being their life contains, in order to save others. Her death enhances her life's meaningfulness, not by rendering her future more meaningful by enabling her to attain ends she already values. (Metz 2014, 103). She divests from her future in order to enhance the meaningfulness of her life to that point, but thereby forgoes future opportunities for additional meaningfulness. Such examples suggest that reasons of meaningfulness and reasons of well-being are distinct inasmuch as they can push in opposite directions with respect to the rationality of ending one's life. At the very least, these two sets of reasons are not co-extensive.

Phenomenologically, meaninglessness also seems to register differently from negative well-being. Suicide oriented around meaningfulness is rationalized not by the agent's belief that her future is not worth investing in because it will be *bad* but because it will, so far as her agency goes, have no *point*. Such an agent may retain *conditional* desires, desires predicated upon her continuing to live (desires not to undergo pain, for instance). But the absence of *categorical* desires to 'propel' her into the future and justify her continued existence *qua* agent (Williams 1973, 85–88) will represent, for many agents, a world in which her 'deepest self' has no place (Calhoun 2018, 52). She may well retain her powers of rational agency, but she will suffer from a sense that such powers are superfluous, once-useful appendages that lie dormant, something akin to a screwdriver in a world full of nails. Such a state is likely to be profoundly disorienting, unsettling, or dispiriting for many agents. Meanwhile, time—the resource necessarily expended in our exercises of agency—will continue to pass for such agents without being expended (in Calhoun's sense) in meaningful ways by such an agent. Such time will inevitably feel like time spent in opposition to one's agency or will.

An agent confronting such meaninglessness suffers a profound sense of loss, I would venture, and so has reason not to endure that stretch of life in which such loss is evident to her. It is this state that many of those who contemplate assisted suicide near the end of life seek to avoid. Talk of 'dignity' is notoriously slippery, but many individuals contemplating assisted suicide who report concern about the loss of dignity near the end of life explicate that concern in terms of the lack of control over their circumstances, the inability to exercise their autonomy in efficacious ways, and alienation from their identities (Rodríguez-Prat et al. 2016). Such fears echo the link between selfhood, agency, and time that Calhoun suggests undergirds living meaningfully.

Of course, those who believe meaningfulness is an element of well-being may respond that, because this condition of finding one's own agency superfluous *feels* bad, it represents a liability against one's overall well-being. Alternatively, perhaps such a condition represents a kind of *harm*, a state of unwilled passivity in which a person must endure the thwarting not of the exercise of their wills but of lacking a context in which exercising those wills can matter (Shiffrin 2012, 26–27). Again, I have no decisive argument against those who would incorporate meaningfulness into well-being such that the reasons that, as I have argued here, bear on the rationality of suicide are in fact reasons of well-being. But such reasons at least fit somewhat uncomfortably under the banner of well-being. For agents evaluating whether their futures are meaningful enough to justify continuing to live are not evaluating whether their futures will be good or evil *simpliciter* but whether the rational pursuit of good and evil will even be intelligible in their future lives.

6. Conclusion

I have argued that understanding suicidal decision as temporal divestment and understanding meaningfulness in life in terms of whether a person has grounds for temporally investing their agency in the future help explain how the latter could provide practical reasons relevant to the former. While the notion of meaningfulness evoked here, much indebted to Calhoun, is controversial, its potential for making sense of how meaningfulness can provide reasons relevant to suicidal decision is a mark in its favour. Partisans of other philosophical theories of life's meaningfulness should thus attempt to show how their theories can make sense of the claim, vindicated both intuitively and by empirical research, that meaningfulness makes a difference to the rationality of suicide.

In making the case for meaningfulness's relevance to the rationality of suicide, I have not addressed the very considerable obstacles we face in determining, in any given case, whether a person's suicide is or would be rational for her. Judgements about whether one's future is worth investing in can err in many ways. For instance, a person can err about what ends she may find worthy of pursuit, either currently or in the future; about whether the pursuit of those ends would justify her investing her agency in the future; or about how much time she would otherwise have in her lifetime if she did not opt for suicide. Such judgements may also be distorted by psychological conditions such as depression, which tend to lead individuals to focus emotionally on the present and discount or distort their own futures (Brandt 1975, 70–71). Hence, my confidence that I have identified the logical conditions for a suicide to be rational in light of considerations of meaningfulness is not matched by a similar confidence that we can utilize these conditions in an epistemically sound way. Indeed, in my estimation, this reflects how identifying what makes suicide rational is generally easier than identifying its rationality in particular cases (Kagan 2012, 336–344).

These epistemic concerns notwithstanding, I hope also to have shown that the fact that suicide is available to us is a fact we should be grateful for inasmuch as it enables us to craft lives of meaningfulness. For imagine a twist on medical immortality, call it *purely medical mortality*, in which we were impervious to death via human agency, whether suicide or homicide, and could only die of non-agential, 'natural' causes. That the choice to end our lives would not be available to us would be a clear drawback of such a condition inasmuch as it puts an important avenue by which to craft more meaningful lives outside of our reach.[3]

References

Benatar, David. 2017. *The Human Predicament*. Oxford: Oxford University Press.
Bradley, Ben. 2015. 'Existential Terror'. *Journal of Ethics* 19: 409–418.
Brandt, Richard . 1975. 'The Morality and Rationality of Suicide'. In *A Handbook for the Study of Suicide*, ed. S. Perlin, 61–75. Oxford: Oxford University Press.
Brown, D. G. 1970. 'The Value of Time'. *Ethics* 80: 173–184.
Bryan, Craig J., et al. 2013. 'Meaning in Life, Emotional Distress, Suicidal Ideation, and Life Function in an Active Duty Military Sample'. *Journal of Positive Psychology* 8: 444–452.
Calhoun, Cheshire. 2018. *Doing Valuable Time*. Oxford: Oxford University Press.
Camus, Albert. 1955. *The Myth of Sisyphus and Other Essays*, trans. J. O'Brien. New York: Alfred A. Knopf.
Cholbi, Michael. 2011. *Suicide: The Philosophical Dimensions*. Peterborough, ON: Broadview Press.
Costanza, A., M. Prelati, and M. Pompili. 2019. 'The Meaning in Life in Suicidal Patients: The Presence and Search for Constructs: A Systematic Review'. *Medicina* 55: 1–18.
Dowie, Suzanne E. 2020. 'What Is Suicide? Classifying Self-Killings'. *Medicine, Health Care, and Philosophy* 23: 717–733.
Fischer, John Martin. 2020. *Death, Immortality, and Meaning in Life*. Oxford: Oxford University Press.
Frankl, Viktor E. 1992. *Man's Search for Meaning: An Introduction to Logotherapy*, 4th ed. Boston: Beacon Press.
Graber, Glenn C. 1981. 'The Rationality of Suicide'. In *Suicide and Euthanasia: The Rights of Personhood*, ed. S. Wallace and A. Eser, 51–65. Knoxville: University of Tennessee Press.
Heisel, M. J., and G. L. Flett. 2016. 'Does Recognition of Meaning in Life Confer Resiliency to Suicide Ideation among Community-Residing Older Adults? A Longitudinal Investigation'. *American Journal of Geriatric Psychiatry* 24: 455–466.
Heisel, M. J., E. Neufeld, and G. L. Flett. 2016. 'Reasons for Living, Meaning in Life, and Suicide Ideation: Investigating the Roles of Key Positive Psychological Factors in Reducing Suicide Risk in Community-Residing Older Adults'. *Aging and Mental Health* 20: 195–207.

---

[3] I wish to thank John Martin Fischer, Ben Mitchell-Yellin, and Iddo Landau for their helpful feedback on this article.

Hill, D. J. 2011. 'What Is It to Commit Suicide?' *Ratio* 24: 192–205.
Kagan, Shelly. 2012. *Death*. New Haven, CT: Yale University Press.
Khan, R. L., et al. 2018. 'Experimentally-Enhanced Perceptions of Meaning Confer Resilience to the Interpersonal Adversity Implicated in Suicide Risk'. *Journal of Behavioral Therapy and Experimental Psychiatry* 61: 142–149.
Kleiman, E. M., and J. K. Beaver. 2013. 'A Meaningful Life Is Worth Living: Meaning in Life as a Suicide Resiliency Factor'. *Psychiatry Research* 210: 934–939.
Lester, D. 1998. 'Helplessness, Hopelessness, and Haplessness and Suicidality'. *Psychological Reports* 82: 946.
Little, Miles. 1999. 'Assisted Suicide, Suffering and the Meaning of a Life'. *Theoretical Medicine and Bioethics* 20: 287–298.
Martela, F., and M. F. Steger. 2016. 'The Three Meanings of Meaning in Life: Distinguishing Coherence, Purpose, and Significance'. *Journal of Positive Psychology* 11: 531–545.
Metz, Thaddeus. 2013. *Meaning in Life: An Analytic Study*. Oxford: Oxford University Press.
Metz, Thaddeus. 2014. 'Meaning as a Distinct and Fundamental Value: Reply to Kershnar'. *Science, Religion, and Culture* 1: 101–106.
Metz, Thaddeus. 2019. 'Recent Work on the Meaning of 'Life's Meaning': Should We Change the Philosophical Discourse?' *Human Affairs* 29: 414–414.
Nagel, Thomas. 1986. *The View from Nowhere*. Oxford: Oxford University Press.
Orbach, Israel, Mario Mikulincer, Eva Gilboa-Schechtman, and Pinhas Sirota. 2003. 'Mental Pain and Its Relationship to Suicidality and Life Meaning'. *Suicide and Life Threatening Behavior* 33: 231–241.
Pabst Battin, Margaret. 1996. *The Death Debate: Ethical Issues in Suicide*. Upper Saddle River, NJ: Prentice-Hall.
Rodriguez-Prat, A., C. Monforte-Royo, J. Porta-Sales, X. Escribano, and A. Balaguer. 2016. 'Patient Perspectives of Dignity, Autonomy and Control at the End of Life: Systematic Review and Meta-ethnography'. *PLoS One* 11(3): e0151435. doi:10.1371/journal.pone.0151435
Schechtman, Marya. 2014. *Staying Alive: Personal Identity, Practical Concerns, and the Unity of a Life*. Oxford: Oxford University Press.
Scheffler, Samuel. 2013. *Death and the Afterlife*. Oxford: Oxford University Press.
Schnell, Tatjana, Rebekka Gerstner, and Henning Krampe. 2018. "Crisis of Meaning Predicts Suicidality in Youth Independently of Depression." *Crisis: The Journal of Crisis Intervention and Suicide Prevention* 39: 294–303.
Shiffrin, Seana Valentine. 2012. 'Harm and Its Moral Significance'. *Legal Theory* 18: 357–398.
Shneidman, Edwin. 1993. *Suicide as Psychache: A Clinical Approach to Self-destructive Behavior*. Lanham, MD: Jason Aronson/Rowman and Littlefield.
Sinclair, Sungchoon, Craig J. Bryan, and Annabelle Bryan. 2016. 'Meaning in Life as a Protective Factor for the Emergence of Suicide Ideation That Leads to Suicide Attempts among Military Personnel and Veterans with Elevated PTSD and Depression'. *International Journal of Cognitive Therapy* 9, 87–98.
Steger, M. F., P. Frazier, S. Oishi, and M. Kaler. 2006. 'The Meaning in Life Questionnaire: Assessing the Presence of and Search for Meaning in Life'. *Journal of Counselling Psychology* 53: 80–93.
Stokes, Patrick. 2019. 'Are There Dead Persons?' *Canadian Journal of Philosophy* 49: 755–775.
Sullivan, M. D. 2005. 'The Desire for Death Arises from an Intolerable Future Rather Than an Intolerable Present'. *General Hospital Psychiatry* 27: 256–257.

Tan, L., J. Chen, T. Xia, et al. 2018. 'Predictors of Suicidal Ideation among Children and Adolescents: Roles of Mental Health Status and Meaning in Life'. *Child Youth Care Forum* 47: 219–231.

van Wijngaarden, Els, Anne Goossensen, and Carlo Leget. 2018. 'The Social–Political Challenges behind the Wish to Die in Older People Who Consider Their Lives to Be Completed and No Longer Worth Living'. *Journal of European Social Policy* 28: 419–429.

Varelius, Jukka. 2013. 'Ending Life, Morality, and Meaning'. *Ethical Theory and Moral Practice* 16: 559–574.

Varelius, Jukka. 2016. 'Life's Meaning and Late Life Rational Suicide'. In *Rational Suicide in the Elderly*, ed. R. E. McCue and M. Balasubramaniam, 83–98. New York: Springer.

Velleman, J. David. 1999. 'A Right of Self-Termination?' *Ethics* 109: 606–628.

Williams, Bernard. 1973. 'The Makropulos Case: Reflections on the Tedium of Immortality'. In B. Williams, *Problems of the Self: Philosophical Papers 1956–1972*, 82–100. Cambridge: Cambridge University Press.

Wolf, Susan. 2010. *Meaning in Life and Why It Matters*. Princeton, NJ: Princeton University Press.

CHAPTER 29

SUFFERING AND MEANING IN LIFE

MICHAEL S. BRADY

> Man ... was a *sickly* animal: but suffering itself was *not* his problem, but the fact that there was no answer to the question he screamed, 'Suffering for *what*?' ... The meaninglessness of suffering, *not* the suffering, was the curse which has so far blanketed mankind.
> —Nietzsche ([1887] 1992, 284–285)

> (T)here is also purpose in that life which is almost barren of both creation and enjoyment and which admits of but one possibility of high moral behavior: namely, in man's attitude to his existence, an existence restricted by external forces. ... The way in which a man accepts his fate and all the suffering it entails, the way in which he takes up his cross, gives him ample opportunity—even under the most difficult circumstances —to add a deeper meaning to his life. It may remain brave, dignified and unselfish.
> —Frankl (1984, 88)

WHAT is suffering? On my view, suffering refers to a category of negative affective experiences, which includes negative physical experiences such as physical pain, hunger, fatigue, and coldness, and negative mental experiences such as terror, anxiety, loneliness, and disappointment.[1] What makes it the case that these and many other forms of experience count as forms of suffering? I want to maintain that this is so because of two conditions: (1) they are all forms of *unpleasantness*; and (2) they are all forms of

---

[1] To see this view in detail, see the first two chapters of my book *Suffering and Virtue* (2018).

unpleasantness that we *mind*, in the sense that we have an occurrent desire that they cease. In short: suffering is unpleasantness that we want to stop.

It seems clear that suffering, understood in this way, can undermine or destroy the meaning in a person's life. Think of those who experience years of chronic pain or debilitating illness, or who live in crippling poverty, or who are victims of racism or sexism or homophobia, or who suffer physical assault, or who exist in conditions of political oppression. It is not difficult to imagine life lacking meaning for people under these and similar conditions, for such conditions would seem to rule out the possibility or presence of those elements that seem constitutive of a meaningful life. These plausibly include, following Thaddeus Metz, 'certain kinds of intellectual reflection, moral achievement, and artistic creation' (Metz 2013, 60): such elements represent ways in which we transcend our animal self, move beyond seeking pleasure as such, and realize 'conditions worthy of great esteem and admiration' (Metz 2013, 37). They will include things like deep personal relationships, the exercise of autonomy, forging a successful career, a sense of one's own flourishing, physical and psychological health, and community with others.

In this chapter, I'll consider some ways in which suffering can have a *positive* relation to meaning, even in the lives of those who suffer greatly. Indeed, as the quotation from Frankl suggests, meaning is possible even in the absence of very many of the 'estimable and admirable conditions' that Metz highlights (2013, 60). This suggests two approaches to the question of the relationship between suffering and meaning. On the one hand, episodes or experiences of suffering can be (made) meaningful for those who suffer, so that a subject can find meaning in their experiences of suffering, even if their situation is not one that they, or any rational person, would welcome or embrace *all-things-considered*. To anticipate: meaning in such cases can be understood in terms of having the right kind of virtuous attitude towards one's situation.[2] But the value of the virtuous response in such cases does not outweigh the disvalue of the situation itself. It's a great good that a person remains brave, dignified, and unselfish in the face of horrific conditions, of the kind experienced first-hand by Frankl. But clearly the world would be a better place if the horrors inflicted by the Nazis had not come about. The virtuousness of Frankl's response to atrocity does not change this fact. We might put the point as follows: suffering of this kind can allow for a virtuous and meaningful *response*, but plausibly undermines the conditions needed for a meaningful *life*.

On the other hand, there are episodes and experiences of suffering that are central to a meaningful life as a whole, that are rationally welcomed and embraced by the sufferer, and that *make for* a meaningful life all-things-considered. This is because many of the central elements in a meaningful life—including many of the components of such a life that Metz lists—would not be possible without such experiences. Many people

---

[2] I don't mean to suggest that a person can *always* find meaning under any conditions, since it is plausible to assume that some forms of suffering can be so great that, for most people at least, they preclude having the right kind of virtuous attitude. Thanks to Iddo Landau for pressing me to be clearer about this point.

from certain religious traditions will view suffering in this way. But such a perspective is not confined to the faithful. The idea that suffering can contribute to the meaningfulness of a life is, as we shall see, extremely prevalent in secular thinking and behaviour as well. A central part of the argument here is that suffering is a *condition* on the value of a very wide range of activities and ends, many of which constitute the kind of purposeful achievements that give life meaning. It is not just the religious who have an answer to Nietzsche's question, therefore; the non-religious can find meaning in suffering by realizing its centrality to the value of their purposes and goals.

The structure of the chapter is as follows. In section 1, I consider Nietzsche's approach to finding meaning in suffering, and show how it can fit into a more broadly *virtue-theoretical* framework. This suggests that there are central elements to a meaningful life—including psychological health and different forms of virtue—which are possible even in the face of significant suffering. As I'll explain, none of this suggests that our lives are more meaningful all-things-considered as a result of such suffering. But it is to say that even very great suffering does not rule out the possibility of meaning—as Frankl's quotation suggests. In section 2, I turn to religious approaches, and in section 3, their secular counterparts, both of which highlight the centrality of suffering to a meaningful life. Whereas the first section illustrates that suffering does not rule out the possibility of meaning, the second and third sections propose that for many people a meaningful life is one in which suffering plays a central and indeed essential part. The religious argument in section 2 stresses God's purpose in allowing or inflicting suffering on His creatures; the secular argument in section 3 stresses the role that suffering plays as a condition on the value of certain activities. Given the relation between such activities and purposeful *achievement*, and the centrality of achievement to meaningfulness in the lives of many people, then suffering can itself be viewed as a necessary condition on meaningfulness for such people. Suffering is thus essential for a meaningful life all-things-considered, at least for those who are religious, or for those capable of purposeful achievement. Or so, at least, I want to argue.[3]

1. Meaningful Suffering: Nietzsche, Psychological Health, and Virtue

Nietzsche is one of the few philosophers to have written extensively about suffering, and his distinctive and provocative take on the subject is worth examining here. This is not simply of interest for Nietzsche scholars, however. For in Nietzsche's work we can find the basis for the kind of view expressed by Frankl: that the meaning one can find in suffering is a function of one's attitude towards that suffering.

---

[3] For a more detailed account of the value that suffering can have, including chapters on Nietzschean and religious approaches to suffering, see my *Suffering and Virtue* (2018).

The most famous statement about suffering in Nietzsche's writings—indeed, one of the best-known philosophical aphorisms in the Western tradition—comes from *Twilight of the Idols*: '*From the military school of life*: what does not kill me makes me stronger' (Nietzsche [1889] 1968, 33). But the kind of strength Nietzsche is talking about here is important. For Nietzsche, suffering enables us to exhibit or display *psychological strength*, and it is this that is central to the meaning that suffering can have for creatures like us. (Nietzsche rejects the 'ascetic' approach which appeals to the divine in an attempt to make sense of, find meaning in, suffering [Leiter 2002, 263]. We'll look at religious approaches to suffering in the next section.) To see this, note that Nietzsche accepts that suffering doesn't necessarily make someone stronger. He accepts what is a tenet of common sense, namely that suffering can weaken a person, both physically and psychologically. This is why, after all, we might think that suffering is antithetical to a good and meaningful life. Nevertheless, Nietzsche suggests that whereas physical weakness is an 'objective' or 'external' feature of the person's circumstances and condition, psychological weakness is a matter of the wrong kind of internal attitude towards one's suffering, towards these external forces, and is thus a matter of a subjective response to what is objectively happening. (Panaïoti 2013 103) This helps to explain the quotation from Nietzsche at the start of this chapter. The really serious problem with suffering isn't the suffering itself. Instead, it's the lack of meaning for or point of the suffering: '[t]he meaninglessness of suffering, *not* the suffering, was the curse which has so far blanketed mankind' (Nietzsche [1887] 1903, 210). Nietzsche's suggestion, therefore, is that suffering is problematic insofar as we lack a reason or point or purpose which we can appeal to in order to explain and justify it. *That* is what is really bad about suffering.

Now on Nietzsche's view, psychological weakness is a matter of a particular kind of negative response to one's suffering: the psychologically weak person is someone who despairs about their suffering, or resents this fact (Panaïoti 2013, 103). Psychological strength is a matter of the opposite kind of attitude towards suffering: to be psychologically strong is to take a positive attitude towards things like illness, loss, adversity, and misfortune. Indeed, Nietzsche even suggests that the right kind of attitude towards suffering is to welcome or embrace the fact that one suffers, to view it as something to be overcome. On Nietzsche's view, suffering is essential to psychological strength, since it provides the conditions in which one can welcome and overcome adversity: and taking such attitudes *constitutes* psychological strength. On this account, the adoption of such an attitude—our viewing suffering as an opportunity to overcome—makes suffering meaningful for us, provides its purpose or value. It is thus possible to find meaning even in the worst of physical suffering—as Nietzsche did in his own life (Leiter 2002, 131)—by taking up a positive attitude towards such objective and external negative conditions. As a result, Nietzsche thinks that suffering provides the opportunity for a meaningful response, rather than undermining or destroying meaning in one's life.

There is something clearly right about Nietzsche's view. Psychological strength is, after all, one of the elements or components of a meaningful life. Psychological strength would seem to be an 'estimable or admirable condition', to employ Metz's language. It is, moreover, plausible to think that psychological strength is, at least in part, a matter of taking a positive attitude towards difficulty and adversity. This is because psychological strength is best understood not as a fleeting condition of a person's mental life, but as a deep aspect of their character. Strength of character is best understood, therefore, in terms of the possession of certain traits. Since these will be estimable, admirable traits, they can be characterized as *virtues* of character. And virtues of character all seem to involve positive attitudes towards various forms of adversity. Consider, to illustrate, the virtues that arguably constitute strength of character: the virtues of courage, forbearance, fortitude, patience, and resilience. Now consider what some philosophical greats think about these. For Aristotle in the *Nicomachean Ethics*, 'courage is a mean with respect to things that inspire confidence or fear, in the circumstances that have been stated; and it chooses or endures things because it is noble to do so, or because it is base not to do so' (Book 3, §7). So Aristotle thinks that courage is a matter of taking up a positive attitude towards negative external circumstances, of facing up to fear and danger because to do so is noble or beautiful. St. Augustine likewise makes a positive attitude central to one of the virtues which constitute strength of character, when he writes that 'fortitude is love readily bearing all things *for the sake of the loved object*' (St. Augustine 1886, Ch. 15.5). Or consider now another virtue which expresses strength, namely patience—whose Latin root, *pati*, means 'to suffer, endure'. Cicero writes that 'patience is the voluntary and prolonged endurance of difficult things for the sake of virtue or benefit' (quoted in St. Thomas Aquinas 1947, II.II 128.1). Here, too, an admirable or estimable condition is constituted by a positive attitude towards 'difficult things'—those that bring us suffering, adversity, misfortune.

As a result, even if we disagree with Nietzsche's particular identification of the relevant attitude—of welcoming or embracing suffering *because* this provides the opportunity to overcome—the general structure of Nietzsche's attempt to find meaning in suffering seems extremely plausible.[4] Virtuous responses to—and hence positive attitudes towards—suffering are by definition estimable and admirable. They would seem to constitute forms of moral achievement, and so fit in to Metz's characterisation of those elements that are constitutive of a meaningful life.[5] It is, moreover, a kind of moral achievement that is central to Frankl's thinking on suffering and meaning: faced with 'fate and all the suffering it entails', one can, as Frankl did, nevertheless 'remain brave, dignified and unselfish'. Fate and all the suffering it entails does not necessarily undermine the possibility of a meaningful response, therefore. Instead, is possible to

---

[4] Nietzsche's identification might well give us pause, since it seems to reflect a morally questionable attitude towards suffering. There is something morally suspect about regarding my grief at the death of a loved one as valuable *because* it gives me the opportunity to be strong. I ought not to welcome such grief, even if it is entirely fitting or appropriate to the circumstances.

[5] I have focused here on virtues that constitute strength of character. But there are other virtuous responses to suffering that express our vulnerability. These are especially apparent in our responses to illness, and encompass virtues such as adaptability, creativity, compassion, and humility. For a detailed focus on such virtues, see the works by Havi Carel and Ian James Kidd in the References.

find meaning in suffering, if it is possible for one to take up the right kind of (virtuous) attitude towards it.

In the following section we'll move beyond particular instances where one can find meaning in suffering, and consider the role that suffering might have in making a life meaningful *in toto*. Here suffering can be viewed as playing a much more positive role in a meaningful life.

2. SUFFERING AND MEANING: RELIGIOUS PERSPECTIVES

We have seen that positive attitudes towards suffering can be estimable and admirable, and so can contribute to the meaning in someone's life. Nevertheless, it clearly does not follow that a person's life is more meaningful all-things-considered as a result of such suffering. It is difficult to argue that suffering of the kind that Frankl endured in the concentration camps of Theresienstadt, Kaufering, and Türkheim, or the kind of misery which is the daily reality of tens of millions of people living under conditions of extreme poverty, political oppression, violence, and degradation, make for a meaningful life all-things-considered. To put things another way: It is difficult to justify the presence of such horrendous evils, to use Marilyn McCord Adams's term, by appeal to the moral achievements that they make possible (Adams 1990, 211). So although one's response to suffering might be admirable, the overall situation in which one suffers can still have a debilitating effect on one's capacity to live a meaningful life, and so the net benefits of suffering in providing a meaningful response can be clearly outweighed by the very great losses that suffering imposes on other aspects of one's life. One might respond courageously and patiently to years of chronic pain, and be exceptionally estimable and admirable as a result. Still, one would clearly have been better off without the years of chronic pain, since the effects of this on other components of a meaningful life—one's career, one's relationships, one's achievements—can be devastating, both in terms of our flourishing, and in terms of the meaning that we find in our lives.

To think in this way is to adopt what Thomas Hurka calls a 'comparative principle' about our attitudes towards suffering and other evils. Such a principle maintains that '[t]he degree of intrinsic goodness or evil of an attitude to x is always less than the degree of goodness or evil of x' (Hurka 2001, 133). Hurka notes that G. E. Moore held something similar:

> There seems no reason to think that where the object [of an attitude] is a thing evil in itself, *which actually exists*, the total state of things is ever positively *good on the whole*. The appropriate attitude towards a really existing evil ... may be a great positive good on the whole. But there seems no reason to doubt that, where the evil is *real*, the amount of this real evil is always sufficient to reduce the total sum of value to a negative quantity. (Moore 1903, 219)

Even if, therefore, a positive attitude towards suffering is estimable or admirable, and so adds a meaningful element to one's life, the loss of meaning as a result of the suffering might usually or even always outweigh any gain in meaning. Suffering can still reduce the total sum of meaning to a negative quantity, in spite of one's positive and meaningful response.

There are, however, many who think that the presence of suffering in a life makes an all-things-considered positive contribution to the meaning it has; indeed, many think that suffering is central to living a life that is full of meaning. This thought is prominent in many religious traditions, and in particular in Christianity and Islam. In both traditions, the ultimate point or meaning in one's life is a form of righteous behaviour and spiritual development, at the end of which one is reunited with the divine. And in each tradition, suffering is central to this ultimate meaning or purpose in at least two important ways. Let us look at these in turn.

(1) Recall Nietzsche's question, 'suffering for *what*?' Both Christian and Islamic traditions have answered this question by claiming that suffering is punishment for *sin*. The point of suffering, according to each, is that it is divine payment for wrongdoing. This justification for suffering is extremely common in both Christian and Islamic traditions. Thus the Koran states: 'whatever in the way of good befalls you, it is from God; and whatever in the way of evil befalls you, it is from yourselves' (Chapter 4:79).[6] And in Deuteronomy, Moses tells the people of Israel that 'if you do not obey the LORD your God and do not carefully follow all his commands and decrees I am giving you today, all these curses will come on you and overtake you' (Deuteronomy 28:15).[7]

How might such suffering, and this answer to the question, contribute to a meaningful life? The Biblical and Koranic answer seems to be that punishment which is payment for sin and transgression is a matter of divine *justice*. That God is a righteous judge, and imposes suffering as punishment for wrongdoing, is apparent from many passages in the Old Testament. Romans holds that God 'will repay each person according to what they have done' (Romans 2:6); Exodus that 'when the time comes for me to punish, I will punish them for their sin' (Exodus 32:34); and Jeremiah tells us that 'I the LORD search the heart and examine the mind, to reward each person according to their conduct, according to what their deeds deserve' (Jeremiah 17:10). Given this, we also have an answer to the question of how suffering fits into a meaningful life. For *accepting* one's suffering for this reason would seem to constitute a moral *response*; and any subsequent remorse, apologies, and reparations would seem to constitute moral *achievements* on the subject's part. In accepting rightful punishment for wrongdoing in this way, the sufferer therefore evinces morally admirable attitudes and morally estimable behaviour. It is not difficult to see how such responses count as elements in a

---

[6] References to the Koran follow Gustav Flügel's versification, first published in 1834, translated by A. J. Arberry ([1955] 2008).

[7] All Biblical quotations taken from New International Version (UK), https://www.biblegatewaycom/versions/New-International-Version-NIV-Bible/.

meaningful life, therefore, given the prominence of moral achievement and estimable action in such a life.

Accepting divine punishment for wrongdoing does not simply evince an element in a meaningful life, however. In addition to this, both Christian and Islamic traditions hold that unless one accepts one's suffering in this way, and pays penance for sin, one is debarred from entering into the Kingdom of Heaven. Suffering isn't just payment for sin, therefore. The ultimate point of suffering is to ensure that one is spiritually developed enough to be forgiven, and to be rewarded by God in the afterlife. This suggests that suffering, as punishment for sin, is much more central to the meaningful life than the considerations in our first section suggested. For we are all sinners, or so the religious traditions suppose. As a result, unless we suffer for our sins, we are debarred from the one thing that stands to give our life meaning above all else, namely acceptance into God's loving embrace. For sinners like us, suffering is necessary for *ultimate* meaning.

This explanation is well-known, but is subject to an equally well-known objection concerning its scope. For it is not only wrongdoers or the wicked who suffer; suffering can affect the virtuous and vicious alike, the blameworthy and blameless. Abrahamic religions therefore face a problem of the *distribution* of suffering, famously illustrated in the Book of Job, a virtuous man who was made to suffer miserably by Satan (Job 1:1). Even if we are sinners, therefore, our suffering does not always line up neatly with our sinning. We might behave badly and (in this earthly realm) avoid any suffering. We might behave virtuously, and nevertheless suffer greatly. So whereas suffering as a result of wrongful behaviour can be viewed as meaningful by the wrongdoer, suffering that is undeserved, that randomly afflicts the good and the bad alike, fails to have this kind of justification. Isn't suffering of this second kind, suffering that is not plausibly viewed as a punishment or payment for sin, therefore meaningless? Here we encounter our second explanation of how suffering and meaning are related.

(2) Both Christian and Islamic texts respond to the problem generated by the scope of suffering by invoking the idea of suffering having a point or purpose as a *test of faith*. This idea occurs frequently in the Old Testament; Genesis, for instance, relates how God tests Abraham by ordering him to sacrifice his son, Isaac. Equally, the idea is prominent in the New Testament; see for instance the letter of James: 'Consider it pure joy, my brothers and sisters, whenever you face trials of many kinds, because you know that the testing of your faith produces perseverance. Let perseverance finish its work so that you may be mature and complete, not lacking anything. . . . Blessed is the one who perseveres under trial because, having stood the test, that person will receive the crown of life that the Lord has promised to those who love him' (James 1:2–4, 12). It is also expressed in many places in the Koran: 'And we will surely test you with something of fear and hunger and a loss of wealth and lives and fruits, but give good tidings to the patient, who, when disaster strikes them, say, 'Indeed we belong to Allah, and indeed to Him we will return'. Those are the ones upon whom are blessings from their Lord and mercy. And it is those who are the [rightly] guided' (Koran 2:155–157). 'Every soul will taste death. And We test you with evil and with good as trial; and to Us you will be returned' (Koran 21:35).

For those who have faith, undeserved suffering can therefore have meaning—and can, indeed, contribute to the enhancement of a meaningful life—precisely because it is endured and resisted. For the endurance and persistence of faith in the face of suffering is essential to the ultimate point or purpose of the religious life, namely the blessings and eternal life that are the reward of the faithful. By enduring and overcoming, the religious devotee thereby communicates her faith to the divine; she shows that she is faithful and will endure. This idea is also prominent in Koranic teaching: 'Did you reckon that you would enter the garden without God knowing those of you who make an effort and without knowing those who are patient?' (Koran 22:2). On the Islamic picture, God knows who is faithful and who is not by putting his followers to the test, by making them suffer, and rewarding those who respond virtuously. Here too suffering is essential for those who believe, if they are to achieve the ultimate purpose in life. Far from undermining meaning, therefore, (great) suffering is essential to living a meaningful life, in both Christian and Islamic traditions.

Christians and Muslims have at least two answers to Nietzsche's question about why we suffer. By accepting suffering as punishment and repenting, one displays praiseworthy and admirable moral behaviour. By accepting punishment as a test of one's faith, one both develops important virtues and expresses one's love and devotion to the divine, with (so the believer hopes) the result of being joined together with the divine and living a life of eternal bliss. Since this is the ultimate meaning for people of these faiths, suffering is essential to, rather than destructive of, a meaningful life.

So much seems to be true of those who appeal to a supernatural being in search for meaning—both of life in general, and of suffering in particular. But what of those who are without faith? How might they answer Nietzsche's question, and avoid the descent into meaninglessness than suffering threatens?

3. Suffering and Meaning: Secular Perspectives

If we are atheist or agnostic, we will be unable to avail ourselves of the idea that suffering, whether punishment or test, is essential to our living a meaningful life, aimed at ultimate union with the divine. But there might be a different way in which suffering can be central to a meaningful life from a secular perspective. This is as a condition on the value of *achievements*. Achievement, broadly understood, is a vitally important aspect of a meaningful life; indeed, we can note that 'purposeful achievement' might well encompass the kinds of intellectual reflection, moral achievement, and artistic creation that Metz identifies as defining a meaningful life. To see this, however, we first need to focus more closely on what achievement is.

When we initially think about achievement, it is tempting to think of it as having a very high bar, such that only the truly exceptional can achieve. It is easy to veer into this kind of thinking, since the notion of achievement is often illustrated by feats that are only available to a few: writing a great novel, curing a debilitating disease, winning an Olympic medal, and so on. But there are very many things which can constitute achievements, and they are clearly relativized to people's age, character, ability, social circumstances, and many other things. So the bar for what constitutes an achievement needs to be set very much lower, in order to accommodate this obvious fact. Thus, learning to tie one's shoelaces is an achievement for a five-year-old; speaking in a meeting is an achievement for a person who is painfully shy; travelling to another country was an achievement a few hundred years ago, but not nowadays; and so on. Since we want to allow that the five-year-old has achieved something when she learns to tie her shoelaces, then achievements need not be things of exceptional value. Nevertheless, when looked at from the context of meaning in *life*, achievements tend to be the large-scale valuable projects, ones that one looks upon with a sense of pride, ones which bolster one's esteem and standing. Given this, it is plausible to think that achievements are elements in a meaningful life, precisely because they are the kinds of things (following Metz) that merit esteem and pride. So a life of achievement might be characterized by being in a loving relationship and raising a family; a life of devotion to friends, neighbours, community; a life of sporting activity with the occasional moments of excellence; a life devoted to the arts, to music, reading, painting, acting, even if one doesn't make one's career from these things; a life which is characterized by concern and compassion for others; a life of exploration, of travel, of seeing the world and meeting many different people; a life of service to one's institution, community, country; a life where one has displayed integrity, fought for justice, stood up for what is right. Within these and other forms of achievement, there is of course room for a vast degree of different ways and modes of living. There are very many ways in which one can devote oneself to a career (and countless careers), or to one's friends and community (and countless communities), or to loving relationships, or of commitment to the arts. One person's commitment might be stronger than another's, without this meaning that a weaker commitment is incompatible with achievement. One person's commitment to things that constitute achievements might be stronger at some times and weaker at other times within a life, again without this undermining what they achieve.

What does seem true is that a life without any of these things—without any of the vast array of things that constitute achievements, a mode of living that doesn't involve raising a family or a successful career or commitment to justice or to the arts or to sport or to the environment—is a life that would be severely lacking in meaning. The strangely barren and meaningless lives of those who always submit to their strongest fleeting desires, or lifestyle hedonists, or those whose only goal is to amass wealth, are meaningless precisely because they seem to lack anything that could constitute an achievement, any admirable or estimable object or end that their activity has brought about, anything that they can be proud of or praised for.[8] What I now want to claim is that overcoming suffering is in

---

[8] It is no doubt true that amassing great wealth can require great levels of effort, persistence, coping with difficulty, and overcoming obstacles. But my intuition is that it doesn't constitute an achievement

very many cases central to the value of achievements. Moreover, given that achievement can clearly include both the kind of moral responses to value that we discussed in section 1, and lives of religious devotion and faith that we discussed in section 2, then this account of the role that suffering has in meaningful lives constitutes a unifying picture, one that brings together the ideas that we can have meaningful responses to suffering, *and* that suffering is central to a meaningful life.

To make this argument, note that very many of us are—as a matter of psychological fact—motivated to pursue activities that are arduous, difficult, and challenging, activities that, in short, have suffering at their core. It is, after all, a remarkable fact about human beings that many of our activities involve the intentional pursuit of things that involve pain and suffering. Consider, to illustrate, the following activities: mountaineering, mixed martial arts, chess, video gaming, endurance running, doing philosophy, playing the violin, renovating a classic car, Tough Mudder, ballet, learning Mandarin, ice fishing. It is clear that people do these (and many similar) things because they think that they have value, and indeed give a purpose to one's afternoons, weekends, even lives. It is also clear that, as a matter of psychological fact, people pursue most or all of these things in part *because* they are challenging, painful, arduous. Suffering is at the heart of these activities. It is not that at which the activities aim—those who do philosophy or renovate cars are not obviously masochistic—but suffering would seem to be a *condition* on the value that these things have for the people who do them. Part of the point of endurance running is to test oneself, to see how much one can take, how much pain and suffering and discomfort one can experience and overcome and finish the race. The fact that endurance running involves a great deal of physical suffering is part of what makes it worthwhile for those who do it. If it didn't involve pain and suffering, it wouldn't be a challenge, and people wouldn't be attracted by it.

What is true of endurance running is equally true of the other activities listed previously. Mountaineers want difficult, challenging, arduous climbs; they are uninterested in pleasant, easy, lowland walks. Where would be the challenge, or the achievement, in those? No doubt mountaineers are interested in the views when they get to the top, the sense of camaraderie, the stories to relate after the fact. But what they really seem motivated by is the chance to face up to and overcome the extremes of physical and emotional suffering that climbing tall peaks generates. The ability to express grace and beauty while putting your body through physical pain and emotional suffering is central to the discipline of ballet. We admire and esteem ballet dancers not just for their grace and beauty, but—as a condition of our admiration—for what we know it has cost and is costing them. And so on: cavers push themselves to extreme exploration; classical musicians want the challenging, the almost impossible, pieces; the religious devotee

---

precisely because amassing wealth for its own sake fails to constitute a *valuable* project, given that wealth is not, plausibly, an intrinsic good. So the notion of an achievement, in the sense of something that contributes to a meaningful life, is a *normative* concept. Thanks again to Iddo Landau for pushing me to clarify this point.

wants a life that involves sacrifice; and when it comes to philosophy, we want to take on and wrestle with the big, difficult, and utterly perplexing questions. If the process of philosophy was easy, if the answers were simple, I wouldn't be writing this, and you wouldn't be reading it. So it seems clearly true that as a matter of fact people pursue a very great range of activities partly *because* these activities are imbued with pain and suffering and hardship. Suffering isn't the only thing that humans want when we do these things; but it is, nevertheless, a condition on the value that they have for us.

But it is not just a brute psychological fact that many of us are motivated to pursue activities that involve suffering in this way. We can, instead, propose a closer link between suffering and the value of certain achievements, and maintain that many of us are *right* to view suffering as a condition on the value of certain activities. To see this, consider Gwen Bradford's rich and detailed account of the nature of achievement, as described and defended in her excellent book of that name (Bradford 2015). Bradford's basic claim is that achievements have two essential components: they involve *difficult processes*, and result in a product that is *competently caused*. Now the latter element isn't important for the point I want to make here. With respect to the former, Bradford writes:

> One feature that appears to distinguish [an] achievement—and, I will contend, all achievements—is that it is *difficult*. If tying my shoes presented a particular difficulty for me to overcome ... then my success might count as an achievement too. If writing a novel were so easy that anyone could do it, we wouldn't think of it as an achievement. Finding a cure for cancer is turning out to be difficult task. Writing a dissertation, running a marathon, or even smaller scale achievements, such as winning a game of chess, baking a soufflé, or cultivating a bonsai—all of these achievements are difficult to do. Were it the case that any of these activities were easy, we wouldn't think of them as achievements.... This suggests that difficulty is a necessary component for achievements. (Bradford 2015, 12)

What, however, is difficulty? Bradford writes: 'Something is difficult in virtue of requiring some sufficient degree of *effort*. Things require effort in virtue of having certain *features*. Different activities require effort in virtue of various features that they have. Some activities require effort because they are very physically demanding, others require effort because they make use of multiple skills, or a lot of diverse knowledge' Bradford 2015, 28). My proposal is that we can add suffering to this list of features. That is, it requires intense effort to face up to, endure, and overcome suffering, and so such things clearly count as things that are difficult to do. Suffering is thus the condition on the value of certain activities precisely because suffering *makes* those things difficult, and hence as things which are candidates for genuine achievements. So it is not merely a psychological quirk that we are motivated to pursue activities insofar as they involve pain and suffering. Instead, this psychological fact reflects the normative truth—that by facing up to, enduring, and overcoming suffering, we seek to achieve something, and in so doing give meaning to our activities and lives. Since this is a very general point—since, as we have seen, very many activities and ends require enduring and overcoming pain and suffering—then the close connection between suffering and meaning is not simply restricted to religious or moral outlooks. Instead, the connection will be apparent in very many of the things that human beings do. Suffering is thus a condition on meaning in the lives and activities of human beings generally.

4. Conclusion

Suffering can have devastating effects on human beings, and one way in which it can do so is by undermining or destroying the conditions for a meaningful life: a life that embodies and expresses to a large degree the kinds of intellectual reflection, moral achievement, and artistic creation that Metz plausibly claims are central to a meaningful life. However, it is also true that a meaningful response to (great) suffering is possible, given that positive attitudes towards suffering express strength of character and other virtues. Moreover, it is also true that for many people, both religious and secular, suffering is necessary for a life of meaning. Through suffering we atone for sin and express our faith, which are essential for achieving the ultimate purpose according to Christian and Islamic traditions. Through suffering we face up to and overcome difficulty, which is a condition on achievement itself. Indeed, given the importance of achievement in any valuable and distinctively human life, we might propose that a meaningful life is not possible without suffering playing a central role. Far from thinking of suffering as solely destructive to meaning in a life, therefore, we should reflect upon and embrace the positive part that suffering can play in enabling us to live meaningful lives.[9]

References

Adams, M. M. 1990. 'Horrendous Evils and the Goodness of God'. In *The Problem of Evil*, ed. M. M. Adams and R. M. Adams. Oxford: Oxford University Press, 209–221.
Arberry, A. J. [1955] 2008. *The Koran*. Oxford: Oxford University Press
Aristotle. *Nicomachean Ethics*, translated by Sir David Ross, *Oxford World's Classics*. Oxford/New York: Oxford University Press, 2009.
Bradford, G. 2015. *Achievement*. Oxford: Oxford University Press.
Brady, M. S. 2018. *Suffering and Virtue*. Oxford: Oxford University Press.
Carel, H. 2013. *Illness*, 2nd ed. Durham, NC: Acumen.

---

[9] This chapter develops certain ideas from my 2018 book *Suffering and Virtue*. That book emerged from the Value of Suffering project, which ran during 2013–2016 at Glasgow, and was funded by the John Templeton Foundation (Grant ID 44167). I owe great thanks to the Foundation for their generous support, and to my co-investigators on the project, David Bain and Jennifer Corns. Iddo Landau provided very helpful feedback on this chapter, and I am very grateful to him for his comments and support.

Carel, H. 2016. 'Virtue Without Excellence, Excellence Without Health'. *Aristotelian Society Supplementary Volume* 90(1): 237–253
Frankl, V. E. 1984. *Man's Search for Meaning*. New York: Washington Square Press.
Hurka, T. 2001. *Virtue, Vice, and Value*. New York: Oxford University Press.
Kidd, I. 2012. 'Can Illness Be Edifying?' *Inquiry* 55(5): 496–520.
Leiter, B. 2002. *Nietzsche on Morality*. London: Routledge.
Metz, T. 2013. *Meaning in Life*. New York: Oxford University Press.
Moore, G. E. 1903. *Principia Ethica*. Cambridge: Cambridge University Press.
Nietzsche, F. [1887] 1902. *The Genealogy of Morals*, trans. H. Samuel, Edinburgh: T.N. Foulis, 1–212.
Nietzsche, F. [1889] 1968. *Twilight of the Idols*, trans. R. Hollingdale. London: Penguin.
Panaïoti, A. 2013. *Nietzsche and Buddhist Philosophy*. Cambridge: Cambridge University Press.
St. Augustine. 1886. *The Writings against the Manichaeans and against the Donatists*, trans. P. Schaff. New York: Christian Literature.
St. Thomas Aquinas. 1947. *The Summa Theologica*, trans. Fathers of the Dominican Province. New York: Benziger Bros.

CHAPTER 30

PARADOXES AND MEANING IN LIFE

SAUL SMILANSKY

1. Preliminaries

Paradoxes can be said to be the quintessence of philosophy, combining as they typically do the argument form and the radical challenge to the seemingly obvious. Zeno's Parmenidean challenges to common-sense notions of movement are a famous early example. Much like reflection about paradoxes, reflection about meaningfulness *in* our everyday lives and pursuits (MIL), and the meaning *of* a human life overall (MOL), goes back a long way in philosophy. Yet oddly, at least in the Western tradition, reflection about paradoxes and MIL/MOL has hardly been combined, and certainly not to the extent that one could have imagined. Paradoxes are recognized to be central in areas such as logic and the philosophy of mathematics, epistemology, and the philosophy of science, but not in moral philosophy (cf. Smilansky 2007a; Sainsbury 2009, chapter 2; Sneddon 2012) and even less so in the exploration of MIL/MOL.[1] There are good reasons to think that paradoxicality will be important to MIL and the MOL, so this neglect is significant. In this chapter, I explore some widely known apparent paradoxes, together with some lesser known ones, that bear upon MIL and the MOL, and draw out their significance for this topic. I look at what it means to live with paradoxes, and conclude with some general reflections.

It will be important first to consider what paradoxes are, so that we do not exclude significant paradoxes because our understanding of the nature of a paradox is too limited, but at the same time do not render the notion too broad. A paradox need not necessarily

---

[1] Since understanding the world and the idea that life makes sense are important for our topic, if logical theory is 'infected' with paradox, then the very canons of reason by which we make sense of the world are unstable and faulty. Yet in my view the major challenges that paradox poses here follow from the moral and MIL/MOL paradoxes themselves.

involve a strict contradiction, but it will not be convincing, nor will it be fruitful, if we 'lower the bar' and consider as paradoxes much that is merely surprising, odd, or counter-intuitive. The term 'paradox' is often used in some professional contexts, and even more so in popular discussions, in an unhelpfully loose way. W. V. Quine, in his classic essay 'The Ways of Paradox' asks (and replies): 'May we say in general, then, that a paradox is just any conclusion that at first sounds absurd but that has an argument to sustain it? In the end I think this account stands up pretty well' (Quine 1976, 1). This is, in my view, a bit too lax, for sounding absurd 'at first' is not enough: a surprising but (on reflection) *easily acceptable* conclusion is not a paradox. I will follow Sainsbury's elegant definition: 'This is what I understand by a paradox: an apparently unacceptable conclusion derived by apparently acceptable reasoning from apparently acceptable premises' (Sainsbury 2009, 1). Often, we shall see, we will need to keep the sense in which the conclusion is, in some respects, absurd, but overcome our sense that it is, indeed, overall unacceptable.

We hence require another notion, that of an *existential paradox* (Smilansky 2007a, 4–5). The conclusion of the existential paradox is (as far as we can see) true and yet absurd and hence really paradoxical. The fault is not in the assumptions or in the argumentation that leads from them to the paradoxical conclusion, as in the prevalent interpretation of paradoxes, but in the absurdity of the 'reality' this conclusion describes. The paradoxical result is not an indication that we have made a mistake, but a revelation of how things are. A paradox, then, can also be a true, absurd conclusion derived by acceptable reasoning from acceptable premises. Sometimes there will be paradoxicality and absurdity that is worth noting, without quite reaching the level of a strict paradox. In any case, conceptually we can, of course, have absurdity that does not result from paradox, but our focus in this chapter is on paradoxes. And a central claim is that the prevalence of paradox makes life much more absurd than we have realized, and impacts meaning.

What makes for absurdity? To say that a state of affairs is absurd, in the sense that concerns us, is to say something about the fundamentally alien relationship between this state of affairs and human reason, human nature, or our basic expectations about human life and the moral order (cf. Camus 2000, 22–26; Nagel 2012a). Absurdity then means that our conclusions seem not to make sense to us, as they are sharply in conflict with certain firm intuitions and basic expectations. Beyond this broad characterization, we shall leave this notion intuitive, and assume that it will become clearer in the course of our discussion of those paradoxes where it is relevant. Since I shall aim to speak about paradoxes in a robust sense, the corresponding absurdity will need to be substantial.

I will focus upon paradoxes within the analytic side of the Western tradition, and even there, I will be selective and not aim to consider every example.[2] It seems significant that we can reach firm conclusions about paradoxes, absurdity, and MIL/MOL from a

---

[2] For example, I will not consider the theological context, where there are MIL/MOL-related paradoxes; see e.g. Hick (1977); Metz (2019, 41–43). The topic of personal identity is also rife with paradox (e.g. Parfit 1984, Part 3), but we cannot consider these complexities, and will assume here a fairly stable common-sense notion of the self.

tradition that aims at conceptual and argumentative rigor. 'Analytic existentialism' can be built upon firm foundations, in paradoxes about value, morality, and MIL/MOL. I will by and large not consider claims for paradoxes that apply only to certain views (such as utilitarianism, or Kantian deontology); although obviously we will consider paradoxes that emerge from assumptions that not everyone will accept.

We will also consider what it means to live with paradoxes that bear upon MIL and the MOL. The questions here have hardly been explored. The ways of dealing with paradoxes in daily life are complex, and as we shall see, some of them give rise to further meta-paradoxicality.

Wolf (2010) has analysed MIL as having to do with subjective attraction to objective value. Metz (2013, 219–239) has analysed it as having to do with, among others, the domains of the good and the true. Weinberg (Chapter 19 in this volume) has analysed meaningfulness as having to do with, among others, significance, value, purpose, and impact. As we shall see ahead, paradoxes affect many of these and other aspects of MIL and the MOL. And paradoxes will be seen to be salient both for objectivists and for subjectivists.

Population Paradoxes

One sphere in which paradoxes can enlighten us on MIL and the MOL is that of population. A major instance is the *Non-identity Problem* (henceforth NIP) or non-identity effect (the classic here is Parfit 1984, Part 4). Broadly, the NIP is concerned with the way in which our moral evaluation of certain actions is problematized by their existence-giving aspect. Morality has always been assumed to pertain to already existing people, who are then sometimes wrongly harmed. However, it was then realized that, particularly given the fragility of the conditions of coming to be, sometimes actions that intuitively seem to be manifestly morally wrong determine who will be born. Paradoxically, our wrongdoing, even crimes, may then be *victimless*, since everyone alive (and, we are assuming, happy to be alive) will be dependent for their existence on the wrongdoing, and would welcome it rather than complain about it.

There has been a considerable amount of discussion of the NIP, particularly in trying to deal with the basic apparent paradoxicality just explained (see e.g. Boonin 2014). Following Parfit's lead, nearly all of the discussion has focused on its forward-looking implications. One example is Benatar's (2006) radical anti-natalist normative claim that having children is wrong, in the light of certain asymmetries between bringing into existence and not doing so, and because life is systematically all-considered bad. Hence he makes various paradoxical claims relevant to MIL/MOL, such as that abortion in the early months of pregnancy should be the default position, and that the dying out of humanity would be good. Heyd (1992) makes a conceptually even more radical claim, that since all value is person-affecting, neither the continuation of humanity nor its extinction is a matter of value. Both are complex positions, and have generated considerable discussion. I do not find their respective assumptions compelling: in the case of Benatar due to the possibility of comparing non-existence and existence (see later discussion) coupled with the unreasonable negativity of his claims about happiness (see Smilansky 2012a; Landau 2020); although of course happiness and MIL are distinct. Concerning Heyd's view, I find the radical denial of impersonal comparisons totally unconvincing. If I am correct, then these are merely apparent paradoxes, given that we can deny the assumptions or reasoning behind the conclusion.

The largely neglected backward-looking perspective concerning the NIP seems even more fruitful.[3] Thompson pointed out that it seems to threaten integrity, since it makes apologizing for past collective evils, the absence of which would have precluded our consequent existence, unconvincing and hypocritical (Thompson 2000; cf. Levy 2002). Adams has argued that the NIP threatens love, since '[w]hat we prize concretely in our loving presupposes evil as well as good' (Adams 2009, 5). Love is crucial for our sense of MIL, but he says that we need to be as it were existentially ambivalent here. In response, Metz (2009) makes a number of complex moves which seek to allow love to exist in this context, through lowering the required standards of coherence for 'wishing' how things should be. By contrast, I have argued that often we can neither remain ambivalent nor escape the predicament; we have here a 'package deal', and matters are inevitably grim. First, we confront a monstrous paradoxical antinomy: in the commonplace all-considered-preference sense of regret, either we must regret that we and our loved ones exist (and also that nearly everyone who ever lived existed); or we do not regret (and are indeed arguably forbidden to regret) most of the calamities of history, such as slavery and the Holocaust. Second, I then further argue that, when the moral stakes are high enough, we ought to regret our existence and that of our loved ones (Smilansky 2013b; cf. Johnson 2015). Human existence and the meaning that we find in it are morally tainted. Similarly unhappy implications apply to the gratitude we owe, which turns out to be systematically perverse, paradoxical, and meaning-threatening in complex ways (Smilansky 2016).

A further set of implications threatening meaning applies to many of the ways in which human beings react to history, such as in collectively mourning and resenting tragic events or wrongs. Once we recognize that we and the people we care about personally are dependent on those past events, most of the collective mourning and resentment cease to make sense. Without those events, the very existence and nature of our societies, and the content of our culture, would have been transformed beyond recognition (Smilansky 2019a). The narrative meaning of most collectives and the subjective sense of meaning of individuals insofar as their identities are based upon living with such historical narratives are hence severely threatened. Not all backward-looking implications of the fragility of coming into existence and the NIP are, however, grim:

---

[3] Broad discussions of history and population ethics relevant to this chapter are, for example, Wallace (2013); Kahane (2019). One of the few areas that has received attention is that of reparations (e.g. Sher 1981). The neglect of the backward-looking concern with the NIP is a moral lacuna, and part of the more general neglect of what I have elsewhere called 'The Moral Philosophy of History' (Smilansky 2019a).

they also imply that we ought to see each other as inevitable partners in the world, who cannot systematically wish that others had not been born (Smilansky 2020b).

Since we cannot now go back in time and change history (there is therefore no *Ethics of time-travel*), the implications here are largely ones of understanding life in new ways, rather than of practice. However, if one accepts my further recent claims about 'Duties to History' (DTH), we probably have some resultant duties, such as to be good, or even to be happy; and consequent challenges and opportunities for the enhancement of MIL/MOL through the interaction with the past (Smilansky 2021a).[4]

Parfit's paradoxical *Repugnant Conclusion* (henceforth RC) (Parfit 1984, Part 4) is also relevant to meaning. Given reasonable but intricate assumptions which I cannot expand on here, we are led to opt for a world with a huge population, that Parfit calls Z. This world is optimal because there are so many people in it, leading to a maximization of positive value, despite the fact that everyone's lives are just barely worth living. The RC seems compelling for utilitarians, given that Z is the world with the highest overall utility. But the intuitions need not be utilitarian. The very existence of another person who subjectively is glad to be alive and feels that she is living a meaningful life seems to make the world better. It is also good for those additional existing persons: if we were these people, we would clearly be glad that our existence had not been blocked (see e.g. Huemer 2008).[5] Yet then it is unclear what can stop us from descending into repugnancy. There has been a concerted effort to save us from the RC, but no clear success (see e.g. Ryberg and Tannsjo, 2004). We seem unable to rid ourselves of an absurd conclusion that would be destructive to the things that we centrally value. It seems to me that we need to continue and think things through philosophically, and in the meantime remain sceptical, and not proceed to apply the RC in practice. Clearly the absurdity of a conclusion is a reason to be highly skeptical about it. On the other hand, there are cases where in spite of its absurdity, the conclusion, all things considered, should be accepted. There is no formula for distinguishing between these cases, and our view would depend upon the specific discussions.

The RC debate has been phrased in terms of happiness or well-being. There is further room for discussing RC-type issues directly in the context of MIL/MOL, such as the trade-offs between happiness and MIL; and the question whether what matters is having

---

[4] A strong set of paradoxical results will follow if we add concern over benefiting or harming the interests of past people. Numerous awful people's lives may be getting better and better, and can gain meaning after their deaths; a striking example would be Genghis Khan, who was manifestly a moral monster, but has the most direct descendants of any single known past figure. And some people who had short and not terribly positive lives perhaps may turn out to have some of the best and most meaningful lives simply because they will have numerous descendants who each have good lives (Smilansky 2020d). On the ethics of harming the dead, see Smilansky (2018); Boonin (2019).

[5] It might be asked whether I can coherently think that, *for me*, never to have existed would have been bad. For, no one for whom that could have been bad would ever have existed (see e.g., in different ways, Heyd 1988; Benatar 2006; Weinberg 2016). But once I do exist, asking myself prudentially whether I wish not to have been born does make sense. For one who has lived a life of harsh and prolonged suffering unbalanced by any good, to be sorry to exist seems perfectly reasonable. We do seem, then, to think that we can relevantly compare existence and non-existence, even from the first-person perspective.

fewer people with a very high MIL, or a much larger number of people with a lower MIL. This can be asked under both objectivist and subjectivist views about meaning. Combining the NIP, the RC, and questions of MIL/MOL raises fundamental but largely unexplored questions for MIL/MOL research. Seemingly absurd conclusions may well have strong and disturbing arguments in their favour. If meaning is additive, one such conclusion would be a 'Meaning-RC world' with a huge amount of meaning in it, but thinly spread among countless people, each of them living lives that have very little meaning. A second absurd conclusion would be the idea that the irresponsible could become the great contributors to meaning in the world (for example, by having many children whom they then abandon). Having children is a fundamental source of meaning in and of our lives (see e.g. Smilansky 1995; Weinberg 2016), but a 'quantitative' direction will quickly lead to absurdity, threatening the significance, value, and rationality of life, yet it may be difficult to philosophically resist.

Work and Absurdity

Work is both objectively and subjectively important to the quality of people's lives, and offers complex opportunities for leading meaningful lives, together with significant challenges. A possible paradox inheres in Williams's famous discussion of integrity (Williams 1973, 1981; cf. e.g. Dan-Cohen 2008). His case of George (Williams 1973, 93f) concerns a 'contribution' by working in a plant that produces nuclear materials, which is against one's principles. Nevertheless, one can then function *less eagerly* than one's likely replacement, which is likely to limit the damage. Achieving great and unique meaning in one's life, primarily in terms of impact, here requires interpreting integrity perversely, giving up on inner consistency and harmony; and often embracing hypocrisy (cf. Smilansky 1994a; Cohen 2000).

Effective Altruism claims that idealistic people should often avoid choosing a professional life devoted to directly helping others (MacAskill 2014). Instead of, say, training themselves and then devoting years to volunteer work in Third World countries, they should choose a highly lucrative job, which is in itself morally neutral, or even harmful—the resulting high earnings would then enable them to maximize monetary contributions, and make a drastically greater contribution to the very causes they value. Often, indeed, the more morally disturbing would be their choice of career and mode of engagement, the greater could be their earnings, monetary contribution, and consequent impact/MIL. An idealistic life of direct devotion to and engagement in beneficence, by contrast, is paradoxically claimed to be a betrayal of the good causes, and to have much less objective meaning.

Two further large issues follow from people's replaceability at work. My *Paradox of Beneficial Retirement* (Smilansky 2007c; see Lenman 2007; Manheimer 2008; Lang 2014) concerns the predicament of a person such as a medical doctor who realizes that, were he to leave, someone much better would replace him; and this would make a large positive difference for his patients. Note that the argument here is not yet another over-demanding consequentialist injunction, but concerns one's own *integrity* and professional meaning. On the one hand, it is highly unreasonable to expect such a person to leave, given that he has invested so much in becoming a doctor, and that this is central to his identity and the meaning he finds in his life. On the other hand, it seems that this person cannot keep both his profession and his integrity; he can no longer truthfully say that he is a doctor because he cares about people's health, and the meaning in his life relating to his professional identity ceases to make sense. This paradox pertains to a very large number of people (roughly, whenever one's work matters, one is below average, and there are better likely replacements). It casts a previously unrecognized pessimistic shadow on the MIL and MOL of many.

As I show more recently (Smilansky 2021c), replaceability challenges even more broadly the very idea of benefiting and thereby making a meaningful *contribution*. The threat of paradox can to some extent be dealt with, but (in a way that I cannot outline here) this topic brings out surprising and sometimes paradoxical implications, such as about which jobs or positions are worth pursuing for a more meaningful life. Making *irreplaceable* contributions through creativity or unusual caring rather than, say, being in important positions, becomes pre-eminent.

Morality, Luck, and Meaning

An early example here are the so-called Socratic paradoxes, whereby a person who is 'worse', or 'less good', or 'less virtuous' can never harm a better one, and it is better to be wronged than to wrong (Plato 1997, 28, 30c–d). These, however, require assumptions that hardly anyone today will agree with.

The paradox of *Moral Luck* is a more compelling example; since it is widely known, we do not need to explain it in detail (see Statman 1993). The general point that primarily matters for our concern is that, as Bernard Williams showed (Williams 1981; cf. Williams 1985; Nagel 2012b) the desire for the moral evaluation of persons which is *safe* from luck is intimately related to the wish to preserve the idea that life makes sense, and has meaning. The purist ethical Kantian project is intimately connected to such a desire. However, implementing it would quickly lead to absurdity in familiar ways.[6] As Williams's famous discussion of Gauguin shows, the issue is a matter of meaning in one's personal life no less than of ethics.

---

[6] One particularly perverse way in which such hopes for meaning and justice are shattered is through the prevalence of *Teflon Immorality* (Smilansky 2013c), which concerns the numerous paradoxical practical ways in which wrongdoing and wrongdoers can make themselves safe. A vicious libel will not be confronted because doing so will only spread the damage; in many cases the need for compensation will decrease the more the victims are harmed; and dictators will be resisted less the worse they are (as it is perceived that trying to do so may instigate worse reprisals), for example. For a detailed study of compensation as an 'existential paradox', see Smilansky (2013d).

There is, however, scope for, as it were, turning the tables on bad luck, through the paradoxical idea of *'Fortunate Misfortune'* (e.g. Smilansky 2007b; Sainsbury 2009, 27–31). Sometimes apparently tragic circumstances, such as being born with great physical difficulties or into great poverty, actually turn out to have been fortunate. This may occur for example through building the character and motivation of the purported victims, and thereby leading them to triumphs greater than they would have otherwise achieved. It causes perplexity as to the nature of those original challenges. If the people were thrown into those difficulties without choosing, to swim or sink, and overcoming took huge efforts and involved great hardship, pain, or humiliation, so that no one would wish such a predicament upon (say) his children, then these events clearly seem to have been misfortunes. Yet at the same time, in these particular instances the given events actually made the lives of the people much better, in a way that (we are assuming) they acknowledge to have been worthwhile, overall. So, have these events, then, been fortunes or misfortunes? In any case, from the perspective of the people themselves, this can be a way of 'writing their own story' in heroic terms (see Velleman 2005), turning the overwhelming, apparently senseless, brute misfortune into a good fortune, giving it meaning and as it were forcing it to make sense.

Another apparent paradox that has received considerable attention can be called *It makes no difference whether or not I do it*. It concerns the consistent moral expectation for people to do things at some cost to themselves, while (in terms of the expected effects) it hardly matters whether they do so or not, or indeed often does not matter at all (see e.g. Parfit 1984, chapter 3; Glover 1986; Kagan 2011; Smilansky 2012b; Nefsky 2017). Examples such as paying taxes, refraining from watering one's garden in a drought, voting, recycling, and not trying to wriggle out of compulsory military service show the variety and importance of the topic. It is unclear how much of the sense of paradox here appears only given utilitarian-like consequentialist intuitions, and how much of it would remain with deontological, contractual, and virtue ethical views, which can imbue the 'senseless' conformist actions with meaning. Yet even the non-consequentialist directions give a 'Sisyphus-like' quality to much of personal sacrifice, as being ineffective and meaningless in practice.

A sense of the 'foreignness' of morality and its indifference to plain humanity is even more clearly seen from a recent puzzle concerning *the Moral Evaluation of Past Tragedies* (Smilansky 2020a). Seemingly, we cannot justify the 'obvious' idea that morally we should most prefer a situation allowing victims of specific past calamities such as slavery, World War I, or the Holocaust to have been spared to live free and peaceful lives. For, from the perspective of a self-centred personal morality, we prefer that they suffer as they did, lest we not be born (due to the non-identity effect we have noted). And from the perspective of impersonal morality, it would have been preferable that those people had not been born in the first place (since other, earlier calamities would have best been avoided), rather than being born and then not be tormented and killed. Other perspectives are seen to be unhelpful as well. Yet this seems absurd.

Another paradox that is highly relevant to MIL/MOL is *Morality and Moral Worth*. It concerns the inherent tension between moral improvement and the conditions for the attainment of moral worth (Smilansky 2007d). Given that imposing moral requirements on people is legitimate only when there are genuine needs for making such demands, widespread social improvements will decrease the conditions enabling the heights of moral worth. The value achieved through the struggle against extreme poverty, disease, or dictatorship dissipates when these do not exist. Yet clearly we are not morally permitted to spread poverty, disease, and political oppression, just so that people could then attain meaning by struggling against them.[7] When effective, moral worth can eliminate the need for itself, like a mythological animal eating its own tail, hence depriving life of, arguably, the highest form of human value. This 'existential paradox' is a striking example of the phenomena of 'the Good Absurd' (Smilansky 2007a, chapter 11), of paradoxes that indicate that a paradoxical state of affairs is, overall, good; so that the greater the goodness, the greater the absurdity, and *thus here we need to make the world more absurd*.[8]

We typically think that (assuming something like moral realism) there is one true solution to moral dilemmas such as 'Trolley type' cases. To think that firm, contrary evaluations can be true together in the same situation (and not just due to our epistemic limitations, or as pertaining to different aspects) seems paradoxical. However, in 'A Hostage Situation' I have recently showed that, under certain conditions, this is not so; and yet it is not clear how this can be (see Smilansky 2019b). Another radical possibility is for a *Designer Ethics*, where, for instance, in a paradigmatic Trolley type case, the question whether the five or the one are to be saved would depend upon the perceived beliefs and value commitments of those potential victims (Smilansky 2020c). Such an account seems absurd from the conventional perspective of a universal morality, but I argue that it nevertheless has a lot going for it philosophically. These directions would seem to allow a much closer fit between individual notions on MIL and morality. Often one can both choose a moral position (among a variety of acceptable but contrary ones) according to one's values and inclinations; and be treated by others according to one's position; thereby helping us to shape our lives and infuse them with greater meaning.[9]

A number of specific virtues and dispositions also appear to be paradoxical, in a way that bears upon MIL and the MOL. One neglected matter is what I have called *Reactive-Contributions*, the way we contribute to others by benefiting from their contributions (Smilansky 2003a). A more well-known example is the mystery of modesty, in the sense that concerns the self-evaluation and self-appreciation of people (rather than of not presenting one's high self-estimate to others). Here we have the *Paradox of Modesty*: how can an epistemically adequate self-evaluation by the admirable and accomplished

---

[7] Metz (2013, 57) makes a similar point within an individual life.
[8] Another paradox related to moral worth is the *Paradox of Self-Sacrificing Altruism* (SSA), which at least in cases of saving one person arguably appears as a moral mistake. One sacrifices a person who, through that very sacrifice, has become much more valuable than the ordinary person one typically saves (Smilansky 2021b). SSA has often been seen as the highest form of the achievement of moral meaning in and of life, but may be destructive of objective value and thus self-defeating.
[9] For an application of such thoughts in an applied context, see Smilansky (2022).

nevertheless be both genuinely modest and a virtue? If they know their value, how then can they be modest about it? If they do not know their value or deceive themselves about it, how can this be a virtue? Driver (2001, chapter 2) has as it were embraced paradoxicality, and sees modesty (together with a number of other virtues) as 'Virtues of ignorance'. This radical proposal means that a deficient subjective sense of the meaning that they have achieved in their lives inheres in the modest; both virtue and meaning significantly depend upon ignorance or self-deception. Others have resisted this last idea, see e.g. Richards (1988); Flanagan (1990); Statman (1992); Ben-Zeev (1993); Schueler (1997); Smilansky (2003b); but it seems fair to say that no proposal has gained widespread agreement, and the paradox is still having the last laugh.

Further Absurdity

We cannot consider the free will problem in detail here, but absurdity is widespread (see Smilansky 2013a); while the free will debate shows consistent over-optimism (Smilansky 2010). My own view is complex, combining pluralism on the compatibility question and Illusionism (Smilansky 2000, 2022). It is in many ways a pessimistic view, which sees the free will problem as the graveyard of our noblest aspirations and deepest beliefs; and shows life to be profoundly absurd (Smilansky 2000, section 11.5; Smilansky 2022). The implications of the denial of libertarian free will are vast, and this is further enhanced if one also rejects compatibilist forms of free will and moral responsibility. For then, *all one's attainments would ultimately not be to one's credit, but merely an 'unfolding of the given'*. This has severe deflationary implications for one's value and meaning. Moreover, on my view, what this entails for our sense of self-respect, appreciation of others, and indeed the very sense of self is so momentous that it leads to the *positive* need for demeaning forms of self-deception and illusion; which further impacts MIL and the MOL.

A specific paradox concerning free will is *Hard Determinism and Moral Worth*. Belief in hard determinism (or other forms of free will and moral responsibility denialism) has the perverse advantage of potentially making one especially morally worthy, and one's actions particularly meaningful. This is because a hard determinist, who denies desert, blameworthiness, and praiseworthiness, does not then think that his moral worth is at stake in the free will-related ways. If he nevertheless acts well in the face of temptation, the value and meaning of actions may become *greater*, because of the greater 'purity' involved, i.e. the absence of self-concerned, free will-dependent motivation. A further twist is that this value is greater if one chooses morally, believes in hard determinism, but hard determinism is at least partly false and there is, after all, some free will–related moral worth; see Smilansky (1994b); Double (2004); Smilansky (2000, sec 10.1). Here belief in hard determinism can enhance MIL/MOL.[10]

---

[10] For a similar effect outside of the free will context, see Smilansky (1997). For two paradoxical discussions in the free will context, see 'prepunishment' (e.g. New 1992; Smilansky 2007e); and my *reductio 'Funishment'* argument against hard determinism (Smilansky 2011).

Paradoxes of practical reasoning also can have bearing on MIL. Consider for example cases such as those of deaf people, where (1) it seems clear that it would have been better for everyone concerned had their hearing been corrected at birth but; (2) if it is not corrected and those people grow up deaf, then many may be glad that their hearing was not corrected, and that they have their current identity, as deaf people who share in deaf culture and find specific meaning in their deaf lives (Harman 2009; cf. Wallace 2013). This is not plausibly thought of as an example of Fortunate Misfortune, but as a consequence of the role of time and perspective on our evaluations. At the margin we can have clearly mad possibilities, whereby people are radically transformed against their autonomy and interests, even brainwashed, but then come to approve, *post factum*, of the intervention.

Finally, there is reason to think that the future will show a great increase in paradoxicality, particularly due to future technologies (see Smilansky 2007a, Postscript); and this should also have momentous impact on MIL/MOL. Just because the future is likely to be so different, and even more paradoxical, we need to practice recognizing and dealing with paradoxes, and try to prepare for the paradoxicality to come.

'Crazy Ethics' and MIL/MOL Paradoxes

The idea of 'Crazy Ethics' (CE) which I introduced in Smilansky (2013a) has intimate relations and parallels with the 'crazy', absurdity-infused implications of paradoxes concerning MIL/MOL, and hence it would be fruitful to briefly consider it. I focus on 'craziness' within normative and applied ethics, and assume that morality has a stable meta-ethical grounding (various meta-ethical views might suffice here). I use Crazy Ethics as a semi-descriptive term for moral views or descriptions of states of affairs that despite being *true* (or at least plausible) are, in another sense, crazy or absurd. Although the craziness does not present a single common denominator but comes more in the form of a 'family resemblance', the crazy features share the idea that common, important, and seemingly reasonable expectations from morality are disappointed, in significant ways, leading to a surprising, discordant and, to some extent, even irrational situation.

By now the similarity between CE and many of the implications of the paradoxes we have seen will be apparent. Of course, many MIL/MOL paradoxes were also directly about morality and its limitations (such as Moral Luck, and Morality and Moral Worth); would not realistically be implemented or seemed manifestly absurd (Beneficial Retirement and the Repugnant Conclusion, for instance); or indicated that absurdity prevailed in common attitudes to life (such as Self-Sacrificing Altruism and most of the backward-looking implications of the NIP). The prevalence of moral paradox, absurdity, and perversity often severely limit our ability to live a meaningful life. And even when matters were not inherently ethical (such as with Fortunate Misfortune, Reactive-Contributions, some of the significance of the free will problem, or the repeated meta-paradoxical temptations of lack of awareness), they showed characteristics similar to CE.[11]

Living with Paradoxes

Fear of paradox, of complexity, of dissonance, and of non-applicability; the shadow of the senseless and absurd; the threat of the harmful influence of knowledge and awareness, all seem particularly worrisome when we come to consider the meaning in and of our lives, reflect on the possibility for a life of value, and inform people's behaviour towards others. Moral and MIL/MOL paradoxes can threaten our sense that life has meaning, and rock the security of our personal, moral, and social orders. By contrast, contemporary physics seem to give us a radically counter-intuitive and indeed often radically absurd view of the natural world, but this is not perceived by hardly anyone to be threatening, and it is felt that it can be safely left to the physicists.

Many of the paradoxes have pessimistic implications. Again and again, we saw paradoxicality with which it would be very difficult if not impossible to live, which implies that life should be lived in ways that are strongly contrary to common sense. This puts in doubt matters that are crucial for a sense of MIL and MOL, that threaten our sense of coherence and integrity, or which arguably should not be widely known.

Paradoxes have significant implications for MIL/MOL. There is a 'quantitative' matter here, i.e. how many paradoxes there are and how much of life is paradoxical; and a 'qualitative' one, namely, what the paradoxes imply about meaning. We have seen that paradoxes are indeed widely prevalent, and that many of them tell us unhappy things about MIL and the MOL. Moreover, the paradoxes are relevant both for objectivists and for subjectivists on meaning. While my general view is that most people's lives have meaning, and this can be further enhanced (see Landau 2017), most paradoxes show the grim side of reality concerning MIL, and imply that life has less meaning than we have thought. Both the 'good' and the 'true' domains of meaning are affected (see Metz 2013, 227–230). The philosophical understanding of paradoxes gives ample indication of the widespread absurdity and tragedy of life. By and large, the greater the paradoxicality, the greater is the harm to MIL and the MOL. Both our capacity to live lives of value and to think that life makes sense are under threat. Sometimes there is not much that can be done with this largely depressing knowledge, be it about the free will problem and its implications, most of the backward-looking significance of the NIP, or the puzzle about the Moral Evaluation of Past Tragedies. Sometimes we can fight back against the paradoxicality and at least try to limit its influence, as with Moral Luck or Teflon Immorality. In any case, much of human life is seen to be drenched with irrationality, perversity is pervasive, and distasteful results abound.

---

[11] In the moral sphere we seem particularly prone to simplistic pictures, to formulae, and to optimism about individual and social capacities to be morally good and to create reasonably satisfactory moral orders (see e.g. Toulmin 1981; Smilansky 2007a, chapter 12; Hämäläinen 2020).

Beyond this broad result, however, there is room for complexity and nuance, and not all is negative. The idea of the 'Good absurd' of course works in the opposite direction. Morality and Moral Worth, for example, shows some positive aspects of the intimacy between the good and the absurd. Reactive-Contributions are basically positive and life-enhancing. Fortunate Misfortune is an MIL and MOL paradox that can be interpreted in a radically *optimistic* manner: it implies that, perhaps, almost any misfortune can be transformed into good fortune. And even Hard Determinism and Moral Worth may offer a unique opportunity for merit and meaning. Frequently, even when we uncover the negative, we can gain some positive value and meaning by facing up to the grim truths and not deceiving ourselves, and confronting the challenges, even in the face of temptations to avoid doing so.

Some of the paradoxes need to be thought of as philosophical puzzles. While with certain paradoxes we seem to have an adequate understanding, this does not seem to be the case concerning the Repugnant Conclusion; some of the issues of integrity raised by Williams and the supporters of Effective Altruism; Beneficial Retirement; and perhaps the Paradox of Modesty. While continuing to struggle with these conundrums, the proper response may be sceptical and agnostic.

This connects us to another meaning-related worry, about understanding. How can we explain our lives or make sense of them if they are rife with paradox? The paradoxes and the absurdity they generate no doubt challenge any simplistic rationalistic optimism about life. However, our ability to understand paradoxes, and sometimes to offer solutions to them, is in itself a positive indicator of the human ability to make some sense of life, and to gain value through our ability to discover and understand. If we are so often able to do this with the 'black holes' of paradox, this bodes well for the less troublesome areas. That what we discover is often unwelcome and indeed perverse is unfortunate, but it is knowledge and understanding nevertheless, and proves the rational abilities of humanity, and the power of philosophy. There may be non-epistemic limits here, and some corners of our universe may indeed be unfathomable; but it seems too early to form any firm conclusions.

In any case, as we saw, the struggle with paradoxicality can, in itself, add meaning to our lives. Paradoxes need to be understood, to be hopefully resolved, but if unresolved to be borne, and then often to be actively dealt with; all of these open up MIL/MOL-related opportunities. Such challenges can imbue our life with a sense of meaning in various dimensions, such as significance, value, impact, purpose, and point.

Paradoxes cause great complexity, discord, and inconsistency, typically make for disappointment, and thereby harm ideas of MIL and the MOL, such as those involving simplicity, harmony, goodness, rationality, and purity. Yet they also sometimes make or allow for meaning-enhancing variety and diversity, freedom, depth, and challenge and opportunity, which would not otherwise exist. In any case, a sophisticated, more fully aware view of human life, its absurdities and its meaning, cannot disregard the salience of paradoxes.[12]

---

[12] I am very grateful to Aaron Ben-Zeev, David Enoch, Amihud Gilead, Arnon Keren, Iddo Landau, Sam Lebens, Tal Manor, Ariel Meirav, Guy Pinku, Alma Smilansky-Teichner, Daniel Statman, and Rivka

References

Adams, Robert Merrihew. 2009. 'Love and the Problem of Evil'. In *The Positive Function of Evil*, ed. Pedro Alexis Tabensky. Houndsmills, UK: Palgrave Macmillan 1–13.

Benatar, David. 2006. *Better Never to Have Been: The Harm of Coming into Existence*. Oxford: Clarendon Press.

Ben-Zeev, Aaron. 1993. 'The Virtue of Modesty'. *American Philosophical Quarterly* 30: 235–246.

Boonin, David. 2014. *The Nonidentity Problem and the Ethics of Future People*. Oxford: Oxford University Press.

Boonin, David. 2019. *Dead Wrong: The Ethics of Posthumous Harm*. Oxford: Oxford University Press.

Camus, Albert. 2000. *The Myth of Sisyphus*, trans. Justin O'Brien. London: Penguin.

Cohen, G. A. 2000. *If You're an Egalitarian, How Come You're So Rich?* Cambridge, MA: Harvard University Press.

Dan-Cohen, Meir. 2008. 'Luck and Identity'. *Theoretical Inquiries in Law* 9: 1–22.

Double, Richard. 2004. 'The Ethical Advantages of Free Will Subjectivism'. *Philosophy and Phenomenological Research* 69: 411–422.

Driver, Julia. 2001. *Uneasy Virtue*. Cambridge: Cambridge University Press.

Flanagan, Owen. 1990. 'Virtue and Ignorance'. *Journal of Philosophy* 87: 420–428.

Gheaus, Anca, and Lisa Herzog. 2016. 'The Goods of Work (Other Than Money)'. *Journal of Social Philosophy* 47: 76–89.

Glover, Jonathan. 1986. 'It Makes No Difference Whether or Not I Do It'. In *Applied Ethics*, ed. Peter Singer. Oxford: Oxford University Press 125–144.

Hämäläinen, Nora. 2020. 'Inconsistency in Ethics'. *Philosophy* 95: 447–470.

Harman, Elizabeth. 2009. '"I'll Be Glad I Did It" Reasoning and the Significance of Future Desires'. *Philosophical Perspectives* 23: 177–199.

Heyd, David 1982. Supererogation. Cambridge: Cambridge University

Heyd, David. 1992. *Genethics: Moral Issues in the Creation of People*. Berkeley: University of California Press.

Hick, John. 1977. *Evil and the God of Love*. London: Macmillan.

Huemer, Michael. 2008. 'In Defence of Repugnance'. *Mind* 117: 899–933.

Johnson, Sean. 2015. 'Morally, We Should Prefer to Exist: A Response to Smilansky'. *Australasian Journal of Philosophy* 93: 1–5.

Kagan, Shelly. 2011. 'Do I Make a Difference?' *Philosophy and Public Affairs* 39: 105–141.

Kahane, Guy. 2019. 'History and Persons'. *Philosophy and Phenomenological Research* 99: 162–187.

Landau, Iddo. 2017. *Finding Meaning in an Imperfect World*. New York: Oxford University Press.

Landau, Iddo. 2020. 'Two Arguments for the Badness and Meaninglessness of Life'. *Journal of Value Inquiry* 54: 429–442.

Lang, Gerald. 2014. 'Jobs, Institutions And Beneficial Retirement'. *Ratio* 27: 205–221.

Lenman, James. 2007. 'Why I Have No Plans to Retire: In Defence of Moderate Professional Complacency'. *Ratio* 20: 241–246.

Levy, Neil. 2002. 'The Apology Paradox and the Non-identity Problem'. *Philosophical Quarterly* 52: 358–368.

Weinberg for helpful comments.

MacAskill, William. 2014. 'Replaceability, Career Choice and Making a Difference'. *Ethical Theory and Moral Practice* 17: 269–283.

Manheimer, Ronald J. 2008. 'The Paradox of Beneficial Retirement: A Journey into the Vortex of Nothingness'. *Journal of Aging, Humanities, and the Arts* 2: 84–98.

Metz, Thaddeus. 2009. 'Love and Emotional Reactions to Necessary Evils'. In *The Positive Function of Evil*, ed. Pedro Alexis Tabensky. Houndsmills, UK: Palgrave Macmillan 28–44.

Metz, Thaddeus. 2013. *Meaning in Life: An Analytic Study*. Oxford: Oxford University Press.

Metz, Thaddeus. 2019. *God, Soul, and the Meaning of Life*. Cambridge: Cambridge University Press.

Nagel, Thomas. 2012a. 'The Absurd'. In *Mortal Questions*. Cambridge: Cambridge University Press 11–23.

Nagel, Thomas. 2012b. 'Moral Luck'. In *Mortal Questions*. Cambridge: Cambridge University Press 24–38.

Nefsky, Julia. 2017. 'How You Can Help, without Making a Difference'. *Philosophical Studies* 174: 2743–2767.

New, Christopher. 1992. 'Time and Punishment'. *Analysis* 52: 35–40.

Parfit, Derek. 1984. *Reasons and Persons*. Oxford: Oxford University Press.

Plato. 1997. 'Apology'. In *Plato: Complete Works*, ed. John M. Cooper and D. S. Hutchinson. Indianapolis: Hackett 18–36.

Quine, W.V. 1976. *The Ways of Paradox and Other Essays*. Cambridge, Mass.: Harvard University Press.

Richards, Norvin. 1988. 'Is Humility a Virtue?' *American Philosophical Quarterly* 25: 253–259.

Ryberg, Jasper, and Torbjorn Tannsjo, eds. 2004. *The Repugnant Conclusion: Essays on Population Ethics*. Dordrecht: Kluwer Academic.

Sainsbury, R. M. 2009. *Paradoxes*, 3rd ed. Cambridge: Cambridge University Press.

Schueler, G. F. 1997. 'Why Modesty Is a Virtue'. *Ethics* 107: 467–485.

Sher, George. 1981. 'Ancient Wrongs and Modern Rights'. *Philosophy and Public Affairs* 10: 3–17.

Smilansky, Saul. 1994a. 'On Practicing What We Preach'. *American Philosophical Quarterly* 31: 73–79.

Smilansky, Saul. 1994b. 'The Ethical Advantages of Hard Determinism'. *Philosophy and Phenomenological Research* 54: 355–363.

Smilansky, Saul. 1995. 'Is There a Moral Obligation to Have Children?' *Journal of Applied Philosophy* 12: 41–53.

Smilansky, Saul. 1997. 'Moral Accountancy and Moral Worth'. *Metaphilosophy* 28: 123–134.

Smilansky, Saul. 2000. *Free Will and Illusion*. Oxford: Oxford University Press.

Smilansky, Saul. 2003a. 'Reactive-Contributions and Their Significance'. *Public Affairs Quarterly* 17: 349–357.

Smilansky, Saul. 2003b. 'Free Will and the Mystery of Modesty'. *American Philosophical Quarterly* 40: 105–117.

Smilansky, Saul. 2007a. *10 Moral Paradoxes*. Malden, MA: Blackwell.

Smilansky, Saul. 2007b. 'Fortunate Misfortune'. In S. Smilansky, *10 Moral Paradoxes*. Malden, MA: Blackwell 11–22.

Smilansky, Saul. 2007c. 'The Paradox of Beneficial Retirement'. In S. Smilansky, *10 Moral Paradoxes*. Malden, MA: Blackwell 23–32.

Smilansky, Saul. 2007d. 'Morality and Moral Worth'. In S. Smilansky, *10 Moral Paradoxes*. Malden, MA: Blackwell 77–89.

Smilansky, Saul. 2007e. 'Determinism and Prepunishment: The Radical Nature of Compatibilism'. *Analysis* 67: 347–349.
Smilansky, Saul. 2010. 'Free Will: Some Bad News'. In *Action, Ethics and Responsibility*, ed. Joseph Keim Campbell, Michael O'Rourke, and Harry S. Silverstein. Cambridge, MA: MIT Press 187–201.
Smilansky, Saul. 2011. 'Hard Determinism and Punishment: A Practical *Reductio*'. *Law and Philosophy* 30: 353–367.
Smilansky, Saul. 2012a. 'Life Is Good'. *South African Journal of Philosophy* 31: 69–78.
Smilansky, Saul. 2012b. 'On the Common Lament, That a Person Cannot Make Much Difference in This World'. *Philosophy* 87: 109–122.
Smilansky, Saul. 2013a. 'Free Will as a Case of "Crazy Ethics"'. In *Exploring the Illusion of Free Will and Moral Responsibility*, ed. Gregg Caruso. Lanham, MD: Lexington Books 103–119.
Smilansky, Saul. 2013b. 'Morally, Should We Prefer Never to Have Existed?' *Australasian Journal of Philosophy* 91: 655–666.
Smilansky, Saul. 2013c. 'Why Moral Paradoxes Matter: 'Teflon Immorality' and the Perversity of Life'. *Philosophical Studies*, 165: 229–243.
Smilansky, Saul. 2013d. 'A Difficulty Concerning Compensation'. *Journal of Moral Philosophy* 10: 329–337.
Smilansky, Saul 2016. 'Gratitude: The Dark Side'. In *Perspectives on Gratitude*, ed. David Carr. New York: Routledge 126–138.
Smilansky, Saul. 2018. 'Punishing the Dead'. *Journal of Value Inquiry* 52: 169–177.
Smilansky, Saul. 2019a. 'The Good, the Bad, and the Nonidentity Problem: Reflections on Jewish History'. In *Jewish Philosophy in an Analytic Age*, ed. Sam Lebens, Dani Rabinowitz and Aaron Segal. Oxford: Oxford University Press 307–324.
Smilansky, Saul. 2019b. 'A Hostage Situation'. *Journal of Philosophy* 116: 447–466.
Smilansky, Saul. 2020a. 'The Moral Evaluation of Past Tragedies: A New Puzzle'. *Journal of Moral Philosophy*, 17: 188–201.
Smilansky, Saul. 2020b. 'We Are All in This Life Together'. *Iyyun* 68: 85–93.
Smilansky, Saul. 2020c. 'Should We Sacrifice the Utilitarians First?' *Philosophical Quarterly* 70: 850–867.
Smilansky, Saul. 2021a. 'The Idea of Moral Duties to History'. *Philosophy* 96: 155–179.
Smilansky, Saul. 2021b. 'A Puzzle about Self-Sacrificing Altruism'. *Journal of Controversial Ideas* 1, doi:10.35995/jci01010007.
Smilansky, Saul. 2021c. 'Contribution, Replaceability and the Meaning of Our Lives'. *Theoria*, 87: 1481–1496.
Smilansky, Saul. 2022. 'Illusionism'. In *The Oxford Handbook of Moral Responsibility*, ed. Derk Pereboom and Dana Nelkin. New York: Oxford University Press, forthcoming.
Smilansky, Saul. Forthcoming. 'Normative Pluralism and Autonomous Vehicles'. In *AV Ethics: Beyond the Trolley Problem*, ed. Ryan Jenkins, Tomáš Hříbek and David Černý. New York: Oxford University Press.
Sneddon, Andrew. 2012. 'Recipes for Moral Paradox'. *American Philosophical Quarterly* 49: 43–54.
Statman, Daniel. 1992. 'Modesty, Pride and Realistic Self-Assessment'. *Philosophical Quarterly* 42: 420–438.
Statman, Daniel. 1993. *Moral Luck*. Albany: State University of New York Press.
Thompson, Janna. 2000. 'The Apology Paradox'. *Philosophical Quarterly* 50: 470–475.
Toulmin, Stephen. 1981. 'The Tyranny of Principles'. *Hastings Center Report* 11: 31–39.

Velleman, J. David. 2005. 'The Self as Narrator'. In *Autonomy and the Challenges to Liberalism*, ed. John Christman and Joel Anderson. Cambridge: Cambridge University Press 56–76.

Wallace, R. J. 2013. *The View from Here*. Oxford: Oxford University Press.

Weinberg, Rivka. 2016. *The Risk of a Lifetime*. Oxford: Oxford University Press.

Williams, Bernard. 1981. 'Moral Luck'. in B. Williams, *Moral Luck*. Cambridge: Cambridge University Press 20–39.

Williams, Bernard. 1985. *Ethics and the Limits of Philosophy*. London: Fontana.

Williams, Bernard, and J. J. C. Smart. 1973. *Utilitarianism: For and Against*. Cambridge: Cambridge University Press.

Wolf, Susan. 2010. *Meaning in Life and Why It Matters*. Princeton, NJ: Princeton University Press.

CHAPTER 31

EDUCATION AND MEANING IN LIFE

DORET DE RUYTER AND ANDERS SCHINKEL

Introduction

HUMAN beings have the unique ability to give meaning to their lives. This is both a blessing and a curse, for it provides us with the opportunity to make something of our lives that is not predetermined by our nature, but it also gives us a (sensed) responsibility to do that well. This felt responsibility is, however, not alien or imposed. As stated by Viktor Frankl ([1946] 1985), we have a need to have meaning in life; without meaning, we will not be able to live a fully human life. We were therefore surprised to read that the inhabitants of the Netherlands are the most likely to say that their life has no meaning (Froese 2016, 62).[1] Paul Froese attributes this outcome to characteristics of our country that actually seem to be quite beneficial to people: 'The Netherlands is a highly modern and pluralistic country. It has a long history of liberalism and openness to new ideas, and it is currently one of the ten richest countries in the world. Secular, check. Wealthy, check. Open to newness, check. Seems like a perfect hot house for meaninglessness' (Froese 2016, 62). We return to Froese's counter-intuitive depiction of our country in our discussion on upbringing in families and education in schools, although he does note a few pages later that specific groups indicated in the Gallup World Poll that they don't believe their life has an important purpose or meaning, namely elderly and poorer

---

[1] We were surprised because we do not have the impression that the Dutch are not living a fully human life. Furthermore, Dutch children are the happiest in the world (Adamson 2013), their (self-reported) well-being has remained the highest for several decades (Unicef 2020) and almost 90 percent of Dutch adults are satisfied with their lives (see https://www.cbs.nl/nl-nl/nieuws/2019/13/90-procent-tevreden-10-procent-sombert). Finally, it is plausible to assume that having meaning in life is necessary for being satisfied with one's life or experiencing feelings of happiness. So, if the Dutch are that happy, we also presume they have meaning in life.

Dutch citizens, and suggests that they have special reasons for this evaluation, like relative deprivation (2016, 65).

We begin with a concise clarification of the meaning of 'meaning in life', as we understand it, which leads to an exploration of the ways in which education and the relationships between adults and children/youth can contribute to having meaning in life. The relation between education and meaning in life can be understood both as a constitutive and a contributive relation. In the first case, it is defended that whatever makes life meaningful also gives education its (ultimate) point (e.g. Allen 1991, 50; Puolimatka and Airaksinen 2001, 318). We adhere to the second view, namely that education plays an important role in (developing) meaning in life, but that meaning in life is not the final end or justification of education. It is among the various aims of education, which also include the acquisition of knowledge and skills and the socialization of the younger generation. The ultimate or final aim of education is, in our view, the dual, interrelated aim of the flourishing of human beings and the world.

THE MEANING OF MEANING IN LIFE

Meaning in life is investigated in both psychology and philosophy and there is much overlap in their understandings of the concept, although in both there is also diversity on (a) what 'meaning in life' means precisely or what constitutes meaning in life; (b) what can be regarded as (proper) sources of meaning in life; and (c) whether meaning in life is subjective, i.e. dependent on and defined by a person herself or if there are (also) objective criteria for meaning in life and what those could be. We briefly address these three points in this section. We will do so in terms of meaning in life, though without thereby implying a categorical difference with what is commonly termed *the* meaning *of* life (e.g. Schinkel 2015). That is to say, 'meaning in life' here stands for the whole range of possible meaning, from the experienced everyday meaningfulness of our activities, relationships, and so on, to possible answers to ultimate questions concerning (our) existence. That said, 'meaning in life' as we understand it here, does imply a focus on the meaning *in persons' lives*, rather than an abstract meaning of life as a metaphysical principle in itself.

What Constitutes Meaning in Life

In previous work (Schinkel, De Ruyter, and Aviram 2016), we distinguished two dimensions of meaning in life, namely a descriptive cognitive and a valuative cognitive-emotional dimension. The first we can concisely describe as the idea that people have meaning in life when their own life, as well as the environment in which they live, makes sense to them—their life has a certain coherence and they understand the world around them to the level that they can meaningfully interact with others and the cultural and natural world. With the psychologists Frank Martela and Michael Stegler (2016) and Login George and Crystal Park (2016), we agree that it is helpful to divide the valuative dimension into two distinct aspects, namely purpose and significance or mattering.

Purpose primarily looks to the future. People can be said to have meaning in life when they have and are able to pursue aims that are meaningful to them, aims that provide them with a reason to live their life (in a certain way). Purpose has been interpreted more strictly by various authors (e.g. Damon 2009; Moran 2018), suggesting that aims need not only be meaningful to the person herself but also lead to action that intends to have a positive impact beyond the person.

Significance or mattering primarily looks to the past and the present. People experience meaning in life when they believe their existence makes a difference—that they and what they do has some import and that this is recognized by others. Thus, significance or mattering comprises two sub-aspects: first, that one is engaged in activities or relationships that one believes to be worthwhile, and, second, that one is recognized by others—one's existence matters to others. Mattering draws our attention to an issue that is relevant to the topic of this chapter: while significance is primarily a construction of the person herself, although influenced by the values and circumstances of one's environment, that one matters is primarily attributed by other persons, although the person must pick up these signals and interpret them correctly. This shows that meaning in life is an inherently relational concept: one finds meaning in life by contributing something of value to the lives of others or the state of the world and by receiving the response of the other.

Sources of Meaning in Life

People find or construct meaning in life through various sources. These sources can be described in terms of the spheres of life that provide people with opportunity for finding meaning: relationships with, for instance, family, friends, community members, or the natural world and activities like volunteering, activism, education, art, and play. Also the self—who one is and could become—can be a source of meaning in life, e.g. discovering one's true self and actualizing one's potentialities, as humanist psychologists like Maslow or Rogers suggest (see Baumeister 1991, 77–115; Froese 2016, 68–98). Baumeister (1991) distinguishes four needs for meaning in life: purpose, values, efficacy, and self-worth. These needs can also be regarded as sources that provide meaning in life. Finally, some authors interpret the previously described dimensions or aspects of meaning in life as sources of meaning, e.g. that purpose in life contributes to meaning in life.

The way in which sources contribute to a person's meaning in life not only depends on a person's characteristics and abilities and on the possibilities of the environment but is also influenced by a meaning framework, 'a complex web of propositions that we hold about how things are in the world and how things will be' (George and Park 2016, 206), which consists of a person's beliefs, worldview, and expectations (see also De Ruyter 2002, 36, 37). This meaning framework, which could also be regarded as a source of meaning in life by itself, as Baumeister and Froese suggest, gives direction to all three aspects of meaning in life (George and Park 2016, 207, 208).

Is Meaning in Life Subjective?

We underwrite the hybrid view of meaning in life, i.e., that meaning in life is not a completely subjective evaluation, but that there are (also) objective criteria that need to be fulfilled for a person to be justified in saying that one's life has meaning. This is relevant for a description of the qualities of education that are conducive to finding meaning in life, for in the case of subjective interpretation, educators would (aim to) be value neutral in their approach or value that children discover their own 'authentic' meaning in life, while if one believes there are objective criteria, educators would want and have to attempt to make sure that children adopt particular values, as these would be necessary for leading a meaningful life.

Our interpretation of meaning in life is similar to that of Susan Wolf, who suggests that meaning in life 'arises from loving objects worthy of love and engaging with them in a positive way' (Wolf 2010, 8), involving 'subjective and objective elements, suitably and inextricably linked' (Wolf 2010, 9). In her other, more often quoted, words, meaning arises 'when subjective attraction meets objective attractiveness' (e.g., Wolf 2010, xii). We agree with Wolf that it is notoriously difficult to define what is objectively valuable, and follow her proposal that it be interpreted 'simply' as non-subjective: value needs to be found outside oneself—it lies in the object of one's action (which can also be a person).

Thus, we suggest that meaning is not merely dependent on an individual's taste or feelings; relationships and activities need also be good for others or at a minimum not harmful to others or the (social and natural) environment. This does not mean that people may not or should not spend time on activities that do not have this outside-the-self quality, like playing solitary games or unwinding on the couch, but that these are not their only activities or primary sources of their meaning in life. Nor does it imply that their activities and relationships should not be pleasurable to them, but it does mean that they are not only focused on their own well-being. This idea resonates with William Damon's definition of purpose, namely that 'purpose is a stable and generalized intention to accomplish something that is at the same time meaningful to the self and consequential for the world beyond the self' (Damon 2009, 33).

With this groundwork about the meaning of life's meaning in place, we can begin with our explication of the relation between education and meaning in life. We will do so for two spheres in which children are educated, namely the family and the school.

Meaning, Upbringing, and Family Life

Family life is a profound source of children's meaning in life, and both the children's relationships within the family and their upbringing influence all aspects of their future meaning in life.

First, parents are the first and most often the primary adults who contribute to children's sense of who they are and who introduce them into the world. For instance, from the remarks of their parents, children learn that they are (regarded as being) friendly, smart, or conscientious, or sluggish or impatient. Children also pick up from their parents ideas about their abilities and the possibilities their parents believe they will have in life: parents tend to have ideas and ideals with regard to the (level of) education that children should receive, the type of work that they hope their children will get, their involvement in communities and society, and, last but not least, the types of relationships they will be able to form and maintain. On the basis of implicitly and explicitly given guidance and (emotional) responses, children begin to make sense of themselves, what their life could be, and what the world looks like and could look like. This guidance is not value-neutral. Parents' meaning framework(s) influence their interaction with their children and their upbringing. A powerful example can be found in Tara Westover's memoir *Educated* (2018), which describes her upbringing in a Mormon family closed from the wider world.

Second, as Westover's book also starkly illustrates, parents normally want to pass on their meaning framework to their children. With this meaning framework, children (begin to) develop their ideas about their purpose in life, as well as which types of relationships and activities are significant. With the rise of liberal philosophy of education that defends autonomy as an aim of education, discussions about parents' entitlement to bring up their children to endorse their conception of the good life also emerged. For instance, in the 1980s there was a lively debate in the *Journal of Philosophy of Education* among Terence McLaughlin (1984, 1985, 1990), David Bridges (1984), Eamonn Callan (1985), and Peter Gardner (1988), and in the 2010s we find a similar discussion between, among others, Harry Brighouse and Adam Swift (2014) and Matthew Clayton (2015). The central question is if upbringing within a conception of the good life necessarily infringes upon the child's right to an open future (Feinberg 1980), which in the context of this chapter can be interpreted as the ability and freedom to choose a meaning framework that the child believes should inform her meaning in life.

We suggest that parents as adults should have the freedom to live their lives in a way that is meaningful to them, influenced by the values they hold dear. In practice, this will influence family life as well: the family will have certain customs related to their worldview, attend community gatherings, and friends of the family will tend to have similar convictions (e.g. McLaughlin 1984). This not only gives parents the opportunity to live a meaningful life as they see it, but also offers children the opportunity to acquire a conception of the good with which they can begin to construct their own meaning framework (but see Callan 1985 and Clayton 2015 for an opposite position). However, in line with McLaughlin (1984, 1985, 1990) and Brighouse and Swift (2014, 2016; see also Schinkel, De Ruyter, and Aviram 2016), we do want to argue that there is a boundary to this freedom of parents, which is the freedom of children to develop their own conception of the good. After all, parents' particular conception of the good can be a significant source for themselves, but it does not have to be so for their children. Children may come to value another, even conflicting, conception of the good. It is possible that both meaning frameworks meet the criterion of objective worth, while still being incompatible, for instance a religious and an atheistic conception of the good life, or two different deeply held religious ones. Diminishing children's freedom could seriously hamper children's possibility to find meaning in life.

That parents raise their children with a particular conception of the good that guides the children in their quest for meaning in life may actually have become more important in recent years than was the case in the 1980s. Liberalism has triumphed in Western countries, which has provided more (experienced) freedom and openness and has supported increasing pluralism, to which Froese (2016) points. However, freedom and a plurality of options may also come with a loss. Without guidance and an inspiring sense of the good and sense of purpose, available options for life's purpose can be overwhelming and could contribute to depression and anxiety. If so, then the discussion should indeed not be about *whether* parents may raise their children with a conception of the good life, but *how* they should do this. A perspective that supplements our position is offered by Hartmut Rosa's resonance theory. That children need to discover their meaning in life themselves is one of the conditions of modern life that Rosa believes to be problematic: 'the answer to "what kind of life should I strive for?" has become very elusive, shrouded in uncertainty' (Rosa 2017, 41). To this he adds that modern society does give advice, be it unhelpful, namely to acquire the resources to be able to lead a good (or meaningful) life. Thus, people are currently busy with collecting resources—making resources available, accessible, and attainable (what he calls the Triple A Approach)—rather than living a meaningful life by having meaningful relationships and activities. The simple example he gives is that people take thousands of pictures with their phones but don't have the time to reconnect with the experience they had. Against this Triple A Approach, Rosa suggests that we should stand in a resonant relationship to the world and other human beings. Resonance has four elements: (a) the experience of being truly touched: af←fection; (b) the experience of responsive self-efficacy: e→motion; (c) a transformative quality; and (d) an elusiveness—it cannot be controlled in the sense that it cannot be brought about at will (Rosa 2017, 47, 48). While parents are often the adults who promote the Triple A Approach, they are (also) particularly well placed to foster the development of resonance. Although resonance cannot be controlled or forced to appear in everyday family life parents can provide ample opportunities (time, space, and place) to experience resonance in relationships with others and the world. We have to be realistic, though. Neoliberalism has seeped into the fibres of contemporary life, and counteracting it takes more than a few parents. Furthermore, those parents who wish to foster resonant relationships might also become anxious that they actually diminish their children's future quality of life if they did not prepare them for the rat race, thereby experiencing conflict regarding their duties.

Third, empirical research shows that families are an important source of meaning in life (e.g. Lambert et al. 2010, 2013). Lambert et al. (2013), for instance, argue that a person's sense of belonging, which denotes both having positive relationships and the feeling that one is fully accepted (which goes beyond simply having social relationships), is particularly satisfied in families. An explanation for this could be the unique way in which family relationships satisfy the needs for belonging of its members (Lambert et al. 2010, 374, 375). The value of family life for children's (developing) sense of purpose and significance as well as the profoundness of their primary caregivers' recognition are hard to miss; many children whose parents are engrossed in their own lives, for instance because of an addiction, come to believe that they do not matter. The relationship with their children and raising them are also special sources of meaning for most adults, though not all adults want to start a family.

The importance and unique contribution of the family for meaning in life of both children and parents provides powerful reasons to respect the autonomy of families. The so-called dual interest position, as defended in philosophy of education and political philosophy (e.g., Brighouse and Swift 2014, 2016; Clayton 2006; Sypnowich 2018), stresses that the interests of both children and parents should be taken into account in reflecting on the relative autonomy of families, because both have interests in upbringing as a significant activity and in their unique relationship. Focusing on children's interests only could easily become too demanding on parents, or a reason to claim that children should be raised by the best carers, which affects the source of meaning in life of parents. On the other hand, children should not be seen as their parents' property with which they can do whatever they want, as this affects children's meaning in life, as we described under the second point in this section. We agree with the dual interest position but do want to stress that autonomy is relative, because parents can seriously harm children, which justifies intervention by outsiders. But as importantly, autonomy should not be interpreted as complete self-sufficiency. All families need support from outsiders, and this is particularly true for disadvantaged families. If families make the significant contribution to children's meaning in life as is suggested, then children should have parents who are not overwhelmed by financial worries or who have to have two jobs to be able to make a decent income, but who have time and energy for engaging with their children (see also Brighouse and Swift 2016), which contributes to parents' meaning in life as well.

Thus, we argue that families and parental upbringing have a profound influence on children's experienced meaning in life and their developing ideas about themselves and the world as well as their purpose in life, which are influenced by the meaning framework of their parents. However, when children mature, other social relationships gain import as well. The school is a particularly important environment where children and youth can increase their understanding of the world, develop a purpose in life, and explore which relationships and activities are significant to them. Schools are also places that can build up or confirm, but also deny or diminish, children's experience that they matter. We therefore now turn to schools and explore how the education of teachers and school life (should) impact children's meaning in life.

Meaning, Education, and Life in Schools

Children between the ages of four and eighteen spend a considerable portion of their lives in schools. These formal educational institutions are designated places for children to get to know the world in some of its many aspects. They are also supposed to be places where children become equipped for life—not least of all a working life—in adult society, for citizenship, and for political participation. Finally, schools are often charged with a role in helping children develop their identity and become responsible, self-governing adults; as citizens, they are supposed to become critical thinkers, not uncritical conformists. One may well wonder how realistic these expectations are. Schools can be critiqued for 'failures' of many kinds. Much that is learned in school turns out to have little relevance beyond the test and is soon forgotten. Preparation for the labour market tends to dominate over concerns for broader kinds of meaningfulness. Even apart from such considerations, it is easy to overestimate the influence of schools relative to families, peers, and the wider society (existing social relations as well as cultural influences). Finally, we must keep in mind the reality of the classroom, which much of the time is not an ideally hospitable climate for meaningful teaching and learning, for instance because of a lack of order, a lack of attention on the part of students, a lack of motivation to teach or learn, difficulties in bringing controversial issues to the table, and so on.

That said, if compulsory education can in principle be justified in spite of the preceding points (and we will here assume that it can), it seems that its justification must include reference, at some level, to what makes life meaningful. As education makes up a significant portion of people's lives, *and* is supposed to make people better equipped for life, education that would be oblivious to what makes life meaningful or would even detract from its meaningfulness would be deeply problematic.

So it should at least be an aim of education to contribute to the meaning in people's lives. Given the hybrid view of meaning we accept, it can in theory do so by contributing to the objective meaningfulness of children's lives (now or in their future) and by contributing to the subjective meaningfulness of their lives; but for any such contribution to be complete, the objective and the subjective would (at some point) have to meet (Wolf 2010). This meeting does not have to occur immediately. Apparently 'useless' stuff learned long ago can sometimes turn out to be—or can become—meaningful after all. But education's contribution to meaning in life is not limited to such chance events and should be built into what education is or aims at and how it is organized.

Thus, we do think it is worth reflecting on the possible role of schools in contributing to the meaning in people's lives, and in doing so we start from two premises: (a) any meaning or lack of meaning children (will) experience in their (future) lives stems from their particular lives and life situations; and therefore (b) education that aims to contribute to meaning in life will have to take account of this.

First of all, since education is by its very nature concerned with increasing children's knowledge and understanding of the world, it can hardly fail to have an impact on the first dimension of meaning we distinguished: the cognitive dimension, the dimension of understanding or sense-making. There are reasons to be sceptical about (the nature of) schooling's actual impact; Reber (2019, 453), for instance, refers to the criticism that the curriculum is too fragmented to provide coherence. But these are reasons to criticize a particular form of education, rather than the very real possibility of education having an impact. At any rate, insofar as the curriculum helps children to understand their world in greater breadth and depth, it will also help them orient themselves in it and give them a measure of control over their environment (if not always actual control, then still intellectual control [understanding]). A growth in understanding of one's world will in principle help diminish meaning deficits that arise from an inability to make sense of one's world and/or oneself in relation to that world. For example, education can transform aimless anxiety caused by randomly picked up scraps of information about global warming and environmental crises into a more coherent and calmer perception of the situation (dire as it is). That said, nothing is ever simple, and this example may also serve to demonstrate this: to be better informed about our ecological situation may also mean to be *more* likely to panic, to feel *less* control, and to experience the world as in many ways *beyond* sense. The implication is not that it is better to keep children less informed (though naturally we need to consider carefully what to introduce to children and when) but rather that the dimension of understanding or sense-making should not be divorced from the valuative dimension(s) of purpose and significance.

Before we turn to those, however, it is important to look at the notion of 'understanding the world' or 'being able to make sense of the world' a bit closer. For the difference between 'the world', on the one hand, and 'one's world' or 'your world', on the other, is quite important here. The more schooling entails that children are being taught about the world in ways that do not connect to *their* world, the less children will be able to make sense of their school experience in general. There is thus a close connection between meaningfulness of the curriculum to the children and experienced meaning in life. The climate strikes initiated by Greta Thunberg are a case in point; for some children, climate change is, understandably, a source of existential concern (Thunberg 2019). What is the point of being in school if you may not have a future? What is the point of it, in particular, if what you're asked to learn in school has little relevance to the ecological problems that threaten this future and their causes? Connecting the curriculum to children's own (life)worlds does not necessarily mean, however, that a substantive connection is made with something that already interests them deeply; it may be enough if children trust that what they are learning (or, more broadly, their school experience as a whole) will have future relevance, even if they do not perceive it now.

If even that is absent, all is still not lost, for it may be that what is taught is 'objectively' meaningful and that the children will, at some point in their lives, discover this—but in that case, this cannot redeem the school experience as one lacking in meaning (see Reber 2019, 448, 450). Judgements about education's contribution to the sense-making dimension of meaning in life will therefore always be complex. In between the extremes of utter meaninglessness and the ideal harmony of subjective and objective meaning, now and in the future, lies the whole of education in the real world.

As said, the descriptive cognitive dimension of understanding or sense-making cannot be seen as entirely separate from the valuative cognitive-emotional dimension with its aspects of purpose and significance or mattering. The school strikes for climate change clearly show how understanding and a sense of purpose can go together—though in Thunberg's case, the understanding and the awareness of the ecological crisis were gained not in school but through self-education. By drawing students' attention to societal problems or things of beauty and value that require protection, and by developing their understanding of these issues, schooling can also help children discover a purpose and develop a sense of purpose. In this case, the meaning of education is connected with meaning in life or the meaning of life—why they are in school makes sense in light of why they are there at all (Damon 2009, 173). Education and a sense of purpose can thus mutually support each other, since a sense of purpose, combined with awareness of the person one needs to become in order to be able to fulfil that purpose (including what knowledge, understanding, and skills one needs to develop, or even what qualifications it requires), can be strong motivators of learning in school (Moran 2018, 149). We will return to education's possible contribution to children' purpose and significance or mattering, but here we briefly wish to mention one other perspective that shows understanding and the valuative dimensions of meaning to be closely connected. From the perspective of Hannah Arendt's (educational) philosophy, teaching should both stem from and foster *amor mundi*, a love for the world that inspires (taking) responsibility for the world. 'World' here means the human and, in particular, the public, political world, the order we have created together, which must be continually maintained and renewed—which means people will have to take up the responsibility to do so. In Arendt's educational philosophy, teachers' authority depends on their taking responsibility for the world (even if it is not as they would like it to be); children's ability to take responsibility for the world and, in turn, to renew it depends on having acquired an understanding of that common world as it is, as well as 'love' for that world in the sense of a commitment to saving it, making it better, as opposed to an inclination to turn away from it in disappointment or despair. Importantly, for Arendt, the world is *plural*, because people are different and their perspectives on the good life and the good society differ. Therefore, love of the world must include recognition of plurality, rather than an effort to get rid of difference in pursuit of unity. In other words, education for meaning in life requires that we strive to help children accept that in the real world, meaning will always be plural; moreover, recognition of this plurality is at the same time a way of confronting the complexity of the world (Arendt 1958, 2006; and, for instance, Gordon 2001; Vlieghe and Zamojski 2019; Zuurmond 2016).

Following on from the previous point, in school children can and often do become acquainted with different worldviews, religions, and visions of the good life. Thus, a third way in which schooling, through its main purpose, can contribute to meaning in life is by offering children a means to orient themselves explicitly with regard to this very issue of meaning in life. This is often phrased in terms of enabling children to choose for themselves between worldviews and conceptions of the good life, or to make autonomous decisions about what they believe (e.g. Gardner 1988; Brighouse 2006; see Warnick 2012 for more examples), but this is much too simplistic—it caricaturizes the way in which people come to adhere to a (religious) worldview, or conception of the good life. It is closer to the truth to say that acquainting children with worldviews may help to create conditions for a (more) reflective way for them to relate to their own beliefs and convictions. It may irritate, stir something in the mind, by creating or heightening awareness of the contingency of beliefs that were until then perhaps seen as self-evident. Yet, in practice, the presentation of other worldviews often remains abstract, meaning they are in a poor position to compete with—i.e. become plausible alternatives for—children's homegrown worldviews. Moreover, they can come across as exotic, as curiosities rather than live options for making sense of the world and one's place in it. Serious worldview education needs to overcome these challenges; and at the same time it should take care not to be too successful at this too early, since children have an interest in developing a stable initial identity first, before they are confronted with a plurality of options that would otherwise be bewildering and result in 'identity diffusion' (Ackerman 1980; McLaughlin 1984; MacMullen 2007; Schinkel, De Ruyter and Steutel 2010, 283) and/or relativism (and possibly nihilism). An example of religious education pedagogy that aims to prevent exoticism and relativism was proposed by John Hull (1996). In the 'gift approach' or 'gift to the child approach', a *numen*—a religious item that 'occupies a more or less distinct position within the life and faith of the religion', 'is charged with numinous power, or with the sense of the sacred or with the power of devotion', and 'has gifts to offer children' (Hull 1996, 174-175)—is presented to (young) children in a careful way. The lesson goes through stages of engagement, exploration, contextualization, and reflection. Children are gradually familiarized with the item, which becomes revealed to them as an item of worship (for some), but first and foremost remains an educational object: 'The child has a spiritual right to come close to religion but also a spiritual right not to come too close' (Hull 1996, 178). In the contextualization stage, the numen—for instance, a figure of Ganesha—is treated as holy by all, 'but only a child who belongs to Ganesha may approach him' (Hull 1996, 177). What this example of a religious pedagogy suggests is not that a religious education that enables children to 'choose' for themselves what (not) to believe is possible after all, but rather that religious education can contribute to children's education and spiritual development exactly when it does *not* present religions as options that are on a par with each other for each individual child.

Part of this more or less direct engagement with questions of meaning should also be that schools—and in particular teachers—respond sensitively to children's sense-making and other meaning questions (e.g. around the death of a grandparent or a news story about a school shooting), that they anticipate such (future) questions, and that they expand the range of possible meaning questions and experiences, for example through art education (and aesthetic learning more generally; see Reber 2019, 456) and engagement with nature. Nature education, or outdoor education, offers great possibilities to foster wonder and awe—modes of experience that generally speaking tend to heighten children's sense of meaning, provide experiences of resonance (Rosa 2017), or at any rate promote their engagement with questions of meaning (Schinkel 2017, 2018; Washington 2018; Kristjánsson 2020).

As said, schools can also contribute to children's (current and future) sense of purpose. A very concrete way in which schools may (attempt) to do this is through service-learning. Moran (2018, 149) suggests that service-learning 'is the most likely educational experience to make salient all four dimensions of purpose because, by definition, it is engagement in actions expected to positively impact others and the common good'.[2] Again, we must be aware of possible divergences between theory and practice. Community service can also come to serve perverse purposes: it can become an instrument of résumé-building and popularity competitions, can become 'evidence' of one's own righteousness or moral superiority, and can become problematic even by becoming primarily a way to enhance one's *own* meaning in life. Some of these risks come along with particular (theoretical) models of service-learning, which may also suffer from more fundamental issues. The philanthropic model, for instance, is vulnerable to critique for ignoring issues of social justice and power inequalities (Marullo, Moayedi, and Cooke 2009; Speck and Hoppe 2004): rather than highlighting that poverty and deprivation are injustices to be addressed on a collective level, a philanthropic model in which the rich and fortunate bestow benefits on the less well-off risks reaffirming inequalities in wealth and power and creating dependencies of the less fortunate on the goodwill of the advantaged.

It is worth noting the interconnections between purpose and significance or mattering. Contributing to the common good or to the lives of others through caring, community projects, or research—and finding a purpose in this—can also be a way of coming to experience that you matter, because you make a difference. But teachers and the curriculum can also contribute to the third dimension of meaning in life more directly. The two most obvious ways in which schools can and should do so are by communicating to individual students that they matter and by communicating to socially recognized or distinguished groups that they matter (ethnic minorities, cultural minorities, different genders, and so on). A teacher who not only knows your name but actually sees you and responds to you with pedagogical tact (Van Manen 2016) recognizes your existence and your worth, and this contributes to your subjective sense of meaning in life. A textbook of US history that does not acknowledge the role of slavery in the origins of the American Civil War—and in the development of the United

---

[2] The four dimensions are: personal meaningfulness, future intention, active engagement, and beyond-the-self-impact (see also Damon 2009).

States as such—commits not just a historical error, but also a failure of recognition toward African Americans.

The organization and ethos of the school can contribute to individual and group recognition, and thus to the dimension of significance, in similar ways—in short, by giving or withholding from individuals or groups a voice—but also through the message they communicate about what matters in life, for example the pursuit of knowledge and understanding, but also equality, caring, and mutual respect. This is just one example of a message communicated implicitly and explicitly through the ethos of the school, i.e. through the values embodied in its ceremonies, procedures, rules and regulations, mission statement, and so on. It is impossible to quantify the effect of such messages on children's (future) outlook on life and where they seek and find meaning. It stands to reason that a small-scale community school based on ecological principles that attaches significance, ultimately, to educational outcomes such as caring for the community and for nature will have a different influence on its pupils than a large-scale urban school whose primary focus is academic achievement and winning in competition with other schools. It also stands to reason that their influence will differ from one pupil to another, depending on their temperament and character, family background, and other circumstances. However great or small the effect may be, it is important for schools (and school leaders and teachers) to be aware of what their effect *would* be, if indeed it lingered, and particularly to reflect on what they actually do in schools, which may well detract from, rather than contribute to, children's meaning in life.

It should be clear, then, that whether, and the extent to which, children's educational experiences contribute to the meaning they experience in their lives depends on various factors; but teachers play an important role in many of them. The meaning that education contributes to children's lives is to a considerable extent up to the teachers. This is, at the same time, one of the main reasons why education can also contribute to teachers' meaning in life. Teaching can be considered a meaningful profession, in the sense that it offers the opportunity to contribute positively to the lives of children as well as, indirectly, to benefit society (Damon 2009; Fourie and Deacon 2015). A passion for a particular subject and a sense of wonder about the world are other reasons why teaching is meaningful to many in the profession. The degree to which teachers can actually experience their work as meaningful does in part depend on circumstances; in particular, it depends on the extent to which the conditions in which they have to work allow them to actually teach and to do so in a meaningful way (Tomic and Tomic 2008; Johnson and Down 2013; Ainsworth and Oldfield 2019).

Conclusion

In this chapter, we have described the possible positive and unique contributions of family life and parental upbringing, as well as of students' participation in schools and teachers' education, to children's (future) meaning in life. We have also mentioned at several points that we need to be realistic in our expectations. It is all too easy to write a coherent theoretical explication and normative proposal, while losing sight of the real world. Meaning in life is a complex matter, influenced by various sources.

Families and schools can and normally do contribute to children's (ability to find) meaning in life as children and adults, but there are many other sources and enablers of meaning, as well as possible detractors. Life circumstances and conditions, such as one's actual opportunities to realize goods like meaningful work and fulfilling relationships, and inequalities in the distribution of such opportunities, bear significantly on the valuative dimensions of meaning. Social media, access to (fake) news, dominant cultural narratives, and discrepancies between the latter and one's personal experience and opportunities in life are examples of factors that impact the cognitive as well as the valuative dimensions of meaning. However, precisely given the unique position of parents and teachers, we do believe that they have to take responsibility, preferably in a collaborative relationship, to (a) open the complex world in a way that helps children to find their way; (b) present a meaning framework that provides a standpoint from which to evaluate what is significant, while also giving sufficient freedom to engage with other values, ideals, and beliefs that may inform children's own meaning framework; and (c) develop relationships with children or students that foster their feelings that they matter, while at the same time instilling a desire and sense of responsibility to matter to others. Although these are big words, small gestures can have a profound impact, and individual recognition does not require complex methods or magical qualities.

References

Ackerman, Bruce A. 1980. *Social Justice in the Liberal State*. New Haven, CT: Yale University Press.

Adamson, Peter. 2013. *Child Well-Being in Rich Countries: A Comparative Overview*. Innocenti Report Card 11. Florence: UNICEF Office of Research.

Ainsworth, Steph, and Jeremy Oldfield. 2019. 'Quantifying Teacher Resilience: Context Matters'. *Teaching and Teacher Education* 82: 117–128.

Allen, R. T. 1991. 'The Meaning of Life and Education'. *Journal of Philosophy of Education* 25(1): 47–57.

Arendt, Hannah. 1958. *The Human Condition*. Chicago: University of Chicago Press.

Arendt, Hannah. 2006. 'The Crisis in Education'. In H. Arendt, *Between Past and Future*, 170–193. New York: Penguin Books.

Baumeister, Roy F. 1991. *Meanings of Life*. New York: Guilford Press.

Bridges, David. 1984. 'Non-Paternalistic Arguments in Support of Parents' Rights'. *Philosophy of Education* 18(1): 55–61.

Brighouse, Harry. 2006. *On Education*. London: Routledge.

Brighouse, Harry, and Adam Swift. 2014. *Family Values: The Ethics of Parent-Child Relationships*. Princeton, NJ: Princeton University Press.

Brighouse, Harry, and Adam Swift. 2016. 'The Goods of Parenting'. In *Family-Making: Contemporary Ethical Challenges*, ed. Françoise Baylis and Carolyn MacLeod, 11–28. Oxford: Oxford University Press.

Callan, Eamonn. 1985. 'McLaughlin on Parental Rights'. *Journal of Philosophy of Education* 19(1): 111–118.

Clayton, Matthew. 2006. *Justice and Legitimacy in Upbringing*. Oxford: Oxford University Press.

Clayton, Matthew. 2015. 'Anti-Perfectionist Childrearing'. In *The Nature of Children's Wellbeing: Theory and Practice*, ed. Alexander Bagattini and Colin Macleod, 123–140. Dordrecht: Springer.

Damon, William. 2009. *The Path to Purpose: How Young People Find their Calling in Life*. New York: Free Press.

De Ruyter, Doret J. 2002. 'The Right to Meaningful Education: The Role of Values and Beliefs'. *Journal of Beliefs and Values* 23(1): 33–42.

Feinberg, Joel. 1980. 'The Child's Right to an Open Future'. In *Whose Child? Children's Rights, Parental Authority, and State Power*, ed. William Aiken and Hugh LaFolette, 124–153. Totowa, NJ: Adams.

Fourie, Mandi, and Elmari Deacon. 2015. 'Meaning in Work of Secondary School Teachers: A Qualitative Study'. *South African Journal of Education* 35(3): 1–8.

Frankl, Viktor E. [1946] 1985. *Man's Search for Meaning*. New York: Washington Square Press.

Froese, Paul. 2016. *On Purpose: How We Create the Meaning of Life*. Oxford: Oxford University Press.

Gardner, Peter. 1988. 'Religious Upbringing and the Liberal Ideal of Religious Autonomy'. *Journal of Philosophy of Education* 22(1): 89–105.

George, Login S., and Crystal L. Park. 2016. 'Meaning in Life as Comprehension, Purpose, and Mattering: Toward Integration and New Research Questions'. *Review of General Psychology* 20(3): 205–220.

Gordon, Mordechai, ed. 2001. *Hannah Arendt and Education: Renewing Our Common World*. Boulder, CO; Oxford: Westview Press.

Hull, John M. 1996. 'A Gift to the Child: A New Pedagogy for Teaching Religion to Young Children'. *Religious Education* 91(2): 172–188.

Johnson, Bruce, and Barry Down. 2013. 'Critically Re-Conceptualising Early Career Teacher Resilience'. *Discourse: Studies in the Cultural Politics of Education* 34(5): 703–715.

Kristjánsson, Kristján. 2020. *Flourishing as the Aim of Education: A Neo-Aristotelian View*. Oxon: Routledge.

Lambert, Nathaniel M., Tyler F. Stillman, Roy F. Baumeister, Frank D. Fincham, Joshua A. Hicks, and Steven M. Graham. 2010. 'Family as a Salient Source of Meaning in Young Adulthood'. *The Journal of Positive Psychology* 5(5): 367–376.

Lambert, Nathaniel M., Tyler F. Stillman, Joshua A. Hicks, Shanmukh Kamble, Roy F. Baumeister, and Frank D. Fincham. 2013. 'To Belong Is to Matter: Sense of Belonging Enhances Meaning in Life'. *Personality and Social Psychology Bulletin* 39(11): 1418–1427.

MacMullen, Ian. 2007. *Faith in Schools? Autonomy, Citizenship, and Religious Education in the Liberal State*. Princeton, NJ; Oxford: Princeton University Press.

Martela, Frank, and Michael F. Steger. 2016. 'The Three Meanings of Meaning in Life: Distinguishing Coherence, Purpose, and Significance'. *The Journal of Positive Psychology* 11(5): 531–545.

Marullo, Sam, Roxanna Moayedi, and Deanna Cooke. 2009. 'C. Wright Mills' Friendly Critique of Service Learning and an Innovative Response: Cross-Institutional Collaborations for Community-Based Research'. *Teaching Sociology* 37(1): 61–75.

McLaughlin, Terence H. 1984. 'Parental Rights and the Religious Upbringing of Children'. *Journal of Philosophy of Education* 18(1): 75–83.

McLaughlin, Terence H. 1985. 'Religion, Upbringing and Liberal Values: A Rejoinder to Eamonn Callan'. *Journal of Philosophy of Education* 19(1): 119–127.

McLaughlin, Terence H. 1990. 'Peter Gardner on Religious Upbringing and the Liberal Ideal of Religious Autonomy'. *Journal of Philosophy of Education* 24(1): 107–125.

Moran, Seana. 2018. 'Purpose-in-Action Education: Introduction and Implications'. *Journal of Moral Education* 47(2): 145–158.

Puolimatka, Tapio, and P. Juhani Airaksinen. 2001. 'Education and the Meaning of Life'. In *Philosophy of Education 2001*, ed. S. Rice, 311–319. Urbana-Champaign (Il.): Philosophy of Education Society.

Reber, Rolf. 2019. 'Making School Meaningful: Linking Psychology of Education to Meaning in Life'. *Educational Review* 71(4): 445–465.

Rosa, Hartmut. 2017. 'Available, Accessible, Attainable: The Mindset of Growth and the Resonance Conception of the Good Life'. In *The Good Life beyond Growth: New Perspectives*, ed. H. Rosa and C. Henning, 39–53. London: Routledge.

Schinkel, Anders. 2015. 'Education and Ultimate Meaning'. *Oxford Review of Education* 41(6): 711–729.

Schinkel, Anders. 2017. 'The Educational Importance of Deep Wonder'. *Journal of Philosophy of Education* 51(2): 538–553.

Schinkel, Anders. 2018. 'Wonder and Moral Education'. *Educational Theory* 68(1): 31–48.

Schinkel, Anders, Doret J. De Ruyter, and Roni Aviram. 2016. 'Education and Life's Meaning'. *Journal of Philosophy of Education* 50(3): 398–418.

Schinkel, Anders, Doret J. De Ruyter, and Jan Steutel. 2010. 'Threats to Autonomy in Consumer Societies and their Implications for Education'. *Theory and Research in Education* 8(3): 269–287.

Speck, Bruce W., and Sherry L. Hoppe, eds. 2004. *Service-Learning: History, Theory, and Issues*. Westport, CT; London: Praeger.

Sypnowich, Christine. 2018. 'Flourishing Children, Flourishing Adults: Families, Equality and the Neutralism-Perfectionism Debate'. *Critical Review of International Social and Political Philosophy* 21(3): 314–332.

Thunberg, Greta. 2019. *No One Is Too Small to Make a Difference*. N.p.: Penguin Books.

Tomic, Welko, and Elvira Tomic. 2008. 'Existential Fulfilment and Burnout among Principals and Teachers'. *Journal of Beliefs and Values* 29(1): 11–27.

UNICEF Innocenti. 2021. 'Worlds of Influence: Understanding what shapes child well-being in rich countries'. *Innocenti Report Card 16*. Florence: UNICEF Office of Research.

Van Manen, Max. 2016. *Pedagogical Tact: Knowing What to Do When You Don't Know What to Do*. New York: Routledge.

Vlieghe, Joris, and Piotr Zamojski. 2019. *Towards an Ontology of Teaching: Thing-Centered Pedagogy, Affirmation, and Love for the World*. Cham: Springer.

Warnick, Bryan R. 2012. 'Rethinking Education for Autonomy in Pluralistic Societies'. *Educational Theory* 62(4): 411–426.

Washington, Haydn. 2018. *A Sense of Wonder towards Nature: Healing the World through Belonging*. London: Routledge.

Westover, Tara. 2018. *Educated: A Memoir*. New York: Random House.

Wolf, Susan. 2010. *Meaning in Life and Why It Matters*. Princeton, NJ: Princeton University Press.

Zuurmond, Anouk. 2016. 'Teaching for Love of the World: Hannah Arendt on the Complexities of the Educational Practice'. In *Complexity in Education: From Horror to Passion*, ed. Cok Bakker and Nicolina M. Montessori, 55–74. Rotterdam: Sense.

CHAPTER 32

VIRTUAL REALITY AND THE MEANING OF LIFE

JOHN DANAHER

1. INTRODUCTION

LOTS of people are anxious about virtual reality. This anxiety is often represented in popular media. Consider two classic films of the 1990s. In *The Truman Show*, the eponymous lead character lives his entire life on a complex TV set populated by paid actors. Eventually, Truman realizes that there is something not quite right with his life. He exposes the ruse and escapes into the real world. In *The Matrix* the lead character Neo encounters a band of rebels who make him aware of the fact that his entire life has been lived inside a hyperrealistic computer simulation. In one of the central scenes of the film, Neo is offered a choice of two pills: a blue pill that will allow him to continue to live his life in the simulation, blissfully unaware of what is really going on; and a red pill which will reveal the uncomfortable truth. He takes the red pill.

In both of these films, the suggestion seems to be that we should sympathize with the lead characters' choices to abandon their illusions and find out what the real world is like. To live inside the illusion would, it is hinted, is to live a less meaningful life. This is an idea with deep philosophical roots. The traditional interpretation of Plato's allegory of the cave, for example, is that one of the goals of the well-lived life is to shake free the shackles of illusion and get closer to reality. If this is right, then it seems to scotch any claim that a meaningful life can be lived inside virtual reality.

In this chapter, I will challenge this view and defend two major claims: (1) that the binary choice facing the protagonists in *The Truman Show* and *The Matrix* is too simplistic and that it is not really possible to choose to live entirely in the real world or in a virtual world because our lives tend to blend elements of both; and (2) it is possible to pursue meaning in a virtual world. I will defend these claims in four main stages. First, I will say a few brief words about the conditions that need to be satisfied in order to live a meaningful life. Second, I will discuss the nature of virtual reality, examining both its recent technological forms and its deeper historical roots. Third, I will present four arguments for thinking that meaning is possible in a virtual world. Fourth, I will explain and respond to four major objections to this claim.

2. Some Assumptions about Meaning in Life

Other chapters in this book have discussed the classic philosophical questions about the meaning of life. In this chapter, I will skirt these questions and make a few assumptions.

I will start with the assumption that it is possible for human beings to live a meaningful life. In doing so, I will assume a pluralist theory of the conditions of meaning (cf. Danaher 2019, chapter 4). According to this pluralist theory, a meaningful life is one that satisfies a set of subjective and objective conditions of value (Campbell and Nyholm 2015). On the subjective side, the individual living the life must be satisfied and fulfilled by what they are doing. They must achieve things through their actions and perceive that their actions have value (Luper 2014; Bradford 2013, 2016; Wolf 2010). On the objective side, the individual must make some positive difference to the world around them (Smuts 2013). In other words, they must contribute something of value to the world through their lives. What exactly must they contribute? Following Metz and others, I assume that contributions to the good, the true, and the beautiful are the obvious pathways to meaning (Metz 2011). An individual can live a meaningful life if they do something that is morally good for the world, develop some form of knowledge or insight, or produce something of aesthetic value. I also assume that among the things that can be morally good for the world is developing one's own moral virtues, building satisfying relationships with others, and developing skills and abilities that can be used to produce things of objective value. To this extent, I assume that there can be a close connection between human well-being and meaning, even though it is common to see these as distinct aspects of the well-lived life.

I will not assume that meaning is a binary property. Lives are not either meaningful or not. Lives can, on my understanding, be more or less meaningful depending on the number of conditions of meaning that are satisfied within that life and also the degree to which any particular condition of meaning is satisfied.

These assumptions affect the analysis that follows. When assessing whether or not meaning is possible in a virtual reality, I will be assessing whether or not it is possible to satisfy the plural conditions of objective and subjective meaning in such a world.

3. What is Virtual Reality?

To assess whether meaning is possible in virtual reality (VR), it is important to have some handle on what VR is. This is tricky since it is a slippery and nebulous concept.

Nevertheless, I think we can distinguish between two major visions of VR: the *technological vision* and the *anthropocentric vision*.

The Technological Vision of VR

The technological vision of VR holds that a *virtual reality* is a *computer-simulated reality*. A VR *life* is, consequently, one that is lived inside such a simulation. This is a common view of VR. In most people's minds, use of the phrase 'virtual reality' will conjure up the image of someone donning a headset ('head-mounted display' or HMD to use the jargon) that will project this computer-simulated reality directly into their eyes. This is sometimes combined with suits or gloves or other objects that allow people to project their bodily movements into the simulated space. It is also possible that people could use haptic technology to experience and transmit touch-like sensations through the computer simulation.

This technological vision is captured by one of the most popular definitions of VR from Michael Heims (1998, 221):

> Virtual reality is a technology that convinces the participant that he or she is actually in another place by substituting the primary sensory input with data produced by a computer.

The key thing about this definition of VR is that it requires a technology that enables some degree of *immersion* into the simulated space. In other words, it requires a technology that creates an illusion, which can be more or less convincing, for the user that they really inhabit the computer simulation.

If we adopt a slightly looser technological definition of VR, we could abandon this need for immersive technology and include any technology that enables a person to live and act (if only temporarily) in a computer-simulated environment. Thus, we could say that people playing computer games and online multiplayer games, such as *World of Warcraft*, live and act in a VR. We could say the same about people who spend time in virtual worlds such as *Second Life*, which are not game-worlds but, rather, open-ended computer-simulated social spaces. This is despite the fact that people access these worlds through keyboards and computer controllers, and act via onscreen avatars, and not by wearing immersive headsets and suits. It may make sense to loosen the definition in this way since some users and creators of these platforms—perhaps most noticeably the users and creator of *Second Life*—often describe them as a form of VR.

We could also include other variations on the technological vision of VR. For example, the fictional Holodeck in *Star Trek* depicts a form of immersive VR in which the user does not wear any head-mounted display but, rather, walks into a large a room in which computer-simulated people, objects, and environments are projected—through some technological MacGuffin—into the room around them. Whether such a technology is possible is unclear, but if it were it would surely count as a type of technologically mediated VR.

Similarly, there is nowadays an increased interest in *augmented* reality technology. This involves projecting computer-simulated objects or characters onto our experiences of the existing physical reality. At the time of writing (the year 2021), the current generation of smartphones come with augmented reality features as standard, and there are a variety of games that make use of augmented reality applications. Augmented reality technology is interesting because it involves using technology to blur the boundaries between computer-simulated worlds and the real world.

Whatever the precise technological form, the distinguishing feature of this technological vision of VR is that of the computer-simulated world. It is this computer-simulated environment that provides the 'virtual' aspect of the reality inhabited by the user. With computer simulations it is, in principle, possible for people to create vast fictional worlds that are free from many of the constraints of the real world. They can also interact with other humans who share the computer-simulated space or with wholly computer-programmed or artificial characters. These features of the technological vision of VR become important when it comes to assessing the possibility of finding meaning in VR.

The Anthropocentric Vision of VR

The anthropocentric vision of VR takes a different perspective. Instead of seeing VR as something that is computer-simulated and accessed through technology, it sees VR as something that is made possible by the human mind, sometimes assisted by culture and technology, and with much deeper roots in the human condition. In his expansive history of human ideas, Felipe Fernandez-Armesto (2019) makes the case that the imagination is the most distinctive human trait. Memory gives us access to past experiences; anticipation allows us to predict future experiences; imagination is what happens when both of these things fail. Imagination is what allows us to see what isn't there; to invent fictional worlds and beings; and to interact with them.

Fernandez-Armesto doesn't make the connection between the history of human imagination and VR explicit in his writings, but others have. André Nusselder (2014), for example, points out that ever since we have had the power of symbolic thought, we have had to power to live in two worlds: the virtual world created by our minds and the physical reality in which we are embodied. Nusselder also argues that leading schools of philosophical thought have highlighted this duality. For example, he argues that Kantianism is explicitly founded on the notion that there is a natural world—a world of necessity and scientific law, partly constructed by our minds—and a moral world—a world in which we use our wills to create a new reality (Nusselder 2014, 73–74). Similarly, he argues that existentialism is premised on the idea that we are beings that can imagine new realities and bring them about through our actions. We thus have one foot in each reality at all times: the virtual world of our imaginations and the natural world around us (see also Kreps 2014 on the links between critical theory, postmodernism, and VR).

We can narrow the gap between the imagined virtual world and the natural world in two ways. We can create cultural and social constructions that we layer over our experiences of the natural world. For example, we can create social institutions such as corporations, money and marriage that are not really 'out there' in the real world but are, rather, in our minds and made possible through collective agreement (Searle 1995, 2010). We can also use technologies to narrow the gap between our imaginations and the physical world. One of the problems our early ancestors faced was that they had active imaginations but limited means of making those imaginations a reality. Modern humans have sophisticated and powerful technologies for making their imaginations a reality. Computer simulations are perhaps the most extreme manifestation of this technological capacity. They allow us to create wholly new worlds, free from many (though not all) of the limitations of the physical world. They are a blank canvas for the imagination.

One of the writers who has done the most to advocate this anthropocentric vision of VR is Yuval Noah Harari. He argues that humans have always lived large portions of their lives in VR, projecting things from the mental world onto the physical world. He singles out religious beliefs and practices as perhaps the most obvious example of this (Harari 2016, 2017). He then uses this observation to make the point that those who argue that our lives will be robbed of meaning if we live inside a computer simulation are wrong. We have been doing this for millennia anyway. The technology changes nothing fundamental; it just narrows the gap between imagined and physical realities.

It's time to lay my own cards on the table. In general, I agree with the proponents of the *anthropocentric vision*. The idea of a VR is not new. It is something that has been with us ever since we developed the capacity for imaginative symbolic thought. Since then, we have always lived in two worlds. Technology can make the distinction between the two worlds less phenomenologically noticeable, but unless humans transcend their physical, biological bodies (as some transhumanists and futurists hope), we will remain tethered in the physical world. We will always have one foot in both worlds and will never live *completely virtual* lives. This tethering to physical reality may prove important when it comes to assessing the possibility of living a meaningful life in VR.

4. How Meaning Might Be Possible in VR

Now that we have a clearer conception of VR in place, we can turn to the main question: 'Can we find meaning in a virtual reality?' The popular consensus appears to be against this idea, but let me offer four arguments in favour of meaning in VR.

Argument 1: The 'No Difference' Argument

The first argument in favour of VR is that it is 'no different' from our current reality. If we grant, for the sake of argument, that it is possible for humans to live meaningful lives right now, and that our ancestors have lived meaningful lives before us, and if we accept the basic thrust of anthropocentric vision of VR, then we should accept that it is possible to find meaning in VR. To make the logic more explicit, the argument would look something like this:

(1) Humans can live meaningful lives right now and have lived meaningful lives in the past.
(2) Much of human life as it is currently constituted (including the parts to which we attach most value and meaning) is lived inside virtual realities.
(3) Therefore it is possible for humans to live meaningful lives in virtual reality.

The first premise is relatively uncontroversial. It is not claiming that *all* human lives are meaningful. Many may not be. It is just claiming that it is possible for us to live meaningful lives right now and that at least some of our ancestors—Einstein, Florence Nightingale, Jonas Salk, and so on—have lived meaningful lives. The second premise is the controversial one since it relies on the accuracy of the anthropocentric vision of VR. The idea is that, perhaps unbeknownst to yourself, you and your ancestors have already been spending your lives engaging with virtual ideas, concepts, and things, and deriving meaning from those engagements. Why would you worry about the new technological manifestations of VR? There is no significant difference between them and what is already possible.

As mentioned in the previous section, Yuval Noah Harari is perhaps the most vocal proponent of this view. He has argued that 'the meaning we ascribe to what we see is generated by our own minds' (Harari 2017). In other words, meaning always has and always will depend on the virtual (imagined) world.

Is this a compelling argument? Since I have already declared myself to be a fan of the anthropocentric vision of VR, I do find it somewhat compelling. I think Harari and other proponents of this view are right to say that large portions of our current lives are virtual, and so to the extent that we already derive meaning from them we shouldn't worry too much about the new wave of VR technologies and the kinds of lives they might enable. Nevertheless, I do think one can go too far in pushing the 'no difference' argument.

In particular, I think it is wrong to assume that there is no difference between the forms of VR that were possible in the past and the forms that will be possible in the future with digital technology and artificial intelligence. These phenomena lie on a continuum, and there is no sharp break between what our ancestors did and what we might do in the future, but this does not mean that there are not and will not be significant differences. While we have always had the power to imagine outlandish and fantastical worlds, our capacity to phenomenologically inhabit those worlds has been limited by our technologies. The level of technological control and freedom that is made possible by the new wave of VR technologies makes it possible to phenomenologically inhabit imaginary worlds in a new way. It may no longer be just those with strong imaginations or access to psychedelics drugs who can experience a vivid form of VR. It may now be possible for anyone with access to the relevant technology.

Argument 2: The Conditions of Meaning Argument

The second argument in favour of VR is that it is possible to satisfy the conditions of meaning in virtual spaces. Recall from earlier that the conditions of meaning are both subjective and objective in nature. You have to be subjectively satisfied and fulfilled by what you are doing, and you have to do something of objective value and worth. This second argument then claims that within a virtual world it is possible to satisfy both sets of conditions.

In Danaher (2019, chapter 7) I argued that there are several ways in which this was possible. For one thing, in virtual worlds we can develop real friendships and alliances with other people who inhabit those virtual worlds. We can engage in moral actions with them—for example, acts of charity, helping, and the alleviation of suffering—by providing them with resources in the virtual world and conversing with them about problems they may be having through the virtual interface. We can develop skills and abilities in virtual spaces. For example, in a virtual game-world we can hone our skills at the game. We can look at it as a craft (Sennett 2008). The game provides an external structure that includes objective standards of performance. We can adapt our skills and abilities to those standards. There can also be great aesthetic beauty to these skilled performances (Dreyfus and Kelly 2011). We can also develop deeper knowledge of the game and how it works. This can enlighten and uplift ourselves and other players of the game. We can also see virtual worlds as opportunities to hone and develop our moral virtues. Many philosophers of sport, for example, have argued that sports are like moral laboratories or dramas (McNamee 2008). Virtual worlds—including computer-simulated worlds—could perform the same function. In short, it seems possible that we can attain a version of the good, the true and the beautiful in virtual worlds as well as in physical reality.

There are some obvious objections to this argument. The most obvious is that a virtual life, for all its benefits, is missing something—namely, 'reality'. We will deal with this objection in more detail in the next section. As a preliminary to this, however, we can turn to current and historical analogues of virtual life to bolster the argument. Consider, for instance, the lives of great sport stars or actors. To a large extent, the central focus of their lives is a virtual arena: the sport field, the stage, the movie screen, and so on. In those arenas, the individual either lives a fantasy life (in the case of the actor) and accepts a constructed and arbitrary set of constraints upon their actions (in the case of the sport star). Can these people live meaningful lives? It seems obvious enough that they can. They can achieve things within the respective arenas and derive a lot of personal satisfaction from these achievements. They can also create performances of great aesthetic beauty and diversity that have the power to uplift and alleviate the suffering of those who watch and take pleasure in those performances.

Argument 3: The (Meta)-Utopian Argument

Another argument in favour of the virtual life is that it makes possible a utopian style of existence. We tend to think of utopians as naive and Polyannaish, at best, or dangerous, at worst. The great massacres of the twentieth century are, for example, sometimes attributed to misguided utopian projects (Popper 2002, chapter 18). As Yorke (2016) describes it, one of the main problems with these historic utopian projects is how they tried to impose a fixed blueprint of the ideal society on a reluctant population. There is, however, an alternative ideal of utopia that focuses on trying to improve society and ensuring a dynamic and open future (Danaher 2019, chapter 5; Yorke 2016). This ideal moves away from the 'blueprint' model of utopianism toward a 'horizontal' model, according to which there is no fixed destination for humanity but, rather, an unending project—or, indeed, multiple projects—of improvement (Wilde 1981). Being part of those ongoing projects can be a source of meaning.

This third argument, then, is that VR is to be welcomed because it enables us to pursue these utopian projects. At the most basic level, VR allows us to imagine a better world and, through technology or social constructions, to narrow the gap between the reality we currently inhabit and our imaginations. On top of this, modern VR technology, with its scope for endlessly diverse computer-simulated worlds, opens up a vast horizon of possible worlds for us to explore. We can thus use VR technology to pursue a more ambitious set of utopian projects.

Related to this, it is possible to argue that VR technologies can make Robert Nozick's vision of the 'meta-utopia' a more practical reality (Nozick 1974; Bader 2011). Nozick's meta-utopia is a distinctive take on what the utopian project should be. Nozick argues that a utopian world is one that is judged by its members to be the best possible world. But it is impossible to create a single utopian world: values are plural, and people have different preference rankings over the set of plural values. So, instead of trying to create a single utopian world, we should focus on creating a world-building mechanism that allows people to create and join worlds that best match their own preferences. This world-building mechanism would be the meta-utopia. Nozick himself argues that a libertarian minimal state is the closest real-world analogue to the meta-utopia. But there are problems with this: there is limited space in the physical world, and policing the boundaries between different libertarian associations can be difficult. It's possible that moving into computer-simulated spaces would alleviate some of these practical problems. Computer-simulated spaces allow for relatively unlimited expansion of virtual worlds, and it is easier to separate and keep the peace between the different virtual worlds.

Argument 4: The Virtual Sublime Argument

The final argument in favour of VR is a little bit different from the preceding ones. Whereas they focused on the possibility of humans having better (or at least no different) experiences in VR, this one focuses on the possibility of them having worse experiences. How could this provide the basis for meaning? Answer: because it could give humans visceral phenomenological access to the sublime. Hunter and Mosco (2014) have argued that the idea of the *sublime* is a key idea in philosophical and religious thought. The sublime is something that is both awe-inspiring and terrible. It transports us from the mundanities of life to something radically different and astonishing.

Having experiences of the sublime is attractive to human beings. Some of the most celebrated artworks, for example, depict awe-inspiring and terrible realities. Hunter and Mosco point, specifically, to the paintings of Hieronymus Bosch, which depict hellish and terrifying landscapes. One of the things that attract us to such depictions, however, is that they are relatively safe to experience. We want to get close to the sublime, but we don't want to be at risk.

If we grant that having experiences of the sublime is something that can contribute to a meaningful life, then we can make an argument in favour of VR, particularly in the form of immersive, but dystopian, computer-simulated worlds. These worlds can be astonishing and terrifying. They can transport us away from and transcend the mundanities of the real world. They can, as Hunter and Mosco put it, 'offer a type of sublime transcendence that allows people to deal with horror, without "actually" having to experience it' (Hunter and Mosco 2014, 727).

5. Objections to VR

In this section I will discuss four major objections to the idea that meaning is possible in VR.

Objection 1: The 'It's Not Real' Objection

The most obvious objection to the idea of meaning in VR is that VR, by its essence, is not fully real. It is a simulation of reality or a poor, imaginative, cousin of reality. It's not the proper thing. We need the proper thing in order to live a meaningful life.

One of the most famous thought experiments in philosophy—Robert Nozick's *Experience Machine* thought experiment—highlights the basic problem (Nozick 1974, 1989; Bramble 2016). In that thought experiment, Nozick asks us to imagine that we have the option of plugging ourselves into an experience machine—i.e. a highly sophisticated and realistic VR simulator. Once plugged into the machine, we can have whatever experiences we would like to have. We can live out our fantasies and dreams and forget about the lives we leave behind. If we had that choice, would we plug ourselves into the machine? Nozick's intuition is that we wouldn't. Nozick uses this intuition to make the case against hedonism because he thinks it shows that having good experiences is not all that matters in living the good life. But it can also be used against the idea of meaning in VR insofar as it suggests that most people think there is something important missing from a wholly simulated life (Metz 2019, 404–405).

There are four things to be said in response to this objection. First, as should be clear from the earlier discussion, VR is an ontologically slippery concept. It's not quite fair or true to say that the things we do or the experiences we have inside a VR are not real. There is a blurry boundary between VR and physical reality. On the anthropocentric vision of VR, we always inhabit both realities. It is not easy to separate out the real from the virtual elements. Furthermore, even on the technological vision of VR, any computer simulations we might inhabit are going to be highly dependent on and interactive with physical reality. Our bodies will remain tethered in physical reality. We will perform actions with them and interact with other physically tethered users of the virtual worlds. We can, consequently, have real interactions, conversations, and friendships with humans through the virtual medium.

Second, there is a technical point to be made about the ontological nature of different kinds of things. Some things are purely *physical kinds*: they depend for their existence on the presence of certain physical properties. Chairs, tables, and apples would seem to be physical kinds. Other things are functional kinds: they are defined by the role they perform and not by their physical properties. Functional kinds break down into two sub-categories: physical functional kinds, which require a reasonably specific physical instantiation to exist (e.g. a lever); and non-physical functional kinds, which do not. Non-physical functional kinds are capable of existing—in a real form—in digital or computer simulations. A classic example is money. Money performs a function in human society and is often tracked and counted using physical tokens (notes, coins). But it does not need those physical tokens to perform its function. It can exist in a purely digital or, indeed, mental form. As long as people believe it exists, and they can keep track of its volume and exchange, it *really* exists. This is important because it highlights the fact that some kinds of things don't need a specific physical presence in order to really exist. Their simulated existence can be just as real as their physical existence. The philosopher Philip Brey (using previous work done by John Searle) has argued that large chunks of our social realities are of this form and they can *really* exist inside digital simulations (Brey 2014; Searle 1996, 2010). Consequently, the 'it's not real' objection doesn't work against all the kinds of things that exist in VR.

Third, there is experimental evidence to suggest that the phenomenological experiences that people have inside VR simulations can stimulate the same emotional and physiological responses as those experiences might have in the real world. This is possible because the human brain naturally constructs a virtual model of the real world based on a handful of perceptual cues (Slater and Sanchez-Vives 2016). VR environments can exploit this feature of human cognition and trick us into thinking that unusual things are happening to us (Meehan et al. 2002; Madary and Metzinger 2016). Thus, there is some phenomenological weight to the experiences we have in VR, which improves the more immersive the VR happens to be. This means that virtual experiences can take on a significance and importance in our lives that enables them to feel important and significant to us. This could suffice for practical meaning in VR, even if the phenomenological weight may not be enough to satisfy philosophers such as Nozick.

Fourth, and finally, there are some specific problems with Nozick's thought experiment. In the way in which it was originally described, Nozick's thought experiment biased the anticipated intuitive response in various ways. For example, by assuming that we would go from our current reality to a new, simulated one, Nozick may have been appealing to loss aversion (a bias in favour of maintaining the status quo), rather than any strong negative intuition against a simulated life. Several researchers have now run experiments in which they test people's reactions to alternative versions of the thought experiment that play around with these biasing features (e.g. getting people to plug out from their current reality and so forth). When they do so, the results are quite mixed, suggesting that there isn't as strong an intuitive resistance to living inside a simulation as Nozick supposed (De Brigard 2010; Weijers 2014). Relatedly, Nozick's thought experiment could be criticized for blurring the boundaries between irreversible deception and voluntary simulation. We might balk at the idea of being deceived into thinking that VR is the same thing as physical reality—like Neo in the *Matrix* or Truman in the *Truman Show*—but if there is no deception, if we freely choose to live inside the virtual world, and if we retain the freedom to 'plug out' at any moment, then things may not be so bad.

All this said, it is still important that there are some differences between virtual worlds and the physical world. Without those differences, the creativity and innovation that are possible in the virtual would cease to exist. Likewise, we wouldn't have access to the digital sublime if the terrifying experiences we had in a virtual world put us at some real risk. But just because there are differences between what happens in virtual worlds and what happens in the physical world does not mean that the former is somehow less real, or less conducive to a meaningful life, than the latter.

Objection 2: The Immorality Objection

A second common objection to a virtual life is that it would be a playground for immorality: in virtual worlds people will believe that they are free from the ordinary requirements of morality and that they can do as they please. In book 2 of the *Republic*, Glaucon presents a thought experiment involving the mythical 'Ring of Gyges', a ring that grants its wearer invisibility. Glaucon argues that if we had the power of invisibility we would engage in the most heinous and unjust acts because we would be free from the threat of punishment. Some authors have suggested that digital environments create something like the Ring of Gyges effect on their users, allowing them to act with moral impunity and anonymity (Vallor 2016, 188). This is also a long-standing trope in science fiction. This is perhaps best illustrated by the novel, movie, and TV series *Westworld*, which depicts a virtual playground that allows users to engage in wanton acts of cruelty, rape, and murder.

There are three things to say in response to this objection. First, the assumption that life in a virtual world will be free from the ordinary constraints of morality needs to be questioned. In response to the previous objection, I made the point that on both the anthropocentric and technological visions of VR there is a close relationship between the virtual and the real. Some things that happen in the virtual world are every bit as real as they would be in the physical world; and many things that happen in virtual worlds are dependent on and interconnected with what happens in the physical world. If this is right, then many of the actions we perform in virtual worlds will have the same properties that would render them moral or immoral if performed in the physical world (Tillson 2018; Ostritsch 2017). For example, relationships of trust and dominance can exist in virtual worlds. The norms we apply to such relationships in the physical world would continue to apply in the virtual world. Likewise, things we do in virtual worlds can be really traumatizing or harmful to people in the physical world due to the phenomenological weight of these experiences (Soraker 2010; Danaher 2018a). Similarly, the assumption that acts in virtual worlds will necessarily be anonymous or free from the threat of punishment is one that can be questioned. Many digital platforms, for example, have internal governance structures and codes, have the capacity to track and trace users, and apply punitive sanctions to them (e.g. banning them from the platform). Indeed, depending on their design, there may well be less anonymity and impunity in digital virtual spaces than there is in the real world.[1]

Second, to the extent that virtual worlds have a 'game-like' aspect to them, they may well be freed from some of the ordinary constraints of morality. This is a common phenomenon. Many sports and games allow us to do things that would, outside of the game context, count as immoral. For example, contact sports such as rugby or American football permit acts that would otherwise count as physical assault. Likewise, games of chance and strategy, such as Poker and Diplomacy, encourage and reward deception. This is part of the fun. Nevertheless, this does not mean that these games are free from all moral constraints. For one thing, there is often an *internal morality* to the game, one that determines virtuous and fair play (MacIntyre 2007). There are also limits to how much moral freedom can be afforded to gameplayers. For example, if actions within games have harmful effects beyond the boundaries of the game, then this can sometimes provide reason to change their internal rules.

Third, although what I have just said implies that virtual worlds are not playgrounds for immorality, there is perhaps one interesting quirk when it comes to morality in a virtual world. This quirk applies specifically to computer-simulated forms of VR. In simulations, people act through avatars in computer-projected spaces. Sometimes those avatars can interact in ways that simulate physical violence to other simulated characters

---

[1] Some digital spaces do encourage and facilitate anonymity, but this is a design choice. If we are worried about people treating these spaces as playgrounds for immorality, we can design against this.

and objects. However, this damage is often easily repairable and replaceable. You could 'kill' my virtual avatar and I could quickly restore it from a backup copy. You could steal my virtual property, but I could replace it with equivalent property in the blink of an eye. The freedom that comes with our control over the digital environment means that the consequential harms of actions within those environments are often trivial. According to most moral theories, the consequences of our actions do matter to some extent. We may then worry that living a virtual life strips away something normatively significant from our actions. This may well be true and may mean that morality within virtual worlds is necessarily more deontological in nature than morality in the physical world. It may mean that virtual morality is more focused on the intrinsic nature of the virtual acts and less on their consequential harms. But this does not mean that virtual worlds are playgrounds of immorality; nor does it undermine the point that some actions in computer-simulated spaces have spillover effects in the real world. For any action with such spillover effects, consequential harms will, again, become a relevant moral constraint.

Objection 3: The Nihilism Objection

A third objection to life in VR is that, far from fostering meaning, it may facilitate nihilism. The term 'nihilism' is multiplied ambiguous. Broadly construed, it signifies some scepticism about the possibility or practicality of value in different domains. Beyond that, there is considerable disagreement about its exact parameters (Joyce 2013). Two versions of the nihilism critique are worth considering here.

The first focuses on *passive nihilism*. This is a form of nihilism that features in the work of Nietzsche and Sartre. It arises from an inability to shape one's own destiny and take responsibility for the values that guide one's own life. Instead of actively shaping who we are, we passively accept values imposed on us by others. Nolen Gertz (2018) has recently argued that technology in general and VR in particular encourage passive nihilism. The problem is that technology fragments our attention and gives us too many options. We are encouraged to 'tune out' from reality; to watch endless streams of entertainment; to live inside virtual bubbles in a wanton and hypnotic state; and to become alienated from our true selves. We are consequently overstimulated, listless, and compliant. We cannot become the masters of our own fate.

Gertz's worries about technology have been echoed by many others, myself included (Frischmann and Selinger 2018; Vallor 2016; Danaher 2019). They are worth taking seriously, but they are not fatal to the prospect of meaning in VR. The argument I have developed in this chapter is that VR doesn't *necessarily* undermine meaning, but particular manifestations of VR very well could do so. If Gertz and other technology critics are correct, then current trends in VR technology could be counter-productive to meaning insofar as they encourage passivity, lack of autonomy, listlessness, overstimulation, fragmentation of attention, and so forth. There are no easy fixes for these problems. But two points are worth bearing in mind. First, they are, to at least some extent, problems that can be rectified through good design and regulation of VR technology. Second, as per the anthropocentric vision of VR, not all forms of VR are reliant on modern digital technologies. There are other ways of accessing virtual spaces that can still be highly conducive to meaning.

The second way of running the objection focuses on *metaphysical nihilism*. This is the more radical thesis that there is no objective value in the world at all. If true, then our hopes of living meaningful lives are forlorn because we cannot realize the appropriate conditions of value in our lives. One might be inclined to think that metaphysical nihilism is either true or not. Nothing about VR or VR technology could possibly change that. This is probably true. Still, there are some forms of metaphysical nihilism that might become more practically salient as a result of technology.

Consider, for example, Thomas Nagel's analysis of the absurdity of life (Nagel 1971). According to Nagel, our lives are absurd because everything we do within them is contingent and questionable. We can always take the view from nowhere and question the worthwhileness of what we are doing. All the constraints we seek to impose on our lives are challengeable from this perspective. Now, in a sense, Nagel's analysis is either correct or it is not. But, in another sense, the practical significance of Nagelian absurdity might be heightened by technological advances. If we can live inside simulated worlds that are unconstrained by physical reality, then everything we do is not just contingent and re-negotiable in theory; it is also contingent and renegotiable in practice. There is no stable, external structure that can provide meaning in our lives.

This could be a major practical problem for proponents of a meaningful life in VR: users of VR simulations may experience a more profound sense of the absurd than others. That said, it is somewhat extreme. At least for the time being, any manifestation of VR will be constrained by physical reality in some respect. We will remain embodied physical beings with one foot in physical reality. This tethering to the physical world will provide some limits on the re-negotiability of our lives. In addition to this, as discussed earlier, some moral norms or constraints may apply irrespective of how we choose to live our lives. These could continue to provide the stable structure that we need for meaning (Danaher 2014).

Objection 4: Political and Social Fragmentation

A final objection to VR is that it could create significant social and political problems. These problems are somewhat orthogonal to the question of whether meaning is possible in VR, but could have some bearing on it. The primary concern here might be that if we can each choose to live in the virtual world that best matches our own preferences—à la the Nozickian meta-utopia—then this will lead to increased political polarization and social isolation. We won't need to interact with others anymore. We won't need to tolerate others, compromise with them, or reach mutual agreement. For many people, this is a problem since improving our social and political interactions is at least part of what it takes to live a meaningful life.

As with Gertz's fears about passive nihilism, there is something worth taking seriously in this objection. But two points should be borne in mind. First, many people will not choose to live inside their own virtual world. They will choose to live with others and will have to fashion some mutual *modus vivendi* with them. Second, and perhaps more importantly, creating the technological infrastructure that would allow for the creation of something akin to the Nozickian meta-utopia would not obviate the need for political and social agreement. On the contrary, it would probably require more political and social agreement to govern and maintain such an infrastructure. Indeed, contra Nozick, sustaining the meta-utopia might well require a larger and more powerful government than any we have ever created before.

6. Conclusion

In conclusion, in this chapter I have suggested that there are at least two different visions of what a virtual life might be: the technological vision, according to which a virtual life is a life lived inside a computer-simulated world; and the anthropocentric vision, according to which a virtual life has always been a core part of human existence, fashioned by our minds and our cultures. The distinction between these two visions is not sharp and they ultimately blur together. Taking this onboard, and working with a pluralistic conception of the conditions that need to be satisfied in order to live a meaningful life, I have argued that it is possible to find meaning in VR.

References

Bader, R. 2011. 'The Framework for Utopia'. In *The Cambridge Companion to Nozick's Anarchy, State and Utopia*, ed. R. Bader and I. Meadowcroft, 255–288. Cambridge: Cambridge University Press. References in text are to the following version: http://users.ox.ac.uk/~sfop0426/Framework%20for%20utopia%20%28R.%20Bader%29.pdf.

Bradford, G. 2013. 'The Value of Achievements'. *Pacific Philosophical Quarterly* 94(2): 202–224.

Bradford, G. 2016. *Achievement*. Oxford: Oxford University Press.

Bramble, B. 2016. 'The Experience Machine'. *Philosophy Compass* 11(3): 136–145.

Brey, P. 2014. 'The Physical and Social Reality of Virtual Worlds'. In *The Oxford Handbook of Virtuality*, ed. M. Grimshaw, 42–54. Oxford: Oxford University Press.

Campbell, S., and S. Nyholm. 2015. 'Anti-Meaning and Why It Matters'. *Journal of the American Philosophical Association* 1(4): 694–711.

Danaher, J. 2014. 'Hyperagency and the Good Life—Does Extreme Enhancement Threaten Meaning?' *Neuroethics* 7(2): 227–242.

Danaher, J. 2018a. 'The Law and Ethics of Virtual Sexual Assault'. In *The Law of Virtual and Augmented Reality*, ed. W. Barfield and M. Blitz, 363–388. Cheltenham, UK: Edward Elgar.

Danaher, J. 2018b. 'Towards an Ethics of AI Assistants'. *Philosophy and Technology* 31: 629–653.

Danaher, J. 2019. *Automation and Utopia*. Cambridge, MA: Harvard University Press.

De Brigard, F. 2010. 'If You Like It, Does It Matter If It's Real'. *Philosophical Psychology* 23(1): 43–57.
Dreyfus, H., and S. D. Kelly. 2011. *All Things Shining: Reading the Western Classics to Find Meaning in a Secular Age*. New York: Free Press.
Fernandez-Armesto, F. 2019. *Out of Our Minds*. London: OneWorld.
Frischmann, B., and E. Selinger. 2018. *Re-engineering Humanity*. Cambridge: Cambridge University Press.
Gertz, N. 2018. *Nihilism and Technology*. London: Rowman and Littlefield.
Harari, Y. N. 2016. *Homo Deus*. London: Harvill Secker.
Harari, Y. N. 2017. 'The Meaning of Life in a World Without Work'. *The Guardian*, 8 May 2017.
Heims, M. 1998. *Virtual Realism*. Oxford: Oxford University Press.
Hunter, A, and V. Mosco. 2014. 'Virtual Dystopia'. In *The Oxford Handbook of Virtuality*, ed. M. Grimshaw, 727–737. Oxford: Oxford University Press.
Hurka, T. 2006. . *Proceedings of the Aristotelian Society* 80: 217–235.
Joyce, R. 2013. 'Nihilism'. In *International Encyclopedia of Ethics*, ed. H. LaFollette, 3606–3010. Oxford: Wiley-Blackwell.
Kreps, D. 2014. 'Virtuality and Humanity'. In *The Oxford Handbook of Virtuality*, ed. M. Grimshaw, 712–726. Oxford: Oxford University Press.
Lanier, J. 2017. *The Dawn of the New Everything*. New York: Macmillan.
Landau, I. 2017. *Finding Meaning in an Imperfect World*. Oxford: Oxford University Press.
Levitas, R. 1990. *The Concept of Utopia*. London: Phillip Allan.
Luper, S. 2014. 'Life's Meaning'. In *The Cambridge Companion to Life and Death*, ed. S. Luper, 198–212. Cambridge: Cambridge University Press.
Macintyre, A. 2007. *After Virtue: A Study in Moral Theory*, 3rd ed. South Bend, IN: University of Notre Dame Press.
Madary, M., and T. K. Metzinger. 2016. 'Real Virtuality: A Code of Ethical Conduct. Recommendations for Good Scientific Practice and the Consumers of VR-Technology'. *Frontiers in Robotics and AI* 3(3). doi: 10.3389/frobt.2016.00003.
McNamee, M. 2008. *Sports, Virtues and Vices: Morality Plays*. London: Routledge.
Meehan, M., B. Insko, M. Whitton, and F. Brooks. 2002. 'Physiological Measures of Presence in Stressful Virtual Environments'. *ACM Transactions on Graphics* 21: 645–652. doi:10.1145/566654.566630.
Metz, T. 2011. 'The Good, the Grue, and the Beautiful: Toward a Unified Account of Great Meaning in Life'. *Religious Studies* 47: 389–409.
Metz, T. 2013. *Meaning in Life: An Analytic Study*. Oxford: Oxford University Press.
Metz, T. 2019. 'Recent Work on the Meaning of "Life's Meaning"'. *Human Affairs* 29: 404–405.
Nagel, T. 1971. The Absurd. *Journal of Philosophy* 68(20): 716–727.
Nozick, R. 1974. *Anarchy, State and Utopia*. New York: Basic Books.
Nozick, R. 1989. *The Examined Life*. New York: Simon and Schuster.
Nusselder, André. 2014. 'Being More than Yourself: Virtuality and the Human Spirit'. In *The Oxford Handbook of Virtuality*, ed. M. Grimshaw, 71–85. Oxford: Oxford University Press.
Ostritsch, S. 2017. 'The Amoralist Challenge to Gaming and the Gamer's Moral Obligation'. *Ethics and Information Technology* 19(2): 117–128.
Popper, K. 2002. 'Utopia and Violence'. In K. Popper, *Conjectures and Refutations*, 2nd ed., 477–488. London: Routledge.
Pinker, S. 2002. *The Blank Slate*. London: Penguin.
Searle, J. 1995. *The Construction of Social Reality*. New York: Free Press.

Searle, J. 2010. *Making the Social World*. Oxford: Oxford University Press.

Sennett, R. 2008. *The Craftsman*. London: Penguin.

Smuts, A. 2013. 'The Good Cause Account of Meaning in Life'. *Southern Journal of Philosophy* 51(4): 536–562.

Slater, M., and M. V. Sanchez-Vives. 2016. 'Enhancing Our Lives with Immersive Virtual Reality'. *Frontiers in Robotics and AI* 3: 74. doi: 10.3389/frobt.2016.00074.

Soraker, Johnny. 2010. *The Value of Virtual Worlds and Entities: A Philosophical Analysis of Virtual Worlds and Their Impact on Well-being*. Inskamp: Enschede.

Strikwerda, L. 2015. 'Present and Past Instances of Virtual Rape in Light of Three Categories of Legal Philosophical Theories of Rape'. *Philosophy and Technology* 28(4): 491–510.

Suits, B. [1978] 2005. *The Grasshopper: Games, Life and Utopia*. Calgary: Broadview Press.

Tillson, J. 2018. 'Is It Distinctively Wrong to Simulate Wrongdoing?' *Ethics and Information Technology* 20: 205–217 DOI: 10.1007/s10676-018-9463-7.

Vallor, S. 2016. *Technology and the Virtues*. Oxford: Oxford University Press.

Weijers, D. 2014. 'Nozick's Experience Machine Is Dead, Long Live the Experience Machine!' *Philosophical Psychology* 27(4): 513–535.

Wilde, O. 1981. 'The Soul of Man under Socialism'. *Fortnightly Review* 292.

Wolf, Susan. 2010. *Meaning in Life and Why It Matters*. Princeton, NJ: Princeton University Press.

Wu, T. 2017. *The Attention Merchants*. London: Atlantic Books.

Yorke, C. 2016. 'Prospects for Utopia in Space'. In *The Ethics of Space Exploration*, ed. J. Schwartz and T. Milligan, 61–71. Dordrecht: Springer.

Yorke, C. 2017. 'Endless Summer: What Kinds of Games Will Suits's Utopians Play?' *Journal of the Philosophy of Sport* 44(2): 213–228.

Index

For the benefit of digital users, indexed terms that span two pages (e.g., 52–53) may, on occasion, appear on only one of those pages.

absurd, 96–97, 149, 393, 440, 441–42, 447, 475, 521. *See also* futility; meaninglessness
accidentality, 94–95, 103–4, 223, 226, 279n.3, 289n.9, 349. *See also* chance; luck
accomplishment, 59, 61n.6, 63–64, 65, 114–18, 119, 132, 153, 169–70, 200, 220, 319–20, 337n.17, 389–90, 423–24, 495. *See also* achievement; challenge
achievement, 29, 58, 103–4, 103n.8, 106, 114–19, 121, 122, 136, 145–47, 179–80, 235, 237–38, 240, 314, 325–26, 327–28, 349–50, 363, 385, 389–91, 394–95, 398, 401–2, 411, 443, 462–63, 465–66, 467–68, 469–73, 482–83, 514–15. *See also* accomplishment; challenge
Adams, Marilyn McCord, 184, 466
Adams, Robert Merrihew, 224–25, 478
admiration, 94–95, 96–97, 99–100, 102, 105, 271–72, 274–75, 462, 464–66, 471–72
adoption, 311–12, 313, 316–17
Adorno, Theodor W. 185
aesthetics, 146, 255–56, 378. *See also* beauty; value: aesthetic
afterlife, 39, 130, 217, 221–25, 229–30, 231, 240–41, 314, 468
aim. *See* goal; purpose
alienation, 268, 294, 349, 364, 389–91, 411–12. *See also* self-alienation
altruism, 211–12, 217, 406, 455–56, 480, 483n.8
amare bonum bonus, 66–68
ambivalence, 395
Angelou, Maya, 167
anger, 182–83, 184, 295–96, 372–73, 386, 412–13
angst. *See* anxiety
animal nature. *See* animal self

animal self, 94–95, 99, 336–37, 349n.6, 362, 462
animals, 30–32, 99, 116–17, 149, 160, 207, 208, 324, 362, 418–19, 432, 440, 450
anxiety, 103, 136, 164–65, 206, 207, 209, 211–12, 344, 350–51, 461–62, 497–98
appreciation, 98, 101–2, 389–90, 403–4, 411–14
arbitrariness, 245, 264, 266
arc of the moral universe, 185–86
Arendt, Hannah, 299–300, 301–2, 304–5, 501
Aristotle, 90, 146–47, 151, 154, 213, 272, 331, 362, 363, 464–65
atheism. *See* theism and atheism
Audi, Robert, 221, 224
authenticity and inauthenticity, 77–78, 160–63, 210–11, 303–4, 388, 494
autonomy, 130–31, 135–36, 138, 139, 140, 150, 409, 456–57, 462, 496–97, 498, 520–21

bad faith. *See* authenticity and inauthenticity
Baier, Kurt, 330–31
Baumeister, Roy, 352, 494–95
beauty, 308–9, 373–74, 412, 471–72, 501, 514. *See also* aesthetics
Beckett, Samuel, 378–79
belonging, 135, 325, 390, 425–26, 498
Benatar, David, 94, 105n.11, 201n.13, 244, 317–18, 477–78
Bergson, Henri, 248, 254–55
binary categories. *See* dualism
bliss, 223–24, 314, 469
boredom, 117, 118, 218, 218n.3, 219–20, 278, 311, 333, 344, 348, 365–66
Bradford, Gwen, 472–73
Bramble, Ben, 189, 199
Brännmark, Johan, 319

Brentano, Franz, 250
Brey, Philip, 517
brotherhood of pain, 217
Buddhism, 147

Calhoun, Cheshire, 348, 451–55, 456–57
Camus, 116n.10, 222n.11, 385, 398n.11, 447–49
categorical desires, 456
cave, allegory of, 508
challenge, 60–61, 64, 65–66, 67, 68, 118, 217–18, 271, 365–66, 380–81, 426, 471–72, 487
chance, 119, 136, 174–75, 404n.2, 499. *See also* accidentality; luck
Christianity, 147, 184, 217, 229–30, 248, 392–93, 424, 467, 468–69
Cicero, 464–65
cipher, 251–57
commitment, 145, 150, 159, 160–62, 167–69, 182, 210, 219, 220–21, 267–68, 348, 372, 373, 375, 376–77, 381–83, 409–10, 469–70, 501
communities, 185, 219, 221, 269, 299n.4, 325–26, 380, 390, 391, 407–8, 462, 469–70, 503–4
compassion, 69, 332, 394, 397–98, 465n.5
compatibilism, 174, 175–77, 179, 484
competence, 115–16, 135–36, 138, 139, 140, 394
Confucianism, 219
consequentialism, 47–48, 96, 102, 189, 200, 330–31
Cooper, David, 246–47, 249–50
Cottingham, John, 225–26, 244, 245
courage, 90, 272, 464–65
Craig, William Lane, 222–23, 224–25, 324, 440
creativity, 349, 481, 518
Csikszentmihalyi, Mihaly, 218
cynicism, 390, 411

Damon, William, 495, 501
Darwall, Stephen, 329n.8, 376–77
de Bres, Helena, 346, 353, 380
death, 46, 117, 118–22, 136, 140, 217, 221–22, 229–31, 311, 327–28, 333, 350, 361–62, 412–13, 449, 450–51, 453–54, 502–3. *See also* afterlife; suicide
depression, 83, 138, 148–49, 332, 348, 351–52, 364, 390–91, 394–95, 397, 423, 457–58, 497–98

despair, 184, 209, 233, 300–1, 303–4, 464, 501
destination. *See* goal
destructiveness, 117, 391–92, 461–62
detachment, 411–12
devotion, 327–28, 469–70, 502
Dewey, John, 185, 247
Di Paola, Marcello, 280
dichotomy. *See* dualism
Dickens, Charles, 146
dignity, 221, 439, 456–57
direction, 116–17, 136, 159, 160, 161, 164–65, 347–48, 445–46. *See also* goal; purpose
distress, 164, 369
Drake Equation, 234–35, 241
dread, 213, 350
Driver, Julia, 483–84
dualism, 244–45, 247, 251–52
   body-mind, 128, 130, 152, 153, 154–55, 156
   subject-object, 247, 249, 250, 251–52
dullness. *See* boredom

Ecclesiastes, 1n.2, 148
effective altruism, 480
effort, 60, 97, 103n.8, 117, 196, 319–20, 373, 389–90, 454, 472–73
Eliot, T. S. 252
Ellis, Fiona, 244
emotions, 129, 133, 137–38, 152–53, 173, 182–83, 332, 351–52, 372–75, 422, 517–18
empathy, 332, 403
emptiness, 300–1, 344
end. *See* goal
Epictetus, 83. *See also* stoicism
Epicurus, 120–21
equanimity, 184
esteem, 33, 94–95, 102, 392–93, 396, 406, 422, 462, 469–70. *See also* self-esteem
evil, 60n.5, 62–63n.10, 67, 84, 104, 115n.9, 145–46, 147, 170–71, 184–86, 212–13, 286, 297, 466
evil, problem of, 184–85
existentialism, 1–2, 213, 511–12
experience machine, 27–28, 52, 98–99, 516–17

faith, 185, 210–11, 469, 473
Feder Kittay, Eva, 396
Fernandez-Armesto, Felipe, 511–12
Fischer, John Martin, 120–21, 176

flourishing, 90, 119, 319, 466, 493. *See also* fulfilment; happiness; welfare; well-being
flow, 217–18, 348
Frankfurt, Harry, 71n.16, 93n.2, 160–62, 218, 266–67, 327, 358, 369, 376, 388
Frankl, Viktor, 1–2, 145, 219, 423, 445, 454–55, 461, 462, 463, 465–66, 492–93
Freud, Sigmund, 221, 425
Fricker, Miranda, 296, 298–99
friendship, 113–14, 115, 146–47, 152, 170, 181–83, 293, 363, 390, 397, 406, 407, 408, 420, 494, 514, 517
Froese, Paul, 492–93
fulfilment, 64, 71, 213, 214–15, 349–50. *See also* flourishing; happiness; welfare; well-being
fundamentality theory, 48, 271n.4, 333–34
futility, 63, 149, 350, 431–32, 447. *See also* absurd; meaninglessness

Gadamer, Hans-Georg, 252–53, 255–56
Gertz, Nolen, 520–21, 522
Gilgamesh, Epic of, 1n.2
goal, 29, 83, 95–96, 115n.9, 116, 117, 133, 145–46, 190, 196–97, 200–1, 213, 214–15, 272, 327–28, 343–44, 345, 347–48, 350, 423, 494. *See also* project; purpose; pursuit; teleology
  vs. desire, 116–17
  of life, 205
  orientation, 319–20
  regulative vs. terminative, 145–46
  satisfaction, 425
  self-propagating, 61–63
Gödel's theorem, 208
grief, 149, 293–94, 327–28, 408–9, 465n.4

Haidt, Jonathan, 217–18
happiness, 59, 97, 99–100, 114–15, 116, 121–22, 145, 293, 366, 381, 382, 425–26, 477–78, 492n.1. *See also* flourishing; fulfilment; welfare; well-being
Harari, Yuval Noah, 512, 513
harmony, 210, 214–15, 219, 249
Hauskeller, Michael, 331
heaven. *See* afterlife
Hegel, George Wilhelm Friedrich, 185
Heidegger, Martin, 206, 248, 256, 388n.3
Heims, Michael, 510

Hemingway, Ernest, 226, 385
Herostratus, 104
Heyd, David, 477–78
Hobbes, Thomas, 212–13
Hofmannsthal, Hugo von 11–12, 248–50, 251, 253
hope, 152, 185–86, 199, 209, 210–11, 300–3, 348, 453, 454
humility. *See* modesty
Hurka, Thomas, 331–32, 333, 336n.16, 432, 466
Husserl, Edmund, 246–47, 250
hybridism, 245, 247, 268–69, 282–83, 294, 329n.9, 334–35, 376–77, 391, 411–12, 495

immortality. *See* afterlife
inauthenticity. *See* authenticity and inauthenticity
infinity, 208, 209, 210, 223–24, 231, 240–41, 441–42. *See also* afterlife
intensity, 231, 366, 375, 392
intersubjectivism, 329n.8, 350–51
irrationality. *See* rationality and irrationality
Islam, 184, 217, 229–30, 467, 468–69

James, Henry, 83
James, William, 83–84, 87–88, 246, 254, 328–29
Jaspers, Karl, 247, 251–53, 254
Jenner, Edward, 434–35, 443
Jonas, Silvia, 246–47
Judaism, 184, 217, 229–30
Julian of Norwich, 147, 208
Junger, Sebastian, 217

Kafka, Franz, 122
Kahane, Guy, 233–36, 237–38, 238n.12, 441
Kant, Immanuel, 155–56, 206–7, 301n.7, 409
Kauppinen, Antti, 50n.6, 66, 363, 363n.3, 380–81, 382
Kekes, John, 334
Kierkegaard, Søren, 87–88, 182, 213
King, Martin Luther, Jr. 186
Klemke, E. D. 327
Kołakowski, Leszek, 246–47, 248
Korsgaard, Christine, 160, 161–62

Landau, Iddo, 115n.8, 136, 224, 243–44, 279, 318n.18, 324, 411, 412, 440–41
Langer, Susanne, 254–55

Lear, Jonathan, 347
Lewis, C. S. 209, 223–24
Locke, John, 79
love, 31–32, 152–53, 181–83, 210, 217, 221, 267, 268–69, 293, 308–9, 310, 327–28, 332–33, 362, 363, 397, 408, 420, 469, 478, 501
   God's, 240n.15
   of God, 244
luck, 93–94, 223, 225–26, 349–50, 367, 481–84. *See also* accidentality; chance

MacIntyre, Alasdair, 213
Mallarmé, Stéphane, 255–56
Marcel, Gabriel, 247
Marcus Aurelius, 89. *See also* stoicism
Mawson, T. J. 38, 39, 224–25
May, Simon, 207
McDowell, John, 214
McGeer, Victoria, 296, 302, 303
meaning
   great (*see* meaning: ultimate)
   having vs. searching for, 139, 422–23
   illusory, 147, 157
   objective, 43, 60–61, 134–36, 139, 157, 230, 245, 247, 263, 271–72, 275–76, 282, 283, 294, 329n.9, 330–34, 349–50, 364–70, 376–77, 390–91, 401–2, 416–17, 435, 493, 495, 500–1, 509, 514–15 (*see also* objectivism)
   subjective, 43, 136, 146–47, 245, 263, 264–66, 275–76, 294, 327–30, 364–70, 376–77, 390, 401–2, 416–17, 418, 435, 493, 495, 500–1
   superlative (*see* meaning: ultimate)
   ultimate, 28, 39, 65–66, 68–73, 94, 101–2, 205–6, 222–23, 246, 308–10, 313–15, 318–21, 438–39, 440, 467–68
   undesirable, 37–39, 40, 229
meaninglessness, 52–53, 148–49, 218n.3, 222–25, 264–65, 313–15, 343–44, 350–51, 379, 396, 437–43, 453–54, 464, 492–93, 520–21. *See also* absurd; futility
Meister Eckhart, 248
Merleau-Ponty, Maurice, 252–53, 255–56
Metz, Thaddeus, 48–49, 53–54, 94, 99n.3, 189, 200, 220, 243–44, 245, 271n.4, 278–79, 282n.5, 326n.4, 331, 332–34, 336n.16, 397, 442n.4, 462–63, 478, 509

Mill, John Stuart, 59, 61, 148
Milton, John, 181–82
Mintoff, Joe, 97, 334, 336
modesty, 392–93, 394–95, 465n.5, 483–84
Montaigne, Michele de, 78n.9, 86, 146–47, 394–95
Moore, Adrian, 205
Moore, G. E. 466
morality
   objective, 214, 224–25, 263, 264
   subjective, 263–64, 265–66

Nagel, Thomas, 44n.1, 96–97, 103, 293–94, 305, 314–15, 441–42, 521
Nahmias, Eddy, 180
narrative justification, 346–47
narrativity, 36, 74, 164–66, 213, 214, 271–72, 273–75, 319, 329–30, 346–47, 378–80, 381–82, 423–25, 445–46. *See also* personal narratives
Nielsen, Kai, 330–31
Nietzsche, Friedrich, 122, 461, 463–66, 467
nihilism, 130, 209, 343, 350–51, 446–49, 502, 520–21. *See also* pessimism
Nozick, Robert, 29, 97, 98–99, 114–15, 312n.11, 314–15, 436, 515, 516–18, 521–22
numbness to value, 155, 411
Nussbaum, Martha, 293–94, 299–300
Nusselder, André, 511–12

objectivism, 43, 245, 247, 282, 283, 329n.9, 330–34, 390–91, 509, 514–15. *See also* meaning: objective; significance: objective; value: objective
objectivity of attitude, 182–83, 293–94
obligations to ourselves, 273
Ogawa, Seiji, 150–51
optimism, 302–3, 318–21, 411, 431, 486n.11, 487. *See also* nihilism; pessimism

pain. *See* suffering
Parfit, Derek, 110n.1, 477–80
Parker, Theodore, 185–86
Pascal, Blaise, 224
Pater, Walter, 146–47
personal narratives, 378–80, 381–82
pessimism, 1–2, 201, 431, 485–87. *See also* nihilism; optimism

Pieper, Joseph, 207
Pihlström, Sami, 246–47
Plantinga, Alvin, 184
Plato, 481, 508, 518–19
pluralism, 37, 318–21, 337, 492–93, 497–98, 501, 502, 509
Plutarch, 89
pride, 78n.7, 94–95, 99–100, 103–4, 118, 349–50, 372–73, 392–93, 396, 411, 469–70
principle of recursion. See *amare bonum bonus*
project, 58–61, 62–63, 66, 68–73, 162, 168–69, 313–15, 319, 363, 367, 382, 452. *See also* goal; purpose
Pseudo-Dionysius the Areopagite, 248
purpose, 32, 94–95, 116, 133, 145–46, 159, 161, 162–63, 205–6, 223, 308–9, 311, 352, 353, 401–2, 403, 417–18, 423–24, 431–34, 445–46, 464, 493–94, 500, 501, 503–4. *See also* goal; project
pursuit, 59–67, 117, 168–69, 205–6, 313–14, 450. *See also* goal; project; purpose
Purves, Duncan, 330–31

Quine, W. V. 475–76

Rahner, Karl, 207, 208, 211
Ratcliffe, Matthew, 348
rationality and irrationality, 30, 48, 65, 152, 157, 162, 176, 183, 207, 214–15, 247, 249, 250–51, 325–26, 331–32, 333–34, 336–37, 361, 372–73, 374, 422, 447, 453–55, 457–58, 487
Rawls, John, 60n.5, 365
religion, 1, 3, 32–33, 34, 39, 87–88, 130, 184, 402n.1, 420, 463, 466–69, 502. *See also* Buddhism; Christianity; Confucianism; Islam; Judaism; supernaturalism and naturalism; theism and atheism
result machine, 97, 103n.8
Ricoeur, Paul, 87–88
ring of Gyges, 518–19
Romantic movement, 1–2
Rosa, Hartmut, 497–98
Russell, Bertrand, 233, 366

Sainsbury, R.M., 475–76
Saint Augustine, 121–22, 206, 464–65
Saint Thomas Aquinas, 207, 212–13, 214–15, 464–65
Salinger, J. D. 386–87, 390n.5, 395n.9
Salk, Jonas, 443
Sartre, Jean-Paul, 77–78, 245, 388n.3, 439
Scheffler, Samuel, 311, 318n.18
Schopenhauer, Arthur, 63, 121–22, 201n.13
Schroder, Timothy, 358
Seachris, Joshua, 346
self improvement, 219
self-actualization, 494
self-alienation, 78, 88, 213
self-deception, 88, 386–87, 389, 484
self-discovery, 162–63, 168
self-esteem, 118, 212, 403, 406, 422
self-expression, 426
self-interestedness, 389, 392–93. *See also* selfishness
selfishness, 367–68. *See also* self-interestedness
self-sacrifice, 29, 99n.4, 114–15, 116, 145–46, 147, 217, 327–28, 364, 408–9, 455–56, 483n.8
self-seclusion, 391
self-transcendence, 94–95, 105, 107, 145–46, 150, 189, 333–34, 462, 512
Shakespeare, William, 78, 148, 375–76, 379, 382, 383
Shklar, Judith N. 396
significance
    objective, 230, 232–33, 241
    subjective, 230, 231, 240n.15, 241
Singer, Peter, 113n.5, 218–19, 245, 442n.4
Sisyphus, 29, 47–48, 63–64, 69–70, 82, 116n.10, 216, 217, 218–19, 447, 448, 482–83
Smith, Quentin, 331
Smuts, Aaron, 47–48, 218, 279, 330–31
Socrates, 76
Spinoza, Baruch, 173, 174, 208
Steiner, George, 255–56
Stoicism, 184. *See also* Epictetus; Marcus Aurelius
Strawson, Galen, 159–60, 164–66, 381
Strawson, P. F. 182–83, 293–94, 299–300, 305
striving, 122, 132, 190, 208, 209, 211, 426
Stump, Eleonore, 212–13
subjectivism, 43, 72, 245, 247, 253, 390, 391. *See also* meaning: subjective; significance: subjective; subjectivity

subjectivity, 134–35, 327
suffering, 1, 64, 114–15, 121–22, 149, 184, 218–20, 361, 364, 445, 454, 455–56, 461
suicide, 119n.11, 120–21, 385, 422, 445
supernaturalism and naturalism, 39, 155, 225, 243–45, 327n.5, 401–2. *See also* religion; theism and atheism
survivor guilt, 394–95, 408–9

Tartaglia, James, 201n.13
Taylor, Charles, 213, 365n.6
Taylor, Richard, 218, 264–65, 435n.2
teleology, 117, 151, 153, 154, 211–15, 223, 378–79
The Matrix, 508, 518
The Truman Show, 232–33, 508–9, 518
theism and atheism, 39, 130, 205, 216, 229, 244–45, 253, 434, 438–43. *See also* religion; supernaturalism and naturalism
Thomas, Joshua, 330–31
Thompson, Janna, 478
Thoreau, Henry David, 274
Thunberg, Greta, 277, 500–1
Tillich, Paul, 248, 250–51
Tillman, Pat, 221–22
Tolstoy, Leo, 148–49, 223–24, 385, 391n.6
transcendent sphere, 205, 209–11, 244–45, 247, 251–52, 516
transformation, 298, 497–98
true self. *See* authenticity and inauthenticity
trust, 210, 302, 390, 403, 406, 408, 519
Turgenev, Ivan, 343–44

utility monster, 97, 102n.7

Valéry, Paul, 255–56
value
  aesthetic, 44–45, 46–47, 54, 509, 514
  extrinsic, 218–20, 231
  final, 27–28, 29, 37, 66, 95–96, 98, 106–7, 313–14, 348, 362, 420, 451–52
  instrumental, 65–66, 94–96, 100–1, 359, 451
  intrinsic, 48–49, 58–59, 67, 95–96, 217, 218, 234, 348, 349, 358–59, 451–52, 453, 455
  narrative, 271–72, 273–75
  objective, 58–61, 72–73, 162, 214–15, 219–20, 224–25, 231, 232–33, 241, 252–53, 294, 349–50, 364–70, 376–78, 380, 381–82
Velleman, David, 319
view from nowhere, 293–94, 305, 521
virtue ethics, 265n.2, 269, 272

Waghorn, Nicholas, 231n.4, 238n.12
Weil, Simone, 248
welfare, 110–16, 121–22, 219, 333n.14. *See also* happiness; fourishing; fulfilment; well-being
well-being, 1–2, 45, 90, 110–14, 139, 217, 331, 334, –64, 367, 368, 446, 455–57, 492n.1, 509. *See also* happiness; flourishing; fulfilment; welfare
Westover, Tara, 496
wickedness. *See* evil
Wielenberg, Erik J. 48–49, 234–35n.7
Williams, Bernard, 85n.21, 122, 230, 233–34, 235–36, 237–38, 480, 481, 485–86
Williams, Clifford, 211–12
Wittgenstein, Ludwig, 129, 131, 206–7, 254–56, 364, 394–95
Wolf, Susan, 47–48, 50–51, 52, 53–54, 99, 115n.8, 189, 219–20, 268–70, 272, 324, 334–35, 364, 365, 376–77, 495
Wong, Wai-hung, 329–30, 380
Woodard, Christopher, 283–89, 290

Yates, Robert, 385, 391n.6
yearning. *See* striving
Young, Julian, 256

Zeno, 209, 475
Zuckerman, 221